STATISTICAL EVIDENCE
IN LITIGATION

STATISTICAL EVIDENCE IN LITIGATION
Methodology, Procedure, and Practice

DAVID W. BARNES
Professor of Law and Economics
Syracuse University College of Law
Maxwell School of Citizenship and Public Affairs

JOHN M. CONLEY
Associate Professor of Law
University of North Carolina Law School

LITTLE, BROWN AND COMPANY
Boston and Toronto

Library of Congress Catalog Card No. 85-50292

ISBN 0-316-08148-5

MV

Published simultaneously in Canada
by Little, Brown & Company (Canada) Limited

Printed in the United States of America

To Carol, Lisa, and law school deans
who support faculty research.

D. W. B.

As always, to Paula.

J. M. C.

SUMMARY OF CONTENTS

CONTENTS

CHAPTER ONE

Statistics, Statisticians, and What Lawyers Need to Know About Them   1

CHAPTER TWO

Data Acquisition and Analysis   37

Contents   xi

CHAPTER THREE

Statistical Inference Generally   83

CHAPTER FOUR

The Significance of Numerical Differences   117

CHAPTER FIVE

Analyzing Numerical Differences Among Categories 197

CHAPTER SIX

Collecting and Analyzing Sample Data   249

CHAPTER SEVEN

Proving Associations Between Variables: The Correlation Coefficient 331

CHAPTER EIGHT

Estimation and Prediction: Techniques for Assessing the Influences of Multiple Factors   403

CHAPTER NINE

Presenting and Attacking Statistical Evidence   497

CHAPTER TEN

Cases Involving Statistical Evidence 545

APPENDIX A

Standard Statistical Tables   597

APPENDIX B

Mathematical Symbols   629

APPENDIX C

Selected Equations   633

TABLE OF EXHIBITS

PREFACE

This book describes and explains the variety of ways statistical tools are used as proof of factual issues relevant to legal disputes. It is designed both as a treatise on the use of statistical evidence in litigation and as a reference book for the litigator. Various chapters discuss trial strategy and evidentiary rules, illustrate the application of statistical methodology and the calculation and interpretation of statistical results, and describe the process of data acquisition and statistical analysis using computers.

The reader might consider reading the first three chapters as an introduction to the use of statistical evidence. Taken together they summarize the contents of the book. Chapter 1 introduces the reader to various litigation applications of statistical techniques and some basic terminology with which the litigator employing statistical methods must be familiar. Chapter 2 describes problems associated with assembling data and with choosing a form of statistical analysis, and Chapter 3 introduces a variety of tools of statistical inference. The next five chapters discuss specific problems in litigation that are amenable to statistical resolution: establishing the significance of numerical differences (Chapter 4), analyzing numerical differences among categories (Chapter 5), collecting and analyzing sample data (Chapter 6), proving associations between variables (Chapter 7), and assessing the influences of multiple factors on an event of interest (Chapter 8). In each of these "tools" chapters, the statistical methodology used in inferential analysis is presented initially without the distraction of complex formulas and equations in order to emphasize how the tools are used and interpreted. For most of the techniques discussed, however, the methods by which the associated statistics are calculated are illustrated by numerous examples in the final part of each chapter. Tables necessary for evaluating the statistical significance of each result are presented in the Appendix of Tables at the end of the book. Except for some of the more arcane computations related to multiple regression (discussed in Chapter 8), those that are much more easily calculated by computer, this book is a self-contained reference work providing all of the formulas and tables necessary to perform the statistical analyses discussed. Chapter 9 contains a discussion of evidentiary rules relevant to the submission of statistical evidence and a discussion of strategic considerations useful in assisting factfinders in understanding offerings of quantitative evidence. In Chapter 10, reported decisions in selected substantive law areas are compiled and discussed to suggest to litigators how the techniques explained in the preceding chapters might be useful in practice.

Throughout the book each statistical concept is illustrated by numerous examples of applications or interpretations of the concepts in reported decisions of courts and administrative agencies. The book is designed for lawyers with no previous statistical training. Each chapter is replete with cross-references designed to simplify discussion and to refer the reader to appropriate portions of the book where important concepts are discussed in more detail.

ACKNOWLEDGMENTS

Lavish praise must go to Carol Bronson, who was responsible for typing innumerable drafts of this book. Acting above and beyond the usual duties of a secretary, Carol organized and maintained the hundreds of exhibits and equations appearing throughout this book. Asking an ace legal secretary to immerse herself in the drudgery of typing arcane mathematical formulas is asking for trouble, but Carol seemed to thrive on the challenge of keeping all of this work and one of the authors in order. Ten thousand thanks.

Lisa Ivy Cohen, research assistant extraordinaire, has put several years of effort into this work, performing tasks from researching the hundreds of cases annotated in this book to making valuable editorial comments. A large portion of the footnotes are hers, as is credit for editorial changes in some of the early chapters. In addition to being a willing and able worker, she is a most pleasant sounding board. Strong suspicions exist that Lisa and Carol conspired to control the writing of this book.

Other research assistants who contributed to this book include David Sadofsky, Douglas McCusick, Jeff Carl, and Ruth Kaufman of Syracuse University College of Law, as well as Barbara Ball of the University of New Mexico School of Law. Susan Lederman, Doris Stoddard, Gayle Fletcher, and Camille Pompeo also assisted in secretarial chores. Professor Rod Surratt of Syracuse University kindly reviewed Chapter 9 from the point of view of an evidence professor and Professors Gary LaFree and Chad McDaniel of the University of New Mexico generously reviewed portions of Chapter 8 from the perspective of social science methodologists. Many thanks to all of these contributors.

We gratefully acknowledge the financial support of the Center for Interdisciplinary Legal Studies of the Syracuse University College of Law. This book will add to the growing body of published interdisciplinary research that their grants have supported in endeavoring to advance the commingling of law and related disciplines in legal education and scholarship. Valuable support was also obtained from the Syracuse University Senate Research Fund. The University of New

Mexico School of Law postal and copying budgets suffered greatly on our behalf while I was a visitor at U.N.M. during the final stages of manuscript preparation. The enthusiasm of law school deans for faculty research makes such projects feasible.

We are grateful to the Literary Executor of the late Sir Ronald Fisher, F.R.S., and to Dr. Frank Yates, F.R.S., and to the Longman Group, Ltd. of London for permission to reprint Tables II, III, IV, VII, VII I, and XXXIII I from their book, Statistical Tables for Biological, Agricultural and Medical Research (6th ed. 1974).

Last, we recognize the bounteous moral support from the academic colleagues, judges, and practicing lawyers who enrich and inform our judgment, who have made their offices available to us, and who have shared their wisdom with us during our research.

David W. Barnes

I wish to acknowledge the contributions made by my wife, Paula, and my children, Rebecca, John, Robin, and Christina, who, at various times and in various combinations, put up with me, encouraged me, and scribbled on the manuscript; my mother, who taught me long division when I was absent from school having my tonsils out, and the Sisters of Notre Dame, who taught me almost everything else I know about mathematics; Barbara Smith, my former legal secretary, who prepared early drafts of much of the manuscript carefully and cheerfully; and the alumni of my law and social science seminars at the University of North Carolina and Boston College, whose interest in the field has continually renewed my own.

John M. Conley

We owe a tremendous debt to David W. Peterson, statistician, president of Personnel Research Inc., which serves litigators in formulating and presenting statistical evidence, professor of management at the Fuqua School of Business at Duke University, and friend. This book would not be the same without his inspiration, stimulation, and chastisement. Any errors exist due to our ignorance and thickheadedness rather than to David's attempts to educate us. His most direct contribution to this book is Chapter 2, Data Acquisition and Analysis, in which his analytical expertise and depth of experience are apparent.

David W. Barnes and John M. Conley

January, 1986

STATISTICAL EVIDENCE
IN LITIGATION

CHAPTER ONE

Statistics, Statisticians, and What Lawyers Need to Know About Them

§1.0   Introduction

Few scientific terms inspire such strength of reaction as the word *statistics*. Frequently the reaction is fear and loathing: fear of an occult science and loathing of its practitioners' apparent ability to influence events. At the other extreme, the observer may be seduced by the magic of numbers and drawn into uncritical acceptance of any proposition carrying the aura of quantitative science.

On this score lawyers and judges are quite like the rest of men (and women) although, like their pharisaic predecessors, they may not see themselves as such. Any lawyer with experience in complex litigation can recall instances of courts rejecting sound scientific evidence because it looked and felt strange, and thus was untrustworthy. Conversely, an alert statistician reading the Title VII case law can find abundant examples of otherwise forceful judges who have meekly accepted dubious scientific propositions because they were advanced by people called experts. Behind both sets of circumstances, of course, are lawyers who were insufficiently persuasive on the merits of their scientific evidence or too credulous to detect artifice masquerading as science.

The purpose of this book is to facilitate finding the middle ground between statistical luddism and credulity. Reduced to its Latin root, statistics means nothing more than the description of the way some entity looks and works. If the reader remembers anything from this book, it should be that for all its modern elaborations statistics still means nothing more.

To achieve their purpose, the authors do three things:

1. Introduce the reader to a number of important statistical concepts and techniques through the use of concrete and realistic examples;
2. Illustrate the adaptation of these techniques to recurring legal problems; and
3. Offer practical advice on how to use appropriate statistical techniques in the courtroom and how to discover and attack those techniques that are inappropriate.

To explain and illustrate the statistical concepts and methods introduced in the text, the authors use examples drawn largely from reported cases, which have been selected for their utility in illustrating statistical issues and do not necessarily represent the current state of the law in their subject areas. Some of the cases illustrate more than one statistical issue and are therefore repeated at different points in the text. Chapter 10 presents a review of leading statistical evidence cases organized by legal subject matter. Some readers who are concerned with a particular legal problem may wish to consult Chapter 10 first in order to find examples of cases similar to their own.

The book presumes on the part of the reader only common sense and enough mathematical background to manage a checking account and a credit card, and it demands nothing more than attention and a willingness to venture into unfamiliar areas.

This chapter is designed to illustrate the general utility of statistical evidence and to describe the lawyer's role in the preparation and execution of a case involving statistics and statistical expert witnesses. Sections 1.1 through 1.3 explore the chronological expansion of the role of statistics in litigation. Sections 1.4 and 1.5 discuss the statistician's role in the litigation process from background assistance in development of the case to expert testimony. Statisticians are likely to provide the most effective assistance if the lawyer understands the language and methodology of statistics and can serve as an intermediary between the legal and statistical worlds. Sections 1.6 through 1.9 describe several specific aspects of the lawyer's role in the preparation and presentation of a case involving statistical evidence. Sections 1.10 through 1.15 illustrate by simple examples three broad categories of problems arising in litigation to which statistical methodology is applied and present some of the concepts that are basic to the art of drawing conclusions from data.

A. THE STATUS OF STATISTICAL EVIDENCE IN COURT

In 1897, Oliver Wendell Holmes, then a Justice of the Massachusetts Supreme Judicial Court, predicted a glorious future for statistical evidence in the courtroom: "For the rational study of law the black letter man may be the man of the present, but the man of the future is the man of statistics and the master of economics."[1]

Holmes's future has arrived slowly and with a halting gait, if indeed it has arrived at all. As a number of authors have observed, the reception of statistical evidence in the courtroom has been cautious at

---

§1.0   [1] Holmes, The Path of Law, 10 Harv. L. Rev. 457, 469 (1897).

best and uninformed at worst; the nonuse and misuse of statistics have been more common than its use.[2]

§1.1   Origins of Statistical Evidence in Court

The earliest efforts to apply statistical theory to legal problems date back to the Enlightenment. In 1785, the French mathematician Condorcet discussed the probability of error in group decisions, including those made by juries.[1] The same topic was pursued by other French mathematicians, most significantly Poisson.[2] As was Condorcet, Poisson was interested primarily in using mathematics to assess the probability that judgments were correct. As one of the leading contemporary exponents of statistical evidence has noted, Poisson's work "has become a cornerstone of modern probability theory, with an enormous range of scientific application . . . but the law itself has remained virtually immune to its influence."[3] In the two centuries since the publication of Condorcet's essay, the law has done virtually nothing to act on the suggestion that probability theory could assist in assessing the fairness and efficiency of the legal process.[4]

A thoroughly unenthusiastic reception was given to the earliest attempts to make direct use of statistical analysis as evidence. The first such effort in an American courtroom may have occurred in the case of *Robinson v. Mandell*,[5] popularly known as the *Howland's Will* case.

---

[2] For a useful summary of the history of statistical and other social science evidence in the courtroom, see Michelson, Rosen, & Washby, History & Status of the Art of Applied Social Research in the Courts, in The Use/Nonuse/Misuse of Applied Social Research in the Courts (M. Saks & C. Baron eds. 1980).

§1.1   [1] M. Condorcet, Essai Sur L'Application de L'Analyse à La Probabilité des Decisions Rendues à La Pluralité des Voix, De l'Imprimerie Royale, Paris (1785).

[2] S. Poisson, Recherches Sur La Probabilité Des Jugements En Matière Criminelle et En Matière Civile, Précédés des Règles Générales du Calcul des Probabilités, Bachelier, Paris (1837).

[3] Finkelstein, The Application of Statistical Decision Theory to the Jury Discrimination Cases, 80 Harv. L. Rev. 338, 339 (1966).

[4] For a recent review of the use of probability theory in legal proceedings, see Imwinkelried, The Standard for Admitting Scientific Evidence: A Critique from the Perspective of Juror Psychology, 28 Vill. L. Rev. 554, 562-563 & nn.57-58 (1982-1983). For a more technical discussion, see Kaplan, Decision Theory and the Factfinding Process, 20 Stan. L. Rev. 1065 (1968). While the law has been less than enthusiastic about probability theory, statisticians have continued to be fascinated by the possibilities. See, e.g., Gelfanda & Solomon, A Study of Poisson's Models for Jury Verdicts in Criminal and Civil Trials, 68 J. Am. Stat. Assn. 271 (1973).

[5] 20 F. Cas. 1027 (D. Mass. 1868)(No. 11,959).

The plaintiff, Hetty Robinson, was the niece of the deceased, Sylvia Ann Howland. Hetty alleged that she and her Aunt Sylvia had agreed to make mutual wills in which each named the other as beneficiary. According to Hetty, Aunt Sylvia's purpose in making this agreement was to ensure that if Hetty were to predecease her father the father would receive none of the property that Hetty had inherited from her mother, Aunt Sylvia's sister.

When Aunt Sylvia died, Hetty came forward with a multipage document that she claimed was the will Aunt Sylvia had executed pursuant to the agreement. Mandell, Aunt Sylvia's executor, produced a second will, inconsistent with the alleged agreement, that he claimed was her true last will and testament.

Included in Hetty's version of the will were a noncontroversial first page containing an admittedly authentic signature of Aunt Sylvia, and a second page listing the key provisions and bearing a signature that the executor claimed to be a forgery. The executor argued that the admitted signature on the first page of Hetty's version was unnaturally similar to that on the contested second page. Such similarity, he said, went well beyond what might occur by chance over the lifetime of the average person.

In support of his position, he introduced the testimony of Benjamin Peirce, a professor of mathematics at Harvard. Peirce examined the two signatures and somehow calculated that the chance of genuine occurrence of such identity was one in one thousand six hundred sixty-six million of millions of millions of times. The court apparently permitted this testimony to be introduced but did not rely on it in deciding the case, since a point of contract law rendered the forgery issue immaterial. Circuit Justice Clifford, who heard the case, regrettably had nothing to say about the merits of the proffered statistical evidence, except to offer the tantalizing comment that "some of the questions discussed were new, and it must be admitted that they are highly important as affecting the rules of evidence."[6]

Almost 50 years later probability theory was still knocking with hesitation at the courthouse door. In *People v. Risley*,[7] the subject again was forgery. Risley, a Utica lawyer, was convicted in the trial court of altering an evidentiary document by inserting the words "the same" in

---

[6] Id. at 1032. The reported decision does not describe Peirce's testimony. The testimony is referred to in an annotation in 3 Am. L. Rev. 377 (1868-1869) and in the later case of People v. Risley, 214 N.Y. 75 (1915).

[7] 214 N.Y. 75 (1915).

a witness's affidavit in a prior civil action, a change that had materially improved his client's position.

The key issue on appeal was the testimony of a university professor of mathematics named Snyder. The prosecution had introduced a typing sample from Risley's office typewriter containing the words "the same" and had emphasized the apparent identity between the type in the sample and in the allegedly altered document. First, two experts on typewriters described the defects and the idiosyncrasies in the type produced by Risley's machine. The mathematician, who then testified, began with the assumptions that all such defects and idiosyncrasies had occurred independently and that the chances of occurrence and nonoccurrence of a given defect were equal. He multiplied together the respective probabilities of occurrence for all the defects and idiosyncrasies (as just noted, the probability was assumed to be 50% in every case) and concluded "that the probability of these defects being reproduced by the work of a typewriting machine, other than the machine of defendant, was one in four thousand million."[8]

The New York Court of Appeals reversed the conviction on the basis of the admission of this testimony. The majority opinion took the witness to task because, among other things, he

> was not qualified as an expert in typewriting; he had never made a study of such work, or the machine claimed to have been used for the purpose of interpolating words in the document offered in evidence, nor did he take into consideration in arriving in his result the effect of the human operation of such a machine; that is, whether the same defects would always be discernible, no matter who was the individual operating the machine.[9]

A concurring judge went further, hitting at least implicitly upon the two major statistical flaws in the professor's testimony. First, the concurring judge was apparently aware that the probabilities of the occurrence of each of the observed defects and idiosyncrasies were undoubtedly not equal, noting that "of the 13 similar defects testified to by him, two were variable and concededly may be eliminated."[10] Second, it was not reasonable to assume that the occurrence or nonoccurrence of each of the defects was an independent event; one defect might be the cause of another or a series of defects might occur

[8] Id. at 85.
[9] Id.
[10] Id. at 88.

together as a result of a single flaw in manufacturing. In summary, "the problem was sought to be determined by a so-called law of mathematical probability, regardless of actual experience, physical facts, or the element of human agency, and on the assumption manifestly false that a given thing was as liable to happen as not to happen."[11]

The *Howland's Will* and *Risley* cases, primitive as they now seem, reflect problems that even today are endemic to the use of statistical evidence. Lawyers and their witnesses, beguiled by the promise of statistics, continue to ignore its limitations and to proffer quantitative evidence without proper factual foundation. And many judges, suspicious of being victimized by that practice, continue to throw out the good with the bad.

§1.2 Transitions to Modern Uses of Statistical Evidence

Although the widespread acceptance of statistical evidence by the courts was more than half a century away, the Supreme Court's 1908 opinion in *Muller v. Oregon*[1] represents a turning point in the acceptance of social science evidence generally. At issue in *Muller* was an Oregon statute that limited the working hours of women. To defend the statute the state had only to show that it was reasonably based. To make this point Louis Brandeis included in the brief he submitted on behalf of the state what the Court termed "a very copious collection"[2] of authorities on the purported physical and mental differences between the sexes and on protective legislation enacted in other states and countries. The Court accepted and relied on these authorities, inviting twentieth century science into the judicial process with almost insouciant understatement: "It may not be amiss, in the present case, before examining the Constitutional question, to notice the course of legislation as well as expressions of opinion from other than judicial sources."[3] Working from Brandeis's brief, the Court found "that women's physical structure and the performance of maternal functions place her at a disadvantage in the struggle for subsistence,"[4] and that there is an "inherent difference between the two sexes, and in the

[11] Id. at 89.
§1.2 [1] 208 U.S. 412 (1908).
[2] Id. at 419.
[3] Id.
[4] Id. at 421.

different functions in life which they perform,"[5] and upheld the statute.

The invitation extended by the Court in *Muller* was largely ignored. In fact, social science evidence via the "Brandeis brief" did not play a major role in a Supreme Court case until *Brown v. Board of Education of Topeka*[6] in 1954. In *Brown,* the renunciation of the separate-but-equal doctrine turned in large part on inferences drawn from sociological and psychological studies of the impact on black children of separate education. Even prior to *Brown,* however, statistics had lurked unobtrusively in the back of the courtroom and had played a significant part in at least one line of cases, beginning with *Norris v. Alabama.*[7]

In *Norris,* an effort was made to reverse the convictions of several black defendants on the basis of discrimination against blacks in the selection of grand and petit jurors. In addressing the issue of the process by which the defendants were indicted, the Court considered the fact that although blacks comprised 7.5% of the adult male population of the county where the indictments had been handed down, no witness recalled ever having seen a black serve on a grand or petit jury. The Court found that this constituted a "prima facie case of the denial of the equal protection which the Constitution guarantees."[8] A similar conclusion was drawn about the trials, which were held in a county where the adult male population was 18% black, but where no black had ever been called for jury service, even though many qualified.

No statistical analysis was presented, and none was necessary, given the blatancy of the underrepresentation and the admission by county officials that their policy was not to call the blacks for jury duty. Nonetheless, the *Norris* opinion suggested that a case could now be made for the importance of quantitative comparisons, and other litigants soon came forward with similar theories but with less compelling evidence.

In *Cassell v. Texas,*[9] for example, a black convicted of murder challenged his conviction on the basis of the exclusion of blacks from Dallas County grand juries: of the 21 grand juries that preceded his indictment, 17 had contained one black; the other four, none. Thus

[5] Id. at 423.
[6] 347 U.S. 483 (1954).
[7] 294 U.S. 597 (1935).
[8] Id. at 591.
[9] 339 U.S. 282 (1950).

only 17 of the last 252 grand jurors, or 6.7%, had been black, while blacks constituted 15.5% of the population of the county. However, since blacks represented only 8.5% of those paying the poll tax, a requirement for jury service, the Court concluded that "without more it cannot be said that Negroes have been left off the grand jury panels to such a degree as to establish a prima facie case of discrimination."[10]

A final example is the 1965 case of *Swain v. Alabama*,[11] in which a black had been convicted of rape. As evidence of exclusion of black jurors he showed that while 26% of all adult males in the county were black, only 10 to 15% of the grand and petit jurors empanelled since 1953 had been black. The Court rejected these data as inconclusive:

> We cannot say that purposeful discrimination based on race alone is satisfactorily proved by showing that an identifiable group in a community is underrepresented by as much as 10% . . . . The overall percentage disparity has been small, and reflects no studied attempt to include or exclude a specified number of Negroes.[12]

The transition period was thus characterized by a willingness on the part of the Supreme Court at least to consider evidence of a quantitative or social science nature,[13] but until the decision in *Brown*

---

[10] Id. at 285-286. The Court ultimately reversed the conviction on the basis of the distribution of the 17 blacks on the grand juries. While statistical analysis might have been helpful to show the extreme improbability, in the absence of discrimination, of two blacks never having sat together on a grand jury, it was apparently not offered.

[11] 380 U.S. 202 (1965).

[12] Id. at 208-209. In reading a case such as *Swain*, the reader should be aware of the distinction between percentage point difference and percentage difference. This distinction is discussed in greater detail in Sections 4.2 and 4.3. A percentage point difference is the raw difference between one percentage and another. Thus in *Swain*, since blacks constituted 26 percent of all adult males in the relevant population but only 15 percent of jury panel members, there was a difference of 11 percentage points between the observed and the expected representation of blacks on juries. A percentage difference is the discrepancy between the observed and expected percentages divided by the expected percentage. Using the figures from *Swain*, the percentage difference would be 11 divided by 26, or 42.3%.

[13] A general standard for the admission of scientific evidence was established by the District of Columbia Circuit in Frye v. United States, 293 F. 1013 (D.C. Cir. 1923). The *Frye* standard requires that the expert testify that both the theory and the instrumentality employed are reliable and have gained general acceptance in the relevant scientific community. While the Federal Rules of Evidence have undermined the *Frye* standard, and a number of states have done so by decision or statute, it remains the majority rule at the state level. See Imwinkelried, The Standard for Admitting Scientific Evidence: A Critique from the Perspective of Juror Psychology, 28 Vill. L. Rev. 554, 556-559 (1982-1983). General evidentiary problems are considered in more detail in Section 9.3.1.

v. Board of Education[14] this willingness was rarely tested. Prior to the explosion of Title VII litigation in the 1970s, proffered statistical evidence seldom went beyond the type of probability analyses introduced in *Risley*[15] and the *Howland's Will* case,[16] and such evidence was poorly received by the courts.[17] This trend has reversed itself over the last 10 to 15 years. Section 1.3 discusses the impressive range of statistical techniques that the courts now find acceptable.

§1.3   The Current Multiplicity of Uses of Statistical Evidence

Since the varied uses of statistical evidence is the central theme of this book, no effort will be made in this section to catalog those uses exhaustively. For introductory purposes, suffice it to mention briefly some of the major areas of law in which statistical proof has become particularly important: it has long been used in employment discrimination cases and is becoming increasingly common in antitrust, tort, tax, food and drug, and unfair competition law. Chapter 10 provides a more thorough survey of these and other substantive areas of the law in which statistical evidence has been presented.

Most readers will probably associate statistical proof with employment discrimination, and it is in that area that it has undergone its most sophisticated development and has had its most decisive influence. The Supreme Court opened the door to statistical proof in its 1971 decision in *Griggs v. Duke Power Co.*,[1] which dealt with employment testing. The *Griggs* Court held that Title VII of the Civil Rights Act prohibits not only overt discrimination but also testing and other practices that are fair on their face but have a discriminatory impact. This meant that the plaintiff was no longer required to prove discrim-

---

[14] 347 U.S. 483 (1954).
[15] 214 N.Y. 75 (1915).
[16] 20 F. Cas. 1027 (D. Mass. 1868)(No. 11,959).
[17] Similar efforts to use probability theory are found in a number of later cases. The best known of these is People v. Collins, 68 Cal. 2d 319, 66 Cal. Rptr. 497 (1968), in which a mathematician attempted to quantify the probability of more than one set of persons having the characteristics of the alleged perpetrators of a particular crime. This evidence was rejected by the California Supreme Court in *Collins*, however, and similar evidence has been almost uniformly criticized by the courts. See Imwinkelried, at 562 n.58, cited in Section 1.2 note 13, and, generally, Stripinis, Probability Theory and Circumstantial Evidence: Implications from a Mathematical Analysis, 22 Jurimetrics 59 (1981).
§1.3   [1] 401 U.S. 424, 432 (1971).

inatory intent in the traditional, qualitative fashion. *Griggs* held that he or she need only make a numerical demonstration that the protected group fared less well than the majority under the suspect procedure.

This principle was confirmed six years later in *Hazelwood School District v. United States,*[2] in which the Supreme Court held explicitly that appropriate statistical evidence is sufficient to establish a prima facie case that the defendant has engaged in a pattern or practice of employment discrimination. In another case decided the same year as *Hazelwood, Teamsters v. United States,*[3] the Court held that once a prima facie case has been established by statistical proof, the burden falls on the defendant to show that such proof is either inaccurate or insignificant. The Court warned employers that the rebuttal of the plaintiff's statistical case must be specific and must consist of more than general affirmations of good faith.[4]

Statistical evidence had finally arrived, sufficient in and of itself to establish a prima facie case and requiring rebuttal on its own terms. In other employment discrimination cases discussed in the chapters that follow a variety of federal courts have given their approval to such specific concepts as standard deviation, statistical significance, and regression analysis.

Statistical techniques have also found wide acceptance in antitrust cases as proof of both liability and damages. The *Corrugated Container* litigation, discussed in greater detail in Section 1.12, is typical: the statistical analysis introduced in that series of cases was relevant to both the existence of a price-fixing conspiracy and the extent of damages. Statistical analysis has also been used to calculate the damages sustained as a result of monopolistic practices by a manufacturer,[5] and less sophisticated quantitative data in the form of market share analyses have long been a key element of proof in monopoly and merger cases.[6]

Statistical evidence has also been used in tax cases. In one frequently cited case, the owner of a number of television stations sought to depreciate its network affiliation contracts, raising the issue of

[2] 433 U.S. 299, 307-308 (1977).
[3] 431 U.S. 324, 339 (1977).
[4] Id. at 342 and n.24. See also Trout v. Hidalgo, 517 F. Supp. 873, 881 (D.D.C. 1981), *modified sub nom.* Trout v. Lehman, 702 F.2d 1094 (D.C. Cir. 1983).
[5] See, e.g., Coleman Motor Co. v. Chrysler Corp., 376 F. Supp. 546 (W.D. Pa. 1974), *vacated,* 525 F.2d 1338 (3d Cir. 1975).
[6] Perhaps the classic example of the use of market share data to determine whether monopoly power exists is Brown Shoe Co. v. United States, 370 U.S. 294 (1962).

whether the agreements had a determinable useful life.[7] The tax-payer sought to prove that the termination of the various contracts would follow certain mathematical laws applicable to the spacing of randomly occurring events. The Tax Court found this line of rea-soning to be highly persuasive, but the court of appeals rejected it out of hand because it ignored "the facts of life of the television broad-casting industry."[8] The Court of Claims has also rejected statistical evidence that certain assets have determinable useful lives.[9] In other recent cases, statistical analyses have been offered to prove that a discount should be applied to a stock's market value in determining a value for tax purposes,[10] and to establish reasonable rates of compen-sation for corporate executives.[11]

Tort litigation is yet another area in which statistical analysis is playing an increasingly important role. Using regression analysis and other techniques, plaintiffs have attempted to demonstrate what their lifetime earnings would have been but for the injury in dispute and thus to establish a criterion against which their reduced earning ca-pacity is to be measured. Statistical evidence has also been used in the liability phase of tort cases in an effort to eliminate chance and other exculpatory explanations for events at issue. While the increasing prevalence of such evidence is obvious to the practitioner at the trial level, thus far the appellate courts have done little to establish the standards under which it should be received and weighed.[12]

----

[7] Indiana Broadcasting Corp. v. Commissioner, 41 T.C. 793 (1964), rev'd, 350 F.2d 580 (7th Cir. 1965).

[8] Id. at 583.

[9] Burlington Northern, Inc. v. United States, 80-2 U.S. Tax Cas. (CCH) ¶9,781 (Ct. Cl. 1980) (taxpayer introduced regression analysis to show that assets had determinable useful lives; analysis rejected by court).

[10] Campbell v. United States, 661 F.2d 209 (Ct. Cl. 1981) (regression analysis as evidence of proper value of unregistered stocks received by trust).

[11] News Publishing Co. v. United States, 81-1 U.S. Tax Cas. (CCH) ¶9,435 (Ct. Cl. 1981) (excess salary disallowed as deduction; competitive salary shown by regression analysis).

[12] The case law dealing with the use of statistical analysis in tort cases is poorly developed. In Barnes v. United States, 525 F. Supp. 1065 (N.D. Ala. 1981), the plaintiff argued, and the defendant conceded, that there was a statistical correlation between the occurrence of a neurological disorder and the receipt of a governmentally adminis-tered swine flu shot. Although its finding for the plaintiff was apparently based in large part on this correlation, the court formed its conclusion without analyzing the statistical evidence. Administrative and judicial proceedings instituted to enforce product safety laws have proven more informative on the issue of using statistical evidence to prove tort-like liability. See, e.g., United States v. Ford Motor Co., 453 F. Supp. 1240 (D.D.C. 1978) (statistical analysis of failure rate of a mechanical part); United States v. General Motors Corp., 377 F. Supp. 242 (D.D.C. 1974) (similar issue).

A final area in which statistical evidence has played a key role is administrative law and procedure, where quantitative evidence has been of particular importance in proceedings to license drugs and food additives.[13] Both drugs and food additives are tested on animals for safety, and drugs are then tested on human patients for efficacy. On questions of safety, it is literally vital to know whether the death of a certain number of animals during the test period is possibly related to the substance being tested or is comfortably within the range of what would have been expected on the basis of chance alone. Where efficacy is concerned, statistics are used to assess whether apparent relationships between the use of a drug and improvement of symptoms are likely to be real or due to random phenomena.[14] The use of statistical analyses in drug licensing is so well established that the Food and Drug Administration has promulgated regulations to guide statistical effectiveness studies done on new drugs.[15]

Statistical evidence has also played a key role in adjudicating claims of unfair advertising.[16] In truth-in-advertising proceedings, the dispositive question is usually whether the advertisement tends to mislead the public,[17] and survey data are commonly relied on to prove or disprove the point. Statistical techniques are used to assess the adequacy of the sample size, the appropriateness of the process for selecting the sample, the legitimacy of the questionnaire used and the significance, if any, of patterns observed in the responses.[18]

There is at present virtually no area of the law in which properly conceived and executed statistical proof cannot be admitted as evidence. In employment discrimination cases, where the battle for

---

[13] E.g., Certified Color Mfrs.' Assn. v. Mathews, 543 F.2d 284 (D.C. Cir. 1976) (safety of Red Dye No. 2).

[14] In re Pfizer, Inc., 81 F.T.C. 23 (1972) (efficacy of over-the-counter burn remedy compared to placebo).

[15] 21 C.F.R. §312.111(a)(ii)(a)-(e) (1982).

[16] E.g., In re Coca Cola, Inc., 83 F.T.C. 746 (1973) (vitamin C content of fruit drink); In re ITT Continental Baking Co., 83 F.T.C. 865 (1973) (healthfulness of Wonder Bread).

[17] See In re Warner-Lambert Co., 86 F.T.C. 1398, 1461 (1975), *modified*, 562 F.2d 749 (D.C. Cir. 1977), *cert. denied*, 435 U.S. 950 (1978) (Listerine case; Commission examined manufacturer's studies of efficacy in determining whether advertisements have a "tendency and capacity to deceive"); P. Lorillard Co. v. F.T.C., 186 F.2d 52 (4th Cir. 1950) (claim of "lowest tar and nicotine" among tested cigarette brands literally true but nonetheless deceptive because actual difference in levels was negligible).

[18] See In re Kroger Co., 98 F.T.C. 639 (1981) (analysis of survey of competing grocery store prices); In re California Milk Producers Advisory Bd., 94 F.T.C. 429 (1979) (analysis of survey designed to measure attitudes toward advertisement). Surveys, sampling, and techniques for analyzing samples are discussed in Chapter 6.

acceptance was begun and fought tenaciously, the litigator will find well-defined rules for the admissibility and assessment of particular statistical techniques. That does not mean, however, that the battle cannot and should not be fought on less familiar terrain. As the examples presented in this book will repeatedly demonstrate, the keys to gaining acceptance for statistical evidence in new areas are (1) to convince the court that the factual foundation is sound, and (2) to establish intellectual and psychological links between the statistical proof advanced and the commonsense methods of reasoning to which the court would otherwise resort.

B. THE STATISTICIAN AS A RESOURCE

Quantitative data have no value in and of themselves; they assume probative force only when, after appropriate analysis by a skilled user, they prompt well-reasoned inferences by an educated factfinder. From the first day of his or her retention as an expert, the statistician in litigation must not only be that skilled user but also ensure that the factfinder is sufficiently educated to draw the appropriate inferences. The statistician must also ensure that the retaining lawyer is able to understand, evaluate, and present the case. In turn, the lawyer must understand how the statistician views his or her role in the legal process. Section 1.4 deals with the need for cooperation and mutual understanding between lawyer and expert, and Section 1.5 identifies several stages of case preparation and presentation during which the statistical expert may be particularly helpful.

§1.4   The Statistician's Concept of Self:
Scientific Idealism Versus Legal Pragmatism

For many scientific experts the greatest problem in participating in litigation is accommodating their own professional goals and standards to those of the law. As its etymology suggests, science is the search for knowledge. Ideally, that search is unfettered. The ethical scientist propounds theories and hypotheses to explain the workings of the world around him; when his theories are confounded by events in the world, he so acknowledges and seeks new explanations. As

Galileo, Thomas Huxley, John T. Scopes, and others might attest, reality often wanders far from the ideal. Nonetheless, it is probably an accurate generalization that most contemporary scientists, including statisticians, hold the ideal of science as their own and strive to attain it. The law shares with science the ultimate objective of truth, but in the legal process the search is far from unfettered. Anglo-American law long sought the truth not by objective search but by subjecting the contestants to physical ordeal, which much later evolved into the verbal competition we know as the trial. From this competition in the courtroom, the law has come to assume that the truth will emerge.

Another significant difference between the legal and scientific truth-seeking processes lies in the scope of the evidence considered. In a careful scientific investigation, anything having any conceivable relevance is scrutinized. The law also considers all things that are relevant, but *relevancy* is a term of art, and its meaning in particular situations is not always congruent with a scientist's view of what ought to be considered.[1]

The scientist in the courtroom may thus be uncomfortable in two respects: first, he or she may be disturbed at the transformation from dispassionate analyst to advocate and feel that the only reasonable way to proceed is to sit down with the other side's expert and work out whatever differences in assumptions, data, or analytical techniques may have lead to divergent conclusions. The lawyer, on the other hand, is ethically obligated to present those facts supportive of his client's position in the strongest light possible and is limited only by

---

§1.4 [1]The problem with divergent definitions of *relevance* is illustrated by an example from personal experience. In an eminent domain case tried by one of the authors, Fairbairn v. Town of Barnstable, No. 37547 (Barnstable County, Mass. Super. Ct., unpub. op., Aug. 3, 1981), the issue was whether the presence of a large supply of pure groundwater beneath the property that had been taken should be considered in valuing the property. Under the applicable legal standard, natural resources could not be assigned value unless they had been used prior to the taking or were to be used in the near future. Because there was no market for the water in the surrounding area at the time of the taking, the evidence of the groundwater's value was not admitted because no one could testify to actual or planned use.

The plaintiff's hydrological expert took the view that market conditions at the time of the taking were not an accurate measure of the groundwater's true value. In his opinion, a more important consideration was that population growth in the vicinity and the attendant likelihood of pollution of existing water supplies made future marketability a virtual certainty. Thus, he concluded, the groundwater was extremely valuable by the standards of both science and common sense. Under controlling common law, however, such evidence of future marketability, which the hydrologist viewed as the single most significant consideration in the case, was held "irrelevant" and thus inadmissible.

considerations of good faith and fairness. Second, the scientific expert is frequently frustrated by the limitations imposed by the rules of evidence. Often, the factor that in the expert's mind best explains the dispute is immaterial to the lawsuit as it has been framed or is otherwise inadmissible.

Neither of these concerns is easily addressed, but the impact of both can be minimized. A lawyer sensitive to the problem of experts' reluctance to act as advocates can emphasize that while the processes of science and the law are fundamentally different, they are not inconsistent. The expert can be reassured that he or she will initially be asked to do nothing more than conduct a scientific investigation employing his or her own standards and methods, and if the results of that investigation support the client's position, the expert will then be asked simply to present them in the most effective way possible. Weaknesses will not be hidden but will be considered in advance, explained where possible, and otherwise acknowledged forthrightly. Where the results of the investigation are adverse they will be fully discussed and taken into consideration in deciding whether to press the claim or defense or to compromise or capitulate; in no event will the expert be asked to testify to a conclusion not supported by the investigation. Above all, the expert will never be asked to argue or advocate but merely to present the results and let those in the business of advocacy argue from them.

The second type of concern presents greater problems. It may well be that an immaterial factor best explains the facts in dispute or that a proper scientific investigation would take into consideration evidence that the law deems inadmissible. There is little to be done except to lay out the problem at the earliest stages of the litigation and permit the expert to decide whether he or she can conduct a valid investigation and reach a meaningful conclusion within the confines of the law of evidence. If the answer is no, the lawyer will want to consider retaining another expert; if other experts give a similar response, the issue of the feasibility of raising the statistically proved claim or defense will have to be confronted.

§1.5 What Statisticians Do for Lawyers

Assuming that philosophical agreement between lawyer and expert can be reached, the question becomes what specific services the expert can provide and how they can be most usefully rendered. The services will usually fall into three categories: background assistance with the case as a whole, preparation of the lawyer for cross-examination, and testimony as an expert witness.

§1.5.1 Background Assistance

Any lawyer with experience in cases that turn on technical evidence will recognize that few mistakes are more serious than waiting too long to retain an expert. This is nowhere more true than in a case that will turn on statistical evidence. In the employment discrimination area many claims have been brought or fought on the basis of superficially compelling but ultimately baseless allegations, with an expert being retained only as an afterthought. Similarly, many antitrust lawyers will recall cases where there is strong circumstantial evidence of collusion on prices, but where belated statistical analysis shows that the alleged collusion could not have contributed to higher prices.

On the plaintiff's side, the expert should be retained before the complaint; on the defendant's, the expert should be retained before a binding decision to resist or to settle. As soon as a lawyer assumes responsibility for a case that may involve statistical evidence, he or she should begin interviewing statisticians and should retain one with demonstrated technical and analytical skills and with obvious promise as an educator and communicator. The lawyer should then put at the disposal of the statistician all quantitative data that appear to have any relevance to the issue being litigated.

Working from these initially disclosed data, the statistician can do at least the following:

(A) Assess the adequacy of the data and determine whether and how they can be analyzed;

(B) Evaluate the technical sophistication of the lawyer and educate him or her about the methods to be employed, focusing as much on their limitations as on their potential;

(C) Bring to the lawyer's attention other sources of relevant data that may exist and assist the lawyer in framing appropriate inquiries and, later, discovery requests;

(D) Assist the lawyer in identifying, interviewing, and retaining other types of experts that may be needed; and

(E) Perform a preliminary analysis of available data to enable the lawyer to judge whether the claim or defense should be raised in the first place and to make a preliminary evaluation of the settlement value of the case.

§1.5.2   Cross-Examination Preparation

In any technical case it is critical for the trial lawyer to be able to confront the other side's expert intelligently, at least on those few issues that are pivotal in the case. On cross-examination the lawyer must initially demonstrate sufficient grasp of the opposing expert's concepts and jargon to generate credibility and lure the expert into a confrontation. (See Section 9.2.1, where methods of presenting and attacking statistical evidence are discussed.) Thereafter, questions directed at the weaknesses in the opponent's case must be framed in such a way that they are brought across to the finder of fact. The ability of the lawyer to achieve these objectives will depend in large part on the statistician's ability as an educator.

Ideally, the lawyer will have some familiarity with general statistical concepts and may even have some training or experience with the particular techniques being used in the case. Almost invariably, however, each case will involve some new statistical wrinkle that is beyond the capabilities of even the most scientifically knowledgeable trial lawyer. The expert must take the lawyer as he finds him or her and guide counsel in detail through each of the pertinent statistical issues. While it may be sufficient on direct examination to rely on the statistician to communicate the case, effective cross-examination requires a high level of genuine understanding of the issues involved. Once this has been achieved, the expert can further assist by identifying specifically the most vulnerable areas in the opponent's case. While the final framing of questions must ultimately be left to the lawyer (and questions written out in advance are an invitation to disaster in any event), the statistician can contribute by proposing key words and phrases and formulating hypotheticals that will be particularly unsettling to the opposing expert.

§1.5.3   The Statistician as an Expert Witness

Expert testimony in court is the tip of the iceberg that is the role of the statistical expert. (See Chapter 9, generally.) But like the tip of the iceberg, it is the most visible part of the total package. Accordingly, potential for success in the courtroom is the single most important criterion in selecting an expert.

Among those attributes that are good predictors of success are broad knowledge of the field; practical as well as academic experience; the ability to communicate complex ideas in straightforward, noncondescending, and persuasive language; and character and integrity, both in fact and in appearance. Previous trial experience tends to be greatly overrated. A history of earlier testimony seldom has any positive effect on judges or jurors, and, in any event, it is no substitute for knowledge, experience, credibility, and communication skills. Too much experience as a witness can backfire when a skillful cross-examiner evokes the "hired gun" syndrome.[1]

The essence of good expert testimony is effective teaching. With few exceptions, the statistical expert will be introducing the judge and jury to a new and perhaps threatening field. In the course of a few hours (Polonius might have been talking about expert testimony when he observed that brevity is the soul of wit)[2] the expert witness will be required to interpret background concepts such as sampling, probability, and significance; to explain and justify the particular methodology applicable to the case; and to present the results persuasively. The expert can be made to feel more comfortable with this multifaceted task by a reminder that direct testimony is nothing more than a seminar for intelligent but technically unsophisticated lay people. Strategies such as inviting the expert to lecture briefly on very simple concepts early in the testimony can serve to acclimate him or her to the courtroom environment and to establish an effective teaching style before the difficult and controversial material begins. (See

---

§1.5 [1] In areas of the law where expert testimony is routine, such as medical malpractice and eminent domain, many experts prepare and give expert testimony as a full-time job. In one particularly skillful cross-examination observed by one of the authors, it was brought out that a real estate appraiser had spent the entire month preceding the trial giving expert testimony for substantial fees in several different cases, and that expert testimony had been his sole occupation for most of his adult life. While the authors are aware of no relevant scientific studies, it seems reasonable to assume that credibility is enhanced if an expert is shown to be an active practitioner in a particular field who, in deference to his expertise, is called upon occasionally to render opinions in court. Statistical evidence is still sufficiently rare that a cadre of full-time experts seems not to have developed, although that will undoubtedly change.

[2] The reference is to Act II, scene ii of *Hamlet*. Polonius's greatest failing, of course, was his inability to follow his own advice. Regrettably, that failing is shared by all too many experts.

Section 9.2.2, Maximizing the Persuasiveness of the Statistical Expert.)

Technical cases frequently turn on the competing experts' ability to withstand cross-examination. If each expert is truly knowledgeable, is an effective communicator, and is testifying to a defensible result, then he or she will withstand cross-examination. An inexperienced expert may not believe this; therefore, repeated moot cross-examinations directed at the major weaknesses in the case may be of considerable help in instilling a sense of confidence. Above all, the expert must be encouraged to perceive the coming cross-examination as he would an intellectual debate in his own discipline. The statistician can best enhance his credibility on cross-examination by holding tenaciously to the essence of his findings, by dealing openly and fairly with weaknesses, and by resisting efforts to personalize the cross-examination, keeping his remarks on a calm and dispassionate level.

With the increasing popularity of alternative dispute resolution procedures, the visible part of the expert's role often extends beyond the courtroom. It is sometimes helpful to include experts in settlement conferences, to explain the strengths of their own case, and to raise questions about the opponent's weaknesses. Experts can also play a prominent role in "mini-trials," in which encapsulated versions of the opposing cases are presented in an informal setting before decisionmakers for the two sides. A mini-trial may involve an abbreviated version of the traditional direct and cross-examination. In a highly technical case, however, it may be more productive to allot limited speaking time to an expert for each side and then to permit the two to question each other, all in the presence of the decisionmakers. The purpose of this is to enable the decisionmakers to make an objective assessment of the relative strengths and weaknesses of their cases in an atmosphere that lacks the inhibiting artificiality of the courtroom. Having done so, they can move on to a private settlement conference, with the experts remaining on call to resolve technical questions. For a more extensive discussion of the role of experts in a case's pre-trial stage, see Section 9.4.

§1.5.4 The Statistician as a Computer Expert

Litigation in which computers are involved has become far more common in the last few years as a result of expanded use of quantitative evidentiary techniques and the proliferation of personal and business computers. Every case involving statistical evidence is likely to be a "computer case" in the sense that a computer will have been used for the collection, storage, and analysis of the relevant data, which may have been retrieved from the opposing party's computer. See Section 2.2, where the use of data gathered by adversaries is discussed. Accordingly, the case may require a computer expert to explain and justify the reliance on other than firsthand investigative work. More often than not, this need can be filled by the statistician who is supervising the analysis.

From an evidentiary standpoint, the statistician will be required briefly to establish his or her familiarity with and supervisory responsibility for the reception of the data and their organization, coding, entry, storage, analysis, and retrieval. Unless an untested or otherwise unusual computer system has been employed, the expert need do no more than describe it in very general terms and comment on the routine use of comparable systems by others in the field. The expert must allay any concerns about the delegation of work by emphasizing that the delegation is routine and in fact essential. See Section 9.3.1, where evidentiary considerations are discussed in more detail. If the expert is qualified to choose the system and supervise its operation, he or she will be more than qualified to give the background testimony. This testimony will, incidentally, afford the expert yet another opportunity to become comfortable with the business of testifying and to demonstrate to the finder of fact the extent of his or her knowledge and teaching skills.

C. WHY LAWYERS NEED TO KNOW STATISTICS

Each of the aspects of the statistician's role as defined in Section 1.5 envisions some degree of cooperation and participation on the part of the lawyer, which in turn presume some understanding of statistics. Whatever the lawyer's initial level of understanding, he or she must have the willingness to improve it and must bring to that effort the same dedication that a good trial lawyer brings to more traditional legal tasks.

Sections 1.6 through 1.9 describe the lawyer's role in a statistical case. The lawyer must be able to assess the weight of the statistical evidence for settlement purposes, plan the strategy of presentation of the evidence, relate factual issues involved in a particular case to the expert's credentials in qualifying him or her as a witness, and assist the expert in translating statistical evidence for the finder of fact. Each of these sections might be viewed as an argument for the lawyer's acquiring a minimum level of competence in statistical methodology.

§1.6 The Lawyer's Duty to Evaluate the Case

Every trial lawyer has an ongoing duty to his or her client to evaluate the case objectively for settlement purposes, a duty that begins at the very first meeting with the client and continues through the final disposition of the appeal. Obviously, the lawyer who cannot understand the essential proof in the case cannot offer a meaningful evaluation. While the lawyer's evaluation of any case will become more refined as the facts and the law are more fully developed, an experienced trial lawyer usually can offer right at the start a rough approximation of what issues need to be resolved and what a claim may be worth. In a case that turns on statistical evidence, this skill is directly proportional to the lawyer's grasp of statistical theory. A lawyer who does not know enough about statistics to make an informed judgment on whether the case ought to be brought in the first place may be well advised to decide at least that it ought to be brought by someone else.

§1.7 Considerations of Presentation and Strategy

A reasonable grasp of statistical method and theory is particularly helpful in deciding how the case will be tried. The statistician is an expert in quantitative analysis but not necessarily in persuasion. Unless, however, the lawyer can participate knowledgeably in structuring the statistician's presentation, the determination of trial strategy, the essence of the advocate's role, will fall to the statistician by default.

If the lawyer has gone through the effort of learning the basic principles of statistics and the specifics of those applications that are important to the case, he or she is in a unique position to frame a presentation that will be comprehensible, meaningful, and perhaps even entertaining to a lay audience. The knowledgeable lawyer can recall the hurdles encountered in his or her own learning process, as well as the breakthroughs that occurred and the illustrations and aids that facilitated them. The less painful the learning process can be made for the trier of fact, the more likely a statistical case will prove persuasive. (See Section 9.2.2, Maximizing the Persuasiveness of the Statistical Expert.)

§1.8 Evidentiary Considerations

The rules of law governing expert testimony are deceptively simple. Rule 702 of the Federal Rules of Evidence provides only that "If scientific, technical, or other specialized knowledge will assist the trier of fact to understand the evidence or to determine a fact at issue, a witness qualified as an expert by knowledge, skill, experience, training or education, may testify thereto in the form of an opinion or otherwise."[1] On its face, the rule suggests that the testimony of a reasonably competent expert ought to be admissible in almost any case, but in practice, trial judges are likely to be far more restrictive: many of them require that a specific relationship be shown between the witness's training or experience and the issue at hand, and some may insist on a detailed explanation of the probative value of the expert's analysis.[2] See Section 9.3.1, which considers evidentiary problems.

§1.8 [1] Fed. R. Evid. 702.

[2] The practical problems likely to be encountered are illustrated by the case of Presseisen v. Swarthmore College, 442 F. Supp. 593 (E.D. Pa. 1977). In *Presseisen*, the plaintiffs introduced a statistical study called regression analysis (see Chapter 8) in an effort to show sex discrimination in salary among the Swarthmore faculty. The plaintiff's expert, Dr. deCani, then chairman of the statistics department at the University of Pennsylvania, testified that women took longer on the average than men to reach a given faculty rank and had salaries that were significantly lower than those of comparably qualified men. The court cited several reasons for rejecting Dr. deCani's analysis and for finding for the defendants. Its final and perhaps most telling criticism was that "[a]lthough there is no question that Dr. deCani is an eminently qualified statistician, we do not believe that his expertise extends into the discipline that governs what goes into the factors to be considered in assessing the amount of an individual's salary in a college." Id. at 616. The court suggested that the plaintiffs might have laid a foundation for Dr. deCani's testimony by bringing in an academic dean from an institution comparable to Swarthmore to discuss the subjective and qualitative factors that went into hiring and promotion. (The Swarthmore provost had testified for the defendant.)

It is hoped that after completing this book the reader will appreciate that the court's critique is flawed in many respects. Much oversimplified, Dr. deCani's purpose was to disregard the subjective factors the court thought so important and to analyze salary in light of the objective factors (such as age, degree, and experience) that were available from Swarthmore's records. Nonetheless, the problem illustrated is a recurring one, and the trial lawyer must take care to give the statistical expert a meaningful education in the nonstatistical facets of the case.

Once again, the lawyer who is not well grounded in statistical theory will be unprepared to overcome these obstacles. One who is unfamiliar with statistics will be hard pressed to explain to an incredulous judge why an epidemiologist is now qualified to express an opinion about employment discrimination, and the uninitiated lawyer will have equal difficulty in persuading a judge that a model of price behavior is anything more than rank speculation. On the other side of the coin, the lawyer who is statistically well prepared will be ready, willing and able to advise the court when the opposing expert's background bears no relation to his present testimony or when the other side's mathematical model is based on demonstrably false premises.

§1.9 The Lawyer as an Intermediary

In any technical case the trial lawyer's most important role is as intermediary among the scientific, legal, and lay worlds. It is the lawyer who must bridge the logical and linguistic gaps between the expert witness and the finder of fact. On direct examination of his own expert, it is the lawyer's responsibility to see that the testimony moves smoothly and unhesitatingly from the simplest, most readily understandable concepts to the more complex and obscure. The lawyer must also work with the expert to choose a style of presentation that is comprehensible without being condescending. It is important that the finder of fact is introduced to statistical terminology gradually and without any irritating failures to explain unfamiliar terms. The lawyer plays a similar role on cross-examination, first by demonstrating a mastery of the subject matter and then by ensuring that the judge and jury will be able to grasp weaknesses in the opposing expert's case. (See Section 9.5, where problems arising in the cross-examination of the statistical expert are considered in more detail.)

Although the expert has primary responsibility for the development of the facts, it is the sole responsibility of the lawyer to see that there is a proper fit between the facts and the applicable law. The lawyer must have sufficient grasp of statistical theory and methods to understand what has happened in the precedents on which he now relies and to ascertain that the proof he is about to offer is consistent with those precedents. He or she must be able to bring to the attention of the statistician aspects of the proposed proof that have been rejected or criticized in prior cases and must work with the expert to meet anticipated attacks. It is up to the lawyer to understand the burden of persuasion in the case at hand and to decide whether the statistical presentation designed by the expert is adequate to meet that burden. None of this is possible, of course, if the lawyer can do no more than hand the problem to the statistician and then at trial invite the expert to state his or her findings.

D. HOW MUCH STATISTICAL THEORY LAWYERS NEED TO KNOW

By now it should be clear that lawyers trying cases involving statistical evidence ought to know something about statistical theory; just how much is a more difficult question. Clearly, any lawyer who takes on a case involving statistics needs to be able to understand and explain at least the elementary concepts alluded to in this chapter, including sampling, probability, significance, chance explanation, relationships and differences, and modeling. The lawyer should also know how to acquire more specific knowledge and be willing to do so. By the time of trial, he or she must be able to understand in some detail the theories and methods that the statistician proposes to use. This does not mean that the lawyer must be able to do the mathematical analysis, although experimenting with simple data is not a bad idea. He or she should, however, be able to explain each of the steps involved on a general conceptual level and should understand the mathematical details of the analysis to the extent required to cross-examine specific weaknesses in the opponent's case.

This may sound extremely demanding, but in fact it is not. Trial lawyers regularly demonstrate an admirable capacity to understand such diverse fields as anatomy and structural engineering; there is no reason why they cannot do the same with statistics. While the difficulty of the effort will be less than anticipated, the results should exceed expectations. Because so few have undertaken the effort, the grasp of elementary statistics will add an exotic and powerful weapon to the trial lawyer's arsenal of methods of persuasion.

The remaining sections in this chapter illustrate three types of problems that can be addressed by statistical methodology and introduce concepts that form the basis for drawing conclusions from data. Sections 1.10 and 1.11 describe situations in which statistical methods can be used to demonstrate that two numbers or sets of numbers are different from or are related to one another in some fashion, while Section 1.12 illustrates the power of statistical methods to predict future values of numbers that are relevant to a lawsuit. Sections 1.13, 1.14, and 1.15 illuminate the mystery of how statisticians determine how much weight to place on their statistical findings.

§1.10 Demonstrating the Significance of a Difference

Numerical evidence is often introduced to show that two things are different. To take a simple example, it might be introduced to show that two pieces of property have different values, or in a more complex situation, to demonstrate that a certain group of people within a population is underrepresented in some body that has been drawn from that population. Assuming that a raw numerical underrepresentation can be shown, the practical question becomes whether that difference can reasonably be attributed to chance factors, as the following example illustrates.

> *The Case of the Biased Board:* The enabling legislation for a state university in the Southwest empowers the governor to appoint 20 members per year to five-year terms on the 100-member board of overseers. A Hispanic-American legal defense group has brought a lawsuit charging the governor with discriminating against Hispanics in his appointments, in violation of the antidiscrimination provisions of the enabling legislation. The legal defense group relies in large part on the numerical data set out in Exhibit 1.10(a).

EXHIBIT 1.10(a)
Data for the Case of the Biased Board

	1977	1978	1979	1980	1981	1982	1983
Hispanic % in Population	10.2	9.8	10.3	10.7	11.2	11.4	11.7
Hispanics on Board	9	10	9	8	9	8	9

The plaintiffs point out that in six of the seven years of the incumbent's term, the percentage of Hispanics on the board has been less than their percentage of the total population. However, common sense would dictate that a court determine whether the observed disparities are in some sense significant before interfering in the operation of the executive branch.

From a practical standpoint, the disparities are highly significant to the Hispanic plaintiffs. For certain categories of important decisions, 10% of the board members voting together can block action and require the proposal under consideration to be reformulated by the administration. In six of the seven years the Hispanics lost the block voting veto they would have had if their representation on the board had precisely matched their percentage of the population.

The defendants respond, however, that the disparities are meaningless because they are *statistically insignificant.* That is, the observed fluctuations in Hispanic membership on the board are nothing more than what one would expect as a matter of chance, assuming that the governor's actual intent was to exercise his appointment authority in an entirely nondiscriminatory manner.

The question at this point is whether statistics can provide a means to resolve the dispute, and the answer is a qualified yes. Statistical evidence cannot illuminate the governor's state of mind, nor can it assist the court in deciding what constitutes actionable discrimination. Statistical techniques are available, however, that permit one to evaluate differences between expected (in an ideal world) and observed frequencies and to quantify the likelihood that such differences would be found (again in an ideal world) purely as a matter of chance. These limited determinations, properly made and presented, may constitute circumstantial evidence from which inferences can be drawn about such things as state of mind and the magnitude of legally material discrepancies. The evaluation of the significance of differences is discussed throughout this book, primarily in chapters 4, 5, and 6.

§1.11 Demonstrating Relationships

Numerical evidence can also be used to show that two things appear to be related; for example, it might suggest that the rate of small business failure rises as the prime interest rate rises. The practical question is whether the apparent relationship reflects causation or is merely a chance observation.

EXHIBIT 1.11(a)
Hiring Test Scores v. Performance Scores

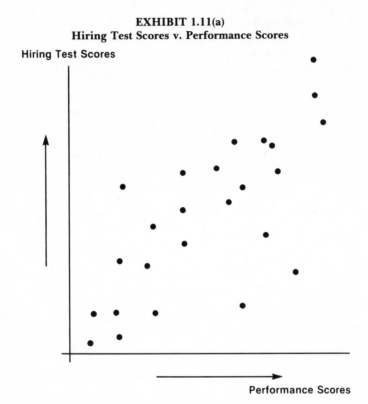

Testing Employment Tests: In many employment discrimination cases, the burden ultimately falls on the defendant employer to show that a particular test or other selection criterion is meaningfully related to job performance. Assume here that the employer is trying to justify a written mechanical aptitude test that is given to machine operator applicants. Each year the employer gives each operator on the payroll a quantitative evaluation, which is based primarily on the number of parts completed per day and the percentage of the individual operator's completed parts that are rejected by quality control.

As Exhibit 1.11(a), a graph of the scores, suggests, there does seem to be some relationship between an operator's score on the hiring test and his or her subsequent performance: those who got the lowest test scores at the time they were hired are clustered at the bottom of the performance scale, while most of the more efficient workers seem to have had high test scores. There are, however, a few exceptions: some operators who scored poorly when hired turned out to be very efficient and vice versa.

The question again is whether statistics can somehow assess and pass judgment on the significance of the apparent relationship, and the answer is once again a qualified yes. Calculation of a statistic called the *correlation coefficient* will permit the relationship between the two quantities to be expressed in numerical fashion (e.g., .637 or .891). Reference to appropriate tables will permit the statistician to make a further statement about the likelihood that the observed relationship is attributable to chance rather than to a real relationship between test scores and performance.

Regardless of the results, however, the statistician will not be able to say that there *is* a causal relationship between test scores and job performance — only that the apparent relationship is most unlikely to have occurred as a matter of chance alone. So-called spurious correlations do occur. Consider, for example, the well-publicized and usually unerring correlation between the performance of the stock market and the conference of the Super Bowl winner.[1] But where the likelihood of the observed correlation being attributable to chance is very small (e.g., one or two in 1,000), common sense and sound judicial discretion should enable some reasonable conclusions to be drawn about the job-relatedness of the test. The correlation coefficient is the subject of Chapter 7.

§1.12 Describing and Predicting Behavior

Statistical evidence is sometimes used to describe how an industry or other system works at a given point in time. Such a description is often referred to as a *model* and may be used to predict how the system will work at some other time. The key to the accuracy of the prediction is, of course, the accuracy of the original model.[1] The following example illustrates that models can be used to inform judgments and that they can be used to mislead.

---

§1.11 [1] Between 1967 and 1978, there was a perfect correlation between the original league of the Super Bowl winner and the performance of the stock market. Each year in which the Super Bowl winner in January had originally been a National Football League team, the stock market finished the year higher, and each year the winner was originally an American Football League team, the market finished lower. While this correlation is perfect in a statistical sense, the authors hesitate to recommend that the reader base his or her investment decisions on it. See L. Koppett, Viewpoint, Sports Illustrated, Apr. 23, 1979, at 8.

§1.12 [1] See Chapter 8 for a discussion of methods for determining the reliability and accuracy of predictions resulting from statistical models.

Corrugated Container Litigation, *The Plaintiffs' Case:*[2] In this private antitrust action, the plaintiffs, who were purchasers of corrugated cardboard containers, alleged that during the years 1963 to 1974 the manufacturers of the containers had kept prices artificially high through an illicit agreement. At trial the plaintiffs sought to show, through statistical evidence, that during the "conspiracy period" the container prices were significantly higher than what one would have expected in a competitive market.

Using data from that period, 1963 to 1974, the plaintiffs' expert designed a statistical model that incorporated the influences on prices of production costs, demand, availability of raw materials, price trends in the economy as a whole, and the fact that price controls were in effect from 1971 to early 1974. This model accounted for prices during the 1963-1974 conspiracy period with considerable accuracy.

The plaintiffs' next step was to use the model to predict prices for the period following the alleged conspiracy. Their theory was as follows: since the model appeared to describe price behavior accurately, it should predict prices in the years following 1974, the year in which the alleged conspiracy ended, as accurately as it predicted prices during the conspiracy years. If the model failed to predict prices during the post-conspiracy period, the factors influencing prices must have changed.

In fact, the actual prices after 1974 dropped below the predicted prices. The plaintiffs' expert concluded that since the model had predicted well during the earlier period there must have been a change in circumstances, which he identified as the end of the conspiracy that had artificially inflated prices in the 1963-1974 period.

As with other areas of statistical analysis, the interpretation of results derived from models cannot be left to statistical techniques alone. Common sense and good judgment are the ultimate check on

---

[2] In re Corrugated Container Antitrust Litig., 441 F. Supp. 921 (J.P.M.D.L. 310, 1977). This litigation followed a Supreme Court decision in favor of the government in an earlier civil price-fixing action, United States v. Container Corp. of Am., 393 U.S. 333 (1969) and a grand jury investigation of price fixing in the industry in the mid-1970s. The discussion in the text draws on M. Finkelstein and H. Levenbach, Regression Estimates of Damages in Price Fixing Cases, 46 Law and Contemporary Problems 145 (1984), and on discussions with Dr. Robert Larner of Charles River Associates, Boston, Mass., and Dr. Michael Mann of the Department of Economics, Boston College. Dr. Larner's firm consulted with the defendant in the *Corrugated Container* litigation.

For a reported case involving an analysis similar to that discussed in the text, see Spray-Rite Service Corp. v. Monsanto Co., 684 F.2d 1226, 1240-1241 (7th Cir. 1982). It is noteworthy that in *Spray-Rite* the court of appeals made only passing reference to the plaintiff's regression analysis, even though that analysis was the basis of the substantial damage award, one of the major issues on appeal.

the possibility of being misled. From a statistical standpoint the plaintiffs' argument in *Corrugated Container* seemed persuasive: the chosen factors explained price behavior quite adequately during the conspiracy; when these factors ceased to explain price it was reasonable to attribute their failure to the end of the conspiracy. The defendant's statistician was unpersuaded, however, and countered with a model of his own.

> **Corrugated Container Litigation,** *The Defendant's Case:*[3] The defendant's model for explaining price behavior was like the plaintiffs' model in that essentially the same explanatory factors were used and predicted prices were compared to actual prices. The defendant's expert based his model, however, on actual prices during the later *competitive* period rather than the conspiracy period. He then predicted prices backward in time into the conspiracy period. Comparing actual and predicted prices during the alleged conspiracy period, he found that the actual prices were noticeably *lower* than what his model had predicted. In other words, the prices predicted by his model of a competitive, nonconspiratorial market exceeded those actually charged in the allegedly conspiratorial market.

The net result of the battle of the experts was that one found prices to be unexpectedly high during the conspiracy period and the other found them to be unexpectedly low. The jury found for the defendant. While it is always dangerous to speculate about cause and effect in jury verdicts, perhaps the defendant's counter-analysis alerted the jurors to the fallibility of statistical inferences.

In the *Corrugated Container* case, two groups of reputable experts used accepted statistical techniques on carefully gathered data and reached directly opposite conclusions. There is nothing wrong with either model in a mathematical or theoretical sense; both account for observed events with reasonable accuracy. The problem lies in making the leap from accounting for the known to predicting the unknown. In making this leap the statistician must assume that no unexpected new influences on price behavior have been introduced between the two time periods being compared.

Consider a model designed to account for American gasoline prices during the years 1965 through 1972. The influences on prices presumably would include such factors as general economic perfor-

---

[3] In re Corrugated Container Antitrust Litig., 441 F. Supp. 921 (J.P.M.D.L. 310, 1977).

mance, the volume of car sales, the amount of new oil discovered, and transportation costs. The model would probably account for gasoline price behavior during the designated period with considerable accuracy.

Now attempt to use such a model to predict gasoline prices in 1973 and succeeding years. Its predictive value would be negligible, since history had introduced new and controlling factors such as the politics and respective states of mind of the rulers of Egypt, Syria, Iraq and Saudi Arabia, the prevailing view of Israeli national security in the Knesset, the level of terrorist activity in the Middle East, and the stability of the Iranian monarchy. By the same token, a post-1973 model that included these new factors would utterly fail to account for price behavior in the age of relative innocence before the first Arab oil embargo.

This is precisely the dilemma that bedeviled the competing experts in the *Corrugated Container* case. Each model seemed adequate on its own terms, but the world had changed during the period under investigation: new influential factors not identified by either expert had apparently intruded themselves and rendered meaningless the original models. The moral of the story is that while statistical modeling may suggest or confirm judgments, numbers do not make judgments; people do.

§1.13   Chance as an Explanation for Observed Phenomena

The fundamental goal in many statistical procedures is to determine whether chance alone can explain the results. Only if a chance explanation can be ruled out with a fair degree of certainty does it become reasonable to suspect that the statistical results are caused by some other factor. The following example illustrates the problem.

Sampling Yankee Stadium: Assume that 50,000 people are seated in Yankee Stadium. Assume further that the group has been specially selected to include 25,000 adult men and 25,000 adult women. The particular 25,000 men and 25,000 women chosen have been selected at random, such as by social security number.

Out of this stadium crowd, 100 people are then selected at random (for example, the 8th person in the 4th row of each of the first 100 sections). In such a sample, the commonsense expectation is that there would be about 50 men and about 50 women. If the breakdown were

55/45, or even 40/60, we would not be terribly surprised and would probably ascribe the discrepancy to "chance." If, however, the composition by sex turned out to be 75/25 or 80/20, we might begin to suspect that the total crowd was not as evenly divided as we had been led to believe, or that the seating arrangement within the stadium had something to do with sex. We would become particularly suspicious if similar breakdowns were observed in subsequent groups of 100.

The difficult question is at what point we should abandon our assumption that an observed deviation from the expected 50/50 breakdown is merely a random fluctuation. This assumption is usually called the *null hypothesis,* the hypothesis that the observed results are the product of chance, and is the working assumption in every inferential statistical analysis.[1] A number of techniques permit the precise measurement of the likelihood, or *probability*, that the observed results would occur if the null hypothesis were true. This probability is called a *p*-value[2] and is expressed as a decimal number less than or equal to one. Thus, if we found that the probability that an 80/20 sex breakdown would occur in a truly unbiased sample was less than one in 100, we would say that the *p*-value was less than .01 ($p < .01$).

The calculation of the *p*-value provides a means of quantifying the probability that an observed discrepancy or relationship is attributable to chance, but this calculation alone does not tell us when to abandon the null hypothesis. Once again, a judgment is required.

At the start of many statistical research projects, the investigator determines how low the *p*-value will have to be before the results of the research will be accepted. For example, it might be determined that the results will not be accepted unless the probability of occurrence by chance is less than 1 in 50, that is, unless the *p*-value is less than .02. When the statistical analysis yields a *p*-value that is less than the predetermined criterion, the results are deemed *statistically significant.*[3] If the results are not statistically significant, they are rejected

§1.13 [1] See generally, R. Winkler and W. Hays, Statistics: Probability, Inference and Decision 414 (2d ed. 1975).

[2] Id. at 442.

[3] Many scientific disciplines have established conventions for the acceptance of research results. In the social sciences (psychology, sociology, and anthropology, for example), research results are often deemed to be statistically significant if the *p*-value is less than .05. See D. Baldus and J. Cole, Statistical Proof of Discrimination 291 (1980). This convention has also been recognized for certain purposes by the Equal Employment Opportunity Commission. See Documentation of Impact and Validity Evidence, 29 C.F.R. §1607.15(B)(5) (1982).

because of the unacceptably high probability that they occurred as a matter of chance.[4]

Other circumstances can be imagined in which a much finer level of tolerance would be required. If, for example, 600 members of a group of 1,000 persons testing a new drug experienced amelioration of their symptoms over the test period, one would want to have a high degree of certainty that those results were not attributable to chance before permitting advertising and distribution of the drug.

The appropriate level of statistical significance is thus a matter of choice, perhaps on the part of the investigator and perhaps on the part of the recipient of the investigator's report. The choice will not be arbitrary; it will depend on the extent to which error is acceptable. While a 1-in-20 chance of error might be acceptable if the only consequence is the erroneous acceptance of an anthropological theory, a chance of error of 1 in 1,000 might be far too high if the consequence is a hazard to human health.

The same principles are applicable to the assessment of chance as an explanation for more complex statistical results. For instance, the process of assessing observed relationships involves hypothesizing that the relationship, such as that between test scores and job performance in the example in Section 1.11, is due merely to chance. An evaluation is then made of the probability that the observed relationship would be found if the null hypothesis were true. Depending on the purpose of the analysis, a p-value can be established below which the null hypothesis will be rejected and an inference drawn that the observed relationship is attributable to something other than chance.

§1.14 Interpreting the Significance of Statistical Evidence

The fact that a discrepancy or a correspondence turns out to be statistically significant does not mean that it has *practical* significance. *Statistical* significance means that the probability that the observed event was due to chance is below a predetermined standard. For a

---

[4]The complement of the level of statistical significance is sometimes termed the *confidence* level. Thus, if it is found that the p-level is less than .05, it is sometimes said that the confidence level for the analysis is 95%. The use of the term confidence level, while widespread, is rather misleading, because the calculation of a p-value does nothing more than yield the probability that a particular result would occur as a matter of chance; it says nothing about alternative explanatory hypotheses.

finding to be practically significant, it must have some influence on a legal decisionmaker faced with a choice among alternative explanations for the event.

Consider again the data presented in Exhibit 1.10(a). It might well be the case that the pattern of discrepancies between observed and expected Hispanic representation on the board of overseers would yield a *p*-value that a statistician would consider statistically significant. It is another question, however, whether a judge or other decisionmaker would consider a discrepancy of only one or two board members to be of practical significance. Practical significance is thus that magnitude of disparity or that degree of correspondence that will be persuasive to a decisionmaker. It is not a statistical concept, but rather an imprecise term whose meaning is determined on a case-by-case basis.

A closely related idea is that of *legal* significance, which is that magnitude of discrepancy or degree of correspondence that will cause a statistical analysis to be accepted by a court as probative evidence. Like practical significance, legal significance has no precise statistical definition. In the employment discrimination context, some courts have attached legal significance to particular levels of statistical significance,[1] but for the most part its determination will depend on a court's ad hoc assessment of such factors as the adequacy of the data, the comprehensiveness of the analysis, and the credibility of the expert witnesses.

§1.15 The Concept of Probability and Its Relationship to Causation

The adversary process is designed to decide ultimate issues of fact by juxtaposing opponents' explanations of the circumstances giving rise to the legal action: in a discrimination case, the circumstances may be an observed absence of minority employees; in an antitrust

---

§1.14 [1] See Castaneda v. Partida, 430 U.S. 482, 496 n.17 (1976); Contreras v. City of Los Angeles, 656 F.2d 1267, 1273 (9th Cir. 1981); NAACP v. Siebels, 616 F.2d 812, 817 n.13 (5th Cir. 1980). The *Siebels* case is particularly interesting because it adopts a standard of significance from a sociology textbook without discussing why what is significant to a sociologist should be significant to a court. For an illustration of a court attempting to reconcile conflicting notions of statistical significance, "human reason," and legal effect, see Johnson v. Shreveport Garment Co., 422 F. Supp. 526, 539-540 (W.D. La. 1977), *aff'd*, 577 F.2d 1132 (5th Cir. 1978).

case, a decline in sales, allegedly due to a competitor's trade practices; in a products liability case, the occurrence of an automobile accident. In each case there is at least one explanation that would be sufficient to relieve the defendant of liability, such as a dearth of qualified minority workers in the relevant geographic area, a general business downturn affecting industry-wide sales, or misuse of the vehicle that caused it to crash. Inculpatory explanations would be intentional discrimination by the employer, illegal tie-in sales by the competitor, or defective design by the manufacturer.

Statistical evidence does not prove or disprove particular inculpatory or exculpatory explanations because it cannot show what caused the particular result that is of interest to the factfinder. Statistical testing can, however, indicate the likelihood that a particular history of events could occur by chance. A strong statistical relationship between two events, such as race and the probability of being hired or the commission of an unfair trade practice and a decline in a competitor's sales, tempts the logical mind to infer a causal connection between the events. By eliminating chance as an alternative causal explanation and by showing that there is a weak relationship between other events and the outcome of interest, statistics may support the inference of an inculpatory explanation. The opposing party's task is then to show that there are innocent reasons for the relationships observed, or that the circumstantial evidence offered as proof by the other party is otherwise unpersuasive.

Thus, while statistical evidence cannot be used to prove causation, it can be used to support or attack theories of causation by eliminating alternative explanations for the observed phenomenon. To provide the strongest inference, statistical evidence must be based on accurate, relevant, and appropriate data and be of high statistical significance. When no substantial exculpatory explanations remain, the factfinder may be willing to take an additional logical step and conclude that the prohibited activity must have caused the outcome observed.

CHAPTER TWO

Data Acquisition and Analysis*

*This chapter was prepared by David W. Peterson, Ph.D, statistician, president of Personnel Research, Inc., Adjunct Professor of Business Administration, Fuqua School of Business, and Senior Lecturer, Duke University Law School.

§2.0   Introduction

Chapter 1 outlines in broad terms the utility to litigators of statistics, statisticians, and statistical analysis. Statistical analysis using any of the approaches discussed in the following chapters requires data. In this chapter we consider general problems related to the acquisition and analysis of data and describe some of the common features of statistical analyses, particularly those analyses involving substantial amounts of data. The goal of this chapter is to alert the litigator to several phases of the data acquisition and analysis process that might not be anticipated by one overseeing such a project for the first time.

Statistical analysis often begins with a collection of one or more sets of data. Because the scope, quality, and completeness of the data collected exert an enormous influence on the form an analysis can take and on the interpretation one can place on the results, great care must be taken to ensure that the data underlying a study are as complete and reliable as possible. Problems arising in the data acquisition phase of a statistical analysis are considered in Sections 2.1 and 2.2.

Once the data are in hand, chances are that they will not be in a form convenient for analysis. If the body of data is large, it may be most efficient to use a computer to assist in the analysis, even though this requires that the information be converted into a form suitable for use by a computer. Entering the data into a computer and checking their accuracy once entered make up the second phase of data analysis, discussed in Sections 2.3 and 2.4.

After the information has been entered into the computer, the statistical calculations are undertaken in accordance with one or more computer programs. In some circumstances the creation of a program is a major task. Sections 2.5 and 2.6 highlight features of this task and characteristics of programs especially important to litigators.

The fourth and final phase considered in this chapter is the choice of a type of analysis. Whether or not a computer is used, the analysis of the data must be governed by some theory or logical process that is consistent with the litigant's legal theory and with sound numerical and statistical principles. Different types of analysis having varying data requirements are discussed in Sections 2.7, 2.8, and 2.9. Section 2.10 describes the way in which statisticians construct models of a process, formulate questions that are testable by statistical methods, and draw conclusions from the analysis. This section leads into Chapter 3 and the subsequent chapters, which describe the statistical methods useful in addressing specific factual problems of proof in litigation.

A. THE DATA ACQUISITION PHASE OF STATISTICAL ANALYSIS

Since a statistical analysis requires data, the litigant using statistics is nearly always faced with tasks or questions relating to the acquisition of suitable data. Two types of data acquisition situations can be distinguished. In the first situation, suitable data have not been collected or are unavailable, and it is necessary to acquire information from *primary sources* such as interviews or experiments (see Section 2.1). In the second, all or most of the data have already been collected, in which case the process by which they were collected must be examined to determine their usefulness. (See Section 2.2).

§2.1 Gathering Your Own Data

Gathering data from original or primary sources is in many respects the ideal way to commence a statistical analysis. Advantages to collecting data from primary sources include being able to specify precisely the size of the group or number of items to be surveyed or measured, or to specify the precise time-span, geographic coverage, or other relevant qualities of the measurements. Another advantage is in prescribing the variable to be measured, i.e., the exact measurement to be taken, question to be asked, or instrument to be used. Furthermore, primary source data acquisition allows one to choose whether the information is recorded initially on paper, audio tape, photographic film or some other medium, and whether it is recorded in the form of an essay, a set of numerical values, a short answer selected from a list of possible answers, or some other format. Control over the details of the data collection process permits custody of the data from the collection through the analysis phases and ensures that any anomalies appearing late in the analysis phase can be traced back to particular incidents during the data collection.

Data collection can, on the other hand, be very expensive and time-consuming. One probably would not, for example, seriously consider surveying all households in the state of Michigan to determine the racial composition of the group of residents who would be willing to work in automobile assembly plants. Even though such information might be of vital importance to a litigant in Michigan, the cost of acquiring it might be too great. Rather, information from a decennial United States census might be used, despite the fact that such data would reveal only the composition of persons *working* in assembly plants and not necessarily of the persons *desiring* to work there.

Another disadvantage is that data collection is also subject to challenge on the grounds that it was done in a biased way. A litigant may, for instance, argue successfully that the opponent's survey questions were worded in such a way as to evoke a self-serving response. Bias might also be shown where the group of people surveyed or the time period covered by a set of measurements was inappropriate.

In re Litton Industries, Inc.:[1] Litton conducted a survey of independent consumer and commercial appliance service agencies to elicit opinions as to the quality of microwave ovens. The list of agencies questioned was based on Litton's list of authorized service agencies. The survey was defective because

(A) a substantial number of those interviewed were servicing dealers of Litton microwaves and their responses could be biased;[2]

(B) it systematically excluded one-sixth of the group of agencies Litton claimed to have surveyed, namely those that serviced Litton but were not on the authorized service list;[3]

(C) it purported to survey technicians, but really surveyed agencies and obtained the opinion of only one technician at each agency;[4]

---

§2.1 [1] 97 F.T.C. 1 (1981), *modified,* 100 F.T.C. 457 (1982).
[2] 97 F.T.C. at 26-28.
[3] Id. at 28-29.
[4] Id. at 30.

(D)   it included opinions of technicians who had but limited experience with brands other than Litton.[5]

In re MacMillan, Inc.:[6] A survey was conducted to determine whether graduates of LaSalle Extension University correspondence schools were in demand and were successful in increasing their earnings. The survey was deemed biased because the cover letter for the questionnaire indicated that the information was for Federal Trade Commission use[7] and some of the questions were leading and did not provide for responses in sufficient variety.[8]

A question of bias also arises when the collected information does not correspond exactly to that desired because of the failure of data-recording devices or the inadvertent loss or destruction of portions of the data. Sometimes it is not apparent at the time the data are collected that a recording device failure has occurred, and it is only later, when the data from that time are compared with others, that it becomes evident that such a failure *may* have occurred. Under these circumstances the analyst faces the dilemma of excluding data that may be relevant or else relying on data that are quite unrelated to the phenomena of interest. Because this departure from the ideal could affect the conclusion of the study, the study is subject to a challenge that it is self-serving, particularly when the collector of the data has or should have had control over the exclusion of items in the data set. Thus, while gathering data fosters a deep appreciation of their reliability and shortcomings, it encumbers one with the responsibility of defending the neutrality and objectivity of the process.

In the two sections that follow, two special sets of circumstances involving data collection are discussed. In the first, an exhaustive collection effort is infeasible; a partial or sample collection is used instead. The second set of circumstances involves not just data collection, but the construction of an experiment in such a way that the data collected permit one to discover causal relationships.

§2.1.1   Sampling from a Large Population

If information concerning the job preferences of Michigan residents is needed and the investigator is unwilling to assume that the

[5] Id. at 31-32.
[6] 96 F.T.C. 208 (1980).
[7] Id. at 283-284.
[8] Id. at 286.

questions asked by the decennial census takers adequately captured this information, she might have to identify a representative sample of residents and ask them about their job preferences. If information about securities transactions at a bank is needed but examining the entire voluminous file of papers recording these transactions is too burdensome, a representative sample of the papers might be selected for study. In either case, if the sample is chosen in proper fashion and is of sufficient size, an analysis based on the sample can be almost as informative as one based on an exhaustive tally. Chapter 6 discusses statistical aspects of sampling in more detail.

> **United States v. Nissan Motor Corp.:**[9] The defendant collected sales invoices covering six years from its dealers in 14 states, an enormous task that cost nearly a million dollars and netted about 40,000 invoices. Later, to save on further costs, a representative sample of only about 12% of these invoices was used by the defendant in completing its studies. Professors Rubinfeld and Steiner,[10] in reviewing the statistical aspects of the case, replicated certain of the defendant's studies using all 40,000 invoices. There was no practical difference between their results and those of the defendant.

In these examples, the residents of Michigan and the voluminous file of papers are called *populations,* and the persons interviewed and the papers selected for study are called *samples.* The selection of a sample from a population requires great care because a sample should be as representative as possible of the population. For example, if the Michigan residents are to be interviewed by telephone, the sample will include only people who can be reached by telephone. To the extent that job preferences of people without telephones differ from those of people with telephones, and to the extent that there are many people without telephones, the sample will not be representative of the job preferences of the population. Furthermore, if residents only of Ann Arbor, Michigan, are included in the sample (perhaps to save on long distance telephone charges), the sample may not be representative of the population because Ann Arbor is the site of a large university, and the job preferences of the residents in that city may be atypical of those in the population statewide. If within Ann Arbor 1000 people are called in the order of their listing in the

---

[9] See In re Nissan Motor Corp., Antitrust Litigation, 552 F.2d 1088 (5th Cir. 1977).
[10] D. Rubinfeld & P. Steiner, Quantitative Methods in Antitrust Litigation, 46 Law and Contemporary Problems 69 (1983).

telephone book, starting with Arne Johnson, the sample may contain disproportionately many Scandinavians, and disproportionately few blacks, Orientals, Irish, and Jews. To the extent that job preferences vary among persons of different ethnic origins and to the extent that ethnic origin is reflected in one's name, the sample may also fail to be representative. Determining the best way to sample the population of Michigan residents is sufficiently complex that almost any method can be alleged (though perhaps not proved) to result in some sort of bias.

Not all sampling problems are as complex as that of choosing a representative group of Michigan residents. For instance, determining the best way to sample the population of securities transactions is much easier, because all members of the population can be identified, and each can be analyzed with equal ease. One probably would not choose the sample of transactions only from the first file drawer, for those might be just the ones occurring in December, possibly a nonrepresentative month, or they might be the ones involving short-term municipal bonds, possibly a nonrepresentative type of security. One way of ensuring a representative sample is to number the papers in sequence (assuming now that each sheet corresponds to a separate transaction), select them in the order in which their numbers appear in a standard table of random digits, and stop when the desired sample size is reached. A sample drawn in this fashion is called a *simple random sample.*[11]

There are sometimes circumstances that permit one to improve on the simple random sample, in the sense that the resulting sample is even more likely to be representative of the population. If, for example, securities transactions of different types were maintained in different file drawers, one could modify the sampling method to ensure that a prescribed number of transactions from each file drawer were included in the sample. This would remove the possibility that the simple random sample, due to the luck of the draw, would contain few if any transactions from a given drawer. This modified sampling method is termed *stratified sampling* (see Section 6.4).

A stratified sample differs from a simple random sample in that "subsamples" are taken from preselected portions of the population. The stratified sample is made up of simple random samples of each subpopulation, i.e., each drawer. These subgroups are selected to ensure that all important groups are adequately represented in the sample.

---

[11] See Section 6.2, Simple Random Samples, for a further discussion of the use of a random number table.

United States v. General Motors Corp.:[12] The government surveyed a stratified random sample of the 1,319 owners of trucks
identified by General Motors as having reported wheel failures. The
survey had as its goal the collection of affidavits from owners detailing
the number of wheel failures that had occurred on their trucks. The
survey resulted in 154 affidavits, disclosing 393 failures. The results of
the survey were extrapolated to yield the conclusion that if all 1,319
owners were to be asked to submit affidavits, it is 95% probable that at
least 670 would respond with affidavits, and it is 95% probable that at
least 1,400 failures would be reported in such a survey.[13]

How large should a sample be to be reliable? It is impossible to
answer this important question without knowing a great deal about
the exact circumstances. If one just wants to know the proportion of
Michigan residents willing to work in an automobile assembly plant
who are blacks or the proportion of securities transactions that involved special concessions on commissions, a sample that is a tiny
fraction of the whole population can supply an answer that is adequate for most purposes. If one wants to know how residents' job
preferences vary by location within Michigan for various ethnic
groups, or how commission concessions varied over time by type of
security, the sample must be larger than in the former case, because
the questions to be resolved are more detailed. In either case, an
increase in the sample size generally increases the likelihood that the
sample is representative, but the influence of successive increases in
the size diminishes as the sample grows. In determining sample size,
one must strike a balance between the cost of gathering more data
and the influence such data will have on the sample. The issue of
sample size is discussed further in Section 6.13.

§2.1.2 Designing an Experiment

Occasionally there arise in litigation special situations in which
one has the opportunity not only to collect data, but also to control the
circumstances under which the data arise. Consider for example a
situation in which the alleged efficacy of a certain drug is in question.
One convincing way of testing the drug is as follows: First, find people
willing to participate as subjects who are in similar health and assign

[12] 377 F. Supp. 242 (D.D.C. 1974).
[13] Id. at 251.

each at random to one of two treatment groups without informing them of the type of treatment they are to receive. To each member of one group, administer the drug, and to each member of the other, appear to administer the drug, but in fact administer some other drug or inert substance. After a suitable delay, have the health of each member of each group evaluated by someone appropriately qualified but who does not know the treatment in fact given to any subject. If the health of the subjects in one group is found to be systematically different from that of the other subjects, one may infer that the difference was caused by the drug. A test of this sort is called a *designed experiment.*

In re Alleghany Pharmacal Corp.:[14] The Federal Trade Commission alleged that Alleghany's product, Hungrex, containing phenylpropanolamine hydrochloride (P.P.A.), was ineffective as an appetite suppressant, contrary to its advertisement. Alleghany had experts conduct a quadruple blind study; a sample was divided into four groups and neither the participants nor the personnel administering the capsules had knowledge of the contents of any of the capsules given to the four groups. Eighty-one patients were selected for the test and, presumably, assigned arbitrarily to one of the four groups. About an hour before each meal, each patient swallowed a capsule of a type characteristic of the group with which he or she was associated. The patients in the first group were given P.P.A. at a dosage level of 25 milligrams (mg). The patients in the second group were given 50 mg. of P.P.A. The patients in the third group were given a prescription drug called dextroamphetamine, known to be an appetite depressant. The patients in the fourth group were given a placebo, a capsule composed of inert ingredients. There was no restriction on the caloric intake of any patient during the course of the six-week study. Alleghany contended that in Group 1, 14 out of the 19 patients lost anywhere from one to ten pounds in weight.[15] 17 of the 21 patients taking the prescription drug in Group 3 lost from one to ten pounds, and 13 of 21 patients in Group 4 who took the placebo gained weight. Therefore, Alleghany concluded that P.P.A. was an appetite suppressant, as was reflected in Groups 1's loss of weight, and that Hungrex was properly advertised.

In re Stauffer Laboratories:[16] Stauffer advertised the "Magic Vibrating Couch" as an effective means to reduce weight and firm and tone muscles. A physician at George Washington School of Medicine

[14] 75 F.T.C. 990 (1965).
[15] Id. at 1005.
[16] 64 F.T.C. 629 (1964), *aff'd,* 343 F.2d 75 (1965).

conducted a study by having a number of obese employees of George Washington University Hospital use the Magic Couch in the hospital for ten weeks. The results of the study showed that the Magic Couch had no effect on weight or dimensions.[17]

Data from designed experiments are subject to many of the same criticisms as data gathered using other collection methods.

In re Warner-Lambert Co.:[18] One issue in this case was whether the respondent's product, Listerine, was effective in preventing colds.[19] One test conducted by the respondent was faulted because both the subjects and the evaluators could tell whether Listerine was being used by the subject, a condition that could have influenced either the behavior of the subject or the opinion of the evaluator.[20] A second test conducted by the respondent was also unreliable in part because the division between those subjects treated with Listerine and those treated differently was not random.[21]

§2.2   Using Someone Else's Data

Many litigation situations calling for statistical analysis involve use of a body of data that the analyst has no hand in assembling. The employment history records maintained by an employer, the tape listing the prices at which stocks on a major exchange traded last year, books containing general social and economic characteristics of the northern New Jersey populace as compiled in the last decennial national census — all are collections of someone else's data. Since these data are not compiled for trial purposes, they have a certain facial validity that the results of a special survey may lack. On the other hand, they may be lacking in detail, comprehensiveness, or accuracy, shortcomings that may make data of this type only marginally useful in illuminating the issues of interest.

Below are mentioned some sources of data that may be valuable in litigation. The list is far from complete and serves only to suggest the variety of alternative sources. Also mentioned are some problems typically encountered in using data from these sources.

[17] 64 F.T.C. at 636.
[18] 86 F.T.C. 1398 (1975), *modified,* 562 F.2d 749 (1977).
[19] 86 F.T.C. at 1405.
[20] Id. at 1427-1428, 1431-1432.
[21] Id. at 1437.

§2.2.1   Sources of Data

Two distinct types of data that may be available to a litigant are those under the control of the opposing party or parties, and those under the control of parties not involved in the litigation. The opponent's data generally are found and obtained during the discovery phase of the litigation, but since the opposing party usually has little interest in facilitating the release of its data to its antagonists, it can be difficult for the litigant to find out even the nature of the data available from this source. In complex cases, a coordinated program of interrogatories and depositions may be needed to discover not only the nature of the data but the manner in which they are stored and can be retrieved from an opponent's files. Interrogatories and depositions may be used to determine the kinds of files the opposing party maintains, the filing media and organization used, facilities used to access and manipulate files, routines according to which data are collected and entered into files, methods used to ensure file accuracy and completeness, routines used for retrieving data, and the identity of people who have knowledge of these facts. One may also use these discovery techniques to find out the nature of reports generated routinely from the opponent's files, and the details of the record structure within each file, including the physical position of each item of information on a record and the meanings of any abbreviations used.

While getting useful data from an opposing party can be frustrating because of the party's reluctance to help, acquiring them from a neutral source can also be frustrating because of the difficulty of locating the right source. If it is crucial to establish the characteristics of the 1979 market for toothpaste in Cincinnati, the incidence of employee illness attributable to air quality at plants engaged in the manufacture of certain industrial chemicals, or the job preferences and skills of the unemployed in Michigan in the early 1980s, the task of locating and acquiring the necessary data can be formidable.

A university research library may be the best starting point for finding a source for this type of general data. Such libraries maintain in their collections data distributed by numerous agencies of the federal government, such as the Department of Commerce, the Department of Labor, and the National Safety Council, and large amounts of statistical data published at regular intervals by private organizations such as the American Hospital Association, Dun and Bradstreet, and the Dow Jones Company. In addition, scholars in infinite variety analyze these data on their own and report their conclusions in books, reports, and journals often found in these libraries.

Much useful statistical information is also found at university computing centers, which tend to acquire a variety of large and important statistical data sets. Access to these may be restricted to students and faculty affiliated with the university, but access to written descriptions of the data sets tends to be less restricted and can provide valuable clues to the existence and source of suitable data.

Not to be overlooked are commercial data suppliers who, for a fee, will provide data concerning securities markets, the economy, demographics, and a host of other topics. Several such suppliers can furnish data by telephone directly into a customer's computer or on a magnetic disk or tape that can be read by a computer.

Once the most promising sources are identified, it may be necessary to contact each source, be it an agency or private organization, to seek more specific information about the data: one may want to know, for example, whether data more directly related to the interests of the litigant are available as well as how the relevant data were collected. Discussions with scholars who have worked with the data can also be helpful in identifying the inferences that may reasonably be drawn.

§2.2.2 Problems with Using Someone Else's Data

Much as it might be desirable to construct a data base especially tailored to the issues in a particular case, time and money considerations often dictate that an existing data set serve, perhaps with minor modification. In such a case the analyst may not have had complete control over or have knowledge about the process of constructing the data set and may face a variety of uncertainties that affect the amount of time an analysis will take and the ultimate credibility of the results. These uncertainties arise from various stages in the development of the already established data set, some of which are described below.

Data Collection: Data collection practices have an obvious influence on the scope and completeness of the data set. It is important that the system used for the collection be one that yields objective and accurate data and permits analysis of the legal theory of interest. For example, if an employer is accused of racial discrimination in its disciplinary practices concerning lateness and absenteeism, a data set based on timecards with mechanically stamped check-in and check-out times could be an extremely valuable basis for determining objectively the merit of the allegation. On the other hand, if the instances of lateness and absenteeism are recorded only at the initiative of supervisors, it may well be that they tend to report the lateness of employees of one race more faithfully than those of another, and thus the data set is of little use in addressing the merit of the allegation, for it may be tainted by the very practice being challenged.

Gay v. Waiters' and Dairy Lunchmen's Union, Local No. 30:[1] In this hiring discrimination case one issue was whether the data reflecting the history of applications for positions as waiters were a reliable guide to the proportions in which a nondiscriminating employer would have hired blacks. The applications data were disregarded by the court for the following reasons, among others:

(A) the race coding on the record of applicants was unreliable, leading the court to believe, in light of other testimony, that relatively more black applicants than nonblacks had their race recorded incorrectly;
(B) the records were kept only intermittently and hence were not complete with respect to the numbers of applicants;
(C) the application procedures used may have discouraged relatively more blacks than nonblacks from becoming registered in the log;
(D) the records did not include applications made orally to managers by temporary employees seeking transfer or promotion.[2]

Ambiguity about the population to which the data set pertains may also lead to uncertainty regarding the validity of conclusions to be drawn from analyzing the data.

1980 Census Challenges:[3] The 1980 United States Census data underwent several court challenges because of alleged undercounts of people in certain geographic areas. Though the census is intended to encompass all persons residing in the United States, it cannot achieve that ideal for a variety of reasons, including people's travel, living arrangements, literacy, and willingness to be counted. Because the population intended to be covered is somewhat different from the actual population, there is the possibility that some characteristics of the whole population are not accurately reflected in the published data.

§2.2 [1] 489 F. Supp. 282 (N.D. Cal. 1980).
[2] Id. at 312.
[3] See, e.g., Young v. Klutznick, 652 F.2d 617 (6th Cir. 1981).

When using data collected through someone else's survey, it is often important to determine how the questions were asked and how the responses were recorded. When collecting data the surveyor should anticipate and control the range of possible responses without distorting the respondent's meaning. For example, a mail survey seeking the occupation of an individual may either ask the respondent to classify her job as one in a list of job titles or else permit her to supply any title she might choose. There is more latitude for a playful and distorting response in the latter situation, and a study of occupations of the population thought to be represented by the respondents might consequently suffer. Data from each questionnaire should be reviewed to determine whether the answers given seem consistent and reasonable. Those that seem odd should be verified to the extent possible by (1) returning to the data source, (2) contacting the person surveyed, or (3) repeating the measurement. Before relying on someone else's survey data, the litigator would be well advised to determine the extent to which any aberrant responses were verified.

Coding: Data are nearly always recorded in abbreviated form and must therefore be decoded in order to be understood. The coding method or set of abbreviations chosen early in the collection phase exerts an enormous influence on the range of issues that can be illuminated through study of the data. A personnel data set recording the number of years of education possessed by each newly hired employee may be useful in a study of how college graduates were placed at their time of hire compared to high school graduates. If the issue is whether graduates of engineering colleges were placed differently than were English and history majors, however, more information is required.

Data sets maintained over a prolonged period of time may change coding systems at some point, introducing a new hazard to the analyst. The decennial census, for example, changes its definitions of census tracts rather regularly, making it difficult sometimes to compare characteristics of small geographic areas from one census to the next. Also changed from time to time are the job categories to which people are assigned by virtue of their job titles and the geographic definitions of major metropolitan areas on the basis of which many summary statistics are compiled. Employers who maintain personnel history data sets also tend to change coding systems. For instance, old codes may be modified to accommodate new kinds of jobs, perhaps through the assignment to a newly created job of a code previously used to designate a job now no longer staffed. Especially distracting are instances in which new employees are assigned payroll numbers formerly assigned to former employees, a practice that may make it difficult for the analyst to track an employee's history. Even the venerable Dow Jones index undergoes changes of this sort: as new industries gain in importance and others fade, the index is occasionally redefined in such a way as to reflect the price level of currently representative major securities. An analyst unaware of these changes could be led far astray.

Verification: All too often one starts to work with a large data set only to discover after some effort that it contains numerous errors of which the creators and regular users are apparently quite unaware. On some occasions the difficulty may be traced, for instance, to the fact that the nucleus of the data set had been assembled and keyed into the computer by loosely supervised students on summer break from college, people with little knowledge of the company's record-keeping system or the structure of its departments, job grades, or pay and promotion systems. If little is done to check the comprehensiveness or accuracy of the data selected and keyed, the project may be well along before the data are discovered to be too unreliable to use. A data set received from almost any source should be checked for consistency internally, with other data sets, and, whenever possible, with its ultimate source. (See Section 2.3, Checking the Accuracy of the Data.) It is very risky to presume that a data set is exactly as its donor describes it.

Updating: One can also be unpleasantly surprised when verifying a data set to discover that there were serious flaws in the manner in which it was maintained. Large sets used in the ordinary course of business tend to grow and change as the business unfolds, and the manner in which these changes take place can have a substantial effect on the usefulness of the data for litigation purposes.

Consider, for example, a personnel history file in which the educational attainments of employees at their time of hire are recorded. If some employees go to school nights, finish their degree work, or take correspondence courses, these additional attainments may not be recorded. Some employers make no attempt to keep educational data current; others will put changes into the file if an employee insists; still others try very hard to keep up with employees' latest educational attainments. The user of such a history file needs to know the practices of the employer involved.

As another example, one employer kept an extensive personnel history file for current employees, dutifully adding each change in status to the employee's records within one to three weeks of the pertinent event. At the end of each year a copy of the entire current file was recorded on magnetic tape and stored in the company archives. A problem arose because every year there were a number of employees who left the company sometime in December whose termination records were not entered into the file until January, thus causing the company to miss getting the final record on the year-end archive tape. Each summer, as part of the file maintenance procedure, however, all records of employees terminated during the previous year were automatically deleted from the current file. It thus appeared from the year-end archive tapes that as of the end of a year certain employees were apparently alive and employed and, as of the next, they had vanished without trace.

As a final example of the untrustworthiness of data received from sources beyond one's control, consider the employer who used a computer program to update its personnel files, and that program contained a hidden error. The employer occasionally made retroactive adjustments in pay grade and pay, not a common type of entry, but one that would occur over a dozen times a year. It was only this type of record change for which the updating program was faulty, but the fault was impressive: it obliterated all of the employee's previous records, making it appear that he or she had always been in the same department and at the same pay grade. Over a period of six years an error of this sort could ruin a data set for litigation purposes, and, once again, an analyst unaware of the process by which the data set evolved could be seriously misled.

Documentation: As the preceding several sections suggest, an analyst cannot go forward supplied only with a data set; it is also necessary to have a description of the process by which the data set was built, for this may have an important influence on the analyst's treatment of the data. Although the description is a vital aspect of its documentation, so too are a code book and a record layout. A *code book* defines each of the abbreviations used in the data set. For example, the numbers 1 through 5 may be used to indicate the racial category of the individual to whom the record pertains. The code book would register the fact that 1 denotes Caucasians, 2 denotes blacks, and so forth. The *record layout* of a data set is a document indicating the exact location within a data record of specific types of information, such as an employee's name and date of birth. It seems obvious that a record layout, a code book, and a data set history are aspects whose accuracy and completeness are every bit as important as those of the data set itself, yet on at least one occasion an analysis collapsed on the day of trial because of a record layout error. In a case in which the heights of people hired was the central issue, height in inches somehow got interchanged with the last two digits of the year of hire.

B. ENTERING DATA ON A COMPUTER

When a statistical analysis of a large body of data or when a variety of analyses of even a small body of data are required, it often is most economical to use a computer. Unless the data are obtained in a form permitting them to be fed directly into a computer, substantial effort may be necessary to get them in. Two phases of this process are (a) entering the data into the computer and (b) completing an accuracy check to test for errors made in entering the data.

It is usually desirable to obtain the data chosen for analysis on magnetic tape or some other medium permitting rapid and accurate entry into a computer. Data recorded on such media are said to be in *machine-readable form*. Usually any source that offers its data in the form of computer printouts can supply the same data in machine-readable form.

When the requisite data are not available in machine-readable form, it may be necessary to enter the data by typing or *keying* them in their entirety. This can be a straightforward process if the printed records are legible and unambiguous and if they are being keyed verbatim. Even so, for a large data set, keying errors are almost certain to occur, and to the extent that the records are ambiguous or illegible, or that the typist is required to extract or summarize data while keying, the possibilities for error increase.

Though reasonable efforts need to be made to ensure that these conversion errors are not numerous, one cannot assume that any measures are completely effective in eliminating them and must therefore be prepared to cope with them at later stages in the analysis. There are at least two facets to a program of coping with such errors, a series of consistency checks (discussed in Section 2.3) and a permanent audit trail (see Section 2.4).

§2.3   Checking the Accuracy of the Data

To check the accuracy of data for *data conversion* (i.e., typing) errors one may use a variety of consistency checks. One way involves comparing the original data source with the data newly recorded on the computer for any anomalies; another is to have the data set keyed twice in its entirety by two different people and then to compare the resulting machine-readable data sets using a computer program. Wherever the two data sets are different, the original data source is consulted and the appropriate corrections are made. Though for a large data set this can mean an enormous increase in effort, it is a widely used method of checking and usually catches and corrects a substantial number of errors.

For large data sets, though, this method usually will not find all keying errors, because occasionally the same keying mistake is made both times the original is keyed or an error is made in correcting a discrepancy between the two keyed sets. And sometimes, despite plans to the contrary, a portion of the data set may get keyed only once and therefore not get checked. Such possibilities call for further checks.

Another simple and effective check is to have the computer print out all of the different values that a variable takes and the frequencies with which these values are taken. If, for example, such a tally is done for data set entries supposedly recording birth months, the values listed should include nothing beyond the usual 12 months, and the number of people born in any one month should be about the same as the number born in any other. Any departures from this expected pattern should be investigated, and either explained or corrected. In a tally done on the names of the departments in which people work, department names that occur relatively few times in the data set should be checked back against the source documents to see if they are correctly spelled.

Another kind of check takes advantage of redundancy in the data set. If, for example, both age and date of birth are part of each person's record, the computer should be requested to calculate age from the birthdate information and point out any instances in which the calculated age differs from the age that was keyed. Instances of disagreement should be checked against the original data source to determine the reason for the discrepancy.

Data set redundancy can be exploited in other ways to point out possible errors. For example, if commodity prices as recorded in the source data set are known generally to change by a small amount from one time period to the next, the computer can be used to detect those instances in which large changes are recorded so that they may be verified against the source.

Aside from these tests of internal consistency of the machine-readable data set, one should also verify the data against external sources: if they share some elements in common with other machine-readable data sets known to be reliable, these corresponding parts should be compared using the computer. A data set keyed from an employer's personnel history records might be checked against a machine-readable file containing annual earnings information to detect errors in names or social security numbers or instances in which particular historical records were inadvertently excluded. If it is possible to reproduce reports or summaries already published by an independent source, they should be prepared from the data set and compared with their counterparts. For example, a survey to determine the demand for health care facilities by age bracket of the population would yield data that, when aggregated, would indicate a demand by the population as a whole. If this has already been estimated and published by a state or federal agency or a health care association, it should be compared with the demand aggregated from the keyed data. Any disparity may be the result of keying errors, and should be traced to its source.

One of the most important checks for an analyst to make is with people who are familiar with the phenomena to which the data pertain. Charts, tables, cross tabulations and statistical analyses derived from the machine-readable data set may be reviewed by experts who would be able quickly to spot data quirks that would otherwise escape detection. A personnel manager, for instance, would know at once whether the number of persons hired as indicated in the keyed data is approximately correct; a sales manager would spot quickly any major error in the volume of sales attributed by the keyed data to a particular geographic region.

§2.4 Tracing Computer Data to Their Sources

In order to check the machine readable data set against its source, one must be able to trace back quickly and surely to that source. Each of the original papers from which the computerized file of data was keyed should be marked with a page number or *control number.* Each control number should be keyed simultaneously with the other elements of the source page. When a question arises about the accuracy of a particular entry in the machine-readable data set, the control number can be used to identify the sheet of paper from which it was taken. Control numbers can be checked for order and gaps as one of the internal checks of the accuracy and completeness of the data conversion.

In the process of checking the data set, it is not unusual to discover errors in the source papers from which the data were keyed. In such cases, these papers (uncorrected) are no longer the entire authority for the data set, and the task of tracing each component of the data set to its origin is compounded. It is of great importance to make note of instances in which the original papers are in error, the consequent correction used in the machine-readable data set, the date it is made, and the authority on which it is based. Without such records, it may not be possible at some later date to determine why the data set differs from the papers from which it was keyed, nor to determine whether a particular tabulation done in the past incorporated the correction.

Sometimes a machine-readable data set must undergo some reformatting or mixing with other data sets before it is in a form suitable for analysis. It is desirable to have these operations done with a computer program that serves to document the exact steps in the modification process. Making changes through a word processor or other editing process for which no permanent record is made is highly undesirable, for one cannot then verify at a later date the exact source of an item in the machine-readable data set.

C. THE COMPUTER PROGRAMMING PHASE OF STATISTICAL ANALYSIS

Computers have been used in connection with the litigation process in a variety of ways and have a range of important roles to play. Their usual role is to assist in calculations, and occasionally it is only through the use of a computer that the myriad calculations can be accomplished. They have also been used to help manage the documents pertinent to litigation, to scan them for key phrases and retrieve them according to a variety of descriptions of their content. But despite the power and versatility of computers and despite their ability to perform many clerical tasks quickly and without error, there are many possibilities for error in choosing an analysis and in writing the instructions to the computer describing the desired analysis. Errors of either type may make the results of a computer analysis suspect or even meaningless.

Instructing the computer is called *programming*. In the sections that follow, attention is focused on characteristics of programming that may seem unusual to someone who has never programmed (Section 2.5) and then on a very important by-product of programming, the audit trail provided by a well-written program (Section 2.6).

§2.5   The Iterative Nature of Computer Programming

A brief on a point of law is usually not written in a single draft. An outline, perhaps several outlines, and several drafts are required for an author to capture and focus the diverse elements of fact, law, and argument for a good brief. At some stages in the process, sections of the draft may be cast aside in favor of a more clearly written passage, or simply omitted because they do not fit the flow of logic. Writing a computer program has much in common with writing a legal brief. While it is possible to write and revise a computer program without using a computer, one can often learn more efficiently about a program draft by running it on a computer and inspecting the results. Indeed, it is common programming practice to write computer programs that, when run, reassure the programmer that all is well or indicate the part of the program that is faulty.

For example, a program might be required to prepare a chart comparing market survey results to data reported by the United States census. Several computational steps must precede the drawing of the chart in order to summarize both the market survey and census data for people residing in each of several counties. This task involves many different steps, an error in performing any one step may make the results of all subsequent steps meaningless. A cautious programmer will include program commands that direct the computer to print out some of the results of each step so that they can be checked for correctness.

Two points about this method of testing may seem odd (and unduly expensive) to litigators exposed to it for the first time: when a program does not run satisfactorily to completion, the programmer is likely to mention without blush that it contains one or more errors (and indeed, the computer may use just this term to point out places where corrections are needed). It seems contrary to usual professional practice to expect a client to pay for a mistake, and yet under these circumstances it may be quite appropriate to do so. It is simply convention that we do not consider preliminary drafts of a brief as containing errors; they are merely "preliminary drafts," but in writing programs the term *error* does not carry the same negative connotation found in many other contexts. Programming errors are a standard part of the writing of computer code, and a good programmer is likely to have the computer run many "erroneous" or draft versions in the process of perfecting it. The practice of having the computer help identify areas needing revision greatly speeds up the process of creating a final, working program.

The second point about programming practices that may raise doubts about their efficiency pertains to programmers' tendency to make programs print out many pages of intermediate calculations in order to reassure themselves that the programs are working properly. This appears to be requiring the computer to do more than is necessary in order to meet the client's needs and thereby unnecessarily increasing the cost of analysis. Although this process may result in more pages being printed out and more computing being done, these intermediate printouts may be justified because they (1) detect errors that might otherwise escape notice, and (2) help the programmer and client gain confidence in the nature and correctness of the calculations performed by the computer. Both of these matters are of great importance, and consequently a good programmer makes it a practice to have a program provide regular samples of the results of intermediate calculations.

§2.6 The Computer Program as a Record of Computations

A computer program's primary function is often viewed as specifying to a computer the exact sequence of operations to perform on one or more sets of data. However, after a program is run it also serves as a record of the operations undertaken to produce the printed results. The printed version and results are sometimes called an *audit trail*, a printout of the sequence of instructions together with the record of operations the machine performed in response to each instruction. An audit trail is invaluable in reconstructing the steps that lead to a summary table or chart, in discovering whether certain special cases are included or excluded from a given tally, or verifying that it is the June rather than the July data that serve as a basis for the calculations. Furthermore, the audit trail can be reviewed to determine if any errors were made in handling the data and sometimes will provide information regarding the characteristics of the data sets used (such as size, structure, date of last change, and method of creation).

An audit trail can be powerful evidence that a given exhibit is a correct and comprehensive summary of a given body of data and can be the vehicle through which litigants describe in complete detail the calculations they think most appropriate to sustain their position.

D. CHOOSING A TYPE OF ANALYSIS

Having discussed three phases in which data are collected and processed, we turn to the fourth phase, in which the researcher examines the data to see what information they reveal. There are four distinct types of analysis that are commonly used on statistical data. One type is used to summarize a large body of data such as the progress of monetary inflation in the United States over the last decade, the costs to private subscribers of local telephone calls both before and after the breakup of AT&T, or the hiring practices of a firm. The second type explores data to help detect patterns or relationships within a data set: placing age and salary data on a graph, for instance, may reveal that salaries decline on average after the age of 50 rather than continuing to rise until retirement. This knowledge might affect the way an analyst chooses to model or describe an employer's salary determination practices. Statistical analysis can also be used for estimating quantities or qualities that cannot be directly measured or observed, such as forecasting future sales or estimating those that would have occurred but for the actions of a competitor. Yet a fourth use of statistical analysis is in making inferences about the relationships among two or more variables, which can help determine, for example, whether an employee's pay depends at least in part on gender. These four types of statistical analysis are discussed in Sections 2.7 to 2.10.

§2.7   Summary Description of Data

Numerical summaries are in such common use that one scarcely distinguishes them from the qualitative parts of conversations and announcements. Notwithstanding their varying degrees of complexity, one feature they all have in common is that they reflect only certain aspects of a body of data. For example, news reports note that unemployment increased or decreased last month by a certain percentage, a summary that does not distinguish a decrease in Detroit from an increase in Boston, nor the extent to which the change was uniform with respect to the population's age, race, or gender. As another example, drivers are reminded of the number of traffic deaths that have occurred recently in their state. This is another summary of a large and complex body of data, but it reveals nothing about highway conditions attendant to the accidents or characteristics of the drivers involved. Finally, a court may hear that an unfair trade practice has cost a plaintiff a certain volume of business, a summary that may encompass a large number of transactions spread over many states and many years, and which conveys nothing of the enormous variability in the level of business over time and from one region to another.

Sometimes a summary is more than a single number. Newspapers and magazines often use charts or graphs to indicate how the purchasing power of the dollar has changed and how various geographic areas differ in population, employment, weather, and so forth. Such summaries are in effect collections of numbers rather than single numbers but are still simplifications of a vastly more complex reality.

Summary analyses run the gamut from a simple measure like an average (see Section 2.7.1), to differences or trends (see Section 2.7.2), to graphic displays (see Section 2.7.3).

§2.7.1   Averages, Medians, Standard Deviations, and Ranges

There are many single-number summaries of data sets in everyday use. Perhaps the most familiar is the *average*, the sum of a collection of numbers divided by the number of numbers in the collection. The average of a group of numbers is never smaller than the smallest member of the group, nor larger than the largest; it is representative of the center or location of the number group. If the numbers in a group fall more or less symmetrically to either side of their average value, then the average may be an adequate summary of the group, but if the numbers in a group are asymmetrical, perhaps with many members being slightly less than the average and a few being substantially more than the average, then a different measure of the center or location of the group may be more informative. One such measure is the *median,* the middle number in the group when its members are arranged in ascending order, or the average of the two middle numbers when the number of numbers in the group is even. In the asymmetrical case mentioned above, the average exceeds most of the numbers in the group, while the median falls squarely in the middle of the group.[1]

Often a group of numbers is representative of a much larger group that for various reasons cannot be studied in its entirety. If the group under study was drawn at random from the larger group (especially if the smaller group has been distorted or contaminated by copying or measuring errors), the average can be misleading as an indicator of the center of the larger group of numbers. Under such circumstances, a better indication of the center may be obtained by excluding several of the largest and smallest values from the smaller group in the calculation of the average. This type of average is called a *trimmed average.* The median is an extreme case of a trimmed average, one in which all but the middle one or two numbers are discarded.

In addition to having a single number represent the center of a group of numbers, it is sometimes convenient to have a single-number indicator of the spread or *range* of the group. One obvious measure of this would be the numerical difference between the largest and smallest numbers in the group.[2] A less obvious but often more useful measure is the *standard deviation,* calculated by subtracting from each number in the group the average for the group, squaring each result, calculating the average of the squares and then the square root of this average. This is explained more fully in Section 4.7. Though it smacks of alchemy, the standard deviation has the interesting and useful property that, for many groups of numbers, about two-thirds of the members of the group will fall within one

---

§2.7 [1] For example, if the group of numbers is 1, 2, 3, 4, 15, and 25, the average is 8.3 (50 divided by 6) and the median is 3.5, the average of the two middle numbers, 3 and 4.

[2] For example, in note 1 the range is 24 (25 minus 1).

standard deviation of the average value and about 95% will fall within about two standard deviations of the average (see Section 4.10, Useful Properties of the Standard Deviation).

§2.7.2   Differences and Trends

A more complex summary analysis displays differences or trends in statistical data. An issue in litigation often involves two sets of data, one demonstrating the chief consequences of the defendant's actions, the other being a standard to which the first data set is compared. Ideally, the two sets are structured in such a way that if the defendant's actions were legal, the two sets would be similar, while illegal actions would tend to cause the data sets to differ. If in fact the data sets are quite different, the disparity may be regarded as evidence of the defendant's culpability. Under these circumstances, interest attaches not so much to the characteristics of the two data sets individually as it does to the differences between them.

In the simplest case, the important difference might be summarized as a single number, as when the plaintiff-retailer's sales volume for a certain period of time is compared with what it would have been but for the allegedly unfair trade practices of the defendant. In other cases, the difference may be an array or distribution of numbers, as when the ages of people dismissed during an employer's reduction in labor force are contrasted with the ages of the retained employees. A much more complicated example involves a case in which a computer program is allegedly derived without proper authorization from another, copyrighted program. Comparison of the two programs may reveal many different types of distinctions, some so qualitative that they do not lend themselves to computations.

Two of the most common ways of characterizing a *difference* between two numbers are (a) showing the numerical result of subtracting one from the other, and (b) expressing this difference as a percentage of one or the other of the original numbers. These two methods may convey vastly different impressions: the loss of a million dollars in sales due to an unfair trade practice sounds very substantial, but much less so if it represents one tenth of one percent of total sales for the period. On the other hand, twenty thousand dollars lost by another company could amount to a much more significant-sounding eighty-five percent of total sales.

Not only can one's impression of a simple difference between two numbers be affected by which of the above methods is used to express it, it can also be influenced by the data collection process from which the numbers were derived. If, for example, it is unreasonable to suppose that total sales could be estimated with confidence to within one tenth of one percent, it is scarcely evidence of an unfair trade practice to find that the difference between actual and projected sales is of this magnitude, even if the difference is a million dollars. In general, the practical significance of a difference is diminished whenever there is uncertainty as to the accuracy of one or the other of the numbers being compared.

In attempting to deal with these various considerations, statisticians have devised several ways of expressing differences that are alternatives to the two mentioned above. One method that has been used frequently in courtroom proceedings since the early 1970s is based on standard deviations, a widely adaptable unit of measure that can incorporate the effects of uncertainty in each of the two numbers being compared and permits expression of a difference in units so standard that its significance can often be interpreted at once (see Sections 4.10 and 4.11). An alternative is based on probabilities called p-values. p-values are generally more cumbersome to calculate, but they are more widely applicable and reliable and perhaps easier for a nonstatistician to comprehend (see Sections 1.13, where p-values are introduced, and 2.10, where the interpretation of p-values is discussed in greater detail). Both of these methods of representing differences are used extensively in the chapters that follow.

Sometimes an issue turns not on comparison of two data sets so much as on the pattern formed by a sequence of sets. For example, a case disputing the adequacy of a city's pollution control measures might be made by demonstrating by several different measures that its air quality has declined steadily for each of the last six years. The case against the computer program plagiarist might be made by showing that the allegedly infringing program's earliest surviving fragments contain an unmistakable similarity to the copyrighted program from which no copy was authorized and that more recent fragments exhibit a steady pattern of revision away from the copyrighted source. In each of these cases a *trend* in the data is a critical feature.

In the case of the city's pollution control measures, the presence of a trend can be detected and conveyed convincingly by means of a graph showing changes in air quality from one year to the next. Though probably more difficult to comprehend, this same information could be represented in list form. Another way of detecting the trend is by fitting a smooth curve to the data and observing the curve's features.

There are several standard and generally objective ways of describing trends through the use of graphs. Many are based on calculations performed directly on the raw numbers and do not require one even to plot the data beforehand. Indeed, many if not most computer installations have programs in their libraries that can be used to fit various kinds of curves to data. While curves of this sort can be very useful summaries of a data set, there is much that can go wrong when data are analyzed too mechanically. Great care must be exercised to ensure that such a summary does not obscure a feature of signal importance. Numerical methods for fitting curves are discussed in Chapter 8.

§2.7.3 Graphic Methods for Displaying Data

While averages, differences, and trends are very useful ways of summarizing or characterizing data, on some occasions a *graphic display* may be more helpful. A graphic display can effectively communicate information about a data set too complex to be captured by a handful of averages or differences. Through a carefully chosen display sequence an analyst may be able to determine the most effective ways in which to present the key features of a data set, and a litigator will be able to highlight key points of his argument in court. (See Section 9.4, which discusses demonstrative evidence.) Modern computer programs make possible and even simple a variety of ways to display data for such purposes: creating highly informative graphs and charts is no more difficult or time-consuming than performing the statistical calculations displayed. Several standard types of displays are described below.

A *scatter plot* is a widely-used device for showing the association between two variables. An example appears in Exhibit 2.7.3(a), where price of a particular security is plotted against time. It is evident from the plot that the relationship is rather complex, that the price has a seasonal variation, an upward trend, and some sort of sudden shift midway in 1975. If one did not know these features and elected an alternative method to summarize the data, such as using the best-fitting straight line (a method described in Chapter 8), it is evident that much potentially interesting detail would be hidden.

While a scatter plot is very good for showing the relationship

EXHIBIT 2.7.3(a)
Scatter Plot of Security Price v. Time

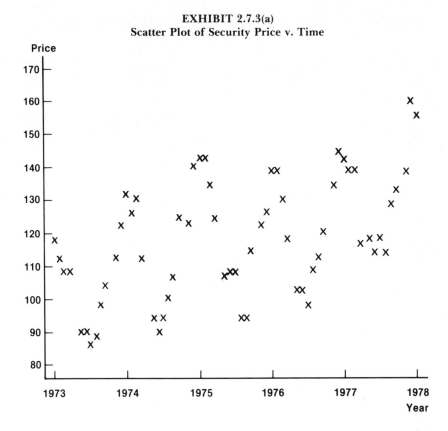

between two variables, there are often times when one would like to know the manner in which a particular variable is associated with two or more other variables. A scatter plot can sometimes be adapted to provide an adequate description of this association, as shown in Exhibit 2.7.3(b). Here the relationship between employee pay, seniority, and type of work is depicted for a particular employer. Pay and seniority are reflected by a point's placement on the page, while the type of work is reflected in the symbol used to register the point.

A *bar chart* is an alternative to the scatter plot and is especially useful when one variable is qualitative rather than numeric and when to each of its values there corresponds but one value of the other variable. Exhibit 2.7.3(c) is example of a bar chart giving the number of days lost per 100 scheduled employee days due to accidents (the quantitative variable) in each of a firm's five departments (the qualita-

EXHIBIT 2.7.3(b)
Scatter Plot of Hourly Pay by Seniority and Job Category

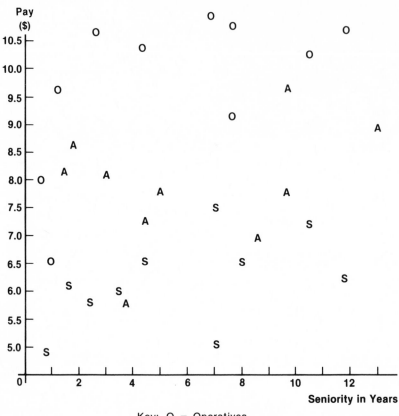

Key: O = Operatives
A = Assembly Workers
S = Service Workers

tive variable). For each department there is but one "number of days lost," and, accordingly, for each department the length of the bar indicates the number of days lost per 100 scheduled employee days. Apparently people in the fabrication department are most susceptible to time lost from accidents, and people in the other departments have a much lower susceptibility.

As with a scatter plot, one can introduce additional factors to depict the relationships among several variables. Exhibit 2.7.3(d) is a bar chart that shows lost time due to accidents indicating association

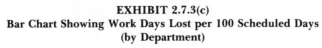

EXHIBIT 2.7.3(c)
Bar Chart Showing Work Days Lost per 100 Scheduled Days
(by Department)

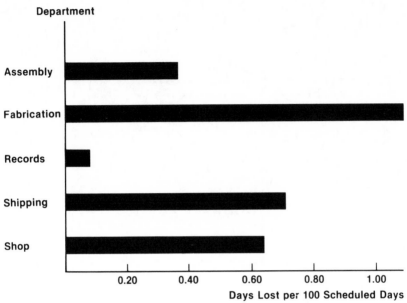

not only with department, but also with the grade range of the job within each department. Viewing the graph, one might note that the reason the accident rate is high in the fabrication department may be related to the fact that there are so many employees in that department in grades one through three.

If instead of seeing the relationship of two or more variables one wishes to view the collection of values taken by a single variable, the *stem and leaf diagram* may provide useful insights. Shown in Exhibit 2.7.3(e) is a stem and leaf diagram for 138 carbon monoxide readings taken at a particular work location in a chemical reduction plant. The stem on this Exhibit breaks down the observations by ranges, 10-14, 15-19, 20-24, 25-29, up to 145-149. The first of these ranges corresponds to the bottom entry on the stem, and successive ranges correspond to entries higher up the stem. On the leaves, which protrude horizontally to the right of the stem, the exact readings within each range are recorded. Thus, within the range 120-124 (indicated by the lower "12" on the stem) are four observations, 121, 121, 123, and 123

EXHIBIT 2.7.3(d)
Bar Chart Showing Work Days Lost per 100 Scheduled Days
(by Department and Grade)

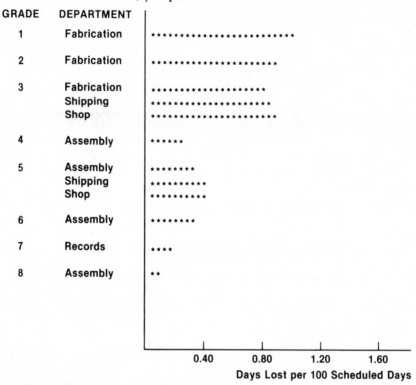

(indicated by the leaves "1 1 3 3" to right of this point on the stem). Within the 30-34 range (indicated by the stem's lower "3") there are 46 observations: 14 readings at 30, nine readings at 31, ten at 32, four at 33, and nine at 34 (as indicated by the leaves). This method of display permits one to see the individual meter readings and, by shifting one's attention to the shape of the figure, to determine the ranges of values most frequently taken and the frequencies with which they are taken. In this diagram, it is apparent that there are two distinctly different conditions at the work location, one that features low carbon monoxide levels and prevails about 90% of the time and one that features generally high but variable levels and prevails about 10% of the time. Details such as these might well go unnoticed if these data are summarized only in terms of a mean and standard deviation.

EXHIBIT 2.7.3(e)
Stem and Leaf Plot of CO Exposure Levels

Stem	Leaf	Number
14	5	1
14	0	1
13	5	1
13		
12		
12	1133	4
11		
11	03	2
10	688	3
10		
9	9	1
9	1	1
8	8	1
8	2	1
7		
7		
6	6	1
6		
5	5	1
5		
4		
4	12	2
3	555556677777888899	18
3	0000000000000011111111122222222222333344444444444	46
2	555555566667777777788888888889999999	36
2	011122333344444	15
1	78	2
1	2	1

```
        |    |    |    |    |    |    |    |    |    |
        5   10   15   20   25   30   35   40   45
```

§2.8 Exploratory Data Analysis

The *exploratory* approach to *data analysis* is a method of learning more about the variables and relationships inherent in a data set that until recently was regarded by many statisticians as rather unsavory and disreputable. Legitimate statisticians, it was held, approached a body of data with a definite theory about the patterns to be found therein and simply confirmed or disproved their theory by performing a sequence of calculations and interpreting the results.[1]

§2.8 [1] This approach is discussed in more detail in the context of modeling relationships among variables. See Section 8.4, Choosing Variables for Regression Analysis.

To use data to suggest a theory and then to use them again to confirm that theory is of course rather circular and is not a reliable method for constructing theories with general applicability. But it is quite evident that there is much to be gained from examining a body of data just to learn what patterns it contains, and it is also evident that statistical methods ought to be useful in detecting such patterns. Recently, several very prominent statisticians have devoted their efforts to the study of exploratory data analysis problems and have provided the field not only with some standard terminology and techniques, but also with an aura of legitimacy.[2] This section highlights a few of the methods that have been suggested for finding patterns in data.

§2.8.1 Numerical Methods for Exploration

Numerical methods for identifying key features of a data set include the calculation and comparison of averages for various subgroups of data, of correlations between various pairs of variables, and of standard deviations of various variables. They include methods of tallying and grouping the data into frequency tables, of sorting and printing various portions of the data set, and of fitting various hypothetical mathematical models to the data to determine the types of idealized structures that best describe relationships within the data set.

Many of the numerical methods are similar, if not identical, to those used to summarize data (see Section 2.7) or to those used for estimation, forecasting, or inference (see Sections 2.9 and 2.10). Averages, medians, and standard deviations are useful in explorations to summarize the characteristics of certain portions of the data set so they may be readily contrasted with other portions, and the mathematical models used in estimation and forecasting can be used in exploration for purposes of detecting relationships among the variables in the data set. Inferential analysis can be used to determine the strength of an apparent relationship or pattern in the data — to assess whether the pattern is enduring and profound or merely a probable consequence of chance.

Numerical methods for exploration owe their variety and ease of use to the digital computer, through which even the most elaborate of analyses can often be conducted efficiently. But even with such

---

[2] J. Tukey, Exploratory Data Analysis (1977); F. Mosteller & J. Tukey, Data Analysis and Regression (1977); E. Leamer, Specification Searches: Ad Hoc Inferences with Nonexperimental Data (1978).

sophisticated help numerical methods may fail to identify the key features of a large data set if they are inartfully applied. Imagine browsing through five years' worth of a local grocery store's item-by-item sales records and how easy it would be to overlook the fact that every year daily turkey sales peaked in late November and again in late December. Unless one has some preconceived ideas about patterns that may exist in the data, there is a good chance that some important patterns will escape notice, a probability that can be reduced if the numerical search for patterns is augmented with a careful selection of graphic displays of the data. (See, for instance, Section 8.13, concerning problems associated with nonlinear data.)

§2.8.2 Visual Methods for Exploration

Pictures of data are an indispensible aid to the analyst in detecting patterns, quite aside from their value in presenting the results of an analysis. A scatter plot (see Section 2.7.3) can convey at a glance a complex relationship between two variables that might never be guessed or detected through numerical techniques. Similarly, a stem and leaf diagram (see Section 2.7.3) can show at once the clusters of predominant values taken by a variable, information that might never be revealed by analyses of averages, medians, and standard deviations.

Other types of diagrams that can be used to detect patterns in data include bar charts (see Section 2.7.3) and histograms, such as the one shown in Exhibit 2.8.2(a), which captures information about the frequency of occurrence of particular carbon monoxide exposure levels in a plant. Maps, tree diagrams, cluster plots, flow diagrams, box and whisker plots — all are visual means of representing salient characteristics of data, and these listed are merely suggestive of the variety of graphic methods used to discover patterns in data.[3]

§2.9 Estimation and Forecasting

Often questions arise that call for some type of *estimation,* an appropriate reconstruction of events that should have occurred but did not. To what extent did the nondisclosure of a material fact inflate

---

[3] A beautiful and thorough book on graphs, charts, and other visually appealing methods for summarizing data in a form useful for analysis is E. Tufte, The Visual Display of Quantitative Information (1983).

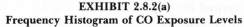

EXHIBIT 2.8.2(a)
Frequency Histogram of CO Exposure Levels

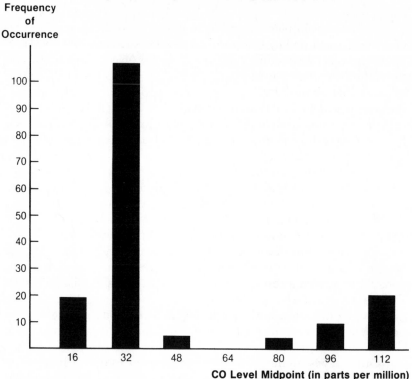

the price of a corporation's common stock? What is the share of the microcomputer statistical software market that a plaintiff company would have captured but for the unfair trade practice it alleges? What are the monetary damages incurred by female employees as a result of their company's sex-biased promotion practices? The analysis of these questions requires the estimation of certain numerical quantities. To determine the schedule of rates that will ensure a particular regulated utility company a fair rate of return on its capital demands *forecasting,* predicting events that have not yet occurred.

Estimation and forecasting techniques range in complexity from very simple calculations of averages, through visual extrapolation of patterns in graphs and charts, to sophisticated mathematical models in which some aspects of the models are determined by the data themselves. Several types of estimation and forecasting methods are described below.

§2.9.1 Informal Numerical Methods for Estimation and Forecasting

One of the simplest instances of estimation occurs when one determines from a poll of 1,000 television watchers that 32.1% of them viewed at least one daytime soap opera during the past week. There is the natural tendency in the absence of any other considerations to estimate that about 32.1% (more or less) of television viewers across the nation watched at least one daytime soap opera last week, and perhaps to estimate that about 32.1% of television viewers watch at least one such show in any given week. These poll results might even lead one to forecast that next week in particular about 32.1% of the television watchers in this country will watch at least one daytime soap opera. These are examples of informal numerical estimation or forecasting. Another such example occurs when one notes that revenues for a particular company have grown at an average annual rate of 14% over the last five years and forecasts that next year's will exceed this year's by 14%. Another occurs when one casually interpolates between numerical entries in an annuity table to estimate the value of an annuity at an interest rate intermediate to those given explicitly in the table.

Many estimation and forecasting methods of this sort involve averaging to remove the effects of variations in the data thought to be of a spurious nature in order that their fundamental underlying characteristics may be understood. These methods also generally result in estimates about whose accuracy one can say little at the time the estimate is made. In the television viewer example, there is some assurance that 32.1% may be the best estimate given the available information, but without further data or assumptions, one does not know whether the true percentage might reasonably be even lower than 20%. Information of this kind is provided by a class of analyses we call formal numerical methods.

§2.9.2 Formal Numerical Methods for Estimation and Forecasting

Formal numerical methods for estimation and forecasting embody a feature that permits an intriguing result: the estimation of the amount of error made in the process of creating the estimate or forecast of interest. For example, in the television viewer example of the preceding section, if one assumes that the 1000 viewers polled are representative of television viewers generally and that the response given by each viewer polled was in no way related to the responses of any other viewer polled, chances are 99 out of 100 that the true percentage of television viewers nationally who watched at least one daytime soap opera last week is between 29% and 35%. Such an estimate, called a *confidence interval*, is described in Section 3.15 and is discussed more completely in Section 6.11.

Confidence intervals can be constructed for a variety of estimates and forecasts. One elegant model resulting in confidence intervals for forecasts is based on *regression analysis*, a process in which the entity to be forecast is presumed to depend on a variety of factors, and the record of past occurrences of these factors and the concomitant entity to be forecast are used not only to estimate a mathematical formula expressing this entity's dependence on the factors, but also to estimate the amount of error inherent in forecasts based on the use of this formula. Along the way, this analysis also provides estimates of the error inherent in each of the weights it assigns to the factors on which the forecast entity depends. (See Chapter 8 for a discussion of regression analysis.)

This ability of certain methods of estimation and forecasting to supply their own critiques comes at the cost of having to rely on certain assumptions, some of which may be difficult to verify. In the case of the television viewers, one must presume that there was no collusion among the poll's respondents and that the persons polled have television-watching habits similar to those of the populace as a whole. A carefully designed method of selecting people to be polled would reduce the chance that such assumptions are violated and make the assumptions believable; still, they might be wrong, thus rendering the confidence interval inaccurate. The assumptions underlying a regression analysis are numerous and complex. The wide array of assertions one can compile rest on a very delicate foundation of assumptions that must be understood in order for regression results to be interpreted correctly. (See Chapter 8.)

§2.9.3 Visual Methods for Estimation and Forecasting

In all but the simplest cases it is generally helpful to display graphically the various aspects of the data being studied. Carefully chosen scatter plots, histograms, bar charts and the like can substantially reduce the chances that some critical factor is omitted in formulating the estimate or forecast. A scatter plot might reveal, for instance, that sales of a certain beverage are about the same every day of the week except Friday, when people buy more to lay in a supply for the weekend. An analysis based only on numerical methods might well overlook this anomaly and substantially underestimate the sales that would have been made on a certain Friday, but for the store having been damaged by fire the night before.

§2.10 Inferring Conclusions from Data

Statistical inference is a mode of analysis that is foreign to most people. Unlike summaries and forecasts, statistical inference is not commonly encountered by the lay person, yet this is the type of analysis that is usually the subject of the basic college statistics course, whether it be taught in the sociology department, the psychology department, or the school of business. In addition it has recently received a great deal of attention in connection with employment discrimination, jury selection, deceptive trade practices, occupational health and safety, and antitrust litigation.

Statistical inference can be used to provide answers to a variety of questions. For example, one may wish to know if a certain vitamin tablet is more effective in preventing colds than a competing product is, whether the 15% decline in demand for a certain firm's product is correlated with the advertising practices of another firm (when suitable allowances are made for the effects of a general economic downturn), or whether among similarly situated employees, nonminority people are generally chosen by the employer for the best assignments. The first step in inferential analysis is to construct a simplified description of the process of interest, capturing and interrelating key features while leaving out unimportant details. This description is called a *model*.

In models constructed for purposes of litigation, one of the primary features is that one or more of the assumptions are often directly related to the culpability of the accused, such as the assumption that there is no correlation between the advertising practices of one firm and the demand for a competitor's product or that non-minority employees have exactly the same chances of being chosen for the most desirable positions as do other similarly qualified employees. When such a model is sufficiently detailed, it can be used to predict results of the process being modeled. Examples of such predictions are the extent to which the economic downturn would produce a decline in demand for a product independent of the advertising practices of a competitor, or the extent to which minority employees due solely to chance might be underrepresented among persons selected for desirable job assignments.

If a model is comprehensive and accurate in relating the essentials of the process and yet, for example, the 15% demand downturn for a product or the number of minority employees selected (e.g., ten) is not within the range predicted, one may infer that the model does not correspond with reality. One reason for this failure may be that the accused is in fact culpable, that the assumptions in the model corresponding to the innocence of the defendant are inaccurate, an interpretation plaintiffs would be inclined to proffer. Another possible reason is that other assumptions are wrong and that the model fails to take account of some important and exculpatory factor in yielding its predictions. If the latter reason applies, no inference of culpability should be drawn from the analysis. This, of course, is the interpretation a defendant would urge.

The results of an inferential analysis are often expressed as a *p*-value. Examples of *p*-value calculations are given in Sections 3.12 through 3.18. The *p*-value is the probability that if the assumptions underlying the model are correct, a record as inconsistent with the model as the one that in fact occurred would occur by chance. (See also Sections 2.10.3 and 2.10.4.) The *p*-value in the advertising case is the probability that if there were no connection between the defendant's advertising practices and the demand for the plaintiff's product, the downturn would have been as great as or greater than the 15% it turned out to be. In the employee selection case, the *p*-value is the probability that if the employer selected employees for favored treatment at random from among persons equally qualified, as few or fewer than ten minority employees would have been chosen. A sufficiently small *p*-value discredits the assumptions in the model because it indicates that there is little chance that the observed data would have occurred if the assumptions were correct.

Substantial injustice can be wrought through misapplication of statistical inference, especially when a court chooses uncritically to rely on the opinion of a statistical expert (see Section 1.12). Formation of a reliable and relevant opinion requires an expert to understand key legal points at issue and a broad range of possibilities for statistical analysis. If the expert's base is too narrow, there is a possibility that the opinion will be ill-founded or even wrong. Most of this book is devoted to discussion of various aspects of statistical inference and its potential use in litigation, with the object of enhancing courts', litigants', and experts' understanding of this potential, and of some pitfalls as well. In the following paragraphs, general characteristics of statistical inference are introduced; specific methods of inference are treated in succeeding chapters.

§2.10.1 Choosing a Model to Describe Events

A good inferential analysis is a compromise among several competing ideals. First, the analysis must rest on a model that reflects reality to an acceptable degree. Since a model is a simplification of reality, the detail that is lost in the simplification can often only be estimated, and reasonable people may disagree as to the importance of the loss. Though in some instances one may be able to conclude that of two given models, one is demonstrably more realistic than the other, there are other cases in which no such determination is possible: of two models, each may possess refinements not possessed by the other.

As an example, consider a situation in which an employer attempts to determine the racial composition of the employees it should have hired in the past three years. From incomplete records of applicants, it appears that 20% of the new hires should have been blacks, but from an analysis of the labor force in the area within commuting distance of the workplace, it appears that 17% of the new hires should have been. Depending on the reliability and completeness of the applicant data and on the method used to obtain the local workforce estimate, neither of these two availability estimates may be more authoritative or trustworthy than the other. In that case, it seems likely that neither 17% nor 20% is the precise standard to which the employer's record should be compared and that the real standard is some unknown percentage near these.

Realism by itself may not dictate the choice of a model. Irrelevant detail should always be excluded in order to focus on the issues of interest and to bring the data to bear on these issues in the most effective manner. Because the requisite data may not be available, a realistic but complicated model may have to be abandoned in favor of a model requiring less detailed data for its implementation: for example, a model requiring information on the occupational categories of residents within each census tract in the Chicago area might have to give way to one based on occupational information within larger geographic regions, or perhaps to one requiring less detail within each tract. Even if the detailed data exist, it is possible that the model would have to be abandoned because of the considerable cost of acquiring and processing the data. The number of calculations required by a model may run well into the millions, making the use of a computer a necessity. Hence the availability of a suitable and affordable computer may be an important factor in the choice of a model.

Sometimes one is faced with choosing between two models, one being more realistic but based on little data, and the other being less realistic but based on much more data. Consider the case of a model that postulates that female employees at a plant be paid, on average, at the same hourly rate as males regardless of skill, job duties, seniority, or performance. Contrast that with one in which the average pay of females should equal that of males who were hired at the same time and with the same skills as the females. Every employee on the payroll has some impact in the first model, because each person's pay is included in one or the other of the averages, but if there were only a few instances in which males and females hired at the same time had similar skills, relatively few employees would influence the averages calculated in the second model.

As a rule, statisticians prefer to incorporate more rather than less data in their models, because under ideal circumstances additional data permit stronger inferences. This desire must be tempered, however, by consideration of the model: in some cases, the incorporation of more data comes only at the expense of an unacceptable decrease in realism.

§2.10.2 Stating Testable Propositions: The Null Hypothesis

The assumptions underlying a statistical model are of two kinds, one called background assumptions and the other the null hypothesis. Ideally the background assumptions are noncontroversial and innocuous and are, under the best of conditions, assumptions that all parties would agree are realistic or otherwise reasonable regardless of whether the null hypothesis is correct. By contrast, the null hypothesis is often very closely linked to the culpability of the defendant, and its accuracy is very much in contest. Under ideal circumstances, the only contested assumption in the model is the null hypothesis, and, by extension, the culpability of the defendant. If the observed data are strongly inconsistent with the model, one infers that the null hypothesis is inaccurate and counts this result as evidence supporting or undermining the defendant's innocence.

In practice, the background assumptions are themselves often controversial, and the fact that the defendant's record is inconsistent with the model may be as much an indictment of the background assumptions as it is of the null hypothesis. Background assumptions can and should be challenged and should be tested empirically whenever possible. As an example of a model with background assumptions and a null hypothesis, consider the situation in which an employer selects for a particular entry-level job 10 new employees from a pool of 100 applicants, of whom 20 are females. Suppose that the employer hires 10 males and no females and in consequence is accused of employment discrimination against females. One analysis of these data is as follows.

Let the background assumptions be that all 100 of the applicants were equally qualified for the ten identical openings and equally desirous of being hired for one of those jobs. It is further assumed that there are no more and no fewer than these 100 applicants and that the employer must fill exactly 10 openings. Take as the null hypothesis the assumption that there is no relationship between an applicant's gender and the likelihood of being hired. In this example, the null hypothesis means that the employer selected the new hires by drawing *at random* the 10 people required from the pool of applicants. Let the measure of the employer's performance be the number of females hired, which in this instance takes the value zero. Given these assumptions, it is apparent that the range of reasonable values for the measure should include the number two because 20% of ten people hired is two. But it is not clear how far to either side of two the range of reasonable values extends nor, in particular, is it clear without further guidelines whether it includes the observed value of zero.

If it is determined that the observed value of zero lies outside the range of reasonable values, one is said to reject the null hypothesis. In the above example, this means that the employer apparently did not select employees at random from the applicants, that there apparently is some relationship between gender and being hired. The new employees may have been selected by order of application or by physical size or on the basis of their gender. Whatever the criterion, it appears to be correlated with gender. If the criterion were demonstrably gender, it is likely that the plaintiffs would prevail, but if some other basis were claimed by the employer and corroborated by the data, the court would have to decide whether the correlation with gender rendered the employer's choices legal or not.

In this example, saying that the null hypothesis has been rejected may be rather inexact. If the employer legitimately distinguished among applicants based on the time they applied or on certain skills they possessed, it is really the background assumptions that have been violated, for not all applicants were equally eligible. Thus, notwithstanding the fact that both sides agree that the null hypothesis has been rejected, as that term of art is used, it does not follow that the employer is culpable: there may be other explanations for why there appears to be a relationship between gender and being hired. In this instance, the background assumption of equal qualification may not have been true.

While it is often the practice among some applied statisticians to accept without question a set of background assumptions, thereby letting the null hypothesis stand or fall based on whether or not the measure of the defendant's performance takes a value consistent with it, this practice must be sharply challenged when encountered in litigation. It is of paramount importance that in an inferential analysis both the background assumptions and the null hypothesis be fully explained and exposed to scrutiny, so that all points at which the assumptions depart from reality can be identified and evaluated for legal significance.

As the above discussion suggests, an analyst has some latitude in choosing the assumptions or model on which an inferential analysis rests. There is also some latitude in the choice of the measure of the extent to which the actual performance record differs from one consistent with the model, though occasionally there is no practical difference between two such measures. One could, for example, use the *percentage* of new hires that were female as the index of an employer's performance, or just as well, the *number* of females that were hired. Sometimes, however, the choice of the index influences the *power* of the statistical analysis to detect a violation of the null hypothesis. The *power* of a statistical test is defined as the probability of rejecting a null hypothesis when it is in fact false. Accordingly, in choosing a model and a measure of the extent to which the defendant's record is consistent with the model, the analyst must, other things being equal, favor methods that have the greatest power to detect legally significant departures of the defendant's record from that expected under the model.

§2.10.3   The Probability of Error in Drawing Conclusions from Data

By accepting or rejecting a null hypothesis, one may err in either of two ways: one may reject the null hypothesis in a situation where it is true or fail to reject it when it is false. The first kind of error is referred to as a *type one error* and the second, a *type two error*. Thus, by rejecting the null hypothesis that there was no relationship between gender and being hired and permitting the inference of discrimination on the basis of gender, one faces the possibility of a type one error. By accepting the null hypothesis, one faces the possibility of a type two error, concluding that the selection process was gender-neutral when in fact it inhibited the hiring of females. In deciding whether to accept or reject a null hypothesis, the evaluator of the data must weigh the chances of each of these types of error occurring and decide which of the two to risk.

The p-value resulting from a statistical analysis can often be interpreted as the probability of making an error given that the null hypothesis is correct and one chooses to reject it. The latter probability is not the same as the probability that the null hypothesis is correct, because, like the p-value, it is calculated under the assumption that the null hypothesis *is* correct. While knowing the probability that the null hypothesis is correct could be very useful in a litigation, there is rarely an objective basis on which to found such a calculation, and one must be content with knowing a p-value. Unfortunately, there is no reason to suppose in general that these two probabilities are similar in magnitude, and hence a p-value need not approximate the probability that the null hypothesis is true.

§2.10.4 p-Values, Null Hypotheses, and Culpability

There is in the law a long tradition of making the presumption that an individual is innocent until proven guilty; unless the evidence is clearly to the contrary, the innocence of the accused is presumed. It is much the same with the statistical method of inference: a set of assumptions regarding the process by which the available data came into being is presumed to be true, unless the data indicate convincingly to the contrary. The Supreme Court has developed this analogy further by calling the finding of an innocent person guilty a type one error[1] and the finding of a culpable person not guilty a type two error.[2]

While the analogy does not always apply even in a statistical case, there are circumstances in which a null hypothesis can correspond closely to the proposition that the accused is innocent, and plaintiffs can attempt to demonstrate through statistical inference and the production of a small p-value that the evidence contravenes that hypothesis and hence also that proposition. In evaluating this argument, a trier of fact should recognize first the distinction between a p-value and the probability that the null hypothesis is false, a distinction discussed in the preceding section. Secondly, the trier should recognize that the calculation of the p-value usually rests not only on the presumption that the null hypothesis is true, but also on the presumption that certain background assumptions are true; if the background assumptions are inaccurate, so too may the p-value be inaccurate. For these two reasons, the trier should be extremely reluctant to identify a p-value with the probability of innocence; the two probabilities are quite distinct philosophically and may be quite different numerically.[3]

§2.10   [1] Ballew v. Georgia, 435 U.S. 223, 234 (1977).
[2] Id.
[3] D. Kaye, Statistical Significance and the Burden of Persuasion, 40 Law and Contemporary Problems 13 (1983); D. Peterson, Preponderance of Evidence, p-Values, and Standard Deviations, Personnel Research Report, Oct. 1983.

CHAPTER THREE

Statistical Inference Generally

§3.0 Introduction

A baffling array of statistical tests is currently offered in courts and administrative tribunals as proof of competing factual positions.

These competing methods may appear to be unrelated to one another and equally valid or invalid, depending on the perspective and predilections of the uninitiated observer. Full utilization of quantitative evidence as a tool of advocacy requires an appreciation of available options. Subsequent chapters distinguish among the statistical tools by examining the questions addressed by each statistical technique, by comparing and contrasting cases in a broad selection of substantive law areas where the tools have assisted courts in making factual determinations, by indicating different data requirements for using the various statistical methods, and by illustrating how statistical results are calculated, interpreted, and attacked.

This chapter has three purposes. The first is to identify the types of problems that can be addressed using statistical methods. Cases in which factual issues amenable to statistical analysis arise are described to provide a background for discussion and a reference point to the lawyer unfamiliar with statistical problems. The second purpose is to introduce the general notion of statistical inference. The analytical approaches to various factual issues arising in the cases described are similar to one another in that all involve drawing inferences from statistical evidence. These similarities are emphasized in order to provide the reader with a simple, intuitive appreciation for the utility of statistical inference generally. The third purpose is to describe selected statistical methods used to address the factual issues raised in the examples. The introduction to specific statistical tools in this chapter enables the lawyer to move to the appropriate chapter in which the tool is described in greater detail.

After reading this chapter, the lawyer should have a better grasp of how quantitative evidence is used and a preliminary understanding of how to interpret statistical findings. Subsequent chapters enable the lawyer to select from among the tools the one most suitable to a particular task, to calculate statistical results, and to expose weaknesses in statistical arguments.

A. INFERENTIAL PROBLEMS ARISING FROM CALCULATED DIFFERENCES

A *difference* is obtained by subtracting one number from another. The difference may be between two measurements of a single variable, such as a factory's observed emission of a pollutant on Wednesday and observed emission on Thursday, or between an observed value and an expected value, such as an observed and an expected number of minority employees. While observed values are usually actual physical measurements, the expected values are often based on historical experience or a legal standard. A difference is also referred to as a *disparity*, particularly when observed and expected values are involved. Often when a difference or disparity is calculated, the question arises whether the difference between the numbers is big enough (or small enough) to have legal significance. Because a difference or disparity might occur by chance, the process of statistical inference is used to determine the probability that the difference occurred by chance in order to eliminate chance as a plausible explanation. This section illustrates how the inferential problems associated with interpreting differences between various types of measurements arise in a wide spectrum of legal contexts.

§3.1 Absolute Differences Between Two Numbers

An absolute difference is calculated simply by subtracting one number from another. Where the magnitude of this difference is essential to the disposition of the legal dispute, courts are presented with the question of whether the absolute difference is large enough to support asserted legal claims.

> **Castaneda v. Partida:**[1] The criminal defendant alleged that Mexican-Americans were underrepresented on grand juries in Hidalgo County, Texas, where he was convicted of burglary with intent to rape. His counsel argued that if Mexican-Americans were represented on juries with the same frequency that they appeared in the population as a whole there would have been 688 Mexican-American grand jurors over the past 11 years instead of the 339 observed.[2] Subtracting the observed number of 339 from the expected number of Mexican-American jurors yields a disparity or difference of 349 jurors.

For purposes of legal proof, the result of subtraction of whole numbers may not be particularly useful because the process is insensitive to the absolute magnitudes of the numbers involved. A difference

§3.1   [1] 430 U.S. 482 (1976).
[2] Id. at 496 n. 17.

between two numbers may or may not appear large, depending on the magnitudes of the two numbers. Subtracting a hypothetical 17,339 observed jurors from 17,688 expected also shows a difference of 349, but this shortfall seems much less serious given the large total number of jurors selected.

§3.2 Differences Between Two Percentages

Percentages are often used to provide a different perspective on the difference between absolute numbers. In Hidalgo County, for instance, 79.1% of the population was Mexican-American while only 39% of people called for jury duty were Mexican-Americans.[1] Whenever one number expressed in percentages is subtracted from another expressed in percentages, the result is a *difference between percentages* (also called a *percentage point difference*) and is expressed in numbers of percentage points between the two numbers.[2] Thus the difference between 79.1% and 39% is 40.1 percentage points. With the larger hypothetical numbers (17,339 observed and 17,688 expected), the difference is only 1.6 percentage points,[3] confirming our intuitive impression that the hypothetical disparity is not as serious as the actual example from *Castaneda*.

United States v. Goff:[4] The defendant alleged that blacks and poor people had been underrepresented on the voter registration list from which federal grand jurors were drawn in the Eastern District of Louisiana. The court discussed disparities between expected and observed percentages of 5.27 percentage points for blacks and 6.17 percentage points[5] for poor people. The *Castaneda* Court found that 40.1 percentage points[6] was a significant disparity evidencing discrimination, while the *Goff* court found 6.17 percentage points insufficient to

§3.2 [1] Castaneda v. Partida, 430 U.S. 482, 486-487 (1976).
[2] The difference between percentages is not to be confused with the percentage difference, which is the ratio of the difference between percentages to one of the original numbers expressed in percentages. Failure to appreciate this distinction and follow the convention adopted in this book can lead to considerable confusion, as illustrated by Supreme Court decisions discussed in Sections 4.2 and 4.3, where the distinction is discussed in greater detail.
[3] 17,688 = .791 × 22,362 and 17,339/22,362 = .775. The percentage point difference is .791 − .755 = .016 or 1.6%.
[4] 509 F.2d 825 (5th Cir. 1975).
[5] Id. at 826-827.
[6] 430 U.S. 482, 495 (1976).

show substantial underrepresentation of poor people. These findings are understandable; 6.17 is a considerably smaller disparity than 40.1.

Board of Education v. Califano:[7] The court found that only .9%[8] of the teachers were black in a New York City school where, had teachers been assigned in a racially neutral fashion, one would expect 5.1%[9] to have been black. This underrepresentation of 4.2 percentage points (5.1% minus .9%) was thought by the court to be substantial and evidence of disparate treatment of whites and blacks.

Why is a calculated difference of 6.17 percentage points insufficient to show discrimination in one case but a difference of 4.2 percentage points sufficient in another? The answer requires more than a knowledge of the relevant law. There must be more underlying these conclusions than simple differences between either absolute numbers or percentages. That something is the answer to the questions "How big is big?" and "Under what circumstances is big significant?" Inferential statistical methods combined with knowledge of the relevant law help to answer these questions.

Certified Color Manufacturers' Association v. Mathews:[10] Scientific studies regarding deleterious effects on laboratory rats were scrutinized by the court in a determination of the carcinogenic properties of Red Dye No. 2. One scientific study concluded that of rats dying before the end of the study, seven of twenty-three rats from the group receiving high dosages of Red Dye No. 2 were found to have cancer while four of thirty rats from the low dosage group had cancer. Is the difference in incidence of cancer between the two groups large enough to establish a link between the dye and the disease? If you conclude that it obviously is, you can easily imagine numbers where the significance of the difference is more questionable.

Some courts have been willing to rely on their own judgment as to the legal significance of a difference without resorting to statistical inference.

United States v. Maskeny:[11] Appellant offered statistics that showed a disparity between the percentage of each allegedly underrep-

---

[7] 584 F.2d 576 (2d. Cir. 1978).
[8] Id. at 584 n. 28.
[9] Id. at 584 n. 29.
[10] 543 F.2d 284 (D.C. Cir. 1976).
[11] 609 F.2d 183 (5th Cir. 1980).

resented group in the community and the percentage of that group on the list from which jurors were chosen was less than 10 percentage points. The Supreme Court in an equal protection case had held that an underrepresentation by as much as ten percentage points did not show purposeful discrimination.[12] A previous opinion of the Fifth Circuit had upheld a system that resulted in an eleven percentage point disparity between the percentage of black people in the population and black people on the jury.[13] Following these precedents in *Maskeny*, Judge Coleman of the Fifth Circuit specifically declined to consider inferential methods and relied on the absolute disparity to say that there was no constitutional violation shown.[14]

Other courts have relied on inferential methods when evaluating the significance of a disparity. (See Section 3.12).

§3.3 *Differences with Multiple Categories*

In addition to the two-group cases, black-nonblack in *Board of Education*[1] or high dosage-low dosage in *Certified Color*,[2] cases arise where there are numerous categories, one or more of which are allegedly subject to different treatment. A disparity can be calculated for each category in such cases. We often wish to summarize the disparities as a group.

Inmates of the Nebraska Penal and Correctional Complex v. Greenholtz:[3] Four racial groups were granted discretionary parole with different frequencies. The plaintiffs were a class of Native American and Mexican-American inmates of a Nebraska prison claiming that the defendant members of the Nebraska Board of Parole denied discretionary parole to class members on racially and ethnically discriminatory grounds. Statistics showed that overall 59.3% of those eligible were granted release by discretionary parole, but while 60.7% of whites and 63.0% of blacks were paroled, only 40.7% of Native Americans and 27.8% of Mexican-Americans were.[4] The difficulty is not in calculating the differences between expected and observed parole rates for each

---

[12] Swain v. Alabama, 380 U.S. 202, 208-209 (1965).
[13] Thompson v. Sheppard, 490 F.2d 830 (5th Cir. 1974).
[14] 609 F.2d 183, 190 (5th Cir. 1980).
§3.3 [1] 584 F.2d 576 (2d Cir. 1978), discussed in Section 3.2.
[2] 543 F.2d 284 (D.C. Cir. 1976), discussed in Section 3.2.
[3] 567 F.2d 1368 (8th Cir. 1977).
[4] Id. at 1371.

subgroup but in determining whether the disparities as a whole are sufficient to indicate unlawful discrimination among the various categories.

§3.4 Differences Between Averages

It is often necessary to compare the averages of two different groups of numbers. Calculating the difference between averages is one way to compare two groups. If the averages are different the groups themselves may be different in some relevant respect. Before calculating the difference, the averages of the two groups must be determined. While this may involve an additional computational step compared to subtraction of absolute magnitudes, the same inferential problem arises: in this context, how big must a difference between averages be to be significant?

In re Forte-Fairbairn, Inc.:[1] In what was essentially a contract claim heard before the Federal Trade Commision, a dispute arose over the identity of certain fibers invoiced as baby llama fibers. The buyer alleged that the fibers shipped were from baby alpacas rather than llamas. Experts who specialized in distinguishing fibers by microscopic examination compared the diameters of fibers taken from the shipment to known samples of alpaca and llama. If the average diameters of alpaca and llama fibers were different, then comparing the average diameter of the delivered fibers to that of known fibers would have identified the shipment. If the average diameters of the two types were numerically close and the diameters of a given type vary from one another, could we still identify the fibers by comparing average diameter to the known sample?

Presseisen v. Swarthmore College:[2] The issue of how big a difference between averages is big enough arose more pointedly where a former assistant professor alleged sex discrimination in promotion practices by her employer college. The average time between receipt of highest degree to promotion or appointment to assistant professor was 3.3 years for males and 5.8 years for females.[3] The difference between averages is 2.5 years. Is this a big enough difference to be significant?

§3.4 [1] 62 F.T.C. 1146 (1963).
[2] 442 F. Supp. 593 (E.D. Pa. 1977), *aff'd,* 582 F.2d 1275 (3d Cir. 1982).
[3] 442 F. Supp. at 609.

The complication presented by *Presseisen* and *Forte-Fairbairn* is that we are not simply summarizing the difference between two absolute numbers such as expected and observed values but are calculating the difference between two averages, statistics that abstract a particular characteristic from a larger group of numbers. It is not surprising that in determining the significance of differences between averages we will want to know how much the individual numbers summarized by these averages vary from the averages. If some men and women with identical characteristics are promoted in the same length of time, how significant is it that many others are not?

§3.5   Differences from Sample Data

Litigators are concerned not only with whether an observed number is significantly different from expected but also whether it is significantly above a legal maximum or below a legal minimum. Often physical measurements combine the difficulty of comparing averages as in *Presseisen*[1] with complexities introduced by a sampling process.

> **Reserve Mining Co. v. EPA:**[2] Governmental agencies and environmental groups sought an injunction to prevent the defendant company from discharging wastes from its iron ore processing plant into the ambient air over Lake Superior. A court-appointed expert witness, Dr. William Taylor, testified that the concentration of asbestiform fibers in the ambient air was 0.0626 fibers per cubic centimeter of air. Since airborne fiber concentrations will vary on different days and in different locations depending on, among other things, the output of the iron processing plants and meteorological conditions, Dr. Taylor averaged the fiber count of five testing sites. In an effort to determine whether the asbestos level in the ambient air was too high, the average from the five sample sites was compared to the only legal standard available for comparison, the level typically associated with occupational exposure to asbestos.[3]

The basic problem in *Reserve Mining* is the same as in *Castaneda:*[4] determining the significance of a difference between two magnitudes. In *Reserve Mining* one of the magnitudes is the average of a subset or

---

§3.5   [1]442 F. Supp. 593 (E.D. Pa. 1977), discussed in Section 3.4.
[2]514 F.2d 492 (8th Cir. 1975).
[3]Id. at 511 n. 34.
[4]430 U.S. 482 (1976), discussed in Section 3.1.

sample consisting of measurements at only five testing sites. An average calculated from sample data is also referred to as a *sample mean.* To evaluate the significance or the difference between sample means and other numbers, we will want to take into account not only how much the individual items in the sample group vary from the sample mean but also the size of the sample group.

This same process has been used to establish a legal maximum.

Marathon Oil Co. v. EPA:[5] One issue discussed was the appropriateness of the method by which the Environmental Protection Agency set its effluent discharge standards for the oil, mud, grease, and soaps that are washed from offshore oil drilling platforms. The EPA set these effluent standards by looking at the average performance of the best existing pollution technology in the business and sampled discharges from some of the plants that were using the technology in an exemplary fashion. At issue in the case was whether this sampling method gave an emission standard achievable 100% of the time by a plant using the best technology. The disparity between the level specified in the standard and the level that could be achieved 100% of the time arose from complexities introduced into the measurement problem by the sampling and averaging processes.

Similar issues arise when comparing an observed value obtained from a sample to a legal minimum.

United States v. General Motors Corp.:[6] The director of the National Highway Traffic Safety Bureau alleged that the automobile manufacturer failed to issue a safety-defect notification to purchasers of a defective wheel used on light trucks. The relevant issue was whether the number of wheel failures was "significant" enough to require customer notification, that is, whether the number exceeded a minimum below which no notification was required. The difference between actual failures and the minimum could not be calculated directly because some customers with defective wheels did not report the failure to the company. As in *Reserve Mining,* where the actual average concentration of asbestiform particles was unknown, the number of wheel failures was estimated by sampling a selected group of customers. Since the number of wheels manufactured was known, the total number could be estimated once the percentage of failures was determined. Calculating the difference between estimated total failures and the minimum num-

---

[5] 564 F.2d 1253 (9th Cir. 1977).
[6] 377 F. Supp. 242 (D.D.C. 1974).

ber triggering the notification requirement is straightforward.[7] Determining the significance of this difference is complicated by the sampling and averaging process.

§3.6 Similarities Among Inferential Problems Arising from Calculated Differences

The examples in Sections 3.1 through 3.5 illustrate simple differences between absolute magnitudes (often, observed and expected numbers), between percentages, between magnitudes and between percentages where there are numerous categories involved, between means calculated from measurements of all members of a group, between sample means, and between means and legal maxima and minima. A recurring problem is to determine the statistical and, ultimately, the legal significance of a difference between two values. As is elaborated on further in Part C of this chapter, statistical inference helps make such determinations.

B. INFERENTIAL PROBLEMS INVOLVING RELATIONSHIPS BETWEEN VARIABLES

This section explores two statistics used to describe how the value of one variable, such as the budget for salaries, varies when the value of another variable, such as the number of employees, changes. These two statistics are the sample correlation coefficient and the sample regression coefficient; both are measures of the correspondences between two variables. The inferential problems that arise from determining the legal significance of these statistics are similar to those arising from the calculation of differences: Instead of asking whether a difference is big enough to be significant, however, we ask whether a correspondence between two variables is strong enough, consistent enough, or, in general, big enough to be significant. We begin with

---

[7] Actually, the requirement of notification is triggered by evidence of a "large number" of failures. How big a "large number" is depends on the facts and surrounding circumstances of each case. Therefore, the legal minimum is the number below which the director or, as in this context, the court feels the number of failures is not large. Id. at 252 n. 28.

correlation coefficients in Sections 3.7 and 3.8 and then discuss regression coefficients in Sections 3.9 and 3.10.

§3.7 Simple Correlation

The *correlation coefficient* is a measure of the consistency with which the values of two variables change in the same direction. If two variables are *correlated,* knowing the value of one helps us to predict the value of the other: knowing the circumference of someone's head, for instance, helps one to infer hat size, and knowing someone's age helps one to predict remaining life expectancy.

When an increase in the value of one variable, e.g., head circumference, leads us to expect an increase in the value of the other, e.g., hat size, we say that there is a *positive correlation* between the two or that the variables are *directly related.* When an increase in the value of one variable, e.g., age, leads us to expect a decrease in the value of the other, e.g., remaining life expectancy, there is a *negative correlation* between the two variables, an *inverse relationship.*

Head circumference and hat size have an almost perfect positive correlation, because when head circumference in inches is divided by 3.14, that is the corresponding hat size as it is customarily measured. Age and remaining life expectancy are negatively correlated but not perfectly so, because there are other factors that determine life expectancy, such as health, family history, evil habits, and occupation.

United States v. City of Chicago:[1] The court examined the relationship between the performance of police sergeants on a written promotion examination and their efficiency ratings on the job. The plaintiffs had proved that there were statistically significant disparities between proportions of blacks and whites selected to be promoted to sergeant, thereby shifting the burden to the defendant to persuade the court that the written exam on which promotions were based was job-related. One would expect that the sergeants with high efficiency and performance records would score well on a well-designed, job-related, written exam, and that those with low records would score poorly. If not, the score on the exam would be a bad predictor of future performance. When a high level of performance by an individual on one scale, e.g., actual performance, is matched with a high level by the same individual on another scale, e.g., the written exam, and an individual

§3.7 [1] 385 F. Supp. 543 (N.D. Ill. 1974).

with low scores on one gets low scores on the other, the scores are positively or directly correlated and if sergeants with high scores on one scale had low scores on the other and vice versa, the scores would be negatively correlated. The scores examined in this case showed a positive correlation for a sample of 176 incumbent sergeants. Generally, though not always, those sergeants with high efficiency ratings scored higher on the written exams than those with low efficiency ratings.

Once we reach the point where we have identified the correspondence as positive or negative, we are back at the same point we were with differences; how big or small does the correlation have to be to support the legal claims involved? In the *City of Chicago* case, how often will we allow highly efficient sergeants to score poorly on the written test and still conclude that the test is job-related? If 5% score poorly on the written test, is that too many? 20%? 80%? The combination of statistical methods and substantive law that tells how big a difference must be to be significant also addresses this issue; how often must there be a positive or negative relationship between the two measurements in order to conclude that there is a statistically significant and legally sufficient positive or negative correlation overall? In *City of Chicago*, the court concluded that even though a positive relationship was shown there was not a statistically *significant* positive correlation overall and that the test was not job related.[2]

Determining the job-relatedness of a test by looking at correlations to actual performance, a process referred to as validation, can be complicated further by separately examining the individual components of a multipart exam. In such an inquiry correlation coefficients may be calculated to reflect the relationship between appropriate portions of the written exam and their corresponding job performance tasks. For each coefficient the questions arise whether the correspondence is significant, and, for the collection of coefficients taken together, whether there are enough large coefficients to permit the conclusion that the exam is job-related. Statistical inference provides some guidance in answering these questions.

Boston Chapter NAACP v. Beecher:[3] The Civil Service sought to validate the use of its firefighters' exam by correlating exam scores with scores achieved by firefighters in each of 13 job-related tasks such as ladder extension, handling a preconnected hose, air mask operation,

[2] Id. at 559.
[3] 371 F. Supp. 507 (D. Mass. 1974).

extinguisher selection, securing lines and knots, and hose and hydrant operations. An expert witness, Dr. Costa, testified that only two of the task scores showed a significant correlation to the exam scores, and those were "barely significant."[4] The court found that the Civil Service had not met its burden of demonstrating that the exam was "in fact substantially related to job performance."[5] The greater the number of correlations calculated, the more often decisions arise as to the statistical significance of the computed correlations.

The calculation of a correlation coefficient is admittedly more complicated than computing a difference, but the interpretation is not difficult. The correlation coefficient always takes a value between -1 (for perfect negative correlations) and $+1$ (for perfect correlations). If the value of one variable, such as exam score, is totally unrelated to the measurement of the other, such as performance score, the coefficient equals zero.

Samples are often used to estimate the extent of the relationship that exists between two variables; if the items chosen are representative of those in the population as a whole, the correlation coefficient calculated from the sample, the *sample correlation coefficient,* is a good estimate of the population correlation coefficient. Once a sample correlation coefficient is calculated, the question remains whether the coefficient is statistically significant, that is, is it different enough from zero (no relationship) that one may infer that there is indeed a positive or negative relationship between the variables in the population, whatever its magnitude may be.

United States v. City of Chicago:[6] Witnesses at one point reported a statistically significant correlation of .247 between police exams and performance scores.[7] Because this coefficient was calculated from a sample of 176 police sergeants, this is an estimate of the relationship between these variables in the population. This correlation, .247, is not very close to $+1$, which would show a perfect positive correspondence between examination and performance scores, but a statistician might nevertheless conclude that it is statistically significant because the correlation has an associated p-value of .02, which indicates that sampling would give a sample correlation coefficient of this size only 2% of the time if the correlation calculated from the entire population were zero.

---

[4] Id. at 517.
[5] Id.
[6] 385 F. Supp. 543 (N.D. Ill. 1974).
[7] Id. at 558.

Why would one conclude that this low correspondence is statistically significant?

In re National Commission on Egg Nutrition:[8] The Federal Trade Commission considered evidence of a correlation between average level of dietary serum cholesterol in each of seven countries and the corresponding number of new deaths from coronary heart disease and definite nonfatal heart attacks. This sample correlation coefficient was equal to .76[9] but was statistically significant only at a 5% level, a p-value of .05. Remember that the lower the significance level or p-value, the greater the statistical significance. Why is a sample correlation coefficient of .247 for the *City of Chicago* case more statistically significant than .76, which appears to be closer to a perfect correlation?

Just as a greater difference between two numbers should show a greater and, hence, more significant disparity, one would expect a correlation coefficient closer to 1 to be interpreted as showing a closer and, thus, more significant correspondence between the values of the variables. As we shall see, however, one key to statistical differences is the number of observations we make of the variables in question. It is not surprising that within certain limits the more measurements we make of a certain event, whether it is selection of jurors, concentration of air pollutants, rates of coronary heart disease, or correspondences between test scores, the more reliable our conclusions will be. Increasing the number of observations will not necessarily increase the degree of correlation, but it will make a given correlation estimate more reliable and, hence, more significant to the legal factfinding process. In *City of Chicago* the sample correlation coefficient was calculated using 176 test scores. In *Egg Nutrition* only seven countries were observed. This large difference in sample size affects the relative reliability of the estimates that result of the respective population correlation coefficients.

Knowing the degree of correlation between measurements of different variables helps to explain how the value of one variable changes when there is a change in the value of the other. The greater the correspondence, the more the changes in one explain changes in the other. The *coefficient of determination* is a statistic calculated by squaring the correlation coefficient and is interpreted as the fraction

---

[8] 88 F.T.C. 89 (1976), *modified,* 570 F.2d 157 (D.C. Cir. 1977), *cert. denied,* 439 U.S. 821.
[9] 88 F.T.C. at 130.

of variation in one variable explained by variations in the other. When values of variables change regularly and systematically in a corresponding way, the correlation coefficient will approach $+1$ or -1, and the coefficient of determination will approach $+1$, indicating that a large fraction of the variation in one variable is mathematically explained by that in the other.

In re National Commission on Egg Nutrition:[10] The increased risk of heart attacks and heart disease in men was examined by exploring its correlation with their consumption of eggs. The trade association of egg manufacturers would have loved to be able to show a zero or even negative correlation between heart disease and the dietary intake of serum cholesterol, which comes from eggs. An expert witness, Dr. Connor, reported a sample correlation coefficient of 0.666 between the coronary heart disease death rate in thirty countries and the associated average daily intake of eggs.[11] To find out how much of the variation in heart disease is mathematically explained by variations in egg consumption, one simply squares the sample correlation coefficient. Thus 44% (.666 × .666) of the variability in heart disease rates is accounted for by variations in egg consumption, according to Dr. Connor. Other testimony revealed that 66% of the variation in the level of new diagnoses of coronary heart disease among men in seven countries and 53% of variation in deaths from coronary heart disease and definite nonfatal heart attacks were accounted for by the variation in mean level of dietary serum cholesterol; the sample correlation coefficients were 0.81 and 0.73 respectively.[12] The coefficient of determination provides some perspective on the relationship between the variables and assists in addressing the problem whether these correspondences are large enough to prove that advertisements praising the healthful properties of eggs are deceptive and misleading.

Note that neither the correlation coefficient nor the coefficient of determination indicates that either variable causes the other variable to change. There is undoubtedly a correlation between the number of clergymen in a community and the number of new births in the community, yet it would be frivolous to suggest that the former caused the latter even though there is a mathematical correspondence between the variables. The documented correlation between the original league of the winner of the Super Bowl and performance of the

[10] Id.
[11] Id. at 130.
[12] Id. at 133.

stock market each year discussed in Section 1.11 note 1 is another example of correlation without causation. One must carefully interpret the correlation coefficient as measuring the mathematical correspondence between changes in the values of the variables. From a high degree of mathematical correspondence one may infer a causal relationship if the connection is sensible and logical, but a high correlation *by itself* does not establish causality.

§3.8   Rank Correlations

It is noteworthy that in order to use correlation coefficients one need not have numerical measurements of the variables: as long as they reflect qualities that can be ranked (from highest to lowest, biggest to smallest, or best to worst) correlation coefficients may be used.

Pennsylvania v. Local Union 542, International Union of Operating Engineers:[1] A class of minority workers alleged employment discrimination in the operation of the union's referral system. The statistical expert prepared two ordinal lists, the first ranking members of the union by how often they were out of work, the second ranking members in the order in which they were actually referred to jobs. The theory was that if the assignments were made on a nondiscriminatory basis members out of work most often would be referred to jobs first. The rank orderings of workers on referral and out-of-work lists were compared by calculating a sample rank correlation coefficient. A perfect positive correspondence between the employees' places on the two lists would give a correlation coefficient of +1 and would be evidence of a nondiscriminatory referral system. The expert prepared 17 pairs of lists representing different job categories and time periods. Sample rank correlation coefficients ranged from .08, showing almost no relationship between the lists for a given time period and job category, to .62.[2] The out-of-work lists, which, if used as a guideline for referral would explain the orderings on the referrals lists, explained from .6% to 38.4%[3] of the referrals, leaving as much as 99.4% and as little as 61.6% unexplained. The court found that this corroborated the plaintiffs' claims of discrimination in that it proved there was much room for arbitrary and standardless selections; "When combined with other statistical disparities considering the race factor directly, this correlation study aids the inference of discrimination."[4]

§3.8   [1]469 F. Supp. 329 (E.D. Pa. 1978), *aff'd mem.*, 648 F.2d 922 (3d Cir. 1981).
[2]469 F. Supp. at 356.
[3]Id.
[4]Id. at 357.

The statistical expert in *Local Union 542* concluded that few of the lists reflecting actual referral rankings showed any statistically significant correspondence to their associated out-of-work list. How much similarity must there be between the lists for there to be a statistically significant correspondence? How big does the coefficient have to be to be big? As we shall see, the statistical significance of a correspondence is determined in a fashion similar to that of a difference, by use of the methods of statistical inference.

§3.9 Simple Regression Coefficients

Correlation coefficients summarize the extent to which the values of two variables change in the same direction at the same time. They do not, however, allow one to predict *how much* the value of one variable changes when there is a change in the value of another variable. Related to the correlation coefficient is the *regression coefficient,* which does provide this information.

South Dakota Public Utilities Commission v. Federal Energy Regulatory Commission:[1] The state utility commission opposed a FERC order permitting an accelerated rate of depreciation for certain facilities owned by Northern Natural Gas. The FERC order was based on a finding that because reserves of natural gas were dwindling, Northern's pipeline equipment would lose its value before its physical life was over. In order to estimate when there would be no natural gas left to transport on the pipeline, the relationship between two variables, time and new discoveries, was examined to project a year in which no new discoveries would be made. The regression coefficient was − 160.16 billion cubic feet per year, which meant that the first variable, new annual discovery, decreased by 160.16 billion cubic feet of gas for a one-year change in the second variable, time. Given the current level of discoveries, calculations projected that no new discoveries would be made after 1981.

The reliability, accuracy, and, therefore, significance of the projection embodied in a regression coefficient will depend, not surprisingly, on the basis from which we derive our prediction. We would not predict winter snowfall for New England by reference only to Arizona's weather, or by looking at just one or two years of New England's weather history. Nor would we attach much significance to

§3.9 [1]643 F.2d 504 (8th Cir. 1981).

our precise estimate of this year's snowfall if historically we observe a wide variation from year to year. The significance of the conclusion will be affected by the logical relationship between the variables, by the number of measurements made, and by the variability among those measurements. Statistical tests involving each of these parameters guide the factfinder in assessing the significance of the conclusion. One can calculate a p-value associated with each such regression coefficient that indicates the statistical significance of the computed relationship between the variables.

§3.10   Multiple Regression Coefficients

The particular utility of regression coefficients is that one can simultaneously estimate the individual effects of numerous variables on the variable one is trying to estimate, predict, or explain, which is referred to as the *dependent variable* because its value depends on the values of the explanatory variables. The explanatory variables are referred to as *independent variables*.

> **Presseisen v. Swarthmore College:**[1] In this sex discrimination case, one expert tried to predict salaries of college teachers (the depencent variable) by summarizing the effects of sex, age, years since highest degree, years teaching at Swarthmore, degree, and academic division (the independent variables). An opposing expert testified that other variables also would affect salary and should have been included in the regression calculations. Additional variables might include measures of scholarship, teaching ability, publications and their quality, quality of degree, duration of career interruptions, and administrative responsibilities.

> **Agarwal v. Arthur G. McKee Co.:**[2] The plaintiff's regression analysis in this typical race discrimination in employment case included the following explanatory variables to explain salary differentials: minority status, years of education, years since receipt of highest degree, age of employee, years of prior experience, and years of employment by the defendant employer.

One can estimate the individual effects of any number of explanatory or *independent variables* on the value of a variable one wishes to

§3.10 [1] 442 F. Supp. 593 (E.D. Pa. 1977), *aff'd*, 582 F.2d 1275 (3d Cir. 1982).
[2] 19 Fair Empl. Prac. Cas. (BNA) 503 (N.D. Cal. 1977).

explain or predict, the *dependent variable*, by simultaneously calculating a regression coefficient for each. No matter how many coefficients are simultaneously calculated, the individual coefficients can be examined one by one. By one expert's testimony in *Presseisen*, for instance, the coefficient describing the relationship between salary, the dependent variable, and gender, one of the independent variables, in 1972 had a value of − 340, which indicated that female teachers on average made $340 less than males with comparable skills.[3] This estimate is the effect on salary of gender alone, when all other independent variables are held constant. This is the coefficient of interest in a sex discrimination suit. The calculation is intended to separate out all the other influences on salary except for the effect of gender. A familiar problem arises, however, in determining the practical and statistical significance of this difference between male and female salaries. Is it large enough to justify the remedy sought by the plaintiff? Is $340 significantly different from zero, given the absolute size of salaries? Not surprisingly, the significance will depend on the number of measurements taken of the variables and the variation among those measurements. If men's salaries differ widely from one another, we would not be surprised to find that the average salary for women differs by some small amount from men's average salary.

The use of multiple regression coefficients is not limited to discrimination cases.

Northshore School District No. 417 v. Kinnear:[4] The ability to explain variations by districts in per pupil expenditures on education was critical to defenders of the Washington state school financing system. The plaintiffs claimed that variations in expenditures were due to the localized method of financing schools. Francis Flerchinger, a statistician from the Office of Superintendent of Public Instruction, tried to explain the dependent variable, the level of expenditures per pupil in each of Washington's 320 school districts, by reference to two independent variables unrelated to the financing scheme, teachers' pay and staff per thousand students in each district.[5] The coefficient on each of these two independent variables describes the effect of variations in the variable on the level of expenditures per pupil, just as sex or race might explain salary differences among teachers. Again, the reliability of the coefficients would have to be tested.

---

[3] 442 F. Supp. at 617.
[4] 530 P.2d 178 (Wash. 1974).
[5] Id. at 186.

The regression coefficient of −340 associated with the sex variable in *Presseisen* is the average difference between salaries of otherwise similar males and females. The regression coefficient explains how the value of one variable changes when there is a change in the value of the other, just as a correlation coefficient does. Both indicate *whether* one variable increases in value as the other does; whether, for example, as ingestion of dietary serum cholesterol increases, the rate of coronary heart disease increases. What a regression coefficient adds is information as to *how much* the value of one variable increases or decreases when the other changes. The regression coefficient −340 tells us not only that as gender changes from male to female salaries decline but that the decline is $340. In *South Dakota Public Utility Commission*[6] the coefficient of −160.16 tells us not only that new discoveries are declining as each year passes, but also that the new annual discoveries of natural gas decrease by 160.16 billion cubic feet on average from the level of the year before.

The *coefficient of multiple determination* summarizes the strength of the association between a dependent variable and one or more independent or explanatory variables. In some instances the relationship is so close that nearly all of the variation in the values taken by the dependent variable can be attributed to variations in the values of the explanatory variables. In other cases the values are quite unrelated to those taken by the explanatory variables. The fraction of the variation in the dependent variable that is accounted for by variations in the explanatory variables is called the coefficient of multiple determination. Possible values of the coefficient range from zero to 1, with the latter corresponding to a regression in which variations in the values taken by the explanatory variables account fully for variations in the dependent variable's values.

Northshore School District No. 417 v. Kinnear:[7] The coefficient of multiple determination was reported by the court to be .75,[8] indicating that average pay for certificated staff and staffing ratio per 1,000 pupils, the independent variables, combined to account for 75% of the variation in expenditure per pupil, the dependent variable.

As with the coefficient of determination discussed in Section 3.7, there are significance tests for assigning *p*-values to the combined

---

[6] 643 F.2d 504 (8th Cir. 1981), discussed in Section 3.9.
[7] 530 P.2d 178 (Wash. 1974).
[8] Id. at 186.

effect on the dependent variable of any selected group of independent variables. Using such a test one can determine whether the coefficient calculated for a particular set of numbers is different enough from zero that it signals some power on the part of the independent variables to explain or account for variation in the dependent variable.

§3.11 Similarities Among Inferential Problems Arising from Calculated Differences and Correlations

For many situations in which regression and correlation coefficients are used we want to know both whether the results are due to some fluke or aberration in the numbers used to calculate them and whether the size of the coefficient is large enough to persuade the factfinder that the proponent's claim is correct. Both types of coefficients are used to summarize the numerical correspondence between variables. If there is none, the values of each coefficient will be zero, though the regression coefficient is not constrained to fall between −1 and +1, as the *South Dakota Public Utility Commission* example[1] illustrates. The question of statistical significance is often whether the calculated coefficient is truly different from zero or whether any difference from zero is due merely to some chance aberration. This statistical issue of significance is conceptually identical to determining whether the *difference* between expected and observed numbers is large. For the discrimination, contract, and environmental law cases described in Part A of this chapter, we were continually questioning the significance of differences such as between expected and observed values, between an observed value and a legal maximum or minimum, or between averages from different samples. Calculating percentages and averages may be mathematically easier than calculating coefficients, but the process of determining their statistical significance is similar. The legal significance of a particular difference or correspondence depends on the state of the relevant case law and the discretion of the judge and jury as influenced by the lawyers and witnesses.

---

§3.11 [1]643 F.2d 504 (8th Cir. 1981), discussed in Section 3.9.

C. SOLUTIONS TO INFERENTIAL PROBLEMS: SIGNIFICANCE TESTING

For each of the cases discussed, a statistical test indicates the significance of the estimate that has been calculated, whether it is a difference, a correlation, or a prediction resulting from a regression. The statistician, by calculating a *test statistic* and taking into account varying sample or group sizes or numbers of categories, estimates a probability, a *p*-value, that the difference, correspondence, or prediction occurred by chance. (See Section 2.10 where *p*-values are discussed.) An estimate with a high probability of random occurrence is called statistically insignificant: one with a low *p*-value is considered to be significant. The following sections briefly describe a number of approaches used to find *p*-values. Chapters 4 through 8 describe which tests are appropriate for which problems, using data that are drawn from or related to cases to illustrate when different approaches are appropriate and how the mathematical calculations are performed.

§3.12 Testing the Significance of Simple Differences

In the *Castaneda*[1] and *Goff*[2] cases, the respective differences in observed and expected percentages of 40.1 and 5.27 percentage points were easily distinguished. Recall that the courts found that 40.1 was a significant disparity but 5.27 was not. A disparity of 40.1 is so large that it seems unlikely to have occurred by chance, while the 5.27 is comparatively small. Why then, in *Board of Education*,[3] was 4.2 percentage points statistically significant?

An appropriate test statistic for determining the significance of simple differences between two numbers or percents is the *Z* statistic, calculated by dividing the difference between the numbers or percents, i.e., the disparity, by the *standard deviation,* a statistic that measures the typical variation of observations around the average. (See Section 4.7, where the standard deviation is discussed in greater detail.) The *Z* Table indicates how probable it is that such a disparity

---

§3.12   [1] 430 U.S. 482, 495 (1976), discussed in Section 3.1.
[2] 509 F.2d 825, 827 (5th Cir. 1975), discussed in Section 3.2.
[3] 584 F.2d 576, 584 nn. 27-28 (2d. Cir. 1978), discussed in Section 3.2.

would occur by chance, i.e., whether it is a statistically significant difference. In *Board of Education*[4] the disparity of 4.2 percentage points gives a Z test statistic of −2.52. The Z Table reveals an associated *p*-value of .0118, indicating that in this group of teachers, the observed underrepresentaion of blacks is likely to occur by chance only 1.18% of the time if the hiring process is really carried out without reference to race. (See Section 4.14, where the calculation of *p*-values from Z test statistics is discussed.)

For other differences, such as the disparity in *Goff*,[5] a mathematical equation called the *binomial formula* is used to calculate the *p*-value directly. (See Section 4.28). The formula is used because the group size under consideration was rather small, a jury of 23 members, compared to the size of the group in *Board of Education*, a school with 129 teachers. The binomial formula in *Goff* indicates a *p*-value of about .42, suggesting that the probability of finding a disparity as large as the one that occurred here just by chance was about 42%.

Thus a court might find that the disparity in *Board of Education*, based on a sample of 129, is statistically significant, that is, not likely to have occurred by chance, while the disparity in *Goff*, based on a group size of only 23, is not statistically significant because it would occur by chance almost half of the time.

§3.13 Testing the Significance of Differences with Numerous Categories

Disparities involving two or more categories can be analyzed using a similar procedure. Recall in *Inmates*,[1] for instance, that there were disparities between observed and expected values for four different racial groups being examined simultaneously. An appropriate test statistic for this case is the *chi-square* statistic,[2] which like the Z statistic, is calculated from the differences between expected and observed values for each category. The chi-square table shows for various numbers of categories the probability of getting values of the chi-square statistic by chance, i.e., the *p*-value. The *p*-value associated with the chi-square test statistic indicates the likelihood that the ob-

---

[4] Id. at 584-585 n. 29, discussed in Section 3.2.
[5] 509 F.2d 825, 827 (5th Cir. 1975), discussed in Section 3.2.
§3.13 [1] 567 F.2d 1368 (8th Cir. 1977), discussed in Section 3.2.
[2] *Chi* is pronounced Kī to rhyme with sky.

served differences in treatment among categories could have occurred by chance. See Chapter 5 regarding the chi-square test.

Certified Color Manufacturers' Association v. Mathews:[3] The chi-
square test statistic for two categories, high dosage and low dosage rats,
equals 1.85.[4] Checking the chi-square table indicates a 10% to 20%
probability that one might observe the same difference in cancer rates
even if there is no relationship between dosage and cancer. This p-value
of .20 to .10 is described as a 10 to 20 percent significance level. Because
the standard relied on by the statistical expert in this case requires a p-
value less than .05, this finding was considered not statistically
significant.

**Inmates of the Nebraska Penal and Correctional Complex v.
Greenholtz:**[5] A chi-square test for the four racial categories, white,
black, Mexican-American and Native American, gives a chi-square
value of 7.49[6] and a p-value between .10 and .05, indicating a probability between 5% and 10% that the parole hearings would have given the
same results even if there had been no discrimination. Because the p-
value was greater than .05, among other reasons, the court concluded
that there was no proof of discrimination sufficient to make out an
equal protection claim.[7]

Chance v. Board of Examiners:[8] Using a chi-square test, the court
found that the probability that the small actual number of minorities
passing the qualifying exam for public school administrators was due to
random factors alone was less than one in a billion and consequently
enjoined administration of the examination.[9]

§3.14 Testing the Significance of Differences Between Sample Means

When numerical calculations are derived from samples rather
than from a measurement of the whole population, an element of

---

[3] 543 F.2d 284 (D.C. Cir. 1976), discussed in Section 3.2.
[4] This figure is calculated for an observed 7 of 27 high dosage rats and 4 of 30 low
dosage rats getting cancer to determine whether there is a significant departure from
the mean cancer rate of 21%. Id. at 290 n. 30.
[5] 567 F.2d 1368 (8th Cir. 1977), discussed in Section 3.2.
[6] This figure is calculated for observed numbers of 358 of 590 whites, 184 of 235
blacks, 24 of 59 Native Americans, and 5 of 18 Mexican-Americans receiving discretionary parole to determine whether there is a significant departure by racial group
from the mean discretionary parole rate of 59.3%. Id. at 1371.
[7] Id. at 1381.
[8] 330 F. Supp. 203 (S.D.N.Y. 1971), aff'd, 458 F.2d 1167 (2d Cir. 1972).
[9] 330 F. Supp. at 212.

uncertainty is introduced and resulting estimates or predictions are inherently less precise. The t test statistic is often appropriate for determining whether the mean calculated for one sample is significantly different from that calculated from another sample. See Section 6.12, Direct Significance Tests for the Differences between Sample Estimates.

> **Presseisen v. Swarthmore College:**[1] The 30 men and 12 women who had been promoted to assistant professor form a sample of all those who might go through the allegedly discriminatory promotion process at Swarthmore. The average time for promotion from instructor to assistant professor was 3.3 years for men, 5.8 years for women. The t statistic permits a determination of the probability that this difference could occur by chance if the men and women came from identical populations and were being treated in a similar fashion. The t statistic for these data equals $-.74$. Reference to the t table indicates a p-value of .50, which means that a disparity between length of time until promotion of this magnitude could occur by chance 50% of the time even if the men and women came from identical populations and were treated in a similar fashion.[2]

§3.15 Testing the Significance of Differences Involving Legal Maxima and Minima

The t statistic is used in calculating the significance of the difference between a sample mean and a legal maximum or minimum. A mean derived from a sample is only an estimate of the true population mean, and thus it is unfair to compare it to a legal maximum or minimum without evaluating the accuracy of the estimate. Using the t table, we can calculate a limit above or below or a range around the sample mean, beyond which the true population mean is unlikely to fall. This range above, below, or around the sample mean is referred to as a *confidence interval*. The confidence interval is used to compare the sample mean to the legal standard. (See Section 6.7).

> **Reserve Mining Co. v. EPA:**[1] The scientist calculated a sample mean airborne asbestiform fiber concentration of 0.0626 fibers per

---

§3.14 [1] 442 F. Supp. 593 (E.D. Pa. 1977), *aff'd*, 582 F.2d 1275 (3d Cir. 1982), discussed in Section 3.4.

[2] The numbers of faculty members in each group are hypothetical; the opinion does not give the actual numbers. They were, however, chosen for realism rather than convenience.

§3.15 [1] 514 F.2d 492 (8th Cir. 1975), discussed in Section 3.5.

cubic centimeter (cc) of air. To adjust for his lack of certain knowledge
that this sampling gave the same mean concentration as was actually
present in the air, he calculated a confidence interval around the estimate of 0.0626 that ranged from .035 fibers per cc (the lower end of the
interval) to .0902 fibers per cc (the upper end of the interval). Thus he
could say that there was only a 5% chance that the population mean was
outside that range. If the upper end of the range was below the legal
maximum concentration for ambient fibers, then it is relatively unlikely
(less than a 5% chance) that the legal standard was being violated. This
range rather than the average alone was used as the estimate for the
concentrations. Using a range rather than a sample mean for an estimate neatly takes into account the imprecision inherent in sampling.

Marathon Oil Co. v. EPA:[2] The EPA sought to establish a legal
maximum for effluent washing off offshore oil drilling rigs. By observing what actually came off a sampling of rigs specially designed to
minimize effluent, the EPA calculated the effluent's sample mean level.
Since this is only an estimate of the performance of high technology
rigs, the EPA calculated a confidence interval within which the actual
mean for all high technology rigs was likely to fall. Since most high
technology rigs were likely to have effluent levels below the top of the
confidence interval, the EPA adopted the top of the interval as the legal
maximum average amount of effluent that could wash from an oil rig in
a given time period. This would force rigs without sophisticated technology to upgrade their equipment in order to reduce their effluent to
below the legal maximum, that is, to perform like a high technology rig.
In order to find a confidence interval into which the effluent levels of
most high technology rigs would fall, the EPA used a t statistic associated with a p-value of .01. Using this, experts calculated that high technology rigs would violate the legal maximum by chance only 1% of the
time.

United States v. General Motors:[3] The court sought to determine
whether the estimated number of failures of a wheel produced by the
defendant was greater than the legal minimum necessary to trigger the
defect notification procedures. The estimated number was determined
from a sample. A confidence interval around that number indicated a
range within which the actual number of failures was likely to fall. A t
statistic associated with a p-value of .05 was chosen to calculate the confidence interval. There was, therefore, only a 5% chance that the actual
value was outside the interval. Because the low endpoint of the interval

[2] 564 F.2d 1253 (9th Cir. 1977), discussed in Section 3.5.
[3] 377 F. Supp. 242 (D.D.C. 1974), discussed in Section 3.5.

was still above the legal minimum, the court inferred that a sufficient number of wheel failures had occurred to trigger the defect notification requirement.

§3.16 Testing the Significance of Correlation Coefficients

In order to test the statistical significance of the correlation coefficient, denoted by r, one may refer to an r Table, which indicates p-values associated with correlation coefficients for different sample sizes. (See Section 7.4.) As discussed in Section 7.5, a t statistic may also be used to find the associated p-value. A correlation coefficient that is not statistically significant is one that, in the opinion of the analyst, has too high a p-value, that is, too great a probability that the observed correspondence occurred by chance.

It should come as no surprise by now that one correlation coefficient may be larger than another in absolute magnitude yet less statistically significant because it is based on a smaller sample.

United States v. City of Chicago:[1] In a study based on test scores of 176 police sergeants, the sample correlation coefficient, r, between written exam score and performance score was equal to .247.[2] The r table reveals that for a sample of this size the p-value is .02,[3] indicating a mere 2% probability that this correspondence was due to chance, i.e., due to some characteristics of the particular sergeants chosen for the sample.

In re National Commission on Egg Nutrition:[4] With a sample size of only seven countries, the correlation between the mean level of dietary serum cholesterol in each country and the incidence of heart disease in each country was .76.[5] The r table reveals that for a sample of this size, the p-value associated with an r value of .76 is .10, indicating a 10% probability that this sample correlation could occur in the absence of a correlation in the population.

Although a different table must be used the same logic applies to the rank correlation coefficient. This table also reveals the p-value

---

§3.16 [1] 385 F. Supp. 543 (N.D. Ill. 1974), discussed in Section 3.7.
[2] Id. at 558.
[3] Id.
[4] 88 F.T.C. 89 (1976), *modified*, 570 F.2d 157 (D.C. Cir. 1977), *cert. denied*, 439 U.S. 821.
[5] 88 F.T.C. at 130.

associated with correlation coefficients of various sizes calculated from different sized samples. (See Section 7.11.)

Pennsylvania v. Local Union No. 542, International Union of Operating Engineers:[6] The rank correlation between out-of-work lists and referral lists was computed. The legal theory was that if these lists were positively correlated, it would mean that the union was using the greatest length of time out of work as a criterion for who should be referred first to a new job. To have a p-value of .05, the rank correlation coefficient must exceed .36 if there are 40 union members on each list and .89 if there are only six members on each list. Thus sample size does make a big difference to statistical significance. In this case the correlation coefficients for 17 different pairs of lists ranged from .08 to .62.[7] Because there were more than 40 union members on each list and because most coefficients were greater than .36, most correspondences were statistically significant. Because many of the correlation coefficients were not practically significant, however, the court concluded "this correlation study aids the inference of discrimination."[8]

Thus the statistical significance of a correlation coefficient depends not only on the size of the estimated coefficient, but also on the size of the sample from which the estimate was calculated. While a correlation of .247 (based on a sample size of 176) may have a lower p-value than a correlation of .76 (based on a sample size of seven), the increased statistical significance does not necessarily imply increased practical significance. Experience informed by a thorough grounding in statistics will best enable the litigator to determine the persuasive value of the statistical evidence. The practical significance of a result depends on, among other things, the absolute size of the estimated correlation, the other proof that has been submitted in the case, and nature of the factual issues to be resolved in a particular lawsuit.

The *coefficient of determination*, r^2, discussed in Section 3.10, may aid the intuition in deciding the question of the practical significance of a particular correlation coefficient. Even though an r of .249 in *City of Chicago*[9] is statistically significant, only 6.2% of the variation in written scores was accounted for by the correspondence to performance scores. In *Local Union No. 542*, a rank correlation coefficient of

---

[6] 469 F. Supp. 329 (E.D. Pa. 1978), *aff'd mem.*, 648 F.2d 922 (3d Cir. 1981), discussed in Section 3.8.
[7] 469 F. Supp. at 355.
[8] Id. at 357.
[9] 385 F. Supp. 543, 558 (N.D. Ill. 1974), discussed in Section 3.7.

.38 for one of the pairs of lists may have been statistically significant, but time out of work explained only 14% (.38 × .38) of the order of referral, leaving open the possibility that factors such as arbitrary exercise of discretion by the union could account for much of the variation. The use of the correlation coefficient is best thought of as a two-stage process: first, determining the statistical significance by use of an appropriate significance test and second, determining the practical significance by an examination of the practical implications of the statistical results.

§3.17 Testing the Significance of Regression Results

The practical utility of regression results depends on the reliability of the estimates and predictions produced, and reliability of results depends on two related factors, the extent of each independent variable's influence on the dependent variable and the cumulative explanatory power of the independent variables. These highlight the two uses of regression analysis and are examined separately in the following two sections. (See also Sections 8.2 and 8.3, which discuss these uses of regression analysis in greater detail.)

§3.17.1 Testing the Separate Influence of Each Independent Variable

Regression analysis is used to estimate how much influence one variable, such as race, has on a second variable, such as salary. We are not as interested in predicting salary as we are in determining whether an employee's race has an influence on his salary. Our focus in significance testing is whether the regression coefficient, which quantifies the relationship between the variables of interest to the factfinder, is big enough to support the legal claims of the proponent. The first step is to determine whether it is statistically significant. The less statistically significant a calculated coefficient is, the less convincing is the estimated regression coefficient as evidence of a correspondence.

South Dakota Public Utilities Commission v. FERC:[1] The parties used a regression approach to determine when natural gas reserves

§3.17 [1]643 F.2d 504 (8th Cir. 1981), discussed in Section 3.9.

would run out in order to establish for depreciation purposes when the gas pipeline equipment would no longer have any utility. They estimated a yearly decline of 160.16 billion cubic feet in new discoveries of gas. Because this number is based on a sample, it is only an estimate of the average annual change in reserves. We want to know whether the regression coefficient of − 160.16 is big enough to be significantly different from zero. If not, we cannot be reasonably certain that there is any predictable change in additions to annual reserves of natural gas (the dependent variable) over time (the explanatory or independent variable). The test procedure is similar to that for testing whether disparities between numbers or percentages are significant, as was done in *Castaneda*,[2] *Goff*,[3] and *Inmates*.[4] Here the disparity is between the calculated value of the regression coefficient, − 160.16 billion cubic feet, and zero, because we are testing whether this coefficient is significantly different from zero, just as we tested whether the observed number of minority group members was different from the expected number. We use the t test in this situation to test the significance of the difference.

The t test statistic for the regression coefficient describing the correspondence between time and the accumulation of new reserves of natural gas was calculated to be − 2.209. The t table for a sample size of ten years from which data were taken reveals a p-value of .05. This may be taken as evidence of a statistically significant decline in additions to reserves each year.

If there are many independent variables used to explain variations in the dependent variable, the t test is applied separately to the regression coefficient for each independent variable. The t test indicates the statistical significance of each variable's independent contribution to explaining the variation of the dependent variable. See Section 8.8 for a more detailed discussion of this test.

Presseisen v. Swarthmore College:[5] A t test applied to the regression coefficient of − 340 dollars calculated for the independent variable of sex, one of several used to explain variations in faculty salaries, indicates only whether sex had a significant part in the salary determination process; it would not indicate whether all of the variables taken together give a reliable salary prediction. Dr. Iverson, expert witness for the defendant, testified that his estimate that salaries for women

[2] 430 U.S. 482 (1976), discussed in Section 3.12.
[3] 509 F.2d 825 (5th Cir. 1975), discussed in Section 3.12.
[4] 567 F.2d 1368 (8th Cir. 1977), discussed in Section 3.13.
[5] 442 F. Supp. 593 (E.D. Pa. 1977), *aff'd*, 582 F.2d 1275 (3d Cir. 1982), discussed in Section 3.10.

were 340 dollars lower than for men in comparable positions was not statistically significant.[6] He testified that the probability of chance occurrence of the negative values for the coefficient on the sex variable varied from 37% to 66% for different years in which the coefficient was calculated. For no year did the probability of random occurrence, the p-value, drop to 5% or below. The court refused to find that sex had a discriminatory impact on salary determination.[7]

§3.17.2 Testing the Collective Explanatory Power of the Independent Variables

When the emphasis shifts from the statistical significance of each independent variable to the cumulative explanatory power of several variables taken together, an F test is substituted for the t test. The calculated F statistic is compared to an F table which, for varying sample sizes and numbers of independent variables, shows the reliability of the prediction generated by the regression analysis as a whole. As with other significance tests, a p-value is associated with this conclusion. The p-value indicates the probability that we would observe as much explanatory power as is indicated by the coefficient of multiple determination if there were no actual relationship between the dependent variable and any of the independent variables. See Section 8.12, where applications of the F test are discussed in greater detail.

Northshore School District No. 417 v. Kinnear:[8] Dr. Flerchinger, a statistical witness for the defendant, sought to explain variations in per pupil expenditures (the dependent variable) by estimating the effects of two independent variables, teachers' pay and certified staff per thousand students.[9] His purpose was to show that it was these variables rather than the state's allegedly unconstitutional school finance system that resulted in differences in expenditures per student. The coefficient of multiple correlation, R^2, was .75, which, as the witness testified, indicated that these two variables accounted for 75 percent of the variation in expenditure per pupil.[10] The F statistic corresponding to this R^2 indicates a p-value of less than .01. From this level of statistical

[6] 442 F. Supp. at 616-617.
[7] Id. at 619.
[8] 530 P.2d 178 (Wash. 1974), discussed in Section 3.10.
[9] Id. at 186.
[10] Id.

significance one could infer that average pay for certified staff and staffing ratio per 1000 students combined to be a reliable predictor of variations in expenditures per pupil because the probability of finding an R^2 as large as .75 if there was no actual relationship between the dependent variable and these independent variables was less than 1%. The practical significance of this high calculated F value was that it served as one piece of evidence designed to demonstrate the constitutionality of the school finance system. The plaintiffs had alleged that it was the method of financing education that caused the variations in expenditures; the defendants wanted to prove that something else explained the variations. The defendants' argument was that the variations were explained by constitutionally acceptable differences in average pay and staffing ratios rather than unacceptable factors.

§3.18   Summary

Inferential statistical methods indicate the likelihood that a particular measurement occurred by chance. We are interested in why certain results occur because causation is an issue in many cases and because factfinders are interested in the reliability of numerical estimates. Statistics do not prove what caused a particular result, although they may eliminate chance as a plausible explanation and may indicate correspondences between factors relevant to a particular alternative causal theory. A difference or relationship that is likely to have occurred by chance is not statistically significant, but evidence of a high probability of random occurrence may have tremendous practical significance to the parties involved in a lawsuit because it may provide evidence that one of the parties did not cause the outcome. The various statistical tools measure different kinds of relationships — differences and correspondences — and test for the probability that the relationship occurred by chance. These tests all involve two key factors: (1) the size of the group involved or the number of categories in the group involved or the sample size and (2) the diversity or variation within that group or sample. Each test reveals a p-value that is the basic information on which statistical conclusions are based. Thus all tools and all tests are interrelated. The validity of competing methods depends on the care with which measurements are made and the statistical and legal validity of the factual theories being tested. The validity of measurement techniques is traditionally the statistician's province, and the plausibility of factual theories is traditionally the litigator's. Understanding statistical proof is a matter of appreciating the relationship between the two.

Subsequent chapters discuss one by one the uses and limitations of each statistical tool, starting as this chapter does with simple differences and working up to multiple regression. Each chapter discusses how the tool has been used in a variety of cases and describes how to calculate various summary and test statistics and find their associated p-values. The final two chapters discuss particular evidentiary problems that arise when using quantitative evidence and indicate particular problems that arise in different substantive law areas.

CHAPTER FOUR

The Significance of Numerical Differences

§4.0   Introduction to the Problem of Analyzing Differences

When it is necessary to prove not only that an event occurred but that it had a legally relevant consequence, comparisons of numerical measurements taken before and after the event may indicate its effect. The event might be a vehicular accident causing a decrease in the victim's earning power or a merger causing an increase in the merged corporation's market share. In both of these situations, the before-and-after comparisons of income or market share are relevant. If no event of legal consequence has occurred, the "before" measurement leads us to expect an "after" measurement of a given size. It is by comparing the observed "after" measurement to the expected measurement that we may measure the effect of the event.

Similarly, whenever behavior departs from a legal standard, that standard forms the basis for comparing the expected measurement with an observed measurement in order to determine the effect of the behavior. In discrimination cases the legal standard of proportionality or nondiscriminatory treatment provides a standard to which the observed outcome of the selection process is compared. Statistical analysis provides a mechanism for determining whether a significant departure from the expected outcome has occurred.

This chapter presents methods of statistical inference used to analyze how different an observed numerically measurable outcome is from the outcome expected on the basis of historical experience or a legal standard. The first sections discuss the relevance of numerical differences in litigation contexts and explore situations in which the result of simple subtraction alone fails to convey important aspects of differences. Subsequent sections describe how various statistical concepts can be used to draw additional legally relevant information out of numerical differences that may enhance the arguments a lawyer can use to establish or to discount the significance of a difference. As will be the practice throughout this book, the final sections of the chapter describe how statistical results discussed within the chapter are calculated.

A. THE RELEVANCE OF NUMERICAL DIFFERENCES

A *difference* describes how far apart numerically two measurements of a single variable are from one another. The measurements may be actual physical measurements or numerical estimates, or one number may be an observed measurement and the other an expected measurement. The differences may be expressed in terms of the units of measurement themselves (Section 4.1, Absolute Differences) or in percentage terms (Section 4.2, Percentage Point Differences and Section 4.3, Percentage Differences).

§4.1 Absolute Differences

An *absolute difference* is the difference between two numbers expressed in terms of their units of measurement. This difference is often referred to as the *disparity* between the measurements, particularly when an observed number is compared to an expected number. The presence or absence of a significant disparity may be crucial to the resolution of a legal issue.

Grant v. Schweicker:[1] Qualification for social security disability benefits depended on the extent to which the claimant was able to work and support himself. Social security regulations establish a legal

§4.1   [1] 699 F.2d 189 (4th Cir. 1983).

framework for evaluating claims that includes an examination by a vocational evaluator who quantifies various aspects of a claimant's work-related capabilities. Eligibility depends on the difference between the claimant's measured abilities and those of typical nonphysically impaired individuals. In this type of situation the typical capabilities are an expected measurement to which the observed measured abilities of the claimant are compared.

Brown v. Vance:[2] The holding that Mississippi's statutory fee system for compensating justice court judges violated constitutional guarantees of due process rested on proof of significant disparities between the number of cases filed in courts of judges with various predispositions towards the police and towards creditor-plaintiffs. A judge's compensation depended on the number of cases filed in the judge's court. The plaintiffs alleged that police officers favor judges who more frequently convict defendants and that collection agencies and other creditors favor judges who more frequently find in their favor. This possible temptation to judges violates a defendant's right to a "neutral and detached judge."[3] Some of the differences cited by the court showed the division of traffic tickets between judges in various districts within the state.[4] In District II, for instance, Judge Vance handled 421 cases in one six-month period while Judge Condia handled only two, an impressive difference. In District III, Judge Sims handled 160 cases while none were brought to Judge Hines. The court described the differences as "startling."[5] In this case two actual measurements are compared rather than an expected and observed measurement.

In re American Telephone and Telegraph Co.:[6] One consideration determining whether AT&T's application for a general increase in interstate telephone rates would be granted was the rate of return AT&T should receive on its equity. One factor discussed by the Commission was the difference in risk between AT&T's business and other investments.[7] Here the disparity would be between AT&T's riskiness and a standard or average level of riskiness of other investments. A positive disparity resulting from greater riskiness of AT&T's investments compared to average risks taken by utilities would help justify a higher than average rate of return.

---

[2] 637 F.2d 272, 285 nn. 16-18 (5th Cir. 1981).
[3] Ward v. Village of Monroeville, 409 U.S. 57 (1972), *construed in* Brown v. Vance, id. at 279.
[4] 637 F.2d at 280 n. 11.
[5] Id. at 281.
[6] 86 F.C.C. 2d 257, 268 (1981).
[7] Id. at 276.

Castaneda v. Partida:[8] In deciding that Mexican-Americans had been discriminated against in the selection of grand jurors in Hidalgo County, Texas, the Supreme Court relied on a disparity of 349 jurors between the expected number of Mexican-American jurors (688, based on the percentage of Mexican-Americans in the population) and the observed number selected over an 11-year period (339). The Court concluded, "The mathematical disparities that have been accepted by this Court [in other jury discrimination cases] as adequate for a prima facie case have all been within the range presented here."[9]

§4.2 Percentage Point Differences

Numerical differences may also be presented in terms of difference between percentages. Subtracting one percentage from another yields a difference between percentages called a *percentage point difference*, not to be confused with a percentage difference (discussed in Section 4.3). Understanding the distinction is important if confusion is to be avoided.

In some cases, a difference can be expressed as either an absolute difference or a percentage point difference, though the meanings conveyed are not identical. For example, if it is known that a space shuttle is attempting reentry with eight fewer heat reflecting tiles than planned, it is more informative to know that the missing tiles are only .03% of the usual complement. The absolute difference does not reveal the proportion of tiles that are missing.

Castaneda v. Partida:[1] The absolute disparity between observed and expected numbers of Mexican-American jurors was 349 jurors. Since we expected 688 this seems intuitively to be a large disparity. But if we had expected 10,688 Mexican-American jurors, a shortfall of 349 jurors would not be so remarkable. Absolute differences fail to account for the magnitude of the expected and observed numbers.

Computing expected and observed percentages and percentage point differences sometimes eliminates the misperception created by absolute differences. Following the space shuttle example, a loss of only

---

[8] 430 U.S. 482, 496 and n. 16 (1977).
[9] Id. at 496.
§4.2 [1] 430 U.S. 482, 486 n. 17 (1976).

.03% of the heat reflecting tiles (e.g., eight divided by 30,000) does not seem great, but loss of 80% (e.g., eight divided by ten) does.

Castaneda v. Partida:[2] Because 79.1% of the population in Hidalgo County, Texas was Mexican-American, we would expect 79.1% of jurors to be Mexican-American if there was no discrimination. Eight hundred seventy jurors were chosen during the relevant 11-year period. Of these, 339 or 39% (339 divided by 870) were Mexican-Americans.[3] We would have expected 79.1% or 688 (.791 times 870) to be Mexican-Americans. The percentage point disparity is 40.1 (79.1 minus 39), which seems rather large. If we had expected 10,688 Mexican-American jurors on the basis of 79.1% of the total (13,512 jurors = 10,688 divided by .791) and we had an absolute disparity between expected and observed of 349 (as in the actual case), the percentage point disparity would tell a different story. Instead of 40.1 the percentage point disparity would be 2.6 (79.1 minus 76.5) because the observed number of 10,339 (10,688 minus 349) is 76.5% of the total (10,339 divided by 13,512). A 2.6 percentage point disparity seems rather insignificant.

Courts evaluating the significance of disparities in discrimination cases often rely on percentage point differences instead of absolute differences.

Castaneda v. Partida:[4] The Supreme Court compared the 40.1 percentage point disparity to those disparities in other cases where prima facie cases of discrimination had been made out: *Turner v. Fouche*[5] (60% blacks in the population compared to 37% on the grand jury lists, for a disparity of 23 percentage points (60 − 37)), *Whitus v. Georgia*[6] (blacks listed in tax digest are 27.1% of taxpayers, but blacks are only 9.1% of those on the grand jury venire, a disparity of 18 percentage points), *Sims v. Georgia*[7] (24.4% of tax lists, 4.7% of grand jury lists, a 19.7 percentage point disparity), and *Jones v. Georgia*[8] (19% of tax lists, 5% of jury list, a 14 percentage point disparity). The percentage from the general population or that portion eligible for jury service (e.g., those on the tax lists) provides the expected percentage.

---

[2] Id. at 486 n. 6.
[3] Id. at 487 n. 7.
[4] Id. at 495-496.
[5] Id. (*construing* Turner v. Fouche, 396 U.S. 346 (1978)).
[6] Id. (*construing* Whitus v. Georgia, 385 U.S. 545 (1967)).
[7] Id. (*construing* Sims v. Georgia, 389 U.S. 404 (1967)).
[8] Id. (*construing* Jones v. Georgia, 389 U.S. 24 (1967)).

The jury lists provide the observed percentage to which the expected percentage is compared.

§4.3   Percentage Differences

A *percentage difference* is a fraction obtained by dividing the disparity by a base number, often the expected number. A *percentage point difference* is the disparity alone, obtained by subtracting one percentage number from another. The disparity and base value used in calculating the percentage difference may be either absolute numbers or percentage numbers, though one may not mix the two in the same fraction.

Castaneda v. Partida:[1] The percentage difference between observed and expected is 50.7%. The disparity is 349 jurors or 40 percentage points, which is divided by the expected absolute number or percentage of Mexican-American jurors, 688 or 79.1 percentage points. Either calculation gives 50.7% (349 divided by 688 gives the same result as 40 divided by 79.1: both equal .507 or 50.7%).

Note that percentage differences are indicated by a percentage sign following the differences, e.g., 50.7%, while a percentage point difference is indicated by the words "percentage points", e.g., 40 percentage points. This convention avoids the confusion that often arises between the concepts.

Castaneda v. Partida:[2] The Supreme Court described the disparity between 79.1% Mexican-Americans expected and 39% observed as a "difference of 40%". Under the convention described in this section this is clearly incorrect. Correctly stated this is a difference of 40 percentage points or a difference of 50.7%.

Swain v. Alabama:[3] The importance of the difference is clear from cases citing *Swain*, in which the Supreme Court held, "We cannot say that purposeful discrimination based on race alone is satisfactorily proved by showing that an identifiable group in the community is underrepresented by as much as 10%." If they had meant to indicate a percentage difference below which a claim of discrimination is not

§4.3   [1] 430 U.S. 482 (1976).
[2] Id. at 495 (1976).
[3] 380 U.S. 202, 208-209 (1965).

proved, the Supreme Court should not have relied on the two cases they cited. In the first, *Akins v. Texas*,[4] the expected percentage of black jurors was 15% and the observed percentage was only 8.35%, a 6.65 percentage point difference, to be sure, but a 42% underrepresentation. In *Cassell v. Texas*,[5] the second of the cases, the difference between expected and observed percentages was 8.8 percentage points (15.5 minus 6.7 equals 8.8 percentage points), but blacks were underrepresented on grand jury panels by 57% ((15% minus 6.7%) divided by 15.5%). A rule that a prima facie case of discrimination is shown by a 10% disparity is quite different from a rule requiring a ten percentage point disparity. The latter is the one actually followed by many courts who do not use more sophisticated statistical analysis,[6] and that the Supreme Court apparently intended to articulate in *Swain*.

B. PROBLEMS WITH NUMERICAL DIFFERENCES

Numerical differences, whether they are absolute, percentage point, or percentage differences, may fail to measure the significance of a difference. In addition, differences may conceal information that might be relevant to factfinding. These two problems call for more sophisticated statistical tools.

§4.4 Failure to Measure the Significance of a Difference

The various numerical measures discussed in Section 4.1 through 4.3 all have the common problem that they may fail to measure the significance of a difference. Section 4.2 noted the failure of absolute differences to account for the size of the measurements involved, and Section 2.2 commented on the fact that threshold levels of percentage point disparities and percentage point differences themselves sometimes fail to account for the differences between outcomes of cases. We compared two cases dealing with percentage point differ-

---

[4] Castaneda v. Partida, 430 U.S. 482 (1976) (*construing* Akins v. Texas, 325 U.S. 398, 405 (1945)).

[5] Id. (*construing* Cassell v. Texas, 339 U.S. 282, 284-85 (1950)).

[6] See, e.g., United States v. Maskeny, 609 F.2d 183 (5th Cir. 1980).

ences illustrating what appeared to be an inconsistency among courts. In *Board of Education v. Califano*[1] the court found an underrepresentation of 4.2 percentage points was substantial, while in *United States v. Goff*[2] the court found an underrepresentation of 6.17 percentage points was not substantial. Without inferential statistical methods, it is difficult to explain the numerical distinctions between these cases and why a particular threshold level is appropriate.

In addition, although we have suggested that a 2.6 percentage point underrepresentation is trivial when 79.1% are expected, (See Section 4.2) 2.6 percentage points may not be trivial if a minority group makes up only 2.6% of the population and we never see any of that group selected. Percentage point differences alone do not provide any way to distinguish these two situations.

Courts do not regularly rely on percentage disparities, perhaps because these disparities are so greatly affected by the absolute magnitude of the measurements. A 50% underrepresentation might, for instance, be caused by having one fewer minority member than expected where the expected number is two or by having 700 fewer than expected where the expected number is 1400. A more useful statistic would take both the absolute measurements and the percentages into account and combine useful inferential properties that enhance their utility in determining the significance of a difference. (See Sections 4.9 through 4.11 on the standard deviation.)

It should be noted that while absolute differences, percentage point differences, and percentage differences may not be very useful in explaining the significance of a disparity, an awareness of the distinctions between them make them useful tools of advocacy. A disparity that seems large in absolute terms may be made to seem small by using percentage terms, and a disparity that is large in percentage terms may appear small in absolute terms.

§4.5 Failure to Capture Subtle Differences — Differences and Averages

Every statistic hides something if it condenses a lot of information into a single number (see Section 2.7). The average monthly income for your law office may be the same for two years (so there is a

§4.4 [1] 584 F.2d 576 (2d Cir. 1978).
[2] 509 F.2d 825 (5th Cir. 1975).

disparity of zero) but that fact may not show that there was tremendous fluctuation in income each month during one year and a steady, regular flow of income during the other year. In a litigation context this distinction that is hidden by the difference between averages may be important.

> **In re Forte-Fairbairn, Inc.:**[1] The issue was the identity of certain fibers shipped by the seller under a contract for the sale of baby llama fibers, which the buyer, wishing to reject the shipment, claimed were baby alpaca fibers. The problem was to identify the fibers. Although there is no difference in the appearance or average diameter of baby llama and alpaca fibers the expert witnesses were able to identify the fibers on the basis of how much variation there was in each of the two samples around the average diameter and determine that there is more variation in the diameters of llama fibers than in those of alpaca fibers.[2] Thus, by calculating a statistic that summarized the variation in diameter for the shipped fibers the experts were able to compare a relevant measurement of those fibers to known fibers and identify the shipped fibers as significantly different from alpaca fibers but not significantly different from llama fibers. This statistic was the standard deviation.[3]

C. DESCRIPTIVE STATISTICS: VARIANCE, STANDARD DEVIATION, AND COEFFICIENT OF VARIATION

Averages, medians, and other such summaries of groups of numbers (discussed in Section 2.7) are often called descriptive statistics; they describe certain features of the numbers on which they are based and suppress others. Three measures commonly used to describe the variability among numbers within a group of numbers are the *variance*, the *standard deviation,* and the *coefficient of variation.* In the next three sections these measures are described in turn.

§4.5 [1] 62 F.T.C. 1146 (1963).
[2] Id. at 1167.
[3] Id.

§4.6   Variance

The term *variance* is often used as a synonym for disparity or difference: if there is a difference of 15 between the observed number of minority employees and the expected number, one might say that the variance between observed and expected is 15 employees. In many statistical discussions, however, *variance* is used in a technical sense, and its meaning is quite different from the one just mentioned.

Technically, the *variance* is a statistic that describes the diversity within a group of numbers. If a group of numbers contains many that are much larger or much smaller than the average, we say that there is a great deal of variation in the group. The variance is correspondingly large. If a group of numbers contains relatively few that differ very much from the average, we say that there is little variation. The variance is correspondingly small.

> **In re Forte-Fairbairn, Inc.:**[1] The F.T.C. sought a way of measuring fibers that would distinguish baby alpaca fibers from baby llama fibers. One measure, the average diameter, was identical for both fibers, 20.6 microns,[2] and therefore of little use in distinguishing the fibers. Fiber experts found, however, that in a sample of llama fibers there was more variation around that average diameter of 20.6 microns; some were much wider, some much narrower. The calculated variance was 42. Baby alpaca fibers had a variance of 20, indicating that typically there was less variation among alpaca fibers. Armed with this information, the experts tested a sample of unknown fibers, calculated a variance around 40, and concluded that these must be baby llama fibers.[3]

The variance is a difficult number to interpret, as the following exhibit illustrates. Exhibit 4.6(a) shows hypothetical data describing net income of a law office each month for two years. Note that there is much greater fluctuation in income in the first year than in the second, yet both have the same average monthly income and the same total income.

The variance for year one, 350,469, is much greater than for year

---

§4.6   [1] 62 F.T.C. 1146 (1963).
[2] One micron is one thousandth of a millimeter or four one-hundred thousandths of an inch.
[3] The experts did not rely on the variance, as later examples illustrate, but the case illustrates the idea of variance from a mean value.

EXHIBIT 4.6(a)
Variance in Law Office Income

	Income Year 1	Income Year 2
January	$ 300	$ 450
February	1900	500
March	200	700
April	400	560
May	600	670
June	500	800
July	700	400
August	1500	620
September	100	450
October	800	700
November	200	650
December	50	750
Total Income for Year	$7250	$7250
Average Monthly Income	$ 604	$ 604
Variance	350,469	15,557
Standard Deviation	$ 592	$ 125

two, 15,557, indicating a greater variation from month to month in year one. Looking at a variance by itself conveys little information because it is out of proportion to the numbers whose deviations it summarizes. The individual deviation of each number from the average is squared and then the variance is calculated by averaging the squared deviations. See Section 4.21.2. The squaring process makes the variance disproportionate to the numbers themselves.[4]

§4.7 Standard Deviation

The square root of the variance is called the *standard deviation*. Taking the square root eliminates the disproportionality of the variance. Compare the standard deviations and variances for the two lists

[4] The variance is not always disproportionately larger than the numbers themselves: if the disparities between the mean and the individual items on a group are fractional, i.e., less than one, the squaring process gives a variance that is disproportionately small.

in Exhibit 4.6(a). The standard deviation can be thought of as a measure of the typical or expected variation of the numbers in a group from their average. Interpreted as the typical variation, the standard deviation is an intuitively understandable concept and an entity one can relate easily to the numbers it summarizes. The monthly incomes in year one in Exhibit 4.6(a) have an average of $604 and exhibit considerable variation from that average. February was about $1200 higher than average; December, the lowest, was $542 lower than average. The standard deviation of $592 summarizes all of these departures from the average. The typical variation from the average value is almost as large as the average, $604, indicating a great deal of fluctuation even without reference to year two. In contrast, in year two the standard deviation, $125, is substantially smaller than the average, $604.[1]

In re Forte-Fairbairn, Inc.:[2] The F.T.C. used standard deviations to distinguish baby llama and baby alpaca fibers in a deceptive practices action in which a buyer alleged that a seller had shipped the wrong type of fibers. Even though the alpaca and llama fibers tested had the same average diameters, 20.6 microns, llama fibers show greater variation in their diameters, a standard deviation of 6.5 microns. The alpaca fibers have a standard deviation of 4.4 microns, indicating less variation in diameter. With this knowledge experts were able to identify a sample of unknown fibers as llama fibers because the calculated standard deviation was about 6.5 microns.

Driessen v. Freborg:[3] The court considered the constitutionality of a public school labor contract clause requiring pregnant teachers to take a leave of absence after the seventh month of pregnancy. The court held that the clause violated due process as an unreasonable presumption but held that the school could impose reasonable requirements for pregnancy leaves of absence to prevent disruption and ensure continuity of instruction.[4] The statistical problem was to determine how far ahead of the expected due date pregnant teachers should have to leave. One study introduced into evidence showed that the average duration of a pregnancy was 279 days but that the typical variation or standard

---

§4.7 [1]Sometimes the standard deviation is presented as a percentage of the mean. A high percentage indicates substantial variation while a low percentage indicates little. See Section 4.8, Coefficient of Variation.
[2]62 F.T.C. 1146 (1963).
[3]431 F. Supp. 1191 (D.N.D. 1977).
[4]Id. at 1196.

deviation from this average was about nine days.[5] If most births occurred within nine days of 279 days, the court reasoned, then very few would be pregnant for a period further from the average than two standard deviations, or 18 days, and thus a requirement that teachers take a leave of absence 18 days before the expected birth date was not unreasonable.[6] The standard deviation is a convenient way of summarizing the typical or expected deviation from the mean.

Alabama Hospital Association v. Beasley:[7] A regulation setting standards for Medicaid reimbursements stated that the maximum amount of reimbursable costs for each class of hospitals under the Alabama State Medicaid plan was average operating costs plus one standard deviation. Hospitals reported their costs on a uniform reporting sheet. The costs for each hospital in a class were averaged and a standard deviation was calculated. Designers of the regulation figured that all hospitals with below average costs or costs only slightly above average, that is, within one standard deviation, would be fully reimbursed, while hospitals with costs substantially above average would not, presumably because they were relatively inefficient. The comparable standard for nursing home reimbursements was average costs plus one-half standard deviation.[8] Thus a smaller percentage of those with above average costs were fully reimbursed.

The average duration of pregnancies in *Driessen* and the average level of cost in *Alabama Hospital* provide "expected" values around which departures from the norm are likely to occur. Slight departures are likely, radical departures are less likely. The standard deviation in each example measures the degree of departure from the norm or expected value that is typical.

§4.8   Coefficient of Variation

The importance of a standard deviation of a given size sometimes depends on the size of the average value used in its calculation. For instance, in the law firm described in Section 4.7, the standard deviation in monthly revenues is $592 in the first year, nearly as large as the monthly average. This indicates that the monthly swings in income

---

[5] Id. at 1194.
[6] Id. at 1196.
[7] 702 F.2d 955, 956 (11th Cir. 1983).
[8] See Alabama Nursing Home Assoc. v. Califano, 465 F. Supp. 1183 (N.D. Ala. 1979), *rev'd*, 617 F.2d 388 (5th Cir. 1980).

are so great that one might reasonably expect occasional months with little or no income. Statisticians compare the standard deviation to the average by calculating the *coefficient of variation* (C.V.), a statistic that expresses the amount of variation within a group of numbers as a percentage of the average value. Thus, by dividing the standard deviation of incomes for the different months in year one, $592, (see Exhibit 4.6(a)) by the average monthly income, $604, we find that the typical variation is 98% ((592/604) × 100%) of the average. The coefficient of variation for year two in Exhibit 4.6(a) is only 21% ((125/604) × 100%).

Putting the variation in percentage terms facilitates the comparison of the variation to the average. The utility of the coefficient of variation is more obvious in a case where the averages from the two groups of numbers (e.g., the monthly income data in Exhibit 4.6(a)) are different. We might, for instance, want to compare the relative variability of income for a large firm and a small firm. Assume that the large firm has a standard deviation of $15,000 for its monthly income in a sample year and the average monthly income is $125,000. Is this more or less variation than for the small firm with a standard deviation of $125 and an average monthly income of $604? The coefficient of variation for the large firm is 12%, less than for the small firm, 21%, so by this measure there is relatively more variation in the small firm's income.

As with other descriptive statistics, coefficients of variation appear in a variety of substantive law areas, but it does not appear to be referred to very often in reported opinions.

B. F. Goodrich Co. v. Department of Transportation:[1] National Highway Traffic Safety Act standards for testing automobile tires under the tire quality grading regulation required that the manufacturing of tested tires be subject to quality controls with coefficients of variation below 5%. Although a tire is designed to certain specifications, due to inconsistencies in the manufacturing process there might be slight variations in specifications such as tire weight or circumference or tread depth. The coefficient of variation measures the percentage variation around that specification for each quality characteristic observed. From measurements of actual tread depth of newly manufactured tires, for instance, a standard deviation can be calculated. The testing agency required that this standard deviation, that is, the typical variation around the specification, be no more than 5% of the specification.

§4.8   [1]541 F.2d 1178 (6th Cir. 1976).

Thus, if the specifications called for a tread depth of one-half inch, the standard deviation could be no greater than 5% of 0.5 inches, or 0.025 inches. By stating the quality standard in terms of a single coefficient of variation, the testing agency avoided having to state different standard deviation requirements for each specification.

Taylor v. Weaver Oil and Gas Corp.:[2] The plaintiff alleged sex discrimination on the grounds that female employees were given smaller raises than their male counterparts. Recognizing that some variation in salary increases among employees was inevitable, given different skills and experience, the defendant's expert compared a summary measure of the variation in raises for a period in which there could have been no sex discrimination (because there were no men) to the measure for the period at issue in the lawsuit. The defendant's theory was that if sex discrimination was a factor in setting raises during the second period, then the coefficient of variation would show greater relative variation in raises during the second period. The coefficients of variation were in fact the same for both periods, and the defendant prevailed. Note that a comparison of standard deviations alone would not have been revealing in this case because the average raises were different during the two periods involved.

In re Forte-Fairbairn, Inc.:[3] Despite the fact that the average diameters of two types of fibers were the same, thus enabling an identification of fiber type by standard deviation alone, the experts presented their data in terms of the coefficients of variation for the diameters of the two types. Baby alpaca fibers have a C.V. of 22% (standard deviation equals 4.5 microns, average diameter equals 20.6 microns) while baby llama fibers have a C.V. of 31.5% (standard deviation equals 6.5 microns, average diameter equals 20.6 microns).[4] The unknown fibers to be identified in this case had a C.V. of around 34% and were therefore identified as baby llama fibers. Note that a comparison of standard deviations would have been enough. The expert witnesses were, however, undoubtedly accustomed to thinking in terms of percentage variation and therefore reported their findings in terms of the coefficients of variation.

---

[2] 18 Fair Empl. Prac. Cas. (BNA) 23 (S.D. Tex. 1978).

[3] 62 F.T.C. 1146 (1963).

[4] The experts calculated C.V.'s and standard deviations for several samples of fibers. The numbers used here are drawn from those results for purposes of illustration. The average diameter was calculated by dividing the reported standard deviation for llama fibers by the reported C.V. for llama fibers (6.5/.315 = 20.6). Id. at 1168-1169.

D. THE STANDARD DEVIATION AS AN INFERENTIAL STATISTIC

As a descriptive statistic, the standard deviation provides a measure of typical variation in values of the numbers in a group. As an inferential statistic it provides information useful in determining the degree of significance of a particular disparity or difference. Recall from Section 1.14 that there are two aspects of the significance of an observed event such as a difference, namely the *practical significance* of the difference and the *statistical significance*. Arguments as to practical significance are not inferential statistical arguments even though statistics may be used to support them. We focus in this section on the aspect of statistical significance, whether a particular disparity or difference is likely to have occurred by chance.

§4.9 Statistical Significance and Randomly Occurring Differences

Significance testing reveals the probability that a particular observed outcome could have occurred by chance under certain idealized circumstances. Significance testing is relevant to determining the legal effect of a difference because if the difference could reasonably have been the result of chance or random factors, it is difficult to attribute it to some unlawful act.

Grant v. Schweicker:[1] Eligibility for social security disability benefits depends on the difference between the claimant's measured job-related abilities and those of a nonimpaired individual. Small differences might occur by chance; there is some random fluctuation in abilities even among nonimpaired individuals. It is necessary to ensure that the difference between claimant's abilities and the average ability level is significant enough so that we can be sure it is due to disabilities rather than random fluctuation, that is, chance.

Brown v. Vance:[2] The difference in number of cases brought to different judges was alleged to have been due to the way in which judges were paid. A judge's compensation depended on the number of

§4.9 [1] 699 F.2d 189 (4th Cir. 1983).
[2] 637 F.2d 272 (5th Cir. 1981).

cases filed in the judge's court. Allegedly, more cases were filed in courts of judges who were favorable to police officers and creditors, the complainants who initiated most of the cases. Was the difference due to the compensation scheme's effect on the justice court judge's incentives or due to chance? It would be useful for the opposing parties to establish whether the calculated difference in cases filed in the various courts was due to chance or not.

Alabama Hospital Association v. Beasley:[3] Under state standards for Medicaid reimbursements, only hospitals with costs significantly above average were not fully reimbursed for Medicaid services performed. The theory behind the standard was that full reimbursement should go only to cost-efficient hospitals. This approach implicitly suggests that hospitals with costs around average are cost-efficient, a source of contention in this case. The standard recognizes that some hospitals might be cost-efficient but have incurred costs that are slightly above average due to random factors other than mismanagement. The standard fully compensates such hospitals. How great a departure from average must there be to indicate that something other than chance, such as inefficient operation, is causing the higher costs? It would be useful in standard setting to be able to define this point.

Gay v. Waiters' and Dairy Lunchmen's Union, Local No. 30:[4] Based on relevant characteristics of the San Francisco area population, the court determined that of 390 hirings of waiters at a hotel, one would expect 43 blacks. There actually were only 38 blacks hired.[5] Was this disparity between the expected number of blacks and observed due to discriminatory practices during the hiring process or just due to chance? A disparity of 40 blacks would be more suggestive of discrimination while a disparity of only one would seem like a random occurrence. The use of the standard deviation as an inferential tool helps draw the line between chance and discrimination as alternative explanations for a particular disparity. Significance testing will test the plausibility of an assertion that this difference is a random occurrence.

§4.10   Useful Properties of the Standard Deviation

The standard deviation has mathematical properties that make it particularly appropriate for determining the probability that an ob-

---

[3] 465 F. Supp. 1183 (1979), *rev'd,* 702 F.2d 955 (11th Cir. 1983).
[4] 489 F. Supp. 282 (N.D. Cal. 1980).
[5] Id. at 308.

served difference occurred by chance. These properties come from the part of probability theory that is concerned with how measurements of observed events are distributed in populations.[1]

A difference or disparity is said to be statistically significant if it is unlikely to have occurred by chance. An observation that is within one standard deviation of the mean is quite likely to have occurred by chance. Conversely, an observation many standard deviations from the mean is unlikely to have occurred by chance. The properties of particular distributions allow us to be much more specific. For many useful distributions, observations more than one standard deviation from the mean occur by chance about one-third of the time. That is a fairly large percentage so we should not be too surprised to see such observations just by chance. Observations more than two standard deviations from the mean occur by chance only about 5% of the time, and observations more than three standard deviations from the mean occur only about .27% of the time. The inferential utility of these properties is that if we observe a measurement that is more than three standard deviations from the mean or expected value, we should be suspicious of the claim that it occurred by chance, because such great variations from the expected outcome occur only rarely, which may lead us to believe that there is some other explanation for the disparity. These probabilities of random occurrence are only rough approximations and depend on a variety of factors. Sometimes they are so rough that more precise inferential statistics are necessary. These factors and alternative inferential statistics appropriate to various types of differences are discussed in Part E of this chapter.

§4.11 Inferential Application of the Standard Deviation

Two of the most frequently cited cases that use standard deviations to demonstrate the significance of disparities are *Castaneda v.*

§4.10 [1] The study of the distribution of measurements in a population involves an examination of where within the range from the smallest possible measurement to the largest most observations appear. Are the potential observations clustered around the mean of all the measurements with fewer and fewer observations appearing towards the extreme ends of the range or are they evenly dispersed throughout the range? Most of the observations might be at the small end of the range with just a few at the large end or vice versa. For a detailed discussion of three particularly useful distributions see Sections 4.13, 4.15, and 4.17.

Partida[1] and *Hazelwood School District v. United States.*[2] Both were discrimination cases: *Castaneda* was a jury discrimination case brought as an equal protection claim, and *Hazelwood* was a "pattern or practice" of employment discrimination case brought under Title VII of the Civil Rights Act of 1964.[3] A note in *Hazelwood* describes the inferential use of standard deviations as "a precise method of measuring the significance of such statistical disparities" like those observed between expected and observed numbers of blacks on the Hazelwood teaching staff.[4] Following the methodology explained in *Castaneda*[5] and describing the standard deviation as " a measure of predicted fluctuations from the expected value of a sample,"[6] the Court in *Hazelwood* concluded that "[t]he difference between observed and expected values was more than six standard deviations in 1972-1973 and more than five standard deviations in 1973-1974."[7] The Court then quoted *Castaneda* to the effect that "[a]s a general rule for such large samples, if the difference between the expected value and the observed number is greater than two or three standard deviations then the hypothesis that teachers were hired without regard to race would be suspect."[8] The Court concluded that the demonstrated differences (63 expected versus 16 observed in 1972-1973 and 70 expected versus 22 observed in 1973-1974) "were on their face substantial"[9] and sufficient to establish a prima facie case.

The Court in *Castaneda* had really only concluded that a disparity greater than two or three standard deviations would make a social scientist suspicious of the hypothesis that the selection of people was neutral with respect to race. As other courts have suggested,[10] the *Castaneda* Court may very well have based its holding on an absolute disparity of 40 percentage points rather than a calculation of standard deviations, but the "*Castaneda* rule," sometimes referred to as the "two or three standard deviations rule" has taken on a life of its own and is

---

§4.11   [1]430 U.S. 482 (1976).
[2]433 U.S. 299 (1976).
[3]42 U.S.C. §2000e (1976).
[4]433 U.S. at 308-309 n. 14.
[5]430 U.S. at 496-497 n. 17.
[6]433 U.S. at 308-309 n. 14.
[7]Id.
[8]Id.
[9]Id. at 308-309.
[10]See, e.g., United States v. Maskeny, 609 F.2d 183 (5th Cir. 1980).

widely quoted as the standard threshold for a prima facie case, particularly in Title VII litigation.[11]

In both of these cases the *random variable* was the observed number of ethnic group members selected, either as jurors or teachers. The value of the random variable for Hazelwood was 16 in 1972-1973 and 22 in 1973-1974 because that was the observed number of black teachers on the teaching staff of the school district. This observed number was compared to the *expected number* of black teachers, 63 in 1972-1973 and 70 in 1973-1974. For the respective years, the expected numbers are the means for the group of all teachers on the Hazelwood teaching staff. Calculations of these expected numbers are discussed in Section 4.21.1. Briefly, however, we expected 63 black teachers in 1972-1973 because black members made up 5.7% of the pool of qualified teachers in the geographic area[12] and Hazelwood hired 1105 teachers. The expected value for the random variable in 1972-1973 was .057 times 1105, or 63 black teachers.

E. INFERENTIAL STATISTICAL TESTS OF SIGNIFICANCE OF A DIFFERENCE

In this chapter we are concerned with significance testing in order to determine the probability that an observed disparity or difference occurred by chance. Using a variety of statistical methods, one can estimate for any collection of observations the extent to which a particular observation is peculiar or unusual. The degree of peculiarity is expressed as a probability called a p-value, which indicates an improbable or unusual observation. This part of the chapter describes a variety of approaches for calculating p-values for differences.

The differences discussed in this chapter are those referred to in Section 3.12 as simple differences. Illustrations of simple differences, that is, differences between absolute numbers or percentages, appear throughout this part. Discussion of statistical tools used to analyze differences among multiple categories (see Section 3.13) is deferred

---

[11] W. Connolly & D. Peterson, Use of Statistics in EEO Litigation, §11.08 (1983); and D. Baldus & J. Cole, Statistical Proof of Discrimination 294 (1980) and pp. 106-108 of the 1984 Cumulative Supplement.
[12] 433 U.S. 299, 308 (1976).

to Chapter 5, and discussion of tools used to analyze differences between sample estimates (see Section 3.14) and between sample estimates and legal maxima and minima (see Section 3.15) is deferred to Chapter 6.

§4.12   The Chebychef Approach to Calculating p-Values

In many cases of interest to litigators, factfinders are concerned with processes that result in one of a number of possible outcomes. A process or mechanism that is determined only by chance and whose exact outcome it is impossible to predict in advance is called a *random experiment*. Such a process generates a *random event*, an occurrence that can sometimes be represented as a numerical value. That representation is a variable because there are a number of possible outcomes of the experiment. The numerical representation of a random event is referred to as a *random variable* because it was determined by chance. Examples of random variables might include the height of a randomly selected individual (the numerical value for which comes from a physical measurement) or the number of members of a particular racial group among a group of recently hired employees (the numerical value for which comes from counting).[1] Often the application of statistical methods to litigation problems involves treating the outcome that resulted as a random variable and using a statistical test to determine the probability that the *observed value* of the random variable could occur by chance. That probability is the *p*-value.

Chebychef, a Russian mathematician, developed a mathematical inequality for calculating *p*-values. To apply Chebychef's inequality to the calculation of *p*-values, one must first calculate the mean and standard deviation of the random variable. The formulas for the mean and standard deviation of a variety of different types of ran-

---

§4.12   [1] The mean calculated from a sample of heights of different subjects or the proportion of a group with a particular racial identification can also be random variables because they are numerical values that may result from random experiments. Chapter 6 discusses tools appropriate for the analysis of means and proportions as random variables. The methods discussed in Chapter 6 are useful for determining the probability that a particular sample mean could occur by chance given information about the value of the population mean. Of greater interest, because often the population mean is unknown, is the question of how precise an estimate is the sample mean of the unknown population mean. Litigation applications of statistical methods designed to answer this question are the main focus of Chapter 6.

dom variables are presented in Section 4.21. The mean in this context is also called the *expected value* of the random variable, which is not literally a value that we expect to occur; it is instead a mathematical average of all of the possible outcomes weighted by the probability of their occurring. Thus, if blacks make up 17% of the applicant pool for an employer who wishes to hire 23 people, the *expected number* of blacks among those hired will be 3.91 (using Equation 4.21.1(c) discussed in Section 4.21.1) even though it would be impossible to hire exactly 3.91 people of any race.[2]

Subtracting the mean value from the particular observation of interest gives the disparity or difference between the observed and expected values. Dividing this disparity by the standard deviation yields the number of standard deviations the observed value is from the mean (see Section 4.23, where this disparity in terms of numbers of standard deviations is calculated with examples). Thus a difference of 25 between the observed and expected numbers of minority jury members, for instance, divided by a standard deviation of 16.67, would indicate that the observed value of the random variable, the number of minority jury members, was 1.5 (25/16.67) standard deviations from the expected number.

Chebychef's inequality says that the probability of an observation *less* than k standard deviations from the mean occurring by chance is *at least* $1 - 1/k^2$. Accordingly, the probability of observing a value of the random variable that is k or *more* standard deviations from the mean is *at most* $1/k^2$.[3] Thus the p-value for an observation one and one-half standard deviations from the mean is *at most* $1/(1.5)^2$ which equals 1/2.25, or .44. Observations as much as one and one-half standard deviations from the mean value will occur *at most* 44% of the time. By contrast, an observation differing from the mean by as much as 12 standard deviations will only occur *at most* $1/12^2$ or .69% of the time.

This use of Chebychef's inequality is applicable as an inferential statistical tool for all types of data from all kinds of distributions drawn from large samples or small. All subsequent statistical tests are merely efforts to be more precise about the p-value. All other tests apply only under restricted conditions, but when these are met they yield p-values that are in practical cases always smaller than those

---

[2] Expected numbers are not necessarily whole numbers. *Expected number* is a term of art only loosely related to an actual number.

[3] The letter k must be a number of standard deviations greater than or equal to 1 for Chebychef's inequality to be informative.

given by Chebychef's inequality. Remember that the inequality says that observations of a particular size occur *at most* a certain percentage of the time; under specific conditions the frequency of a particular observation is often much lower. Appreciating those conditions enables the analyst to determine the *p*-value more precisely. The sections that follow indicate the various conditions under which different statistical tests provide more accurate *p*-values than are given by Chebychef's inequality. The sections are organized by different types of probability distributions. A *probability distribution* shows the possible values of a random variable and the corresponding probability that each value will occur. We begin with the one that is perhaps most familiar to nonstatisticians, the normal distribution.

§4.13   p-*Values for Normally Distributed Random Variables*

A *normal population* of numbers has most of its members clustered near the mean, and the density or relative frequency of the numbers decreases with increasing distance from the mean. If the frequencies with which the numbers in the normal population appear as the result of random experiments are plotted on a graph, the figure resembles a bell-shaped curve. On a bell-shaped curve, the highest point of the bell appears over the mean or expected value, indicating the value for the random variable around which most observations are clustered. The curve descends on either side of the peak, showing the decreased likelihood of observations for values for random variables further from the expected value.

Exhibit 4.13(a) shows the bell-shaped curve that represents the relative frequency of various values for the random variable, the diameter of a llama fiber. This curve would indicate the frequency of various values in the population if we had measured every fiber. The various diameters have a mean value that is the arithmetic average of diameters for all fibers actually measured. The mean of the diameters is also the expected value of the random variable. If it is calculated from a sample of the llama fibers, it is an estimate of the population mean and expected value and is referred to as a *sample mean*. The standard deviation could also be calculated from all of the fibers actually measured. If the fibers measured were a random sample of all fibers, the resulting statistic would be referred to as a *sample standard deviation,* an estimate of the standard deviation we would have cal-

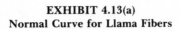

EXHIBIT 4.13(a)
Normal Curve for Llama Fibers

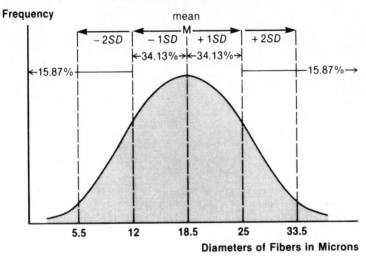

Diameters of Fibers in Microns

culated had we measured every fiber, the population standard deviation. The formulas for calculating population and sample means and standard deviations appear in Sections 4.21.1 and 4.21.3.

Suppose that the graph of frequencies in Exhibit 4.13(a) results from our inspection of a very large number of llama fibers and that we have calculated that their expected value is 18.5 microns. From the measurements of the diameters of all llama fibers we can also calculate the population standard deviation, which we assume for the purpose of illustration is 6.5 microns. With this information it is possible to illustrate a particularly useful property of the normal distribution. As discussed briefly in Section 4.10 and 4.11, approximately 68% of all observations of a normally distributed random variable will be within one standard deviation of the mean. This is true for any random variable that is normally distributed. For our llama fiber example, this means that approximately 68% of all llama fibers observed will be within one standard deviation, or 6.5 microns, of the expected value of 18.5 microns. Thus 68% of the time when we select a llama fiber at random, it will have a diameter between 18.5 minus 6.5 microns and 18.5 plus 6.5 microns. This range, from 12 to 25 microns, is the one standard deviation range on either side of the mean depicted on Exhibit 4.13(a).

This information about the probability distribution of the random variable is useful because it permits inferences regarding the probability of the occurrence of values of the random variable that are further from the mean than the one standard deviation range. If 68% of fibers have diameters within the one standard deviation range from 12 to 25 microns, then 32% (100% minus 68%) must have diameters outside of that range. Another way to phrase this conclusion is to state that there is a 32% chance of observing a fiber with a diameter either smaller than 12 microns or larger than 25 microns.

Because the bell-shaped curve is symmetrical around the mean, i.e., if there are as many fibers with diameters greater than the mean as there are with diameters less than the mean, 50% of the time a randomly selected fiber will have a diameter greater than 18.5 microns and 50% of the time a randomly selected fiber will have a diameter less than 18.5 microns. The symmetry of the normal distribution allows us to add additional detail to the conclusion that 32% of llama fibers will have diameters outside of the 12 to 25 micron (plus or minus one standard deviation) range. Half of these fibers beyond the one standard deviation range, or 16%, will have diameters less than 12 microns and 16% will have diameters greater than 25 microns. Thus there is only a 16% chance that the random variable will take a value less than 12 microns and a 16% chance that it will take a value greater than 25, as illustrated in Exhibit 4.13(a).

There are two ways to express the p-value for a value of the random variable that is outside of the one standard deviation range. A *two-tailed test* indicates the probability of being outside of the range without distinguishing whether the observed value is greater than the upper boundary of 25 or less than the lower boundary of 12 microns. The two-tailed p-value for an observation one standard deviation from the mean is equal to .32 because 32% of observations fall outside of the range. A *one-tailed test* indicates the probability of being below the range (or, alternatively, above the range). Thus an observed diameter of less than 12 microns would occur 16% of the time and the p-value for a one-tailed test would be .16. Similarly, an observed diameter of more than 25 microns would occur 16% of the time and the p-value for a one-tailed test is again .16.

The p-value for any observed value of the random variable can be estimated by reference to a Z Table, also called a Normal Table. A Z Table appears in the Appendix of Tables at the end of this book. The preliminary step is to determine how many standard deviations the observed value is from the expected value of that random variable.

This is accomplished in the same way as for the Chebychef approach. The expected value is calculated (see Section 4.21.1) and subtracted from the observed value to determine the difference between them, which is then divided by the standard deviation. The resulting number is the number of standard deviations by which the observed and expected values differ. The Z Table shows, for selected numbers of standard deviations, probabilities from which one- and two-tailed p-values can be calculated.

§4.14   Using the Z Table for Hypothesis Testing

This Section illustrates the use of the Z Table to calculate p-values for hypotheses related to the significance of a difference between observed and expected values of a random variable that is normally distributed in the population. As Exhibit 4.13(a) illustrates, for an observation that is one standard deviation from the expected value, the area under the normal curve is divided into four relevant parts: the left tail of the bell-shaped curve below 12 microns, the area between 12 microns (one standard deviation below the expected value) and the expected value, the area between the expected value and one standard deviation above the expected value, and the area above the one standard deviation mark of 25 microns in the right tail of the distribution. Because the curve is symmetrical, only one of these areas needs to be known for the other three to be determined. The Z Table indicates the areas between the expected value and a specified number of standard deviations from the expected value (either above or below) for selected fractional numbers of standard deviations from zero to four.

There are three parts to the Z Table reproduced in this book. Down the left hand side of the Table are numbers of standard deviations, also called Z scores, to one decimal place, from 0.0 to 3.9. To the right of these Z scores are the probabilities associated with them. Thus for a Z score of 1.0 the value of .3413 appears to the immediate right. This means that 34.13% of the observations of a normal random variable lie within the range from its expected value to 1.0 standard deviations above its expected value. From this we can calculate that 34.13% of observations of such a random variable lie in the range from its expected value to 1.0 standard deviations below its expected value, that 15.87% (50% minus 34.13%) lie beyond 1.0 standard deviations below the expected value, and that 15.87% lie beyond 1.0 stan-

dard deviations above the expected value. Thus, the one-tailed
p-value for an observation 1.0 standard deviations below the mean is
.1587. If the mean is 12 microns, as in the llama fiber example,
15.87% of observed fibers are likely to have diameters more than 1.0
standard deviations below the mean. Similarly, for an observation two
standard deviations below the expected value the area corresponding
to a *Z* score of 2.0 is .4773, indicating that 47.73% of the observations
of a normal random variable lie between the expected value and 2.0
standard deviations above the expected value. A similar percentage
lies in the 2.0 standard deviation range below the mean, 2.27% (50%
minus 47.73%) lie more than 2.0 standard deviations above the expected value, and a similar percentage lies more than 2.0 standard
deviations below. Thus the one-tailed *p*-value for an observation 2.0
standard deviations above or below the expected value is .0227. The
two-tailed *p*-value takes into account the percentage of observations in
both extremes beyond 2.0 standard deviations and equals .0227 times
2 or .0454.

The numbers across the top of the *Z* Table allow us to determine
the probabilities for fractional parts of numbers of standard deviations to two decimal places. For instance, if one wished to calculate the
probability of the random occurrence of a value of a random variable
that was 3.26 standard deviations below the expected value, one
would trace down the left side of the Table to 3.2 and then over to the
entry underneath 0.06, which is .4994. The one-tailed *p*-value associated with such an observation is 50% minus 49.94% or .0006, indicating that .06% of the values taken by a normal random variable fall
3.26 standard deviations or more below its expected value. The two-
tailed *p*-value is 2 times .0006 or .0012.

The appropriateness of the one- or the two-tailed test is often
dictated by the nature of the question asked. Three general types of
questions arise: (1) is it likely that the observed *overrepresentation* occurred by chance; (2) is it likely that the observed *underrepresentation*
occurred by chance; or (3) is it likely that the observed *disparity* occurred by chance? The first two types of queries are amenable to one-
tailed tests, while the third type is addressed by a two-tailed test. Each
of the first two types allows for only one possibility; an overrepresentation occurs only when the observed number is greater than the
expected, while an underrepresentation occurs only when the observed number is less than the expected. By failing to specify whether
the observed number is greater or less than expected, the two-tailed
test of the probability that a disparity occurred by chance allows for
both possibilities.

Examples from discrimination law illustrate these alternative types of questions. A one-tailed approach would be appropriate to test the hypothesis that the overrepresentation of blacks in the low-paying janitorial position is due to chance alone, and the resulting p-value would indicate that probability that an overrepresentation as large or larger than the one observed would occur by chance if the employees were hired randomly from among those qualified. Similarly, a one-tailed approach would be appropriate to test the hypothesis that the underrepresentation of blacks in managerial positions is due solely to chance, and the key value would indicate the probability of random occurrence of an underrepresentation as large or larger than the one observed. The two-tailed test is associated with a hypothesis that the difference between the observed value of the random variable and its expected value was due solely to chance and, because it allows for the possibility of either an over- or under-representation requires that we calculate the combined probabilities of being either above or below the expected value. Thus, for the two-tailed test we add together the probability of being in the right tail of the distribution and the probability of being in the left tail. A two-tailed test may be appropriate in the discrimination example if the issue is whether the hiring process is neutral with respect to race because it yields a probability that a disparity as large as or larger than that between the observed and expected values would occur by chance.

While the Z test for the significance of differences is probably the most common of all statistical tests used in litigation, no examples have been discovered that employ the test in a situation where the probability distribution of the random variable was known to be normal and the standard deviation of the population was known, as assumed in the discussion in Section 4.13. This apparent contradiction is accounted for by the fact that the Z test is a useful approximation to the results given by other tests based on other (i.e., nonnormal) distributions under certain well-recognized conditions. When statisticians say that one test (usually a more simple, straightforward, test) is a good approximation for another test, they usually mean that the test employed gives a calculated p-value that is negligibly different from what the alternative test would have given.

The principle behind using the Z test for other than normal distributions is embodied in the *central limit theorem*, which states that the probability distributions of some random variables tend to resemble the normal distribution as the size of the sample involved increases. Thus, even if the underlying probability distribution is not normal, the Z test can still be used for many distributions with applications relevant to litigation if the sample size on which the calculations are based is large. In particular, the Z test can be used in certain situations involving the binomial distribution, discussed in Sections 4.15 and 4.16, and the hypergeometric distribution, discussed in Sections 4.17, 4.18, and 4.19. Tests associated with these distributions appear to be the most commonly used inferential tests used in litigation involving differences between numbers. The use of the Z test to approximate p-values given by methods peculiar to these distributions is discussed following the description of those distributions. The apparent lack of litigation applications of the Z test in situations where the probability distribution of the random variable is known to be normal and the population standard deviation is known does not mean that an appreciation of the properties of the normal distribution is not useful to the litigator, as the following case illustrates.

Alabama Nursing Home Association v. Califano:[1] The regulation setting standards for reimbursements from the Alabama Medicaid Services Administration provided that for each class of nursing homes, 60% of all participating facilities are fully reimbursed for allowable costs by the Medicaid plan. The plaintiffs argued that this level of reimbursement was not "reasonably cost related" as required by the Medicaid Act.[2] After performing various statistical tests, the plaintiff's expert determined that the lowest ceiling that would meet the requirement of reasonable cost-related reimbursement would be the mean cost plus one-half standard deviation.[3] Knowledge of the workings of the Z Table allows one to estimate the percentage of nursing homes that would be fully reimbursed under this alternative standard under the assumption that nursing home costs are normally distributed across nursing homes. If the maximum amount of reimbursement were *mean* costs instead of mean plus one-half standard deviation 50% of hospitals would be fully reimbursed. From the Z Table we can see that one-half (or 0.50) standard deviations encompasses 19.15% of the observations on either side of the mean because the Table shows .1915 next to the Z score of .50. Thus, under the alternative standard proposed by the plaintiffs, 50% plus 19.15% (or 69.15%) of the nursing homes would be fully reimbursed rather than 60% as under the regulations then in effect.

Other Medicaid reimbursement schedules are now stated in terms

§4.14   [1] 465 F. Supp 1183 (M.D. Ala. 1979), *rev'd*, 617 F.2d 388 (5th Cir. 1980).
[2] 42 U.S.C. §1396a(a)(13)(E) (1976).
[3] Id.

of standard deviations. See, for instance, *Alabama Hospital Association v. Beasley*,[4] in which the reimbursement regulation for hospitals, mean cost plus one standard deviation, was challenged.

§4.15 p-*Values for Binomial Distributions — The Binomial Formula*

The *binomial distribution* is one of two probability distributions related to dichotomous variables that are of particular importance to litigators concerned with testing the significance of a difference. The other is the hypergeometric distribution, introduced in Section 4.19.

In Section 4.14 we found that normal random variables could take on any value along the measuring scale. The random variable, diameter of a llama fiber, could take on any value, as could a random variable such as the amount of pollution emitted. By contrast, a *dichotomous variable* can take on only two possible values. Dichotomous variables of interest to discrimination law, for instance, are gender and minority group membership. An individual's gender can take on either one of the two possible "names", male or female. Arbitrarily assigning a "1" to males and a "0" to females, we can convert gender to a dichotomous numeric variable. Similarly, minority group membership may be represented as a dichotomous variable if members of the two possible classes, minority and nonminority, are assigned numerical values. The dichotomous variable is a random variable if its value is the result of a random experiment (see Section 4.12, where the concept of a random variable is introduced).

Another random variable associated with dichotomous variables is the total number of observations of a particular type that result from a random experiment, such as the hiring of 20 employees; while the outcome of a single hiring decision (e.g., of either a male or female) might be of some interest to a factfinder, many discrimination cases are concerned with the total number of women hired out of the 20 people hired during a given period. If attention is focused on a single hiring decision, the random variable in this example would be the gender of the particular person hired, with the possible values of 0 and 1, but if attention is focused on the 20 hiring decisions as a group, the random variable of interest would be the number of the particular gender hired. In this latter case, the values the random

[4] 702 F.2d 955, 956 (11th Cir. 1983).

variable could take range from zero women hired to 20 women hired. Under certain circumstances, the number of females hired may be considered a binomial random variable.

For a random variable to have a binomial distribution it must satisfy five conditions. While these conditions appear at first to be rather technical and arcane, they are easy to understand and apply in many cases that the litigator is likely to confront. The requirements are:

1. The random variable must be based on binary outcomes. A hiring decision that is random with respect to gender and that can only result in the hiring of a man or woman is an example of an event that leads to a binary outcome.

2. The random variable must be the total number of events (decisions, in this example) that resulted in a particular outcome. Thus, for the hiring example, the total number of women hired is a variable satisfying this condition, but the *proportion* of hires that were female is not. The binomial random variable, then, can take on any value between zero and the total number of women who could have been hired to fill available positions.

3. The number of binary events must be independent of the outcomes of those random experiments. In the hiring example, this condition is met if it was known at the outset that 20 vacancies, not more or less, had to be filled. It would not be met if the employer simply started picking new hires at random from its applicant pool with the intent of ceasing as soon as the number of females chosen reached ten.

4. The random experiments (hiring decisions in this example) must be independent of one another. This requirement means that the outcome of one random experiment in terms of the characteristic of interest (gender in this example) must not affect the outcome of the next one. Thus, if a man (or a woman) is hired in one hiring decision, that outcome must in no way influence the next hiring decision.

5. The probability of a particular outcome occurring must not change between random experiments. The likelihood of a particular event occurring must be the same for each random experiment. Thus, if people are hired from a pool of applicants, the percentage of women in that pool remaining after each hiring decision must not change from one random experiment to the next in order for the random variable, total number of women hired, to be binomially distributed. If the pool contains thousands of individuals and if only 20 in all are to be hired, it is apparent that the gender composition in the

pool will change by a negligible amount as each new hire is selected and removed from the pool. Under these circumstances, the probability of a female being chosen under random selection is practically constant from one random experiment to the next, so this condition for a binomial random variable is met. If, on the other hand, the pool from which the 20 new hires were selected contained only 25 individuals, the condition would not be met because the gender proportions in the pool can change substantially depending on the genders of the people hired early on.[1]

Often, the binomial random variable of interest in litigation is the number of times a particular characteristic is observed in a sample. Significance testing allows one to compute the probability (*p*-value) that a disparity between the observed value and the expected value of a random variable as large or larger than the one observed would occur by chance. For binomial random variables, this *p*-value can be calculated using the binomial formula (discussed in 4.23). Once the requirements for a random variable to be binomially distributed are met, there are only two factors that affect the probability of observing in a sample a specified number of items with a particular characteristic: the total number of observations made, that is, the sample size, and the percentage of items in the population as a whole that possess that characteristic. There are a variety of alternative methods for calculating the *p*-value, but they all require the same background information and use comparable symbols to identify the three inputs to the calculation: *x*, the number of observed items that possessed a particular characteristic; *n*, the total number of observations made, that is, the sample size; and *P*, the percentage of items in the population as a whole that possess the characteristic.

Antitrust Hypothetical: In a particular growing industry, 10% of all new entrants to the field fail before being in business one full year. One such failed entrant sued an established industry leader on behalf of other new entrants who had allegedly suffered as a result of a conspiracy among the established firms. Among the uncontroverted facts was that, during the year in question, 25 new entrants to the industry had

---

§4.15 [1] The classic example of a binomially distributed random variable is the number of heads that appear as the result of a fixed number of coin flips. The outcomes of each trial, a flip, are binary, either heads or tails; the random variable is the total number of heads. The appearance of a head or tail on one flip does not affect the likelihood of a head or tail on any other flip, and the probability of a head or a tail on any given flip is the same for each trial (and equal to 50% if the coin is fair).

failed. The plaintiff wanted to establish that this unusually high number of failures was due to the trade practices of the industry leaders. The defendant claimed that the high number of failures was due to chance. P is the underlying percentage of firms that possess the characteristics of interest, failure. A dispute over the value of P would involve a question of whether the historical failure rate was 10% or some other figure, higher or lower. Naturally, the plaintiff would want to establish that the historical rate was low while the defendant would want to show it was high. The total number of observations made, n, would be the total number of firms that entered this year, the sample size. A dispute over n would involve a question of how many firms actually entered during the year in question. The plaintiff would naturally want the total entrants to be low (so that the failure rate would be high) while the defendant would want the number to be high. The number of failures, 25, is the number of observations from our sample (n firms) that exhibit failure. While there is no dispute over this value of the random variable, the number of failures, the plaintiff will be better off if this number is high.

The random variable in the antitrust hypothetical is binomially distributed if each firm as of year's end either clearly had or had not failed, if the number of firms entering during the year was not influenced by the number of failures that year, if the failure of one new entrant did not affect the likelihood that another new entrant would fail, and if the probability of failure is exactly the same for each entrant. If any of these background assumptions are not met, the binomial test may not give an accurate p-value from which to draw inferences relating to the hypothesis that there is no relationship between the trade practices of the established firms and the business failures in the industry.

> *Insurance Claim Adjustment:* A shipper inspected 15 beer kegs from a derailed trainload and found that seven had been damaged. Shipper's insurance policy would indemnify the shipper if 20% or more of the shipment were damaged. The insurer claimed that a sample of 15 kegs was insufficient to show a 20% damage rate. Using the binomial formula, the shipper was able to demonstrate that if the underlying damage rate was as low as 20%, the probability of finding as many as seven damaged kegs out of 15 just by chance was only 1.81% and therefore finding so many would be rather unlikely. If the underlying damage rate is even lower, say 10%, the probability of finding as many as seven damaged kegs by chance is lower, .03%. But if the damage rate is greater than 20%, e.g., 35%, the probability of finding seven or more defectives just by chance is greater, 24.52%. This argument suggests

that it is unlikely that the damage rate is 20% or less, which supports the shipper's claim. For any possible underlying damage rate, P equals that rate, x equals 7, and n equals 15.

Litigation frequently is concerned with the choice of the appropriate n, x, or P to be used in the calculation of probabilities (see examples in Section 4.19). The p-values for selected combinations of P, x, and n are also shown in the Cumulative Binomial Table that appears in the Appendix of Tables at the end of this book, which will facilitate computations. The use of this table is compared to the use of the binomial formula in Section 4.23. The resulting p-values, whether calculated by use of the binomial formula or the Cumulative Binomial Table, are always identical because the values on the Table were calculated using the formula.

§4.16 Z Test for Large Sample Binomial Distributions

When the sample size for a binomially distributed random variable is large, the Z test gives an acceptable approximation to the p-value that would be obtained by the binomial formula. This is very fortunate because manipulating the formula becomes very awkward when sample sizes get large, and, as a glance reveals, the Cumulative Binomial Table is very cumbersome for large sample sizes. A general rule is that the normal distribution is an acceptable approximation to the binomial distribution as long as the proportion of the population possessing a specified characteristic, P, and the sample size, n, are such that n times P and n times (one minus P) are both greater than or equal to five.[1] By "acceptable approximation" we mean that the techniques used for determining p-values for normally distributed variables yield p-values for binomially distributed variables that are negligibly different from those that techniques designed specifically for binomially distributed variables yield. Thus, for large samples of a binomially distributed variable the Z test gives the same p-values as the binomial formula. We would not care about this approximation except that the Z test is easier to calculate.

---

§4.16 [1] See, e.g., R. Pfaffenberger & J. Patterson, Statistical Methods 199 (1977). According to some statistical sources, the binomial is accurately approximated by the Z test if SD^2 or n times p times q is greater than or equal to 9. L. Sachs, Applied Statistics, 175 (1981). This test is much more restrictive than the one presented in the text.

When using a Z test for a binomially distributed variable, the greatest precision is obtained through the use of a *correction for continuity*,[2] which adjusts for the fact that a continuous distribution (the normal distribution, see Section 4.13) is used to approximate the p-values of a discrete distribution, the binomial (see Section 4.15).

The degree of additional precision obtained through use of the correction for continuity usually is negligibly small when the sample size is large (see Section 4.20). The correction for continuity can therefore be ignored for sufficiently large samples without affecting the calculated p-values.[3]

A.B. & G. Instrument and Engineering, Inc. v. United States:[4] The Court of Claims examined inspection standards for nose fuse adapters, an artillery shell component, in a case involving rejection of a shipment because too many adapters were defective. The inspection standards required examining 315 adapters before rejecting a shipment as large as 10,001 to 35,000 pieces.[5] One issue was whether the government was entitled randomly to select and test only 20 units and reject the shipment of 20,000 units if all 20 in the sample were faulty. The court found for the government, stating that "it is a fair bet that a larger sample would have revealed an even greater number of disqualifying defects."[6]

Using the binomial formula we can compute the probability of finding as many as 20 defective units in the *Engineering* example just by chance in a sample of 315 adapters. We need to know the underlying probability that a given unit is defective. While the case does not indicate the standard necessary for rejection of the shipment, assume that if 5% of the shipment is defective, rejection by the government is justified. Because the sample is so large (315 adapters) the binomial formula is awkward to use and the tables do not go high enough. The Z test approach can be used, however, for a sample size of 315 and will yield the probability of finding 20 defective adapters out of 315 if 5% of the adapters are defective. If the defective rate is .05 then the expected number of defects is .05 times 315, or 15.75. The observed number is 20 and the disparity is 4.25, which is 1.10 standard deviations from the mean. The probability of observing a disparity this large or larger by chance is 13.57% (see Section 4.24). If the rate of defect is higher, e.g.,

---

[2] See, e.g., R. Pfaffenberger & J. Patterson, Statistical Methods 197-201 (1977).
[3] Id. at 199. An example of the application of the correction for continuity is discussed in Section 4.26.
[4] 593 F.2d 394 (Ct. Cl. 1979).
[5] Id. at 397.
[6] Id.

6%, it is more likely that we would find so many defects, 39.74%. The higher the underlying defective rate the less surprised we are to find 20 or more, and it is very unlikely that we would find 20 or more if the underlying rate is less than 5%. If the underlying rate is only 2%, for instance, we would get 20 or more defectives out of 315 just by chance only .55% of the time. Procedures for making these calculations appear in Section 4.24.

§4.17   p-Values for Hypergeometric Distributions

One of the requirements for using the binomial formula or the binomial table is that the percentage of items with a particular characteristic in underlying population remain constant from one random experiment to the next. A difficulty arises when the drawing of a sample appreciably changes the percentage of items with the relevant characteristic remaining in the population. Consider, for example, an employer about to choose five new employees from a pool of 20 qualified applicants, half of whom are blacks. If the first person hired is chosen at random from the pool, it is apparent that chances are even that a black will be chosen. However, if a black is chosen, the second choice will be made from a pool of 19 applicants, 9/19ths or 47% of whom are blacks. If this second choice is also made at random, it is apparent that a black is less likely to be chosen on this trial than on the first trial. Had the person chosen on the first trial been white, however, chances of drawing a black on the second would be *better* than even. Thus, while one might be tempted to regard the number of blacks among the five new hires as a binomial random variable, this may produce misleading results because the conditions of the binomial model are not fully satisfied; the trials are not independent of one another because the probability of a particular outcome changes between hires.

If the five new hires are chosen at random (either one at a time or all at once — it makes no difference in the probability calculations), the number of blacks chosen among the five is a hypergeometric random variable. The formulas for calculating probabilities, means, and standard deviations are somewhat different for hypergeometric random variables than for binomial random variables (see Sections 4.21.1 and 4.21.3). These differences are most pronounced in cases in which the number of people hired is a significant fraction of the total pool of applicants. If the applicants number 1000 instead of just 20 and only five new hires are selected at random from the pool, the number of blacks among the five would technically be a hypergeometric random variable, but it would also be so nearly binomial that in practice either model could be used.

The selection of new hires from a limited pool is an example of *sampling without replacement*. If an item is drawn out of the population and cannot be drawn again, the remainder of the group of which that item was a member is now a smaller percentage of the population. If the population is large the deletion of one item changes the proportions very little, but as more items are withdrawn the opportunity for significant changes in proportions increases. Whenever sampling without replacement occurs, and this is often the case in discrimination law, the p-values for dichotomous events are accurately calculated using the *hypergeometric*, rather than the binomial, *probability formula*. The procedures for these calculations appear in Section 4.25.

> **Jurgens v. Thomas:**[1] In an employment discrimination case against the Equal Employment Opportunity Commission, plaintiffs examined the defendant's promotion practices between 1975 and 1979. Out of 284 employees, 62 males and 222 females, only three males were promoted while 29 females were.[2] Given the proportions of males and females among those eligible to be promoted, 62/284 or 21.83% and 222/284 or 78.17%, respectively, what is the probability that three or fewer males would be promoted? Using the hypergeometric formula, the probability of so few males being chosen by chance was .0491, or 4.91%.[3] Note that after each person is promoted the proportions change slightly. If the first person is male the proportion of males declines from 62/284 to 61/283 or 21.55%; if the first person selected is female the proportion of males increases from 62/284 to 62/283, or 21.91%.

> **Adams v. Gaudet:**[4] The court examined the probability of adverse statistical impact on blacks and females by comparing their promotion rates to those for whites and males. In one position, for instance, that of assistant principal, there were four females and 18 males. One female and eight males were promoted. A hypergeometric distribution of the selection probabilities is involved here because as soon as the first per-

---

§4.17   [1] 29 Fair Empl. Prac. Cas. (BNA) 1561 (N.D. Tex. 1982).

[2] Id. at 1568-1569 n. 15.

[3] One of the crucial background assumptions for this calculation is that, throughout the period, all of the original 284 employees who had not yet been selected were equally eligible for the next selection. The p-value does not provide any information regarding the validity of this assumption. A factual examination of this assumption is necessary to establish that the model accurately describes the process involved.

[4] 515 F. Supp. 1086, 1140 (W.D. La. 1981).

son from the group of 22 is promoted the proportion of males remaining in the group changes. The hypergeometric formula indicates that the probability that one or fewer women would be promoted given random selection is .45. In another discriminatory hiring aspect of this case, a p-value of .04897 was calculated for a situation where 13 of 128 white applicants for a clerical job were hired while only two of 69 blacks were.[5]

While the hypergeometric formula is appropriate when sampling from a limited population without replacement, such as under the circumstances specified in Sections 4.18 and 4.19, the binomial formula or a Z test may be substituted for the hypergeometric approach. One must appreciate the background assumptions underlying each approach in order to avoid using the wrong one.

§4.18 Binomial Test for Small Sample Hypergeometric Distributions

When the sample size is small relative to the size of the population, the selection of one item out of the population has little effect on the proportion of items with each of the two characteristics and there is very little difference between the hypergeometric and the binomial distributions. That being the case, the binomial test is a good approximation to the hypergeometric test; using a binomial test will give a p-value almost identical to the p-value obtained from the hypergeometric test. As a general rule, whenever the sample size is less than about 5% of the size of the population, the binomial test may be substituted for the hypergeometric test.[1] Other statisticians offer alternative threshold percentages; ratios of sample size to population size ranging from .01 to .20 have been suggested.[2] When in doubt as to the accuracy of the binomial approximation, use the hypergeometric probability formula.

Adams v. Gaudet:[3] Of 41 applicants for administrative staff positions, one of ten blacks and five of 31 whites were promoted. The sample size, six promotions, is by some standards small relative to the

[5] Id. at 1137.
§4.18 [1] See, e.g., R. Pfaffenberger & J. Patterson, Statistical Methods 169 (1977).
[2] See, e.g., D. Baldus & J. Cole, Statistical Proof of Discrimination 109 (Supp. 1983).
[3] 515 F. Supp. 1086, 1141 (W.D. La. 1981).

population size, 41 applicants, being only 6/41 or 14.6% of the applicant pool. Using the binomial formula to test the hypothesis that there is no relationship between race and promotion (which, of course, assumes equal eligibility of all candidates) give a one-tailed p-value of .549. By comparison, the hypergeometric formula gives a p-value of .542. Had the ratio of sample size to applicant pool been smaller, the p-values would have been even closer.

EEOC v. United Virginia Bank/Seaboard National:[4] In a class action, minority members alleged discrimination in employment. Among other disparities noted was an overrepresentation of blacks among the lower-level service employees at the bank: of 14 employees in this job category, 11 were black.[5] The percentage of employees in this occupation group throughout the metropolitan area who were black was 50%, leading one to expect that if 14 employees were to be hired at random, 7 of them (.50 × 14) would be black. The issue was whether there was a significant disparity between 11 observed and 7 expected. This can be treated as a binomial distribution because the random variable, number of blacks hired, is based on a counting of binary outcomes, black/nonblack; the selections are assumed to be independent; and the number selected, 14, is fixed and is a very small proportion of the total eligible population in the metropolitan area. The value of the random variable is the number of blacks, 11, in the sample of 14 employees. Thus x, the number of observed items possessing the given racial characteristic, is 11, and n, the sample size, is 14. The proportion of the total population exhibiting this characteristic, P, is 50%. Based on the binomial formula the probability that 11 or more blacks would be among 14 people selected at random from the metropolitan area pool is .0287. (See Section 4.23.) This is the p-value used in significance testing.

As the following example illustrates, when the sample size is only one item, the binomial and hypergeometric formulas give identical results because the underlying population proportion has not had the opportunity to change.

Adams v. Gaudet:[6] Of 11 Supervisors of Secondary Education (three black, eight white), one white was promoted. Using either the binomial or hypergeometric formula the p-value associated with this outcome is .727. See Section 4.26, Exhibit 4.26(b), where the relevant calculations are shown.

---

[4] 615 F.2d 147 (4th Cir. 1980).
[5] Id. at 151.
[6] 515 F. Supp. 1086, 1141 (W.D. La. 1981).

§4.19 Z Test for Large Sample Hypergeometric Distributions

According to the guidelines set forth in Section 4.18, the binomial formula is a good approximation to the hypergeometric test when the sample size is small relative to the population size. From the discussion of the binomial test we know that the Z test gives a good approximation to the binomial distribution for a sufficiently large sample size, n. Consequently, the Z test also gives a good approximation to the hypergeometric p-values for large samples, provided they are a small proportion of the entire population. Criteria for judging when a sample size is large enough for substituting the Z test for the binomial formula also apply here. The proportion of the group possessing a particular characteristic is given by N_1/N where N_1 is the number of members possessing that characteristic in the group of size N. We use N_2 to indicate the number not possessing that characteristic. The comparable criteria for large sample size is that n (the sample size) times N_1/N and n times N_2/N must both be greater than or equal to about 5. In applying the Z test, the hypergeometric formulas are used for calculating the mean and standard deviation of the random variable, and then the number of standard deviations by which the observed and expected values of the random variable differ is calculated to obtain a Z score. The Z Table indicates a p-value associated with the calculated Z score, as discussed in Section 4.14. (See Section 4.27 for examples.) This approximation is accurate only where the sample size is large in absolute terms but small relative to the population size (see Section 4.27).

Castaneda v. Partida:[1] The large sample consisted of 870 jurors selected from the population of Hidalgo County, Texas over an 11-year period. Assuming that no one served twice, the relevant population was the eligible population of Hidalgo County, approximately 80,000 people.[2] The sample was only about 1% of the population so the binomial model closely approximates the hypergeometric. Since the sample size is so large, the Z test is a good approximation to the binomial test without correction for continuity. It yields a p-value of 1 times 10^{-140}, indicating that it is very unlikely indeed that so few Spanish-surnamed jury members would have been selected had their selection been random.

§4.19 [1] 430 U.S. 482, 496 n. 17 (1976).
[2] Id. at 488 n. 8.

These normal and binomial approximations to the hypergeometric formula are very useful because calculations based directly on the hypergeometric probability formula are exceedingly cumbersome except in cases involving small populations or small samples. Using the binomial or hypergeometric probability formulas for the calculation of the standard deviation necessitates a factual determination of the appropriate numbers to be used in the calculation. These numbers present litigable issues. Specifically, the sample size, n, the percentage of the population as a whole possessing a particular characteristic, P, in the binomial formula, or N_1/N, in the hypergeometric formula, and the observed number in the sample possessing the characteristic, x, in the binomial formula, or N_1, in the hypergeometric formula, become important facts to be proved.

EEOC v. United Virginia Bank/Seaboard National:[3] The EEOC claimed that since 27% of the local labor force was black, 27% of the defendant bank's office and clerical positions should be filled by blacks. The court concluded that 14% was a more appropriate value for P, the underlying population proportion of blacks, because only a portion of the black labor force was qualified to perform office and clerical tasks. The 14% figure was obtained by examining the percentage of blacks in different occupational categories in the metropolitan area from which the bank drew its employees. The plaintiff who attempts to show a discriminatory impact of a hiring practice will usually argue for the highest plausible value for the underlying population percentage because that will make the disparity larger and the p-value lower (see Section 4.27).

The sample size, n, was also an issue in this case. EEOC figures showed 336 employees in office and clerical positions at the defendant bank. The court noted that in preparing its figures the EEOC had included employees hired prior to the effective date of Title VII. Because pre-Title VII hiring practices are not relevant in Title VII litigation,[4] the pre-Act hires had to be deleted from the sample. When the 33 white pre-Act hires and two black pre-Act hires are eliminated the sample size is reduced by 35. Changing this sample size increased the one-tailed p-value from .0091 to .0217.

It is more typically the case that when the sample size changes, the observed frequencies of the characteristic change so that there is a change in n and x. Such was the case in *Castaneda* when the dissent

[3] 615 F.2d 147 (4th Cir. 1980).
[4] Hazelwood School District v. United States, 433 U.S. 299, 309 (1976).

suggested that the appropriate sample to examine for evidence of discrimination in jury selection was not those jurors selected during the preceding 11 years but rather those selected during the two and one-half year period while the jury selection process was supervised by the same judge who supervised the selection of the jury for the defendant-appellant. Switching from the 11-year period to the two and one-half year period reduced the number of jurors in the sample, n, from 870 to 220 but also reduced the observed number of Spanish surnamed jurors from 349 to 100. Such changes inevitably alter the resulting p-values.

§4.20 Summary of Decisions Relevant to the Choice of Significance Tests of Numerical Differences

The procedure to follow in determining the significance of a difference between an observed value of a random variable and its expected value begins with the determination of the distribution of that random variable. Probability distributions are discussed generally in Section 4.13, and features distinguishing normal, binomial, and hypergeometric situations are discussed in Sections 4.13, 4.15, and 4.17. If the population is normal, the statistical significance of the difference between observed and expected values can be expressed as a p-value, obtained from a Z Table by way of the Z test.

If the distribution of the random variable is binomial, the binomial formula or Cumulative Binomial Table yields the p-value for the difference between observed and expected values. A Z test can be used to give an accurate approximation for the p-value for the difference between observed and expected values of a binomial random variable for large samples. For this purpose a sample is often considered sufficiently large if n (the sample size) times P (the proportion of observations possessing a particular characteristic) and n times $(1 - P)$ are both greater than about five. If the Z test is substituted for the binomial test, a correction for continuity should be used unless the sample size is quite large (see Section 4.24, where the calculations for the correction for continuity are presented). Exhibits 4.24(c) and (d) in the calculations portion of this chapter illustrate the effect of omitting the correction for continuity when the sample size is 75. As the sample size gets larger for the same P the difference between p-values gets smaller.

If the distribution of the random variable is hypergeometric, the

EXHIBIT 4.20(a)
Guidelines for Determining an Appropriate Significance Test
for Numerical Differences

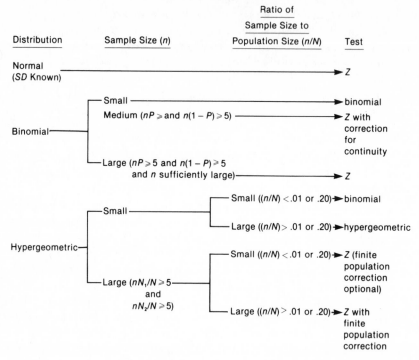

hypergeometric formula must be used to calculate p-values, though if the sample size is much less than the population size, the binomial formula gives an accurate approximation. The ratio of sample size to population sizes (n to N) at which the binomial formula becomes an acceptable substitute depends on the accuracy required by the investigator. Exhibits 4.26(a) and 4.26(b) compare the p-values resulting from a situation in which the ratio of sample size is relatively small (6/41 = .15) and a situation where the ratio is relatively large (10/13 = .77). In the smaller ratio example, the binomial formula yields a p-value of .549, while the hypergeometric formula yields a p-value of .542. In the larger ratio example, the binomial yields .3321 while the hypergeometric yields .2028. If, in addition to a small sample size to population size ratio, the sample size is large, the Z test can be used to give accurate approximation to the p-value obtained using the hypergeometric formula. Exhibit 4.20(a) summarizes the decisions concerning the choice of a significance test for differences.

F. COMPUTATIONAL PROCEDURES RELATED TO ANALYZING DIFFERENCES

The following notation is used in formulas in this section. The numbers in parentheses followng each definition indicate the section where the term was first introduced. Note that upper case letters indicate population values while lower case letters indicate sample values. A lower case symbol in parentheses that follows a similar symbol being defined is the sample equivalent of a population symbol.

k — in Chebychef's inequality, a number of standard deviations from the arithmetic mean to be specified in calculating the proportion of measurements that will lie in the specified numerical range, which is the arithmetic mean plus or minus k standard deviations (4.12)

M_X (m_x) — the mean of a population (sample) of possible observations of the variable X (x) (4.21.1)

M_Y (m_y) — the mean of a population (sample) of possible observations of the variable Y (y) (4.21.1)

N (n) — the number of numbers or items in the population (sample) (4.21.1)

N_1 — in the hypergeometric formula, the number of items in the population from which the sample was drawn that possess the characteristic of interest (4.25)

N_2 — in the hypergeometric formula, the number of items in the population from which the sample was drawn that do not possess the characteristic of interest (4.25)

P — in the binomial formula, the underlying proportion of observations in the population that possess a particular characteristic (4.21.1)

p_o — an observed proportion of observations that possess a particular characteristic

Q — in the binomial formula, the underlying proportion of observations in the population that do not possess a particular characteristic (4.21.1)

Σ — the arithmetic summation of the terms that follow (4.21.1)

SD^2 (sd^2) — the variance of a population (sample) (4.21.2)

SD_X (sd_x) — the population (sample) standard deviation of X (4.21.3)

SD_Y (sd_y) — the population (sample) standard deviation of Y (4.21.3)

X (x) — a variable that takes on numerical values (4.21.1)

X_i (x_i) — the ith value in a sequence of observations of X (x) (4.21.1)

x_0 — an observed frequency with which a particular characteristic appears as a result of n successive trials (4.23)

Y (y) — a variable that takes on numerical values (4.21.1)

Y_i (y_i) — the ith value in a sequence of observations of Y (y) (4.21.1)

Z — the number of standard deviations between an observed and expected value. Also, an inferential test statistic referred to as a Z score (4.13) (4.22)

! — the factorial sign indicates that the number preceding it is to be multiplied by every positive integer less than that number (4.23)

§4.21   Descriptive Statistics: Calculations

In this section simple descriptive statistics are calculated and a substantial portion of the most basic symbolic notation used throughout this book is introduced.

§4.21.1   Mean — Calculations

The mean is the arithmetic average of a group of numbers. A member of the group or list of numbers is represented symbolically by an uppercase letter, such as X or Y, if the group contains all of the items in the population or a lowercase letter, such as x or y, if the group consists of a *sample* of such items from some even larger population. X, x, Y, and y are called *variables,* and they represent characteristics of the population (or sample) under study that can take on two or more values among the items in the population.[1]

A particular item from the list of measurements of a particular variable is referred to symbolically by a number indicating its position

---

§4.21   [1] See, e.g., R. Pfaffenberger & J. Patterson, Statistical Methods 18 (1977).

on the list. The position on the list is generally described by a lower-case letter, usually i or j, so that an unspecified single observation of the variable X would be referred to as X_i. A specific observation is referred to by its number in the subscript; e.g., the fifth observation of the variable X is referred to as X_5. Sometimes the numbers in a population or sample are considered in a sequence corresponding perhaps to the natural order of their magnitude or to the order in which they were encountered in a series of measurements. In each case the subscript indicates the observation's position on a list of measurements.

The Greek upper case sigma, Σ, is the symbol for the mathematical operation of addition and is referred to as the summation sign. The Σ in an equation indicates that everything that follows is to be added together. Thus "ΣX_i for all i" indicates that the measurements for all of the observations of the variable X are to be added together. Similarly, "$\Sigma(X_i - 27)$ for all i" indicates that the differences between each observation of the variable X and 27 should be added together; that is, first subtract 27 from each observed measurement, then add the differences together.

Equations 4.21.1(a)[2] and (b)[3] give formulas for the means for populations and samples while (c)[4] and (d)[5] give the formulas for the means of binomially and hypergeometrically distributed random variables, respectively.

$$\text{mean (finite population)} = M_X = \frac{\Sigma X_i}{N}$$

4.21.1(a)

$$\text{mean (sample)} = m_x = \frac{\Sigma x}{n}$$

4.21.1(b)

$$\text{mean (binomially distributed random variable)} = M_X = nP$$

4.21.1(c)

$$\text{mean (hypergeometrically distributed random variable)} =$$

$$M_X = \frac{nN_1}{N_1 + N_2} = n\frac{N_1}{N}$$

4.21.1(d)

---

[2] Id. at 214. Technically, this formula applies only to finite populations, populations whose members can be counted.
[3] Id.
[4] Id. at 164.
[5] Id. at 167.

Exhibits 4.21.1(a), (b), and (c) show calculations of sample means for each of these three distributions.

EXHIBIT 4.21.1(a)
Calculation of Sample Mean

Variable: diameters of llama fibers $= x$

Observations of the Variable x

$x_1 = 20$ microns	$x_6 = 28$ microns
$x_2 = 17$ microns	$x_7 = 18$ microns
$x_3 = 21$ microns	$x_8 = 22$ microns
$x_4 = 23$ microns	$x_9 = 16$ microns
$x_5 = 19$ microns	$x_{10} = 19$ microns

$$m_x = \frac{\Sigma x_i}{n} =$$

$$\frac{20 + 17 + 21 + 23 + 19 + 28 + 18 + 22 + 16 + 19}{10} =$$

$$\frac{203}{10} = 20.3 \text{ microns}$$

EXHIBIT 4.21.1(b)
Calculation of Mean for Binomially Distributed Variable

Variable: number of fibers with diameters greater than 15 microns among 20 fibers

The underlying population proportion of fibers with diameters greater than 15 microns is 56% or .56.

$$M_X = nP = 20 \times .56 = 11.2 \text{ fibers}$$

EXHIBIT 4.21.1(c)
Calculation of Mean for Hypergeometrically Distributed Variable

Variable: number of women promoted out of eight promotions

The underlying proportion of women in the eligible group of employees is .33. There are 33 women in the eligible group of 100 employees. Thus,

$$N_1 = 33, N_2 = 67, \text{ and } n = 8$$

$$M_X = \frac{8 \times 33}{33 + 67} = 2.64 \text{ women}$$

§4.21.2 Variance — Calculations

The variance describes how much the observations vary from one another using the mean or expected number as a reference point from which to measure disparities (see Section 4.6). The formulas for the variance of a finite population and a sample from a population appear in Equations 4.21.2(a)[6] and (b)[7] respectively.

$$\text{variance (finite population)} = SD^2 = \frac{\Sigma(X_i - M_X)^2}{N}$$

4.21.2(a)

$$\text{variance (sample)} = sd^2 = \frac{\Sigma(x_i - m_x)^2}{n - 1}$$

4.21.2(b)

Exhibits 4.21.2(a) and (b) show how these equations are applied. The

EXHIBIT 4.21.2(a)
Variance for a Finite Population

Variable: monthly law firm income in year 1

(see Exhibit 4.6(a))

Month	X_i Income	$X_i - M_X$	$(X_i - M_X)^2$
January	$ 300	− 304	92,416
February	1900	1296	1,679,616
March	200	− 404	163,216
April	400	− 204	41,616
May	600	− 4	16
June	500	− 104	10,816
July	700	96	9,216
August	1500	896	802,816
September	100	− 504	254,016
October	800	196	38,416
November	200	− 404	163,216
December	50	− 554	306,916

Total Income for Year $= \Sigma X_i = \$7250 \qquad \Sigma(X_i - M_X)^2 = 3,562,292$

$$M_X = \frac{\Sigma X_i}{N} = \frac{\$7250}{12} = \$604$$

$$SD^2 = \frac{\Sigma(X_i - M_X)^2}{N} = \frac{3,562,292}{12} = 296,858$$

[6] See, e.g., R. Pfaffenberger & J. Patterson, Statistical Methods 41 (1977). Technically, this formula applies only to finite populations.
[7] Id. at 248.

EXHIBIT 4.21.2(b)
Variance for a Sample from a Population

Variable: monthly law firm income in year 1
(sample of 5 months)

Month	x_i Income	$x_i - m_x$	$(x_i - m_x)^2$
January	$ 300	-310	96,100
April	400	-210	44,100
August	1500	90	792,100
October	800	190	36,100
December	50	-560	313,600

$$\Sigma x_i = \$3050 \qquad \Sigma(x_i - m_x)^2 = 1,282,000$$

$$m_x = \frac{\Sigma x_i}{n} = \frac{\$3050}{5} = \$610$$

$$sd^2 = \frac{\Sigma(x_i - m_x)^2}{n - 1} = \frac{1,282,000}{4} = 320,500$$

symbol for the variance of a population is SD^2. For a sample, the symbol for the variance is sd^2. Note that the formula for the variance of a population is slightly different than for the formula for the variance of a sample.

Formulas for the variance of binomially and hypergeometrically distributed variables appear in Equations 4.21.2(c)[8] and (d)[9] and are illustrated in Exhibits 4.21.2(c) and (d) respectively.

$$\text{(binomial) } SD^2 = nPQ$$

4.21.2(c)

EXHIBIT 4.21.2(c)
Variance for a Binomially Distributed Variable

Variable: the number of fibers with a diameter greater than 15 microns among 20 fibers

The underlying population proportion of fibers with diameters greater than 15 microns is 56% or .56. Thus,

$$P = .56 \text{ and } Q = 1 - .56, \text{ or } .44$$
$$SD^2 = nPQ = 20 \times .56 \times .44 = 4.9$$

[8] See, e.g., G. Ferguson, Statistical Analysis in Psychology & Education 86 (1976); R. Pfaffenberger & J. Patterson, Statistical Methods 164 (1977).
[9] See, e.g., R. Pfaffenberger & J. Patterson, Statistical Methods 167 (1977).

The variance for a binomially distributed random variable reflects the degree of diversity in the population. The closer the population proportion of each characteristic is to 50%, the greater is the variance. Thus, for a sample of 20, if $p = .50$ the variance is 5, while for $p = .25$, $SD^2 = 3.75$ and for $p = .90$, $SD^2 = 1.8$. As noted in Section 4.6, the greater the diversity, the greater is the variance.

Equation 4.21.2(d) presents the formula for the variance of a hypergeometrically distributed random variable.

$$\text{(hypergeometric) } SD^2 = \left(\frac{N-n}{N-1}\right) n \frac{N_1}{N} \frac{N_2}{N}$$

4.21.2(d)

The factor $(N - n)/(N - 1)$ is the *finite population correction factor* (see Section 4.27, where the hypergeometric distribution finite population problem is described and the relevance of the correction factor is discussed). For a sample of eight people drawn from a pool of 97 eligible employees, of whom 32 are female and 65 are male, the variance, as calculated in Exhibit 4.21.2(d), is 1.64.

EXHIBIT 4.21.2(d)
Variance of Hypergeometrically Distributed Variable

Variable: number of females promoted out of eight promotions

The eligible group size, N, is 97 eligible employees, of whom 32 are female (N_1) and 65 are male (N_2). Sample size, n, is 8.

$$SD^2 = \left(\frac{N-n}{N-1}\right) n \frac{N_1}{N} \frac{N_2}{N} =$$

$$\left(\frac{97-8}{97-1}\right) \times 8 \times \frac{32}{97} \times \frac{65}{97} = 1.64$$

§4.21.3 Standard Deviation — Calculations

The standard deviation is a more convenient measure of the typical variation of a random variable around its expected or mean value. The standard deviation of a population, sample, or random variable is the square root of its variance.[10] The standard deviation formulas for a finite population (Equation 4.21.3(a)), a sample from a population (Equation 4.21.3(b)), a binomially distributed random

[10] See also id. at 214.

variable (Equation 4.21.3(c)), and a hypergeometrically distributed random variable (Equation 4.21.3(d)) reflect this fact.

$$SD = \sqrt{SD^2} = \sqrt{\frac{\Sigma(X_i - M_X)^2}{N}}$$

4.21.3(a)

$$(\text{sample}) \ sd = \sqrt{sd^2} = \sqrt{\frac{\Sigma(x_i - m_x)^2}{n - 1}}$$

4.21.3(b)

$$(\text{binomial}) \ SD = \sqrt{SD^2} = \sqrt{nPQ}$$

4.21.3(c)

$$(\text{hypergeometric}) \ SD = \sqrt{SD^2} = \sqrt{\left(\frac{N - n}{N - 1}\right) n \frac{N_1}{N} \frac{N_2}{N}}$$

4.21.3(d)

Using the example of the variances from Section 4.21.2, the intuitive meaning of the standard deviation for each distribution can be explained.

For either a sample or a population, the standard deviation indicates a typical departure from the mean within the collection of measurements. Thus, for Exhibit 4.21.2(a) the population standard deviation is equal to the square root of 296,858, or $545, which indicates that the typical variation around the mean monthly income of $604 is plus or minus $545; some variations are larger while others are smaller. The standard deviation calculated from the sample data in Exhibit 4.21.2(b) is equal to the square root of 320,500, or $566, a typical variation around the sample mean of $610. The sample standard deviation, $610, is an estimate of the population standard deviation, $566.

The standard deviation for the binomial random variable in Exhibit 4.21.2(c) is the typical variation around the expected number of fibers with a diameter greater than 15 microns. The standard deviation is the square root of 4.9, which is 2.2. If we were to take samples of 20 fibers we would expect many of them to have 11.2 (the mean) plus or minus 2.2 fibers, that is, between 9 and 13.4 fibers, with diameters greater than 15 microns. Like the variance, the closer to the 50-50 point the split of items is within the underlying population, the greater is the expected spread around the mean. As P gets smaller or larger than .50, the standard deviation gets smaller.

In some reported cases[11] the standard deviation for a binomial

---

[11] See, e.g., Board of Education City of New York v. Califano, 584 F.2d 576, 584 n. 29 (2d Cir. 1978).

random variable as a percentage of the group size is calculated by simply dividing the standard deviation by n, the sample size, as illustrated in Equation 4.21.3(e).

$$\text{(binomial) } sd \text{ as percentage of group size} = \frac{sd}{n} = \frac{\sqrt{PQn}}{n} = \sqrt{\frac{PQ}{n}}$$

4.21.3(e)

This typical deviation in percentage terms is then divided into the difference between observed and expected percentages (instead of observed and expected numbers) to obtain the Z score used in a Z test to estimate a p-value (see Sections 4.24 and 4.27, especially Exhibits 4.24(f) and 4.27(c), where such calculations are illustrated).

The standard deviation for the hypergeometric data in Exhibit 4.21.2(d) is a typical variation around the expected number of women to be among eight people promoted. The expected number is 2.64. The square root of the variance is 1.28, indicating that often by chance there will be as few as 1.36 and as many as 3.92 women in this group. As with the variance for a hypergeometric probability, the finite population correction factor $((N - n)/(N - 1))$ comes very close to one and therefore has little effect as the population size, N, expands relative to the sample size; the whole fraction gets closer to one and its effect on the formula is negligible. Under such circumstances, the binomial formula produces almost equivalent results. The precise conditions under which the binomial formula may be usefully substituted are outlined in Section 4.18.

§4.21.4   Coefficient of Variation — Calculations

The coefficient of variation (CV) describes how much variation there is in a population or a sample as a percentage of the mean or expected value. Thus, for any distribution the coefficient of variation is calculated by Equation 4.21.4(a).[12]

$$CV = \frac{SD}{M} \times 100\% \text{ or } \frac{sd}{m} \times 100\%$$

4.21.4(a)

[12] See, e.g., C. Clark & L. Schkade, Statistical Methods for Business Decisions 67 (1969).

In *Taylor v. Weaver Oil and Gas Corp.*[13] the coefficient of variation for a particular year is the standard deviation of the salaries divided by the mean of salaries for that year times 100%. In *Forte-Fairbairn*[14] the coefficient of variation for the diameters of a particular fiber type was the standard deviation of those diameters divided by the mean diameter times 100% (see Section 4.8).

§4.22   Chebychef's Inequality — Calculations

Chebychef's inequality is used to estimate an upper limit on the probability that a disparity as large or larger than the observed disparity could occur by chance. This is useful because it provides a measure of how uncommon a particular observation is if chance is the only factor influencing its outcome. A formal statement of Chebychef's inequality appears in Exhibit 4.22(a).[1]

EXHIBIT 4.22(a)
Chebychef's Inequality

Chebychef's inequality: Given a set of observations of a variable, at least $(1 - 1/k^2)$ of the measurements will lie within k standard deviations of their mean values for any value k greater than or equal to one.

If the mean of a set of measurements is $604 and the standard deviation is $125, then at least $1 - 1/1.6^2$ or 61% of the observations will be within 1.6 standard deviations of $604; that is, at least 61% will be within plus or minus $125 × 1.6 of $604. In fact, as the list of measurements in Exhibit 4.6(a) illustrates, there may be more than 61% of the observations within that range. For year one, the mean monthly income is $604, the standard deviation is $125, and 92% of the months fall in the range of $404 ($604 − (1.6 × $125)) to $804 ($604 + (1.6 × $125)). For year one, with a mean of $604 and standard deviation of $545, 83% (10/12) of the months fall in the range of $268 ($604 − 1.6 × $545) to $1476 ($604 + 1.6 × $545).

The same logic is used to apply this to a binomial or hypergeometric distribution. Using the example in Exhibit 4.21.1(c), where

---

[13] 18 Fair. Empl. Prac. Cas. (BNA) 23 (S.D. Tex. 1978), discussed in Section 4.8.
[14] 62 F.T.C. 1146 (1963), discussed in Section 4.8.
§4.22   [1] See, e.g., R. Pfaffenberger & J. Patterson, Statistical Methods 50 (1977).

the expected number of promoted females was 2.64 and one standard deviation was 1.33 women, we would expect that at least 88% $(1 - 1/3^2)$ of the time when eight people are to be promoted, between 0 (2.64 − (3 × 1.33)) and 6.63 (2.64 + (3 × 1.33)) of them will be women.

§4.23 Binomial Probabilities — Calculations

The binomial formula for the calculation of probabilities is shown in Equation 4.23(a).[1]

$$\text{binomial probability of } x_0 = \frac{n!}{x_0! \, (n - x_0)!} P^{x_0} Q^{(n - x_0)}$$

4.23(a)

To use the binomial formula to give p-values, it is necessary in principle to calculate and sum the probabilities of all possible values of the random variable as different or more different from the mean than the observed value. As indicated in Equation 4.23(b), for an observed frequency, x_0, of a particular characteristic appearing that is greater than the expected frequency, we add the probability of that frequency occurring by chance using Equation 4.23(a)[2] to the probabilities of all other frequencies that are greater, up to the sample size, n.

$$\text{binomial } p\text{-value (one-tail)} =$$

$$\sum \frac{n!}{x! \, (n - x)!} P^x Q^{(n - x)} \text{ for all } x \text{ from } x_0 \text{ to } n$$

4.23(b)

The sum of these probabilities is the same as the probability of a frequency occurring by chance that is as far or further above the mean frequency as the frequency actually observed.

The binomial test can also be used to calculate the probability of occurrences below the expected value. Equation 4.23(c)[3] gives the p-value describing the probability of a randomly occurring frequency as far or further below the mean as the observed frequency.

$$\text{binomial } p\text{-value (one-tail)} =$$

$$\sum \frac{n!}{x! \, (n - x)!} P^x Q^{(n - x)} \text{ for all } x \text{ from } 0 \text{ to } x_0$$

4.23(c)

---

§4.23 [1] See, e.g., R. Pfaffenberger & J. Patterson, Statistical Methods 161 (1977).
[2] Id.
[3] Id.

In the binomial formulas, we have used the *factorial notation*, "!". When a number is followed by an exclamation point, that number is to be multiplied by every integer smaller than itself down to one. Thus 5! equals 5 times 4 times 3 times 2 times 1. Equations 4.23(d),[4] (e), and (f) indicate the general interpretation for $n!$, $x!$, and $(n - x)!$. Note that 0! equals 1, by definition.

$$n! = n \times (n - 1) \times (n - 2) \ldots (\text{down to}) \ldots (n - (n - 1))$$

4.23(d)

$$x! = x \times (x - 1) \times (x - 2) \ldots (\text{down to}) \ldots (x - (x - 1))$$

4.23(e)

$$(n - x)! = (n - x) \times (n - x - 1) \times (n - x - 2) \ldots (\text{down to}) \ldots$$
$$((n - x) - (n - x - 1))$$

4.23(f)

The probability that a binomial random variable will take a particular value is calculated in Exhibit 4.23(a), using Equation 4.23(a), which demonstrates the use of the factorial. Exhibit 4.23(a) shows that the probability of selecting exactly four items out of six that possess a particular characteristic is .296 when the underlying proportion of items in the population possessing that characteristic is .75. Exhibit 4.23(b) shows the calculation of the p-value for an observed frequency of 18 in a sample of 20 where the underlying population percentage is

EXHIBIT 4.23(a)
Binomial Probability of a Single Event

n = 6 (sample size)
x = 4 (observed frequency)
P = .75 (underlying population percentage)
Q = .25 $(1 - P = 1 - .75)$

$$\text{probability of event } x_0 = \frac{n!}{x_0! \, (n - x_0)!} \, P^{x_0} Q^{(n - x_0)}$$

$$\text{probability of event } x = 4 = \frac{6!}{4! \, (6 - 4)!} \times .75^4 \times .25^2$$

$$= \frac{6 \times 5 \times 4 \times 3 \times 2 \times 1}{(4 \times 3 \times 2 \times 1)(2 \times 1)} \times .75^4 \times .25^2$$

$$= \frac{720}{24 \times 2} \times .316 \times .0625$$

$$= .296$$

[4] See, e.g., C. Clark & L. Schkade, Statistical Methods for Business Decisions 136 (1969).

.20. The calculation indicates that the probability of 18 *or more* items with this characteristic being selected is very small indeed.

EXHIBIT 4.23(b)
Calculation of p-Value of Binomial Probabilities: $x_0 > M_X$

n = 20 (sample size)
x = 18 or more (observed frequency)
P = .20 (underlying population percentage)
Q = .80 $(1 - P = 1 - .20)$

p-value $= \sum \dfrac{n!}{x! \, (n-x)!} p^x q^{(n-x)}$ for all x from x_0 to n

$\quad = \sum \dfrac{20!}{x! \, (20-x)!} \times .20^x \times .80^{(20-x)}$ for all x from 18 to 20

$\quad = \dfrac{20!}{18! \, (20-18)!} \times .2^{18} \times .8^{20-18}$

$\quad + \dfrac{20!}{19! \, (20-19)!} \times .2^{19} \times .8^{20-19}$

$\quad + \dfrac{20!}{20! \, (20-20)!} \times .2^{20} \times .8^{20-20}$

$\quad = 3.19 \times 10^{-11}$

$\quad = .0000000000319$

Exhibit 4.23(c) illustrates the calculation of the probability of frequencies of two or less in a group of 20 and an underlying population percentage of .20.

EXHIBIT 4.23(c)
Calculation of p-Value for Binomial Probability: $x_0 < M_X$

n = 20 (sample size)
x = 2 or less (observed frequency)
P = .20 (underlying population percentage)
Q = .80 $(1 - P = 1 - .20)$

p-value $= \sum \dfrac{n!}{x! \, (n-x)!} p^x q^{(n-x)}$ for all x from 2 to 0

$\quad = \dfrac{20!}{2! \, (20-2)!} \times .2^2 \times .8^{(20-2)}$

$\quad + \dfrac{20!}{1! \, (20-1)!} \times .2^1 \times .8^{(20-1)}$

$\quad + \dfrac{20!}{0! \, (20-0)!} \times .2^0 \times .8^{(20-0)}$

$\quad = .13691 + .05765 + .01153$

$\quad = .2061$

Exhibit 4.23(d) illustrates the calculation in the Insurance Claim Adjustment example from Section 4.15, where the probability of finding as many as or more than seven damaged kegs out of 15 when the underlying damage rate is 20% is the probability of seven plus the probability of eight, nine, ten, . . . , up to 15 damaged kegs. The expected number of damaged kegs is three, calculated using the binomial mean formula in Equation 4.21.1(c). The result, .0181, is the probability that if the population damage rate were 20%, seven or more kegs among 15 selected at random would be damaged. If the

EXHIBIT 4.23(d)
p-Value Calculation
Binomial Insurance Example

n = 15 (sample size)
x = 7 or more (observed frequency)
P = .20 (underlying population percentage)
Q = .80 ($1 - P = 1 - .20$)

$$p\text{-value} = \Sigma \frac{n!}{x!\,(n-x)!} P^x Q^{(n-x)} \text{ for all } x \text{ from 7 to 15}$$

$$= \frac{15!}{7!\,(15-7)!} \times .20^7 \times .80^{(15-7)}$$

$$+ \frac{15!}{8!\,(15-8)!} \times .20^8 \times .80^{(15-8)}$$

$$+ \frac{15!}{9!\,(15-9)!} \times .20^9 \times .80^{(15-9)}$$

$$+ \frac{15!}{10!\,(15-10)!} \times .20^{10} \times .80^{(15-10)}$$

$$+ \frac{15!}{11!\,(15-11)!} \times .20^{11} \times .80^{(15-11)}$$

$$+ \frac{15!}{12!\,(15-12)!} \times .20^{12} \times .80^{(15-12)}$$

$$+ \frac{15!}{13!\,(15-13)!} \times .20^{13} \times .80^{(15-13)}$$

$$+ \frac{15!}{14!\,(15-14)!} \times .20^{14} \times .80^{(15-14)}$$

$$+ \frac{15!}{15!\,(15-15)!} \times .20^{15} \times .80^{(15-15)}$$

$$= .0138 + .0035 + .0007 + .0001 + .0000 + .0000$$

$$+ .0000 + .0000 + .0000$$

$$= .0181$$

population damage rate were less than 20%, this observed number of damaged kegs would be even more unlikely.

It is obvious from Exhibit 4.23(d) that binomial probability calculations can become very tedious for sample sizes even as small as 15. The Cumulative Binomial Table provides a simple way to calculate p-values for events whose underlying population probabilities, P, are multiples of .05. The Cumulative Binomial Table included in this book presents the probabilities associated with the random occurrence of any number of events, x, in samples of 25 or less where the underlying population percentage, P, is equal to .05, .10, .15, .20, .25, .30, .35, .40, .45, or .50.

For the insurance claim example illustrated in Exhibit 4.23(d), one calculates the p-value associated with a sample size, n, of 15, observations of 7 or more, and an underlying population percentage of .20, by looking down the rows of n and x values on the left hand side of the table to find n equals 15 and x equals seven. Moving over to the column under $P = .20$ gives the probability of seven or more observations with a particular characteristic in a sample of 15 and an underlying percentage of .20 equal to .0181, the same result as illustrated in Exhibit 4.23(d). If the underlying population percentage is .10, the p-value can immediately be ascertained from the table. The p-value is .0003 when n equals 15, x equals 7 or more, and P equal .10.

There are three limitations to using the Cumulative Binomial Table to calculate p-values: the first is that the table only gives p-values for selected underlying population percentages. It is possible, however, to estimate p-values for unreported population percentages by the process of interpolation, which is fairly straightforward and is discussed in detail in Section 4.28. In Exhibit 4.28(a) this process is applied to a binomial probabilities problem.

The second limitation is that the entries are all probabilities of an observed frequency of occurrence *or more*, e.g., the probability of seven *or more* damaged kegs in the insurance claim example in Exhibit 4.23(d). A simple subtraction, however, enables us to use the table to give the probability of a particular frequency of occurrence or less.

Consider the problem in Exhibit 4.23(c). We are interested in finding the probability of observing two or fewer items in a group of 20 when the underlying population percentage is .20. In this problem n equals 20, x equals two or fewer and $P = .20$. The Table shows a value of .9308 for these values, but that is the probability of 2 or more. For three or more the Table shows a value of .7939. Logically, if the probability of having three or more is 79.39%, the probability of having less than three, that is, two or less, is 100% minus 79.39%, or 20.61%, the same answer as in Exhibit 4.23(e). The general rule for using the Cumulative Binomial Table to find the p-value of an observation, x_0, below the mean or expected value is to subtract the p-value for x_0 plus one from 1.00. For the example in Exhibit 4.23(c) the observation, x_0, equals two. The probability of two or less observations is 1.00 minus .7939, the p-value associated with three ($x_0 + 1 = 2 + 1 = 3$).

The third problem with the Cumulative Binomial Table is that it only presents underlying population percentages of a characteristic of interest up to 50%, .50. What does one do when P exceeds .50? This problem is overcome by calculating the p-value associated with the observed frequency of occurrence of the other dichotomous possibility, which must necessarily have a population percentage, Q, less that .50 if P is greater than .50. For instance, the probability of observing six or more items out of 20 that possess a given characteristic is the same as the probability of observing 14 or fewer items that do not possess that characteristic.

The binomial formulas and Cumulative Binomial Table can also be used to calculate p-values for two-tailed tests. Two-tailed tests reveal the probability of random occurrence of a disparity of a given size above or below the expected value. Equation 4.23(g) shows the formula for calculating the p-value for a two-tailed test.

$$\text{binomial } p\text{-value (two-tail)} = \sum \frac{n!}{x!\,(n-x)!} P^x Q^{(n-x)}$$

$$\text{for all } x \text{ from 0 to } (M_X - |x_0 - M_X|) \text{ and from } (M_X + |x_0 - M_X|) \text{ to } n$$

4.23(g)

The expected value, M_X, is subtracted from the observed value, x_0, to find the disparity. Equation 4.23(g) indicates that the independent probabilities of those events as far below *and* above the expected value as the disparity indicates are added together. Thus, if women are 50% of a large group of persons eligible for each of ten jobs but they only receive two of those jobs, the disparity between observed, two, and expected, five, is three. To obtain the two-tailed p-value we add together the probabilities for the zero, one, and two hirings for women (those from zero to $M_X - |x_0 - M_X|$, which is $5 - |2 - 5| =$ two) as well as eight, nine, and ten promotions (from $M_X + |x_0 - M_X|$ which is $5 + |2 - 5| = 8$, to n, which is 10). Exhibit 4.23(e) illustrates this calculation.

EXHIBIT 4.23(e)
p-Value Calculation
Two-Tailed Binomial Promotions Example

n = 10 (sample size)
x = 0 to 2 and 8 to 10 (disparity equal to or greater than observed)
P = .50 (underlying percent of women)
Q = .50 (underlying percent of men)

$$p\text{-value} = \sum \frac{n!}{x! \, (n-x)!} P^x Q^{(n-x)} \text{ for all } x \text{ from 0 to 2 and 8 to 10}$$

$$= \frac{10!}{0! \, (10-0)!} \times .5^0 \times .5^{(10-0)}$$

$$+ \frac{10!}{1! \, (10-1)!} \times .5^1 \times .5^{(10-1)}$$

$$+ \frac{10!}{2! \, (10-2)!} \times .5^2 \times .5^{(10-2)}$$

$$+ \frac{10!}{8! \, (10-8)!} \times .5^8 \times .5^{(10-8)}$$

$$+ \frac{10!}{9! \, (10-9)!} \times .5^9 \times .5^{(10-9)}$$

$$+ \frac{10!}{10! \, (10-10)!} \times .5^{10} \times .5^{(10-10)}$$

$$= .0010 + .0098 + .0439 + .0439 + .0098 + .0010$$

$$= .1094$$

Using the cumulative Binomial Table, as indicated above, to determine the probabilities for n equals ten and x values of two or less added to those for x values of eight or more gives the same two-tailed p-value as shown in Exhibit 4.23(e).

§4.24 The Z Test — Calculations for Large Sample Binomial Distributions

As discussed in Section 4.16, for large samples the Z test gives an accurate approximation to p-values for binomially distributed variables. For medium-sized samples the correction for continuity is applied to the calculation of the number of standard deviations between expected and observed as illustrated in Exhibit 4.24(a). The Z test approach gives a p-value of .5552 for a two-tailed test, .2776 for a one-tailed test. By comparison, the one-tailed p-value using the binomial formula in Equation 4.23(c) is .2552, as illustrated in Exhibit 4.24(b).

EXHIBIT 4.24(a)
p-Values for Binomially Distributed Variables Using Z Test and Correction for Continuity: $x_0 < M_X$

n = 40 (sample size)
x = 6 (observed frequency)
P = .20 (underlying population percentage)
Q = .80 $(1 - P = 1 - .20)$
$sd = \sqrt{n \times P \times Q} = \sqrt{4.0 \times .2 \times .8} = 2.53$
$M_X = nP = 8$
disparity = $x_0 - M_X = 6 - 8 = -2$
disparity corrected = $x_0 - M_X + .5 = 6 - 8 + .5 = -1.5$
number of standard deviations = $(x_0 - M_X)/sd = -1.5/2.53$
   = $-.593$
area under the normal curve for $Z = .59$ = .2224

Two-Tailed Test
22.24% from mean to .59 sd above the mean
+ 22.24% from mean to .59 sd below the mean

100% − 44.48% = 55.52% beyond .59 sd from mean
p-value = .5552

One-Tailed Test
22.24% from mean to .59 sd below the mean
+ 50.00% above the mean

100% − 72.24% = 27.76% beyond .59 sd below the mean
p-value = .2776

EXHIBIT 4.24(b)
p-Value for Binomially Distributed Variable — Binomial Formula and Z Test Comparison: $x_0 < M_X$

n = 40 (sample size)
x_0 = 6 $(m = np = 40 \times .2 = 8)$ (observed frequency)
P = .20 (underlying population percentage)
Q = .80 $(1 - P = 1 - .20)$

p-value = $\sum \dfrac{n!}{x!\,(n-x)!} P^x Q^{(n-x)}$ for all x from 0 to x_0

$= \dfrac{40!}{6!\,(40-6)!} \times .2^6 \times .8^{34} + \dfrac{40!}{5!\,(40-5)!} \times .2^5 \times .8^{35}$

$+ \dfrac{40!}{4!\,(40-4)!} \times .2^4 \times .8^{36} + \dfrac{40!}{3!\,(40-3)!} \times .2^3 \times .8^{37}$

$+ \dfrac{40!}{2!\,(40-2)!} \times .2^2 \times .8^{38} + \dfrac{40!}{1!\,(40-1)!} \times .2^1 \times .8^{39}$

$+ \dfrac{40!}{0!\,(40-0)!} \times .2^0 \times .8^{40}$

$= .1246 + .0547 + .0475 + .0205 + .0065$
$+ .0013 + .0001$
$= .2552$

Exhibit 4.24(c) illustrates the calculation of a p-value for a binomial model with a medium sized sample for an observed frequency greater than the expected frequency. The difference between this example and the previous one is that when the observed value, x_0, is greater than the expected value, the correction of .5 is subtracted from the disparity (see Exhibit 4.24(c)). When the observed value is less than the expected number, the correction factor of .5 should be added to the disparity (see Exhibit 4.24(a)).

EXHIBIT 4.24(c)
p-Value for Binomially Distributed Variable Using Z Test and Correction for Continuity: $x_0 > M_X$

n = 75 (sample size)
x_0 = 25 (observed frequency)
P = .18 (underlying population percentage)
Q = .82 $(1 - P = 1 - .18)$
$sd = \sqrt{nPQ} = \sqrt{75 \times .18 \times .82} = 3.33$
$M_X = nP = 75 \times .18 = 13.5$
disparity $= x_0 - M_X = 11.5$
disparity corrected $= x_0 - M_X - .5 = 11.5 - .5 = 11$
number of standard deviations $= (x_0 - M_X - .5)/sd = 11/3.33$
     $= 3.306$
area under the normal curve for $Z = 3.31 = .4995$

Two-Tailed Test
p-value $= 1.00 - 2(.4995) = .001$

One-Tailed Test
p-value $= 1.00 - (.4995 + .5000) = .0005$

Given the values of n and P chosen for the examples in Exhibit 4.24(c), the problem may qualify for the large sample approach because n times P equals 13.5 and n times $(1 - P)$ equals 61.5, both greater than five, and n is rather large. The rules outlined in Exhibit 4.20(a) indicate that perhaps the continuity correction factor can be ignored without making much difference. Exhibit 4.24(d) illustrates that the p-values obtained from the Z test without correction for continuity are substantially identical to those obtained with the correction (see Exhibit 4.24(c)).

The illustration, *A.B.&G. Instrument and Engineering, Inc. v. United States*,[1] in Section 4.16, presents the problem of calculating the

§4.24   [1] 593 F.2d 394 (Ct. Cl. 1979).

EXHIBIT 4.24(d)
_p_-Value for Binomially Distributed Variable — _Z_ Test Without
Correction for Continuity

n = 75 (sample size)
x_0 = 25 (observed frequency)
P = .18 (underlying population)
Q = .82 $(1 - P = 1 - .18)$
sd = $\sqrt{nPQ}$ = 3.33
M_X = nP = 75 × .18 = 13.5
disparity = 11.5
number of sd = 11.5/3.33 = 3.45
area under the normal curve for $Z = 3.45$ = .4997

Two-Tailed Test
p-value = 1.00 − 2(.4997) = .0006

One-Tailed Test
p-value = 1.00 − (.4997 + .5000) = .0003

probability of finding 20 or more defective nose fuse adapters in a
sample of 315 if 5% are defective overall. In this problem, n equals
315, x_0 equals 20, and P equals .05, so Q equals .95. The calculation,
using a one-tailed Z test with no correction for continuity (because the
sample size is so large), is presented in Exhibit 4.24(e), and the associated p-value is .1357.

EXHIBIT 4.24(e)
_p_-Value Calculation Using _Z_ Test Without
Correction for Continuity
A.B.&G. Engineering Example

n = 315 (sample size)
x_0 = 20 (observed frequency)
P = .05 (underlying population)
Q = .95 $(1 - P = 1 - .05)$
M_X = 315 × .05 = 15.75
sd = $\sqrt{315 × .05 × .05}$ = 3.86
disparity = 20 − 15.75 = 4.25
number of standard deviations = 4.25/3.86 = 1.10
area under the normal curve for $Z = 1.10$ = .3643

One-Tailed Test
p-value for 20 or more = 1.00 − (.3643 + .5000) = .1357

Exhibit 4.24(f) illustrates the same calculation using the standard deviation as a percentage of sample size to calculate the Z score (see Section 4.21.3). For this illustration we are calculating the probability of getting a defective rate of 6.35% or more (20/315 = .0635) when the expected rate is 5%. Either this approach or the equivalent approach in Exhibit 4.24(e) gives exactly the same Z score and p-value.

EXHIBIT 4.24(f)
p-Value Calculation Using Proportional Binomial Approach and Z Test Without Correction
A.B.&G. Engineering Example

n = 315 (sample size)
p_0 = .0635 (observed proportion) = 20 defects/315 items in the sample
P = .05 (underlying population proportion)
Q = .95 ($1 - P = 1 - .05$)

$$\frac{sd}{n} = \sqrt{\frac{PQ}{n}} = \sqrt{\frac{.05 \times .95}{315}} = .0123$$

disparity = .0635 − .05 = .0135
number of sd = .0135/.0123 = 1.10

Z for 1.10 is the same as in Exhibit 4.24(e) = .3643, thus p-value is same, .1357

§4.25 Hypergeometric Probabilities — Calculations

When sampling without replacement from a binomially distributed population (see Section 4.17), the hypergeometric formula must be used to calculate p-values. Like the binomial formula, the hypergeometric formula, shown in Equation 4.25(a),[1] yields the probability that a particular observed frequency will occur just by chance. And

$$\text{hypergeometric probability of } x_0 = \frac{\dfrac{N_1!}{x_0! \, (N_1 - x_0)!} \times \dfrac{N_2!}{(n - x_0)! \, (N_2 - (n - x_0))!}}{\dfrac{N!}{n! \, (N - n)!}}$$

4.25(a)

§4.25 [1] See, e.g., R. Pfaffenberger & J. Patterson, Statistical Methods 248 (1977).

like the binomial formula, it is necessary to know the relative proportions of each of the two characteristics in the underlying population. Unlike the binomial formula, the relative sizes of the two groups are expressed not in percentages, by P and Q as in the binomial formula, but in whole numbers of members in each group with N_1 indicating the number of items in the population as a whole that possess the characteristic of interest and N_2 indicating the number of items in the population as a whole that do not have that characteristic of interest. The total population size, N, is the sum of N_1 and N_2.

Exhibit 4.25(a) illustrates the calculation of the probability that of eight people promoted at random out of a group of four women and 18 men, just one of the eight would be a woman. (See the example in Section 4.17).

EXHIBIT 4.25(a)
Hypergeometric Probability Calculation
Adams v. Gaudet **Example**

n = 9 (the sample size of those promoted out of N, the whole group)
N = 22 (4 women and 18 men made up the eligible group)
N_1 = 4 (women in the eligible group)
N_2 = 18 (men in the eligible group)
x_0 = 1 (woman selected)

$$\text{Probability of } x_0 = \frac{\dfrac{N_1!}{x_0!\,(N_1 - x_0)!} \times \dfrac{N_2!}{(n - x_0)!\,(N_2 - (n - x_0))!}}{\dfrac{N!}{n!\,(N - n)!}}$$

$$= \frac{\dfrac{4!}{1!\,(4 - 1)!} \times \dfrac{18!}{(9 - 1)!\,(18 - (9 - 1))!}}{\dfrac{22!}{9!\,(22 - 9)!}}$$

$$= \frac{\dfrac{4!}{1!\,3!} \times \dfrac{18!}{8!\,10!}}{\dfrac{22!}{9!\,13!}}$$

$$= .352 \text{ or } 35.2\%$$

In significance testing we are generally concerned with the probability of getting a disparity of a given size or larger, which can be done in a one-tailed or two-tailed test with the hypergeometric formula. For a one-tailed test, when we observe a disparity, we use the hypergeometric test to calculate a one-tailed probability that the observed frequency, of women in this example, could be as far below what was expected, in which case Equation 4.25(b) is used, or, alternatively, could be as far above what was expected, in which case Equation 4.25(c) is used.

hypergeometric p-value $(x_0 < M_X)$ (one-tailed test) =

$$\sum \frac{\dfrac{N_1!}{x!\,(N_1 - x)!} \times \dfrac{N_2!}{(n - x)!\,(N_2 - (n - x))!}}{\dfrac{N!}{n!\,(N - n)!}}$$

for all x from 0 to x_0

4.25(b)

hypergeometric p-value $(x_0 > M_X)$ (one-tailed test) =

$$\sum \frac{\dfrac{N_1!}{x!\,(N_1 - x)!} \times \dfrac{N_2!}{(n - x)!\,(N_2 - (n - x))!}}{\dfrac{N!}{n!\,(N - n)!}}$$

for all x from x_0 to N_1 or n (whichever is smaller)

4.25(c)

Using the formula for the hypergeometric mean from Equation 4.21.1(d), the p-value for the *Adams v. Gaudet*[2] example is calculated using Equation 4.25(b) because the observed frequency, x_0, is one woman while the expected number is 1.64 ($M_X = n(N_1/N) = 9(4/22)$). Exhibit 4.25(b) illustrates this p-value calculation. There is a 45% chance that one or fewer women would be promoted given these facts.

[2]515 F. Supp. 1086, 1140 (W.D. La. 1981).

EXHIBIT 4.25(b)
p-Value Calculation Using Hypergeometric Formula: $x_0 < M_X$

n = 9 (the sample size of those promoted out of N, the whole group)
N = 22 (4 women and 18 men made up the eligible group)
N_1 = 4 (women in the eligible group)
N_2 = 18 (men in the eligible group)
x_0 = 1 (1 woman selected)

$$p\text{-value} = \sum \frac{\dfrac{N_1!}{x!\,(N_1 - x)!} \times \dfrac{N_2!}{(n - x)!\,(N_2 - (n - x))!}}{\dfrac{N!}{n!\,(N - n)!}} \quad \begin{array}{l} \text{for all} \\ x \text{ from} \\ 0 \text{ to } 1 \end{array}$$

$$= \frac{\dfrac{4!}{1!\,(4 - 1)!} \times \dfrac{18!}{(9 - 1)!\,(18 - (9 - 1))!}}{\dfrac{22!}{9!\,(22 - 9)!}}$$

$$+ \frac{\dfrac{4!}{0!\,(4 - 0)!} \times \dfrac{18!}{(9 - 0)!\,(18 - (9 - 0))!}}{\dfrac{22!}{9!\,(22 - 9)!}}$$

$$= .352 + .098 = .450$$

Exhibit 4.25(c) illustrates the use of the hypergeometric formula in an example where the observed number of promoted women, x_0 equals three, is greater than the expected number, 1.64, using the same figures from the *Adams* problem in Exhibit 4.25(b).

EXHIBIT 4.25(c)
p-Value Calculation Using Hypergeometric Formula: $x_0 > M_X$

n = 9 (the sample size of those promoted out of N, the whole group)

N = 22 (4 women and 18 men made up the eligible group)

N_1 = 4 (women in the eligible group)

N_2 = 18 (men in the eligible group)

x_0 = 3 ($> M_X = 9 \times \dfrac{4}{22} = 1.64$)

$$p\text{-value} = \sum \frac{\dfrac{N_1!}{x! \, (N_1 - x)!} \times \dfrac{N_2!}{(n - x)! \, (N_2 - (n - x))!}}{\dfrac{N!}{n! \, (N - n)!}}$$

for all x from 3 to 4 (the top value equals N_1, 4, rather than n, 9, because there are only 4 women available to be promoted)

$$= \frac{\dfrac{4!}{3! \, 1!} \times \dfrac{18!}{6! \, 12!}}{\dfrac{22!}{9! \, 13!}} + \frac{\dfrac{4!}{4! \, 0!} \times \dfrac{18!}{5! \, 13!}}{\dfrac{22!}{9! \, 13!}}$$

$$= .149 + .017 = .166$$

A two-tailed test may also be performed to determine the probability of observing an outcome as far from the expected value (either greater than or less than) as occurred. For this purpose Equations 4.25(b) and (c) are combined as shown in Equation 4.25(d).

$$\text{hypergeometric } p\text{-value (two-tailed test)} =$$

$$\sum \frac{\dfrac{N_1!}{x! \, (N_1 - x)!} \times \dfrac{N_2!}{(n - x)! \, (N_2 - (n - x))!}}{\dfrac{N!}{n! \, (N - n)!}}$$

for all x from 0 to $(M_X - |x_0 - M_X|)$

and from $(M_X + |x_0 - M_X|)$ to N_1 or n (whichever is smaller)

4.25(d)

As for the two-tailed binomial test, the disparity is calculated by subtracting the expected value from the observed value, $x_0 - M_X$. Then the independent probabilities of those events as far below and above the expected value as the disparity indicates are added together. Thus a two-tailed test of the example in Exhibit 4.25(c) would find a disparity between the observed, 3, and expected, 1.64, of 1.36. The only outcome as far as 1.36 below the expected outcome would be zero women. The possible outcomes as far as 1.36 above the expected outcome are three or four women. The hypergeometric probabilities of arriving at zero, three, or four women are added together to get a two-tailed p-value of .264, as illustrated in Exhibit 4.25(d).

EXHIBIT 4.25(d)
p-Value Calculation Using Two-Tailed Hypergeometric Formula

n = 9 (the sample size of those promoted out of N, the whole group)

N = 22 (4 women and 18 men make up the eligible group)

N_1 = 4 (women in the eligible group)

N_2 = 18 (men in the eligible group)

x_0 = 3 (observed women promoted)

$$M_X = 9 \times \frac{4}{22} = 1.64$$

disparity $= 3 - 1.64 = 1.36$

$$p\text{-value} = \sum \frac{\dfrac{N_1!}{x! \, (N_1 - x)!} \times \dfrac{N_2!}{(n - x)! \, (N_2 - (n - x))!}}{\dfrac{N!}{n! \, (N - n)!}}$$

for all x from 0 to $1.64 - 1.36$, i.e., 0, and from $1.64 + 1.36$, i.e., 3 to 4.

$$= \frac{\dfrac{4!}{0! \, 4!} \times \dfrac{18!}{9! \, 9!}}{\dfrac{22!}{9! \, 13!}} + \frac{\dfrac{4!}{3! \, 1!} \times \dfrac{18!}{6! \, 12!}}{\dfrac{22!}{9! \, 13!}}$$

$$+ \frac{\dfrac{4!}{4! \, 0!} \times \dfrac{18!}{5! \, 13!}}{\dfrac{22!}{9! \, 13!}}$$

$$= .098 + .149 + .017 = .264$$

§4.26   Binomial Approximations — Calculations for Small Sample Hypergeometric Distributions

When the sample size is small relative to the population size (n/N < .01 to .20), the binomial formula gives results approximately equal to those given by the hypergeometric formula (see Section 4.18). Exhibit 4.26(a) illustrates this with data from *Adams v. Gaudet*[1] showing that one of ten eligible blacks and five of 31 eligible whites were promoted to administrative staff positions (see Section 4.18, where this case is discussed). The hypergeometric approach for this sample size of six with a sample size to population size ratio of 6/41, or 14.6%, yields a one-tailed *p*-value of .542, while the binomial approach yields a *p*-value of .549.

EXHIBIT 4.26(a)
Binomial and Hypergeometric Calculations Compared: *n/N* Small

Binomial	*Hypergeometric*
n = 6 (sample size)	n = 6 (sample size)
x_0 = 1 (observed number)	N = 41 (10 blacks and 31
P = 10/41 = .244 (underlying	whites comprise the
population	eligible group)
proportion)	N_1 = 10 (black applicants)
Q = 1 − .244 = .756	N_2 = 31 (white applicants)
M_X = 1.46 (expected value)	x_0 = 1 (observed number)

Binomial *p*-value $= \sum \dfrac{n!}{x!\,(n-x)!} P^x Q^{(n-x)}$ for all x from 0 to x_0

$$= \frac{6!}{0!\,(6-0)!} \times .244^0 \times .756^{6-0}$$

$$+ \frac{6!}{1!\,(6-1)!} \times .244^1 \times .756^{6-1}$$

$$= .187 + .362 = .549$$

Hypergeometric *p*-value $= \sum \dfrac{\dfrac{N_1!}{x!\,(N_1-x)!} \times \dfrac{N_2!}{(n-x)!\,(N_2-(n-x))!}}{\dfrac{N!}{n!\,(N-n)!}}$

for all x from 0 to x_0

$$= \frac{\dfrac{10!}{0!\,(10-1)!} \times \dfrac{31!}{(6-0)!\,(31-(6-0))!}}{\dfrac{41!}{6!\,(41-6)!}}$$

$$+ \frac{\dfrac{10!}{1!\,(10-1)!} \times \dfrac{31!}{(6-1)!\,(31-(6-1))!}}{\dfrac{41!}{6!\,(41-6)!}}$$

$$= .164 + .378 = .542$$

§4.26 [1] 515 F. Supp. 1086, 1133 (W.D. La. 1981).

Exhibit 4.26(b) illustrates the rule that the p-value obtained from either the binomial or hypergeometric formula is the same if the sample size equals one, using data from *Adams v. Gaudet*,[2] which show one white promotion (n) and zero black promotions out of three blacks and eight whites eligible. Using either method the one-tailed p-value is .727, indicating a 72.7% probability that this outcome could occur by chance.

EXHIBIT 4.26(b)
Binomial and Hypergeometric Calculations Compared: $n = 1$

Binomial	*Hypergeometric*
n = 1 (sample size)	n = 1 (the sample size of those promoted out of N, the whole group)
x_0 = 0 (observed frequency)	
P = .273 (underlying population percentage)	
Q = .727 ($1 - P = 1 - .273$)	N = 11 (3 blacks and 8 whites made up the eligible group)
M_X = .273	
	N_1 = 3 (the blacks in the eligible group)
	N_2 = 8 (the whites in the eligible group)
	x_0 = 0 (0 blacks selected)

Binomial p-value $= \sum \dfrac{n!}{x!\,(n-x)!} P^x Q^{(n-x)}$ for all x from 0 to 0

$$= \dfrac{1!}{0!\,1!} \times .273^0 \times .727^1 = .727$$

Hypergeometric p-value $= \sum \dfrac{\dfrac{N_1!}{x!\,(N_1-x)!} \times \dfrac{N_2!}{(n-x)!\,(N_2-(n-x))!}}{\dfrac{N!}{n!\,(N-n)!}}$

for all x from 0 to 0

$$= \dfrac{\dfrac{3!}{0!\,3!} \times \dfrac{8!}{1!\,7!}}{\dfrac{11!}{1!\,10!}} = \dfrac{1 \times 8}{11} = .727$$

When the small sample is large relative to the population size, the approximation of the binomial to the hypergeometric distribution is not as close, as Exhibit 4.26(c) illustrates.

[2] Id. at 1141.

EXHIBIT 4.26(c)
Binomial and Hypergeometric Calculations Compared: n/N large

Binomial	*Hypergeometric*
n = 10 (sample size)	n = 10 (the sample size of those promoted out of N, the whole group)
P = .31 (underlying population percentage)	
Q = .69 ($1 - P = 1 - .31$)	N = 13 (4 blacks and 9 whites made up the eligible group)
x_0 = 2 (observed frequency)	
	N_1 = 4 (the blacks in the population)
	N_2 = 9 (the whites in the population)
	x_0 = 2 (2 blacks selected)

Binomial p-value $= \sum \dfrac{n!}{x! \, (n - x)!} P^x Q^{(n-x)}$ for all x from 1 to 2

(note that we do not go from 0 to 2 because it is not possible for 10 promotions to yield 0 blacks since there are only 9 whites)

$$= \frac{10!}{2! \, 8!} \times .31^2 \times .69^8 + \frac{10!}{1! \, 9!} \times .31^1 \times .69^9$$

$$= .2222 + .1099 = .3321$$

Hypergeometric p-value $= \displaystyle\sum \dfrac{\dfrac{N_1!}{x! \, (N_1 - x)!} \times \dfrac{N_2!}{(n - x)! \, (N_2 - (n - x))!}}{\dfrac{N!}{n! \, (N - n)!}}$

for all x from 1 to 2

$$= \frac{\dfrac{4!}{2! \, 2!} \times \dfrac{9!}{8! \, 1!}}{\dfrac{13!}{10! \, 3!}} + \frac{\dfrac{4!}{1! \, 3!} \times \dfrac{9!}{9! \, 0!}}{\dfrac{13!}{10! \, 3!}}$$

$$= \frac{54 + 4}{286} = .2028$$

The Cumulative Binomial Table can also be used when the binomial formula is substituted for the hypergeometric formula. In the example drawn from *EEOC v. United Virginia Bank/Seaboard National*[3] in Section 4.18, 11 of 14 employees in the service jobs category were black while three were white. The underlying population percentage

---

[3] 615 F.2d 147 (4th Cir. 1980).

of blacks was 50%, leading us to expect only seven blacks in this category. What is the probability that 11 or more of the 14 employees would be black? The table reveals that for n equals 14, x equals 11 or more, and P equals .50, the p-value is .0287. This is also the probability of finding three or fewer whites.

§4.27   The Z Test — Calculations for Large Sample Hypergeometric Distributions

When the sample size for a hypergeometrically distributed random variable is large, the Z test gives an acceptable approximation to the hypergeometric formula calculation of probabilities (see Section 4.19). The calculations involved in computing p-values for a large sample using the hypergeometric formula would be very lengthy; the Z test provides a straightforward alternative. The number of standard deviations between observed frequency and expected frequency needed to calculate the p-value is obtained by dividing the disparity by the standard deviation, which is calculated using the hypergeometric standard deviation formula in Equation 4.21.2(d).

> **Castaneda v. Partida:**[1] In order to use the Z test, the Court calculated the standard deviation for the dichotomous variable, race, which had two categories, Spanish-surnamed and not Spanish-surnamed, using the binomial formula.[2] The sample size, n, was 870 jurors selected from the population of Hidalgo County, N, approximately 80,000 people.[3] The population percentages of Spanish-surnamed people was 79.1%, P, therefore non-Spanish-surnamed people made up 20.9% of the population, Q. The binomial standard deviation formula, Equation 4.21.3(c), gives a standard deviation of 11.99. The hypergeometric formula would have given a value of 11.93. This difference is too small to have made any difference to the Court's ultimate finding of discrimination.

While it is always correct to use the hypergeometric formula for the standard deviation of a large sample with hypergeometrically distributed probabilities, the binomial formula is commonly used as an approximation when the sample size, although large, is small relative

§4.27 [1] 430 U.S. 482 (1976).
[2] Id. at 496 n. 17.
[3] Id. at 488 n. 8.

to the population as a whole. Thus Exhibit 4.20(a) indicates that the use of the finite population correction factor is optional when n/N is small.

It is easy to tell how much difference use of the correction factor will make on the calculation of a standard deviation. Using the hypergeometric formula will give a standard deviation that is less than the binomial formula by the amount of the square root of $(N-n)/(N-1)$. Thus a sample that is 50% of the population size will have a hypergeometric standard deviation that is equal to approximately 71% (square root of 50%) of the binomial standard deviation. If the ratio of sample size to population size is 20%, 10%, or 1%, the hypergeometric formula will give a standard deviation that is approximately 89%, 95%, or 99% of that calculated using the binomial formula.

EXHIBIT 4.27(a)
Z Test Approximation to Hypergeometric Formula
***Castaneda* Example**

$N = 80,000$

$n = 870$

$P = .791 = N_1/N = \dfrac{63,280}{80,000}$

$Q = .209 = N_2/N = \dfrac{16,720}{80,000}$

observed = 339
expected = 688
disparity = 349

standard deviation $= \sqrt{\left(\dfrac{N-n}{N-1}\right)n\dfrac{N_1}{N}\dfrac{N_2}{N}}$

$= \sqrt{\dfrac{80,000-870}{80,000-1} \times 870 \times \dfrac{63,280}{80,000} \times \dfrac{16,720}{80,000}}$

$= 11.93$

number of standard deviations = 349/11.93 = 29
area under the normal curve for $Z = 29$ standard deviations = .0000

Two-Tailed Test
0% of items beyond 29 standard deviations from the mean
p-value = .0000

One-Tailed Test
0% of items beyond 29 standard deviations below the mean
p-value = .0000

Exhibit 4.27(a) uses the hypergeometric formula for the standard deviation to calculate the p-value associated with a disparity of 349 jurors in the *Castaneda*[4] case. Note that the Z table only reports percentages up to 3.99 standard deviations from the mean. The probability of an observation that far below the mean is negligibly small. The precise p-value in this case, 1×10^{-140}, is so small it cannot be determined from this table or with many hand-held calculators. To calculate the p-value for this case by hand using the hypergeometric formula would be very cumbersome; a computer would be most helpful.

The methodology used in Exhibit 4.27(a) is so commonly used that it is worth presenting additional examples with different fact situations in Exhibits 4.27(b) and (c). Note that the binomial formula for the standard deviation is used in these examples.

EEOC v. United Virginia Bank/Seaboard National:[5] In this case the underlying population percentage of blacks was one of the factual issues to be resolved. The EEOC argued for a value of P equal to .27 because blacks made up 27% of the metropolitan workforce.[6] The court concluded that .14 was a more appropriate figure because blacks constituted 14% of the metropolitan workforce qualified for the office and clerical positions involved in this case.[7] Exhibit 4.27(b) illustrates the calculation of one-tailed p-values obtained by using these alternative underlying population percentages and demonstrates why plaintiffs in discriminatory impact cases argue for the highest value for P because it gives a lower p-value.

Exhibit 4.27(c) illustrates the effect of changing the sample size from 336 to 301, as was done in *United Virginia Bank*[8] (see Section 4.19). We have altered the observed number of blacks in the pre-Act exclusion group so that the observed percentages stay the same. The calculations are carried out in percentage terms, again illustrating the use of the standard deviation as a percentage of sample size, as discussed in Section 4.21.3.

[4] Id.
[5] 615 F.2d. 147 (4th Cir. 1980).
[6] Id. at 149.
[7] Id. at 150 n. 2.
[8] Id.

EXHIBIT 4.27(b)
Effect of Choice of *P* on *p*-Value
United Virginia Bank **Example**

$n = 336$ office and clerical employees

Plaintiff's View	*Court's View*
$P = .27$	$P = .14$
$Q = .73$	$Q = .86$

observed = 32 black employees

expected = $.27 \times 336 = 90.72$

disparity = $32 - 90.72 = -58.72$

standard deviation =
$\sqrt{336 \times .27 \times .73} = 8.14$

number of *sd* = $-58.72/8.14 = 7.21$

area under the normal curve for
$Z = 7.21 = .0000$

expected = $.14 \times 336 = 47.04$

disparity = $32 - 47.04 = -15.04$

standard deviation =
$\sqrt{336 \times .14 \times .86} = 6.36$

number of *sd* = $-15.04/6.36 = 2.36$

area under the normal curve for
$Z = 2.36 = .4909$

One-Tailed Test

p-value = $1.000 - (.5000 + .5000)$
$= .0000$

p-value = $1.000 - (.5000 + .4909)$
$= .0091$

EXHIBIT 4.27(c)
Effect of Choice of *n* on *p*-Value
United Virginia Bank **Example**

$n = 336$

$P = .14$

$Q = .86$

observed = 32

observed percentage = 32/336
$= .095$

expected percentage = $.14$

sd proportional = $\sqrt{\dfrac{.14 \times .86}{336}}$
$= .019$

disparity = $.095 - .14 = -.045$

number of *sd* = $.045/.019 = 2.37$

area under the normal curve for
$Z = 2.37 = .4911$

$n = 301$

$P = .14$

$Q = .86$

observed = 28.66

observed percentage = 28.66/301
$= .095$

expected percentage = $.14$

sd proportional = $\sqrt{\dfrac{.14 \times .86}{301}}$
$= .020$

disparity = $.095 - .14 = -.045$

number of *sd* = $.045/.020 = 2.25$

area under the normal curve for
$Z = 2.25 = .4878$

One-Tailed Test

p-value = $1.000 - (.5000 + .4911)$
$= .0089$

p-value = $1.000 - (.5000 + .4878)$
$= .0122$

§4.28   Interpolation — Calculations

Tables are useful because they eliminate the need to use complicated formulas such as the binomial or hypergeometric equations, but their utility and accuracy is limited by the particular significance levels or *p*-values that are listed. *Interpolation* is the mathematical process of estimating an unknown value that lies between two known values listed on a table. The known values between which we most commonly need to estimate an unknown value in the context of determining the significance of a difference are *p*-values, appearing on the Cumulative Binomial Probabilities Table.

For binomial probabilities the table presents *p*-values for selected underlying population percentages appearing across the top of the table. These selected percentages are multiples of five. Interpolation can be used to estimate the *p*-value for the random occurrence of a given frequency of a characteristic that occurs in the population at some other percentage, such as 17%. This 17% figure lies between *P* equals .15 and *P* equals .20. Not surprisingly, the corresponding *p*-value will lie somewhere between the appropriate *p*-value for .15 and that for .20. The method of estimating the unknown *p*-value has three steps:

(1)   Divide the difference between the unlisted percentage figure and the lower of the two listed percentages on either side of it by the difference between the two listed percentages.

(2)   Multiply the difference between the listed *p*-values associated with the two listed percentages for the appropriate *n* and *x* by the fraction calculated in step (1).

(3)   Add the result of step (2) to the *p*-value for the lower of the two listed percentages. This gives an estimated *p*-value for the unlisted percentage.

Exhibit 4.28(a) illustrates the use of interpolation as a substitute for the binomial formula when we want to know the probability of randomly observing six or more items with a particular characteristic in a sample of 10 items where the underlying population percentage is .17.

EXHIBIT 4.28(a)
Interpolation of a p-Value from a Binomial Table

$n = 10$
$P = .17$
$x = 6$ or more
lower listed percentage $= .15$
higher listed percentage $= .20$
p-value for $n = 10, P = .15, x = 6$ is .0014
p-value for $n = 10, P = .20, x = 6$ is .0064

Step 1:
    (a) Difference between unlisted percentage and lower listed percentage $= .17 - .15 = .02$
    (b) Difference between listed percentages $= .20 - .15 = .05$
    (c) Difference in (a) divided by difference in (b) $= .02/.05 = .4$

Step 2:
    (a) Difference between known p-value $= .0064 - .0014 = .0050$
    (b) Difference in (a) multiplied by result of Step 1 $= .0050 \times .4 = .0020$

Step 3:
    Result of Step 2 plus p-value for lower listed percentage $= .0020 + .0014 = .0034$

p-value for $n = 10, x = 6$ or more, $P = .17$ is .0034

CHAPTER FIVE

Analyzing Numerical Differences Among Categories

§5.0 Introduction

Much of this book is devoted to the assessment of the significance of observed relationships or discrepancies between or among categories that can be described numerically. One might want, for example, to assess the significance of an observed relationship between average family income and tax funds expended in a number of school districts or an observed discrepancy between the average salaries of men and women in certain departments of a large corporation. Ultimately, of course, a lawyer will want to evaluate whether the observed discrepancy or relationship is likely to have any legal significance. Before making that judgment, however, he or she must determine whether the observed discrepancy or relationship has statistical significance; that is, whether a discrepancy or relationship of the magnitude observed is unlikely to have occurred as a matter of chance alone. If statistical significance is found and chance is excluded as a plausible explanation, attention can be focused on other potential explanations that the law specifically deems inculpatory or exculpatory. The subject of this chapter is the *chi-square test*, one of the most commonly used methods for assessing the statistical significance of differences or relationships between two categories of numerical information or among multiple categories.

In approaching the chi-square or any other test of statistical significance, one should bear in mind that the test is a means for making a comparison. The comparison is between the actual distribution of the characteristic being investigated and the distribution that would have been predicted as a matter of chance alone. For example, in assessing the significance of observed discrepancies between men's and women's salaries, a comparison is being made between the salaries as they are actually distributed and as we would expect them to be if they had been set on a random, nondiscriminatory basis. If the observed discrepancy between average men's and women's salaries is minimal such that the observed salary distributions correspond almost exactly to the random predictions, an appropriately applied test of statistical significance will yield a high p-value. That is, comparing the observed and the expected distributions, we will conclude that there is a substantial likelihood that the discrepancy between the observed and the predicted distributions occurred simply as a matter of chance. If, however, the average salaries are widely divergent and relatively few women's salaries are as high as even the lowest of the men's salaries, it is more likely that an appropriate statistical comparison between the observed and expected distributions will yield a low p-value. A low p-value means, of course, that it is highly unlikely that a discrepancy of the magnitude observed would have occurred as a matter of chance. Consideration of other, more legally significant explanations for the observed discrepancy will be appropriate.

Since a significance test is a comparison between an observed distribution and a distribution that would be expected if chance were the only operative causal factor, the choice of the appropriate significance test is in effect a judgment about the form of the distribution that one would expect to result from chance alone. The nature of the distribution will be determined by a number of criteria related to the type of phenomenon being investigated, the way in which it is described, observed, and measured, and the relationship among the observations. This chapter will describe a number of situations in which measurable phenomena can be expected to follow a *chi-square distribution* or one that does not differ materially from the chi-square distribution. For such phenomena, the chi-square test of statistical significance will provide an appropriate means for determining the likelihood that an observed discrepancy or relationship would have occurred as a matter of chance.

Sections 5.1 through 5.3 discuss the analysis that must precede the application of the test and describe in some detail two contexts in which the chi-square is an appropriate test of the significance of numerical differences or relationships. Sections 5.4 through 5.15 present a number of examples of proper application of the chi-square test in each of the two contexts. These sections include discussions of the assessment and organization of the data to be studied, the preparation of the data for testing, responses to problems likely to be encountered, and alternatives to the chi-square test. Sections 5.16 and 5.17 deal with some of the practical considerations involved in presenting and attacking chi-square results. As in the other chapters dealing with substantive statistics, the final sections (Sections 5.18 through 5.21) cover the calculations necessary to apply the statistical techniques presented in the chapter.

A. ANALYSIS OF DATA USING THE CHI-SQUARE TEST

As noted in Section 5.0, certain types of measurable phenomena can be expected to follow a chi-square distribution. The chi-square test is a formula for measuring the statisical significance of differences between the observed distribution of such phenomena and the distribution that one would expect on the basis of chance alone. As is explained more fully in Sections 5.18 through 5.22, application of the chi-square formula to a suitable set of observations yields a test statistic known as the *chi-square value*. Once the chi-square value and other factors, including sample size, are known, examination of a *chi-square table* (such as the one in the Appendix of Tables at the end of this book) will reveal a *p*-value for the particular relationship or discrepancy being investigated.

As a matter of arithmetic the chi-square formula is one of the simplest tests to apply. This accounts in substantial part for its wide use and for the fact that it is usually one of the first tests of significance taught to beginning students of statistics. The more difficult problem is identifying the circumstances under which it is appropriate to use the chi-square test: there are few situations in which a measurable phenomenon actually follows a chi-square distribution but a number of situations in which phenomena follow distributions that differ only slightly from the chi-square distribution. Any resulting differences, moreover, are likely to be minimized if a large number of observations are made. In many such situations, application of the chi-square test will yield a *p*-value that is virtually identical to that which a more technically correct test of significance would yield. Under these circumstances, familiarity and ease of calculation often lead to the selection of chi-square as a simple, not incorrect, and thus acceptable alternative. In this sense, the chi-square test is a little like a typical vice-presidential candidate: an inspiration to few, yet tolerable to all, and thus a perfect second choice. The following three sections illustrate a number of situations in which the chi-square alternative may properly be chosen.

§5.1 Two Contrasting Applications of the Chi-Square Test

Use of the chi-square formula to test the significance of relationships or discrepancies is appropriate in two contexts. In the first a population is broken down into two or more groups. The members of the various groups are then evaluated in reference to a particular *discrete variable*, which is a variable that can take only a few values. A discrete variable that can take only two values is called a *dichotomous variable*. An example of a dichotomous variable is the result of a test that each taker either passes or fails. The results obtained for the various groups are then compared to each other in an effort to determine whether the observed distribution of results differs from the distribution that would have been expected on the basis of chance alone. The use of the chi-square test in this context will be referred to as a *contingency table analysis*.

In the second context the performances of two or more groups on some variable of interest are compared to a fixed external standard rather than to each other. The question to which the chi-square test is directed is again whether the observed distribution of values associated among the groups differs significantly from what would have been expected on the basis of chance. Since the purpose of this latter type of analysis is to determine how well an observed distribution fits a set of expectations derived from data external to the group being investigated, it is termed a *goodness-of-fit analysis*. Hypothetical applications of these two types of chi-square tests are presented in Sections 5.2 and 5.3.

§5.2 Contingency Table Analysis

Three simple examples will illustrate the use of the chi-square test in the contingency table context.

EXHIBIT 5.2(a)
Contingency Table for Test Takers
Unlimited Passes

	Pass	Fail	
Minority Candidates	5	20	25
Nonminority Candidates	20	5	25
	25	25	

Pass-Fail Test — No Limits: Assume that 50 people take a test. Twenty-five of them are white, and 25 of them are members of minority groups. The test has a fixed passing score, and there is no limit on the number of people who can pass. Five of the 25 minority group members pass, while the other 20 fail; of the nonminority takers, 20 pass while five fail. The question is whether the discrepancy between the pass rates for the two groups is statistically significant.

The variable of interest in this example is the test result. The observed values for this variable (i.e., the test results) can be summarized in a table such as that depicted in Exhibit 5.2(a). The top row describes the performance of all the minority takers, while the bottom row contains information about the performance of nonminority candidates. The first column includes all those who passed, while the second column includes all those who failed. Exhibit 5.2(a) is called a *two-by-two contingency table.* Information can be organized into such a table where two categories of items are being observed (here, minority and nonminority test-takers) and the variable being measured (the test results) is dichotomous, meaning that each observation yields one of two outcomes (that the person passed or the person failed). Where data can be organized into a two-by-two contingency table, a chi-square test is often an appropriate method for evaluating the significance of a discrepancy or relationship between the categories depicted on the table.

If chance (and not ethnic origin) were the only factor that influenced the test results, we would expect the pass rate for one group to be about the same as for the other. For each member of each group, the test would be like a coin toss, an event whose outcome is independent of the outcomes of other tosses. In this case, whether or not one individual passes the exam in no way influences whether or not other people pass. The number of members of each group who pass the test is said to be *binomially distributed* (see Section 4.15). Therefore, to assess the significance of any deviation of the observed distribution from the expected distribution of the variable, the most accurate method is the calculation of a p-value using a formula associated with the binomial distribution.

The binomial calculation is difficult. It happens, however, that the p-value resulting from the calculation is approximately the same as that based on a chi-square distribution. This congruence is particularly close where a large sample is being examined. The standards for determining an acceptable minimum sample size are discussed in Section 5.5.

It should be emphasized that while chi-square is an acceptable subsitute for the binomial model, it is not a perfect one: while chi-square will detect a significant discrepancy, it is blind to the direction of the discrepancy. In the Pass-Fail Test example, assume that we have posed the question of significance because we suspect that the test has a disparate impact on minorities. The chi-square will tell us with reasonable accuracy the probability that the observed discrepancy between minority and nonminority pass rates could have occurred as a matter of chance, but it will not tell us whether a significant p-value is attributable to minorities passing at a very high or very low rate. The chi-square test is thus sensitive to raw numerical discrepancies but not to the direction they take. In most instances the statistician can live with this shortcoming. When the analysis yields a low p-value, the investigator need only look at the raw data to determine whether that result is in fact attributable to a deviation in the suspect direction.

The next example is similar to the first, except that a limit is now imposed on the total number of people who can pass the test. Despite this difference, the chi-square test again will often be acceptable as a simple substitute for the more technically correct test. As in the first example, the data can be organized in a two-by-two contingency table.

Pass-Fail Test — Limit on Passing Scores: Assume the same facts as in Example 1, except that here there are a fixed number of openings, nine. The nine jobs will be given to the nine people who score highest on the test. Since there are only nine people who can "pass" the test, the sum of the numbers in the first column of the contingency table (see Exhibit 5.2(b)) is already fixed at nine. Since the sums of the two rows (the respective numbers of minority and nonminority people who are

EXHIBIT 5.2(b)
Contingency Table for Test Takers
Limited Passes

	Pass	Fail	
Minority Candidates	2	23	25
Nonminority Candidates	7	18	25
	9	41	

taking the test) are already known, the total number of people who will fail the test can also be calculated and entered at the bottom of the second column. With this information, once we can enter a value in any one of the four boxes in the table, we can immediately calculate the values for each of the other three boxes.

If individual test results were determined by chance alone, independent of the ethnicity of the test takers, we would expect the proportion of nonminorities passing to be the same as the proportion of minorities who pass. Unlike the prior example, however, each taking of this test does not exactly resemble a coin toss, since any one test outcome (that is, pass or fail) is now partially dependent on all of the other outcomes. Any individual applicant's chances for getting hired will be strongly influenced by how well all the other applicants did on the test. Because of this interdependence, the number of people within each ethnic group who pass the test is not binomially distributed, but *hypergeometrically distributed* (see Section 4.17).

The technically correct way to assess the significance of any deviation from the expected results would be to use a formula associated with the hypergeometric distribution. Here again, however, the technically correct formula is difficult. Since *p*-value calculations based on the chi-square distribution often approximate those based on the hypergeometric distribution, the chi-square formula provides a reasonably accurate and far simpler alternative. As in the previous example, the accuracy of chi-square improves with increasing sample size. Sensitivity to the direction of the discrepancy is lost here as well, but reexamination of the data should resolve any questions in most instances.

The next example presents a situation in which three categories of people are evaluated with respect to a dichotomous variable. Despite the involvement of the additional category, the analytical approach is the same as that taken in the previous two examples. Once again chi-square is an appropriate substitute for a more technically correct test of significance.

> *Promotion to Tenure:* Assume that a state university has 500 faculty positions. Because of budgetary restrictions imposed by the legislature, the number of tenured positions is frozen: 250 of the 500 positions are tenured, and 250 are untenured. The tenured faculty enjoy permanent job security, higher salaries and benefits, and reduced teaching loads. All of the 500 faculty members either black, white, or Asian. Within each ethnic group there is a similar representation of older and younger faculty members, and tenure opportunities are equally available in all university departments. A claim is made that the university unlawfully favors whites in promoting faculty members to tenured rank.

The first step in assessing this claim might be to ask whether there are statistically significant differences among the tenure rates for the three racial groups (that is, the percentage of faculty members in each group who have tenure). The available data include the numbers of tenured and untenured faculty members of each race. One way of organizing these data would be to group them in a contingency table such as that depicted in Exhibit 5.2(c). This table presents the results of evaluating three categories of people (black, white, and Asian) with respect to a dichotomous variable (tenure status). The top row contains the number of tenured faculty members in each racial group, while the bottom row contains the number of untenured faculty. The sums at the end of the rows are the total numbers of tenured and untenured faculty; the sums at the bottom of each of the three columns indicate the total numbers of faculty members in each of the three racial groups. A table such as this that compares multiple

EXHIBIT 5.2(c)
Contingency Table for Promotion to Tenure

	Black	White	Asian	
Tenured	30	205	15	250
Untenured	70	145	35	250
	100	350	50	

categories with respect to a dichotomous variable is called a *multiple* or *two-by-*n *contingency table.*

In comparison to the previous examples, it is somewhat more difficult to hypothesize here what the tenure rates would be if tenure decisions were made on the basis of chance alone. With the facts given we might assume that each group would have a share of the 250 tenured positions that corresponded to that group's representation on the faculty as a whole. Another way of saying the same thing is that, within each group, approximately half the members would be tenured and half would be untenured. As in the second example, the variable of interest (tenure status) is hypergeometrically distributed because in both examples the members of the categories being compared are competing for a limited number of slots (nine "passes," 250 tenured positions), with the result that any individual outcome is affected by and itself affects all the other outcomes.

In this example, however, the expected hypergeometric distribution is far more complex than in the previous example. There simply is no single technically correct method for assessing the significance of a discrepancy between the observed and expected distributions of tenure status across the three categories; there are instead a number of alternatives, each of which will do only part of the job. In this case chi-square merges these various partial solutions and yields a result that is fairly comprehensive and reasonably accurate.

It should be noted that in this multiple contingency table the three categories being compared (the three racial groups) are merely different; they cannot be ranked in order of preferability. The chi-square test is best applied to a multiple contingency table when the multiple categories being compared are merely different and are not subject to rank-ordering.

Contrast this situation with a two-by-three (or three-by-two; the orientation of the table is irrelevant) contingency table that displays the respective numbers of whites and nonwhites in three job categories that can be ranked in order of good, better, and best. (Note that race of job holders is the variable of interest and that the three job categories are being evaluated with respect to this variable). While the chi-square test can be used as a test of significance, it is generally less informative and less powerful than one that is able to take into account the rank status of the multiple categories.[1]

---

§5.2   [1] In the example just posited, the Mann-Whitney and Wilcoxon rank tests would be preferable alternatives because they take into account the rank status of the categories. See Section 5.9.

§5.3 Goodness-of-Fit Analysis

The preceding section presented three examples of the use of the chi-square test in the contingency table analysis context. Chi-square can also be used to test the significance of differences or relationships where each of two or more categories of information is compared to some external standard rather than to the other categories. This is called *goodness-of-fit analysis*. The logic and methodology of the analysis are the same regardless of how many categories are being compared. The following example illustrates the use of the chi-square test in a multiple category goodness-of-fit analysis.

Grand Jury Selection: In a certain jurisdiction, grand jurors are supposed to be drawn at random from a census list that contains the names of all the adult residents of the jurisdiction. One-third of the people appearing on the census list are white, one-third are Hispanic, and one-third black. We would therefore expect that about one-third of the jurors on any particular randomly selected 18-member grand jury would be white, one-third Hispanic, and one-third black. We would further expect that, while individual juries might deviate widely from the expected composition, the average representation of each ethnic group over a large number of grand juries would be about 33%.

A political group representing minorities believes that blacks and Hispanics have been substantially underrepresented on recent grand juries and suspects that the random system called for by law is not being followed. The group undertakes to collect data to support its position. It ascertains the total representation of Hispanics, blacks, and whites on the ten most recent grand juries. The observed distribution of the three ethnic groups on the ten juries is depicted in Exhibit 5.3(a).

The question once again is whether this observed distribution deviates significantly from the distribution that would be expected on the basis of chance alone. Here, since each ethnic group constitutes 33% of the population from which the jurors are drawn (theoretically at random), our a priori expectation would be that each group would constitute about one-third of the grand jurors. Since the selection of

EXHIBIT 5.3(a)
Ethnic Representation on Ten 18-Member Grand Juries

White	Black	Hispanic	
120	30	30	180

each juror should be an independent event and since the odds for drawing a juror from any of the three groups on any particular selection are the same (one in three), the variable of interest (the number of grand jurors from the various ethnic groups) is binomially distributed, like the coin toss discussed in Section 5.2.

In the three examples in the preceding section, the object was to compare the rates at which members of various groups were allocated to either of two statuses: pass or fail on a test, or tenured or untenured faculty positions. Put somewhat differently, each member of each group faced alternative outcomes. The analysis yielded an internal comparison of the way in which those outcomes worked out across the various groups. In predicting the distribution of outcomes that would have resulted from chance alone, we made no reference to information beyond that appearing on the table.

Here, by contrast, the performance of three groups on a variable of interest (representation on grand juries) is being compared to an external standard. The distribution that would be expected on the basis of chance alone is determined not from the observations included in the analysis, but by reference to a larger, external population. The purpose of the analysis is, in effect, to see how well the observed distribution "fits" the external standard that has been chosen. For this reason, the type of analysis described in the grand jury example is termed a *goodness-of-fit analysis*.

As with the various contingency table examples, chi-square is a reasonable second choice for testing significance in this situation as well. To be technically correct, one would use a formula associated with the binomial distribution to derive a p-value. Where sample size is sufficiently large (see Section 5.5), the chi-square analysis will yield a similar p-value. The p-value derived from the chi-square test will, of course, be equally affected by an overrepresentation or an underrepresentation of minorities, but an examination of the data should clarify any ambiguities.[1]

The application of chi-square to a goodness-of-fit problem is equally appropriate whether there are only two categories of information or multiple categories, as was the case in the grand jury example (data on three different ethnic groups were included). The theory is

---

§5.3   [1] Having determined that there was a statistically significant deviation from the expected racial composition of grand juries, one would simply look at the raw data to infer whether this statistical finding was attributable to over- or underrepresentation of minorities.

the same, and the calculations differ only slightly (see Section 5.22). Regardless of how many categories are being compared, the principal requirements are: (1) that the individual events being tallied be unrelated to each other, as in the case of rolling dice or selecting a few people randomly from a much larger population; and (2) that the external standard against which the observations are compared be based on an entire population or a population mean.

B. APPLICATIONS OF THE CHI-SQUARE TEST TO CONTINGENCY TABLE ANALYSIS

Drawing on a number of reported cases, Sections 5.4 through 5.10 illustrate the application of the chi-square test in the contingency table context. The reader will recall from Section 5.2 that in a contingency table analysis the performance of two or more groups with respect to a dichotomous variable is measured and recorded. One example used was the performance of black and white applicants on a pass-fail employment test. The scores attained by the groups were then compared to each other in an effort to determine whether the observed distribution of passes and fails differed significantly from what might have been expected on the basis of chance alone.

The first and perhaps most critical step in a contingency table analysis is to assess the data to be studied in order to decide whether the chi-square test is an acceptable test of significance. Once this decision is made, it is then necessary to organize the data to permit proper application of the test. The processes of assessment and organization of data are the subject of Section 5.4. These processes will be carried out in the same way regardless of the number of groups being compared. Section 5.5 deals with the determination of the expected numbers against which the observed results will be compared. Section 5.6 introduces the concept of *degrees of freedom,* which is essential to the interpretation of chi-square results. Sections 5.7 and 5.8 suggest partial solutions to the problems often encountered when small groups are being studied, and Section 5.9 reviews a number of alternatives to chi-square that may be appropriate in particular contexts. Section 5.10 briefly distinguishes the t test, an inappropriate substitute for chi-square analysis.

§5.4   Assessment and Organization of Data for Contingency Table Analysis

The first steps in any contingency table analysis are (1) to assess whether the available data are suitable for this method of analysis and (2) to organize the data so that the chi-square test can be properly applied.

Consider three examples from the areas of employment discrimination, environmental law, and food and drug law. Each case contains data that can be organized into a two-by-two contingency table and subjected to chi-square testing.

> **Chance v. Board of Examiners:**[1] This was a class action brought on behalf of black and Puerto Rican candidates for supervisory positions in the New York City school system. The plaintiffs attacked the discriminatory impact of a set of examinations that candidates had to pass before being listed as qualified for the various positions. In an opinion in support of the issuance of a preliminary injunction against the examinations, the court considered a broad range of statistical evidence. Of interest here is a survey done by the plaintiffs' expert that showed the following: during the three preceding years 5,092 whites and 818 nonwhites (blacks and Puerto Ricans) had taken the supervisory examinations; 257, or 31.4% of the nonwhites passed the exams, while 2,256, or 44.3% of the whites passed.[2] The court noted that the white pass rate was almost one and one-half times the nonwhite pass rate but did not indicate that any analysis of the significance of these figures had been done.[3]

The data reported by the court can readily be organized into a two-by-two contingency table. There are two categories of people being compared (whites and nonwhites) with reference to a dichotomous variable (test results). Each person in each category therefore falls into one of two conditions (pass or fail). As depicted in Exhibit 5.4(a), the left column of the table shows the number of candidates of each race who passed, while the right column shows the number who

---

§5.4   [1] 330 F. Supp. 203 (S.D.N.Y. 1971), aff'd, 458 F.2d 1167 (2d Cir. 1972).
[2] 330 F. Supp. at 210.
[3] The court did describe an analysis by the plaintiffs' expert of two individual examinations. On one examination, 61.37% of the whites and 45.26% of the minorities passed; on the other, 48.82% of the whites and 25.60% of the minorities passed. The expert calculated the probabilities of such disparities occurring as a matter of chance at one in a million. Id.

EXHIBIT 5.4(a)
Contingency Table
Chance Example

	Pass	Fail	
White	2,256	2,836	5,092
Non-White	257	561	818
	2,513	3,397	

failed. Since, like a coin toss, each individual taking of the test was independent of every other taking (there was a cutoff score, but no limit to the number of people who could pass), the variable of interest (the number of people in the two groups who passed the test) is binomially distributed (compare the first example in Section 5.2). The numbers in the individual cells in the table are sufficiently large, however, that use of the chi-square test to compare the observed and expected distributions would be reasonably accurate.

Dow Chemical Co. v. Blum:[4] The chemical company sought to stay the enforcement of an Environmental Protection Agency emergency order that banned the use of certain herbicides. In issuing its order, EPA had relied in part on a study of spontaneous abortion rates at hospitals in sprayed and unsprayed areas. The company's experts attacked this study, contending that the application of a chi-square test showed that there was no "statistically significant relationship between hospitalized spontaneous abortions and the spraying" of the suspect chemical.[5] The court accepted the company's criticism, but did not describe the manner in which the chi-square test had been utilized.[6]

It is not clear from the court's opinion just how the data were organized or how the chi-square test was applied. One can, however, readily hypothesize a situation in which the available data could have been organized into a two-by-two contingency table. Presumably the hospital data for each of the two study areas (sprayed and unsprayed) reflected the raw numbers of spontaneously aborted pregnancies and unaborted pregnancies. If so, these numbers could have been orga-

[4] 469 F. Supp. 892 (E.D. Mich. 1979).
[5] Id. at 905.
[6] Id.

EXHIBIT 5.4(b)
Contingency Table
Dow Chemical **Example**

	Aborted	Unaborted	
Sprayed Area	20	80	100
Unsprayed Area	5	95	100
	25	175	

nized as depicted in Exhibit 5.4(b). Hypothetical numbers have been inserted into the various cells. The numbers used give grounds for suspecting a relationship between spraying and the abortion rate. Two categories are being examined (sprayed and unsprayed areas), and each observed pregnancy in each group falls into one of two conditions (aborted and unaborted).

Since the result of each observation is independent of every other observation, the distribution of the variable being studied (pregnancy outcomes) is binomial. Assuming adequate numbers of observations in each cell, the chi-square test would be an appropriate way to calculate the probability that the apparent relationship between location in a sprayed area and frequency of spontaneous abortions resulted from chance alone. As will be explained in Section 5.5, an expected distribution could be developed from the data contained in the table.

In re Kroger Company:[7] The issue in this case was whether Kroger's "Price Patrol" advertisements were deceptive. The Price Patrol was a price list of a number of items sold in Kroger supermarkets. The items included on the list changed from week to week at the discretion of certain Kroger personnel. Kroger ran advertisements in which prices for Price Patrol items were compared to the prices charged by its competitors for the same items.

The FTC reviewed a study of the Price Patrol Program done by a public interest lobbying group. This group's study considered the relative representation on a number of Price Patrol lists of items whose prices had been raised just before listing and whose prices had been lowered before they were listed. Overrepresentation of recently lowered items would support a finding of deception, since Kroger would have been misrepresenting the overall cost of shopping at its supermar-

[7] 98 F.T.C. 639 (1981), *modified*, 100 F.T.C. 573 (1982).

EXHIBIT 5.4(c)
Contingency Table
Kroger Example

	Recent Increase	Recent Decrease	
Price Patrol	50	100	150
Non-Price Patrol	75	75	150
	125	175	

kets. This is in fact what the study showed, and a chi-square test confirmed that the deviation from the expected distribution was statistically significant. The Commission did not disclose the underlying data or describe the manner in which the chi-square test had been applied.[8]

Once again, although the reported decision does not describe the statistical analysis in detail, reasonable inferences can be drawn about the organization of the data and the application of the chi-square test. The study presumably included a number of observations for each of two categories, Price Patrol items and non-Price Patrol items. Each observation apparently fell into one of two conditions, price *increased* prior to listing or price *decreased* prior to listing. Exhibit 5.4(c) illustrates how the data could be organized, using numbers that tend to suggest an overrepresentation of recently decreased items.[9] If each decision to list an individual item were made independently, the selection process would resemble a series of coin flips, and the distribution of the variable of interest (price changes) would be binomial. Assuming a sufficient number of observations, the chi-square test would yield a reasonable approximation of the probability that the discrepancy between the observed and the expected distribution of price changes could be attributed to chance alone.[10]

---

[8] 98 F.T.C. at 692.
[9] As a matter of logic, one might expect a third condition, no change prior to listing. Insofar as can be determined from the Commission's decision, a third category was not included in the study. Had there been a third category, the chi-square test might also have been appropriate, but the analysis would have been in the form of a two-by-three contingency table, such as the third example in Section 5.2.
[10] As the reader may have noted, these data could also have been subjected to a goodness-of-fit analysis (see Section 5.3). The two groups being compared would again be Price Patrol and non-Price Patrol items, and the variable of interest would again be

The *Chance, Dow Chemical,* and *Kroger* cases involved two-by-two contingency tables, which reflect the comparison of two groups with respect to a dichotomous variable. It is also possible to compare more than two groups in the same fashion. In a multiple or two-by-n contingency table analysis, the members of three or more groups are evaluated with respect to a dichotomous variable, and the observed results are organized in a table having two rows and a number of columns equal to the number of groups. Chi-square can be used here as well to test the significance of any discrepancy between the observed and expected distribution of results, subject to the same considerations that apply to two-by-two contingency table analyses. The next two cases illustrate the assessment and organization of data in a multiple contingency table context.

In re MacMillan, Inc.:[11] The issue in this Federal Trade Commission proceeding was whether Lasalle Extension University had issued misleading advertisements concerning the career opportunities for its graduates. The major piece of evidence in the case was an extensive survey of Lasalle graduates. One of the questions bearing on the validity of the survey was whether there were any patterns in who chose to respond and who did not that might impart a bias to the results. In partial response to this concern, the experts taking the survey compared response rates in the various geographic regions that the survey covered. Using a chi-square test, they concluded that there were no statistically significant differences in response rate among the various regions. The experts took this as an indication that the survey results were unlikely to have been biased by systematic differences between those who responded and those who did not.[12] The Commission criticized the latter inference.[13]

Leaving aside the permissible scope of the inferences to be drawn from the analysis, the study of response rate by region provides a good example of the use of the chi-square test in a multiple contin-

---

price change status (recently increased or decreased). Here, however, the comparison would be made to an external standard based on the distribution of recent price changes in the population made up of all items sold by Kroger. This analysis would be similar logically to comparing the minority representation in a particular employer's workforce to that in the population from which that workforce was drawn. See Section 5.11.

[11] 96 F.T.C. 208 (1980).

[12] Id. at 275.

[13] The Commission observed that "[p]ersons with a grievance or a latent dissatisfaction are more likely to respond to a mail survey and thus select themselves." Id. at 284.

EXHIBIT 5.4(d)
Contingency Table
MacMillan Example

	Region					
	1	2	3	4	5	
Respondents	45	50	60	52	46	253
Non-Respondents	55	50	40	48	54	247
	100	100	100	100	100	

gency table situation. Although the reported decision does not set out the data, presumably the numbers of respondents and nonrespondents were known for each of several regions. If we assume that five regions were surveyed, the data could be organized in the manner depicted in Exhibit 5.4(d). Each column represents one of the five regions surveyed. The hypothetical numbers across the top row are the numbers of respondents, while those in the bottom row are the numbers of people who did not respond.

Note that each of the observed events (each decision to respond or not to respond) was theoretically independent. If in fact there were no systematic biases among either the respondents or the nonrespondents, and if each decision were thus governed purely by chance, each observed event would be exactly like a coin toss. Collecting response rate data from five regions would be analogous to collecting the result from tossing five different coins. Accordingly, in each of the five regions, the variable of interest (number of responses) would be binomially distributed.

With an adequate sample size, a p-value calculation based on the five binomial distributions would approximate one based on chi-square distributions fairly closely. Accordingly, the experts in *MacMillan* properly concluded that chi-square was a reasonably accurate method for testing the significance of any discrepancy between the observed and expected distribution of results.

Chance v. Board of Examiners:[14] Earlier in this section, certain data from this case (pass rates for whites and nonwhites taking examinations for supervisory positions in the New York schools) were sub-

[14] 330 F. Supp. 203 (S.D.N.Y. 1971), *aff'd*, 458 F.2d 1167 (2d Cir. 1972).

EXHIBIT 5.4(e)
Multiple Contingency Table
Chance **Example**

	Pass	Fail	
Black	127	151	278
White	718	453	1,171
Puerto Rican	2	5	7
	847	609	

jected to a two-by-two contingency table analysis. The court also considered data comparing three categories: black, white, and Puerto Rican applicants. On the 1965 assistant-principal examination, for example, the results were as follows: 1,171 whites took the test and 718 passed (61.3%) while 453 failed (38.7%); of 278 blacks taking the test, 127 passed (45.7%) and 151 failed (54.3%); of seven Puerto Ricans taking the test, two passed (28.6%) and five failed. According to the plaintiff's expert, the probability of such a distribution occurring as a matter of chance was one in a million.[15]

These data from *Chance* can readily be organized into a multiple contingency table in the form depicted in Exhibit 5.4(e). Each of the rows represents one of the three groups being compared. The left column indicates the numbers in each group who passed; the right column indicates the numbers who failed. Since there were no limits on the number of people who could pass the test, the collection of pass-fail data from the three ethnic groups can be compared to observing the results of tossing three different coins. For each of the three ethnic groups, the distribution of the variable of interest (number of people passing the test) is thus binomial. Given a sufficiently large number of observations, the chi-square test will be a reasonably accurate measure of the significance of any difference between the observed and the expected numbers of passing scores.

To complete this discussion of multiple contingency table analysis, two further points should be emphasized. First, the chi-square test is most effective when the categories being compared are merely different and are not subject to hierarchical ordering. In both *Chance*

---

[15] 330 F. Supp. at 210.

and *MacMillan* the categories being compared (ethnic groups and geographical regions) clearly met this criterion. (Contrast this with a situation in which the three categories being compared are three job groups distinguished by salary. See Section 5.9.3.) Second, it is once again true that the chi-square test will not indicate the direction in which a discrepancy lies. In *MacMillan*, a statistically significant finding could have been attributed to any one of ten different conditions, namely, substantially higher or lower response rates in any of the five regions. In many cases, however, examination of the raw data will reveal in a general way the source of a significant finding.

§5.5 Expected Numbers for Contingency Table Analysis

The purpose of every chi-square analysis is to compare the observed distribution of some variable of interest with the distribution that might have been expected on the basis of chance alone. In calculating a chi-square value from a contingency table, the analyst must posit an expected value to compare with each of the observed values recorded in the table (these calculations are discussed in detail in Sections 5.18 and 5.19). In a contingency table chi-square analysis, the expected values must be derived from an average of the observed values recorded in the table.

The following case can be used to illustrate how expected values are determined in a two-by-two contingency table analysis.

Certified Color Manufacturers' Association v. Mathews:[1] This case involved a laboratory analysis of the safety of Red Dye No. 2. One study put in evidence involved 53 rats. Twenty-three were given a high dosage of red dye, and 30 were given a low dosage. Of the high-dosage rats, seven developed cancer and 16 did not; four of the low-dosage rats developed cancer while 26 did not. These data can be organized in a contingency table such as that depicted in Exhibit 5.5(a).

In *Certified Color*, the objective was to compare the observed incidence of cancer in two categories of rats (high and low dosage) with the incidence of cancer that might be expected on the basis of chance alone. As Exhibit 5.5(a) reflects, each rat in each group has been

§5.5 [1]543 F.2d 284 (D.C. Cir. 1976).

EXHIBIT 5.5(a)
Contingency Table
Certified Color **Example**

	Cancer	No Cancer	
High Dosage	7	16	23
Low Dosage	4	26	30
	11	42	

observed with respect to a dichotomous variable (occurrence or nonoccurrence of cancer); the Exhibit tallies these observations. Each of the observed values recorded in Exhibit 5.5(a) must be compared to an expected value. These expected values are those one would expect to find if chance were the only factor contributing to the distribution of cancer rates between high-dosage and low-dosage rats; in other words, they are the values one would expect if in fact there were no correlation between dosage and cancer rates (that is, if the null hypothesis were true; see Section 2.10.4).

As noted above, the expected values must be derived from an average of the observed values. Here, 53 rats were studied; 11 got cancer. Thus the cancer rate for all rats, regardless of dosage, was slightly less than 21%. If it is assumed that dosage and cancer rate are not correlated (the null hypothesis), then every rat, regardless of the dosage it received, should have had approximately a 21% chance of getting cancer. Accordingly, among the high-dosage rats, 21%, or 4.8, could be expected to have developed cancer, while slightly more than 79%, or 18.2, could be expected to be cancer-free. The corresponding numbers for the low-dosage rats are 6.2 and 23.8. In Exhibit 5.5(b), the expected values have been added to the table.

A similar averaging process would be employed in each of the

EXHIBIT 5.5(b)
Contingency Table with Expected Values
Certified Color **Example**

	Cancer	No Cancer
High Dosage	7 (4.8)	16 (18.2)
Low Dosage	4 (6.2)	26 (23.8)

cases discussed in the preceding section. In the *Chance* case, summarized in Exhibit 5.4(a), it can be seen that 2,513 of a total of 5,910 takers passed the examination, for an average pass rate of 42.5%. On the basis of this rate, one would have expected 348 out of the 818 nonwhite applicants to have passed and 2,164 out of 5,092 of the white applicants. (These are expected values, and those in the remainder of this section have been rounded to the nearest integer.) In *Dow Chemical* (Exhibit 5.4(b)), we would calculate an aggregate abortion rate for all pregnancies both inside and outside the sprayed area (25/200, or 12.5%) and then apply this rate to all pregnancies occurring within the sprayed area (20 + 80 = 100) and all pregnancies occurring outside the sprayed area (5 + 95 = 100). The result would be expected numbers of aborted and unaborted births within each of the two areas. Similarly, in *Kroger* (Exhibit 5.4(c)), it would be necessary to calculate an average rate of recent price increases for all items surveyed and represented in the table. This would be done by dividing the total number of recently increased items in both the Price Patrol and non-Price Patrol categories (125) by the total number of items in the table (300). If we express this rate as a percentage (41.7%) and subtract it from 100%, the result would be the average rate of recent price decrease for all items (58.3%). Application of these rates to the total number of Price Patrol and non-Price Patrol items would yield expected numbers of recently increased and decreased items in each category.

The process for deriving expected values in a multiple contingency table analysis is the same. As in the case of a two-by-two contingency table analysis, there must be an expected value to correspond with each observed value. Consider again the second set of data from the *Chance* case, summarized in Exhibit 5.4(e). As in any contingency table analysis, the expected values must be computed by averaging the observed values. In the absence of bias or any other factors that tended to create systematic differences in results among black, white, and Puerto Rican applicants, one would expect the pass rates in the three groups to be relatively similar. The method for translating this expectation into a set of expected values is to compute an overall pass rate and then to apply this rate to the total number of applicants from each of the three ethnic groups.

The row and column totals in Exhibit 5.4(e) indicate that 1,456 people took the test and 847, or 58.2%, passed. If chance were the only factor working to create differences among groups, one would expect each group to approximate the 58.2% pass rate. Thus, among

EXHIBIT 5.5(c)
Multiple Contingency Table with Expected Values
Chance **Example**

	Pass	Fail	
Black	127 (162)	151 (116)	278
White	718 (682)	453 (489)	1,171
Puerto Rican	2 (4)	5 (3)	7
	847	609	

the whites one would expect approximately 58.2% of the 1,171 applicants to have passed. The expected values calculated in this fashion have been entered beside the observed values in Exhibit 5.5(c).

Expected numbers are the basis for determining whether enough observations have been made to permit use of the chi-square test. As a general rule chi-square is appropriate where each expected value entered in the contingency table is at least five. Note that in the *Chance* data presented in Exhibit 5.5(c) the expected values in the Puerto Rican row are less than five. The use of the chi-square test is therefore suspect. Two partial solutions to the problem of small numbers are discussed in Sections 5.7 and 5.8.

§5.6 Degrees of Freedom for Contingency Table Analysis

After the data have been organized and expected numbers have been calculated, one additional piece of information is required before the chi-square formula can be applied and the *p*-value can be read from the Chi-Square Table. This item is number of *degrees of freedom*. The concept is a difficult one in the abstract but simple to apply in most cases. For the usual two-by-two contingency table analysis, the number of degrees of freedom will equal one. In a multiple contingency table analysis, the number of degrees of freedom equals the number of rows in the table, less one, times the number of columns in the table, less one. In the case of the *Chance* data summarized in Exhibit 5.4(e), the numbers of columns equals three (black, white, Puerto Rican), the number of rows equals two (pass, fail), and (3 − 1)

$\times$ (2 − 1) = 2. Accordingly, there are two degrees of freedom in the *Chance* example.

§5.7   Small Numbers: The Yates Correction

It was noted in Section 5.5 that a chi-square contingency table analysis is generally recommended only when each expected value in the table is at least five. In a two-by-two contingency table analysis, however, it is not always necessary to abandon the use of chi-square because one or more of the expected values is less than five. Under some circumstances it may be possible to use a modification of the chi-square formula called the *Yates Correction*.

It should be noted at the start that the Yates Correction has no clear theoretical basis. It is used because under some circumstances it works, but it is difficult to characterize the precise situations in which it is advantageous. With small expected numbers, it sometimes improves the accuracy of the *p*-value that the chi-square formula yields, and it seems to be particularly helpful where the true distribution of the variable being studied is hypergeometric. Because it is a source of some confusion even among experienced statisticians, the Yates Correction should be used with caution, if at all, by the beginner. The calculation of the Yates Correction is described in Section 5.20.[1]

§5.8   Small Numbers: Combining Categories in Contingency Tables

Small numbers of observations that yield unacceptably small expected values also create problems in multiple contingency table analyses. Here, however, there is a partial solution that is simpler in concept and application than the Yates Correction that is sometimes used in the two-by-two context. In Section 5.5 expected values were computed for the comparison made in the *Chance* case among pass rates for blacks, whites, and Puerto Ricans (see Exhibit 5.5(e)). It was noted that in the Puerto Rican row both expected values fall short of five. The accuracy of the chi-square test will thus be suspect.

---

§5.7   [1] For a scholarly discussion of the Yates Correction and the problems associated with it, see 2 M. Kendall & A. Stuart, The Advanced Theory of Statistics 586 (4th ed. 1979).

One alternative is simply to abandon the chi-square analysis and make the technically correct although considerably more difficult calculations associated with the binomial distribution. In the multiple contingency context another option is to combine two of the categories. Using the *Chance* data, it would be possible to combine the black and Puerto Rican applicants to create a new category having 285 members, 129 of whom passed the test and 156 of whom failed. The expected values for this merged category are derived by adding the expected values for the original categories; thus one would expect 166 people to have passed and 119 to have failed.

If the *Chance* categories are combined in the manner described, the requirement that each expected value be at least five will be met. Some explanatory power will be lost, however, since the resulting analysis will test the significance of any observed discrepancy only between the majority group and the minority applicants taken as a whole. This loss of analytical power may be problematical where two of three categories are being merged, and the largest of those is only slightly more numerous than the smallest. In *Chance*, however, one can reasonably conclude that any finding of significance across all three categories will be due primarily to differences between black and white pass rates.

Two or more categories can be combined any time that three or more categories are being compared. In all cases, the analyst needs to make a commonsense evaluation of the likely impact of the combination on the results. Generally, the smallest categories should be combined first, and categories should be combined only to the extent necessary to ensure that all expected values are at least five. It should be remembered that the number of degrees of freedom will be reduced by the number of categories that have been lost.

§5.9 Alternatives to Chi-Square for Contingency Tables

A recurring theme in this chapter has been that chi-square is most often used as a substitute for another test of significance that is more nearly correct but more difficult to apply. The formula associated with the binomial distribution has been mentioned as an example of such a technically correct but sometimes unwieldly test. This section discusses two additional tests that may be alternatives to chi-square in the two-by-two contingency table context. They are the

Fisher Exact Test (Section 5.9.1), which is associated with the hypergeometric distribution, and the Z test (Section 5.9.2), which is associated with the normal distribution. The section concludes with a discussion of the comparative absence of alternatives to chi-square in the multiple contingency context (Section 5.9.3).

§5.9.1 Fisher's Exact Test as an Alternative to the Chi-Square Test

The reader may recall from Section 5.2 that a hypergeometric distribution will result when two categories are compared with respect to a dichotomous variable and there is a limit on the number of times that one of the values of that variable can occur. The second example in Section 5.2 presents a situation in which a variable of interest will be distributed hypergeometrically. That example involves the relative success of black and white applicants on an employment test. The most significant fact in the example is that there are a limited number of job openings and thus a limited number of "passing" grades available to those taking the test. Since the number of people who can pass is predetermined and a passing score obtained by one candidate will therefore affect the odds facing each of the other candidates, each observed event (each taking of the test) is not independent. Because of this factor the variable of interest (passing scores) is said to follow a hypergeometric distribution (see Section 4.17).

The chi-square test was described as an appropriate second choice in such a situation. The more correct method for assessing the probability that a discrepancy or relationship is attributable to chance when the variable in question is hypergeometrically distributed is called *Fisher's Exact Test*. Although it is more difficult to calculate than chi-square, Fisher's Exact Test offers both increased accuracy and the ability to determine the direction in which a statistically significant discrepancy lies. The calculation of Fisher's Exact Test employs the hypergeometric formula, which is discussed in detail in Section 4.25.

§5.9.2 The Z Test as an Alternative to the Chi-Square Test

Recall the first and second examples from Section 5.2. Both involve comparison of pass rates on an employment test for black and white applicants; in the first example, there are no limits on the number of people who can pass; in the second, only a limited number of "pass" slots are available. In the first example the true distribution of the variable being studied is binomial, while in the second example it is hypergeometric. In both instances it is noted that the chi-square distribution is a reasonable approximation of the actual distribution as long as there is an adequate sample size.

It is also true in both instances that with an adequate sample size the normal distribution can be used to obtain a reasonable approximation of the true p-value. The sample size requirements for use of the normal distribution are similar to those for use of the chi-square distribution.

The Z test, which is discussed more fully in Section 4.14, is used to assess the significance of the deviation of an observed value of a normally distributed random variable from its expected value. In a two-category comparison where the distribution of the variable of interest is binomial or hypergeometric, the Z test can be substituted for the technically correct test under approximately the same conditions as chi-square. The Z test generally provides the same information as the chi-square test, but the Z test also identifies the direction in which a discrepancy lies.

In the *Dow Chemical* and *Kroger* cases discussed in Section 5.4, the Z test and the chi-square test could be used almost interchangeably. In the *MacMillan* case (also discussed in Section 5.4), however, the Z test would be inappropriate, since the analysis involves comparison of multiple categories.[1] In the *Certified Color* case, discussed in Section 5.5, use of either the Z test or the chi-square test is suspect, since one of the expected values in the contingency table falls short of five. For further examples of use of the Z test, see Sections 4.16 and 4.19.

§5.9.3   Alternatives to Contingency Table Analysis for Multiple Categories

In most multiple contingency table situations (see, for example, the *MacMillan* and *Chance* cases discussed in Section 5.4), there is no single alternative that will duplicate or improve on chi-square as a measure of the significance of a discrepancy between an observed and

§5.9   [1]The Z test could be used to compare geographic regions on a two-by-two basis.

an expected distribution. The Z test, for example, generally cannot be used where more than two categories are being compared. There may be situations, however, in which the primary question is not whether there is an overall discrepancy between the observed pattern and the expected pattern. This is likely to be true where the three or more categories being compared can be ranked in some sort of order of preferability. Consider, for example, a two-by-three contingency table that compares the racial makeup (minority versus nonminority) of the incumbents in each of three job categories. Assume further that the three job categories can be arranged in order of most desirable, less desirable, and least desirable.

The chi-square test would reveal whether there was a significant overall discrepancy between the observed racial makeup of the three departments and the racial makeup that might be expected on the basis of chance alone. One might well be interested in asking more refined questions, however, such as just how the distribution of minorities among the three ranked categories compares with the distribution of nonminorities; that is, are minority employees consistently assigned to less preferable jobs than their nonminority counterparts? A detailed statistical profile of the workforce would provide a more revealing look at the employer's job assignment practices than would a simple statement that the two racial groups do not appear to be distributed randomly among the three categories. Under such circumstances the chi-square test fails to answer the questions that are of the greatest practical significance. The Mann-Whitney and Wilcoxon rank tests should be considered as alternatives.[2]

§5.10 The t Test and the Chi-Square Test Compared

The chi-square test is an appropriate test of significance in two contexts: contingency table analyses, in which two or more groups are compared to each other with reference to their performance on a dichotomous variable; and goodness-of-fit analyses, in which the numbers of members of two or more groups who fall into a particular status (e.g., blacks and whites working for a particular employer) are compared to an external standard. Consider next a situation in which

---

[2] See R. Pfaffenberger & J. Patterson, Statistical Methods for Business and Economics 665-680 (1981) and 2 M. Kendall & A. Stuart, Advanced Theory of Statistics 529-533 (4th ed. 1979), where these tests are discussed.

two groups are being compared to each other, as in a contingency table analysis, but with respect to their performance on a variable that can take a range of values, called a *continuous variable*.

> **Booth v. Board of Directors of National American Bank:**[1] The issue here was whether the defendant bank practiced racial discrimination in its treatment of clerical employees. One piece of evidence was an analysis of "the average pay at hire of all clerical employees hired by defendant in 1976."[2] The plaintiff's expert "found the distinctions between black and white pay to be statistically significant, using the Chi-Square test, the *T*-test, and the Mann-Whitney Test."[3] The court gave this analysis little weight because the expert admitted "that his statistical analysis of pay at hire does not account for any skill differences between individual clerical jobs, nor does it account for differences in skill or experience between individual employees which might affect pay at hire."[4]

Of interest here is the apparent simultaneous use of the chi-square test and *t* test. The data cannot be organized in a contingency table, since each member of the two groups is not being relegated to one of two statuses but is being assigned a score on a continuous variable (salary). Nor can the study be organized as a goodness-of-fit analysis, since the groups are being compared to each other rather than to an external standard. This situation thus seems inappropriate for the application of the chi-square test but clearly appropriate for use of the *t* test. The *t* test is discussed more fully in Sections 6.10 and 6.12.

C.   GOODNESS-OF-FIT ANALYSIS

This chapter has thus far focused on use of the chi-square test to make internal comparisons of the performance of two or more groups on such dichotomous variables as passing or failing a test or responding or not responding to a survey. In other contexts one may want to compare two or more groups with reference to some external standard. The chi-square test may be an appropriate method to test

§5.10   [1] 475 F. Supp 638 (E.D. La. 1979).
[2] Id. at 644.
[3] Id.
[4] Id.

the significance of observed differences or relationship between the groups, if the variable on which they are being compared follows a distribution that approximates the chi-square distribution. This type of analysis, termed a goodness-of-fit analysis, differs conceptually from a contingency table analysis. Rather than comparing the performances of two or more groups on a dichotomous variable to each other, the goodness-of-fit analysis compares the numbers of members of two or more groups who fall into a certain status (e.g., the numbers of men and women in a randomly selected sample) to an external standard (e.g., the population from which the sample was drawn). Thus, the expected values used in the analysis are not derived from averaging the observed results that are recorded in the table. Instead, a judgment is made that a particular external data set is representative of the conditions one would expect to find if chance were the sole determinant of the distribution of the groups. As will be seen, because of this judgmental factor the selection of expected values is an important source of error in goodness-of-fit analyses.

The sections that follow present several examples of the use and misuse of the chi-square test in the goodness-of-fit context. Section 5.11 reviews the process of assessing and organizing data prior to performing a chi-square test. Section 5.12 deals with the derivation of expected numbers for use in the analysis, while Section 5.13 explains how the number of degrees of freedom is determined in a goodness-of-fit analysis. Section 5.14 suggests a partial solution to the problem of inadequate sample size, and Section 5.15 gives a brief overview of available alternatives to the chi-square test.

§5.11 Assessment and Organization of Data for Goodness-of-Fit Analysis

As with contingency table analyses, the first steps in conducting a goodness-of-fit analysis must be (1) the assessment of the data to determine whether use of the chi-square test is appropriate, and (2) the organization of the data in preparation for the application of the test. Consider the use of the chi-square test in the following case.

Chinese for Affirmative Action v. FCC:[1] Citizens' groups promoting better employment opportunities for Chinese-Americans appealed from orders of the FCC that renewed the licenses of several broadcast-

§5.11 [1] 595 F.2d 621 (D.C. Cir. 1978).

ers. The court considered allegations of discrimination against Asian-Americans but concluded that the Commission had properly rejected such claims because the broadcasters had employed substantial numbers of them during the prior term of the license, had reasonable representation of minorities in general, and had conducted an affirmative action program.

In a lengthy dissent, Judge Spottswood Robinson commented on "statistical disparities that naturally give rise to an inference of purposeful racial bias."[2] Of interest here is evidence that there were only ten Asian-Americans among the 249 people employed at one licensee station for various lengths of time during the prior term of the license. According to the plaintiffs, 6.9% of the labor force in the relevant Standard Metropolitan Statistical Area (SMSA) consisted of Asian-Americans. Thus, they argued, one could have expected that 6.9%, or 17 of the 249 employees, would be Asian-American. On the basis of a chi-square test, the plaintiffs concluded that there was only a 1-in-27 probability that so great a disparity between observed and expected representation would have occurred solely by chance.[3] Judge Robinson was persuaded that this analysis "generated an inference of calculated employment discrimination."[4]

The data reported by Judge Robinson are suitable for a two-category goodness-of-fit analysis. The object of the analysis is to compare the observed numbers of two categories of people (Asian-Americans and non-Asian-Americans) in the licensee's workforce with the numbers we might have expected on the basis of chance alone. As always, the pertinent question is whether the observed numbers deviate significantly from the expected numbers.

Had chance been the only factor influencing the station's 249 hiring decisions (there were 249 employees in the sample, each of whom represented the outcome of a hiring decision), and had each decision been independent of the others, the hiring decisions would have resembled a series of coin tosses in which the coin was weighted according to the availability of candidates from the two ethnic groups. Over the course of a large number of decisions, the ethnic composition of the workforce should have come to resemble the composition of the pool of available candidates. Under such circumstances, the variable of interest will follow a binomial distribution. Given an ade-

[2] Id. at 636.
[3] Id. at 648-649.
[4] Id. at 648.

EXHIBIT 5.11(a)
Jury Venire Pools

	1	2	3	4	5	6	7	8	9	10		Voter List %
Anglos	28	19	20	20	29	15	20	63	31	21	226	30
Blacks	8	10	9	8	6	10	7	9	6	8	81	20
Chicanos	7	9	11	12	7	10	9	9	5	8	87	20
Orientals	4	7	5	8	3	10	6	6	5	7	61	20
Other	3	5	5	2	5	5	8	3	3	6	45	10
	50	50	50	50	50	50	50	50	50	50		

quate sample size, however, the chi-square test will yield a p-value that reasonably approximates the true p-value.

A chi-square goodness-of-fit analysis can also be used when more than two categories are being compared. The method employed is identical to that used in the two-category situation. In both instances the data must be assessed and organized and an appropriate comparative population must be selected. Consider the use of the chi-square test to compare multiple categories in the following example.

> *Jury Selection:* Assume that in a certain jurisdiction, the law requires that jury veniremen be selected at random from the voter list. The area from which the jurors are drawn contains substantial numbers of Anglos, blacks, Chicanos, and Orientals, and a small number of people belonging to other ethnic groups. A prospective client comes to you complaining of ethnic discrimination in the calling of jury veniremen. She presents the data summarized in Exhibit 5.11(a). This Exhibit reflects the percentage representation of the various ethnic groups on the voter list from which jurors are drawn and the actual representation of these groups in the 10 jury pools that have been summoned in the last year. She asks whether these data will provide statistical support for a finding of discrimination.

The statistical question that must be answered is whether the observed distribution of jurors among the various racial categories differs significantly from that which might have been expected on the basis of chance alone. As illustrated in Exhibit 5.11(a), the jurors are

229

divided among five racial categories. In the absence of any sort of bias, one would expect the representation of each of the ethnic groups in the ten jury pools to approximate their representation in the voter list population. Each selection of a juror from the voter list is theoretically independent of every other choice.[5] The analogy here is to rolling a die: each roll is independent of the others, and each roll may yield one of several results (to make the analogy more accurate, assume that the die is weighted to reflect the relative representation of the various ethnic groups in the voter list population). Under these circumstances, the variables being studied (the representation of the various ethnic groups in the jury pools) are said to be *multinomially distributed.* In a multiple goodness-of-fit context such as this, the chi-square test will yield a *p*-value that will be a reasonable approximation of the true probability that the difference between the observed and expected ethnic distributions would have occurred by chance.

Finally, note that the *p*-value that the chi-square test will yield will be an overall *p*-value. That is, it will reflect the probability that the overall discrepancy between the observed and expected distributions of ethnic groups would have occurred as a matter of chance. The chi-square test will not permit the analyst to draw any conclusions about whether the *p*-value is attributable to over- or underrepresentation of any particular ethnic groups, but it should be possible to make commonsense inferences about the source of a statistically significant discrepancy by a re-examination of the raw data. In the jury selection case, for example, our attention would focus immediately on the relative underrepresentation of Orientals in comparison to the lesser underrepresentation of Chicanos and blacks.

§5.12 Expected Numbers for Goodness-of-Fit Analysis

The object of a goodness-of-fit analysis is to compare the observed distribution of some phenomenon to an expected distribution that is based on an external standard. Therefore, once the observed

---

[5] This is true as long as the population from which the choices are being made is very large, with many members of each of the ethnic groups. With a smaller population, as more and more choices are made, we may start to run short of members of some of the groups. As the supply becomes exhausted in this fashion, a particular choice may influence subsequent choices.

data have been collected and organized, the next steps are to decide on the appropriate external standard and to use it to calculate the expected numbers or values to which the observed values will be compared. The steps are the same regardless of how many categories are being compared. The employment discrimination case discussed in the preceding section will illustrate them.

> **Chinese for Affirmative Action v. FCC:**[1] A Chinese-American citizens' group challenged the renewal of several broadcast licenses, in part on the ground that some of the broadcasters had engaged in employment discrimination against Asian-Americans. One of the stations had employed 249 people during the term of its prior license, only ten of whom had been Asian-American. The plaintiffs pointed out that in the Standard Metropolitan Statistical Area (SMSA) in which the broadcaster was located, 6.9% of the labor force was Asian-American. On this basis, they argued, one would have expected 6.9%, or 17 of the 249 employees to have been Asian-American. Using a chi-square test, they concluded that there was only a 1-in-27 chance that so great a disparity between observed and expected representation of Asian-Americans would have occurred as a matter of chance (that is, if the 249 employees had been selected at random from a large pool that was 6.9% Asian-American).

The organization of the data in *Chinese for Affirmative Action* for use in a chi-square goodness-of-fit analysis was discussed in the preceding section and is relatively straightforward. The calculation of expected values, however, required the plantiffs to make judgments on both statistical and practical levels. In calculating their expected values, the plaintiffs apparently chose as the relevant external standard the entire population of the SMSA in which the licensee station was located. They concluded that in the absence of bias the ethnic makeup of the employer's workforce should have approximated that of the entire population of the surrounding community. They therefore took the Asian-American representation in that population (6.9%) as the expected representation in the station's workforce.

In preparing the data for application of the chi-square test, we can express the observed and expected values as either raw numbers or percentages, but raw numbers are preferable because percentages sometimes require the application of a correction factor. In Exhibit 5.12(a) all values are expressed in raw numbers. Expected values have

§5.12   [1] 595 F.2d 621 (D.C. Cir. 1978).

EXHIBIT 5.12(a)
Table for Goodness-of-Fit Analysis
Chinese for Affirmative Action **Example**

	Asian-American	Non-Asian-American	
Observed	10	239	249
Expected	17	232	249

been calculated by multiplying the total number of station employees by .069 and .931, the expected percentages for the two ethnic groups.

As a mechanical proposition, the calculation and entry of expected values is simple. The difficulty lies in making the judgments that precede the mechanics. In *Chinese for Affirmative Action*, the judgment was made that the representation of two ethnic groups in the total population was a reasonable basis for forming expectations about representation in a particular workforce. This judgment is suspect in several respects. First, as the majority opinion noted,[2] we might dispute the definition of the geographic area from which the station drew its employees. Second, since the plaintiffs based their comparison on the total population rather than the workforce within the SMSA, they implicitly assumed that members of the two ethnic groups were more or less equivalent in their willingness and ability to work. This may well have been the case, but it seems unreasonable simply to have assumed that the two groups had comparable percentages of people too young to work, people too old to work, and people disabled from working.

Most significantly, the use of population data as the measure of availability in an employment case reflects the assumption that there are no systematic differences between the two groups with respect to job qualifications legitimately imposed by the employer. In the case of a broadcaster, it is likely that many positions would legitimately require certain levels of education, training, or experience. The plaintiffs can therefore be criticized for having made an unsubstantiated assumption that the members of the two ethnic groups were comparably situated with respect to such requirements.

In *Chinese for Affirmative Action* a strong argument could have been made for more sophisticated computation of expected values.

[2] Id. at 625 n. 7.

First, an analysis could have been done of minimum qualifications for jobs at the station. The jobs at the station might have been grouped on the basis of qualifications. Next, using census reports, the plaintiffs might have identified job grouping within the SMSA[3] that reflected minimum qualifications similar to those legitimately imposed by the station. Comparisons could then have been made between the ethnic makeup of the station's workforce or its constituent job groups and the ethnic distribution of workers in the SMSA job groupings that had been identified as relevant.

The logic or illogic of deriving expected values from a particular population is relevant to the question of how much practical significance should be attached to the chi-square findings. Judge Robinson's dissent in *Chinese for Affirmative Action* presents an example of a set of expected values that are highly suspect. The general question of how expected values are to be derived must be addressed in every goodness-of-fit analysis, however. To avoid the criticisms suggested in the preceding paragraphs, the proponent of a goodness-of-fit analysis must scrutinize the choices being made from a practical as well as a statistical perspective. The issue of expected numbers and their practical significance is discussed further in Section 5.17.

§5.13 Degrees of Freedom for Goodness-of-Fit Analysis

As was the case with contingency table analyses (Section 5.6), it is also necessary in a goodness-of-fit analysis to know the number of degrees of freedom before a p-value can be calculated. In most goodness-of-fit analyses the number of degrees of freedom equals the number of categories being compared, less one. Accordingly, in a two-category goodness-of-fit analysis such as that in *Chinese for Affirmative Action*, there will be one degree of freedom. In an analysis in which five categories are compared (such as the *Jury Selection* example in Section 5.11), there will usually be four degrees of freedom.[1]

---

[3] The Census Bureau prepares reports for each SMSA that break down the total workforce both by ethnic group and by occupational classifications (e.g., office and clerical, technical, sales, etc.). Using these reports, it is often possible to determine how many members of a certain ethnic group are employed within the SMSA in a particular type of job.

§5.13 [1] There are some complex situations in which the number of degrees of feedom will not equal the number of categories less one. For a discussion of these situations, see G. Snedecor & W. Cochran, Statistical Methods 75-77 (5th ed. 1980).

§5.14   Small Numbers: Combining Categories for Goodness-of-Fit Analysis

In both types of chi-square analyses, the general rule is that each expected value should be 5 or greater. When one or more of these is less than five in a two-category analysis, the Yates Correction can sometimes be made so that the chi-square test can still be applied (see Section 5.7). In a multiple category analysis of either type, two or more small categories may be combined so that all remaining categories will have expected values of at least five. Section 5.8 demonstrated this process in the contingency table context. The process is the same in a goodness-of-fit analysis. Two or more categories (usually the smallest) are combined until all expected values are at least five. The number of degrees of freedom is reduced by one for each category that is eliminated. Combining categories is, of course, done at the expense of some explanatory power, since with each successive combination the analysis becomes less accurate as a model of the real world.

§5.15   Alternatives to Chi-Square for Goodness-of-Fit Analysis

This section discusses alternatives to the chi-square test in the goodness-of-fit context. Section 5.15.1 illustrates the use of the Z test as an alternative to chi-square in two-category analyses. Section 5.15.2 deals with the more complex problem of finding a manageable alternative to chi-square in a multiple category situation.

§5.15.1   The Z Test Alternative

In *Chinese for Affirmative Action*, the distribution of the variable of interest (representation of the two ethnic groups in the workforce) was binomial. The chi-square test was employed as an acceptable substitute for the more complex binomial calculation because the sample size was adequate; that is, each expected value was greater than or equal to five. It was noted in Section 5.9.2 in connection with two-by-two contingency table analyses that a binomially distributed variable can be tested using a Z test with the same degree of approximation as is inherent in a chi-square test. This statement is equally true in the context of a two-category goodness-of-fit analysis. Accordingly, whenever two categories are being compared, whether in a goodness-of-fit or a contingency table context, the Z test is largely interchangeable with the chi-square test. The conditions that permit one to be substituted for the technically correct binomial test (principally, a sufficiently large sample) also permit the substitution of the other. As noted, the Z test is often somewhat more informative than the chi-square test, in that it permits the determination of the direction in which a significant effect lies, while the chi-square test does not. In *Chinese for Affirmative Action*, as in most cases, however, we would only have to look back at the raw data to determine whether a significant finding had been caused by an over- or underrepresentation of the protected category.

§5.15.2 Alternatives in Multiple Category Cases

In a multiple category goodness-of-fit analysis, as in a multiple contingency table analysis, there is no single test that is clearly preferable to chi-square. Use of the t test is inappropriate, since multiple categories are being compared simultaneously to an external standard (see Section 5.10; compare Section 6.7, where a sample mean is compared to an external standard). Another possible alternative, the Z test, is inappropriate where multiple categories are being compared (see Section 5.9.2). If the question is whether the overall distribution of observed values differs from the expected distribution, chi-square is likely to be the preferred alternative, but when we are interested not merely in whether there is a significant difference between two distributions but in the source of that difference, other tests may be appropriate. Consider the following example.

Age Discrimination in Hiring: An employer has been accused of discriminating against middle-aged people by refusing to hire otherwise qualified applicants who are 36 to 50 years old. The plaintiff's theory is that the employer is willing to hire young workers because they do not command high salaries and older workers because they tend to be more loyal and thus more stable, but is reluctant to hire middle-aged people because they command high salaries but are far more mobile than their older counterparts.

One way to investigate the plaintiff's allegations statistically might be to group all the people that the defendant has hired during the relevant time period into three categories: those aged 20 to 36, those aged 36 to 50, and those older than 51. The results would be the observed distribution by age group of people hired. For purposes of comparison, one might consider all the people in the area accessible to

235

the defendant's place of business who had the relevant job qualifications. By breaking this population down into the same three age
groups, computing percentages, and then applying these percentages
to the total number of people hired by the defendant, it would be
possible to calculate expected values for each of the three age groups.

Application of the chi-square test would determine whether the
discrepancy between the observed and the expected distributions was
statistically significant. If a significant difference were found, however, chi-square would reveal little about the source of the difference;
it would yield the same result regardless of whether the discrepancy
was in the form of a large under- or overrepresentation of the middle-aged group, or a comparably large over- or underrepresentation
of either of the other age groups. Chi-square tells us nothing more
than whether the two distributions somehow differ by an amount too
great to be reasonably attributable to chance alone.[1]

D. PRESENTING AND ATTACKING EVIDENCE BASED ON CHI-SQUARE ANALYSIS

General strategic considerations relevant to the presentation of statistical evidence are the subject of Chapter 9. It should be consulted in
preparing to present the results of any of the statistical analyses discussed in this book. The general theme of Chapter 9 is that the trier
of fact should be presented not with an occult science but with a
logical and comprehensible method of reasoning and analysis. This
overall goal dictates three special considerations in the presentation of
chi-square results that are enumerated and discussed in Section 5.16.
Points of particular relevance to attacking evidence based on a chi-
square analysis are discussed in Section 5.17.

§5.16   Presenting Chi-Square Results

First, it must be emphasized that the purpose of a chi-square
analysis is to observe the actual distribution of some variable, to posit

---

§5.15 [1] In the example just discussed, the Kolgomorov-Shmirnov test is a possible
alternative to chi-square for the analyst who requires more refined information. See K.
Bury, Statistical Models in Applied Science 204-208 (1975); R. Pfaffenberger & J.
Patterson, Statistical Methods for Business and Economics 674-680 (1981).

the expected distribution of the variable, to compare the observed and expected distributions, and then to assess the likelihood that a difference between the two as large as the one that actually occurred would have occurred as a matter of chance. This analytical process is straightforward and, the authors submit, readily explicable to an intelligent lay person. Most reported cases (see, for example, those discussed in this chapter) and all too many statistics texts, however, treat the chi-square test as an arbitrary formula that somehow determines whether the numbers it is applied to would have been likely to occur as a matter of chance. The first recommendation is therefore that the nature and purpose of the chi-square analysis not be avoided but be explained in adequate detail; in this context the nuts and bolts of the machine are far less foreboding and thus more credible than its external appearance. See Section 9.1.

Second, the proponent of a goodness-of-fit analysis should devote considerable effort on direct examination to justifying the choice of expected values. For the reasons discussed in Sections 5.17.1 and 5.17.2, the choice of expected values is often the most vulnerable point in a goodness-of-fit analysis. Since the source of this vulnerability is not difficult to understand, it can be exploited by any reasonably skillful cross-examiner. See Section 9.7.3.

The third and final point could be made in any chapter of this book and cannot be overemphasized: the concept of statistical significance should be described in adequate detail and should not be used in ways that overstate its meaning. The often stated abstraction that one can somehow determine mathematically whether an observed discrepancy reflects a discrepancy in the "real world" is both difficult and incorrect. A reasonably detailed explanation of how a p-value is calculated and what it really means is not only more correct but more comprehensible and thus more credible (see Section 9.1). A technically accurate exposition of statistical significance should not only improve the chances that an analysis will be accepted by the trier of fact but should limit the vulnerability of its proponent to cross-examination.

§5.17   Attacking Chi-Square Analysis

Strategic factors to be taken into consideration when preparing to cross-examine a statistical expert are discussed at length in Section 9.7. In addition to these general considerations, when the subject of the testimony is a chi-square analysis, three aspects of the analysis should be investigated with particular care: the original determination to use the chi-square test, the choice of expected numbers, and the problems arising from small samples.

§5.17.1   The Decision to Use Chi-Square

As has been repeatedly emphasized, the chi-square test is appropriate in either of two contexts: contingency table or goodness-of-fit analysis. In the former, two or more groups are compared with respect to their performance on a variable that can have either of two values (e.g., hired or not hired, pass or fail). Expected values are calculated by averaging the values for all the groups. It is important that the groups are compared to each other and not to some external standard. In a goodness-of-fit analysis, by contrast, the numbers of members of two or more groups who fall into a particular status are compared to an external standard. The expected values are derived from observation of a larger, external population to which the groups being studied are presumed to be comparable. In either type of analysis, it is assumed that the events being observed and counted, such as hiring decisions, are truly separate and independent.

In spite of these relatively straightforward criteria for identifying situations appropriate for the chi-square test, the lawyer should be alert for its misapplication. Recall, for example, the *Booth* case,[1] discussed in Section 5.10, in which the expert may have erroneously performed a chi-square analysis of an internal comparison of the values for two groups on a continuous variable (salary). Another common error occurs in situations where the individual events being observed and counted are not truly independent. In another portion of the *Chinese for Affirmative Action*[2] case discussed in Section 5.11, the dissenting judge compared the number of "person-months," which are analogous to man-hours, worked by Asian-Americans and non-Asian-Americans at a radio station.[3] Even if the proper external standard could be found, these would not be appropriate data for a chi-square analysis, since the allocation by the employer of individual person-months is not an independent decision made each month.

---

§5.17   [1] Booth v. Board of Directors of National American Bank, 475 F. Supp. 638 (E.D. La. 1979).

[2] 595 F.2d 621 (D.C. Cir. 1978).

[3] Id. at 649 n. 7. The dissenting judge presented the person-month data but did not indicate whether they were subjected to statistical analysis.

Rather, a decision is made to hire a person, and once such a decision is made, a large block of person-months will automatically go into the Asian-American or non-Asian-American category.

In summary, any lawyer facing a chi-square analysis should initially question the selection of that technique. In consultation with his or her own expert, the lawyer should determine whether the proposed analysis fits into one of the two contexts in which the chi-square test is appropriate. If there does seem to be an appropriate fit, the lawyer should then ask whether each of the criteria for the two contexts discussed in this chapter have been satisfied.

§5.17.2 Expected Numbers

The difficulties encountered in calculating expected numbers have already been discussed in connection with both contingency table and goodness-of-fit analyses (Sections 5.5 and 5.12). In either situation the lawyer preparing for cross-examination should investigate whether the expert has followed the proper procedures for calculating expected numbers. In particular, in a contingency table analysis, the expected values must be derived from an average of all the observations that are entered on the table. When, for example, one is comparing pass rates on a test for two racial groups, as was done in *Chance v. Board of Examiners*[4] (see Section 5.5), the expected figures must be derived from the average pass rate for all those who took the examination rather than from pass rates in another city or from some other external standard. Conversely, in a goodness-of-fit analysis, the expected numbers must be derived from observation of an external population.

In confronting a goodness-of-fit analysis, the lawyer should always look carefully at the external standard that the opposing expert has chosen. As discussed in Section 5.12, when one is comparing the representation of racial groups in a particular job category, the proper external standard is probably not all adults living in the area surrounding the employer's facility, but rather all adults living in the area who have the qualifications that the employer may fairly require. Similarly, in comparing the numbers of blacks and whites who have been selected by a particular judge to serve as grand jury foreperson, the relevant standard is not all adults living within the judicial district

---

[4]330 F. Supp. 203 (S.D.N.Y. 1971), *aff'd*, 458 F.2d 1167 (2d Cir. 1972).

but all adults likely to possess the qualifications the judge may legitimately impose in choosing forepersons.[5] Since the selection of an external standard always involves an element of subjectivity on the part of the statistician, this choice should be given careful scrutiny in the preparation of an effective cross-examination.

§5.17.3 Small Numbers

Statistically significant findings based on small samples are almost invariably vulnerable to effective cross-examination. Even if the p-value is quite low, if the sample size is small the expert may have to admit that a change in just a few observations could push the p-value out of the range of significance. Such situations are not uncommon with chi-square, because the test permits analysis of relatively small samples (expected values need only equal or exceed five) and accepted methods have been developed for dealing with even smaller samples (e.g., the Yates Correction and the combination of categories with small expected values). In preparing for and conducting cross-examination, the lawyer should therefore be alert for overly ambitious claims based on findings that could be undercut by a minor change in the observed results.

E. CALCULATIONS RELATED TO CHI-SQUARE ANALYSIS

The final sections of this chapter present the calculations necessary to perform the analyses that have been discussed. The following notation is used in formulas in Part E. The numbers in parentheses following each definition indicate the section where the notation is first introduced.

---

[5] See United States v. Breland, 522 F. Supp. 468 (N.D. Ga. 1981). In *Breland* the plaintiffs presented a chi-square analysis that showed a statistically significant disparity ($p = .02$) between black representation on grand juries and black representation in the adult population of the judicial district. The court rejected the analysis, in part because "grand jury forepersons are not in fact selected randomly." Id. at 470 n. 9.

χ^2 — the chi-square value (5.18)
E_j — the expected value for the jth observation (5.18)
O_j — the observed value of the jth observation (5.18)

The calculations involved in performing the chi-square test are relatively simple, and the same formula is used in both contingency table and goodness-of-fit analyses. The formula employed is not affected by the number of categories being compared. Section 5.18 presents and explains the general chi-square formula and the use of the chi-square table to derive p-values. Section 5.19 illustrates its application in a contingency table analysis. Section 5.20 discusses the use of the Yates Correction in a two-by-two contingency table analysis and the combination of small categories in a multiple category analysis. Section 5.21 demonstrates the use of the chi-square formula in a goodness-of-fit analysis.

§5.18   The Chi-Square Formula

The chi-square formula is found in Equation 5.18(a).[1]

$$\chi^2 = \sum \frac{(O_j - E_j)^2}{E_j}$$

5.18(a)

The Greek symbol on the left side of the equation is the mathematical symbol for chi-square. Its presence means that the number that the formula yields is termed the *chi-square value,* sometimes referred to as the *calculated* chi-square value. To calculate the chi-square value, the following steps must be taken:

1. $(O_j - E_j)^2$: For each category being compared, the expected value is subtracted from the observed value. The resulting number is then squared, or multiplied by itself.
2. $(O_j - E_j)^2/E_j$: For each category being compared, the result of step 1 must then be divided by the observed value for that particular category.

§5.18   [1] See W. Mendenhall, Introduction to Probability and Statistics, 373-374 (5th ed. 1979).

3. $\Sigma((O_j - E_j)^2/E_j)$: After steps 1 and 2 have been performed for each category, all the results must be added.

Translated into prose, the chi-square formula reads as follows: for each category being compared, subtract the expected from the observed value, multiply that number by itself, and then divide the result by the expected value; when this process has been carried out for each category, add the results, and the sum is the calculated chi-square value. Once the chi-square value has been calculated, refer to a Chi-Square Table like that reproduced in the Appendix of Tables at the end of this book. The table contains a number of *critical values* for chi-square, which will yield certain *p*-values given particular numbers of degrees of freedom. Look, for example, at the top row, which lists the chi-square values associated with certain *p*-values in situations in which there is one degree of freedom (such as two-by-two contingency table analyses): if the analysis produces a chi-square value of 2.706, it can be seen from the table that the *p*-value is .10.

If the analysis yields a calculated chi-square value that happens to correspond to one of the critical values, the *p*-value can be read directly off the table. If the calculated chi-square value falls between two of the critical values, there are two alternative ways to derive the associated *p*-value. In most situations, it will be enough to be able to say that the *p*-value is less than a particular round number. To say, for example, that the *p*-value is less than .05 is to say that a difference as large as the one observed would have occurred as a matter of chance less than one time in 20. If this degree of accuracy is acceptable (as it will be in many legal and social science applications), then one need only find the two critical values between which the actual chi-square value falls and select the higher of the two associated *p*-values. If, for example, the calculated chi-square value is 4.102 and there is one degree of freedom, it can be said that the *p*-value is less than .05.

In those situations where a precise *p*-value is needed, it can be derived through the process of *interpolation*, which is also described in Section 4.28. In general terms, it means finding the relative distance of the calculated chi-square value from each of the critical values between which it lies and then finding the *p*-value that is comparably located between each of the *p*-values associated with those critical values. To illustrate, assume that an analysis with one degree of freedom yields a calculated chi-square of 3.2735. This is halfway between the two critical values of 2.706 and 3.841. Consequently, the *p*-value for this calculated chi-square value will be approximately .075, which

EXHIBIT 5.19(a)
Data for Chi-Square Analysis
Certified Color **Example**

	Cancer	No Cancer
High Dosage	7 (4.8)	16 (18.2)
Low Dosage	4 (6.2)	26 (23.8)

is halfway between the p-values (.10 and .05) associated with the surrounding critical chi-square values.[2]

§5.19 Contingency Table Analysis — Calculations

The following example illustrates the calculation of the chi-square statistic and the determination of the p-value in a two-by-two contingency analysis.

Certified Color Manufacturers' Association v. Mathews:[1] This case, which was discussed in Section 5.5, involved a comparison of cancer rates in rats given high doses of Red Dye No. 2 and those given low doses. The two categories of rats were evaluated with respect to a discrete variable, the presence or absence of cancer. The data are reproduced in Exhibit 5.19(a).

The expected values for each cell in the table were also calculated in Section 5.5. Recall that out of the 53 rats studied, 11 got cancer, yielding an overall cancer rate of slightly less than 21%. If one assumes that dosage and cancer rates are not correlated (the null hypothesis), then every rat, regardless of dosage, should have slightly less than a 21% chance of getting cancer and slightly more than a 79% chance of remaining cancer-free. Multiplying the number of rats in each of the two categories (high dosage and low dosage) by these percentages yields the expected values in each category for rats with cancer and rats without cancer that have been entered in Exhibit 5.19(a).

[2] Similarly, a calculated chi-square value one-third (or, in general, $x\%$) of the way between the lower and higher critical value will have an estimated p-value one-third (or, in general, $x\%$) of the way between the high and low p-values shown.
§5.19 [1] 543 F.2d 284 (D.C. Cir. 1976).

The application of the chi-square formula to these values is demonstrated in Exhibit 5.19(b) without using any correction for the fact that one of the expected values (that for high dosage rats with cancer) is less than five. The formula yields a value for chi-square of 2.26. Since two categories are being compared, there is one degree of freedom. Reading across the top row of the chi-square table, we can see that a chi-square value of 2.26 falls between $p = .10$ and $p = .20$. This means that there is a 10 to 20% probability that a difference between the observed and expected distributions as large as the one discovered would occur purely as a matter of chance. Given that one of the expected values was barely less than five, this result is somewhat suspect. The application of the Yates Correction to this problem is illustrated in Section 5.20.

EXHIBIT 5.19(b)
Calculation of Chi-Square Value
Certified Color **Example**

	Step	*High Dosage with Cancer*	*High Dosage without Cancer*	*Low Dosage with Cancer*	*Low Dosage without Cancer*
	O_j (Observed)	7	16	4	26
	E_j (Expected)	4.8	18.2	6.2	23.8
(1)	$(O_j - E_j)$	2.2	−2.2	−2.2	2.2
(2)	$(O_j - E_j)^2$	4.84	4.84	4.84	4.84
(3)	$(O_j - E_j)^2/E_j$	1.01	0.27	0.78	0.20
(4)	$\Sigma[(O_j - E_j)^2/E_j] = 2.26 = \chi^2$				

The calculation of chi-square is identical regardless of whether two categories or multiple categories are being compared. Once the data have been organized, we simply apply Equation 5.18(a), the basic chi-square formula, remembering to perform the calculation of $(O_j - E_j)^2/E_j$ for each category. The number of degrees of freedom will usually equal the total number of categories being compared less one.

§5.20   *Small Number Corrections — Calculations*

When any of the expected values is less than five, the decision to use the chi-square test is suspect. It was noted in Sections 5.7 and 5.14

that under some circumstances the Yates Correction may improve the results when one or more of the expected values in a two-category analysis is less than five. Use of the Yates Correction involves substituting a modified chi-square formula for the basic formula that is set forth in Equation 5.19(a). The Yates Correction formula is shown in Equation 5.20(a).[1]

$$\text{Yates corrected } \chi^2 = \sum \frac{(|O_j - E_j| - 1/2)^2}{E_j}$$

5.20(a)

In applying the basic chi-square formula, we subtract the expected value from the observed value in each cell, square this number, and then divide the result by the expected value; the results of each of these individual calculations are then totaled to yield the calculated chi-square value. Using the Yates variant, we again subtract the expected value from the observed value in each cell. Next, however, the vertical lines on either side of "$O_j - E_j$" direct that the result be converted into an absolute value. This means simply that if subtracting the expected from the observed value yields a negative number, the minus sign is ignored. When the absolute value has been determined, subtract 1/2 from it, square the result, and then divide this result by the expected value. Perform this calculation for each of the categories being compared and add the results to obtain the Yates-corrected chi-square value. Reference can then be made to the chi-square table in the same fashion as when the basic formula is used.

It should be re-emphasized that statisticians are not in agreement on the precise conditions under which the Yates Correction should be used. As a practical matter, however, it does seem to improve the accuracy of the chi-square analysis under certain conditions involving small samples. Nonetheless, a beginning statistician should be cautious in using it.

The calculation of the chi-square value using the Yates Correction is shown in Exhibit 5.20(a) as applied to the data from *Certified Color*, discussed in Section 5.19. The resulting chi-square value of 1.35 is associated with a *p*-value between .30 and .20.

Remember that the Yates Correction is available only for two-category analyses; it is inappropriate for a multiple analysis. In both types of multiple analyses it is possible, however, to combine the small

§5.20 [1] See 2 M. Kendall & A. Stuart, The Advanced Theory of Statistics 586 (4th ed. 1979).

EXHIBIT 5.20(a)
Yates Correction Applied to Small Numbers
Certified Color **Example**

Step	High Dosage with Cancer	High Dosage without Cancer	Low Dosage with Cancer	Low Dosage without Cancer
O_j (Observed)	7	16	4	26
E_j (Expected)	4.8	18.2	6.2	23.8
(1) $(O_j - E_j)$	2.2	−2.2	−2.2	2.2
(2) $\|O_j - E_j\| - 1/2$	1.7	−1.7	−1.7	1.7
(3) $(\|O_j - E_j\| - 1/2)^2$	2.89	2.89	2.89	2.89
(4) $(\|O_j - E_j\| - 1/2)^2/E_j$	0.60	0.16	0.47	0.12

(5) $\Sigma(\|O_j - E_j\| - 1/2)^2/E_j = 1.35 = \chi^2$

categories where one or more of the expected values is less than five. It should be done in the manner already described in Section 5.8. The combining is done before the chi-square formula is applied, and the new, combined category is treated in the same manner as all the original categories.

§5.21   Goodness-of-Fit Analysis — Calculations

The calculation of the chi-square value in a goodness-of-fit analysis is identical to that in the contingency table analysis; the difference between the analyses lies in the organization of the data and the selection of expected values. Accordingly, the steps here are the same as those described in the preceding section: for each category, subtract the expected number from the observed number, square the difference, and divide the result by the expected number; then add these individual values to obtain the chi-square value. The calculation of the chi-square for the *Chinese for Affirmative Action* data (presented in Exhibit 5.12) is illustrated in Exhibit 5.21(a). The process is identical in a multiple category analysis. In all cases, once a chi-square value has been calculated, a *p*-value can be derived from the table in the manner described in Section 5.18. In most cases, the number of degrees of freedom will equal the number of categories being compared less one.

EXHIBIT 5.21(a)
Calculation of Chi-Square Value
Chinese for Affirmative Action **Example**

	$j = Asian$ American	$j = Non\text{-}Asian$ American
O_j (Observed)	10	239
E_j (Expected)	17	232
(1) $O_j - E_j$	-7	7
(2) $(O_j - E_j)^2$	49	49
(3) $(O_j - E_j)^2/E_j$	2.88	0.21

(4) $\Sigma[(O_j - E_j)^2/E_j] = 3.09 = \chi^2$

CHAPTER SIX

Collecting and Analyzing Sample Data

§6.0   Introduction

When the data needed to present or support a statistical argument are too voluminous to assemble or analyze in their entirety, it is often possible to study only a sample of them and still obtain reliable conclusions. Care must be taken to ensure that the sample is representative of the whole body of data; the method by which the sample is selected is a critical link in the chain of analysis. With a properly drawn sample one can usually estimate precisely the mean or standard deviation of the population or the proportion of the items in the population that possess particular characteristics.

This chapter describes techniques for sampling, methods by which one accounts for the inherent imprecision of sample estimates, grounds for attacking an opponent's evidence derived from a sample, and applications of sampling techniques. The materials cover a wide variety of legal contexts, including reported cases as well as the selection of jurors in voir dire.

§6.1   Samples, Populations, and Statistical Inference

A *population*, for present purposes, is the most complete set of entities to be considered in the course of a study. It is not an absolute construct since a group constituting the population for one study may be but a sample from a much larger population for another study. For example, the people at your home last evening could constitute a population if they are the only people with which the study is concerned. Unless you had out-of-town guests, they were also a sample of the people who live in your town, presumably a much larger group of people who also could be considered a population.

For some small populations, such as the people in your home last night, it is possible to determine in a straightforward fashion the mean and standard deviation of qualities such as their ages, the sizes of their immediate families, and so forth. This is done by noting the relevant particulars of each member and then performing the appropriate calculations. For large populations, such as the people in your state, it may be almost impossible, not to mention prohibitively expensive, to determine exactly the mean and standard deviation of such qualities, given the great numbers of people involved, and their mobility and mortality.[1] To determine a mean, a standard deviation, or some other such quality of a population too large or amorphous to tally exactly, one usually must rely on information contained in a sample from that population. If one is interested, for instance, in the rate at which members of a particular racial group pass a job qualification examination, the population is the entire group of past, present, and future members of that racial grouping. Not only have some of these people never taken the exam, some died hundreds of years before the exam was designed, and many have not yet been born. The best one can do is to estimate this population's pass rate by examining the pass rate of a sample of people who did take the exam.

A population need not be composed of a finite number of elements, nor need the elements be distinct or individual parts. The air in a town's manufacturing district over a week's time may be regarded as a continuous population about which one would like to know the concentration of sulfur dioxide per cubic centimeter. The use of a sample to estimate the population mean concentration is perhaps

---

§6.1 [1] For populations both large and small, the determination of means and standard deviations may be hindered further by the lack of accuracy with which the characteristics of each population member can be measured. While an individual's age and family size are generally unambiguous integers, a person's height and weight vary on a continuous scale and may be reported with a degree of accuracy that depends on the person taking the measurements and on whether the measurement units are pounds or kilograms, inches or centimeters. Section 6.19 discusses the general problems of inaccuracy arising from the collection of data.

mandatory in this case, given the difficulty of obtaining measurements throughout an entire volume of space. If one wishes to know the number of defective fuses in a shipment, the population is the shipment of fuses. If the only way of detecting that a fuse is faulty is by measuring the amount of current that causes it to fail, thereby destroying it, there is an added incentive to use a sample as a basis for estimating a population characteristic.

From measurements of entire populations one obtains precise descriptions of characteristics of the population. From samples one can only approximate that description. Statistical inference involves calculation of probable population qualities based on qualities found in a sample. One might find, for instance, that the pass rate for a sample of minority group members taking an exam was different from that for a sample of nonminority group members. Had all people been tested, one would know for sure whether minorities in the population have a different pass rate from nonminorities. Based on the sample, one can infer a probable range for the population pass rate difference and also calculate the probability (called a p-value) that a pass rate disparity as large as that in the sample would occur if the sample were picked at random from a population in which the pass rates were the same for minorities and nonminorities.

In many legal applications the past performance of a party is viewed as a sample of all outcomes that might have been due to the party's behavior: an employer's past hiring decisions, for instance, might have been dependent on a variety of factors in addition to potentially discriminatory practices. Had the applicants, just by chance, had different skills, or had the skills been distributed differently between men and women, or between minority and nonminority applicants, a different set of hiring decisions might have resulted even with the same underlying practices. A different group of employees from the one actually observed might have resulted had the applicant group been different. Rather than test the employer's practices against all possible applicants, a formidable task since it may not be possible to identify them, we test the practices as applied to a sample, which is made up of those who actually applied. We then examine the effect of the employer's practices on them. Treating past performance as a sample allows us to consider the role of chance in creating the set of hiring decisions that occurred and to separate the influence of random factors such as the composition of the applicant group from the influence of the employer's hiring policy.

This approach to sampling occurs in promotions cases as well. In

Presseisen v. Swarthmore College,[2] the average length of time until promotion for men and for women was treated as a sample mean. The men and women who had been promoted to date were but a sample of the types of people who might have been subject to consideration for promotion at the College during the past.

The use of measures of past performance as a sample on which to base inferences extends to other areas of law as well. In some cases past performance is considered to be representative of what is likely to occur in the future. Thus, in *Spray-Rite Service Corp. v. Monsanto Co.*[3] past sales by Spray-Rite in the market where Monsanto was alleged to have fixed resale prices were treated as a sample of both past and future performance to enable the court to project damages based on sales lost due to the anticompetitive practice.

A. TYPES OF SAMPLES

In designing samples, three goals are of primary importance: minimizing the cost of sampling, choosing a sample that reflects relevant characteristics of the population, and achieving a certain level of precision for the statistical results. A major influence on the precision of estimates is the size of the sample. Because determining sample size requires some knowledge of the statistical concepts to be discussed later in this chapter, the issue of appropriate sample size is deferred to Section 6.13. The current section describes alternative types of samples in sufficient detail to alert the lawyer to various data-gathering techniques and to develop an appreciation for both the complexity and cost of the sampling process. Our goal is to enable the lawyer to discuss sampling techniques with his or her own statistical expert or to depose or cross-examine an opponent's expert intelligently.

§6.2 Simple Random Samples

The *simple random sample* is constructed by drawing elements one at a time from the population in such a way that at each stage every

---

[2] 442 F. Supp. 593 (E.D. Pa. 1977), *aff'd*, 582 F.2d 1275 (3rd Cir. 1982).
[3] 684 F.2d 1226 (7th Cir. 1982), *aff'd*, 104 S. Ct. 1464 (1984).

item remaining in the population has an equal probability of being chosen next. The inferences that can be drawn from a sample depend critically on the method by which the sample is constructed. The analytical tools described in this chapter are used specifically for simple random samples and may be misleading when applied to samples obtained in some other fashion. Attempts to produce simple random samples abound in case law.

A.B.&G. Instrument and Engineering, Inc. v. United States:[1] The producer shipped by rail two lots of nose fuse adapters (an artillery shell component) to the Navy Parts Control Center in Pennsylvania, F.O.B. destination. The contracts "Inspection and Acceptance" provisions specified a random sampling of 315 units for inspection,[2] which meant that each adapter would have an equal probability of being inspected. During shipping the packages shifted, some boxes broke open, and adapters were strewn over the floor of the railroad car. Upon the shipment's arrival, government personnel shoveled the spilled adapters back into their boxes. The shippers alleged that the inspectors examined only those adapters that had spilled. Had that been true, the sample would not have been random because the probability of being selected for inspection would have been unequal between spilled and intact adapters. Instead, the government inspector randomly selected from the entire shipment of adapters.

Johnson v. White:[3] Welfare recipients under the Aid to Families with Dependent Children Program challenged the sampling process that the Commissioner of Welfare of the State of Connecticut used to support a proposed modification of the Connecticut Family Assistance Plan. The commissioner had randomly selected 3,979 families from the total of about 27,000 families to determine need levels and average monthly benefits received.[4] Each unit, whether large or small, containing one or two adults, composed entirely or only partially of eligible people, would have to have an equal probability of being represented in the sample in order for the sample to be a simple random sample.

Kroger Company:[5] The retail food chain advertised survey-based food price comparisons derived from a sampling of prices for its items

---

§6.2   [1] 593 F.2d 394 (Ct. Cl. 1979).
[2] Id. at 397.
[3] 353 F. Supp. 69 (D. Conn. 1972), *modified*, 528 F.2d 1228 (2d Cir. 1975).
[4] 353 F. Supp. at 74-75.
[5] 98 F.T.C. 639 (1981).

and those from competitors' stores. In order to be a simple random sample, each food item would have to have an equal probability of being selected; no food group, such as meat, could be systematically excluded or others, such as private label brands, systematically included.

There are several formal procedures for drawing simple random samples from a population. Some involve assigning numbers to each item in the population and then randomly drawing the numbers to indicate which items are to be examined. For a population with 700 items of which 55 are to be examined, each item might be assigned a number written on a slip of paper, the paper put in a hat and shaken well and 55 of them drawn out. It may be more convenient to refer to a table of random numbers made up of numerals chosen so that there is no systematic relationship between any sequence of numerals regardless of whether the table is read from right to left, left to right, top to bottom, bottom to top, or any other way. A random number table appears in the Appendix of Tables at the end of this book. To select 55 items from a population numbered 1 to 700, choose 55 sequential triples of numbers starting from anywhere in the table, skipping all triples between 701 and 999 and rejecting all repetitions of triples already chosen. The items from the population to be included will be those whose assigned numbers correspond to the 55 three-digit numbers from the table. Using the random number table in this book, the first three triples of numbers starting at the upper right corner of the table are 035, 282, and 807. Since there is no item numbered 807 in our population of 700 items, skip 807 and select the next triple, which is 197. Then continue on until 55 numbers have been selected. For a population size less than 100 and greater than ten items, use sequential two-digit numbers starting from anywhere in the table. Contrived procedures for drawing simple random samples such as using a random number table duplicate informal methods such as reaching into a hat to pick out a number or reaching into a box of parts to pick one for testing.

A *systematic sampling,* such as choosing to include in a sample every 100th person sitting in Yankee Stadium, is often viewed as a type of simple random sampling. Care must be taken, however, that the items chosen are representative of the rest of the population. If Yankee Stadium attendees are sampled to determine beer drinking habits and rows of seats are 25 or 50 seats long, every 100th person will have an aisle seat, perhaps chosen intentionally to be near the beer vendor or the exit. A sample composed in this way might not be representative of the population of attendees. In a systematic sample, the first unit drawn into the sample must be selected randomly and each successive unit is an evenly spaced interval from the previous unit. Just by chance the first and all additional items in a sample drawn according to this rule may still share a common characteristic. The sampling process must be examined in a commonsense way to assess whether bias may result.

> **ITT Continental Baking Co.:**[6] In order to compare the perceptions of TV viewers with those of non-TV viewers regarding the healthfulness of Wonder Bread, the expert for the FTC surveyed individuals whose names were obtained from telephone directories. This process might yield a biased sample if the ownership or nonownership of a telephone corresponds in any way to the views of individuals on the healthfulness of Wonder Bread.

The mathematical calculations associated with simple random samples are presented in the last section of this chapter. While other types of samples are discussed, calculations for various statistical conclusions to be drawn therefrom are omitted. The concepts and caveats that are discussed in all other sections of this chapter apply equally to all types of samples, however, as do all discussions of interpretations of sampling results and their applications in litigation.[7]

§6.3   Clustered Random Samples

When more information is available about the population from which the sample is to be drawn, a sampling technique other than simple random might be preferred in order to save time and expense or to get a more accurate estimate of population values. Additional information may be of two sorts: it may be known that items with different characteristics are evenly scattered throughout the whole population so that any subgroup of the population is likely to be representative of the whole or, alternatively, that certain proportions of the population possess characteristics that might be associated with

---

[6] 83 F.T.C. 865 (1973).

[7] A particularly useful reference for the formulas for analysis of samples that are not simple random samples is E. Clark & L. Schkade, Statistical Methods for Business Decisions, showing stratified samples at 354 and clustered samples at 361-362 (1969).

different properties that are of interest to the sampler. In the first case a *clustered random sample* might save money compared to a simple random sample; in the second a *stratified random sample* might give a more accurate estimate of population measurements (see Section 6.4).

A clustered sample is useful when it would be inconvenient or expensive to conduct a simple random sample of the entire population. Instead of selecting and examining items at random throughout the population, only items in one cluster are examined. A cluster may be made up of those items that are particularly accessible by being in close spatial proximity, for instance. A clustered sample is appropriate only when each cluster selected is thought to be representative of the characteristics of the population as a whole, such as when political pollsters base predicted election results on the outcome of a sample taken in what they think is a typical town. In a clustered sample the probability of a given item being chosen is not independent; it is dependent on whether other items in its cluster have been chosen.

In contract cases the method of sampling to comply with quality requirements for grain shipments is instructive. A hollow tube is inserted into a carload of grain, the bottom end of the tube is closed, and the tube is withdrawn. Before the tube is inserted, each kernel has an equal probability of being selected, but the probability of a given kernel being chosen depends on whether other kernels around it, within a tube's width, and above it and below it are selected. If there is no reason to suspect that the grain in any one part of the car is different from that in any other part, it is an appropriate clustered sample. One or more clusters may be chosen to make up a clustered sample. All items within a cluster or only a random selection may be included in the sample.

Dow Chemical Co. v. Blum:[1] Investigating allegations that a herbicide caused spontaneous abortions in women, the Environmental Protection Agency sponsored a study comparing spontaneous abortion rates along the Oregon coastal range, a forested region where the herbicide had been used, to rates along Oregon's eastern border. This was a clustered sample because the EPA was using hospitals grouped in these two geographic areas as representative of the areas throughout the United States where the herbicide was or was not used. It should be apparent that it was considerably more convenient to collect data from the hospitals in these areas alone compared to sampling hospitals throughout the nation.

§6.3   [1] 469 F. Supp. 892 (E.D. Mich. 1979).

Diamond Alkali Co.:[2] An expert working for the Federal Trade Commission conducted a clustered random sample of customers of cement-producing firms in an 88-county area in order to assist in evaluating the effects of a merger between two cement producers. Rather than randomly sampling customers scattered throughout the states of Michigan, Ohio, Pennsylvania, West Virginia, Maryland, and western New York, the survey sampled views in representative sub-populations to determine customers' buying habits and whether they had experienced adverse effects from the acquisition.[3]

Forte-Fairbairn, Inc.:[4] Fiber experts identified shipments of goods to the complaining buyer as baby llama fibers. Their sampling procedure had several stages: from each of 16 shipments of fibers, a sample of over 1000 fibers was placed in individual boxes; the 16 boxes became clusters from which random samples were drawn, and from each box a sample of fibers was drawn and analyzed.[5]

Warner-Lambert Co.:[6] In order to determine the truth of advertising of the health benefits of gargling with Listerine, officials selected children in a specific school for tests. Hypothesizing that this cluster was a representative sampling of typical kids, the investigators saved resources by focusing their examination on these particular students, who were conveniently located together, and by utilizing the same school doctor, who analyzed the severity of colds suffered by Listerine users and others.

§6.4   Stratified Samples

If additional information enables the researcher to identify population subgroups according to the proportions possessing certain characteristics that may be correlated with the properties to be measured, a more accurate sample may result. Items in a clustered sample are drawn randomly from what might be considered a microcosm of the whole population. When drawing a *stratified sample* one pays special attention to population subgroups that possess particular characteristics of interest. A stratified sample is obtained by identifying

---

[2] 72 F.T.C. 700 (1967).
[3] Id. at 732-733.
[4] 62 F.T.C. 1146 (1963).
[5] Id. at 1161-62.
[6] 86 F.T.C. 1398 (1975), *modified*, 562 F.2d 749 (D.C. Cir. 1977), *cert. denied*, 435 U.S. 950 (1978).

relevant subgroups or strata and taking a simple random sample from each. This method ensures that the subgroup's particular characteristics are reflected in the results of the sample.

United States v. General Motors Corp.:[1] In order to establish that a safety-defect notification must be issued, the National Highway Traffic Safety Bureau sought to prove that a "large number of failures" of a truck wheel manufactured by the defendant had occurred. To establish the number of failures the government conducted a stratified random sample of truck owners who had purchased the wheels in question. There are a number of different subgroups or strata that might have been identified for this sample. To get a fair cross-section of users of the wheels, the sample should include recreational, on-the-road, and off-the-road users, owners of heavy and light trucks, and city and rural users. By identifying the types of use likely to make a difference in the incidence of wheel failure, the surveyor can get a more accurate picture of the pattern of failures.

Anderson v. Banks:[2] A Georgia county school board adopted the California Achievement Test (CAT) as an exit exam that students were required to pass before receiving a diploma. The CAT was chosen because it allowed school administrators to compare their students to a particular norm, established by giving the test to a large stratified random sample of students across the nation. School districts identified as small, large, urban, and rural and from each region of the country were included in the sample to ensure that it was representative.[3] Within each stratum the students were selected by a simple random sample. The court found that while the exam was acceptable, for due process reasons it was unconstitutional as applied.

There are two distinct types of stratified samples. A *proportional stratified sample* is one in which the percentage of the population in each subgroup is identified and the sample is composed of the same percentages. Thus, if a county's electorate is evenly divided among Republicans, Democrats, and right-wing anarchists, and these are the characteristic strata likely to influence the outcome of a sample, the proportions of the three groups in the sample and in the population would be the same.

A *nonproportional stratified sample* is one in which the percentages

§6.4 [1] 377 F. Supp. 242 (D.D.C. 1974).
[2] 520 F. Supp. 472 (S.D. Ga. 1981).
[3] Id. at 488.

of each subgroup in the sample are not the same as in the population. Such a sample is useful when a relevant subgroup is very small compared to other subgroups. A more thorough sampling of that subgroup may allow more precise descriptions of variations within the entire population. Numerical adjustments to calculations of descriptive statistics such as the sample mean must be made, however, to compensate for the disproportionately large number of items from that subgroup.

B. SAMPLE ESTIMATES AND CONFIDENCE INTERVALS

Numerical measures of characteristics such as population means are proportions called *parameters*, which are the numbers we attempt to discover by sampling, and the corresponding numerical measures from a sample are called *statistics* or *point estimates*. A statistic calculated from sample data is usually only an approximation to a corresponding population parameter. In using a sample statistic as an estimate of a parameter's value, one should determine to the extent possible a measure of the precision of the sample estimate. A frequently used indicator of its precision is the *confidence interval,* a numerical range around that point estimate within which one can be fairly certain that the population parameter lies. Because the point estimate alone gives no indication of how likely it is that the corresponding population parameter is similar, finders of fact sometimes reject sample evidence unaccompanied by confidence intervals.

American Telephone and Telegraph Co.:[4] In hearings before the Federal Communications Commission, the telephone company attempted to justify a tariff increase for its message telecommunications service (MTS) by forecasting demand for those services. These forecasts were based on samples of relevant economic variables such as the price elasticity for MTS and were presented as point estimates of the demand that would exist in the future. Future demand was the population parameter. The F.C.C. found that because the forecasts were based on samples and therefore were only estimates of the future values, confidence intervals were needed to indicate a range within which the

[4]86 F.C.C. 2d 956(1981).

factfinders could be relatively certain the future values would fall. The FCC ordered that all future tariff filings contain confidence intervals.[5]

In order to understand the methodology for calculating and interpreting confidence intervals, it is necessary to learn more about the values point estimates are likely to take. The next sections describe cases in which sample means and proportions are used and the ways in which these point estimates are distributed in different samples from the same population.

§6.5   The Distribution of Sample Means

It is generally agreed that the mean of a random sample provides the best estimate of the mean of the population from which the sample was drawn. If a second sample is drawn from the same population and a sample mean calculated, however, the means for the two samples may or may not be equal and there is no way to tell which of the two is the better estimate of the population mean. If we calculate the means for many samples from the same population, however, most of those sample means will be close to the population mean.

One can study the distribution of sample means in the same way the distribution of measurements of a random variable was examined in Section 4.13. A statistical proposition called the *Central Limit Theorem* holds that sample means for large samples[1] will be approximately normally distributed around the population mean. This implies that the means calculated from different samples are clustered around a central value, the population mean, with fewer sample means found for values further from the population mean. This is true no matter what population the samples are drawn from, as long as they are simple random samples.

This property of sample means is useful because it allows one to estimate, from a sufficiently large sample, an interval within which the population mean probably lies.

---

[5] Id. at 968.

§6.5   [1] How large a sample must be for the central limit theorem depends on how closely the distribution from which the samples are taken approximates the normal distribution. Because the closeness varies with different sampling distributions, it is difficult to provide a general guideline indicating how large a sample must be.

Reserve Mining Co. v. Environmental Protection Agency:[2] The EPA estimated the concentration of asbestiform fibers in the ambient air by measuring fiber concentrations in four locations, which were then averaged to get a sample mean. Because this sample mean is only an estimate of the population mean concentration of asbestiform fibers in the air, the EPA wanted to know the likelihood that the population mean was much greater or much less than the estimate. The normal distribution of sample means reveals that most are fairly close to the population mean. Accordingly, the population mean is likely to be fairly close to any given sample mean. How likely and how close are questions that can be resolved by reference to the normal distribution.

§6.6   Standard Error of Sample Means

In Sections 4.10, 4.11, and 4.14 we discussed statistical properties of the standard deviation, which measures the typical variation of all the numbers in a group from the mean for those numbers. There exists a standard deviation for the group of all possible sample means that could be drawn from the same population called the *standard error of the sample mean*. The standard error of the sample mean measures the typical variation in sample means one is likely to observe if repeated samples are taken from the same population. The more the sample means are likely to differ from one another, the greater is their standard error.

The standard error of the sample mean depends on two factors:[1] the standard deviation of the population and the size of the sample. Sample means will vary greatly from one another if the items in the population do so. If the population is quite diverse, random samples are more likely to be dissimilar. The usual measure of diversity or variation is the standard deviation: thus the greater the population standard deviation, the greater the variation among samples and their sample means and, therefore, the greater the standard error of the sample means. As the samples get larger, they are increasingly likely to include a representative selection of items in the population and are more likely to be similar to one another. As the sample sizes get larger, the means are likely to be closer to one another, so the standard error of the sample means gets smaller. The equation for the

---

[2] 514 F.2d 492 (8th Cir. 1975).

§6.6 [1] The standard error of the sample mean for hypergeometrically distributed random variables also depends on the size of the population.

standard error of the sample mean, discussed in Section 6.21.1, reflects these properties. The standard error of the sample mean, which is denoted by se_m, decreases as the population standard deviation decreases or sample size increases. Often, when it is clear from the context that we are referring to the standard error of the mean, we refer to it simply as the standard error.

One can use properties of the normal distribution and the standard error of the sample mean to determine how close the sample mean is to the population mean whenever the sample is sufficiently large. The normal distribution indicates that approximately 68% of sample means will be within one standard error of the population mean, about 95% will be within two, and about 99.5% will be within three.

Reserve Mining Co. v. Environmental Protection Agency:[2] To evaluate the effect of effluent from the defendant's plant, an expert measured the airborne concentration of asbestiform fibers by taking measurements at several locations. The sample mean concentration was 0.0626 per cubic centimeter, and the standard error was 0.014. The calculation of this standard error is shown in Section 6.21.1. Thus approximately[3] 68% of sample means were *within* plus or minus 0.014 fibers (one standard error) of the population mean concentration of fibers, 95% are *within* 0.028 fibers (two standard errors), and 99.5% are *within* 0.042 fibers (three standard errors). Alternatively, 32%, 5%, and .5% of sample means are *more than* one, two, or three standard errors, respectively, from the population mean.

§6.7   Confidence Intervals for Sample Means

One purpose of calculating a sample mean is to estimate the population mean. Properties of the normal distribution, illustrated in Section 6.6, allow one to predict the percentage of sample means that will be within a given distance of the population mean; for instance, 95% will be within two standard errors. An alternative way to state this is that there is a 95% probability that a particular sample mean will be within two standard errors of the population mean or that

---

[2] 514 F.2d 492 (8th Cir. 1975).

[3] This is not a very accurate approximation because the sample size, four, is so small. Alternative approximations appropriate for small samples are discussed in Section 6.21.1. This example is nevertheless illustrative of the application of properties of the normal distribution to the estimation of population parameters.

there is a 95% probability that the population mean will be within two standard errors of any mean calculated from a random sample from that population. We can, therefore, start with a sample mean, calculate its standard error, and find that 95% of the time the population mean will be within two standard errors of the sample mean.

Reserve Mining Co. v. Environmental Protection Agency:[1] The sample mean concentration of asbestiform fibers in the air was 0.0626 per cubic centimeter. If the standard error is 0.014 and if the sample is large there is approximately a 95% chance that the population mean is within 0.028 fibers of that sample mean of 0.0626 fibers, that is, between 0.0346 (0.0626 minus 0.028) fibers and 0.0906 (0.0626 plus 0.028) fibers per cubic centimeter.[2] This conclusion is often stated as follows: "At a 95% confidence level, we estimate the population mean to be between 0.0346 and 0.0906 fibers per cubic centimeter." This range is called a 95% *confidence interval.*

One can calculate confidence intervals for any probability or level of confidence one desires; there is nothing that limits the analysis to 95% confidence intervals.

Eovaldi v. First National Bank of Chicago:[3] A plaintiff class of credit card holders was damaged by the bank's changing its billing cycle, which caused customers to incur extra finance charges. The defendant bank appealed from a judgment against it for damages of $127,899. To support its contention that actual damages were lower, the bank employed an expert to conduct a random sample of accounts to estimate total excess finance charges incurred. Average damage per sampled customer was calculated and then multiplied by the number of customers to find total damages. By calculating the standard error of the sample mean, the expert was able to offer the court a maximum above which actual damages were unlikely to fall. The point estimate for total damages was $22,567. The expert indicated the probability associated with his maximum damages estimate by stating that "Odds are 99 to 1 that the true amount will not be larger than $27,898."[4] This was apparently a 99% confidence interval. A related calculation from this case is shown in Section 6.22.1.

---

§6.7   [1]514 F.2d 492 (8th Cir. 1975).
[2]In Section 6.22.1 a calculation of a confidence interval for this example is based on a very small sample for purposes of illustration and contrast.
[3]596 F.2d 188 (7th Cir. 1979).
[4]Id. at 192. See Section 6.9 regarding one-tailed intervals.

Johnson v. White:[5] In order to justify its changes in the state program for Aid to Families with Dependent Children, the commissioner of welfare randomly sampled 3,079 assistance units out of a total of 27,000 to produce estimates of monthly average needs. The sample mean is once again only an estimate of the population mean for all aid recipients and therefore a 95% confidence interval around this point estimate was calculated. With this range indicated, the finder of fact could conclude that there was only a 5% probability that, just by chance, the population mean would be outside the range.

Marathon Oil Co. v. Environmental Protection Agency:[6] The Water Pollution Control Act requires that the EPA set effluent limits based on the average performance of the best practicable control technology currently available (BPCTCA). The EPA collects effluent discharge data from those plants in the relevant industry that utilize the BPCTCA in an exemplary fashion. As the court points out, a standard could be computed by merely averaging each plant's effluent quality (measured in milligrams per liter) if emission quality from each plant were constant. However, the plants sampled showed considerable variation, e.g., from 1.1 milligrams per liter one day to 86.5 another day, with considerable variation between these figures.[7] The variation around the average was measured in standard deviation terms, converted into standard error of the sample means, and used to calculate the range, a confidence interval, within which an exemplary plant would fall most of the time. For the two effluent limitations confidence intervals of 99% and 97.5% were used. Thus the exemplary plant could be expected to be able to comply with the standard 99% (or 97.5%) of the time. The actual average effluent discharge would be outside the range just by chance, rather than due to the behavior of the polluter, 1% (or 2.5%) of the time.

§6.8 Confidence Intervals for Sample Proportions

The parameters estimated by a sample statistic are often population proportions.[1] Whether one wishes to know, for instance, the

---

[5]353 F. Supp. 69 (D. Conn. 1972), *modified*, 528 F.2d 1228 (2d Cir. 1975).

[6]564 F.2d 1253 (9th Cir. 1977).

[7]Id. at 1266 and n. 36.

§6.8   [1]A proportion might be interpreted as a special case of a mean. Sample proportions are treated separately here and throughout this chapter because many applications of confidence intervals in a variety of substantive law areas involve estimates of population proportions, because sample proportions from repeated samplings

proportion of the employees at a company who are minority members, of the market supplied by a given producer, or of people responding a given way on a survey question, the sample proportion is generally acknowledged to be the best estimate of the population proportion. The sample proportions resulting from repeated samples of the same population are approximately normally distributed around the population proportion for large sample sizes.[2] The computation of confidence intervals for proportions is discussed in Section 6.22.2. The *standard error of the sample proportion* depends, as does the standard error of the sample mean, on the standard deviation of the random variable in the population and the sample size. As with the standard error of the sample mean, the standard error of the sample proportion decreases as that of the population decreases and as sample size increases.

By calculating the standard error of the sample proportion and utilizing properties of the distribution of sample proportions, a confidence interval around a sample estimate can be calculated to indicate a range within which one can be fairly certain the population proportion falls. The probability that the population proportion falls outside of the range indicated just by chance can be estimated.

Warner-Lambert Co.:[3] The manufacturer of Listerine was accused of false advertising in claiming that Listerine was effective in preventing colds. Product Q studies, which result from sampling viewers' perceptions of advertising, were offered as evidence of the effect of ads on the television-watching public. In this instance, they were used to estimate the proportion of people in the population who recalled the advertising message that Listerine was effective for colds and sore throats. The sample proportion for Fall 1963 was .68, or 68% who did remember that theme. In order to determine how close that sample statistic is likely to be to the population proportion, the standard error of the sample proportion is computed and a confidence interval is calculated. The hearing examiner reported that "The percentages expressed in the Product Q reports would vary only 5 or 10 [percentage] points in either direction with a band of confidence at the .05 level of significance."[4] If

---

of the same population have a different distribution from that of sample means, and because the calculation of confidence intervals for sample proportions involve different formulas and present different computational problems.

[2] See Section 6.5 n. 1.

[3] 86 F.T.C. 1398, 1469-1472 (1975), *modified*, 562 F.2d 749 (D.C. Cir. 1977), *cert. denied*, 435 U.S. 950 (1978).

[4] 86 F.T.C. at 1469.

the variation for the 68% estimate for those who recalled the advertising theme "effective for colds and sore throat" were 5 percentage points, then a 95% confidence interval for this sample statistic would be from 63% (68% − 5%) to 73% (68% + 5%). The .05 level of significance indicates that there is only a 5% probability that the population proportion lies outside this range. Because the standard error varies inversely with the sample size, if the standard deviation in the population is known or can be estimated the sample size can be chosen so as to produce a confidence interval of any given size such as 5 or 10% at any level of confidence, such as the .05 significance level chosen by the Product Q surveyors. The process of selecting sample size is discussed in Section 6.13. A confidence interval calculation based on these facts appears in Section 6.22.2.

Teleprompter Corp.:[5] Teleprompter, a cable television system, wished to merge with Westinghouse Broadcasting Company. One factor in determining whether Federal Communications Commission cross-ownership rules applied was whether Teleprompter was a "significantly viewed station" in the same area where four other stations licensed by Westinghouse were broadcasting. Viewing habits are demonstrated in such cases by surveys of viewers to determine what proportion watches a given station. FCC regulations[6] require that to be a significantly viewed station in an area, the audience share must be "one standard error above the required viewing level." This statement of the standard recognizes that the sampling proportion viewing a particular station is only an estimate of the population proportion. When the audience share is estimated from a sample, the standard error of the proportion can be calculated in order to compute a confidence interval around the sample proportion. For a large sample, the population mean will be within one standard error of the sample proportion approximately 68% of the time. If no confidence interval was drawn around the sample proportion, there might, just by chance, be erroneous findings that a station was significantly viewed. Requiring that the sample proportion be a given number of standard errors above the required level reduces the probability that the population proportion could, just by chance, actually be less than the required level.

Equal Employment Opportunity Commission v. H. S. Camp and Sons, Inc.:[7] The defendant's expert in this employment discrimination case used confidence intervals to attempt to show that the racial compo-

[5] 91 F.C.C. 2d 146 (1982).
[6] 47 C.F.R. §76.54.
[7] 542 F. Supp. 411 (M.D. Fla. 1982).

sition of the workforce was due to chance alone and not discrimination. The expert calculated the proportion of blacks in the department of the employer's firm and, using the standard error of the proportion, constructed a 95% confidence interval around it. Due to the normal distribution of sample proportions around the population proportion, there is a 95% probability that the actual percentage of blacks in the relevant labor pool would fall within the calculated confidence interval. Thus, if there were 139 employees in the food and kindred products division of this company and 23% of them were black, the standard error for this proportion would be .036, or 3.6%. A 95% confidence interval around the sample proportion of .23 would be from .160 to .300. (These calculations appear in Section 6.22.2.) There is a 5% probability that the actual population proportion would have fallen outside this range even if the employer had not been discriminating. The court, considering the relatively small probability of the population proportion being outside this range by chance, would give little weight to defendant's claim of no discrimination if the actual percentage of blacks in the population from which the employer hired for this division, the relevant labor pool, did fall outside the range.

The factual finding regarding the actual proportion of blacks in the relevant labor pool is critical in this case because it is that actual proportion that is compared to the interval. If the relevant labor pool contained 35% blacks, as estimated by the number of blacks applying for the jobs, for instance, it would be relatively unlikely that qualified employees were randomly hired into the department, because the population percentage of .35 falls outside the calculated interval from .160 to .300.

§6.9   Significance Testing with One- and Two-Tailed Confidence Intervals

The examples in the previous sections illustrate that confidence intervals not only supply a convenient range for judging the precision of a sample estimate, but also provide a means of testing the significance of a difference between a sample estimate and some external standard. The confidence interval provides a range to which we can compare an outside standard such as the known population proportion of blacks in *EEOC v. H. S. Camp and Sons, Inc.* (Section 6.8), a legal minimum such as the audience share to qualify a broadcast station as significantly viewed in *Teleprompter Corp.* (Section 6.8), or a legal maximum. As with other statistical tests for the significance of a difference (see Sections 4.14 through 4.19), the confidence interval can be used to perform one-tailed tests of whether a sample statistic is significantly greater or less than an external standard or a two-tailed test of whether the statistic is significantly different from (either greater or less than) an external standard.

The examples discussed thus far have all involved two-tailed confidence intervals, those which set both upper and lower limits beyond which the population parameter is not likely to fall. A one-tailed confidence interval sets a limit above which or, alternatively, below which the population parameter is unlikely to fall. A one-tailed confidence interval is appropriate whenever a sample estimate is compared to an external standard such as a maximum allowable amount of pollution, a minimum amount of pollution abatement, a maximum number of allowable defects in a product, or a minimum amount in controversy for jurisdiction. In each of these contexts we are not interested in whether there is a significant difference between the point estimates and the external standard but whether the population parameter exceeds a legal maximum or falls short of a legal minimum.

As an example, consider an estimate of the discharge from a portland cement plant. Environmental Protection Agency regulations forbid the discharge of any gases containing particulate matter in excess of an average of 0.15 kg per metric ton of feed to the kiln[1] and specify the sample size in terms of time and volume of flow of discharge from the kiln.[2] If a sample of this discharge yielded an average of 0.16 kg per metric ton, we could not be certain that the discharge rate for the entire period of operation was in excess of 0.15 kg per metric ton. This sample statistic is only a point estimate of the corresponding population parameter. Using a one-tailed confidence interval we could determine how likely it is that the mean discharge exceeded this external maximum of 0.15 kg per metric ton. This probability depends on the variation within the sample (which reflects the variation within the population) and the sample size. The standard error of the mean captures both of these influences. If the standard error were equal to .02 kg per metric ton, then we could be approximately 99% certain that the average discharge rate for the entire period was greater than .11 kg per metric ton, which is not enough to show a violation. If, on the other hand, the standard error of the mean were only .003, we could be approximately 99% certain

---

§6.9   [1] 40 C.F.R. §60.62(a)(1).
[2] 40 C.F.R. §60.70(b)(1).

that the actual average discharge was greater than .152 kg per metric tons, which does exceed the standard. The basic difference between this and a two-tailed interval is that here we are establishing a limit *below* the sample mean beneath which the population mean is unlikely to fall (a 1% probability in our example). For a two-tailed interval one establishes limits both *above and below* the sample mean beyond which, in either direction, the population mean is unlikely to fall.

Teleprompter Corp.:[3] The survey sampled television viewers' habits to estimate the proportion of the audience that viewed a particular cable television system's broadcasts. A two-tailed confidence interval would provide a range on either side of the sample estimate within which the population proportion was likely to fall with a given probability. A one-tailed confidence interval would be useful to compare the sample proportion to the "required viewing level" necessary to categorize the system as a "significantly viewed station." If, for instance, a station must have a 30% share to be significantly viewed and the sample revealed a 32% share, the standard error of the sample proportion could be calculated to determine a range beneath 32% within which the actual share was likely to fall. If the standard error was 3%, then we could not be 95% sure that the population percentage was greater than 30%. The regulation requires only that we be approximately 70% certain, however,[4] and we can be 70% certain that the population proportion is greater than 30.4%, which exceeds the requisite minimum of 30%. It can be shown that we can be about 75% certain that the audience share is greater than 30%. (These calculations appear in Section 6.22.2.)

Marathon Oil Co. v. Environmental Protection Agency:[5] In order to establish effluent discharge standards, the EPA samples the performance of plants using the best practicable control technology currently available (BPCTCA). Since the EPA's goal is to calculate a maximum allowable discharge standard with which exemplary plants will be able to comply, a one-tailed confidence interval was used to set a maximum level below which the average discharge of exemplary plants was likely to fall. The sample mean was calculated and the standard error of the sample mean was used to determine a one-tailed range above the sample mean within which actual average performance was likely to fall

[3] 91 F.C.C.2d 146 (1982).
[4] 47 C.F.R. §76.54. This section requires that the sample proportion be at least one standard error above the minimum level. For large samples, approximately 68% of the time the sample mean will fall within one standard error of the population mean.
[5] 564 F.2d 1253, 1266 (9th Cir. 1977).

99% of the time. This standard required that the daily discharge of produced water be less than 9.25 pounds per day.[6] If one standard error of the sample mean was .70 pounds per day for the sample, then the sample mean must have been about 7.43 pounds per day. (The calculation for the one-tailed confidence interval discussed in this example appears in Section 6.22.1.)

Section 301(b)(1)(A) of the Federal Water Pollution Control Act[7] requires that the EPA set standards that are achievable by those using BPCTCA technology. Plaintiffs here argued that the standard set using a 99% confidence interval was stricter than that allowed by §301 because even high technology plants would fail to meet the standard, just by chance, 1% of the time.

United States v. General Motors:[8] Under the National Traffic and Motor Vehicle Safety Act, manufacturers of automobiles are required to issue notifications of defects whenever a "large number of failures" of a manufactured part occur. The issue in this case was whether a large number of failures of a truck wheel had occurred. To estimate the number the government constructed a stratified random sample of truck owners. By calculating the average number of wheel failures per owner, the statistician could estimate how many would be observed by all owners of trucks with those wheels. A two-tailed confidence interval would indicate a range within which the population average number of failures would be likely to fall. Because the legal concern is whether the number of failures reaches the minimum above which notification is necessary, a one-tailed confidence interval would be useful. If there were 2000 truck owners with these wheels, the sample mean number of failures per person were two, and the standard error for the sample mean were .07, then we could be 90% certain that the population average number of failures was less than 2.09 and that in total there were probably less than 4180 (2000 × 2.09) failures. A one-tailed test directed the other way would indicate that we could be 90% certain that the population average number of failures was greater than 1.91 and that in total there were probably more than 3820 (2000 × 1.91) failures. A two-tailed 90% confidence interval, given these same facts, would be from 3770 to 4230 failures. (These calculations are shown in Section 6.22.1.) Referring to the one-tailed interval would indicate whether we could be relatively certain that the number of failures was greater than whatever was considered large enough to require notification.

---

[6] Id. at 1259.
[7] 33 U.S.C.A. §§1251-1376 (West 1978).
[8] 377 F. Supp. 242 (D.D.C. 1974).

§6.10   Direct Significance Testing for Point Estimates

Using appropriate statistical methods it is sometimes possible to test more directly the statistical significance of the differences between sample statistics and the types of external standards, legal maximums and minimums, described in Section 6.9. The approach is quite similar to that used in Sections 4.14, 4.16, and 4.19 to test the significance of differences. The general approach is to calculate the disparity between the sample statistic, either a mean or a proportion, and the external standard, then divide by the appropriate standard error. This process yields a calculated Z or t test statistic, which is compared to a table of critical values of Z or t, which in turn reveals a p-value indicating the probability that a disparity of the magnitude observed could occur by chance. Calculations for direct significance tests appear in Section 6.23.

> **Teleprompter Co.:**[1] If the population proportion is less than 30% (which we assume is the required audience share necessary to qualify a television station as being "significantly viewed"), the probability of finding a sample proportion as large as 32% with a sample size of 1289 is no more than 6%. One may calculate the p-value by subtracting 30% from 32% and dividing by the standard error of 1.3%, which gives 1.54. The Z Table indicates a corresponding one-tailed p-value of about .06.

As with other tests of the significance of a difference (see Chapter 4), one sometimes sets a p-value threshold. The p-value that corresponds to the calculated Z or t value, as in the *Teleprompter Co.* example, is then compared to the threshold. If the calculated p-value is smaller, then one- or two-tailed hypotheses regarding the sample proportion may be rejected.

> **Teleprompter Co.:**[2] If the threshold to which our calculated p-value is to be compared is .05, then we must conclude in this example that the evidence does not show that the population mean is greater than the required 30% audience share, because the calculated p-value is about .06. The one-tailed confidence interval approach led us to this same conclusion. In this case the Federal Communications Commission has implicitly recognized that a p-value of about .32 will be the chosen level of comparison. By that standard the population mean audience

§6.10   [1] 91 F.C.C. 2d 146 (1982).
[2] Id.

272

share estimated by the sample will be judged to be significantly greater than the minimum 30%.

Portland Cement Plant Emissions: In this example[3] the external standard was a maximum allowable emission of 0.15 kg of particulates per metric ton of feed to the kiln. The sample mean was 0.16 kg, and the standard error of the mean was .02 kg. If the standard error of the mean had been .003, dividing the disparity of .01 kg by the standard error would yield a critical Z value of 3.33. For a large sample, the associated p-value is .0004, sufficiently small that one might reasonably infer that the average emission for the kiln, the population mean, exceeded the maximum allowable. Since the standard error was in fact .02, however, the associated p-value is .31, indicating a 31% chance that the population mean did not exceed the maximum allowable even though the sample mean did.

Equal Employment Opportunity Commission v. H. S. Camp and Sons, Inc.:[4] The proportion of black employees in one division of the employer-defendant's company was .23, or 23%. If these employees are considered a simple random sample from a qualified labor force of which 35% are black, the standard error of the sample proportion would be .040 (see Section 6.23). The disparity is 12 percentage points (23% − 35%). Dividing the disparity by the standard error of the proportion yields 2.97 standard deviations and an associated p-value of .0015, obtained from a Z Table (see Section 6.22). Using a .05 threshold or significance level (one-tailed test) as a cutoff for rejecting the hypothesis of random selection, this would provide the plaintiff with some evidence of discrimination. The one-tailed confidence interval approach would lead to the same conclusion.

C. SIGNIFICANCE OF DIFFERENCES BETWEEN SAMPLE ESTIMATES

In Sections 6.9 and 6.10 we illustrated methods for comparing a sample mean or proportion to an external standard such as a legal maximum or minimum. Occasionally it is useful to test the significance of an observed difference between two sample means

[3] See Section 6.9.
[4] 542 F. Supp. 411 (M.D. Fla. 1982).

instead of the difference between a sample mean and an external standard. The procedure involved in such a test is only slightly more complicated. With one sample estimate, its standard error was of considerable importance. In the comparison of two sample statistics the standard errors of both must be involved in the computations. This complexity aside, statistical tests for the significance of differences between sample estimates is approached much like other inferential tests of differences. A test statistic is calculated by dividing the difference between the means by the *standard error of the difference between the sample means*. This new statistic is discussed in detail in Section 6.22.3. Confidence intervals may also be used to test the significance of differences between sample estimates. Because the logic of direct significance testing is based on confidence intervals, we consider that approach first.

§6.11   Using Confidence Intervals to Test the Significance of the Difference between Sample Estimates

Using a one-tailed confidence interval it is possible to estimate a limit above or below a sample estimate beyond which the population parameter is unlikely to fall, provided the sample is drawn randomly from the hypothesized population. If confronted with two sample estimates, one greater than the other, it is possible to calculate a range above the smaller and below the larger of the two estimates within which the population parameters corresponding to them are likely to fall. If the intervals overlap, we cannot be certain (at whatever level of confidence underlies the intervals) that there is a statistically significant difference between the estimates. This is one way to test the statistical significance of a difference.

Presseisen v. Swarthmore College:[1] The plaintiff, a former assistant professor who was denied reappointment, alleged that the college had discriminated against women in several areas, including promotions. The sample estimates are mean times for men and women from receipt of highest degree to appointment or promotion to associate professor. The mean time for men was 7.6 years with a sample standard deviation of 3.77 years, while the mean time for women was 16.4 years

§6.11 [1] 442 F. Supp. 593 (E.D. Pa. 1977), *aff'd*, 582 F.2d 1275 (3d Cir. 1982).

with a sample standard deviation of 14.03 years. Assume that there were 30 men and 12 women who had been promoted to associate professor. Treating the 30 men as a sample of all men who might be exposed to the promotion process, the sample mean of 7.6 years has an associated sample standard error of .69. The sample mean for the 12 women has an associated sample standard error of 4.05. One-tailed 95% confidence intervals indicate that 95% of the time the population mean time to promotion is less than 8.77 years for men and greater than 9.13 years for women. (Calculation appears in Section 6.22.3). From this evidence we might infer that men and women are not treated in an identical fashion in the promotions process, which might be due to discrimination or to differences in their qualifications.

It is also possible to calculate a confidence interval for the difference between the two estimates rather than for the two estimates separately. If the confidence interval around this difference includes zero, we cannot conclude that the difference in estimates is so great as to be unlikely to occur if the underlying population means were equal.

Presseisen v. Swarthmore College:[2] Assuming a sample mean time to promotion of 7.6 years and a sample standard deviation of 3.77 years for men and a sample mean time to promotion of 16.4 years and a sample standard deviation of 14.03 for women, the difference between sample means is 8.8 years (16.4 − 7.6). A 95% two-tailed confidence interval around this difference gives a range from 3.43 to 14.17 years. Since this range does not include zero years, there is less than 5% chance that if the population mean times to promotion are identical for men and women, such a difference as exists between the two samples could occur just due to chance factors in the drawing of the sample. (Calculations appear in Section 6.22.3.)

Equivalent methods may be used to draw inferences regarding the significance of differences between sample proportions, as illustrated in Section 6.22.3. When calculating a confidence interval around the difference between two sample means or proportions, the standard error used is not the standard error of the mean or proportion but rather the *standard error of the difference between the sample estimates*. The formulas for this standard error are discussed in Section 6.21.3.

[2] Id.

§6.12   Direct Significance Tests for the Difference Between Sample Estimates

Using the standard error of the difference between two sample estimates it is possible to test directly the statistical significance of the difference between those estimates, as shown in Section 6.23. This process yields a calculated t statistic or Z value, which is compared to a table of critical t or Z values. The table reveals a p-value, indicating the probability that the observed difference between the estimates could appear even if there were no difference between the population parameters.

> **Presseisen v. Swarthmore College:**[1] If the mean time for promotion of 30 men to associate professor is 7.6 years with a sample standard deviation of 3.77 years and the mean time for promotion of 12 women to associate professor is 16.4 years with a sample standard deviation of 14.03 years, the standard error of the difference between the means is 2.74. Dividing the difference, 8.8 years, by the standard error, 2.74, yields a calculated t value of 3.21, which shows that this difference is statistically significant at a p-value less than .01 for a two-tailed test. There is thus less than a 1% probability that such a disparity or difference could occur by chance under random selection from a common population.

An equivalent procedure can be used to test the statistical significance of differences between sample proportions, as illustrated in Section 6.23.

D.   ESTIMATING APPROPRIATE SAMPLE SIZES

An *appropriate* sample size is one that gives an estimate that is precise enough for the intended use to be made of the inferences that will be drawn from the sample. As described in Section 6.6, the precision of the point estimate from a sample depends on two factors: (1) the variation that exists among items in the population as measured by the population standard deviation and (2) the size of the sample. One has no control over the standard deviation in the population, but the

§6.12   [1] 442 F. Supp. 593 (E.D. Pa. 1977), *aff'd,* 582 F.2d 1275 (3d Cir. 1982).

size of the sample can be chosen so as to influence the precision of the estimate. There may be situations where the variation in the population is so great that no practical sample size will give the precision required. In such a case the entire population must be examined or another approach used. Section 6.13 describes the process by which appropriate sample size is determined.

§6.13   Determining Sample Size

It is convenient to think of the precision of a sample estimate such as a sample mean in terms of how close it is to the population parameter. A more precise sample mean is one that is closer to the population mean. When the population parameter is unknown, however, a confidence interval is often used to indicate a range around the sample estimate within which the parameter is likely to fall. Each confidence interval has an associated significance level that indicates the likelihood that the population parameter falls outside of that range due to random selection of items to include in the sample (see Sections 6.7 and 6.8 on confidence intervals). For a given significance level, a more precise estimate will have a smaller range or interval than a less precise estimate. For instance, an estimated mean level of pollutants might be 25 parts per million. If a 95% confidence interval around this mean ranged from 23 to 27 parts per million, the estimate is more precise than if it ranged from 15 to 35 parts per million.

Because confidence intervals are used to describe the precision of the estimate, a statement of the required precision for the sample estimate must include (1) an indication of the acceptable size of the interval around the point estimate (such as plus or minus 10 parts per million) and (2) an indication of the level of confidence with which one wishes to assert that the population parameter falls within that range (such as 99%).

Reserve Mining Co. v. Environmental Protection Agency:[1] An expert measured the ambient air concentration of asbestiform fibers, measured in fibers per cubic centimeter (cc). The sample mean was 0.0626 fibers per cc with a 95% confidence interval of 0.626 ± 0.0276 fibers per cc. The "± 0.0276" combined with the "95% confidence interval" describe the precision of the sample estimate.

§6.13   [1] 514 F.2d 492 (8th Cir. 1975).

Warner-Lambert Co.:[2] In this deceptive advertising case Product Q reports were offered as evidence of the effect of advertisements on the television-watching public. Confidence intervals for the sample proportions calculated in some of these reports estimated that the population proportion was within 5 percentage points of the sample proportion at a .05 significance level. Thus an estimated proportion such as .60 might have an associated 95% confidence interval from .55 to .65. By increasing sample size, the precision of this estimate could be increased, which would be reflected in a shorter interval or in an increased level of confidence or both.

To estimate appropriate sample size, one works backwards from the calculation of a confidence interval. The range in a confidence interval depends on two factors, a critical value for the test statistic, either Z or t, and the standard error of the sample estimate. See Section 6.22, Calculation of Confidence Intervals. The critical value is determined by the confidence level chosen. The standard error of the sample estimate is usually calculated from the standard deviation of the sample and the sample size. For a given confidence level and standard deviation, a sample size can be calculated to yield any chosen range.

Warner-Lambert Co.:[3] If the 95% confidence interval for Product Q reports was achieved at a sample size of 73 with a range of ± ten percentage points, a 99% confidence interval could be obtained for the same range with a sample size of 125. This is an increase in the confidence level without a change in the range. Alternatively, the range can be made smaller, e.g., ± three percentage points for the same confidence level, 99%, by increasing the sample size to 1383.

Often the question is asked, how big a sample is needed to have a given range, for example, of ± 5 percentage points, with a given confidence level of 95%. If the standard deviation is known or can be estimated, the appropriate sample size can be estimated. These calculations appear in Section 6.24.

Reserve Mining Co. v. Environmental Protection Agency:[4] To estimate the concentration of asbestiform fibers in the air with a 90%

---

[2] 86 F.T.C. 1398 (1975), *modified*, 562 F.2d 749 (D.C. Cir. 1977), *cert. denied*, 435 U.S. 950 (1978).
[3] Id.
[4] 514 F.2d 492 (8th Cir. 1975).

confidence interval and an accuracy of ± .001 fibers per cc., we could calculate the necessary sample size using the formulas in Section 6.24. As always, it is necessary to know or have an estimate of the standard deviation of the population. If this is estimated to be .024, then the desired level of precision, a range of ± .001 fibers per cc., can be achieved with a sample size of 1559 observations.

For each example it is necessary to have at least an estimate of the standard deviation of the population. It would be best if the population standard deviation were known, but the usual procedure is to conduct a small sample, often referred to as a *pilot study*, from which a point estimate of the population standard deviation, the sample standard deviation, can be calculated (see Section 6.20.3, Sample Standard Deviation — Calculations). This procedure of sampling in order to find out how large the sample should be is somewhat simplified if the population parameter to be estimated is a proportion rather than a mean: the standard error of a proportion can be estimated quite easily. This enables us to present a table of estimated sample sizes needed to achieve a given level of precision for selected proportions. See Exhibit 6.24(a).

Sometimes a pilot study will be needed to estimate the population proportion or the population standard deviation in order to then estimate sample size. Sometimes a guess (as to the percentage in a minority group, for instance) may give some idea as to the sample size required, and approximations may also be available from previous studies or published data, or data collected for other purposes may give a good estimate. It should be remembered, however, that the quality of the estimate of necessary sample size depends on that of the standard deviation. Once an estimate of the population standard deviation is obtained, determining the appropriate sample size is simply a matter of choosing the level of precision desired and performing the necessary calculations, as illustrated in Section 6.24.

E. SAMPLING METHODS FOR SELECTING JURORS IN VOIR DIRE

The examples discussed thus far in this chapter involve estimates of variables relevant to the factual issues to be resolved at trial. There are several pretrial stages during which statistical sampling techniques may also be useful. Some are discussed briefly in this section in order to alert the lawyer to their availability and, more important, to relate the techniques developed in this chapter to them. In this section the use of sampling techniques to aid in the selection of jurors during voir dire is discussed, and references to more exhaustive treatment of the subject are supplied.

§6.14 Techniques for Informing the Jury Selection Process

For centuries lawyers have been using the process of *voir dire* to impanel jurors most favorably predisposed towards their clients. Statistical approaches to jury selection began to gain notice with a number of highly publicized and politically charged trials during the 1970s. It is not surprising that lawyers in trials with political overtones were among the first to make use of survey techniques because sampling techniques are generally used to determine attitudes of different segments of the population. One expects that potential jurors have fairly well-developed political predispositions prior to hearing any evidence, which seems reasonable whether the defendants are Philip Berrigan and other draft protestors or John Mitchell and Maurice Stans of Watergate fame. In these and other trials statistical information about attitudes assisted defense lawyers in selecting jurors.

As with its evidentiary uses statistical findings provide only part of the information a lawyer needs in pursuing his or her client's interests. Critics of statistical methods of jury selection assert that lawyers are trained by experience to make the right decisions when it comes to picking juries and that a good, experienced lawyer can do a much better job of selecting an effective jury than a team of social scientists.[1] Social scientists would be rash indeed to suggest that statistical methods alone could select the perfect jury, but they point to studies that illustrate the unreliability of intuitive, instinctive judgments relative to more systematic approaches.[2] Nor are statistical sampling techniques the only aids: the literature on jury selection

§6.14 [1]See, e.g., W. Jordan, Jury Selection at 295 (1980).
[2]See, e.g., M. Saks, The Limits of Scientific Jury Selection, 17 Jurimetrics Journal 3, 8 nn. 19, 20 (1976).

discusses use of experts in the analysis of body language, speech habits, eye contact, and in the development of questions that reveal a profile of the juror's personality.[3] The experienced lawyer's intuitive approach to jury selection incorporates many of these types of analysis done in an informal way; specialists merely add a formal and systematic approach to the process. The notion of statistical significance, for instance, may only add information as to whether it is worthwhile to try to obtain a particular piece of demographic information from a potential juror. If the percentage of self-employed business people with a particular attitude is not significantly different from the percentage of students with that attitude, the limited time and questioning opportunities available to the lawyer should not be wasted in determining a juror's occupation.

At the very least a lawyer's knowledge of a jury's attitudes toward a client can only be improved by the complementary use of intuitive and scientific methods. Attitudinal questions are often not allowed by the court, and veniremen may resent such questions.[4] A lawyer familiar with correspondences between attitudes and objective characteristics such as age, sex, or occupation can circumvent such procedural obstacles and avoid any tendency on the part of potential jurors to misrepresent their attitudes. Jurors may misrepresent their views either maliciously or because of an honest though mistaken belief that the justice system requires them to come to jury duty with a completely open mind devoid of values and preconceptions.

§6.15   Attitudinal Surveys and Jury Selection

In the jury selection context an *attitudinal survey* may elicit objective characteristics and subjective opinions of members of the population from which the jury is drawn, and responses to the survey are studied to determine whether there are systematic relationships between people's objective characteristics and their views. The use of statistical analysis of attitudinal surveys assumes that there are systematic relationships between objective, demographic characteristics of individuals and their attitudes on matters relevant to a trial, that individuals can be identified by this information, and that the characteristics, once isolated, can be used to predict a juror's behavior. An

---

[3] See the references cited in footnotes to this and the following section.
[4] W. Jordan, Jury Selection at 298 n.3.

article in the American Journal of Trial Advocacy suggests the following types of objective information that can be elicited from a potential juror in a criminal trial during voir dire: race, sex, age, occupation, juror's experience with crime, marital status, children, awareness of pretrial publicity, community activities, law enforcement connections, military connections, previous jury experience, membership in civil rights organizations, and housing conditions.[1] Other commentators have added to the list television viewing habits, income, newspaper reading habits,[2] and political party registration.[3] One guide to jury techniques describes these demographic characteristics as "indicators of how and by whom people have been socialized and the material conditions that contribute to their perspectives and attitudes."[4] The possible variables are not limited to any prescribed list but may include any that the imaginative lawyer thinks may provide useful correlations to relevant attitudes and that the judge will tolerate. Once objective characteristics are ascertained, the lawyer may be able to use the results of the attitudinal survey to predict the relevant attitudes of each potential juror.

The objective information that cannot be obtained through questioning may be obtained from jury services that sell indexes of available information on prospective jurors gleaned from public records, which are also available to the lawyer directly, of course, from tax or voter registration lists, phone books, court records, and city directories. Moreover, variables such as income or home ownership might be inferred from address or educational level from occupation. Statistical methods can be used to make these inferences more rigorous.

A survey to establish attitudinal relationships must elicit the demographic information that will provide useful objective indications and must contain questions that reveal attitudes. In many respects the design of questionnaires is a science in itself, relying on statistical methods but constituting a separate discipline. Expertise in this field may be obtained from the testing services department of a university or from those involved in academic or professional disciplines where

---

§6.15   [1] D. Ryan & P. Neeson, Voir Dire: A Trial Technique in Transition, 4 Am. J. Trial Adv. 523, 533 (1981).

[2] N. Winston & W. Winston, The Use of Sociological Techniques in the Jury Selection Process, 6 Natl. J. of Criminal Def. 79 (1980).

[3] Arne Werchick, Method Not Madness: Selecting Today's Jury, 18 Trial (No. 12) 65, 66 (1982).

[4] B. Bonora & E. Krauss, General Editors, Jury-work: Systematic Techniques, National Jury Project (1979).

questionnaires are used regularly, such as marketing. Many are familiar with professional polling agencies who specialize in estimating public attitudes. The National Jury Project is an organization that provides advice and consultation to lawyers using surveys for jury selection.

General guidelines have been developed to determine the time necessary to conduct a survey. It has been estimated, for instance, that a telephone survey of 300 people will take 450 hours of interviewers' calling time plus an additional 75 to 150 hours to translate the results of the interview into a form that can be put into a computer.[5] The time involved in collecting and coding the data may be greater than that involved in determining what information should be collected and in analyzing the results. The cost of designing and reproducing the questionnaire, making phone calls, and hiring computer time and operators should not be overlooked in projecting whether a survey would be worthwhile.[6]

The size of the sample depends on the variability within the population and the degree of precision desired (see Section 6.13). If the measure of interest is the proportion of people in each of several occupation categories that favors the death penalty or that thinks big corporations are cheating consumers and the degree of precision desired is plus or minus 2 percentage points at a 95% confidence level (a common degree for national public opinion polls), then the sample must contain enough members of each occupational category to reach this degree of precision. Thus sample size must be geared to the variation within the smallest subgroup about which conclusions are to be drawn. A proportional or nonproportional stratified sample might be necessary to ensure that adequate information is collected (see Section 6.4).

The appropriate group from which this sample is drawn is the total population eligible to serve on the jury, and rules and practices vary among jurisdictions: a rule may state that all literate citizens between the ages of 18 and 75 without felony records are qualified to serve. The appropriate population would be restricted to such adults unless the practice in the jurisdiction was to draw eligible jurors from the voter registration list, in which case the population to be sampled would include only those registered to vote.

The data collected and assembled from the sample will reveal for

[5] Id. at 120.
[6] Id.

every individual a measurement for each objective variable, such as "*M*" for gender, "$15,000" for income, "bus driver" for occupation, and for each attitudinal variable, such as "yes" for "believe in death penalty" or "no" for "feels hostile towards police." The most straightforward type of analysis of such a survey is the sample proportion. Exhibit 6.15(a) has been taken from an article reporting the results of a survey on attitudes toward the death penalty.[7] For each income range, there is a sample proportion of yes's and no's. This information might be used in selecting jurors who might be more favorable to the defendant. The data show that people with lower incomes are somewhat more opposed to the death penalty. For incomes less than $6,000, the sample proportion of yes's is 26%, and a two-tailed 95% confidence interval for the population proportion is 26% ± 7.3 percentage points. A sample size of 1848 would have been necessary to reach a level of precision of ± 2 percentage points. A smaller sample proportion, 11%, of people with higher incomes is personally opposed to the death penalty suggesting that a lawyer representing a client accused of a crime for which the death penalty might be imposed would prefer to have jurors from the lower end of the income scale. Occupational information about the potential jurors might enable the defense lawyer to exclude those with higher incomes. The question remains whether it would be worthwhile to use one's juror challenges to exclude higher income people in particular, since only one in four of the poorest class shares the defense's attitude.

EXHIBIT 6.15(a)
Survey Results for Voir Dire

Question: "Are You Personally Opposed to Capital Punishment?"

Income (range)	Number Responding Yes	Number Responding No	Percentage Responding Yes	Percentage Responding No	Total Number
Less than $6,000	36	104	26	74	140
$6,000 to 9,999	34	135	20	80	169
$10,000 to 14,999	40	158	20	80	198
$15,000 to 24,000	36	105	15	85	241
$25,000 and over	16	126	11	89	142

[7] N. Winston and W. Winston, The Use of Sociological Techniques in the Jury Selection Process, 6 Natl. J. of Criminal Def. 89 (1980).

§6.16 Statistical Tools Relevant to Making Juror Challenges in Voir Dire

While the question of when to use one's challenges is ultimately best answered by the lawyer's balancing of other concerns, there are statistical methods that might assist in making this judgment. A test to see whether there is a significant difference between the proportions of any two income groups was discussed in Section 6.12. The Z test for the difference between sample proportions indicates, for instance, that the probability that the observed difference in proportions between those responding "yes" in the $15,000 to $24,999 group (15%) and those responding "yes" in the $25,000-and-over group (11%) occurring by chance is greater than 28%, so one might not want to place too much weight on this difference. Another way to look at the data would be to combine those with incomes under $14,000 into one group and those over $15,000 into another. The sample proportions would then be 22% (for the low income group) and 14%. The Z test for the difference between these indicates that the probability that the difference occurred by chance is less than 1%. Combining the observation into two broad categories suggests a significant difference between the high and low income group but obscures the fact that people just above $15,000 and people just below $15,000 may have very similar attitudes. Common sense must be used in interpreting these results. Practically speaking the difference is still small — only eight percentage points.

The *correlation coefficient,* which is the topic of Chapter 7, is a way of summarizing the degree to which two variables, such as income and opposition to capital punishment, change in response to each other. An overall negative relationship is observed between income and opposition: individuals with higher incomes generally have lower opposition to capital punishment. The scale on which correlation coefficients vary is between + 1 and − 1, with the negative numbers reflecting a negative relationship. For the capital punishment data, the correlation coefficient might be − .18 indicating a negative relationship between income and opposition but not a strong one. A relationship or correspondence is said to be stronger as the correlation coefficient approaches + 1 or − 1, or gets further from zero. The particular variants of the correlation coefficient that may be most appropriate for this attitudinal survey example are found in Sections 7.8 and 7.9, which discuss correlations between one or more dichotomous variables. When only a weak relationship appears, the lawyer may search for other variables that have more influence or for a set of variables that when observed together are a good predictor of behavior.

Multiple regression, the subject of Chapter 8, is also a useful tool in interpreting attitudinal surveys in the juror selection process. If it is hypothesized, for instance, that sex, income, years of education, and age combine to be a good predictor of attitude, multiple regression techniques estimate not only the average effects of each variable on one's attitude but also the combined effect of all the variables taken together. Multiple regression can be useful in a situation in which a juror possesses several desirable characteristics but not all of them. What is lost when one selects a person with a college education (an undesirable characteristic from some viewpoints) who is a renter rather than an owner of his own home? Regression methods assign weights to such factors and indicate the extent to which they reinforce or nullify one another.

Those who have performed statistical analyses of attitudes in jury selection contexts caution that the correlations between attitudes and objective characteristics are likely to vary among communities.[1] The science is too new for proponents to have analyzed how views may vary systematically from one jurisdiction to another. For this reason some existing surveys are merely referenced here rather than described in detail.[2] The practitioner is cautioned to be alert to specific characteristics of the relevant jurisdiction and to note that the attitudes correlated with objective factors may only be predispositions. The evidence presented during the trial is more likely to influence the ultimate outcome. Moreover, while jurors with certain occupations, ages, and income levels may have certain predilections, it is often suggested that the one most frequently observed is that jurors identify with witnesses and experts having objective characteristics similar to their own, regardless of their own subjective views.[3]

---

§6.16   [1] M. Sax, The Limits of Scientific Jury Selection: Ethical and Empirical, 17 Jurimetrics 3, 15 (1976).

[2] Costantini, Mallary, & Yapundich, Gender and Juror Partiality; Are Women More Likely to Prejudge Guilt?, 67 Judicature 120, 121 (1983); M. Saks, The Limits of Scientific Jury Selection: Ethical and Empirical 17 Jurimetrics 3, 15 (1976); N. Winston and W. Winston, The Use of Sociological Techniques in the Jury Selection Process, 6 Nat. J. of Criminal Def. 79 (1980); W. Jordan, Jury Selection at 302 (1980).

[3] W. Jordan, Jury Selection at 302.

F. ERRORS ASSOCIATED WITH SAMPLE ESTIMATES

Statistics calculated from samples are often estimates of population parameters. Two categories of errors, sampling and nonsampling, make sample statistics inaccurate estimates. Previous sections of this chapter have discussed statistical techniques for determining the difference between the sample statistic and the measurement that would result if observations were made of every item in the population. Even if measurements are taken, recorded, and analyzed without any mistakes being made, sample statistics are often only estimates, which may or may not be very close to the population parameter. The difference between the estimate and the parameter due to the fact that only a portion of the population was observed is referred to as the *precision* of the sample estimate. Lack of precision results solely from the fact that all items in the population were not observed and is also referred to as *sampling error*, which is a term of art. It does not refer to all types of errors made in the course of sampling, such as incorrectly reading a measurement. Sampling error is inevitably associated with any sample size that is smaller than the entire population, although the size of the sampling error, the precision of an estimate, can be affected by choice of sample size, as discussed in Section 6.13.

To understand the difference between sampling error and nonsampling error, it is essential to appreciate the difference between the true population parameter and the measurement that would result if observations were made of every item in the population. Measuring things and making calculations involves the potential for error even if all items are measured. Using a ruler that is not exactly 12 inches long, for instance, will result in error no matter what one is measuring. Thus, due to the inaccuracy in measuring devices, the measurement that would result if observations were made of every item in the population would be erroneous in the sense that it does not give an exact measurement of the true population parameter. Because this type of error may result from measurement whether or not one is taking a sample, it is referred to as *nonsampling error*. The term *accuracy* encompasses both sampling errors, described in the previous paragraph, and nonsampling errors, those that may result from the process of data-gathering and analysis, whether one is gathering data about a sample or the entire population.

The subject of this section is nonsampling errors, those arising from the process of data-gathering and analysis. Data-gathering techniques encompass the design of a sample and the randomness of the selection of items for the sample, as well as methods of collecting and analyzing observations of the items in the sample. Each of these sources of inaccuracy is discussed in turn in the following sections. Perhaps the most serious nonsampling errors are those that result in *bias*, which results when measurements or estimates tend to depart systematically from true population parameters. As in law, we say that statistical evidence is biased if it tends toward one direction (or viewpoint) without regard to the true state of affairs. Sometimes when analyzing the randomness of a sample or the methods of collecting and analyzing data, we will be able to identify the direction of the bias and reject the sample evidence on that basis. At other times a lack of randomness or an improper data collection method may lead us to suspect the accuracy of the sample estimates even though we cannot identify the direction of the bias. In some cases we may wish to reject the evidence altogether or try to determine whether there is a bias by employing further statistical tests. The possibilities are discussed in examples in Sections 6.17 through 6.19.

Nonsampling errors may result from the design or execution of a data-gathering process. Section 6.17 discusses errors that can be avoided by attention to sample design while Section 6.18 focuses on problems of nonrandomness or nonrepresentativeness of samples. Section 6.19 identifies concerns associated with the data collection process itself.

§6.17   Errors Arising from Inappropriate Sample Design

In this section we review a variety of problems in the design of samples that have caused sample evidence to be rejected. Most are commonsense problems that could easily have been avoided. Others are more subtle because they illustrate the failure to take into account the differences in perspective between a factfinder and a scientist. A factfinder in the litigation process may have a narrower set of concerns than a scientist reviewing the same evidence.

The first error is a failure to design experiments to test the precise proposition of interest to the factfinder. In some circumstances a scientist may be more willing to extrapolate from a study of an analogous situation than is a judicial or administrative factfinder.

> **Viobin Corp:**[1] The distributors of Viobin Wheat Germ Oil advertised that their product was beneficial to health in that it "Helps Heart Action — Improves Strength — Vigor." Claiming these advertisements were deceptive, the FTC engaged an expert to test the effects of the Viobin preparation and of a placebo on the physical strength, vigor, and endurance of the participants in the test as detected by electrocardiogram and on measurements of blood cholesterol.[2] The critical error of the experimenter was failure to ensure that the wheat germ oil preparation used was one manufactured by Viobin. There was evidence that Vitamin E was used as the test substance instead. It might very well have been that this vitamin was the only active ingredient in Viobin that was of any potential benefit, but experimenter's failure to test the exact substance led to a dismissal of the complaint,[3] even though a scientist might have been willing to conclude by analogy that the product had no beneficial effect.

Neglecting to build appropriate statistical tests into an experiment might also be construed as design failure. The failure to use confidence intervals noted in the discussion of the rate proceeding in *American Telephone and Telegraph Co.,*[4] is an example. The point estimates reported by AT&T's statisticians did not give any indication of just how precise they were. The FCC insisted that future submissions contain this information. Just as failing to test the exact proposition at issue may result in rejection of the findings as proof of the matter asserted, so may failure to provide information such as point estimates in a meaningful form, such as confidence intervals.

A related design error is the imprecise identification of the variables that are relevant to a legal issue. The failure here may be due to the unavailability of data that are more directly on point, but it may also be due to a misperception of what the finder of fact views as the legal issue. Litigators are aware that it may be difficult to identify the precise concerns of a particular factfinder, and it may not be until appellate review that the problem becomes apparent.

---

§6.17   [1] 66 F.T.C. 733 (1964).
[2] Id. at 742.
[3] Id. at 745.
[4] 86 F.C.C.2d 956 (1981).

James v. Stockham Valves and Fittings Co.:[5] The plaintiffs alleged that the employer denied equal opportunities in earnings to its black employees. The defendant's expert statistician pointed to differences between blacks and whites in a number of productivity variables that accounted, he claimed, for the apparent disparities in pay. While the district court found for the defendant, the court of appeals reversed, questioning the relevance of the productivity variables. For instance, the defendant relied on differences in the level of education despite the fact that education was not a requirement for the positions. Differences in the variables of skill level and "merit rating by supervisor" were rejected because they hid discriminatory practices rather than accounted for them. The expert also offered evidence as to the earnings of employees at Stockham compared with earnings in other companies, changes in earnings of company employees over time, and relative changes in the earnings of company employees recently hired. The appellate court rejected all of this evidence because it did not meet the point that wage differences between blacks and whites were explained by discriminatory job assignments.

Better communication between the lawyers and their experts may avoid design errors of this sort and might save the expense of gathering immaterial or irrelevant data.

Eastland v. Freeman:[6] In this case, the plaintiffs' variables were insufficient to account for differences in jobs that paid different salaries and had disproportionate representation of blacks and whites. Where education, training, skill and experience did play a role in assignment to job categories and were not included in the plaintiffs' analysis, the evidence "can be given little weight in light of the many important variables excluded."

A third design error is one that is likely to lead to bias. Food and Drug Administration guidelines for the submission of biostatistical evidence require that studies of suitability of drugs employ a control group so that the effects on those to whom the test drug is administered can be compared to those who take a placebo.[7] When control groups are used it is essential that the individual who is measuring the effects of the group not know who the subjects are and who the controls are. In order to avoid bias, referred to as *experimenter bias,*

---

[5] 394 F. Supp. 434 (N.D. Ala. 1975), *rev'd,* 559 F.2d 310 (5th Cir. 1977).
[6] 528 F. Supp. 862, 878 (N.D. Ala. 1981).
[7] 21 C.F.R. §314.111(a)(5)(ii)(c) (1983).

interjected by the researcher, the persons doing the measurements are not informed as to the identity of the controls. This ignorance, referred to as *blindness*, is a necessary part of experimental design. It is also necessary that subjects not know whether they are taking the drug or the placebo, because psychological responses may occur. Thus *double blindness* is often a desired, if not required, feature. Studies where the design failed to incorporate procedures to ensure blindness are sometimes rejected as unreliable due to this nonsampling error.

Warner-Lambert Co.:[8] In response to a complaint of deceptive advertising, a test was designed to demonstrate the efficacy of Listerine in lessening the severity of colds. Students gargled daily with either a colored water rinse or Listerine and were examined by a doctor when they contracted colds. The doctor then recorded the severity of the cold for comparison of the two gargling groups. Because the doctor could smell Listerine on the breath of any complaining student who was in the Listerine test group and could not smell it on the breath of those in the colored-water group, the potential for bias arose. Because the students could tell from the flavor whether they were gargling with Listerine or with water, and because television advertisements might have affected their perceptions of the relative efficacy of the two gargles, bias might have arisen in the students' reporting of the symptoms' severity. Both parts of the required double blindness had been destroyed due to inappropriate design. For this and other reasons, the FTC found that the test lacked probative value to support the manufacturer's advertising claims.

Like other design errors, lack of blindness can usually be avoided by commonsense reflection on the ways in which bias might creep into a study. This is not to say that it is always easy to avoid. A technique used in sampling that appears useful to data collection might backfire unexpectedly.

MacMillan, Inc.:[9] The complaint alleged that MacMillan had misrepresented the job potential for graduates of their trade school. A questionnaire designed to collect information about the graduates' success was accompanied by a cover letter with a letterhead of the Federal Trade Commission, Chicago Regional Office. The letter began with the

---

[8] 86 F.T.C. 1398, 1428 (1975), *modified*, 562 F.2d 749 (D.C. Cir. 1977), *cert. denied*, 435 U.S. 950 (1978).
[9] 96 F.T.C. 208, 283 (1980).

statement that "The Bureau of Consumer Protection is gathering information from people who enrolled in LaSalle Extension University correspondence courses [subsidiary of MacMillan] to determine if any action is warranted." The letter was interpreted by the FTC as creating bias because it suggested to the subjects of the survey that they needed protection, which implied wrongdoing by MacMillan. Bias was viewed as anything that suggested one answer as opposed to another. This cover letter was thought to increase the likelihood of response from dissatisfied students, thus systematically leading away from the true measure of student success. Whenever one relevant subgroup of the population to be sampled is more likely than another to respond to a questionnaire, the problem is referred to as *self-selection*. This is a name for another form of bias. As a result of this and other defects in the survey, the hearing examiner found that "Neither firm conclusions or confident findings can be based on [this] survey."[10]

As indicated in *MacMillan*, questionnaires are particularly susceptible to attack. Should a questionnaire be the only available means of proof, a specialist in this form of testing should be employed.

§6.18   Nonrepresentativeness in Samples

Statistical conclusions based on sample estimates rely on the assumption that an unbiased attempt was made either to gather a sample as much like the population as possible in all relevant characteristics or to offer each item in the population an equal chance of being part of the sample. While the mechanism for selecting those items included in a sample is an element of sample design, the problem of nonrepresentativeness is serious enough to deserve separate treatment.

Allegations of nonrandomness may arise when the population from which a random selection is fairly chosen is not the population about which the factfinder desires proof, when the sampling is inadequate, or when the sample is designed either intentionally or by inattention so as to favor one party's view.

Sampling from an inappropriate population is a problem referred to as having a "faulty universe."[1] Because sample statistics are

---

[10]Id. at 289.
§6.18 [1]See, e.g., Hans Zeisel, The Uniqueness of Survey Evidence, 45 Cornell L.R. 322, 340 (1960) and *MacMillan, Inc.*, 96 F.T.C. 208 (1980).

merely estimates of population parameters, the problem of a faulty universe can easily be understood as measuring the appropriate characteristic of an inappropriate group.

Smithkline Corp. v. FDA:[2] The producer of Dexamyl sought approval from the Food and Drug Administration to market its product for the treatment of obesity. In support of its application it offered the results of a study of 30 anxious and obese patients. The FDA argued that these studies offered no proof that the drug would provide some of the claimed benefits in patients who were obese but not anxious, and the court agreed. Smithkline implicitly accepted an alteration of its product labeling so that it was addressed to anxious, obese people only. The problem with this study is easily identified as sampling from a group that is not the population about whom the factfinder is initially concerned.

The problem of a faulty universe also appears in more explicit attempts to extrapolate from one population to another.

Maxwell v. Bishop:[3] The petitioner claimed that the death penalty was discriminatorily imposed against him, a black man convicted of rape. In support of this claim, an expert conducted a study of 19 Arkansas counties that included 47% of the state's population. He examined the outcomes of rape trials during the 1945-1965 period and focused on their disposition according to the race of the rapist and victim. While the expert argued that the findings showed a disparate impact of the sentencing procedure, two fatal flaws of the faulty universe sort were noted by the court in its rejection of the evidence. The first was that the county in which this defendant was sentenced to death was not a test county in the survey, which might not have been a fatal flaw if the counties tested had been similar in relevant characteristics, but apparently they were not. The counties sampled were in the eastern and southern parts of the state, where most of the black population of Arkansas is located. Thus, any findings based on these areas might not apply to other parts of the state.

The benefit of large sample size is that it more precisely captures variations that exist in the population. Failure to recognize these variations may lead to a sample that does not accurately represent the

---

[2] 587 F.2d 1107, 1121 (D.C. Cir. 1978).
[3] 398 F.2d 138 (8th Cir. 1968), *vacated,* 398 U.S. 262.

population as a whole. The failure is exacerbated when variations exist but findings are based on very small samples.

National Lime Association v. EPA:[4] The Environmental Protection Agency issued standards for particulate emissions by lime manufacturing plants, based on a sample of three plants that were able to meet the standards consistently using the best available control technology. The study did not account, however, for demonstrable variation in the chemical composition of the limestone raw material in levels of capacity at which various lime kilns are operated, in fuels used to heat the kilns, and in size of the emitted particles, all of which have or may have an effect on the ability of a plant using the best available technology to meet the standard. As a result, the case was remanded to the EPA administrator for further explanation or supplementary data to take into account the potential lack of representativeness of these tests.

Occasionally sample evidence is submitted which is of adequate size to capture any variations and is taken from a subset of the correct population, but which is based on a sampling that appears so far from random that the objectiveness of the method by which items were chosen for inclusion in the sample is suspect.

Kroger Co:[5] Kroger, a retail food chain, advertised survey-based price comparisons that demonstrated that Kroger's prices for 150 food items were lower than prices at other retail food markets. Two sources of nonrandomness entered the sample: one had obvious potential for biasing the result, and the other might have been demonstrated to be the source of bias. The first was that store employees knew when setting prices which items were included in the survey. This enabled them to raise the prices of items they knew were not in the survey and lower the prices of items to be included. In effect, the results of the survey could have been determined by the survey's proponents, though such tampering was never shown. The second problem was that significant categories of food items, meats, produce, and dairy products, were omitted altogether, leading one to suspect that perhaps Kroger had higher prices on these items. This selection of categories combined with control of prices on survey items theoretically allowed Kroger to have higher prices in fact, even though the surveys showed lower prices. The defect in this sample design might be characterized as follows: pricing of an item was not blind with respect to its presence in the survey, and

---

[4] 627 F.2d 416, 435 (D.C. Cir. 1980).
[5] 98 F.T.C. 639 (1981), *modified,* 100 F.T.C. 573 (1982).

all food items did not have an equal probability of inclusion in the sample.

Litton Industries, Inc.:[6] This manufacturer of microwave ovens advertised that "76% of the independent microwave oven service technicians surveyed recommend Litton." The survey, conducted by an independent testing agency, included 234 technicians who worked for independent service agencies authorized to service Litton microwave ovens and who serviced at least one other microwave brand.[7] The FTC charged that the survey did not support this and related advertising claims. The error in the sampling was that the surveyed technicians were all employed at Litton service agencies appearing on a list given by Litton to the testing agency. Some of the dealers were included on this list of authorized agents at their insistence as a precondition to their selling Litton ovens on a retail level. Litton knew, or should have known, that the list was tainted by the inclusion of agencies that, because of their combined sales and service functions, might have a bias toward a particular oven.[8] Litton was ordered to cease the advertisements that were based on the survey.[9]

Allegations of nonrepresentativeness that have some minimal intuitive appeal appear to make offered survey evidence useless. It is possible, however, to rebut such allegations by demonstrating that the distribution of survey responses by those overrepresented in a sample do not differ significantly from those who are underrepresented. A chi-square test (see Chapter 5) is particularly useful for this purpose. The chi-square test indicates the probability that any observed difference between responses of two or more categories of respondents is due to chance as opposed to being due to an actual difference between those in the various categories. The application of the chi-square test is not always easy to interpret.

MacMillan, Inc.:[10] The issue raised was whether nonrespondents to a survey regarding success of trade courses would be systematically different from those who did respond. Most of the nonrespondents had moved, leaving no forwarding address. The group who conducted the survey used a chi-square test to determine whether there was a

---

[6] 97 F.T.C. 1, 15 (1981), *modified,* 100 F.T.C. 457 (1982).
[7] 97 F.T.C. at 16.
[8] Id. at 26-28.
[9] Id. at 55.
[10] 96 F.T.C. 208 (1980).

significant difference in responses between those who had left the area where they took the courses and those who had not, the theory being that some may have left because the trade courses had failed to produce a job in the area. The chi-square test yielded no significant difference.[11] Note, however, a statistically significant difference would only allow an inference that region of residence was related to views on the survey. This is only circumstantial evidence of the views of nonrespondents. Without making an extra effort to solicit the views of those who did not respond to the survey, this test would not prove or disprove claims of bias in the form of self-selection.[12]

A more straightforward application of the chi-square approach to test randomness can be illustrated by reference to the *Kroger* case. Recall the allegation that the survey was not random because meat, produce, and dairy items were excluded. Using a chi-square test one could compare the distribution of price increases among these items to the distribution of price increases on other food items. To test whether those selected were representative in terms of price increases, a comparison of the distribution of increases on survey items could be compared to the distribution of increases on a random selection of nonsurvey items. In either case the chi-square test would estimate the probability that the price increases were randomly assigned.

§6.19 Problems Arising in Data Collection

The need to take care in collecting data is rather obvious and need not be elaborated upon in detail. The lawyer should be made aware, however, that the process of locating, translating, and recording data is fraught with opportunity for mistakes. Even the most seemingly straightforward data collection mission may present obstacles. For examples of recording errors, the reader should refer back to Sections 2.1 and 2.2, which discuss errors in data collection. A brief survey illustrates the variety of related problems that may arise.

Dow Chemical Co. v. Blum:[1] A manufacturer, challenging an emergency ban of its herbicide, asserted that the Environmental Protection Agency study supporting the ban was flawed by improper data-

[11] Id. at 275.
[12] Id.
§6.19 [1] 469 F. Supp. 892, 905 (E.D. Mich. 1979).

gathering procedures. The study recorded rates of spontaneous abortions in two geographic regions in Oregon, one in which the herbicide had been used extensively and one where it had not. The data gathered from hospitals were flawed, not only because some hospitals would not provide all of the requested information but also because the diagnoses recording whether or not a spontaneous abortion had occurred were not reliable. Relying on such a study might raise questions, though in this case the deference paid to the administrative agency saved the day for the EPA.

Agarwal v. Arthur G. McKee and Co.:[2] In an employment discrimination case, the plaintiff relied on personal files of approximately 700 employees to compile a data base. The court identified three problems of relevance: first, many of the files had missing data and the plaintiff's statistical expert could not say that the gaps had no effect on the quality of the data; second, the expert had the data from the files transferred to computer cards in a series of steps, each of which created the possibility for error due to the need for making subjective judgments in coding; and third, the plaintiff's expert might have verified the accuracy of the data in the personnel file but did not. Some of these problems, particularly the second and third, might have been resolved by sampling the transferred data to verify its accuracy.

The problem of subjective judgments arising in collecting and transferring data from the original file to a computer readable form should be taken seriously.

McCleskey v. Zant:[3] The expert in this habeas corpus case had employed teams of law students to record characteristics of murder defendants, their offenses, and their trials, in an attempt to determine whether sentencing practices in Georgia had a discriminatory impact on blacks. The court, while paying great deference to the enormity of the task confronting the researcher, his law students, and his statistical expert, had difficulty relying on the conclusions because of problems with the data collection process. The judge identified problems such as failure to collect information on variables relevant to the sentencing process, credibility of the witnesses who had testified at the trial, failure to provide enough spaces on the data collection forms for special circumstances surrounding the murder, inconsistencies in coding data between two data gatherers who had examined the same case, and significant numbers of observations on over 100 variables for which the

[2] 9 Fair Empl. Prac. Cas. (BNA) 503 (N.D. Cal. 1977).
[3] 580 F. Supp. 338 (N.D. Ga. 1984).

data were recorded as "unknown." While the petitioner's experts attempted to deal with each problem by modifying the analysis in some way, the judge was not convinced that the results of the analysis had sufficient accuracy to be reliable.

G. COMPUTATIONAL PROCEDURES RELATED TO ANALYZING SAMPLES

The following notation is used in the formulas in this section. The numbers in parentheses following each definition indicate the section where the term is first introduced in this section and in this book. Note that upper case letters indicate population values while lower case letters indicate sample values. A lower case symbol in parentheses that follows a similar symbol to be defined is the sample equivalent of the population symbol.

$d.f.$ — the number of degrees of freedom (6.22.1)

m_x — the mean of a sample of possible observations of a variable (6.20.1)(4.21.1)

n — the number of observations in a sample (6.20.1)(4.21.1)

n_1 — the number of observations in the first sample (6.21.3)

n_2 — the number of observations in the second sample (6.21.3)

N_1 — the number of observations in a sample that possess a particular characteristic (6.22.2)

N_2 — the number of observations in a sample that do not possess a particular characteristic (6.22.2)

P (p) — the proportion of observations in the population (sample) that possess a particular characteristic (6.20.2)(4.21.1)

p_1 — the proportion of observations in the first sample that possess a particular characteristic (6.21.3)

p_2 — the proportion of observations in the second sample that possess a particular characteristic (6.21.3)

Q (q) — the proportion of observations in the population (sample) that do not possess a particular characteristic (6.20.3) (4.21.2)

q_1 — the proportion of observations in the first sample that do not possess a particular characteristic (6.21.3)

q_2 — the proportion of observations in the second sample that do not possess a particular characteristic (6.21.3)

SD (sd) — population (sample) standard deviation (6.20.3) (4.21.3)

sd_1 — the standard deviation of the first sample (6.21.3)

sd_2 — the standard deviation of the second sample (6.21.3)

$se_{diff.\ m.}$ — the standard error of the difference between the sample means (6.21.3)

$se_{diff.\ p.}$ — the standard error of the difference between the sample means (6.21.3)

se_m — the standard error of the sample mean (6.21.1)

se_p — the standard error of the sample proportion (6.21.2)

x_i — the ith value in a sequence of observations of a variable (6.20.1)(4.21.1)

§6.20 Calculations for Point Estimates from Samples

The formulas for computing sample means, sample proportions, and sample standard deviations are given in Equations 6.20(a), (b), and (c), respectively.

$$\text{sample mean} = m_x = \frac{\Sigma x_i}{n}$$

6.20(a)

$$\text{sample proportion} = p = \frac{N_1}{N_1 + N_2}$$

6.20(b)

$$\text{sample standard deviation} = sd = \sqrt{sd^2} = \sqrt{\frac{\Sigma(x_i - m_x)^2}{n - 1}}$$

6.20(c)

Illustrations of corresponding calculations appear in Chapter 4, Section 4.21, Exhibits 4.21.1(a), (c), and 4.21.3(b), respectively.

§6.21 Calculations for Standard Errors of Sample Statistics

It is necessary to calculate the standard errors of sample means and proportions in order to compute confidence intervals around sample estimates, as discussed in Sections 6.6 and 6.8. It is also necessary to calculate the standard errors of sample means, proportions, and the difference between two sample means and proportions in order to do direct significance testing of these sample statistics, as discussed in Sections 6.10 and 6.12. Standard errors for sample means are calculated in Section 6.21.1, standard errors for sample proportions are calculated in Section 6.21.2, and standard errors for differences between sample means and proportions are calculated in Section 6.21.3.

§6.21.1 Standard Error of the Sample Mean — Calculations

The standard error of the sample mean describes the typical variation among the means of samples drawn from the same population. The formula appears in Equation 6.21.1(a).[1]

$$se_m = \sqrt{\frac{SD^2}{n}} \cong \sqrt{\frac{sd^2}{n}}$$

6.21.1(a)

It indicates that the correct formula for the standard error of the sample mean requires knowledge of the population standard deviation, SD. Because we often do not know the population SD, we rely on an estimate of it, the sample standard deviation, sd. Exhibit 6.21.1(a) illustrates the calculation of this estimate of the standard error of the mean, se_m, for the *Reserve Mining* example in Section 6.6, where a confidence interval is calculated around a sample mean of 0.0626 fibers per cc. The standard error of the sample mean is 0.014.

§6.21   [1]W. Hayes & R. Winkler, Statistics: Probability, Inference, and Decision 284 (1970).

EXHIBIT 6.21.1(a)
Calculation of the Standard Error of the Sample Mean
Reserve Mining **Example**

Asbestiform Fiber
Sample Data

Day	Fiber Concentration (per cc) (x)
1	0.03835
2	0.08685
3	0.06270

$$m = \frac{\Sigma x_i}{n} = \frac{0.03835 + 0.08685 + 0.06270}{3}$$

$$= \frac{0.1879}{3} = 0.0626$$

$$sd^2 = \frac{\Sigma(x_i - m_x)^2}{n - 1}$$

$$
\begin{aligned}
\Sigma(x_i - m_x)^2 = (x_1 - m_x)^2 &= (0.03835 - 0.0626)^2 \\
&= (0.02425)^2 = 0.000588 \\
+ (x_2 - m_x)^2 &= (0.08685 - 0.0626)^2 \\
&= (-0.02425)^2 = 0.000588 \\
+ (x_3 - m_x)^2 &= (0.06270 - 0.0626)^2 \\
&= (0.0001)^2 = 0.00000 \\
&= 0.001176
\end{aligned}
$$

$$\frac{\Sigma(x_i - m_x)^2}{n - 1} = \frac{0.001176}{3 - 1} = \frac{0.001176}{2} = 0.000588 = sd^2$$

$$se_m = \sqrt{\frac{sd^2}{n}} = \sqrt{\frac{0.000588}{3}} = 0.014$$

§6.21.2 Standard Error of the Sample Proportion — Calculations

The standard error of the sample proportion describes the typical variation among sample proportions one observes among samples drawn from the same population. The formula appears in Equation 6.21.2(a).[2]

$$se_p = \sqrt{\frac{PQ}{n}} \cong \sqrt{\frac{pq}{n}}$$

6.21.2(a)

[2] Id. at 190.

Exhibit 6.21.2(a) illustrates the calculation of the standard error of the sample proportion for the *H. S. Camp and Sons* example from Section 6.8. For a sample of 139 employees with a sample proportion, p, of 23% black and 77% nonblack, q, the estimate of the standard error of the sample proportion is 0.036.

EXHIBIT 6.21.2(a)
Sample-Based Calculation of the Standard Error of the Proportion
H. S. Camp and Sons **Example**

Data

n = 139 (sample size)
p = .23 (sample proportion of blacks = 42/139)
q = $1 - p$ = .77 (sample proportion of nonblacks = 107/139)

$$se_{\text{proportion}} = \sqrt{\frac{pq}{n}}$$

$$= \sqrt{\frac{.23 \times .77}{139}} = 0.036$$

If the underlying proportion, P, of eligible blacks in the relevant labor pool is known, then that proportion should be used instead of the sample proportion, p, to calculate the standard error of the proportion. If additional knowledge enables us to make a more precise calculation of the standard error of the proportion, we should use it. Exhibit 6.21.2(b) illustrates the calculation of the standard error using a hypothetical population proportion for blacks of .35 in the *H. S. Camp* case. This is particularly important when engaged in direct significance testing of the difference between a sample proportion and a known population proportion. See Section 6.23.

EXHIBIT 6.21.2(b)
Population-Based Calculation of Standard Error of Proportion
H. S. Camp **Example**

Data

n = 139 (sample size)
P = .35 (population proportion of blacks)
Q = $1 - P$ = .65 (population proportion of non-blacks)

$$se_p = \sqrt{\frac{PQ}{n}} = \sqrt{\frac{.35 \times .65}{139}} = .040$$

§6.21.3   Standard Error of the Difference Between Sample Estimates — Calculations

The standard error of the difference between sample means or proportions describes the typical variation in the differences between two sample means or two proportions that are calculated from samples drawn from the same population. In a case such as *Presseisen*, discussed in Section 6.11, we assume that men and women are part of the same population and, hence, there is no significant difference between the promotion practices with regard to either sex. If this is true, as our hypothesis implies, the population means and standard deviations for the two groups are presumptively identical. The data show different sample means for the two groups and different sample standard deviations. Equation 6.21.3(a)[3] uses the two sample standard deviations, sd_1 and sd_2, and sample sizes, n_1 and n_2, to calculate an estimate of the standard error of the difference between the sample means.

$$se_{\text{difference between means}} = se_{\text{diff.m.}} = \sqrt{\frac{(n_1 - 1)sd_1^2 + (n_2 - 1)sd_2^2}{(n_1 - 1) + (n_2 - 1)}} \times \sqrt{\frac{1}{n_1} + \frac{1}{n_2}}$$

6.21.3(a)

Equation 6.21.3(b)[4] gives the formula for the standard error of the difference between sample proportions for use in significance testing when the samples are large.

$$se_{\text{difference between proportions}} = se_{\text{diff.p.}} = \sqrt{\frac{p_1 q_1}{n_1} + \frac{p_2 q_2}{n_2}}$$

6.21.3(b)

A chi-square test can be used for smaller samples, using the observed frequencies in each group as the values in the contingency tables. See Chapter 5.

Exhibit 6.21.3(a) illustrates the calculation of the estimate of the standard error of the difference between means for the *Presseisen*

---

[3] Id. at 264. (Uses n_1, n_2, rather than $n_1 - 1$, $n_2 - 1$, because illustration is for very large sample.)

[4] R. Pfaffenberger & J. Patterson, Statistical Methods for Business and Economics 349 (1977).

example where the sample mean time until promotion to associate professor for men was 7.6 years, with a sample standard deviation of 3.77 years, and for women was 16.4 years, with a sample standard deviation of 14.03 years. The estimated standard error of the difference between means was 2.74 years. This figure is used in Exhibit 6.22.3(b) to do a direct test of statistical significance on this difference.

EXHIBIT 6.21.3(a)
Calculation of Standard Error of Differences Between Means
***Presseisen* Example**

Data

Men	*Women*
n_1 = 30 men	n_2 = 12 women
sd_1 = 3.77 years	sd_2 = 14.03 years

$$se_{\text{diff.m.}} = \sqrt{\frac{(n_1 - 1)sd_1^2 + (n_2 - 1)sd_2^2}{(n_1 - 1) + (n_2 - 1)}} \times \sqrt{\frac{1}{n_1} + \frac{1}{n_2}}$$

$$= \sqrt{\frac{(30 - 1)(3.77)^2 + (12 - 1)(14.03)^2}{(30 - 1) + (12 - 1)}} \times \sqrt{\frac{1}{30} + \frac{1}{12}}$$

$$= 2.74$$

Exhibit 6.21.3(b) illustrates the calculation of the estimate of the standard error of the difference between proportions. The example is taken from the law of unfair competition. The issue is whether the proportion of new cars (relative to total cars, old and new) sold prior to defendant's unfair trade practice is really greater than that sold after the practice occurred. Before, 25% of the dealer's 400 car sales were new cars; afterwards, only 22% of 296 were. The estimate of the standard error of the difference in these proportions is equal to 0.0324. This information is used to create a confidence interval for the difference or for direct significance testing of the difference between these sample proportions. This standard error is used in Exhibit 6.22.3(c) to do a direct significance test of the difference between proportions.

EXHIBIT 6.21.3(b)
Calculation of Standard Error of Difference Between Proportions
Unfair Competition Example

Data

Prior to Practice	*After Practice*
New Cars = 100	New Cars = 65
Total Cars = 400 = n_1	Total Cars = 296 = n_2
$p_1 = .25$	$p_2 = .22$
$q_1 = .75$	$q_2 = .78$

$$se_{\text{diff.p.}} = \sqrt{\frac{p_1 q_1}{n_1} + \frac{p_2 q_2}{n_2}}$$

$$= \sqrt{\frac{.25 \times .75}{400} + \frac{.22 \times .78}{296}}$$

$$= 0.0324$$

§6.22 Calculation of Confidence Intervals

A confidence interval for a sample statistic indicates a range within which the corresponding population parameter is likely to fall with a specified degree of certainty. For each statistic we consider the general formula for the interval around the statistic, which requires that one add to or subtract from (in the case of a one-tailed interval) or add to and subtract from (in the case of a two-tailed interval) the sample statistic, the product of the standard error of the estimate and a critical t or Z value. Sections 6.22.1, 6.22.2, and 6.22.3 illustrate these calculations for sample means, proportions, and differences.

§6.22.1 Confidence Intervals for Sample Means — Calculations

The formula for the two-tailed confidence interval around a sample mean is shown in Equation 6.22.1(a).[1]

$$\text{confidence interval (means)} = m \pm t_{\text{critical}} \times se_m$$

6.22.1(a)

This formula should be used in cases where the population standard deviation for the variable being observed is unknown. This is the most

---

§6.22   [1] W. Hayes & R. Winkler, Statistics: Probability, Inference, and Decision 343 (1970).

common situation we have discovered in legal practice. The sample mean, m, is calculated by Equation 6.20.1(a), and the standard error of the mean is calculated by Equation 6.21.1(a).

In order to find $t_{critical}$, two pieces of information must be determined: (1) the size of the sample from which the mean was calculated and (2) the degree of certainty with which it is desired that the population parameter fall within the interval. Once this information is obtained, a t Table such as that shown in the Appendix of Tables reveals the appropriate critical t value. This Table presents the relationship among probabilities (p-values), critical t values, and degrees of freedom for one-tailed and for two-tailed intervals. The sample size must be known to calculate the number of degrees of freedom, which, in the case of confidence intervals for sample means is numerically identical to one less than the number of observations in the sample, as indicated in Equation 6.22.1(b).[2]

$$\text{degrees of freedom (conf. int. for mean)} = d.f. = n - 1$$

6.22.1(b)

The level of certainty required, also referred to as the *confidence level*, is a matter for the judgment of or requirements placed upon the researcher, just as is the p-value necessary to reject the null hypothesis. Critical t values vary depending on the confidence level chosen. Across the top, the t Table lists *significance levels*, such as .30, .20, .10, and .05 for one-tailed tests and two-tailed tests. Since we are currently discussing two-tailed tests we will consider for now only the significance levels under the Two-Tailed Test heading. The significance level is interpreted in this context as the probability that the population parameter will be outside the confidence interval. Thus the confidence level, which is 1.00 minus the significance level, is the probability that the population parameter will be inside the interval. Confidence levels of .99, .95, .90, and .80, for instance, correspond to significance levels of .01, .05, .10, and .20.

With this information the critical t value to be used in Equation 6.22.1(a) can be found. If our sample size is ten and we wish to be 99% certain that the population parameter falls within the interval, we find the value on the t Table that corresponds to nine degrees of freedom and a significance level of .01 for a two-tailed test. The critical t values for nine degrees of freedom are shown in Exhibit 6.22.1(a). The

---

[2] Id.

EXHIBIT 6.22.1(a)
Critical *t* Values for Nine Degrees of Freedom

						Significance Level						
						One-Tailed Test						
.45	.40	.35	.30	.25	.20	.15	.10	.05	.025	.01	.005	.0005
						Two-Tailed Test						
.90	.80	.70	.60	.50	.40	.30	.20	.10	.05	.02	.01	.001

Degrees of Freedom												
9	.129	.261	.398	.543	.703	.883	1.100	1.383	1.833	2.262	2.821	3.250	4.781

appropriate critical t value for a significance level of .01, nine degrees of freedom, and a two-tailed test is 3.250.

For the *Reserve Mining* example discussed in Section 6.6, the sample mean concentration of asbestiform fibers was 0.0626 fibers per cubic centimeter, and the standard error of the mean was 0.014 fibers. Exhibit 6.22.1(b) illustrates that if the sample size on which this mean was calculated was three then the two-tailed confidence interval runs from .0024 to 0.1228 fibers per cc. This interval is broad because the sample size is so small.

EXHIBIT 6.22.1(b)
Two-Tailed Confidence Interval
Reserve Mining Example

sample size = 3, thus $d.f.$ = 3 − 1 = 2
m = 0.0626 fibers per cc
se_m = 0.014 fibers
confidence level = .95
$t_{critical}$ for two-tailed test, .05 significance level, and 2 $d.f.$ = 4.303

$$\text{confidence interval} = m \pm t_{\text{two-tailed}, .05, 2\,d.f.} \times se_m$$
$$= 0.0626 \pm 4.303 \times 0.014$$
$$= 0.0626 \pm .0602$$
$$= 0.0024 \text{ to } 0.1228 \text{ fibers per cc}$$

Increasing sample size almost always reduces the width of the interval and tends to reduce the estimate of the standard error of the mean because the se_m is the square root of the standard deviation divided by the sample size. An increased sample size also reduces the critical t value because, as a glance at the t Table illustrates, the critical t values get smaller as the sample sizes and, correspondingly, the degrees of freedom increase. If the sample size in the *Reserve Mining* example were increased to 25, for instance, and if the mean and standard error of the mean do not change, the 95% confidence interval would be from .0337 to .0915 fibers per cc.

When the population standard deviation is known and used in the calculation of se_m, the critical Z value is substituted in the confidence interval equation for the critical t value, as indicated in Equation 6.22.1(c).[3]

---

[3] Id. at 328-331.

$$\text{confidence interval (means)} = m \pm Z_{\text{critical}} \times se_m$$

6.22.1(c)

Equation 6.22.1(c) also gives a close approximation to the Equation 6.22.1(a) (which uses the critical t value) whenever the sample size is large, greater than about 30. This approximation works because critical t values for a given significance level change little as sample size increases above 30. For such large samples the critical t value for any given level of confidence is approximately the same as the critical Z value for the same confidence level. The reason that the critical t values for a given significance level approach the critical Z values as sample sizes increase is that as sample sizes increase the estimated standard deviation obtained from the sample is a better approximation of the population standard deviation. When using the critical Z formula for the confidence interval, the mean, m, and standard error of the mean, se_m, are determined in the same way as for the confidence interval based on t. The critical Z value for any confidence level can be found in a Table of Critical Values of Z such as that reproduced in the Appendix of Tables and in Exhibit 6.22.1(c). Note that the critical Z values do not vary with sample size; they depend only on whether a one- or two-tailed test is being used and what significance level is chosen. These critical Z values correspond to the critical t values shown on the t Table for an infinite number of degrees of freedom. When the population standard deviation is known, it should be used in calculating se_m, and the Z formula rather than the t formula for the confidence interval is appropriate.

EXHIBIT 6.22.1(c)
Table of Critical Values of Z

Significance Level

One-Tailed Test																
.45	.40	.35	.30	.25	.20	.15	.10	.05	.025	.01	.005	.0005
Two-Tailed Test												
.90	.80	.70	.60	.50	.40	.30	.20	.10	.05	.02	.01	.001
.126	.253	.385	.524	.674	.842	1.036	1.282	1.645	1.960	2.326	2.576	3.291

Exhibit 6.22.1(d) illustrates the use of the critical Z in the calculation of a confidence interval in the *Eovaldi* case, discussed in Section 6.7, where the sample size included hundreds of observations. The sample mean damage per customer due to excess finance charges was $22,567, and the estimate of the standard error of the mean was $2,292. Using the critical Z for a 99% confidence level, 2.576, the two-tailed confidence interval was from $16,663 to $28,471.

EXHIBIT 6.22.1(d)
Two-Tailed Confidence Interval
***Eovaldi* Example**

Sample size is large so critical Z is used.
m = $22,567
se_m = $2,292
confidence level = .99
$Z_{critical}$ for two-tailed test, .01 significance level = 2.576

$$\text{confidence interval} = m \pm Z_{\text{two-tailed, .01}} \times se_m$$
$$= \$22,567 \pm 2.576 \times \$2,292$$
$$= \$22,567 \pm \$5,904$$
$$= \$16,663 \text{ to } \$28,471$$

One-tailed confidence intervals can also be calculated with little alteration in the basic formulas presented in Equation 6.22.1(a) and (c). The same conventions regarding degrees of freedom and the choice of t or Z critical values are followed. Once the sample mean and standard error of the mean are calculated, a limit can be calculated above which the population parameter lies with a specified degree of confidence. One should use either Equation 6.22.1(d) or (e), depending on whether a t or Z critical value is appropriate.

$$\text{lower limit} = m - t_{\text{critical}} \times se_m$$

6.22.1(d)

$$\text{lower limit} = m - Z_{\text{critical}} \times se_m$$

6.22.1(e)

A limit can also be calculated below which the population parameter lies with a specified degree of confidence. One should use either Equation 6.22.1(f) or (g), depending on whether a t or Z critical value is appropriate.

$$\text{upper limit} = m + t_{\text{critical}} \times se_m$$

6.22.1(f)

$$\text{upper limit} = m + Z_{\text{critical}} \times se_m$$

6.22.1(g)

As noted in Section 6.9, one tailed confidence intervals are particularly useful in testing the likelihood that a population mean is greater than a legal maximum or less than a legal minimum. From a legal perspective, we want to be certain that, at whatever level of confidence desired, the population parameter being estimated using a sample statistic exceeds the maximum or falls short of the minimum. We can either calculate a one-tailed confidence interval at a specified level of confidence to see whether the range encompasses the legal maximum or minimum or use the confidence interval concept to determine the probability that the population parameter exceeds or falls short of the legal standard. For the latter approach, direct significance testing, see Section 6.23, Procedures for Direct Significance Tests for Sample Estimates.

In the *Portland Cement* example in Section 6.9, we were concerned with ascertaining whether a sample mean of 0.16 kg per metric ton was convincing evidence of a violation of the legal maximum allowable average effluent of 0.15 kg per metric ton of particulates from a cement kiln. The sample mean appears to be larger than the maximum but to test whether we can be certain that the population mean exceeds the standard, a one-tailed confidence interval can be calculated as in Exhibit 6.22.1(e). Because we want a value above which we can be 99% certain the population value falls, we use either Equation 6.22.1(d) or (e). If the population standard deviation is unknown, as is almost certainly the case here, and the sample size is small, the critical *t* value approach in Equation 6.22.1(d) is appropriate. Exhibit 6.22.1(e) illustrates that for a sample size of 22 measurements we can be 99% certain of a violation if the standard error of the mean is .003 kg per metric ton, because we can be 99% certain that the population mean is greater than .152. If on the other hand the standard error of the mean were .02 kg per metric ton, we could not be 99% confident that there was a violation, because the value above which we can be 99% confident that the population mean lies, .110, is below the legal maximum of .15 kg per metric ton.

EXHIBIT 6.22.1(e)
One-Tailed Confidence Intervals for Legal Maximum
***Portland Cement* Example**

sample size = 22
degrees of freedom = 21
m = .16 kg per metric ton
confidence level = .99
$t_{critical}$ for one-tailed, .01 significance level, 21 $d.f.$ = 2.518

If se_m = .003:

confidence interval = $m - t_{\text{one-tail}, .01, 21\,d.f.} \times se_m$
= .16 − 2.518 × .003 = .152 kg per metric ton

If se_m = .02:

confidence interval = $m - t_{\text{one-tail}, .01, 21\,d.f.} \times se_m$
= .16 − 2.518 × .02 = .110 kg per metric ton

In *Marathon Oil,* discussed in Section 6.9, the problem was to find an effluent level *below which* exemplary offshore oil drilling rigs would be likely to fall 99% of the time. With a sample mean of 7.43 pounds of effluent per day and standard error of the mean of .70 pounds per day, Equation 6.22.1(e) is appropriate for a small sample size, assumed in Exhibit 6.22.1(f) to be 16. Exhibit 6.22.1(f) illustrates the calculation of a value, 9.25 pounds per day, below which the average daily effluent of high technology rigs is likely to fall 99% of the time. This figure was proposed by the Administration of the EPA as the legal maximum.[4]

EXHIBIT 6.22.1(f)
One-Tailed Confidence Interval for Setting a Legal Maximum
***Marathon Oil* Example**

n = 16
$d.f.$ = 15
m = 7.43 pounds per day
se_m = .70 pounds per day
confidence level = .99
$t_{critical}$ for one-tailed test, .01 significance level, 15 $d.f.$ = 2.602

confidence interval = $m + t_{\text{one-tail}, .01, 15\,d.f.} \times se_m$
= 7.43 + 2.602 × .70 = 9.25 pounds per day

[4] 564 F.2d 1253, 1259 (9th Cir. 1977).

In the *General Motors* example, Section 6.9, the issue was whether the number of wheel failures exceeded a minimum necessary to trigger the defect notification requirement. For a large sample, with a sample mean number of failures per person of two, and a standard error of the sample mean of .07 failures per person, we can find values above which we can be certain (to whatever degree specified) the population number of failures lies using Equation 6.22.1(e), or below which the population value is likely to fall using Equation 6.22.1(g). Exhibit 6.22.1(g) illustrates this use of the critical Z value in one-tailed and two-tailed confidence intervals. Because we are interested in the total number of failures, we multiply these values by the total number of persons owning such trucks to find a number above or below which we can be 90%, the level chosen for this example, certain that the total number of failures falls.

EXHIBIT 6.22.1(g)
Illustration of One-Tailed and Two-Tailed Tests
for Large Samples
***General Motors* Example**

sample size is large
$m = 2.00$ failures per person
$se_m = .07$ failures per person
Z_{critical} for one-tail, .10 significance level $= 1.282$
population size $= 2000$ truck owners

To find a value above which the total number of failures is likely to fall with 90% confidence,

$$\text{Confidence interval} = m - Z_{\text{one-tailed}, .10} \times se_m$$
$$= 2.00 - 1.282 \times .07$$
$$= 1.91 \text{ failures per person}$$

Total failures is likely to be greater than $2000 \times 1.91 = 3820$.

To find a value below which the total number of failures is likely to fall with 90% confidence,

$$\text{Confidence interval} = m + Z_{\text{one-tailed}, .10} \times se_m$$
$$= 2.00 + 1.282 \times .07$$
$$= 2.09 \text{ failures per person}$$

Total failures is likely to be less than $2000 \times 2.09 = 4180$.

Z_{critical} for two-tails, .10 significance level $= 1.645$

$$\text{Two-tailed confidence interval} = m \pm Z_{\text{two-tailed}, .10} \times se_m$$
$$= 2.00 \pm 1.645 \times .07$$

Interval is from 1.885 to 2.115 failures per person.
Interval for total failures is from 3770 to 4230.

§6.22.2 Confidence Intervals for Sample Proportions — Calculations

Because sample proportions are merely a special case of sample means, many of the comments made in Section 6.22.1 apply here as well. The critical difference is that the Z critical values are used. The approach outlined is appropriate whenever the number of items in the sample from each of two categories whose proportions are being estimated is greater than or equal to five. Mathematically, this means that n times p is greater than or equal to five and n times $(1 - p)$ is greater than or equal to five (where n is the sample size and p is the sample proportion of one of the groups). When the sample size is smaller than necessary to meet this condition, direct hypothesis testing for proportions can be carried out using the methodology developed in Sections 4.15, P-Values for Binomial Distributions, and 4.23, Binomial Probabilities — Calculations.

Equation 6.22.2(a) presents the formula for two-tailed confidence intervals for proportions using Z critical values.[5]

$$\text{confidence interval (proportion)} = p \pm Z_{\text{critical}} \times se_p$$

6.22.2(a)

In the *Warner-Lambert* example discussed in Section 6.8, the public opinion researchers estimated the proportion of TV viewers who recalled Listerine commercials. A two-tailed confidence interval around the sample proportion of 68% who remembered the "effectiveness in cold prevention" theme would indicate a range into which the population percentage was likely to fall, as illustrated by the calculations in Exhibit 6.22.2(a), showing a range from .63 to .73 for a 95% confidence interval.

---

[5] W. Hayes & R. Winkler, Statistics: Probability, Inference, and Decision 332 (1970).

EXHIBIT 6.22.2(a)
Confidence Interval for Proportion
***Warner-Lambert* Example**

sample size, n, is large = 335
sample proportion, $p = .68$ so $q = 1 - .68 = .32$
standard error of sample proportion $= \sqrt{\dfrac{pq}{n}} = \sqrt{\dfrac{.68 \times .32}{335}} = .0255$

$p \times n = .68 \times 335 = 227.8 > 5$ and
$(1 - p) \times n = qn = .32 \times 335 = 107.2 > 5,$
thus Z formula is appropriate

confidence interval $= p \pm Z_{\text{two-tailed, .05}} \times se_p$
$= .68 \pm 1.96 \times .0255$
$= .68 \pm .05$
95% confidence interval from .63 to .73

The sample proportion of black employees in *H. S. Camp*, discussed in Section 6.8, was .23. A two-tailed confidence interval from .160 to .300 around this proportion is calculated in Exhibit 6.22.2(b).

EXHIBIT 6.22.2(b)
Two-Tailed Confidence Interval
with Known Population Proportion
***H. S. Camp* Example**

Data

$n = 139$
$P = .35$ (Population proportion of blacks)
$Q = .65$
$p = .23$ (Sample proportion of blacks)
$q = .71$
$se_p = \sqrt{\dfrac{pq}{n}} = \sqrt{\dfrac{.23 \times .77}{139}} = .036$
confidence level = .95
$Z_{\text{two-tailed, .05 significance level}} = 1.96$

confidence interval $= p \pm Z_{\text{two-tailed, .05}} \times se_p$
$= .23 \pm 1.96 \times .036 = .23 \pm .070$
95% confidence interval from .160 to .300 or 16% to 30%

One-tailed confidence intervals are useful for comparing sample proportions to external standards. In *Teleprompter*, discussed in Section 6.8, the issue was whether the sample proportion of the market share was enough *greater* than the standard so that cross-ownership rules applied. In *H. S. Camp* the issue was whether the percentage of blacks in the defendant's workforce was enough *below* the proportion of blacks in the relevant labor pool that we would say that the disparity was significant. The percentage of blacks hired by defendant can be treated as a sample proportion, and a one-tailed confidence interval can be used to ascertain the proportion below which most workforces hired by defendant would fall. Equations 6.22.2(b) and (c) are the appropriate formulas for one-tailed confidence intervals for Z-based intervals used to determine limits above and below which the population proportion is likely to fall.

$$\text{upper limit} = p + Z_{\text{critical}} \times se_p$$

6.22.2(b)

$$\text{lower limit} = p - Z_{\text{critical}} \times se_p$$

6.22.2(c)

Exhibit 6.22.2(c) illustrates the calculation of a proportion above which the percentage of blacks hired by Camp is unlikely to fall. Using the estimated standard error of the proportion obtained from the sample proportion of 23% blacks in the workforce, we calculated an upper limit of .29 or 29% above which the population proportion is unlikely to fall if the employees were hired without regard to race. Because this upper limit is less than the known population percentage of blacks, 35%, this analysis provides some evidence of nonrandom selection and, hence, of discrimination. Note that even though we know the population proportion of eligible blacks we do not use it to calculate the confidence interval around the sample proportion, because we wish to obtain from the employer's labor force data alone an estimate of the proportion of blacks in the population. The fact that the actual population proportion falls above the upper limit of proportions that would be plausible if the employer selected randomly from eligible applicants suggests that the proportion of blacks among the employees is significantly less than the proportion among eligible applicants.

EXHIBIT 6.22.2(c)
One-Tailed Confidence Interval Calculation
for Sample Proportion
***H. S. Camp* Example**

n = 139 Employees
p = .23 (sample proportion)
q = .77
confidence level = .95
$Z_{\text{one-tailed, .05}}$ = 1.645
se_p = .036

upper limit = $p + Z_{\text{one-tailed, .05}} \times se_p$
              = .23 + 1.645 × .036 = .29

A one-tailed confidence interval for the *Teleprompter* example appears in Exhibit 6.22.2(d), where it is assumed that for cross-ownership rules to apply the sample proportion of viewers watching a given station must exceed 30% and we must be 70% certain that the population proportion is greater than 30%. In this example, based on a sample size of 250 and a sample proportion of 32%, we find that we can be confident at a 70% level that the population proportion is greater than .304.

EXHIBIT 6.22.2(d)
One-Tailed Confidence Interval with Population Proportion
Unknown
***Teleprompter* Example**

p = .32, thus q = .68
n = 250
confidence level = .70
$Z_{\text{one-tailed, .30 significance level}}$ = .524

$$se_p = \sqrt{\frac{pq}{n}} = \sqrt{\frac{.32 \times .68}{250}} = .030$$

lower limit = $p - Z_{\text{one-tailed, .30}} \times se_p$ = .32 − .524 × .030 = .304

70% confident that P (the population proportion)
is greater than .304

In order to determine the probability that the population proportion is greater than .30, we must calculate the Z value necessary to give a lower limit of .300, as shown in Exhibit 6.22.2(e). For a one-tailed interval a critical Z of .67 would give a lower limit of .300. The

Table of Critical Values of Z indicates that a one-tailed interval with a significance level of about .25 (a confidence level of .75) would give this lower limit. The Z Table (discussed in Section 4.13), which appears in the Appendix of Tables, can also be used to find the probability associated with this Z score of .67: The Z value on the Z Table corresponding to a Z score of 0.67 is .2486. Subtracting .2486 from 1.000 gives a one-tailed probability of .7514, or 75.14%. (See Section 4.14 for a discussion of the use of the Z Table.)

EXHIBIT 6.22.2(e)
Probability that Population Proportion Exceeds Legal Minimum
***Teleprompter* Example**

$n = 250$
$p = .32$ (estimated population percentage viewing station)
$q = 1 - p = .68$
$se_p = .030$
lower limit $= p - Z \times se_p$

For lower limit of .30 we must find Z such that
$$.30 = .32 - Z \times .030.$$

The only Z score that satisfies this equation is
$$Z = (.32 - .30)/.030 = .67$$

§6.22.3   Confidence Intervals for the Difference Between Sample Estimates — Calculations

If all parts of a one-tailed confidence interval for one estimate are above or below the one-tailed confidence interval for another estimate, then we can infer (at whatever level of confidence underlies the intervals) that the two estimates are significantly different. Exhibit 6.22.3(a) illustrates two confidence intervals for the *Presseisen* example discussed in Section 6.12, one each for men and women who taught at Swarthmore College. The mean time until promotion to associate professor was 7.6 years for men, and 16.4 years for women. The issue is whether these are significantly different when regarded as the result of random draws from a population. The failure of the confidence intervals to overlap indicates that the probability of getting a difference this large or larger when there is in fact no difference is less than 5%. We can be 95% confident that the population mean for men is less than 8.77 years and that the population mean for women is no lower than 9.13 years.

EXHIBIT 6.22.3(a)
Overlapping Confidence Interval for Men and Women
Presseisen **Example**

Data

Men	*Women*
$m = 7.6$ years	$m = 16.4$ years
$se_m = .69 = \sqrt{\dfrac{3.77^2}{30}}$	$se_m = \sqrt{\dfrac{14.03^2}{12}} = 4.05$
$n = 30$	$n = 12$
$t_{\text{one-tailed, .05, 29 d.f.}} = 1.699$	$t_{\text{one-tailed, .05, 11 d.f.}} = 1.796$
Confidence interval =	Confidence interval =
$\quad m + t_{\text{one-tailed, .05, 29 d.f.}} \times se_m$	$\quad m - t_{\text{one-tailed, .05, 11 d.f.}} \times se_m$
$\quad = 7.6 + 1.699 \times 0.69$	$\quad = 16.4 - 1.796 \times 4.05$
$\quad = 7.6 + 1.17$	$\quad = 16.4 - 7.27$
We can be 95% confident	We can be 95% confident
$\quad M < 8.77$	$\quad M > 9.13$

It is easier conceptually to calculate the interval for the difference itself. If the interval includes zero then we can infer, at whatever level of confidence underlies the confidence interval, that the difference is not statistically significant; if it does not include zero we can infer that the difference is statistically significant. The general formulas for confidence intervals for differences between sample means and proportions are shown in Equations 6.22.3(a),[6] (b)[7] and (c).[8]

$$\text{confidence interval (difference between means)} =$$
$$\text{difference} \pm t_{\text{critical}} \times se_{\text{diff.m.}}$$

6.22.3(a)

$$\text{confidence interval (difference between means)} =$$
$$\text{difference} \pm Z_{\text{critical}} \times se_{\text{diff.m.}}$$

6.22.3(b)

$$\text{confidence interval (difference between proportions)} =$$
$$\text{difference} \pm Z_{\text{critical}} \times se_{\text{diff.p.}}$$

6.22.3(c)

[6] W. Hayes and R. Winkler, Statistics: Probability, Inference, and Decision 348 (1970).
[7] Id. at 347.
[8] R. Pfaffenberger & J. Patterson, Statistical Methods for Business and Economics 349 (1977).

The rules for choosing formulas based on critical t or Z values are the same as outlined in Section 6.22.1. For Equation 6.22.3(a), where critical t values must be determined, the number of degrees of freedom is equal to the sum of the sizes of the samples from which the means or proportions were calculated minus two, as shown in Equation 6.22.3(d).[9]

$$\text{degrees of freedom (difference between two sample means)} =$$
$$n_1 + n_2 - 2$$

6.22.3(d)

Exhibit 6.22.3(b) illustrates the calculation of a confidence interval for the difference between sample means in the *Presseisen* example. Note that zero is not included in the interval from 3.43 to 14.17 years, so we can infer the existence of a significant difference at the 5% level of significance. A one-tailed interval, also illustrated in Exhibit 6.22.3(b), indicates that we can be 95% confident that the difference between mean times to promotion of men and women exceeds 4.27 years.

EXHIBIT 6.22.3(b)
Two-Tailed Confidence Interval for Difference
Between Means
***Presseisen* Example**

difference = 8.8 years
n_1 = 30 men
n_2 = 12 women
degrees of freedom = 30 + 12 − 2 = 40
$se_{\text{diff. m.}}$ = 2.74 years   (see Exhibit 6.21.3(a))
confidence level = 95%

Z_{critical} for two-tails, .05 significance level = 1.96

Confidence interval = difference $\pm$ Z_{critical} $\times$ $se_{\text{diff. m.}}$
= 8.8 $\pm$ 1.96 $\times$ 2.74 = 8.8 $\pm$ 5.37
= 3.43 to 14.17 years

Z_{critical} for one-tail, .05 significance = 1.645

lower limit = difference − Z_{critical} $\times$ $se_{\text{diff. m.}}$
= 8.8 − 1.645 $\times$ 2.74 = 4.27 years

[9] W. Hayes and R. Winkler, Statistics: Probability, Inference, and Decision 348 (1970).

The illustration presented here for the difference between sample proportions is a one-tailed test, although two-tailed tests are equally permissible. The proportions tested are taken from the unfair competition example in Section 6.21.3, where the proportion of new cars sold prior to the unlawful practice was 25% and after the unlawful practice was 22%. A set of equations for one-tailed confidence intervals for differences would look like those shown in Equations 6.22.1(d)-(g) and 6.22.2(b) and (c), with differences substituted for means and proportions. The form of the confidence interval equation used in Exhibit 6.22.3(c) appears in Equation 6.22.3(e).

$$\text{lower limit} = \text{difference} - Z_{\text{critical}} \times se_{\text{diff.p.}}$$

6.22.3(e)

EXHIBIT 6.22.3(c)
One-Tailed Confidence Interval for Difference
Between Proportions
Unfair Competition Example

difference $= .25 - .22 = .03$
$n_1 = 400$ total cars sold prior to unlawful practice, of which 25% were new
$n_2 = 295$ total cars sold after the unlawful practice, of which 23% were new
$se_{\text{diff. p.}} = .0324$ (see Section 6.21.3)
confidence level $= 99\%$
Z_{critical} for one-tail, .01 significance level $= 2.326$

$$\text{Confidence interval} = \text{difference} - Z_{\text{one-tail, .01}} \times se_{\text{diff. p.}}$$
$$= .03 - 2.326 \times .0324 = .03 - .075$$
We can be 99% certain that the difference is greater than $-.045$

The computation in Exhibit 6.22.3(c) indicates a value above which we can be 99% certain that the actual difference lies. For these facts, the value is $-.045$. Because zero is one of the numbers above the indicated value of $-.045$ we cannot infer at a 99% confidence level that there is any difference at all.

An upper limit for the difference between proportions can be calculated using Equation 6.22.3(f). Lower and upper limits for differences between means can be calculated using Equations 6.22.3(g) and (h) when a t test is appropriate and Equations 6.22.3(i) and (j) when a Z test is appropriate.

$$\text{upper limit} = \text{difference} + Z_{\text{critical}} \times se_{\text{diff.p.}}$$

6.22.3(f)

$$\text{lower limit} = \text{difference} - t_{\text{critical}} \times se_{\text{diff.m.}}$$

6.22.3(g)

$$\text{upper limit} = \text{difference} + t_{\text{critical}} \times se_{\text{diff.m.}}$$

6.22.3(h)

$$\text{lower limit} = \text{difference} - Z_{\text{critical}} \times se_{\text{diff.m.}}$$

6.22.3(i)

$$\text{upper limit} = \text{difference} + Z_{\text{critical}} \times se_{\text{diff.m.}}$$

6.22.3(j)

§6.23 Procedures for Direct Significance Tests for Sample Estimates

For each of the examples in Section 6.22, a direct significance test using either a t or Z test, as is appropriate, can be performed to determine whether the sample estimate of a population mean, proportion, or difference between sample means or proportions is significantly different from zero. For each test a t or Z value is calculated using either Equation 6.23(a) or (b).

$$\text{calculated } t = \frac{\text{sample estimate}}{\text{estimated standard error of sample estimate}}$$

6.23(a)

$$\text{calculated } Z = \frac{\text{sample estimate}}{\text{standard error of sample estimate}}$$

6.23(b)

The sample estimate can be either a sample mean, proportion, or difference between sample mean or proportion. The standard error of the sample estimate is calculated using Equation 6.21.1(a), 6.21.2(a), or 6.21.3(a) in Section 6.21. The calculated t formula indicated in Equation 6.23(a) should be used for testing the significance of a difference between sample means unless the population standard deviation is known or unless the total sample size on which the calculation is based is sufficiently large. When the sample size exceeds 30 the t test may still be used to test the significance of a difference between means, but the Z test generally gives an acceptable approximation. When the population standard deviation is known or when the significance of a difference between sample proportions is being tested and the criteria of Section 6.22.2 are met, the Z test is appropriate.

The calculated t or Z value for any test is compared to a critical t or Z value obtained from the t Table or Table of Critical Values of Z for whatever significance level the researcher chooses. One or two-tailed tests may be chosen. In the case of t tests the number of degrees of freedom is the same as for confidence intervals, $n - 1$ for tests of means and proportions, $n_1 + n_2 - 2$ for tests of differences. If the absolute value of the calculated t or Z value is greater than the critical value, we may infer that the population parameter being estimated is significantly different from zero.

This direct significance testing also works when comparing sample estimates to legal maxima and minima or any external standard. Equations 6.23(a) and (b) allow comparison of a difference to zero to test the hypothesis that the estimate is not significantly different from zero.

$$\text{calculated } t = \frac{\text{sample estimate} - \text{external standard}}{\text{estimated standard error of sample estimate}}$$

6.23(c)

$$\text{calculated } Z = \frac{\text{sample estimate} - \text{external standard}}{\text{standard error of sample estimate}}$$

6.23(d)

A more general form of these formulas appears in Equations 6.23(c) and (d), which enable one to test the hypothesis that the estimate is not significantly different from the external standard. In Equations 6.23(a) and (b) the external standard is implicitly zero. In each application of direct significance testing, the calculation of the test statistic requires dividing by the population standard error of the estimate (if it is known) or the estimated standard error (if the population standard error is unknown). Thus, when we are comparing a sample proportion to an external standard, such as a known percentage of blacks in an applicants' pool (see Section 6.22.2, *H. S. Camp* example) or a legal minimum proportion of the population that must watch a particular television station (see Section 6.22.2, *Teleprompter* example), the standard error of the proportion used as a divisor must be calculated using the proportion in the known population or external standard. Using data from the illustrations in Section 6.22 where an inference is called for, Exhibit 6.23(a) shows (1) the estimate of the population mean, m, or proportion, p, that was obtained from the sample; (2) the external standard to which it was compared in the illustration; (3) the sample or population standard error of the estimate, whichever is appropriate according to the rules discussed in the previous paragraph; (4) the t or Z statistic calculated by dividing the difference between the sample estimate and the external standard by the standard error; (5) the degrees of freedom in the illustration if a t test is involved; (6) the significance level used in each illustration; and (7) the critical t or Z value that must be exceeded in each illustration to reach the level of significance indicated in (6).

EXHIBIT 6.23(a)
Direct Significance Testing for Selected Examples from Section 6.22

Exhibit Number	(1) Estimate	(2) External Standard	(3) Standard Error	(4) Calculated t or Z	(5) d.f.	(6) Significance Level	(7) Critical t or Z	(8) p-value
6.22.1(e)	$m = .16$	.15	.003	$t = 3.33$	21	.01	2.518[1]	.005
6.22.1(f)	$m = .16$	.15	.02	$t = .5$	21	.01	2.518[1]	.35
6.22.2(c)	$p = .23$	.35	.040	$Z = 3.00$	—	.05	1.645[1]	.005
6.22.2(d)	$p = .32$	.30	.029	$Z = .69$	—	.30	.524[1]	.25
6.22.3(b)	diff = 8.8	0	2.74	$Z = 3.21$	—	.05	1.96[2]	.01
6.22.3(c)	diff = .03	0	.0324	$Z = .93$	—	.01	2.326[1]	.20

1. One-tailed test
2. Two-tailed test

One may also find the *p*-value for any sample estimate compared to zero or to any external standard by referring to the *t* Table or Table of Critical Values of *Z* to find the critical *t* or *Z* value that is closest to yet not greater than the calculated *t* or *Z* value. This *p*-value is interpreted as the probability that the difference between the sample estimate and zero or the external standard occurred by chance. Exhibit 6.23(a) also reports the associated *p*-value for these illustrations in Column (8).[1]

§6.24 Calculations Related to Sample Size Determinations

The precision of the sample estimate is expressed as a range (interval) around the estimate within which the population parameter is likely to fall with a specified level of confidence. Once the researcher has decided on the acceptable size of the confidence interval and the level of confidence, the sample size necessary to achieve any range can be calculated using the formula in Equation 6.24(a)[1] for a sample mean or Equation 6.24(b)[2] for a sample proportion.

$$\text{sample size} = n = \left(\frac{Z_{\text{critical}} \times SD}{\text{desired range}} \right)^2 \cong \left(\frac{Z_{\text{critical}} \times sd}{\text{desired range}} \right)^2$$

6.24(a)

$$\text{sample size} = n =$$
$$\left(\frac{Z_{\text{critical}}}{\text{desired range}} \right)^2 \times PQ \cong \left(\frac{Z_{\text{critical}}}{\text{desired range}} \right)^2 \times pq$$

6.24(b)

As the equations indicate, it is desirable to know the population standard deviation, *SD*, or the population proportions, *P* and *Q*, in order to calculate *n*, the necessary sample size. If these parameters are unknown, estimates must be obtained. If estimates of these parameters,

§6.23 [1] Chapter 4 also discusses the interpretation of direct significance tests based on *Z* tests.

§6.24 [1] R. Pfaffenberger & J. Patterson, Statistical Methods for Business and Economics 368 (1977).

[2] Id. at 369.

such as sd or p and q, are used, the necessary sample size, n, is only an estimate. Because at least an estimate is necessary for this computation, a pilot study may be needed in order to obtain it.

Exhibit 6.24(a) illustrates the estimation of necessary sample size for the *Reserve Mining* example discussed in Section 6.14. The desired range is ± .001 fibers per cc, the confidence level required for our estimate of the mean concentration of fibers is 90%, and the estimated standard deviation (determined, presumably, by a preliminary sampling) is .024.

EXHIBIT 6.24(a)
Sample Size Determination for a Sample Mean
***Reserve Mining* Example**

Data
desired range = ±.001
desired confidence level = .90
sd = .024
$Z_{critical}$ for two-tailed, .10 significance level = 1.645

$$n \cong \left(\frac{Z_{critical} \times sd}{\text{desired range}} \right)^2 = \frac{1.645 \times .024}{.001} = 1559$$

Exhibit 6.24(b) illustrates the estimation of necessary sample size for the *Warner-Lambert* example discussed in Section 6.14. The desired range is ± 5 percentage points, i.e., .05, the confidence level required is 95%, and estimated p, the proportion of viewers who respond in a particular fashion to the question, is estimated to be equal to .25 (so q = .75). As the exhibit reveals, this range can be obtained with a sample size of 289. Exhibit 6.24(c) provides a table of necessary sample sizes associated with the 95% confidence levels, selected desired ranges, and selected values of the population proportion, P. For a 95% confidence interval with a precision of ± .01 or 1 percentage point, for instance, a sample size of 6147 is necessary if the smaller category of items is estimated to be 20% of the population and 9220 if the smaller group is 40% of the population. When P is greater than .50, the appropriate value of Q should be found on the leftmost column of Exhibit 6.24(c).

EXHIBIT 6.24(b)
Sample Size Determination for a Sample Proportion
***Warner-Lambert* Example**

Data

desired range = ±.05
desired confidence level = .95
p (estimated) = .25, thus q = .75
$Z_{critical}$ for two-tailed, .05 significance level = 1.96

$$n \cong \left(\frac{Z_{critical}}{\text{desired range}}\right)^2 \times pq = \left(\frac{1.96}{.05}\right)^2 \times .25 \times .75 = 288.12$$

EXHIBIT 6.24(c)
Table of Estimated Sample Sizes for 95% Confidence Interval
Selected Ranges and Population Proportions

Population Proportion P (or Q) (whichever is less)	Desired Range ±.10	±.05	±.02	±.01
.05	19	73	457	1825
.10	35	139	865	3458
.15	49	196	1225	4899
.20	62	246	1537	6147
.25	73	289	1801	7203
.30	81	323	2017	8068
.35	88	350	2185	8740
.40	93	369	2305	9220
.45	96	381	2377	9508
.50	97	385	2401	9604

CHAPTER SEVEN

Proving Associations Between Variables: The Correlation Coefficient

§7.0   Introduction to the Problem of Demonstrating Correspondences

It is often necessary for the lawyer to establish whether two variables are related to one another, a relationship that is often called an
association, a *correspondence,* or a *correlation* between the variables.
Whichever of these terms is used, the speaker means that when the
value of one variable changes, the value of the other variable also
changes, and in a predictable way. Variables may be *quantitative,*
reflecting characteristics that can be measured numerically, such as
concentration of a pollutant in the air or the number of minority
employees, or *qualitative,* reflecting characteristics that are not inherently numeric, such as gender, race, or occupation.

Craig v. Boren:[1] An Oklahoma statute prohibiting the sale of 3.2%
beer to males under the age of 21 and to females under the age of 18
was challenged as being a gender-based differential that denied equal
protection to males in violation of the Fourteenth Amendment. To
determine whether there was a substantial relationship between the
classification by gender and the important governmental objective of
highway safety, Justice Brennan examined the evidence "in terms of the

§7.0   [1]429 U.S. 190 (1976).

correlation between sex and the actual activity that Oklahoma seeks to regulate — driving while under the influence of alcohol."[2] The variables in this case are gender and arrest status (whether or not an individual had ever been arrested for driving while under the influence of alcohol), both qualitative variables. The various opinions in this case evaluated the association or correspondence between gender and arrest status. The statistics established that .18% of females and 2% of males in the 18-21 age group had been arrested for that offense.[3]

In re National Commission on Egg Nutrition:[4] The Federal Trade Commission alleged that the national trade association of egg manufacturers was falsely advertising eggs as being beneficial to one's health. To prove falsity, the Commission examined scientific evidence relating the volume of consumption of eggs in different countries to the incidence of heart disease in those countries. Both variables, egg consumption and incidence of heart disease, are quantitative. A high degree of correspondence between the number of eggs consumed and the incidence of heart disease suggests that eggs are not healthful. The scientific studies investigated whether the value of one variable, incidence of heart disease, increased as the value of the other variable, egg consumption, increased. The egg manufacturers would like to have shown that the incidence of heart disease decreased as egg consumption increased.

§7.0.1 Informal Use of the Term *Correlation*

The term *correlation* is sometimes used very casually. In *Craig v. Boren,* the Court noted[5] that a higher incidence of arrest is associated with males than with females for a particular age group and time period. Without engaging in any inferential methods, the Court in *Craig* merely observed an apparent correlation.[6] This informal use of the term is commonplace.

Board of Education v. Califano:[7] The court considered whether students were being assigned to schools that appeared to be designated

---

[2] Id. at 201.
[3] Id.
[4] 88 F.T.C. 89 (1976), *modified,* 570 F.2d 157 (D.C. Cir. 1977), *cert. denied,* 439 U.S. 821.
[5] 429 U.S. 190, 201 (1976).
[6] Id.
[7] 584 F.2d 576 (2d Cir. 1978).

for pupils of a particular race in violation of the Emergency School Aid Act. A casual correspondence between variables was observed by Chief Judge Oaks while viewing the percentages of minority school student enrollment and of minority teachers in selected community school districts (CSD's) in the City of New York, as shown in Exhibit 7.0.1(a).[8]

EXHIBIT 7.0.1(a)
Data for Informal Correlation
***Board of Education* Example**

(1) CSD Number	(2) Percent Minority Student Enrollment	(3) Percent Minority Teachers
1	93.6	10.4
7	99.0	27.9
9	97.7	26.9
14	90.3	14.6
22	29.1	1.7
23	99.6	30.0
24	44.0	5.9
25	29.5	2.6
26	25.8	2.7
27	48.4	7.3

Judge Oaks observed that "correlations between the racial/ethnic composition of the student bodies within those school districts exist."[9] The assignment of a higher proportion of black teachers to schools with a higher proportion of black pupils violated the Emergency School Aid Act. The association between increasing minority student percentage and increasing minority teacher percentage becomes more apparent if we redesign Exhibit 7.0.1(a) by ordering the CSD's so that those with the lowest percentage minority student enrollment come first, as in Exhibit 7.0.1(b). Now the increasing minority teacher percentage in column (3) is quite apparent.

[8] Id. at 584 nn. 26-27.
[9] Id. at 583.

EXHIBIT 7.0.1(b)
Reconfigured Data
Board of Education Example

(1) CSD Number	(2) *Percent Minority* *Student Enrollment*	(3) *Percent* *Minority Teachers*
26	25.8	2.7
22	29.1	1.7
25	29.5	2.6
24	44.0	5.9
27	48.4	7.3
14	90.3	14.6
1	93.6	10.4
9	97.7	26.9
7	99.0	27.9
23	99.6	30.0

But note that the minority teacher percentage does not *always* increase as the minority student enrollment percentage does: among the low minority percentage schools CSD No. 22 has a higher minority student percentage than CSD No. 26 but a lower percentage of minority teachers, and among the high minority percentage schools, CSD No. 14 and CSD No. 1 display the same characteristic.

It is more difficult to conclude casually that a correlation exists when the correspondence is not perfect, when the value of one variable does not always increase (or decrease) systematically as the value of the other variable increases. A more formal approach to correlation provides a precise measure of the degree of association and takes into account the instances in which the correspondence is not perfect.

§7.0.2 Informal Observations of Correlations from Graphs

An alternative to studying a list of data to determine whether a correlation exists is to examine a plot of the information on a graph. The values of the two variables of interest are shown on the two axes of the graph so that one can identify whether high values of one variable correspond to high or low values of the second variable. Exhibit 7.0.2(a) depicts the data from the *Board of Education v.*

EXHIBIT 7.0.2(a)
A Scatter Plot Illustrating a Positive Correlation
***Board of Education* Example**

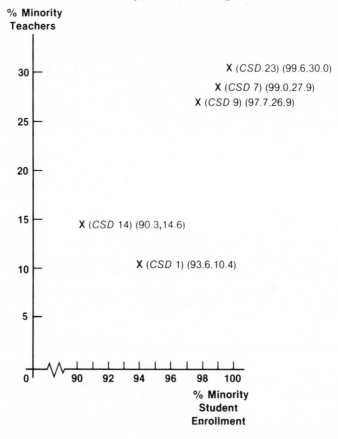

Califano[10] case, indicating the percentages of minority students and teachers in the five community school districts (*CSD*'s) with the highest percentage of minority student enrollment. The minority teacher percentage in a *CSD* is represented on the vertical axis, the minority student percentage on the horizontal axis. Each heavy **X** on this graph represents the minority student and teacher percentages in a single

[10] 584 F.2d 576, 584 nn. 27-28 (2d Cir. 1978).

CSD. Each X is labelled by the *CSD* number it represents and the associated measurements. From this type of graph, which is called a *scatter plot,* one can make casual observations regarding the correlation between the two variables indicated on the horizontal and vertical axes. See Section 2.7.3.

From this scatter plot, as from the exhibits in Section 7.0.1, one can see a correspondence between high percentages of minority teachers and high percentages of minority students. *CSD*'s with lower percentages of minority students (such as *CSD* 14) have a lower percentage of minority teachers. Thus there is an association of high values of one variable with high values of the other and low values of the first variable with low values of the other, which leads us to conclude informally that there is a correlation. We also observe that the association or correspondence does not always hold true: comparing *CSD* 14 with *CSD* 1, we see that while *CSD* 1 has a higher percentage of minority student enrollment, it has a lower percentage of minority teachers, contrary to our general observation. As with tables, it is possible to infer the existence of a correlation from visual inspection of a scatter plot or to detect departures of particular observations from the general association. The more departures, the less we would be willing to conclude that there is a correlation. Scatter plots are quite useful in formulating hypotheses about the correlations between variables, but they usually convey only a subjective indication of the nature and degree of association. The Pearson product moment correlation described in Section 7.1 is one important objective measure of the degree of association between two variables.

A. A SUMMARY MEASURE OF LINEAR ASSOCIATION

It is useful to have a method for measuring the degree of association between two variables. Many such measures are based on the Pearson product moment correlation coefficient. The first portion of this chapter discusses how this correlation coefficient is used in litigation and how it is interpreted as well as the factors that affect the degree of correspondence between two variables: the influence of outside factors (discussed in Section 7.2) and nonproportionality (Section 7.3).

§7.1   The Pearson Product Moment Correlation Coefficient

The *Pearson product moment correlation coefficient* measures the degree of linear association between two variables reflecting the extent to which the values of one variable change in a consistent, predictable fashion as the value of the other variable changes.[1] The degree of linear association between two variables is commonly estimated by sampling. The sample correlation coefficient, given the symbol r, is therefore an estimate of the degree of linear association one would calculate if one were to observe all occurrences of the variables involved. As with other sample statistics, inferences may be drawn regarding the population correlation coefficient from the value of r obtained from a sample. See Sections 7.4 through 7.7, Significance Testing for the Product Moment Correlation Coefficient.

Calculating the Pearson correlation coefficient always gives a value between -1 and $+1$, inclusively. The closer the correlation coefficient is to one of these extremes, the more consistent is the relationship between the variables involved. A correlation coefficient equal to -1 or $+1$ reflects *perfect* consistency in the changes of values of the two variables. If the value of one variable always shows the same *proportionate* increase when the other increases we say that there is a *perfect positive relationship*. If the value of one variable always shows the same *proportionate* decrease when the other variable increases, we say that there is a *perfect negative relationship*.[2] If there is no consistency in the relationship between the variables there is no mathematical association between them and the correlation coefficient is, appropriately, zero. A perfect correspondence, either positive or negative, is

---

§7.1 [1] The Pearson product moment correlation coefficient, developed by Karl Pearson, is the mean of the product of the paired Z scores for the two variables (see Equation 7.21(a)). The Z scores are based on the deviations of the observation of each variable from its respective mean. Deviations are referred to as "moments" by mathematical statisticians, hence the name *product moment*. See C. Spatz & J. Johnston, Basic Statistics: Tales of Distributions 90 (1976). One of the underlying assumptions for drawing inferences from the product moment correlation coefficient is that the two variables involved are normally distributed in the population (see Section 4.13 regarding the normal distribution). A useful discussion of this assumption appears in R. Thorndike, Correlational Procedures for Research, 60-62 (1978).

[2] A proportional relationship between two variables is one in which a one-unit increase in the value of one is associated with change in the value of the other of a magnitude that is the same regardless of the value from which the increase in the first variable was made. See Section 7.3, The Influence of Nonproportionality on the Correlation between Two Variables.

rare in useful applications of the correlation coefficient for two reasons; the value of a variable is likely to be influenced by a variety of factors in addition to the other variable with which we have associated it (including the factor of chance), and the relationship between two variables may not be perfectly proportionate. A zero correlation between two variables is rare because some degree of linear association is likely to occur just by chance. Thus, while it is conceptually possible for the correlation coefficient to take the values, -1, 0, or $+1$, most calculated correlation coefficients lie somewhere between these values.

In re National Commission on Egg Nutrition:[3] A study of thirty countries revealed a sample correlation coefficient, r, of 0.66[4] between the coronary death rate and the average daily intake of eggs in those countries. Because 0.66 is between 0 and $+1$, this is an indication that there may be a positive correlation between coronary death rate and the daily intake of eggs.

In re Sterling Drug, Inc.:[5] A merger between two corporations selling health and beauty aids was challenged by the FTC as violating §7 of the Clayton Act in that the effect was or may have been substantially to lessen competition in several markets. Correlation coefficients showing the extent of association between profitability of firms in the Fortune Directory and the number of five-digit categories in which firms were engaged were offered as evidence of the anticompetitive effects of the merger. The five-digit categories are part of the Standard Industrial Classification System for identifying product classes. A positive correlation would provide some evidence that the more categories in which a firm sold products, i.e., the more diversified is the firm, the higher the profitability. This merger would have resulted in a more diversified firm. The theory was that increased profitability reflected a lessening of competition and therefore the merger should be prohibited.

Orchard View Farms v. Martin Marietta Aluminum, Inc.:[6] In a trespass action, the farmowners sought compensatory damages from the emitter of fluoride particles. To prove that the particles had caused the damage to pine trees, a correlation coefficient was calculated be-

---

[3] 88 F.T.C. 89 (1976), *modified*, 570 F.2d 157 (D.C. Cir. 1977), *cert. denied*, 439 U.S. 821.
[4] 88 F.T.C. at 133.
[5] 80 F.T.C. 477 (1972).
[6] 500 F. Supp. 984 (D. Or. 1980).

tween the variables "amount of scorch" (a blight appearing on pine needles) and "fluorine concentration in the needles." The correlation coefficient between amount of scorch and fluorine concentration was +.50,[7] indicating a positive relationship. Another useful correlation would be between distance from the plant and fluorine concentration. If trees further from the plant had lower concentrations, this would be some evidence that the plant's emissions caused the damage. We would expect a negative correlation coefficient between distance from the plant and fluorine concentration because the flow of air would lead to greater dilution of the emission and concentration would decrease as distance increased.

Anderson v. Banks:[8] The court considered whether exit exams and other practices of the Tattnal County School District in Georgia violated the equal protection clause of the Fourteenth Amendment and other Constitutional and statutory provisions. The plaintiffs attacked the practices by presenting correlation coefficients describing the relationship between a given student's I.Q. and the average percentage of blacks that had been in that student's classes. The calculation for white students showed a negative coefficient, suggesting that the white students with higher I.Q.'s had regularly been placed in classes with fewer blacks. The correlation between race and I.Q. was found to be negligibly different from zero. This statistical evidence formed part of a chain of proof upon which the court relied to find that some of the practices did not pass constitutional muster.

The Pearson product moment correlation coefficient may be the most commonly used form of the correlation coefficient.[9] A typical application involves variables that are *quantitative,* i.e., susceptible to numerical measurement, *continuous,* i.e., can theoretically take any numerical value, and measured on an *interval scale.* Interval scaling means that not only is the order of the numbers important, but also the difference between them. This is sometimes described as a *cardinal* ranking to distinguish it from *ordinal* ranking, where the size of the measurement does not matter beyond providing a way of ranking the items measured from smallest to largest. For example, a list of salaries may be a cardinal ranking: the measured difference in score between an individual with a salary of $95,000 and one with a salary

---

[7] Id. at 998.

[8] 520 F. Supp. 472 (S.D. Ga. 1981).

[9] Other forms of the correlation coefficient are the point biserial, phi, and Spearman rank correlation coefficients, introduced in Sections 7.8, 7.9, and 7.11. See also the part and partial correlation coefficients, introduced in Sections 7.13 and 7.14.

of $85,000 is the same as the difference between $85,000 and $75,000; it is the difference between the salaries that matters. A list of individuals' names starting with the individual with the highest salary and proceeding to the lowest is an ordinal list, which does not reveal *how much* more one person is paid than another. (See also Section 7.10 on distinctions between types of numerical scales.)

Another type of quantitative variable for which product moment correlation coefficients are calculated are *discrete variables,* which like continuous variables can be measured on an interval scale in either a cardinal or ordinal ranking. A discrete variable is limited in the values it can take (such as to whole numbers 1, 2, and 3 rather than all fractions between 0 and 1, for instance). An example of a discrete variable measured on an interval scale is a count of the number of phone calls from clients on a given Tuesday; an example of a discrete variable in an ordinal ranking is the rank of a law firm among firms ordered by size.

In re National Commission on Egg Nutrition:[10] The Federal Trade Commission evaluated scientific studies summarized by correlation coefficients to evaluate allegedly false representations by manufacturers regarding the relationship between eating eggs and increased risk of heart attacks or heart disease. A study of 12,000 men in seven countries revealed a correlation coefficient of 0.73[11] between the mean level of dietary serum cholesterol (a compound found in eggs) in each country and new deaths from coronary heart disease and definite nonfatal heart attacks. The average daily egg consumption and incidence of coronary heart disease are continuous numerical variables, intervally scaled.

Pennsylvania v. Local Union 542:[12] The plaintiffs, minority union members, offered proof that the union's referral system was arbitrary and permitted sufficient discretion by the union to enable it to discriminate against minorities in assigning them jobs. The theory behind the statistical evidence was that a fair referral system would assign union members to job openings depending only on how long the members had been out of work: those who had been out of work the longest would be referred first; those who had most recently been working would be last. Two lists were compiled, the first ranking members in order of the amount of time they had been out of work, the second in

---

[10] 88 F.T.C. 89 (1976).
[11] Id. at 130.
[12] 469 F. Supp. 329 (E.D. Pa. 1978).

the order in which they were referred to jobs. The higher the correlation coefficient between the members' positions on the list, the more correspondence there is between the length of time out of work and the order of referral; the lower the correlation coefficient, the more likely it is that other factors explain the referral order. The out-of-work list and the referral list are *ordinal* because they list members in order of how long they have been out of work, starting with the person out of work the longest, and the order of referral, starting with the person referred first. The numbers on the lists are discrete because one's position on the list may be represented only by a whole number, but the list is not intervally scaled; the difference in time out of work for the first and fifth persons is not necessarily the same as for the eleventh and fifteenth persons. Because the lists are ordinal rankings, this is not a typical application of the Pearson product moment correlation coefficient.[13]

Pennsylvania v. O'Neill:[14] The variables examined in this case were race and the probability of being hired given the presence of relevant job qualification factors. Race as a variable is not inherently numeric, nor is it measured on a continuous interval scale. One may, however, assign numerical values to each race, e.g., 1 to blacks and 0 to whites, but the numbers do not have any cardinal significance. Similarly, one may assign a variable the value of 1 to indicate that an individual was hired and a 0 in case the individual was not. Because of the nature of the variables, this also is not a typical application of the Pearson correlation coefficient.[15]

The Pearson r is used so much more often than any other correlation coefficient that it is referred to as *the* correlation coefficient; when another type is used the special name for the other type is usually attached and a symbol other than r is used.

In many cases r is not exactly equal to -1, $+1$, or 0, suggesting that there is frequently some but not perfect linear association between the variables. Sections 7.2 and 7.3 illustrate how the influence of other factors on the variables' values and how the lack of propor-

---

[13] There are correlation coefficients specifically adapted to ordinal tests, such as the Spearman rank correlation coefficient. While the formula for the Spearman coefficient is equivalent to that of the Pearson, there are differences in their interpretation (see Sections 7.12 and 7.13).

[14] 348 F. Supp. 1084 (E.D. Pa. 1972).

[15] When dealing with variables such as race or gender where observations fit into only one of two possible categories, the point biserial correlation coefficient (discussed in Section 7.8) and the phi coefficient (Section 7.9) provide easily interpreted measures of the degree of association.

tionality in the relationship between two variables affect the correlation coefficient.

§7.2   The Influence of Outside Factors on a Correspondence Between Two Variables

Calculated correlation coefficients close to zero suggest a lack of correspondence between the values of the two variables involved. One reason for this lack of correspondence or any calculated correspondence other than $+1$ or -1 is that factors other than the variables themselves affect their relationship.

Pennsylvania v. Local Union 542:[1] The plaintiff offered correlation coefficients as evidence of arbitrary and discriminatory referral of union members to jobs. On the theory that a nondiscriminatory referral system would give priority in job assignments to those out of work the longest, plaintiff presented correlation coefficients between length of time out of work and order of referral for 17 different groups of employees that ranged from .08 to .62,[2] showing almost no correspondence for some groups and a moderate correspondence for others. The court found that this quantitative evidence corroborated plaintiffs' claims of discrimination because it proved that there was much room for arbitrary and standardless selections.[3] (Note that the coefficients calculated here were rank correlation coefficients. This variation on the Pearson product moment correlation coefficient is discussed in Section 7.11.) Discrimination was a possible "outside factor" influencing referrals.

It is important to note that nonproportionality, discussed in Section 7.3, is also reflected by less than perfect correspondence, and it is often difficult to know whether it is the nonproportionality or the presence of additional explanatory factors that is responsible for the low coefficient. One way to gain some insight into the cause of a low coefficient is to display the data as a scatter plot.

In re Sterling Drug, Inc.:[4] The Federal Trade Commission considered evidence of a correlation between diversification (measured by the

§7.2   [1] 469 F. Supp. 329 (E.D. Pa. 1978).
[2] Id. at 355.
[3] Id. at 357.
[4] 80 F.T.C. 477 (1972).

number of different product classes sold by a firm) and profitability
(measured as the ratio of total profits to total assets). Exhibit 7.2(a)
presents hypothetical data suggested by these facts. Profitability is measured on the vertical axis, and the number of different product classes
is registered on the horizontal axis. Notice that while the general trend
of the data points in the scatter plot is upwards, suggesting a positive
correlation, there are some observations that depart from this trend.
Going from observation (c) to observation (d), we notice a decrease in
profitability (from about 12% to 8%) accompanying an increase in
diversification (from 2 to 3 product classes). This suggests that there are
factors in addition to diversification that influence differences in
profitability among firms. It is easy to imagine some of them: differences in managerial talent, market opportunities, changes in relative
input costs. The result of these outside factors is a correlation coefficient that is less than + 1 but still greater than zero. If, by contrast, the
data appeared as in Exhibit 7.2(b), the correlation would be closer to + 1.

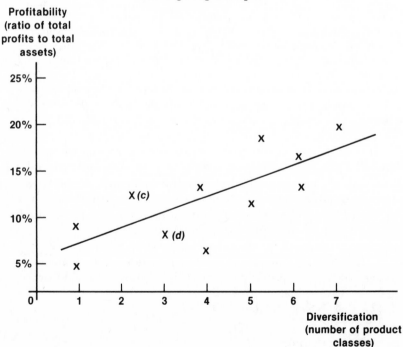

EXHIBIT 7.2(a)
Scatter Plot
Sterling Drug **Example**

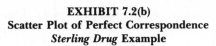

EXHIBIT 7.2(b)
Scatter Plot of Perfect Correspondence
Sterling Drug **Example**

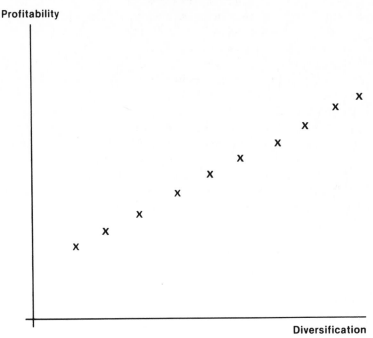

Profitability

Diversification

The greater the variation around the general trend of the data, the less perfect will be the correspondence between the two variables. One cause of this variation is the influence of outside factors.

§7.3 The Influence of Nonproportionality on the Correlation Between Two Variables

One measure of the consistency with which two variables change values in correspondence with one another is whether when the value of one variable goes up the value of the other generally goes down (in the case of a negative correlation) or goes up (in the case of a positive correlation). Section 7.2 considered the possibility that for some observations when one variable goes up in value the other goes up but for other observations the values change in opposite directions. A second part of the measure of consistency is whether the increase or decrease in value is in the same proportion from one change to another. In the *Sterling Drug, Inc.*[1] example in Section 7.2 it might be that adding one more product class always increases profitability by 2%. This is a proportionate increase in profitability for all changes in diversification. In the *National Commission on Egg Nutrition*[2] example, it might be that every country with twice the average egg consumption compared to another always has three times the incidence of heart disease. This is a constant proportionate increase in incidence for all changes in egg consumption. Whenever the relationship between variables is proportionate, the scatter plot of observations will form an approximately straight line. See Exhibits 7.2(a) and (b) as examples.

If the scatter plot forms a curved line, even one with no departures on either side of the curve, the relationship is said to be nonproportional or nonlinear, and the correlation between the two variables is different from $+1$ or -1 due merely to the presence of the nonproportionality quite aside from any effect of outside factors on the values of the variables.

Orchard View Farms v. Martin Marietta Aluminum, Inc.:[3] Exhibit 7.3(a) depicts hypothetical data suggested by the facts of this trespass action. The concentration of fluorine in pine needles is represented on the vertical axis. The distance from the plant emitting fluorine particles is represented on the horizontal axis. We are interested in the correlation between concentration and distance in order to establish that the emissions from this plant caused the damage to the pine trees. Twelve samples of fluorine concentration were taken at different distances and are marked as x's on the scatter plot. Note that as the distance from the plant increases, the fluorine concentration decreases very rapidly at first (up to five miles from the plant) but subsequent decreases in concentration are slower. The proportionate rate of decrease changes as distance from the plant increases. This is evidence that the relationship between the variables of concentration and distance is nonlinear, even though the observed combinations follow a regular and consistent pattern. Typically, the scatter plot will reveal not only a nonlinear relationship such as that depicted in Exhibit 7.3(a) but also indicate the presence and influence of other factors

---

§7.3 [1] 80 F.T.C. 477 (1972).
[2] 88 F.T.C. 89 (1976), *modified*, 570 F.2d 157 (D.C. Cir. 1977), *cert. denied*, 439 U.S. 821.
[3] 500 F. Supp. 984 (D. Or. 1980).

EXHIBIT 7.3(a)
Scatter Plot of an Idealized Nonlinear Correspondence

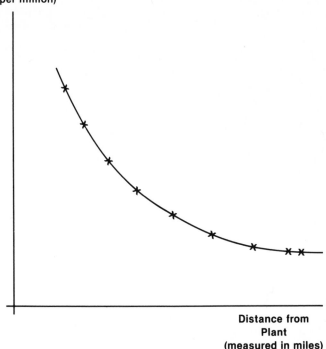

Concentration of
Flourine in Pine
Needles
(measured in
parts per million)

Distance from
Plant
(measured in miles)

(discussed in Section 7.2). Exhibit 7.3(b) indicates a nonlinear relationship that is more realistic, in that the negative relationship between concentration and distance is not perfectly consistent.

Examining a scatter plot is a useful way of detecting the presence of a nonlinear relationship. Imagining the correspondence between concentration of fluorine and distance suggests that it makes sense for that relationship to be nonlinear: most of the effect of the emissions will be felt near the plant, and as we move further away (within a mile or two perhaps) we expect the effects of fluoride emission to fall off quite rapidly. But as measurements are taken at increasing distances

EXHIBIT 7.3(b)
Scatter Plot of Nonlinear Correspondence
Orchard View Farms **Example**

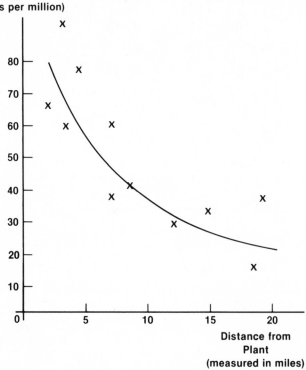

Concentration
of Flourine in
Pine Needles
(measured in
parts per million)

Distance from
Plant
(measured in miles)

farther from the plant, we would expect little change in concentration. A nonlinear association can be predicted from a theoretical consideration of the relationship of interest.

Agarwal v. Arthur G. McKee and Co.:[4] The defendant in this employment discrimination case attempted to explain differences in salaries among employees by demonstrating the relationship between

[4] 19 Fair Empl. Prac. Cas. (BNA) 503 (N.D. Cal. 1977).

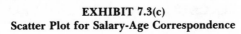

EXHIBIT 7.3(c)
Scatter Plot for Salary-Age Correspondence

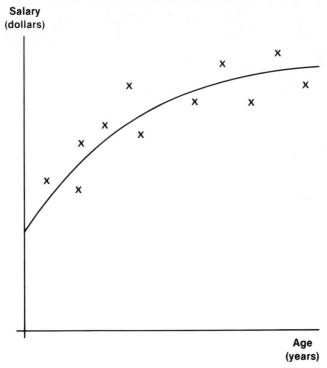

salary and a variety of variables, one of which was age. Labor economics theory suggests that initial increases in salary are large in proportion to one's salary in early years but as one gets older increases are a smaller proportion. If this theory is correct, a scatter plot of ages and associated salaries would appear as in Exhibit 7.3(c). Generally there is a positive relationship between these variables, but the correlation coefficient might not capture the relationship because it is not linear. Thoughtful consideration of the underlying facts suggested to the defendant that a nonlinear technique would give a better estimate of this relationship. The defendant thus presented a nonlinear analysis.

When two variables are associated with one another in a nonlinear fashion, techniques discussed in Section 7.20 may reveal the nature and degree of the nonlinear relationship between them.

B. SIGNIFICANCE TESTING FOR THE PRODUCT MOMENT CORRELATION COEFFICIENT

It is possible in principle to calculate and interpret a correlation coefficient describing the degree of linear association between two variables for either a population or a sample. Calculation of a population correlation coefficient requires measurement of every possible occurrence of the variables in question, e.g., the egg consumption and medical history of every person on earth, the fluorine content of every pine needle, the exam score of everyone who had ever taken a test. The obvious impossibilities suggest that population correlation coefficients are seldom used in law. The difference between population parameters and sample statistics is important to note, however, because the concept of significance testing applies only to sample statistics. The correlation coefficient calculated from a sample taken from a population can be used as an approximation to or estimate of the population correlation, the correlation that would result if the calculation were performed on a perhaps infinite population.

Significance testing enables one to infer the existence of a correlation in the population from the correlation observed in the sample. For example, if one hypothesizes that a population correlation coefficient is zero and obtains a nonzero coefficient from a sample, it is possible to calculate the probability that a sample coefficient so different from zero would result if the population coefficient really were zero. If this probability or p-value is sufficiently small, one infers that the population correlation is likely to be different from zero. In addition it is often possible to infer a range of values within which the population correlation most probably lies. Such p-values and ranges are essential to a litigant or finder of fact in interpreting a sample correlation. The calculation of p-values for sample correlation coefficients is discussed in Sections 7.4 and 7.5. Section 7.6 describes the construction of a confidence interval, a range around the sample correlation coefficient within which the unknown population coefficient is likely to fall.

§7.4 The r Test and the Pearson Correlation Coefficient

The Pearson product moment correlation coefficient, r, is a summary statistic that estimates the degree of linear association between two variables. The r test, which makes use of an r Table such as that appearing in the Appendix of Tables at the end of this book, can be used to test the hypothesis that the population value for the Pearson product moment correlation coefficient is zero. This table contains critical values of r associated with different p-values for one and two-tailed tests across the top of the table, and for different numbers of pairs of observations of the variables down the righthand side. To use this table one compares the calculated r value to the critical r values listed in a row next to the number of pairs of observations used in calculating r. The p-value for the calculated r is indicated at the head of the column containing the critical r value closest to but not greater than the calculated r. The p-value thus obtained is an estimate of the probability that if the population correlation were zero, a sample correlation as different from zero as the one observed on this occasion would occur due simply to the random selection of items for the sample.

   In re National Commission on Egg Nutrition:[1] The Federal Trade Commission reported the correlations shown in Exhibit 7.4(a). Note that all but the first of these correlations is statistically significant at the .05 level, i.e., each has a p-value of .05 or less for two-tailed tests. The effect of sample size on statistical significance can be highlighted by comparing the p-value and r for correlation (1) with those for correlation (9). Even with a substantially lower r value, the correlation in (9) is statistically significant while that in (1) is not, using the .05 cutoff (two-tailed). The difference is due to the sample sizes. For a sample size of seven pairs for correlation (1) the r Table reveals a critical value of .7545 for a p-value of .05. The r for correlation (1) is below that critical value. The r for correlation (9) is also below that critical value for 7 pairs, but .7545 is not the appropriate critical value for 20 pairs of observations, which the table shows as .4438. This critical value and the critical value for a p-value of .02, i.e., .5155, are below the calculated r for correlation (9). The larger the sample size, the lower the r value necessary to ensure statistical significance. Note that for correlations (6) and (7) we have a sample size of 30 and that the critical value for 30 pairs is not shown on the table. A conservative estimate of the appropriate values is obtained by referring to the row for the closest number of pairs shown that is not greater than the sample size. In the case of a sample size of 30, the appropriate critical values are in the row next to 27 pairs. The correlation coefficients in (6) and (7) are both greater

   §7.4   [1] 88 F.T.C. 89, 130-133 (1976), *modified,* 570 F.2d 157 (D.C. Cir. 1977), *cert. denied,* 439 U.S. 821.

EXHIBIT 7.4(a)
Correlation Coefficients
***Egg Nutrition* Example**

Variables	Sample Size	r	p-*value*
(1) mean level of dietary serum cholesterol and new deaths from coronary heart disease and definite non-fatal heart attacks	7 countries	0.73	.10
(2) mean level of dietary serum cholesterol and new diagnoses of coronary heart disease clinical manifestations	7 countries	0.81	.05
(3) percent of calories from fat in the diet and mean level of dietary serum cholesterol	7 countries	0.89	.01
(4) percent of calories from saturated fat and subsequent incidence of coronary heart disease	7 countries	0.84	.02
(5) average daily dietary cholesterol intake and coronary heart disease mortality rates	24 countries	0.83	.001
(6) average daily intake of dietary cholesterol and coronary heart disease death rate	30 countries	0.762	.001
(7) average daily intake of eggs and coronary heart death rate	30 countries	0.666	.001
(8) dietary level of cholesterol and 1964 coronary heart disease mortality rate	20 countries	0.617	.01
(9) percent of calories from saturated fat and 1964 coronary heart disease mortality rate	20 countries	0.546	.02

than the critical r for a p-value of .001. Having found these scientific results to be competent and reliable, the Commission found that the trade association for egg manufacturers "had no reasonable basis for making the representation that dietary cholesterol, including that in eggs, decreases the risk of heart attacks and heart disease."[2] Using a one-tailed test of the null hypothesis that there is no positive relationship between the variables, even the first correlation is statistically significant at the .05 level.

Boston Chapter, NAACP, Inc. v. Beecher:[3] To test the job relatedness of written exams alleged to have a discriminatory impact on minority applicants for firefighting positions, the plaintiffs' expert witness correlated written scores of 88 firefighters with the scores of the firefighters on 13 physical ability performance tests in tasks obviously relevant to the job, such as air mask operation, extinguisher selection, securing lines and knots, hose and hydrant operation, ladder extensions, and handling a preconnected hose. This evidence was presented as 13 separate correlation coefficients, one for each task correlated with the written exam.[4] Even with a sample size of 88 pairs (for which the r Table reveals a critical r value for a two-tailed test of .2172 for a p-value of .05), only two of the correlations (.346 and .313) were statistically significant by this measure. The court concluded that "defendants had not met their burden of demonstrating that the written exam was substantially related to job performance."[5]

The interpretation of the calculated correlation coefficient depends on the outcome of the significance test. If the p-value is small enough, we conclude that this correlation is unlikely to have occurred by chance if the variables are in fact uncorrelated. If the correlation calculated from a sample of the population is unlikely to have occurred by chance, it suggests that there is a correlation in the underlying population, that the two variables really are at least weakly associated in a systematic, consistent, and linear fashion. We draw this conclusion with a level of confidence that depends on the p-value.

If the p-value associated with r is not small then we have not demonstrated a correlation; it *does not mean* that there is no underlying linear association in the population. This significance test is designed not to prove the absence of a correlation in the population, but

---

[2] 88 F.T.C. at 145.
[3] 371 F. Supp. 507 (D. Mass. 1974).
[4] Id. at 516-517.
[5] Id. at 517.

only to indicate its presence. The most we can conclude from a calculated r that is not significantly different from zero is that the evidence presented does not establish a correlation.

> **Boston Chapter NAACP, Inc. v. Beecher:**[6] After finding that most of the correspondences between written exam scores and performance scores were not statistically significant, the court appropriately concluded that the defendant had not shown a relationship between the written and performance scores.[7] It would have been inappropriate for the court to conclude that this demonstrated that the exam was not job related. The most we can infer is that the defendant's rebuttal to this portion of plaintiffs' prima facie case was not convincing.

An alternative way of phrasing the conclusions from the two-tailed r test is to say that we have some evidence that the population correlation is different from zero or, if the r is not significantly different from zero, we could say that the evidence does not contradict the hypothesis that the population correlation coefficient is zero.

§7.5   The t Test for the Pearson Correlation Coefficient

The statistical significance of a calculated r, the sample Pearson product moment correlation coefficient, can also be tested using the t Table. To do so, the summary statistic r is divided by its sample standard error to yield the test statistic, t. This calculated t is compared to the critical values of t shown on the t Table, which has various significance levels across the top for one- and two-tailed tests and degrees of freedom down the side. (The formula for the standard error of r appears in Equation 7.22(a). For more background on critical values and the t Table, see Section 6.23.) The number of degrees of freedom associated with this t test is two less than the number of pairs of observations in the sample. Thus for *Boston Chapter NAACP, Inc. v. Beecher,*[1] with 88 pairs of test scores, we would use the row of critical values next to 86 degrees of freedom if it were given on the table. Since it is not, we use the preceding line on the table, following 60 degrees of freedom. The t table shows p-values for

---

[6] 371 F. Supp. 507 (D. Mass. 1974).
[7] Id. at 517.
§7.5   [1] 371 F. Supp. 507, 516 (D. Mass. 1974).

one- and two-tailed tests. Thus one can estimate the likelihood that the sample correlation coefficient would take a value as far or farther above zero as the one calculated if there were in fact no relationship between the variables, a one-tailed test. Alternatively, a two-tailed test would estimate the likelihood that the sample correlation coefficient would take a value as far or farther from zero as the one calculated if there were in fact no relationship between the variables. See Section 4.14 regarding the difference between one- and two-tailed tests. The t test answers the same questions as are answered by the significance tests using r as a test statistic, gives the same results, and is interpreted the same way. (For more on the difference between one- and two-tailed tests see Sections 4.13, 6.9, and 6.10.) For the appropriate number of degrees of freedom, the p-value is shown at the top of the column above that critical value that is closest to but not greater than the calculated t value.

In re National Commission on Egg Nutrition:[2] The correlations between the variables indicated in Exhibit 7.5(a) can be tested using the t statistic. Note that the p-values using the t test are the same as those derived from using r as a test statistic. Also shown in Exhibit 7.5(a) are the values of t corresponding to a p-value of .05. As observed in Section 7.4, all of these correlation coefficients are statistically significant at the .05 level, that is, their p-values are less than or equal to .05, except for the first.

EXHIBIT 7.5(a)
t Test
***Egg Nutrition* Correlations**

Variables	Degrees of Freedom	Calculated t	Critical t for p-Value of .05	p-Value for Two-Tailed Test
(1)	5	2.37	2.571	.10
(2)	5	3.11	2.571	.05
(3)	5	4.34	2.571	.01
(4)	5	3.50	2.571	.02
(5)	22	7.00	2.074	.001
(6)	28	6.23	2.048	.001
(7)	28	4.73	2.048	.001
(8)	18	3.33	2.101	.01
(9)	18	2.76	2.101	.02

[2] 88 F.T.C. 89 (1976), *modified,* 570 F.2d 157 (D.C. Cir. 1977), *cert. denied,* 439 U.S. 821.

The critical t value decreases as the number of pairs of observations (and, accordingly, the number of degrees of freedom) increases. For samples of about 30 pairs or more, statisticians frequently use as a rule of thumb the critical t value of 2.00 for determining whether a calculated t is statistically significant at the .05 level for a two-tailed test. The justification for this is that as the number of pairs increases above 30, the critical t changes very little and is in all cases nearly two.

§7.6 Confidence Intervals for the Pearson Correlation Coefficient

It is sometimes desirable to prove statistically that the calculated r value is significantly different from a particular number other than zero. The r and t tests as applied thus far only demonstrate whether there is a nonzero correlation between the variables. Confidence intervals can be used to establish that the degree of linear association is probably greater than some legally significant threshold level. This procedure is not much different from that outlined in Sections 6.5 through 6.12. It involves adding to and subtracting from the calculated r an amount sufficiently large to enable us to estimate, with a specified degree of certainty, a range within which the population correlation lies. Once the range is calculated around the estimated r value, any proposed population value falling outside that range can be rejected with the specified degree of certainty.

Boston Chapter NAACP, Inc. v. Beecher:[1] Expert witnesses for both parties agreed that unless the correlation coefficient between written exam score and task performance score exceeded .3,[2] the written exam would not be sufficiently job related to justify its use. Note that this is a measure of practical rather than statistical significance. The experts were agreeing that even if there was a statistically significant linear association between the variables, that is, the r was significantly different from zero, the degree of linear association had to be higher than a minimum level, .3. To test whether the estimated correlation is different from this level, a confidence interval can be computed (as shown in Section 7.23) for each of the 13 correlations calculated in that case. Because only two of the correlations were found to be statistically significant, that is, significantly different from zero, they are the only

§7.6   [1] 371 F. Supp. 507 (D. Mass. 1974).
[2] Id. at 516.

two that could possibly be significantly greater than the .3 minimum. The largest correlation was between the written exam score and task performance score for the air mask operation, where r equalled .346.[3] The range around .346 within which we can be 95% certain that the population value lies is from .15 to .52. The value of .346 for r is significantly different from zero at the .05 level because zero is not within this interval. But we cannot be 95% certain that the population correlation is above .3. Some values less than .3 lie within this two-tailed confidence interval, namely, all of the values between .3 and the lower boundary of .15. There is little support, therefore, for the conclusion that there is a correlation of .3 or more between the exam score and this part of the task performance scores.

The question of whether the degree of relationship is sufficiently high to make a difference to the factfinder requires a determination that is outside the realm of statistics. The degree of relationship required to show practical significance is a subjective judgment. In *Boston Chapter NAACP* the statisticians were experts in psychological testing and presumably drew the .3 rule of thumb from their knowledge of that subject matter. (See Section 7.16 on Practical Significance.)

§7.7 One-Tailed Significance Tests for the Pearson Correlation Coefficient

A one-tailed test of the sample correlation r answers the question, "Is the r significantly *greater than* (or, alternatively, *less than*) zero?" This is slightly different from the issue of whether it is *different from* zero. The only difference in procedure is that the one-tailed critical r or one-tailed critical t must be read from the appropriate table instead of the two-tailed critical value.

In re National Commission on Egg Nutrition:[1] The correlation between the mean level of dietary serum cholesterol and new deaths from coronary heart disease and definite nonfatal heart attacks in seven countries was .73.[2] Using a two-tailed test we could not say with 95%

---

[3] Id. at 517.

§7.7 [1] 88 F.T.C. 89 (1976), *modified*, 570 F.2d 157 (D.C. Cir. 1977), *cert. denied*, 439 U.S. 821.

[2] 88 F.T.C. at 130.

confidence that this was significantly different from zero. We were testing to see whether the population value was *greater than or less than* zero. If we narrow our inquiry and ask only whether the estimate of .73 demonstrates that the population value is *greater than* zero we find that we can be 95% certain it is. The critical r value of .6694 for a one-tailed test is less than the estimated r of .73. The critical t value for a one-tailed test is 2.015 and is less than the calculated t of 2.37. See Section 7.22 for the calculation.

Occasionally there is a need to calculate a one-tailed confidence interval, which provides either a lower boundary above which or an upper boundary below which one can be 95% certain the population correlation lies. The calculations for these intervals appear in Section 7.23.

Boston Chapter NAACP, Inc. v. Beecher:[3] A two-tailed confidence interval around the estimated Pearson correlation coefficient of .346[4] between written exam score and air mask operation score gives a range of .15 to .52, which does not allow us to reject the proposition that the population coefficient is less than .3, a minimum level of practical significance. A one-tailed approach yields a lower boundary above which we can be 95% certain the population coefficient falls. That lower boundary is .18, still below .3. Thus we are unable to reject the proposition that the population coefficient is less than .3.

A particular correlation coefficient may be statistically significant at the .05 level under a one-tailed test but not under a two-tailed test, because a two-tailed test allows for chance occurrences both greater than and less than the hypothesized population correlation. A one-tailed test permits the possibility of an alternative in only one direction, e.g., greater than the hypothesized correlation. As a consequence, the one-tailed p-value associated with a given value of r is, for p-values less than .5, generally about half of the two-tailed p-value associated with that value of r. Thus, in testing the hypothesis that two variables in a certain population are uncorrelated, one might find that the observed r has a one-tailed p-value of .03 and a two-tailed p-value of .06. It is very important in reporting a p-value that one disclose whether it is based on a one- or two-tailed critical value.

[3] 371 F. Supp. 507 (D. Mass. 1974).
[4] Id. at 517.

C. CORRELATIONS INVOLVING DICHOTOMOUS VARIABLES

The applications of the Pearson product moment correlation discussed thus far have variables that may take a variety of values. In other situations, one or both of the variables of interest may be dichotomous, taking only two values. In these cases, it is still possible to calculate a correlation coefficient, but different techniques of either calculation or significance testing are appropriate. This part of the chapter describes variations on the Pearson product moment correlation that arise when the variables involved are dichotomous. One source of these is the conversion of qualitative variables such as race or gender into numerical form. For example, for males the gender variable may be assigned the value of 1, and for females, the value 0. This conversion from qualitative to quantitative variables permits mathematical calculations on them, such as are required in the computation of a sample correlation coefficient. Sections 7.8 and 7.9 discuss the calculation of and significance testing for correlations involving one or two dichotomous variables.

§7.8   Correlations with One Dichotomous Variable

When one of two variables being correlated is dichotomous, a simplified version of the Pearson r formula is used. The *point biserial correlation coefficient*, denoted by r_{pb} is the name given to such correlations.

Anderson v. Banks:[1] The plaintiffs claimed that institution of an exit examination by the school district as a diploma requirement violated constitutional rights and Title VI of the Civil Rights Act of 1964 because blacks were discriminatorily disadvantaged. Validation of the test itself required a correlation between success on each particular question (a dichotomous variable, correct-incorrect) and success on the exam as a whole (a test score that was intervally scaled). If the correlation was low for a particular question, it would be judged to have little validity. An expert from the testing service that designed the exam testified that the point biserial correlation coefficient was used to per-

§7.8   [1] 520 F. Supp. 472, 489 (S.D. Ga. 1981).

form these validity tests and the questions should be discarded if the biserial correlation coefficient was below .30.

Pennsylvania v. O'Neill:[2] A plaintiff class made up of black police officers and unsuccessful applicants for positions in the Philadelphia police department alleged that the department's hiring and promotion practices unconstitutionally discriminated against blacks. Evidence was offered to show the incidence by race of 26 undesirable factors, such as previous arrests, job problems, divorce, and bad credit, that were relevant to the hiring decision.[3] The degree to which these factors were more frequently associated with one race rather than another was presented in a table listing the factors, the percentage of white applicants with a particular factor, and the percentage of black applicants with a particular factor.[4] The point biserial correlation coefficient could have been used to summarize these data and to present a formal measure of the extent to which applicants of one race typically exhibited a greater number of undesirable job related factors. Hypothetical data are shown in Exhibit 7.8(a). "Race of applicant" is a dichotomous variable taking the value 1 for blacks and 0 for nonblacks. The variable "number of undesirable factors present" is an intervally scaled variable. For this small sample of applicants, the r_{pb} is $+.23$, suggesting some small degree of positive linear association. If blacks had been assigned the value 0 and nonblacks the value 1 the correlation coefficient would have been $-.23$.

EXHIBIT 7.8(a)
Data for Dichotomous Variable
***O'Neill* Example**

Applicant No.	Race of Applicant (black = 1) (nonblack = 0)	Number of Undesirable Factors Present
1	1	3
2	0	2
3	1	5
4	1	6
5	0	1
6	0	7
7	0	2

[2] 348 F. Supp. 1084 (E.D. Pa. 1972).
[3] Id. at 1092-1093.
[4] Id. 1097 n.10.

It makes little difference which group is assigned the value 1 and which is assigned 0; switching the dichotomous assignment will change the sign of the coefficient from negative to positive or vice versa. It will be positive if the group having the higher mean value on the intervally scaled variable is assigned the value 1 and the other group, 0. In Exhibit 7.8(a) the mean number of factors present for blacks is 4.66 and for nonblacks, 3. Since blacks have the higher mean value for the nondichotomous variable and are assigned the value 1, r_{pb} is positive.

The significance test of the point biserial correlation coefficient is a test of the proposition that there is no association between the dichotomous variable and the intervally scaled variable; either the r Table or the t Test can be used to test its statistical significance. These procedures are identical to those discussed for the Pearson product moment correlation coefficient in Sections 7.4, 7.5, and 7.22.[5]

> **Pennsylvania v. O'Neill:**[6] Using this method of significance testing, the r_{pb} of .23 between race of applicant and number of undesirable factors present has a p-value higher than .10. For 7 pairs of observations the critical r is .6694 for a p-value of .10. The r_{pb} of .23 is considerably less than this critical value. This small positive correlation could well have occurred by chance even if the population correlation were zero.

§7.9 Correlations with Two Dichotomous Variables

The *phi coefficient*, r_{phi}, is a variation of the Pearson product moment correlation coefficient that is used to indicate the degree of association between two dichotomous variables, which are often derived from qualitative variables with two categories, such as gender (male-female), race (white-nonwhite), or job category (professional-nonprofessional).

---

[5] A test for the statistical significance of a point biserial correlation coefficient is equivalent to a test for the statistical significance of the difference between means of two samples from the same population (see Section 6.12, Direct Significance Tests for the Difference between Sample Estimates) if the nondichotomous variable is normally distributed (see Section 4.13 regarding the normal distribution). When one variable is dichotomous and the other is intervally scaled, it is possible to calculate the mean value for those observations of the intervally scaled variable associated with one of the two dichotomous types and the mean for those observations associated with the other type. Using these means and their associated standard errors, the procedures outlined in Section 6.23 will yield a p-value that is identical to the one that results from the r Table or t test described here.

[6] 348 F. Supp. 1084 (E.D. Pa. 1972).

Craig v. Boren:[1] Justice Brennan referred to the correlation between "maleness" and arrests for driving while under the influence of alcohol, citing reports that .18% of females and 2% of males in the 18-21 age group had been arrested for that offense. Because male-female and arrested-not arrested are two dichotomous variables, the phi coefficient is an appropriate summary statistic for describing the degree of linear association between arrest record and gender. If these figures resulted from a computer survey of the driving records of 20,000 males and females, the correlation between arrest record and gender is .09 if we assign the value 1 to males and to "arrested" or to females and "not arrested." The coefficient is equal to $-.09$ if we assign the value 1 to females and "arrested" or males and "not arrested." A portion of these data might appear as in Exhibit 7.9(a). Without having calculated the phi coefficient Justice Brennan concluded that "Certainly if maleness is to serve as a proxy for drinking and driving, a correlation of 2% must be considered an unduly tenuous 'fit'."[2] Justice Rehnquist, dissenting, attached considerable importance to that fact that arrest statistics demonstrated that a much higher percentage of males were arrested than females.[3] The phi coefficient puts the association between maleness and arrests in perspective. While the correlation of .09 is very low from a practical point of view, it is statistically significant at a .001 level of significance. (See Section 7.17 regarding practical significance.)

EXHIBIT 7.9(a)
Arrest Data
Craig **Example**

Individual No.	Arrested 1 = yes 0 = no	Gender 1 = female 0 = male
1	0	1
2	1	0
3	1	1
4	0	0
5	0	1
.	.	.
.	.	.
.	.	.

§7.9   [1] 429 U.S. 190, 201 (1976).
[2] Id. at 202.
[3] Id. at 223.

Tillery v. Pacific Telephone Co.:[4] Plaintiff alleged racial discrimination in the employer's refusal to transfer him to a sales job. Ultimately a Pearson correlation coefficient between an assessment rating (based on an evaluation of applicant's persuasiveness, behavioral flexibility, originality and other factors) and actual job performance was interpreted as demonstrating that the transfer process was fair.[5] Plaintiff's case might have been assisted, however, by the calculation of a phi coefficient between race (black-not black) and transfer (application granted-not granted). This would require gathering a sample of transfer applications for the company and counting the number of blacks and whites who had and had not had their applications granted. With these data in hand the sample phi coefficient could be calculated. See Section 7.24, where the calculation is explained with examples. A statistically significant coefficient would be evidence of a connection between race and transfer.

In court the two-or-three-standard-deviations rule (see Section 4.11) and the chi-square test (see Chapter 5) are used more frequently than the phi coefficient to determine the probability of a certain distribution among arrestees by gender or transferees by race occurring by chance. However, a test based on r_{phi} yields the same p-value as the analogous test based on the chi-square statistic.

The significance test of the phi coefficient is a test of the proposition that there is no relationship between the dichotomous variables. The r_{phi} value is squared and then multiplied by the sample size to get a chi-square test value, which is compared to critical values on the Chi-Square Table (see Chapter 5) for one degree of freedom. The Chi-Square Table reports critical chi-square values for different p-values. The p-value associated with a given r_{phi} appears above the critical value for one degree of freedom that is closest to yet not greater than the calculated r_{phi}.

Craig v. Boren:[6] The r_{phi} between gender and arrest was .09. The chi-square test statistic is .09 squared (or .0081) times 20,000 (the sample size.) This gives a chi-square value of 1620, which is greater than all of the critical chi-square values shown; for a p-value of .001 the critical chi-square value is 10.827. Despite the small size of r_{phi}, (.09), which varies between -1 and $+1$, the correlation is statistically significant

---

[4] 29 Empl. (CCH) ¶26,650 (N.D. Cal. 1982).
[5] Id. at ¶26,654.
[6] 429 U.S. 190 (1976).

even at the .001 level because of the huge sample size (see Section 7.8 on practical significance).

D. CORRELATIONS INVOLVING RANKED DATA

A variation in the Pearson product moment correlation coefficient is generally used when the data consist of rankings. In Section 7.10 ordinal (ranked) scales are distinguished from the interval scales discussed in the straightforward applications of the Pearson correlation coefficient in Sections 7.1 through 7.3 and the nominal scales used for dichotomous variables discussed in Sections 7.8 and 7.9. Section 7.11 introduces the Spearman rank correlation coefficient, which is used to summarize the degree of relationship between pairs of data ranked on ordinal scales. Section 7.12 discusses significance testing for the rank correlation coefficient.

§7.10   Interval, Nominal, and Ordinal Scales

While dichotomous variables violate the conditions of continuous numbering that is typical of many applications of the Pearson product moment correlation coefficient, a sample with ranked data violates the assumption of interval scaling. The dichotomous variables were "measured" on a *nominal* scale, which means that numbers were assigned only to represent different categories or groups of the variable. These numbers were not measurements in the strict sense; they are better thought of as *names* that allowed us to perform mathematical calculations. For ranked data, the numbers assigned to observations have more interpretive significance because they indicate a place in an *ordering* of the data, e.g., from largest to smallest or shortest to tallest. The particular numbers assigned to the two groups of a dichotomous variable do not make any difference to the absolute value of the correlation coefficient, but in an *ordinal* scaling the numbers do matter. If an observation is assigned the rank of 3 instead of 2 in the ordering from longest to shortest, that indicates there are two longer items instead of one. The order of the numbering has meaning.

    Qualitative variables such as the gender of an individual or the quality of a wine can be represented on nominal scales, assigning 1 to females or good quality wine, 0 to males or bad quality wine. The 1 and 0 do not have any significance except as nominal representation of the group. By contrast, if the relative quality of wines is represented on an ordinal scale from best tasting to worst tasting, the assigned numerical ranking is significant. A wine's position on the list, its rank, depends on its taste rather than an arbitrary assignment of values, so the assignment of numbers to particular wines is not arbitrary.

Quantitative variables are usually measured on an *interval* scale. Not only is the relative order of the numbers important but the distance between the numbers has additional significance, and the concept of *unit distance* is relevant. The difference between any two adjacent integers on an interval scale is the same. For example, observations of how far one city is from another are measured on an interval scale. Two cities that are two miles apart are twice as far apart as two cities that are one mile apart. The unit distance between any two adjacent integers anywhere on this interval scale is identical, one mile. This is not true of the ordinal scale, where the wine with rank 1 may be much better than the wine with rank 2, but that wine may be only slightly better than rank 3 wine. The ordinal scale indicates nothing about the degree of difference between any two ranked items.

The Pearson correlation coefficient formula can be used to calculate coefficients for variables on all three of these scales. Each scale, however, has a simplified version of the formula that is usually employed. Except for the point biserial coefficient (see Section 7.8), the coefficients for these other scales have distinguishable significance testing methods associated with them. The point biserial correlation coefficients and phi coefficient for dichotomous variables and their associated procedures are appropriate for nominally scaled data (as long as there are only two groups and, hence, only two values for the dichotomous variable(s)). The Pearson correlation coefficient and associated procedures are appropriate for intervally scaled data, while the *Spearman rank correlation coefficient* is suitable for ordinally scaled data. Examples of intervally scaled and nominally scaled data have appeared in previous sections. *Local Union 542* is an example of ordinally scaled data.

Pennsylvania v. Local Union 542:[1] The factfinder was presented with evidence describing the process by which members of a union were

§7.10 [1] 469 F. Supp. 329 (E.D. Pa. 1978).

referred to jobs.[2] Two conflicting explanations of the referral process were offered; one was that those union members referred first were those who had been out of work the longest, the other was that some criteria other than length of time out of work were used as the basis for referrals. The plaintiffs argued that race was the criterion for referrals. Because we are concerned with the *order* in which members are referred to jobs, an *ordinal* scaling suggests itself. Union members can be listed according to the order in which they are referred: the member referred first to a job will be given rank 1, the member referred tenth will be given rank 10. The list can be of any length, depending on how many members there are. Note that the difference in terms of time until referral is not consistent throughout the ranking. The unit distance in time between the fourth and fifth referral is not necessarily the same length of time as between the first and second referrals, thus this is clearly not an interval scale. It is reasonable to assume that members are referred to jobs as soon as the jobs become available. The factual issue is the order in which they are referred, and thus an ordinal scale is appropriate.

The ordinal referral list was correlated with an ordinal "out-of-work" list,[3] which ranked members in order of who had been out of work the longest. The member who had been out of work the longest received rank 1. Like the referral list, this is an ordinal list, and like the referral data, an interval-scaled list could have been made out of the length of time out of work, but it is the order on the lists that is important, not the actual length of time out of work or between referrals.

§7.11 The Spearman Rank Correlation Coefficient

The *Spearman rank correlation coefficient*, denoted r_S, is a measure of the degree of association between the ranks of observations on two ordinal lists. If the observations are ranked identically on the two lists, the ranks are said to be perfectly positively correlated and the Spearman rank correlation coefficient is $+1$. When the observations are ranked on one ordinal list in precisely the reverse order of their rank on the other list, the correlation between the ranks is -1. The value of a Spearman rank correlation coefficient is always between -1 and $+1$, inclusively, just like the Pearson coefficient.

---

[2] Id. at 355-358.
[3] Id. at 357.

Pennsylvania v. Local Union 542:[1] Two lists were correlated, the out-of-work list and the referral list. The items on the lists were union members in a single job category. The observed characteristics of each member were, for a given time period, the length of time out of work and the order in which the member was referred to a new job. Those out of work the longest were given the highest rank on the out-of-work list; those referred to jobs first were given the highest rank on the referral list. A positive correlation would indicate a correspondence between positions on the two lists, specifically, those out of work the longest were referred to new jobs first. The closer to + 1 this correspondence is, the more consistent and regular is the assignment of new jobs to those out of work the longest. For the 17 job category groups whose out-of-work lists and referral lists were compared, the correlation coefficients showed correspondences ranging from .08 to .62,[2] suggesting some positive correlation in each of the groups between ranks or orderings on the two lists.

§7.12 Significance Testing for the Spearman Rank Correlation Coefficient

Significance testing for the Spearman rank correlation coefficient is similar to that for the Pearson correlation coefficient except that because the assumptions underlying the Spearman r_S are different, a special table of critical r_S values must be used. The Spearman r Table appears at the end of this book. For the appropriate number of pairs of observations on the ordinal lists, the critical value for r_S is presented on the r_S Table. The p-value associated with a calculated r_S appears at the top of the column above the critical value that is closest to yet not larger than the calculated r_S. A minus sign on the calculated r_S is ignored for significance testing. Both one- and two-tailed tests can be performed on the rank correlation coefficient (see Sections 7.4 through 7.7, Significance Testing for the Product Moment Coefficient). The null hypothesis tested by a two-tailed test is that there is no correlation between the rankings, e.g., that the workers in Local 542 were assigned to jobs at random. A one-tailed test indicates the probability of obtaining such an estimated coefficient by chance if the population coefficient is not greater than (or less than) zero.

§7.11   [1] 469 F. Supp. 329, 355 (E.D. Pa. 1978).
[2] Id. at 355.

A *t* test statistic may also be calculated in order to test the statistical significance of r_S. Because the positions of the items on the ordinal list are not assumed to be normally distributed, (see Section 7.1), the *t* test is recommended only when the sample size is large.[1] Calculations of *t* values for the r_S appear in Section 7.26.

> **Pennsylvania v. Local Union 542:**[2] A rank correlation coefficient was calculated for each of 17 pairs of lists of union members. Each pair of lists had at least 40 union members ranked by length of time out of work and order of referral. The opinion does not indicate the number of individuals on any specific list but if the number of members on list number 4 was 45, the r_S Table shows a critical r_S value of 0.294 for 45 pairs and a significance level of .05 for a one-tailed test. Because r_S for group 4 was only .20, we cannot reject the null hypothesis that there is no positive correspondence between length of time out of work and order of referral. If each of the 17 groups had 45 names on the lists, four of the groups would not have had statistically significant correspondences while 13 would have, by the one-tailed test and .05 significance level. The critical *t* value for a sample of 45, a two-tailed test, and a significance level of .05 is 2.021. The calculated *t* value for group number 4 is 1.338, so the *t* test also indicates a lack of statistical significance for this r_S. Under the two-tailed test we refuse to reject the hypothesis that there is no relationship between positions on the two lists at a .05 level of significance.

E. OTHER MEASURES OF ASSOCIATION

The Pearson, phi, point biserial, and Spearman correlation coefficients are among the measures of association most commonly employed in litigation. Their apparent simplicity in interpretation makes them popular. There are numerous other measures available, several of which deserve mention because of their potential utility to lawyers.

---

§7.12   [1] It is difficult to set a limit on what sample size is sufficiently large to use a *t* test. For a sample of 80 pairs of observations, the Spearman *r* Table and the *t* Table both indicate a *p*-value of .05 for an r_S of .38. However, if the sample size were five and the correlation .89, the Spearman *r* Table would reveal a *p*-value greater than .10, while the *t* Table would give a *p*-value of less than .05.

[2] 469 F. Supp. 329, 355 (E.D. Pa. 1978).

In Sections 7.13 and 7.14 the part and partial correlation coefficients are described.

Seldom is the value of a variable influenced by only one other variable. The fact that a third variable influences the value of one or both of those being correlated means that the coefficient calculated between the first two variables gives a misleading picture of the sources and causes of change in the values of those variables. The part and partial correlation coefficients discussed in these sections provide a way to separate out the individual influences of additional outside factors.

In Section 7.15, several additional correlation coefficients for dichotomous variables are discussed briefly, and reference is made to other measures of association that are useful for analysis of dichotomous relationships.

§7.13   The Part Correlation Coefficient

The *part correlation coefficient* describes the degree of linear association remaining between two variables when any effect of variations in a third variable on the values of just one of the variables is eliminated.[1]

Consider two variables, the first of which, the *explanatory* variable, is thought to explain or cause changes in the value of a second variable. A third variable is also thought to have some effect on the second variable, the one whose value is to be explained. The part correlation coefficient formula eliminates any variation in the second variable corresponding to variations in the third variable and summarizes the degree of association remaining between the second variable and the first variable. The part correlation coefficient, like other correlation coefficients, provides evidence as to the presence or absence of a correlation, and from its existence one might infer a causal relationship between the variables. (See Section 7.16 on Causation.)

Northshore School District No. 417 v. Kinnear:[2] The plaintiffs claimed that unequal educational opportunity resulted from the state's school financing system, violating the Fourteenth Amendment. The

---

§7.13   [1] By contrast, the *partial correlation coefficient* formula eliminates the effect of variation in a third variable on the values of both of the variables. (See Section 7.14).
[2] 530 P. 2d 178 (Wash. 1974).

state offered evidence to prove that factors other than the tax system created disparities among districts in the expenditure per pupil (one measure of educational quality). In particular, the state offered the argument that larger schools could spend less money to achieve the same quality of education as small schools because they were more efficient, but this argument would fail if there were still higher expenditures per pupil in some districts after cost differences were taken into account.

The defendant's statistician presented evidence of a negative correlation between expenditures per pupil and the number of students in a school district, suggesting that rural school districts paid more per pupil, that is, expenditures per pupil go up as number of students goes down.[3] If the increased cost of rural education is due to the fact that each teacher has fewer students, the ratio of teachers to students would be higher in rural areas. To eliminate the cost factors from the correlation between expenditures per pupil (the variables we are trying to explain) and number of pupils (an explanatory variable), one could introduce a third variable into the calculation, the teacher-student ratio (referred to in the opinion as certificated staff per 1000 students).[4]

We expect rural areas to have the smallest numbers of pupils, the highest per pupil expenditures, and the highest teacher-student ratios. Thus we expect negative correlations between the first variable and each of the other two and a positive correlation between the latter two variables. To find the part correlation between the first two variables, we hold the third variable, teacher-student ratio, constant. Assuming that teachers are the only cost difference, this part correlation will indicate the degree of association between number of pupils per district and expenditures per student that is not accounted for by variations in the cost factor. If, for instance, the correlation between expenditures per pupil and number of students is −.86, between expenditures per pupil and certified staff per 1000 students is −.73, and between number of students and certified staff per 1000 students is +.92, the part correlation between expenditures per pupil and number of students in the district is −.48. If this figure is practically and statistically significant, a significant amount of variation in expenditure per pupil is accounted for by the number of students in each district even aside from the cost factors. This might be interpreted as evidence against the economies-of-large-scale-operation argument presented by the state.

[3] Id. at 188.

[4] Id. at 186. Note that our theory is that cost differentials affect expenditures, but we have no reason to believe that they affect the number of students in a district. If the latter theory were true, that cost differentials influenced both other variables, then the partial rather than part correlation coefficient would be the appropriate summary statistic. (See Section 7.14).

§7.14   The Partial Correlation Coefficient

The *partial correlation coefficient* measures the degree of linear association between two variables when the influence of a third variable on *both* of them is removed. The conceptual difference between the *part* and the *partial* correlation coefficients is that the former is used when the third variable is thought to influence the value of only one of the other two variables. The partial correlation coefficient applies when the value of the third variable is thought to influence the values of both other variables. Thus the partial correlation coefficient would be inappropriate for the *Northshore School District No. 417 v. Kinnear*[1] example in Section 7.13 if certified staff ratios might affect per pupil expenditures but would be unlikely to influence the total number of students in the geographical district.

Orchard View Farms, Inc. v. Martin Marietta Aluminum Co.:[2] The court examined evidence of a negative correlation between fluorine content of pine needles and distance from a fluoride emitting plant. If moose droppings also leave a fluorine residue in the needles of pine trees and aluminum plant sites are chosen so as to avoid moose populations, the moose population (per square mile) would influence both plant sitings and fluorine concentration in pine needles. Correlation coefficients between moose population and fluorine concentration might indicate some positive correlation (though undoubtedly small in this fanciful hypothetical) that should be eliminated in measuring the effect of the plant's emissions. The partial correlation coefficient is appropriate rather than the part correlation coefficient because we believe the process of plant siting as well as the fluorine content is influenced by moose population. If the correlation between moose population and distance from the plant is .10, between fluorine concentration and distance from the plant is −.57 and between moose population and fluorine concentration is .20, the partial correlation coefficient that removes the influence of moose from both of the other variables is −.61.

Like the other correlation coefficients, partial correlation coefficients do not prove what *caused* a variable to change its value, but an estimated value for the coefficient might support an inference that a causal connection is likely.

§7.14   [1] 530 P.2d 178 (Wash. 1974).
[2] 500 F. Supp. 984, 998 (D. Or. 1980).

§7.15   Other Measures of Association for Dichotomous Variables

There are numerous additional measures of association for dichotomous variables, some of which are interpreted as correlation coefficients. References in the statistical literature to these techniques often refer to them as methods of cross-tabulations, because data are often arranged in tables in order to facilitate analysis.[1]

Two methods related to the correlation coefficients discussed in this Chapter are biserial correlation coefficients and tetrachoric correlation coefficients. They are useful as estimates of the point biserial and phi correlation coefficients in situations where the data are not truly dichotomous but rather have been *dichotomized.*

Gender and race are truly dichotomous variables because they cannot be numerically measured. It is possible, however, to substitute a dichotomous variable for a continuous one. Salary, for instance, is a continuous, intervally scaled variable but it is possible to dichotomize it by putting salaries into two groups, assigning the value 1 to those over $50,000 per year and 0 to those under $50,000. This salary variable is not truly dichotomous because a continuous variable underlies it, but it is occasionally useful to dichotomize when there are insufficient data to provide numerical measures. A correlation using a dichotomized variable provides an estimate of what the product moment correlation would be if continuous measurements were available. It might provide a clue as to whether it is worth the time and money necessary to make the measurements. When a correlation is calculated between a continuous, intervally scaled variable and a variable that is dichotomized but has an underlying continuous variable, the *biserial* (rather than point biserial) *correlation coefficient, r_b,* is appropriate. As with other correlation coefficients, the r_b is interpreted as the degree of association between the variables.[2]

---

§7.15   [1] See, e.g., G. Upton, The Analysis of Cross-Tabulated Data, Chapters 2 and 3 (1978).

[2] See J. Cohen and P. Cohen, Applied Multiple Regression/Correlation Analysis for the Behavioral Sciences 61-62 for a more detailed discussion of the biserial and tetrachoric correlation coefficients and methods of calculation.

The biserial correlation coefficient can attain values as great as $+1$ or -1, so it is interpreted as the other coefficients are. However, it is possible that some data will yield coefficients with values more extreme than $+1$ or -1. It has been suggested that this can occur only when one of the underlying continuous variables is not normally distributed. (R. Thorndike, Correlational Procedures for Research 85 (1978) and Q. McNemar, Psychological Statistics (4th Ed.) (1969)). See Section 4.13, which describes

In re Sterling Drug, Inc.:[3] Evidence was presented in this Clayton Act Section 7 case that the proposed merger would result in a more diversified company and that diversified companies generally have higher rates of profit. The argument was that higher rates of profit must be associated with noncompetitive market structures and therefore this merger would have anticompetitive effects. Pearson correlation coefficients were calculated between two intervally scaled variables, the number of product classes a company sold and profit rate.[4] The number of product classes was a measure of diversification. If these data are available, the Pearson r provides more information than the biserial r. But if for some reason the detailed data for one of these variables were not available, the biserial r could still be used as long as some information was available. For instance, if it was not possible to determine the number of product classes sold by firms but it was still possible to judge whether a firm was diversified or not, the degree of association between diversification and profits could still be estimated. Hypothetical data for such a calculation appear in Exhibit 7.15(a). The

EXHIBIT 7.15(a)
Data for Biserial Correlation
Sterling Drug **Example**

Firm Number	Diversified (yes = 1) (no = 0)	Profit Rate
1	1	.36
2	1	.22
3	0	.09
4	0	.17
5	1	.14
6	1	.20
7	0	.11
8	0	.19

the normal distribution. When values exceeding $+1$ or -1 are obtained, the biserial correlation coefficient should not be used, but if one is reasonably certain that the underlying distribution of the continuous variable is normal, the biserial coefficient is an appropriate summary statistic.

In evaluating the practical significance of the biserial and tetrachoric coefficients, it should be remembered that they are only estimates of other correlation coefficients. Both coefficients for dichotomized variables are usually larger than the coefficients they estimate and their practical significance should be evaluated accordingly.

[3] 80 F.T.C. 477 (1972).
[4] Id. at 509.

dichotomized variable, diversification, has been given the value 1 for diversified firms and 0 for nondiversified firms. Because we expect more diversified firms to have the higher mean profit rates, we expect the coefficient to be positive. The r_b equals .54, suggesting a positive correspondence.

Lack of data might also lead the attorney to use dichotomous variables to summarize salient characteristics of variables that are inherently not dichotomous. The tetrachoric coefficient is a useful estimate of the product moment correlation coefficient when both of the variables have been dichotomized.[5]

Dow Chemical Co. v. Blum:[6] The use of herbicides 2, 4, 5-T, and Silvex were allegedly associated with an increase in the incidence of spontaneous human abortions. Both variables, amount of exposure to the herbicides and the number of spontaneous abortions, were intervally scaled. The EPA relied on a study showing a statistically significant correlation between spontaneous abortions in the sprayed area and spraying patterns in terms of the pounds of herbicides in that area.[7] This was a Pearson correlation coefficient. If it was only known that a woman had been exposed to 2, 4, 5-T, or Silvex and the spraying pattern was not known, the biserial correlation coefficient could be used with a dichotomous variable (exposure — yes/no) substituted for the level of exposure variable. If the actual number of spontaneous abortions was not known one might be able to substitute some measure of whether there was an unusually high incidence in a particular area — perhaps obtained from anecdotal evidence. The tetrachoric correlation between these dichotomized variables could then be calculated.

F. PRACTICAL SIGNIFICANCE OF CORRELATION COEFFICIENTS

Interpretation of summary statistics has been described as a two-stage process. It is logical first to determine the statistical significance of a particular statistic, because a sample correlation that differs from its

---

[5] See J. Cohen & P. Cohen, Applied Multiple Regression/Correlation Analysis for the Behavioral Sciences 62 (1975).
[6] 469 F. Supp. 892 (E.D. Mich. 1979).
[7] Id. at 896-897.

hypothesized value by an amount so small that it could reasonably be due to chance effects in drawing the sample can hardly be reliable enough to form the basis for concluding that the hypothesized correlation is wrong. Significance testing is best thought of as a threshold test to determine whether it is worthwhile to consider the practical significance of a difference between a sample correlation and its hypothesized value.

The legal importance of a correlation depends on the variables involved and the context in which the evidence of a correspondence is offered. There are two sources of assistance in determining whether a particular correlation is meaningful: the first provides guidance for particular types of variables and is discussed in Section 7.16; the second indicates how much of the variation in one variable is "explained" or mathematically accounted for by variation in the second variable. This statistic, the *coefficient of determination,* is discussed in Section 7.17.

§7.16 Sources of Practical Significance from Other Disciplines

Most of the statistical tools used in law were first applied in other disciplines. The correlation coefficients for dichotomous variables, for instance, have their roots in psychological and educational research. The disciplines in which the tools have been regularly applied have in some cases developed standards for practical significance. Biostatisticians who evaluate the relative efficacies of drugs have a guideline that suggests that there is a practically significant difference between two drugs if a statistically significant difference appears after testing the drugs' effects on 20 to 50 subjects, the theory being that if there is a significant difference it will appear in the test results by the time 20 to 50 subjects have been tested.[1] Using this standard, a Pearson correlation coefficient would have to exceed .4438 (the critical r for a p-value of .05 with 20 pairs and a two-tailed test) or .2732 (for 50 pairs) to reject the hypothesis of no difference between the drugs. For the Spearman coefficient the comparable r's would be .450 and .279. A correlation coefficient exceeding these values would be deemed practically significant according to this convention. This merely reflects the conclusions that the degree of correspondence demon-

___

§7.16 [1] In re Bristol Myers, Co., Slip Op. No. 8917 (F.T.C., Sept. 29, 1979) Finding 393.

strated by these critical values is large enough to be of medical importance.

Cases reveal that experts in the discipline of testing use a rule of thumb that a correlation between exam scores and job performance evaluations must exceed .3 in order for there to be a "satisfactory relationship" between these measures of ability.[2]

> **Boston Chapter, NAACP, Inc. v. Beecher:**[3] The issue was the job relatedness of a written exam for firefighters. Both plaintiffs' and defendants' experts agreed that a correlation coefficient of .3 would be the minimum level to indicate a satisfactory relationship; "a lower coefficient would not be practically significant and would not justify the use of the test."[4] Of the 13 correlations calculated between the written exam score and the 13 task performance scores, only two useful coefficients were statistically significant. Those correlations were .346 and .313 and barely exceeded the minimum level necessary to establish practical significance.[5] The court found that defendants had not met their burden of demonstrating that the allegedly discriminatory exam was substantially job related.[6]

Evidence of conventions regarding practical significance adopted by disciplines in which correlations are analyzed similar to the ones presented in court may be persuasive to the factfinder.

§7.17   The Coefficient of Determination

The *coefficient of determination*, r^2, is a statistic that describes the proportion of variation in one variable that is accounted for by variations in a second variable and is calculated by squaring the correlation coefficient. Neither the correlation coefficient or the coefficient of determination proves what "caused" variation in either of the variables. The coefficient of determination may be a useful general aid to intuition regarding the practical significance of a particular correspondence because it provides an alternative way of looking at the magnitude of the correlation coefficient. In addition to a subjective

---

[2] Anderson v. Banks, 520 F. Supp. 472, 489 (S.D. Ga. 1981).
[3] 371 F. Supp. 507 (D. Mass. 1974).
[4] Id. at 516.
[5] Id. at 517.
[6] Id.

determination of whether the calculated correlation coefficient is close enough to $+1$ or -1, one can examine the percent of variation in one variable that is explained by variation in the other variable by multiplying the r^2 value, such as .09, .53, and .90, by 100%, to get 9%, 53%, and 90%. The percent of variance in the variables not explained by each other is calculated by subtracting the amount that is explained from 100%. The interpretation of the practical significance of a particular r^2 value is still subjective, however, because it adds no factual information to that contained in the r value itself.

Pennsylvania v. Local Union 542:[1] The court examined 17 out-of-work lists paired with 17 referral lists to determine whether referrals were based on a legitimate criterion (length of time out of work) or whether there was room for subjective factors (such as race of the union member) to affect referrals. Of the 17 lists examined, on only one was more than one-third of the referral ordering explained or, in the court's word, "predictable,"[2] based on out-of-work ranking. This one correspondence, for group number 16, was a Spearman correlation coefficient of .62,[3] which when squared gives a coefficient of determination of 38.4%. For another group, number 2, the position on the out-of-work list explained only 0.6% of the referral list ranking. The data are presented as in Exhibit 7.17(a).

§7.17 [1] 469 F. Supp. 329, 355 (E.D. Pa. 1978).
[2] Id.
[3] Id.

EXHIBIT 7.17(a)
Coefficient of Determination
Local 542 **Example**

List Number	Rank Correlation Coefficient r_S	Coefficient of Determination Percent Variance Explained r_S^2	Percent Variance Not Explained $(1 - r_S^2)$
1	.24	5.8%	94.2%
2	.08	0.6	99.4
3	.22	4.8	95.2
4	.20	4.0	96.0
5	.40	16.0	84.0
6	.38	14.4	85.6
7	.55	30.3	69.7
8	.44	19.4	80.6
9	.37	13.7	86.3
10	.52	27.0	73.0
11	.44	19.4	90.6
12	.43	18.5	81.5
13	.46	21.2	78.8
14	.46	21.2	78.8
15	.54	29.2	70.8
16	.62	38.4	61.6
17	.45	20.3	79.7

The court found that an average of 82.5% of the variance in referrals was a result of factors other than order on the out-of-work list.[4] Aware that this analysis did not establish race as the factor causing the lack of correlation, the court nevertheless found that this evidence corroborated plaintiffs' claims of discrimination because it suggested that there was room for "arbitrary and standardless selection."[5]

G. LIMITATIONS AND PROBLEMS

In order to decide whether the correlation coefficient is the appropriate tool for a particular purpose, it is useful to know what the

[4] Id. at 356.
[5] Id. at 357.

coefficients cannot do and do not reveal. Sections 7.18 through 7.20 discuss these limitations.

§7.18   Correlation and Causation

It is most important to be aware that proof of a statistically and practically significant correlation between two variables does not show that changes in the value of one caused changes in the value of the other. Often the variable whose values are thought to be caused by changes in the values of another variable is referred to as the *dependent variable,* because its value is said to depend on the second variable, the *independent variable.* The dependent variable is given the symbol y in our equations for correlation coefficients; the independent variable is given the symbol x. The danger in this approach is that a high correlation between x and y might be taken as proof that x causes y. A high correlation coefficient does not prove causation, as is easily demonstrated by switching the symbols on the variables. Even if the dependent variable is labeled x and the independent variable is labeled y the resulting correlation coefficient is the same. Thus no correlation coefficient can be interpreted as showing a causal relationship between two variables; it only shows a pattern of association. Proof of causal connection between variables may be supported by evidence that there is a high correlation between them but only because we expected causally connected variables to exhibit a pattern of association.

Not all mathematically related (or linearly associated) variables are causally connected. It is quite possible for two variables to have a high degree of linear association but for the value of both variables to have been caused by a third variable. A classic example is the high positive correlation between number of births per year in Norwegian countries at the turn of the century and the stork population each year. Even then it was unlikely that storks caused the increases in births. Study and reflection revealed a third variable, severity of the winters, that was a likely cause of variations in both variables. In severe winters people spend more time secluded cozily inside their homes, increasing the birth rate, and stork offspring, who are born in nests built around chimneys, benefit from the continuously warm fireplaces.

Northshore School District No. 417 v. Kinnear:[1] Plaintiffs challenged the educational finance system of Washington State, claiming that variations in local tax income and expenditures per student resulted in unequal and unconstitutional educational opportunity in the various districts. Underlying their argument was the assumed correlation between expenditures per student and educational quality. The opinion emphasized a search for causes of variations in expenditures. The defendants' statistician reported the greatest cause of variation in costs per pupil was the number of students in each district.[2] Rural schools spent more per pupil than urban districts so there was a high negative correlation between number of pupils and expenditures per pupil. Focusing his attention on this urban-rural difference, Chief Justice Hale found that the variation was due to the economies of large-scale operation available only to the larger, urban school districts. While there was a correlation between revenues raised and costs, higher expenditures were not necessarily correlated with higher educational quality. Thus the plaintiffs' argument failed.

§7.19   Predictive Limits of the Correlation Coefficient

The correlation coefficient measures the consistency with which changes in the values of two variables are proportional to one another. By comparing the calculated coefficient to extreme limits the coefficient takes when the correspondence is perfect, a subjective judgment as to the strength of the linear association can be made. The coefficient of determination provides another way to look at the relationship between the variables by indicating in percentage terms how much of the variation in one variable is accounted for by changes in the other variable. But neither of these statistics permits the statistician to predict the value of one variable given the value of the other. Nor do correlation coefficients alone provide enough information to describe *how much* change in the value of one variable occurs when the value of the other changes. These two features are desirable properties that the correlation coefficient does not possess. Thus, in *Orchard View Farms, Inc. v. Martin Marietta Aluminum,*[1] even if we can calculate a positive correlation between fluoride emissions and fluorine content of pine needles, we do not know how much increase in fluorine con-

---

§7.18   [1] 530 P.2d 178 (Wash. 1974).
[2] Id. at 190.
§7.19   [1] 500 F. Supp. 984 (D. Or. 1980).

tent there would be if the level of emissions were changed. We can predict that the fluorine content would go up if emissions were increased, but we cannot say by how much. In *National Commission on Egg Nutrition*[2] we might be able to predict from positive correlation coefficients that if egg consumption were to increase the incidence of coronary heart disease would increase, but we would be unable to indicate how many more cases of coronary heart disease we would expect if everyone ate three more eggs each week. In *Sterling Drug Inc.*[3] a positive correlation between profit rates and degree of diversification might suggest to stockholders that diversification was a good policy, but it would not tell them how much increased profit they could expect if they doubled the number of product lines they sold.

The *regression coefficient,* which is conceptually related to the correlation coefficient, does provide this information. It is the subject of Chapter 8.

§7.20 The Problem of Nonlinear Correspondence

Pearson correlation coefficients describe the degree of linear association between two variables, but there is no reason to expect that all correspondence will be linear, even if they are consistent and regular. It may be, for instance, that as one variable increases at a constant rate, it causes another variable to increase at an accelerating rate. Such a relationship would not be linear because linearity requires that change in the two variables be consistently proportional, that is, that every one-unit increase in one variable always is associated with the same incremental change in the other.

Agarwal v. Arthur G. McKee and Co.:[1] The plaintiff alleged discrimination in salary determinations, prompting defendant's statistician to attempt to identify the factors influencing salary. A problem of nonlinearity arose in determining the effect of age on salary. Hypothetical data suggested by that case are graphed in a scatter plot in Exhibit 7.20(a). Note that as age increases at a constant rate, salary increases quickly at first but more slowly as workers get older. There are several

---

[2] 88 F.T.C. 89 (1976), *modified,* 570 F.2d 157 (D.C. Cir. 1977), *cert. denied,* 439 U.S. 821.
[3] 80 F.T.C. 477 (1972).
§7.20 [1] 19 F.E.P. Cases 503 (N.D. Cal. 1977).

EXHIBIT 7.20(a)
Nonlinear Data for Salary-Age Relationship
Agarwal **Example**

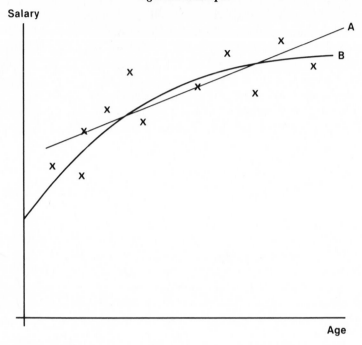

theoretical explanations for this phenomenon: a worker's productivity may increase at a faster rate when he is young, or the employer may not need to give big raises in order to hold on to older workers. Whatever the reason, a straight line, such as *A*, does not describe the relationship between age and salary very well, and a calculated correlation coefficient might be close to zero, understating the degree of relationship between the variables. But we know from looking at the data that there is a consistent though not proportional relationship between these variables. It would be useful to be able to calculate a summary statistic to describe the consistency of this nonlinear relationship.

Because interpreting the Pearson correlation coefficient requires consistency and proportionality, it cannot be used directly to describe accurately the consistency of a nonlinear relationship. There is an indirect approach available, however: the values of the variables may be transformed mathematically so that they do bear a linear relationship to one another. *Linearizing mathematical transformations* are mathematical equations that describe curved lines. By using these equations the nonlinear relationship can be described in a linear fashion, and the degree of association between such linearized variables can be captured in a correlation coefficient.[2] Litigation applications of linear transformations to correlation are not as common as applications to multiple regression. The use of nonlinear techniques is discussed in more detail in Section 8.13, Indicators of Nonlinearity, and Section 8.14, Examples of Nonlinear Specifications.[3]

H. COMPUTATIONAL PROCEDURES FOR THE CORRELATION COEFFICIENT

The following notation is used in the formulas included in this section. The numbers in parentheses following each definition indicate the section where the term was first introduced. Note that upper case letters indicate population values while lower case letters indicate sample values. A symbol in parentheses that follows a similar symbol being defined is the sample equivalent of the population symbol.

$d.f.$ — degrees of freedom (7.22)

M_X (m_x) — mean value of the variable X (x) (4.21) (7.21)

m_{y_0} — the mean of those observations of the continuous variable that are paired with observations belonging to one of the two groups represented by the dichotomous variable (7.24)

m_{y_1} — the mean of those observations of the continuous variable that are paired with observations belonging to the other of the two groups represented by the dichotomous variable (7.24)

M_Y (m_y) — mean value of the variable Y (y) (4.21) (7.21)

N (n) — the number items in the population (sample) (4.21) (7.21)

p — the proportion of sample observations that belong in one of

---

[2] See J. Cohen & P. Cohen, Applied Multiple Regression/Correlation Analysis for the Behavioral Sciences 243 (1975).

[3] L. Sachs, Applied Statistics 453 (1982); J. Cohen & P. Cohen, Applied Multiple Regression/Correlation Analysis for the Behavioral Sciences 243 (1975).

the two groups represented by the dichotomous variable
(7.24)

q — the proportion of sample observations that belong in the
second of the two groups represented by the dichotomous
variable (7.24). q equals $1 - p$ (7.24)

r — the Pearson product moment correlation coefficient (7.1)

r^2 — the coefficient of determination (7.17)

r_{pb} — the point biserial correlation coefficient (7.8)

r_{phi} — the phi correlation coefficient (7.9)

r_S — the Spearman rank correlation coefficient (7.11)

Rx_i — the rank of the ith observation of the x variable (7.25)

Ry_i — the rank of the ith observation of the y variable (7.25)

Σ — arithmetic summation of the terms that follow (4.21) (7.21)

SD_X (sd_x) — the standard deviation of the variable X (x) (4.21)
(7.21)

SD_Y (sd_y) — the standard deviation of the variable Y (y) (4.21)
(7.21)

se_r — the standard error of r (7.22)

X (x) — a variable that takes on numerical values (4.21) (7.21)

X_i (x_i) — the ith value in a sequence of observations of X (x) (4.21)
(7.21)

Y (y) — a variable that takes on numerical values (4.21) (7.21)

Y_i (y_i) — the ith value in a sequence of observations of Y (y) (4.21)
(7.21)

Z_{X_i} (Z_{x_i}) — the Z score associated with the ith value from the list of
observations of X (x) (4.21) (7.21)

Z_{Y_i} (Z_{y_i}) — the Z score associated with the ith value from the list of
observations of Y (y) (7.21)

z' — the Fisher z prime, used in estimating a confidence interval
for r (7.23)

§7.21 The Pearson Product Moment Correlation Coefficient — Calculations

There are several equivalent formulas for calculating the Pearson
correlation coefficient. Each gives exactly the same result and is interpreted in an identical fashion. This section describes four different
methods. Choosing among them will depend on personal preference
and on the summary statistics that have already been calculated. The
formulas given are for coefficients calculated from sample data.

One commonly used formula for r appears in Equation 7.21(a).[1]

$$r = \frac{\Sigma(Z_{x_i} \times Z_{y_i})}{n - 1}$$

7.21(a)

Recall from Chapter 4 that the formulas for the Z scores are as reproduced in Equation 7.21(b) and (c) and the formulas for the standard deviations are as reproduced in Equations 7.21(d) and (e).

$$Z_{x_i} = \frac{x_i - m_x}{sd_x}$$

7.21(b)

$$Z_{y_i} = \frac{y_i - m_y}{sd_y}$$

7.21(c)

$$sd_x = \sqrt{\frac{\Sigma(x_i - m_x)^2}{n - 1}}$$

7.21(d)

$$sd_y = \sqrt{\frac{\Sigma(y_i - m_y)^2}{n - 1}}$$

7.21(e)

Nine separate steps are used to calculate r. To illustrate the calculation, consider the correlation between distance from the fluoride emitting plant (measured in miles) and fluorine concentration in pine needles (measured in parts per million), using hypothetical sample data suggested by *Orchard View Farms v. Martin Marietta Aluminum Corporation*[2] (see Section 7.1). The data and steps are laid out in Exhibit 7.21(a). Exhibit 7.21(b) applies these steps to the data from Exhibit 7.21(a).

---

§7.21 [1] See, e.g., D. Barnes, Statistics as Proof 270 (1983); G. Ferguson, Statistical Analysis in Psychology and Education 105 (4th ed. 1976).
[2] 500 F. Supp. 984 (D. Or. 1980).

EXHIBIT 7.21(a)
Steps for Calculation for Pearson r Using Z Formula

Data

(x)	(y)
Distance (Miles)	*Fluorine Concentration (ppm)*
$x_1 = 5$	$y_1 = 60$
$x_2 = 50$	$y_2 = 10$
$x_3 = 100$	$y_3 = 8$
$x_4 = 1000$	$y_4 = 8$

(1) Calculate the mean of x: $m_x = \dfrac{\Sigma x_i}{n}$

(2) Calculate the standard deviation of x: $sd_x = \sqrt{\dfrac{\Sigma(x_i - m_x)^2}{n - 1}}$

(3) For each x_i, calculate the Z score: $Z_{x_i} = \dfrac{x_i - m_x}{sd_x}$

(4) Calculate the mean of y: $m_y = \dfrac{\Sigma y_i}{n}$

(5) Calculate the standard deviation of y: $sd_y = \sqrt{\dfrac{\Sigma(y_i - m_y)^2}{n - 1}}$

(6) For each y_i, calculate the Z score: $Z_{y_i} = \dfrac{y_i - m_y}{sd_y}$

(7) For each paired x_i and y_i multiply the Z scores together: $Z_{x_i} \times Z_{y_i}$

(8) Add these multiplied pairs together: $\Sigma(Z_{x_i} \times Z_{y_i})$

(9) Divide by $n - 1$ to get r: $r = \dfrac{\Sigma(Z_{x_i} \times Z_{y_i})}{n - 1}$

EXHIBIT 7.21(b)
Calculation of Pearson r Using Z Formula
***Orchard View Farms* Example**

Observation No.	x_i	$x_i - m_x$	$(x_i - m_x)^2$	y_i	$y_i - m_y$	$(y_i - m_y)^2$
1	5	−283.75	80,514	60	38.5	1,482
2	50	−238.75	57,001	10	−11.5	132
3	100	−188.75	35,626	8	−13.5	182
4	1,000	711.25	505,876	8	−13.5	182
Σ	= 1,155		679,017	86		1,978

(Step 1) $\quad m_x = \dfrac{\Sigma x_i}{n} = \dfrac{1155}{4} = 288.75$

(Step 2) $\quad sd_x = \sqrt{\dfrac{\Sigma(x_i - m_x)^2}{n - 1}} = \sqrt{\dfrac{679,017}{4 - 1}} = 475.75$

(Step 3) $\quad Z_{x_i} = \dfrac{x_i - m_x}{se_x}$

$$Z_{x_1} = \frac{5 - 288.75}{475.75} = -.596$$

$$Z_{x_2} = \frac{50 - 288.75}{475.75} = -.502$$

$$Z_{x_3} = \frac{100 - 288.75}{475.75} = -.397$$

$$Z_{x_4} = \frac{1000 - 288.75}{475.75} = 1.494$$

(Step 4) $\quad m_y = \dfrac{\Sigma y_i}{n} = \dfrac{86}{4} = 21.5$

(Step 5) $\quad sd_y = \sqrt{\dfrac{\Sigma(y_i - m_y)^2}{n - 1}} = \sqrt{\dfrac{1978}{3}} = 26$

(Step 6) $\quad Z_{y_i} = \dfrac{y_i - m_y}{se_y}$

$$Z_{y_1} = \frac{60 - 21.5}{26} = 1.48$$

$$Z_{y_2} = \frac{10 - 21.5}{26} = -.44$$

$$Z_{y_3} = \frac{8 - 21.5}{26} = -.52$$

$$Z_{y_4} = \frac{8 - 21.5}{26} = -.52$$

(Step 7) $\quad Z_{x_1} \times Z_{y_1} = -.596 \times 1.48 = -.88$

$\qquad\quad Z_{x_2} \times Z_{y_2} = -.502 \times -.44 = .22$

$\qquad\quad Z_{x_3} \times Z_{y_3} = -.397 \times -.52 = .21$

$\qquad\quad Z_{x_4} \times Z_{y_4} = 1.494 \times -.52 = -.77$

(Step 8) $\quad \Sigma(Z_{x_i} \times Z_{y_i}) = -.88 + .22 + .21 - .77 = -1.22$

(Step 9) $\quad r = \dfrac{\Sigma(Z_{x_i} \times Z_{y_i})}{n - 1} = \dfrac{-1.22}{3} = -.41$

Even though it requires lengthy computations, Equation 7.21(a) is the most intuitively understandable formula for r because it basically includes just two measurements, the Z scores for X and for Y. Recall that a Z score indicates how far from the mean a particular observations is. If two variables are highly correlated then both the x and the y in a pair are likely to be equally far from their respective means. Multiplying the Z scores together to calculate r ensures that the highest r's (closest to $+1$ or -1) will come from data in which the x value furthest from the mean (as measured by the Z score) is paired with the y value furthest from the mean. Adding the multiplied Z scores together ensures that the highest positive r's come from data where x values above the mean of x are paired frequently with y values above the mean of y and that x values below the mean of x are paired with y values below the mean of y. This provides the measure of consistency described in Section 7.2. The highest positive r's result when all multiplied Z values are positive. The highest negative r's result when all multiplied Z values are negative. Note that the size of r does not depend on the size of the sample (n). Even though n appears in the equation for r, it is there merely to cancel out other places where it is hidden, such as in m_x, m_y, sd_x, and sd_y.

Mathematical equivalents to the Z scores formula for r are shown in Equations 7.21(f), (g), and (h).

$$r = \frac{\Sigma(x_i - m_x)(y_i - m_y)/(n - 1)}{sd_x sd_y}$$

7.21(f)

$$r = \frac{\Sigma(x_i - m_x)(y_i - m_y)}{\sqrt{\Sigma(x_i - m_x)^2 \Sigma(y_i - m_y)^2}}$$

7.21(g)

$$r = \frac{n\Sigma x_i y_i - \Sigma x_i \Sigma y_i}{\sqrt{(n\Sigma x_i^2 - (\Sigma x_i)^2)(n\Sigma y_i^2 - (\Sigma y_i)^2)}}$$

7.21(h)

Equation 7.21(f) uses the standard deviations for x and y while 7.21(g) relies exclusively on the deviation of the x and y values from their means. Equation 7.21(h) is a form that is particularly convenient for hand-held calculators.

Exhibit 7.21(b) provides the information necessary to solve Equations 7.21(f) and (g), which is done in Exhibits 7.21(c) and 7.21(d).

EXHIBIT 7.21(c)
Calculation of r Using Equation 7.21(f)

$$\Sigma(x_i - m_x)^2 = 679{,}071$$
$$\Sigma(y_i - m_y)^2 = 1{,}978$$
$$sd_x = 475.75$$
$$sd_y = 26$$
$$n - 1 = 3$$

$(x_1 - m_x)(y_1 - m_y) = -283.75 \times 38.5 = -10{,}924.375$

$(x_2 - m_x)(y_2 - m_y) = -238.75 \times (-11.5) = 2{,}745.625$

$(x_3 - m_x)(y_3 - m_y) = -188.75 \times (-13.5) = 2{,}548.125$

$(x_4 - m_x)(y_4 - m_y) = 711.25 \times (-13.5) = -9{,}601.875$

$\Sigma(x_i - m_x)(y_i - m_y) = -15{,}232.5$

$$r = \frac{\Sigma(x_i - m_x)(y_i - m_y)/(n-1)}{sd_x sd_y} = \frac{-15{,}232.5/3}{475.75 \times 26} = -.41$$

EXHIBIT 7.21(d)
Calculation of r Using Equation 7.21(g)

$$\Sigma(x_i - m_x)^2 = 679{,}071$$
$$\Sigma(y_i - m_y)^2 = 1{,}978$$
$$\Sigma(x_i - m_x)(y_i - m_y) = -15{,}232.5$$

$$r = \frac{\Sigma(x_i - m_x)(y_i - m_y)}{\sqrt{\Sigma(x_i - m_x)^2 \, \Sigma(y_i - m_y)^2}} = \frac{-15{,}232.5}{\sqrt{679{,}071 \times 1{,}978}} = -.41$$

§7.22   The t Test for r — Calculations

The t test statistic for r's calculated from sample data has a straightforward formula shown in Equation 7.22(a).

$$t_{\text{calculated}} = r/se_r$$

7.22(a)

The r is calculated from the sample by one of the formulas in the previous section. The estimated standard error of r is calculated by the formula in Equation 7.22(b).

$$se_r = \sqrt{\frac{1 - r^2}{n - 2}}$$

7.22(b)

Thus the formula for the calculated t may be rewritten as in Equation 7.22(c).[1]

$$t_{calculated} \text{ (Pearson } r) = \frac{r\sqrt{n-2}}{\sqrt{1-r^2}}$$

7.22(c)

For the *Orchard View Farms v. Martin Marietta Aluminum Corp.*[2] example discussed in Section 7.3, the calculated t for the sample r is calculated as shown in Exhibit 7.22(a). The degrees of freedom for this t test are given by Equation 7.22(d) as two less than the number of pairs (n).

EXHIBIT 7.22(a)
Calculation of t Value
***Orchard View Farms* Example**

$$t = \frac{r\sqrt{n-2}}{\sqrt{1-r^2}} = \frac{-.41\sqrt{4-2}}{\sqrt{1-(-.41)^2}} = \frac{-.58}{.91} = -.64$$

$$d.f. \text{ (} t \text{ test for } r) = n - 2$$

7.22(d)

The t Table reveals a p-value of .60 for the two degrees of freedom and a two-tailed test. For a one-tailed test of whether this r is greater than zero, the p-value is .30. By either measure this r is not considered statistically significant under most conventions.

For the *Egg Nutrition* example in Section 7.7 the calculated r was .73 for a sample size of 7. A one-tailed critical t value for five degrees of freedom and a 95% confidence level is 2.015. Using Equation 7.22(c) gives a corresponding calculated t value of 2.39, as shown in Exhibit 7.22(b). Since this calculated t value is greater than the critical t, we reject the hypothesis that r is not greater than zero at a .05 level of significance.

---

§7.22 [1] J. Cohen & P. Cohen, Applied Multiple Regression/Correlation Analysis for the Behavioral Sciences 49 (1975).
[2] 500 F. Supp. 984 (D. Or. 1980).

EXHIBIT 7.22(b)
Calculations for t Test
Egg Nutrition Example

$r = .73$
$n = 7$ countries
$d.f. = n - 2 = 7 - 2 = 5$

$$t_{calculated} = \frac{r\sqrt{n - 2}}{\sqrt{1 - r^2}} = \frac{.73\sqrt{7 - 2}}{\sqrt{1 - .73^2}} = 2.39$$

$t_{critical}$ for 1 tail, .05 significance level, 5 degrees of freedom $= 2.015$

$t_{calculated}$ is greater than $t_{critical}$

§7.23 Confidence Intervals for r — Calculations

Determining a two-tailed confidence interval for r requires the calculation of a range on either side of the estimated r within which the population value for the Pearson product moment correlation coefficient is likely to fall. A one-tailed confidence interval requires calculation of either a lower or upper limit beyond which the population coefficient is unlikely to fall. In either case, the range can be calculated in five steps. These procedures are applicable only for samples of size about 50 or more.[1] To begin, we introduce a new symbol, z', often referred to as the *Fisher z-prime* after Ronald A. Fisher, who developed it. Any value of r may be transformed into a new variable z' by use of an appropriate mathematical equation.[2] The z' has properties that permit one to use the Table of Critical Values of Z to calculate a confidence interval.

Once r has been calculated, a two-tailed confidence interval for the population correlation coefficient can be determined in five steps:

(1) Find the value of z' that corresponds to the r that has been calculated by reference to a z' Transformation of r Table such as the one that appears in the Appendix of Tables at the end of this book.

(2) Find the critical two-tailed Z value from the Table of Critical

---

§7.23 [1] Sir M. Kendall & A. Stuart, 1 The Advanced Theory of Statistics, 419-420 (4th ed. 1979).

[2] The equation is discussed in A. Edwards, An Introduction to Linear Regression and Correlation 86 (1976) and is not presented here because the z' Transformation of r Table is adequate for our purposes.

Values of Z for whatever significance level you may choose, such as .05.

(3)   Calculate the standard error of z' by Equation 7.23(a).[3]

$$se_{z'} = \frac{1}{\sqrt{n-3}}$$

7.23(a)

(4)   Calculate an interval around the z' equivalent to r by Equation 7.23(b).[4]

$$\text{confidence interval} = z' \pm Z_{\text{critical}} \times se_{z'}$$

7.23(b)

(5)   Transform the end points of the z' interval back to r by reference to the z' Transformation of r Table. These are the endpoints for the confidence interval around r.

Using the r equal to .346 calculated in *Boston Chapter, NAACP, Inc. v. Beecher*[5] (see Section 7.6) describing the degree of linear association between written examination scores and task performance scores on air mask operation, we calculate a confidence interval as shown in Exhibit 7.23(a).

---

[3] J. Cohen & P. Cohen, Applied Multiple Regression/Correlation Analysis for the Behavioral Sciences 51 (1975).
[4] Id. at 57.
[5] 371 F. Supp. 507 (D. Mass. 1974).

EXHIBIT 7.23(a)
Calculation of Confidence Interval for r
Boston Chapter NAACP Example

(1) The z' transformation of r table shows a z' (on the borders of the table) of .366 to correspond to an r (in the body of the table) of .345 (the r nearest to .346 shown on the table).

(2) For .05 significance level the critical Z for a two-tailed interval is 1.96.

(3) The standard error of z' is .108.
$$se_{z'} = \frac{1}{\sqrt{n-3}} = \frac{1}{\sqrt{88-3}} = .108$$

(4) The interval is from .149 to .581.
$$z' \pm Z_{\text{critical}} \times se_{z'} = .366 \pm 1.96 \times .108 = .366 \pm .212$$

(5) The r equivalents of $z' = .15$ and .57 from the z' transformation of r table are .15 and .52 respectively. Thus the 95% confidence interval around r is $.15 \le r \le .52$.

The only difference in calculating a one-tailed confidence interval for r is employing a one-tailed critical Z and deciding whether $Z_{\text{(critical)}}$ times $se_{z'}$ should be added to or subtracted from r. If the hypothesis being tested is that r is not greater than a hypothesized value, we can reject this hypothesis whenever that value is lower than the lower boundary of the one-tailed interval, which is given by Equation 7.23(c).

$$z' - Z_{\text{critical}} \times se_{z'} = \text{lower boundary}$$

7.23(c)

If the hypothesis is that r is not less than a hypothesized value, we can reject the hypothesis whenever the value is greater than the upper boundary of the one-tailed interval. That upper boundary is given by Equation 7.23(d).

$$z' + Z_{\text{critical}} \times se_{z'} = \text{upper boundary}$$

7.23(d)

For a significance level of .05, the critical one-tailed Z value is 1.645. Thus, to test the hypothesis that the population correlation is not less than .3 we follow the five steps shown in Exhibit 7.23(b).

EXHIBIT 7.23(b)
One-Tailed Lower Boundary for *r*
***Boston Chapter NAACP* Example**

(1)   The z' transformation of $r = .35$ is $.365$

(2)   The Z_{critical} is 1.645

(3)   The $se_{z'} = \dfrac{1}{\sqrt{88 - 3}} = .108$

(4)   The z' lower boundary is $.1845$
      $.365 - 1.645 \times .108 = .1873$

(5)   The r equivalent of $z' = .1873$ is $.18$, which, being less than $.3$, does not allow us to reject the null hypothesis at a $.01$ significance level.

To test the hypothesis that the population correlation is not greater than $.8$ (arbitrarily chosen for this example) change step (4) and (5) as shown in Exhibit 7.23(c).

EXHIBIT 7.23(c)
One-Tailed Upper Boundary for *r*
***Boston Chapter NAACP* Example**

(4)   The z' interval upper boundary is $.623$
      $.365 + (2.390 \times .108) = .623$

(5)   The r equivalent of $z' = .623$ is $.55$, which, being less than $.8$, allows us to reject the null hypothesis at $p = .01$.

§7.24   Correlation Coefficients for Dichotomous Variables — Calculations

The point-biserial and phi correlation coefficients can be calculated using any of the product moment correlation coefficient formulas given in Section 7.21. It is necessary, however, to assign arbitrary values (such as 0 or 1) to the dichotomous variable(s). Because in the case of the point biserial at least one of the variables is dichotomous and in the case of the phi coefficient both are, a simplified formula can be used. If a computer is doing the calculations, there is no need to use the simplified formula, but using the simplified formula saves time and prevents errors by involving fewer computations to be done by hand. This section illustrates by example the equivalence of the simplified and regular product moment formulas.

When one of the two variables is dichotomous, the Pearson correlation coefficient formula simplifies to that shown in Equation 7.24(a).[1]

$$r_{pb} = \frac{(m_{y_1} - m_{y_0})\sqrt{pq}}{sd_y}$$

7.24(a)

Using the data in Exhibit 7.8(a), the values of m_{y_1}, m_{y_0}, p, q, and se_y are calculated as shown in Exhibit 7.24(a) to produce r_{pb}.

EXHIBIT 7.24(a)
Calculation of Point Biserial Coefficient
***O'Neill* Example**

Observation Number	(x) Race of Applicant (Black = 1) (White = 0)	(y) Number of Undesirable Factors Present	$y_i - m_y$	$(y_i - m_y)^2$
1	1	3	$-.7$	.49
2	0	2	-1.7	2.89
3	1	5	1.3	1.69
4	1	6	2.3	5.29
5	0	1	-2.7	7.29
6	0	7	3.3	10.89
7	0	2	-1.7	2.89
		$\Sigma = 26$		$\Sigma = 31.43$

$$m_y = \frac{\Sigma y_i}{n} = \frac{26}{7} = 3.7 \qquad sd_y = \sqrt{\frac{\Sigma(y_i - m_y)^2}{n-1}} = \sqrt{\frac{31.43}{7}} = 2.12$$

$$\Sigma(y_i - m_y)^2 = 31.43$$

$$p = \frac{3}{7} = .43$$

$$m_{y_1} = \frac{3 + 5 + 6}{3} = 4.\overline{66}$$

$$q = \frac{4}{7} = 1 - .43 = .57$$

$$m_{y_0} = \frac{2 + 1 + 7 + 2}{4} = 3$$

$$r_{pb} = \frac{(m_{y_1} - m_{y_0})}{sd_y}\sqrt{pq} = \frac{(4.\overline{66} - 3)\sqrt{.43 \times .57}}{2.12} = .39$$

§7.24 [1] J. Cohen & P. Cohen, Applied Multiple Regression/Correlation Analysis for the Behavioral Sciences 36 (1975).

The only new calculations in Exhibit 7.24(a) are m_{y_0} and m_{y_1}, the means for the two groups of observations of the continuous variable, y. The two groups are, in this example, those values of y that are for blacks, x equals 1, and those values of y that are for whites, x equals 0. There are three observations for blacks, observations numbered 1, 3, and 4. The y values associated with the x observations numbered 1, 3, and 4 are 3, 5, and 6 respectively. The mean for these three values, M_{y_1}, equals 4.66. A similar procedure is used to calculate M_{y_0}.

Exhibit 7.24(b) displays the calculation using the Pearson formula from Equation 7.21(a), the Z score formula for r. Note that both equations give the same result.

EXHIBIT 7.24(b)
Calculation of r_{pb} Using Z Score Formula
O'Neill Example

Observation Number	x_i	y_i	$x_i - m_x$	$y_i - m_y$	$(x_i - m_x)^2$	$(y_i - m_y)^2$
1	1	3	.57	−.7	.32	.49
2	0	2	.43	−1.7	.18	2.89
3	1	5	.57	1.3	.32	1.69
4	1	6	.57	2.3	.32	5.29
5	0	1	−.43	−2.7	.18	7.29
6	0	7	−.43	3.3	.18	10.89
7	0	2	−.43	−1.7	.18	2.89
$\Sigma = 3$		26			1.68	31.43

$$m_x = \frac{\Sigma x_i}{n} = \frac{3}{7} = .43$$

$$m_y = \frac{\Sigma y_i}{n} = \frac{26}{7} = 3.7$$

$$Z_{x_i} = \frac{x_i - m_x}{sd_x}$$

$$Z_{y_i} = \frac{y_i - m_y}{sd_y}$$

$$\Sigma(x_i - m_x)^2 = 1.68$$

$$\Sigma(y_i - m_y)^2 = 31.43$$

$$sd_x = \sqrt{\frac{\Sigma(x_i - m_x)^2}{n-1}} = \sqrt{\frac{1.68}{7}} = .49$$

$$sd_y = \sqrt{\frac{\Sigma(y_i - m_y)^2}{n-1}} = \sqrt{\frac{31.43}{7}} = 2.12$$

Observation Number	Z_{x_i}	Z_{y_i}	$Z_{x_i} \times Z_{y_i}$
1	1.16	−.33	−.38
2	−.87	−.80	.70
3	1.16	.61	.71
4	1.16	1.08	1.25
5	−.87	−1.27	1.10
6	−.87	1.55	−1.35
7	−.87	−.80	.70
		$\Sigma =$	2.73

$$r_{pb} = \frac{\Sigma(Z_{x_i} - Z_{y_i})}{n} = \frac{2.73}{7} = .39$$

When two truly dichotomous variables are correlated, the calculation is simplified further. The formula for the phi coefficient is shown in Equation 7.24(b).[2]

$$r_{phi} = \frac{BC - AD}{\sqrt{(A + B)(C + D)(A + C)(B + D)}}$$

7.24(b)

With two variables, each with two categories, there are a total of four groupings. We refer to the number of items in each grouping as A, B, C, and D. To calculate the phi coefficient we need to know only the frequencies with which observations appear in each group. A frequency table such as that appearing in Exhibit 7.24(c) is the easiest way to keep the groupings straight. Exhibit 7.24(c) depicts the frequencies for the hypothetical data in the *Craig v. Boren* case[3] discussed in Section 7.9. For that hypothetical we assume that 49% of the people sampled between the ages of 18 and 21 are male and 51% are female. For a sample of 20,000, there are 9,800 males, of whom 2% or 196 had been arrested and 10,200 females, of whom 18 or .18% had been arrested. These frequencies of arrest status by gender provide the information necessary to calculate r_{phi} as shown in Exhibit 7.24(d).

EXHIBIT 7.24(c)
Frequency Table for Calculation of Phi Coefficient
***Craig* Example**

	Male	*Female*	*Total*
Arrested	A = 9,604	B = 10,182	A+B = 19,786
Not Arrested	C = 196	D = 18	C+D = 214
Total	A+C = 9,800	B+D = 10,200	A+B+C+D = 20,000

EXHIBIT 7.24(d)
Calculation of Phi Coefficient
***Craig* Example**

$$r_{phi} = \frac{BC - AD}{\sqrt{(A + B)(C + D)(A + C)(B + D)}} =$$

$$\frac{(10,182 \times 196) - (9,604 \times 18)}{\sqrt{19,786 \times 214 \times 9,800 \times 10,200}} = .09$$

[2] Id. at 37.
[3] 429 U.S. 190 (1976).

§7.25 The Spearman Rank Correlation Coefficient — Calculations

The Spearman rank correlation coefficient can be calculated using Equation 7.21(a) for the Pearson correlation coefficient, provided the values of x_i and y_i are replaced by their ranks, R_{x_i} and R_{y_i} respectively. As for the point biserial and phi correlation coefficients, however, the Pearson formula can be simplified to give an easier formula that yields identical results. Because the ranks are substituted for quantitative measurements in the formulas and because there may be ties in ranks, that is, two or more observations with the same measurement and therefore the same rank, ordinal lists with tied ranks require special treatment in calculation. The computation for the case without tied ranks is described first.

Equation 7.25(a) is a simplified version of the Pearson product moment correlation coefficient formula that is often used to calculate the Spearman rank correlation coefficient.[1]

$$r_S = 1 - \frac{6\Sigma(Rx_i - Ry_i)^2}{n(n^2 - 1)}$$

7.25(a)

Note that Rx_i and Ry_i represent the ranks of the observations on the variables' respective ordinal lists. Exhibit 7.25(a) demonstrates the calculation of the Spearman rank correlation coefficient using hypothetical data suggested by *Pennsylvania v. Local Union 542*,[2] showing the correlation between position on the out-of-work list and order of referral to be .3. For five pairs of observations the Spearman r Table in the Appendix of Tables at the end of this book indicates a critical value for a one-tailed test and .05 significance level of .9. This r_S of .3 is not significantly different from zero at a p-value of .05 because r_S is less than .9000.

---

§7.25   [1]See, e.g., A. Baggaley, Intermediate Correlational Methods 23 (1964).
[2]469 F. Supp. 329 (E.D. Pa. 1978), discussed in Section 7.11.

EXHIBIT 7.25(a)
Calculation of r_S for Case Without Tied Ranks
Local 542 **Example**

Member Number	x_i Days Out of Work	y_i Order of Referral	Rx_i Rank on x list	Ry_i Rank on y list	$(Rx_i - Ry_i)^2$
1	26	1	1	1	0
2	3	4	5	4	1
3	19	5	2	5	9
4	11	3	3	3	0
5	7	2	4	2	4
					$\Sigma = \overline{14}$

$$n = 5$$
$$\Sigma(Rx_i - Ry_i)^2 = 14$$
$$r_S = 1 - \frac{6\Sigma(Rx_i - Ry_i)^2}{n(n^2 - 1)} = 1 - \frac{6(14)}{5(25 - 1)} = .3$$

When two or more observations have the same rank due to having the same underlying measurement (such as the same number of days out of work), the rank to be used in the calculation is the average of the positions occupied by observations with the same values. Thus in Exhibit 7.25(b) members number 1 and 6 were both out of work for the same length of time, 26 days. No one was out of work longer so they would collectively occupy ranks 1 and 2. Because neither ranks ahead of the other, both members are assigned the averaged rank (1.5) on the X list. Members number 5, 7, and 9 were each out of work for seven days. There are six members who were out of work longer so these three members share 7, 8, and 9. The average of 7, 8, and 9 is 8 so each is assigned a rank of 8 on the X list, as shown in Exhibit 7.25 (b). Note that because members 1 and 6 are sharing the first two positions, the rank for the next member, number 8, is 3. Because members 5, 7, and 9 share the ranks 7, 8, and 9, member number 2 takes the rank of 10 even though the next lower assigned rank is 8 (assigned to each of the members 5, 7, and 9). The calculation proceeds as usual for r_S, using the averaged ranks for Rx_i. There are no ties among the y observations in this example, but if there had been they would be treated the same way.

EXHIBIT 7.25(b)
Calculation of r_S for Case with Tied Ranks
Local 542 Example

Member Number	Days Out of Work	Order of Referral	Rank on x list	Rank on y list	$(Rx_i - Ry_i)^2$
1	26	1	1.5	1	0.25
2	3	4	10	4	36
3	19	5	4	5	1
4	11	3	6	3	9
5	7	2	8	2	36
6	26	6	1.5	6	20.25
7	7	8	8	8	0
8	22	7	3	7	16
9	7	9	8	9	1
10	12	10	5	10	25
				$\Sigma =$	144.5

$$n = 10$$

$$\Sigma(Rx_i - Ry_i)^2 = 144.5$$

$$r_S = 1 - \frac{6\Sigma(Rx_i - Ry_i)^2}{n(n^2 - 1)} = \frac{1 - 6(144.5)}{10(100 - 1)} = .12$$

§7.26   Significance Testing for r_S — Calculations

For sample sizes less than about 30 the summary statistic, r_S, should be used in combination with the Spearman r Table for significance testing. For larger samples, the t test statistic can be calculated using Equation 7.26(a), which is similar to Equation 7.22(c) for the Pearson coefficient.[1]

$$t_{\text{calculated}} \text{ (Spearman } r) = r_S\sqrt{\frac{n - 2}{1 - r_S^2}}$$

7.26(a)

The critical t values are found on the t Table for n − 2 degrees of freedom. Thus, for eight sample Spearman rank correlation coefficients and associated numbers of pairs of observations, Exhibit 7.26(a)

§7.26 [1] A useful discussion of significant tests for special forms of the correlation coefficients appears in A. Edwards, An Introduction to Linear Regression and Correlation Ch. 9 (1976).

shows the associated p-values for a two-tailed test. Using either the r_S Table or the t Table, the p-value is found above the critical value (for the appropriate number of degrees of freedom) closest to yet not greater than the calculated r_S or calculated t value. It can readily be seen from Exhibit 7.26(a) that the sample size is an important factor in the statistical significance of Spearman rank correlation coefficients.

EXHIBIT 7.26(a)
Calculation of p-Values for r_S by r and t Tests

r_S	n	$t_{calculated}$	closest smaller critical r	closest smaller critical t	p-value
.36	9	—	< .600	—	> .10
.21	12	—	< .497	—	> .10
.77	8	—	.738	—	.05
.60	23	—	.549	—	.005
.77	47	8.10	—	3.551	.001
.21	82	1.92	—	1.671	.10
.36	31	2.08	—	2.045	.05
.60	106	7.65	—	3.460	.001

CHAPTER EIGHT

Estimation and Prediction: Techniques for Assessing the Influences of Multiple Factors

§8.0 Introduction

It is often useful for the lawyer to describe the relationship between two variables or to predict how much the value of one variable will change when the values of other variables change. The correlation coefficient measures the degree of association between two variables (see Section 7.1) but fails to describe *how much* the value of one variable changes when the value of other variables change. See Section 7.19. This information, provided by *regression analysis,* is sometimes essential to the resolution of factual issues.

South Dakota Public Utilities Comm. v. Federal Energy Regulatory Comm.:[1] In order to establish the useful life of certain pipeline equipment for tax depreciation purposes, it was necessary to predict when the natural gas fields served by the pipeline would be exhausted. One factor influencing gas reserves, that is, the total amount of gas left to be shipped, was the amount added to gas reserves each year by new discoveries. Another factor influencing the reserves was time, because each year more gas was piped out of the fields. In order to predict when the pipeline would no longer be useful, it was necessary to know how much gas reserves decreased on average each year due to shipments out of the fields and increased on average each year due to new discoveries. Regression analysis enabled the parties to make this prediction.

Presseisen v. Swarthmore College:[2] In this employment discrimination case the parties used regression analysis to estimate the effect of

---

§8.0 [1] 643 F.2d 504 (8th Cir. 1981).
[2] 442 F. Supp. 593 (E.D. Pa. 1977), *aff'd,* 582 F.2d 1275 (3d Cir. 1982).

gender on salary. A correlation coefficient between the variables "gender" and "salary" would indicate the consistency with which men received higher salaries than women but would not indicate *how much* higher were men's salaries than women's. Regression analysis enabled the parties to estimate how much higher the salaries were for one gender than for the other.

In *regression analysis* the variable whose value we are trying to predict or explain is referred to as the *dependent variable,* so-called because we expect its value to depend on the values of one or more explanatory factors. These factors are referred to as *independent* variables or *regressors.* In the *Public Utilities* example the quantity of gas reserves is the dependent variable, thought to be influenced by the independent variables of time and new annual discoveries. In *Presseisen* the dependent variable is salary. The plaintiffs argued that the value of salary depended on a number of independent variables such as gender, years of employment, age, academic rank, and department. In regression analysis particular attention can be focused on any one independent variable, such as gender in *Presseisen,* or on the cumulative predictive power of all independent variables taken together, as in *South Dakota Public Utilities.* Applications of regression analysis appear in Sections 8.1, 8.2, and 8.3. Section 8.4 discusses the problem of choosing variables to be included in regression analysis.

As with other statistical tools, once a prediction or an estimate of the effect of one variable on another has been made, its statistical significance can be tested. When using regression analysis for prediction, significance testing is a means of assessing the precision of the prediction or of testing whether the observed cumulative explanatory power of the independent variables is due to the random selection of items to be included in the sample on which the prediction is based. When using regression analysis to estimate the effect of a particular independent variable on a dependent variable, a significance test yields a p-value, which estimates the probability that the difference between the estimated effect and some hypothesized effect (such as zero, which would indicate no effect) was due to chance. Significance testing is discussed in Sections 8.5 through 8.12.

As discussed in Chapter 7, variables may have linear or nonlinear relationships between them. Recognizing the possibility of nonlinearity is as important in regression analysis as it is for correlation coefficients (see Section 7.20). Using the procedures discussed in Section 8.13 one can test for nonlinearity. Section 8.14 discusses regression techniques used to describe nonlinear relationships.

The validity of particular applications of regression analysis depends on a variety of background assumptions (see Section 2.10 on background assumptions generally). Sections 8.15 through 8.17 describe several of these assumptions, how to determine whether they have been satisfied, and what may be done if they are not.

Many computations associated with regression analysis are usually done by computer because they are particularly complicated and are often beyond the capacity of hand-held calculators. The discussion of computations in Sections 8.18 through 8.24 emphasizes calculations used to interpret the estimates that result from regression rather than the calculation of the estimates themselves.[3]

A. THE UTILITY OF REGRESSION ANALYSIS

A regression analysis often begins with a conceptual model of how various influences combine to produce a result. In any given application only a subset of all possible interactive variables are considered, those that might have some effect on the variable of interest to the factfinder or whose effect we wish to describe. This subset of chosen variables is organized in a mathematical equation described in detail in Section 8.1 and illustrated by numerous examples in Sections 8.2 and 8.3. This equation is called a *regression equation* and is a mathematical model of how the variables interact. It might be a small model that describes the interactive relationship between only two variables, one of which, the *dependent variable,* is thought to change in response to changes in the other variable, the *independent variable.* Other regression equations, such as those used in macroeconomic models of the United States economy, have hundreds of independent variables, each of which is thought to influence the value of a dependent vari-

---

[3] The methodology by which regression estimates are calculated is explained in D. Barnes, Statistics as Proof: Fundamentals of Quantitative Evidence (1983), which takes the reader through calculations for regressions with one independent and one dependent variable. When more variables are involved, matrix algebra or linear algebraic techniques are generally used to calculate the relevant statistics. For those familiar with the techniques of matrix algebra, a classic text in the area is T. Wonnacott & R. Wonnacott, Regression: A Second Course in Statistics (1981). S. Chatterjee & B. Price, Regression Analysis by Example (1977), present a very useful, down-to-earth discussion with useful examples of many of the regression techniques described in this chapter.

able. All types of models from the simplest to most complex have been offered as evidence in courts and administrative tribunals.

The cases highlighted in this chapter were chosen to illustrate the variety of uses of regression analysis and the methods by which relationships between variables are modeled. Considerable liberties have been taken with the facts where the reported decisions are not explicit about the form of the model, about all of the variables involved, or about the regression results. Since our goal is to illustrate rather than anthologize, we have simplified other cases for purposes of exposition while preserving the essence of the legal issues involved and the type of evidence presented.

§8.1 The Regression Equation

Regression models may describe the relationships among two or more variables. Section 8.1.1 discusses the *bivariate regression equation,* a mathematical expression involving only two variables, one dependent and one independent. Section 8.1.2 discusses multivariate regression equations, mathematical expressions involving three or more variables, one dependent and the remainder independent.

§8.1.1 The Bivariate Regression Equation

The relationship between two variables can be visualized from a graph on which are plotted the variables' observed measurements. In Exhibit 8.1.1(a), a graph describes the relationship between salary, the dependent variable, and experience, an independent variable that is likely to influence salary. The data represented by these points appear in Exhibit 8.1.1(b). The scatter plot in Exhibit 8.1.1(a) illustrates a general increase in the salary of bridge builders as more experience is acquired, which is measured by the number of bridges an individual has built. Such data are usually obtained from a sample.

EXHIBIT 8.1.1(a)
Scatter Plot for Regression Analysis
Bridge Builder Example

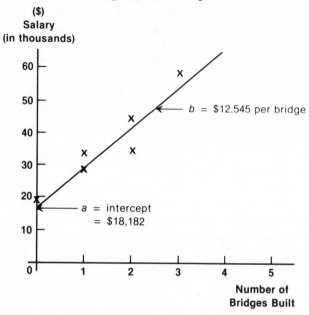

EXHIBIT 8.1.1(b)
Data for Regression Analysis
Bridge Builder Example

Worker Number	Number of Bridges Built	Salary ($)
1	2	45,000
2	1	30,000
3	0	20,000
4	2	35,000
5	3	60,000
6	1	32,000

One statistic that can be obtained from regression analysis is the *regression coefficient,* which indicates the average change in the dependent variable associated with a one unit change in the independent variable. The regression coefficient calculated from a sample, given the symbol b,[1] is an estimate of the average change in the population as a whole. In accord with our conventions for symbols the population regression coefficient is given the symbol B. The sample regression coefficient, b, for our example is equal to $12,545 per bridge. It is an estimate of the population B that we could calculate only if we knew the salary and experience levels for all bridge builders.

The graph also illustrates that even with no experience a bridge builder earns some salary. A second statistic that can be obtained from regression analysis is the *regression intercept,* also called the *constant,* which indicates the average contribution to the value of the dependent variable by factors or variables that are not included among the specified independent variables. The intercept calculated from a sample, given the symbol a,[2] is an estimate of the average contribution in the population to the value of the dependent variable by omitted independent variables, which is denoted by A. The sample intercept, a, for our bridge builder example is $18,182, an estimate of the population constant, A, the amount of salary that is not due to experience, the only independent variable in the equation.

Using the regression coefficient and the regression intercept, the relationship between salary and experience can be described and two uses of regression analysis can be illustrated. We have estimated that salary is related to two factors, "experience" and "all other influences." On average the base salary is $18,182, but it increases by $12,545 for each bridge a builder can claim as experience. We can *predict* salary for a particular individual by adding to a, $18,182, the value of b, $12,545, multiplied by the number of bridges worked on by the individual. These regression results can be expressed in mathematical terms as in Equation 8.1.1(a), which simply repeats that salary equals a base amount, a, plus an increment for experience, b times number of bridges.

$$\text{Salary} = a + b \times \text{Number of Bridges}$$

8.1.1(a)

By convention the dependent variable is often given the symbol y and the independent variable the symbol x. The general formula for a

---

§8.1 [1] Some statisticians refer to and denote the sample regression coefficient by the Greek letter beta.
[2] Some statisticians refer to and denote the intercept by the Greek letter alpha.

bivariate regression equation is shown in Equation 8.1.1(b), where y stands for salary and x stands for number of bridges.[3]

$$y = a + bx$$

8.1.1(b)

When using the regression equation to *predict* a value for y we have to know not only the values of a and b, but also the particular value of x for which we want to estimate a corresponding y value. A particular value of x is denoted by x_j and the corresponding y value is denoted by y_j. Having calculated a and b, we can use the regression equation to calculate a predicted value for the dependent variable, denoted by y_j^*.[4] For predicting y_j^* the regression equation appears as in Equation 8.1.1(c).

$$y_j^* = a + bx_j$$

8.1.1(c)

Using Equation 8.1.1(c) and the calculated value of a and b, we can predict salary for any level of experience, such as x_j equals four bridges, as shown in Equation 8.1.1(d).

$$y_j^* = a + bx_j = \$18{,}182 + \$12{,}545x_j =$$
$$\$18{,}182 + \$12{,}545(4) = \$68{,}362$$

8.1.1(d)

The difference between the observed value of y_j that corresponds to the observed value x_j and the predicted value, y_j^*, is called the *error,* the *residual error,* or the *residual,* and is denoted by e_j. The formula for the error is shown in Equation 8.1.1(e).

---

[3] There are a variety of ways of indicating that two values are to be multiplied together. Frequently we have used the multiplication symbol ($\times$) or the word *times* to indicate that multiplication is required, e.g., 5 $\times$ 3 and $t \times se_m$ or 5 times 3 and t times se_m. A convention often used when symbols or a number and symbols appear next to each other in an equation, such as bx_i or $150m_x$, means that the values should be multiplied together, that is, the particular value indicated by x_i should be multiplied by b, the regression coefficient, or the mean of x, m_x, should be multiplied by 150.

[4] The predicted value for the dependent variable is referred to as "$y - \text{sub } j - \text{star}$."

$$e_j = y_j^* - y_j$$

8.1.1(e)

Recognizing that a prediction involves the potential for error, the general formula for the bivariate regression equation appearing in Equation 8.1.1(b) is often rewritten in the form shown in Equation 8.1.1(f).

$$y = a + bx + e$$

8.1.1(f)

For more on the error term in the regression equation, see Section 8.13.2.

A second use of regression analysis is to *estimate* the effect of an independent variable, such as experience, on the dependent variable, salary, by examining the size of b, \$12,545, in the bridge builder example. The effect of experience on salary seems large for bridge builders. The question of whether this apparently large effect is due merely to those individuals who happened to be selected for the sample remains to be examined (see Section 8.5 through 8.8).

The formula in Equation 8.1.1(b) is the formula for a straight line. The formulas for a and b, when applied to a particular set of observations of two variables, result in the description of a specific line that has important properties. The straight line in Exhibit 8.1.1(a) minimizes the distances between the plotted data points and the line. To be precise, it minimizes the sum of the *squared vertical distances* of the plotted data points from the line. Regression lines such as the line rising from left to right in Exhibit 8.1.1(a) are referred to as *least squares lines*. The mathematical technique by which the formula for the line that minimizes the squared vertical distances is calculated is called *ordinary least squares*, abbreviated *OLS*. Those familiar with geometry will recognize the regression coefficient as the *slope* of the least squares line.[5]

---

[5] It is not necessary to understand the geometry of the regression line outlined in the previous paragraph in order to understand regression analysis. In fact, as soon as the effects on a dependent variable of more than one independent variable are examined, the analogy of the regression equation to a simple line is no longer appropriate. Accordingly, this chapter focuses on the regression equation, rather than its geometric characterization, and on the way in which regression results are interpreted and used as evidence.

§8.1.2   The Multivariate Regression Equation

The extension from a bivariate regression equation with two variables, one dependent and one independent, to a *multivariate* or *multiple regression equation,* with two or more independent variables, is conceptually straightforward. The basic difference is that in multivariate analysis we can simultaneously identify the individual effects of numerous independent variables on a single dependent variable. The statistics calculated for a multivariate regression analysis may include a regression coefficient, *b, for each independent variable,* which indicates the average effect on the dependent variable of a one unit change in that independent variable, as well as an intercept, *a,* which indicates the average contribution to the value of the dependent variable by those influential factors that are not included in the multiple regression equation. With an intercept and one regression coefficient, denoted b_i, associated with each of m independent variables, denoted x_i, the multivariate regression equation has a general form shown in Equation 8.1.2(a).

$$y = a + b_1x_1 + b_2x_2 + b_3x_3 + b_4x_4 + \ldots + b_mx_m$$

8.1.2(a)

After we have calculated the intercept and the regression coefficients we can predict a y value that corresponds to values for the individual x_i's. Thus, if in addition to experience, the first independent variable in a multivariate regression equation, x_i, other influences on bridge builders' salaries include age, x_2, and number of hours of overtime, x_3, the regression equation for bridge builders' salaries would appear as in Equations 8.1.2(b), (c), and (d). In Equation 8.1.2(b) the independent variables are specified.

$$\text{Salary} = a + b_1(\text{Experience}) + b_2(\text{Age}) + b_3(\text{Average Hours of Overtime})$$

8.1.2(b)

In Equation 8.1.2(c) symbols are used to represent the variables: S, E, Ag, and HO stand for salary, experience, age, and hours of overtime.

$$S = a + b_1E + b_2Ag + b_3HO$$

8.1.2(c)

This kind of shorthand is frequently used. In Equation 8.1.2(d) the general formula with y and x's denoting the variables is used.

$$y = a + b_1x_1 + b_2x_2 + b_3x_3$$

8.1.2(d)

If we have taken a sample and calculated an intercept a equal to \$9500 and coefficients b_1 equal to \$12,545, b_2 equal to \$83, and b_3 equal to \$25, we can predict that for a 40-year-old bridge builder who works 250 hours of overtime a year and has built four bridges the annual salary will be \$69,250, as calculated in Equation 8.1.2(e).

$$S = a + b_1E + b_2Ag + b_3HO =$$
$$\$9500 + \$12,545E + \$83Ag + \$25HO =$$
$$\$9500 + \$12,545(4) + \$83(40) + \$25(250) = \$69,250$$

8.1.2(e)

Using the general form of the regression equation from Equation 8.1.1(d), the calculation would appear as in Equation 8.1.2(f).

$$y_i^* = a + b_1x_{1,j} + b_2x_{2,j} + b_3x_{3,j} =$$
$$\$9500 + \$12,545x_{1,j} + \$83x_{2,j} + 25x_{3,j} =$$
$$\$9500 + \$12,545(4) + \$83(40) + \$25(250) = \$69,250$$

8.1.2(f)

The y_j^* indicates a particular predicted value of y that corresponds to particular values of x_1, x_2, and x_3. Those values are indicated by the subscript j, so that in our example $x_{1,j}$ equals four bridges, $x_{2,j}$ equals 40 years of age, and $x_{3,j}$ equals 250 hours of overtime.

These alternative formats are presented to familiarize the reader with the various ways in which regression results are presented. The substantive content of each presentation is identical.

§8.2 Predicting the Value of a Dependent Variable

Prediction involves extrapolating from the known to the unknown. Sample regression coefficients describe the relationships between the dependent and independent variables based on sample data. When values for the independent variables are specified, an estimated value of the dependent variable can be calculated, which enables us to predict its value in situations where actual measurement is difficult or impossible. Often the difficulty is simply that the information is unavailable.

Chewning v. Seamans:[1] In this employment discrimination case the defendant, Energy Research and Development Administration (ERDA), had admitted to statistical disparities in starting salaries and salary advancement between male and female professionals. A problem arose in calculating back pay compensation for those affected because ERDA records and other pertinent sources did not contain enough information to enable each class member to identify the particulars of her claim. One solution to the problem is to compensate each person on the basis of an average treatment for employees with similar credentials, such as time in grade, date of hire, and professional category. The court specifically authorized a court-appointed master to use multiple regression to predict what an average salary (the dependent variable) would be for an individual with a specified set of credentials that gave values to the independent variables. The values for the regression intercept and coefficient would be calculated from a sampling of those records that were complete. The court recognized that multiple regression would give only an average salary that corresponds to a woman's particular professional characteristics and that some women might get more than they deserve and some less. The court concluded that "Nevertheless, the statistical methodology will yield a 'meaningful' result in back pay calculations and may be used where the paucity of records prevents a more individualized determination."[2]

News Publishing Co. v. United States:[3] The issue in this tax case was the deductibility of a bonus paid to the chief executive officer of the company. The IRS claimed that this bonus exceeded the amount of reasonable compensation for services rendered. Because the officer was in a unique position it was impossible to ascertain what was a reasonable compensation level by reference to other salaries in the company. In order to predict what a reasonable level would be, an IRS expert examined data from a sample of similar companies that revealed each chief executive officer's compensation and each company's sales revenue. He used a bivariate regression with total compensation paid to chief executive officer as the dependent variable and annual sales revenue as the independent variable. The theory behind using sales revenue as the

§8.2 [1] 19 Empl. Prac. Dec. (CCH) ¶9153, 20 Empl. Prac. Dec. (CCH) ¶30,158 (D.D.C. 1979).
[2] 20 Empl. Prac. Dec. (CCH) ¶30,158 at 11,826.
[3] 81-1 U.S. Tax Cas. (CCH) ¶9435 (Ct. Cl. 1981).

independent variable was that executive compensation varies with a company's size and that sales revenue was a good proxy for size. The expert calculated the *a* and *b* values necessary to predict an average compensation level for a chief executive officer in a company the size of News Publishing. The court relied on a comparison of this prediction (and other measures) to the actual compensation paid in determining that this bonus was in excess of reasonable compensation for services rendered.

Selig v. United States:[4] The taxpayer in this case was a part owner of the Milwaukee Brewers Baseball Club who sought to depreciate the contracts for his ballplayers. A regression equation was used to predict the expected value of a player's contract, the dependent variable, based on independent variables such as the player's salary level, age, batting average, and times at bat. Values for the coefficients on these variables were obtained by examining contract values, player statistics, and salary levels for a sample group of players. A second equation was used to estimate the player's salary, the dependent variable, based on performance characteristics of the player. For pitchers, for instance, the independent variables were the lifetime ratio of strike outs to walks, the proportion of a team's total innings pitched by the player, the change in those ratios over time, the number of years the pitcher had pitched in the major leagues, the pitcher's age, and a variable that indicated whether the pitcher averaged less than 30 innings pitched per year. Predictions from these equations were compared to a "transaction equation" that predicted the value of a player's contract from the point of view of trading the player to another team. Data for this transaction equation were taken from a Master Chronological List, which listed most transactions in the player market over a relevant ten year period. Changes over time in the value of a player's contract as measured by these equations provided a measure of depreciation in the contract value. While the regression analysis suffered somewhat from problems with data, the approaches used were creative and, moreover, successful in supporting the depreciation deduction claimed by the taxpayer.

On some occasions prediction by means of multiple regression is necessary because the event to be measured will not take place until sometime in the future.

American Telephone and Telegraph Co.:[5] In this rate regulation case, AT&T predicted that its Message Telecommunications Service (MTS) would earn a 12.62% rate of return if the company was allowed a

---

[4] 565 F. Supp. 524, 537-539 (E.D. Wis. 1983).
[5] 86 F.C.C. 956, 965-966 (1981).

16% rate increase for domestic and a 35% rate decrease for overseas MTS. One can imagine several of the independent variables that must go into a prediction of rate of return, the dependent variable. Certainly the prices charged for MTS services and a measure of the demand for those services at various prices must have been included among the explanatory variables. The FCC regularly relies on multiple regression forecasting for predicting future revenues that will result from rate changes but criticized this particular model for incorporating false assumptions about how responsive demand was to price changes.[6]

Shell Oil Co. v. Costle:[7] The Environmental Protection Agency (EPA) used regression analysis to predict the total amount of effluent that would be discharged from a wide variety of types of petroleum refineries. Among the independent variables thought to affect the amount of effluent, the dependent variable, were nine general process categories, such as crude oil processes, cracking processes, lubes and greases production, first and second generation petrochemical production, and asphalt production. By sampling refineries the EPA was able to calculate values for the regression coefficients and predict for a plant with any given collection of these processes how much pollution would be discharged. On the basis of the predictions effluent limitations were set. The issue in this case was whether a specific production process used by the oil company fell into one of the general process categories with lower effluent limitations.

It is often useful to be able to predict the value a dependent variable would have taken if certain intervening events had not occurred. Multiple regression is a useful tool for making such "what if" projections.

Spray-Rite Service Corp. v. Monsanto:[8] The distributor, Spray-Rite, proved that the defendant, a manufacturer of herbicides, conspired with other distributors to fix the resale price of its products. Spray-Rite's expert testified that the unlawful practices caused a decline in their sales from 1968 to 1972 and that in 1972 Spray-Rite was forced out of business. He used regression analysis along with various accounting methods to predict lost profits. One way in which a regression equation could be used to predict the profits Spray-Rite would have earned but for the conspiracy would be to use profit as the dependent variable and both time measured in years and sales in the industry as a

---

[6] Id. at 967-968.
[7] 595 F.2d 224, 226 (5th Cir. 1979).
[8] 684 F.2d 1226, 1240 (7th Cir. 1982).

whole, measured in dollars, as independent variables. The variable of time would capture any trend toward increasing or diminishing profits while the variable of industry sales would capture any trend toward expansion or contraction of the plaintiff's general line of business. Data for these variables would be taken from the years prior to the conspiracy. For particular years and levels of industry sales, profits for years after the conspiracy had begun could be predicted. The result would be predicted values for profit for the conspiracy years as if the conspiracy had not taken place. Equation 8.2(a) shows a hypothetical regression equation for these three variables; y equals profits, x_1 equals time (measured in years), and x_2 equals industry sales (measured in dollars).

$$y_j = a + b_1 x_{1,j} + b_2 x_{2,j} =$$
$$\$27,520 + \$11.7\text{Year} + .0014\text{Industry Sales}$$

8.2(a)

The values for a, b_1, and b_2 were calculated from hypothetical data for the preconspiracy years 1958 to 1968. If industry sales were \$320 million in 1968, the projected profit for Spray-Rite would be \$498,545.60, as shown in Equation 8.2(b).

$$\text{Predicted Profit} = \$27,520 + \$11.7(1968) +$$
$$.0014(\$320,000,000) = \$498,545.60$$

8.2(b)

The actual profit for 1968 would be subtracted from the projected profit figure to calculate the damages for 1968. Repeating the process for each of the years in question would give an estimate of total damages.

Certain assumptions underlie predictions made on the basis of regression results: the assumption arising in *Spray-Rite* is that the relationships between the variables when the data are collected are unchanged at the time for which the prediction is to be made. If new forces are operating in the second time period to influence the value of the dependent variable, the relationships between the variables, as described by the regression coefficient, and the cumulative effect of all factors not included among the independent variables, as described by the regression intercept, may have changed. Whenever any of the coefficients or the intercept changes, a different prediction may result. The ability to predict accurately beyond the time period from which the data were acquired is limited to situations where there has not been a significant change in the way in which explanatory variables influence the dependent variable.

§8.3   Estimating the Influence of Particular Independent Variables

The regression coefficient associated with a particular independent variable describes how much the dependent variable changes on average when there is a one unit change in the independent variable. Multiple regression can be used to isolate the effect of an independent variable on a dependent one even when there are many factors influencing the value of the dependent variable.

B. F. Goodrich Co. v. Department of Transportation:[1] The court reviewed regulations establishing uniform tire quality grading standards for automobile passenger tires, one part of which involved estimating the rate at which the tire lost its tread. The equation used to estimate tire wear was similar to the general bivariate form appearing in Equation 8.1.1(b), $y = a + bx$, where y equals tread depth measured in mils (thousandths of an inch), and x is miles of use after the initial break-in period (two circuits of the test track). We would expect the b, average treadwear rate, to be negative because as miles of use, x, increases there should be less tread remaining, y. The intercept, a, is the amount of tread on the tire when there is no wear beyond the initial break-in period, that is, when x equals 0. The reported decision refers to a as the "reference tread depth" because it provides a reference point from which the tread depth starts declining as more miles of use are put on the tire. The case report includes the graph reproduced in Exhibit 8.3(a) to illustrate declining tread depth as "miles of use" increases.[2] The focus of this simple bivariate regression equation is on the influence of miles of use, the independent variable, on tread depth, the dependent variable, as measured by b, the sample regression coefficient, which is the slope of the line. If the b were equal to $-.0155$, a one unit increase in the independent variable, that is, one more mile of use, decreases the tread depth by .0155 mils.

Anderson v. Banks:[3] Plaintiffs alleged that the requirement that all students perform at the ninth grade level on the California Achieve-

§8.3 [1] 541 F.2d 1178, 1194 (6th Cir. 1976).
[2] Id. at 1202.
[3] 520 F. Supp. 472, 487 (S.D. Ga. 1981).

EXHIBIT 8.3(a)
Bivariate Regression Data Plot
***B. F. Goodrich* Example**

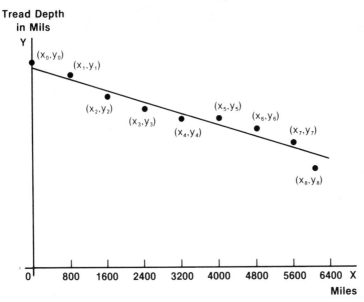

ment Test (CAT) before graduating from high school had a disproportionate impact on black students. The plaintiffs' expert used a multiple
regression analysis to examine the effect of several independent variables on CAT scores. The independent variable "race percent average,"
was the average percentage of black children in a particular student's
classes from the third to the eighth grade. This variable had a large
effect on the ultimate CAT score, a greater effect than IQ score, special
educational placement, or race. The negative regression coefficient on
race percent average describes the average decrease in CAT score associated with a one percentage point increase in the average percentage
of blacks in a student's class.

While common sense suggests that it might be quite reasonable to
conclude that tire use *causes* tread wear, determining that it is the
presence of a substantial number of blacks in the classroom that *causes*
achievement test scores to decline is not. An alternative explanation is
that a third variable, such as the quality of the teacher, may be correlated to both achievement test scores and average percentage of

blacks if less capable teachers are routinely assigned to classes with a higher percentage of blacks. If teaching assignments are made in this way, perhaps the causal factor is teacher quality. Demonstrating a significant relationship between a dependent and an independent variable by means of a significant b value does not indicate a causal relationship in the absence of a thoughtful consideration of alternative possibilities and the mechanism by which causation occurs.

The terms of art used in discussing regression results are sometimes misleading with respect to inference of causation. We describe the regression coefficients as estimating the *effect* of a one unit change in the independent variable on the dependent variable. This "effect," however, is a measure only of how much change there is. If the dependent and independent variables in a bivariate regression equation were switched so that, in the *B. F. Goodrich* example, for instance, miles of use was determined by tread depth rather than the other way around, we could still calculate a b value for tread depth, now the independent variable, despite the fact that the tread depth could not cause the tire to be used. The lesson is that coefficients indicate nothing about causation in the absence of a logical analysis of the underlying processes, even though they might provide evidence that supports such an analysis.

Because a significant regression coefficient, like a significant difference, does not prove causation, regression analysis plays a mostly supportive role in cases where causes are important. In some areas, however, such as employment discrimination, it is enough merely to show that one variable appears to have a strong impact on another.

Paxton v. Union National Bank:[4] Plaintiffs alleged that Union National Bank discriminated against blacks by paying blacks less than whites. Two regression equations were calculated with monthly earnings (E) as the dependent variable. One, shown in Equation 8.3(a), had just one independent variable, race; the other had 12: race (R), years of schooling (YS), B.A. degree (BA), master's degree (MA), months of seniority (S), part time worker (PT), months of bank management experience (BMX), months of other management experience (OMX), months of computer specialist experience (CSX), months of accounting experience (AX), months of collector experience (CX), and months of professional-technical experience (PTX), as shown in Equation 8.3(b). The results of the two equations are shown in Equations 8.3(c) and (d).

[4]519 F. Supp. 136, 163 (E.D. Ark. W.D. 1981).

$$E = a + bR$$

8.3(a)

$$E = b_1R + b_2YS + b_3BA + b_4MA + b_5S + b_6PT +$$
$$b_7BMX + b_8OMX + b_9CSX + b_{10}AX + b_{11}CX + b_{12}PTX$$

8.3(b)

$$E = 854.42 - 213.35R$$

8.3(c)

$$E = -4.19R + 27.51YS + 98.19BA + 135.54MA +$$
$$40.80S + 126.57PT + 83.44BMX + 89.73OMX +$$
$$77.16CSX + 36.23AX + 88.34CX + 24.21PTX$$

8.3(d)

A comparison of the coefficients on race for the two equations shows a striking difference. The bivariate regression, Equation 8.3(a), shows that being black reduces monthly earnings by an average of $213.35, while the multivariate regression, Equation 8.3(b), shows that being black reduces monthly earnings by an average of only $4.19. The difference is that multiple regression separates out the individual influences of various factors such as level of education, seniority, and prior work experience, which may be correlated with race but are legitimate factors for the employer to consider; race is not. The multivariate equation indicates that when legitimate factors are separated from the illegal race factor there is very little influence of race on earnings. The court concluded that blacks and whites who were similar with respect to legitimate variables had essentially equivalent salaries. The salaries of similarly situated blacks and whites differed on average by only $4.19 per month.

The disparities indicated by the bivariate equation in *Paxton* were apparently due primarily to unequal education, seniority, and experience. The coefficient on years of schooling, $27.51, indicates an average increase in earnings of $27.51 for each year of schooling. The coefficient on months of seniority indicates that, on average, a one-month increase in seniority is worth an additional $40.80 per month in earnings, and each month of collector experience is worth $88.34 in additional monthly earnings.

The interpretation of the coefficients for B.A. degree, M.A. degree, and part-time work are only slightly more complicated. These variables are dichotomous in character in that they can take only one of two values, either yes or no. The coefficient for B.A. indicates that its presence on a person's record accounts for an increase of $98.19 in earnings on average; a master's degree accounts for an average of $135.54. A full time worker earns $126.57 more per month than a part-time worker. The treatment and interpretation of dichotomous variables, commonly referred to as *dummy variables*, are discussed at greater length in Section 8.4.2.

In employment discrimination cases involving salaries, parties are regularly reminded by courts that multiple regression is a useful tool for separating the individual influences of relevant variables. The key comparison for proof of disparate treatment is that individuals similarly situated are treated similarly.

> Not surprisingly, where an employer has employees in differing occupations and of different backgrounds, a simple comparison of the average wage of all white employees and all black employees (or all male employees and all female employees) will not be enough to prove salary discrimination.[5]

> The Court believes that the proper inquiry in an analysis of salaries by race should focus on whether black and white employees with the same tenure at the same job are paid the same salaries.[6]

> Plaintiff has submitted evidence showing that blacks were earning less on the average than were defendant's white employees. Such statistics, however, are meaningless without more. Were evidence produced which showed the black employees with the same length of employment and the same qualifications were paid lower rates for similar jobs, . . . this Court might feel compelled to conclude that the disparity was due to racial discrimination.[7]

While multiple regression is in many ways ideally suited to this task, one must be careful to avoid using multiple regression models of the salary determination process to prove more than that of which they are capable. The defendant's expert in *James v. Stockham Valves*[8] used a series of "productivity factors" such as education, skill, build-

---

[5] Vuyanich v. Republic Natl. Bank of Dallas, 505 F. Supp. 224, 280 (N.D. Tex. 1980) *judgment vacated and remanded*, 723 F.2d 1195 (5th Cir. 1984).
[6] Pouncy v. Prudential Ins. Co. of Am., 499 F. Supp. 427, 449 (S.D. Tex. 1980).
[7] Keely v. Westinghouse Elec. Corp., 404 F. Supp. 573, 578 (E.D. Mo. 1975).
[8] 559 F.2d 310, 331 (5th Cir. 1977).

ing experience, craft skill level, and absenteeism to explain that these factors rather than discrimination explained the earnings differences. Circuit Judge Wisdom noted, however, that the wage differences might be best explained by racially discriminatory job allocations. Thus, while the expert may have explained the salary process for individuals once they were placed in a job, it did not model the process by which employees were placed into the higher paying jobs initially. The choice of variables and the choice of the process to be modeled must be approached with a careful eye to the plaintiff's allegations.

Regression analyses, both bivariate and multivariate, used for estimating the influence of particular independent variables, appear in a wide variety of substantive law areas, from administrative to criminal law.

National Citizens Committee for Broadcasting v. Federal Communications Commission:[9] The petitioners sought review of FCC rules relating to cross-ownership of television stations by newspapers operated in the same geographic area. Numerous regression analyses were offered to support and attack policy positions underlying the rules. One study endeavored to explain an alleged 15% higher price for advertising on cross-owned stations by demonstrating that audience size explained the apparent difference in rates. However, a regression analysis with advertising rates as the dependent variable resulted in a coefficient on audience size, the independent variable, that was negligibly small. This evidence suggests that audience size is not a likely alternative explanation for differences in rates.

Shell Oil Co. v. Costle:[10] The Environmental Protection Agency used nine oil refining process categories as independent variables to explain the amount of discharge of effluent from oil refineries. Each of the categories represented a production process in which a particular plant might engage, though not every refinery carried out every process. After sampling a number of refineries in the United States the EPA was able to calculate b values for each process and use the resulting multivariate regression equation to predict the effluent likely to be discharged from any plant. In addition the b values allowed the EPA to determine which of the processes resulted in the greatest discharge. An analysis of the statistical significance of the sample regression coefficients showed that six of the processes had a significant effect on dis-

[9] 555 F.2d 938, 958-959 (D.C. Cir. 1977).
[10] 595 F.2d 224, 226 (5th Cir. 1979).

charge level. Five of the significant b's had positive values, indicating that the presence of that process increased discharge while one, "second generation petrochemical production," had a negative value, indicating that adding this process resulted in a decrease in the production of waste. The other three processes apparently had little or no effect.

McClesky v. Zant:[11] Petitioner's expert witness, Professor David Baldus, endeavored to show that race was a significant factor in sentencing in this habeas corpus review of a death penalty imposed for murder of a policeman in Georgia. In one regression model of the judicial processes leading to sentencing, Professor Baldus included 230 independent variables describing characteristics of crimes, victims, perpetrators, and steps of the judicial process, such as whether plea bargaining was involved. The dependent variable was the probability that the death penalty would be imposed. Of particular interest to the court were the regression coefficients associated with two variables, the race of the victim and the race of the defendant, both of which were equal to .06. The court interpreted the regression coefficient as showing "the average difference in death penalty rate across all cases *caused by* the independent variable of interest."[12] We interpret the "caused by" language to indicate a mathematical correspondence only; since regression results do not prove causation, these coefficients meant that if the victim was white or the defendant black, the death penalty rate was six percentage points higher than if these characteristics were not present. Even the expert described these effects as small but with respect to the first of these two variables testified that "[t]he race of the victim in this system is clearly not the determinant of what happened, but rather that it is a factor like a number of other factors, that it plays a role and influences decision making."[13]

Gregg v. Georgia:[14] In his dissent to the majority opinion affirming the imposition of a death penalty for murder in Georgia, Justice Marshall reviewed a regression analysis that used "execution risk" (the number of executions as a percentage of total convictions) as an independent variable in a multivariate equation designed to evaluate the effect of the death penalty on the dependent variable, "homicide rate." The regression coefficient on execution risk was interpreted as showing that from 1933 to 1967 each additional execution in the United States might have saved eight lives. A variety of criticisms of this study, how-

---

[11] 580 F. Supp. 338, 366 (N.D. Ga. A.D. 1984).
[12] Id. at 369, emphasis added.
[13] Id. at 368.
[14] 428 U.S. 153, 234 (1975).

ever, led Justice Marshall to reject arguments that the death penalty can be justified as a deterrent to crime.[15]

§8.4 Choosing Variables for Regression Analysis

Choosing independent variables for a regression equation involves at least two concerns. The first is a theoretical consideration of what factors are likely to influence a particular dependent variable. This process is discussed in Section 8.4.1. The second is a practical consideration of how to include as variables those factors that cannot readily be measured. This problem, addressed by the use of *dummy variables,* is discussed in Section 8.4.2.

§8.4.1 Theoretical Aspects of Choosing Variables

A regression equation is a model of the relationships one expects to find in the system being analyzed. There are advantages to beginning a regression analysis with a theoretical idea of how the system operates and what variables are likely to be related to others. Many social scientists are insistent that the theoretical construct be developed before any calculations are done to avoid drawing fallacious conclusions regarding causation. As we shall see from an example discussed later in this section, the number of apple trees in a school district may be a good predictor of variations in per pupil expenditure among the school districts of Washington State. Certainly the apple trees do not directly cause variations in per pupil expenditure; it is much more likely that the rural character of the school district, which is positively correlated with the number of apple trees, has a more direct effect. Thoughtful consideration of potentially influential factors and of how the system operates prior to devising a regression equation avoids such patently spurious conclusions as well as more subtle ones and may result in a more complete model.

Presseisen v. Swarthmore College:[1] In the salary equation the plaintiff's expert included sex, age, years since highest degree, years at Swarthmore College, degree, and division. While these independent

---

[15] Id. at 236.
§8.4 [1] 442 F. Supp. 593, 616 (E.D. Pa. 1977), *aff'd,* 582 F.2d 1275 (3d Cir. 1982).

variables appear to capture the basic objective information about a faculty member, one of the defendant's experts testified that additional factors are relevant to the salary-setting process, such as publications record, some assessment of teaching ability, quality of degree, extent of career interruptions, and the presence of administrative responsibilities. While it is not clear that all of these actually do affect salary, at least some of them could. Regression analysis is the tool used to test whether they actually do affect salary, so their inclusion in the equation should be considered.

In *McCleskey v. Zant,* a habeas corpus case, District Judge Forrester stated, "[T]he model must be built by someone who has some idea of how the decision-making process under challenge functions."[2] His admonition is not to be taken lightly. In *Presseisen v. Swarthmore College,* where conflicting regression models of the salary determination process were presented, the testimony of plaintiff's expert was discredited by the fact that even though he was chairman of the Statistics Department at the University of Pennsylvania, he was not qualified as an expert in that area of college administration concerned with the setting of salary.[3] Judge Forrester's comments suggest three kinds of evidence useful in validating the construction of a regression model: (1) direct testimony as to what factors are known to be operating in the system being modeled, (2) testimony as to what factors operate in systems like the one being modeled, and (3) expert testimony as to factors one might expect to operate. In a salary discrimination case the direct testimony might come from the personnel officer or other individual in charge of establishing salaries for the defendant. Additional suggestions as to relevant factors might come from someone in a similar position with another employer, and testimony from an expert in the field of compensation might also be useful.

In cases where the focus is on prediction rather than on the relationship between a particular independent variable and the dependent variable, some departure from the norm of requiring an a priori theoretical notion of what factors should be included is occasionally tolerated.

Northshore School District No. 417 v. Kinnear:[4] Petitioners challenged the constitutionality of the state's system of school financing on

[2] 580 F. Supp. 338, 355 (N.D. Ga. A.D. 1984).
[3] 442 F. Supp. 593, 616 (E.D. Pa. 1977), *aff'd,* 582 F.2d 1275 (3d Cir. 1982).
[4] 530 P.2d 178 (Wash. 1974).

the ground that differences in local tax revenue per student in districts across the state result in unconstitutional inequality in educational opportunity, as reflected in differences in expenditures per student among the districts. The defense was that unequal expenditures did not mean unequal opportunity. A main portion of the defendant's statistical case consisted of the results of a computer search through potentially relevant variables to see if something beside tax revenues would explain the admittedly wide variations in expenditure levels among districts. There appears to have been no testing of a theoretical model of those factors thought to be influential. The testimony suggests that data for a number of potentially relevant factors were entered into the computer and the computer selected the two factors that had the greatest relationship to the dependent variable, expenditures per pupil:[5]

> In this case we are attempting to . . . account for the basic expenditure per pupil and the program selected, the computer selected as the two primary factors the average pay for certificated staff and a staffing ratio per 1,000 pupils as accounting for 75 percent of the variation in the expenditures per pupil.

Testimony indicated that staffing ratios were highest in rural schools where, to cite the example of the smallest school district, there were only five students assigned to the one teacher. The staffing ratio was high and explains the high expenditure per pupil, but the real reason for the difference was the rural character of the district and not the challenged financing scheme. The court found this logic persuasive.

When this kind of exploration is carried out, the theoretical justification for the explanatory variable becomes a potentially very convincing post hoc rationalization. In the *Northshore* example, constitutionally acceptable factors with substantial explanatory power were discovered, even though the resulting variables do not tell us anything more than the fact that expenditures per pupil for staffing constitute a large portion of total expenditures per pupil. There is a deeper underlying cause for high or low staffing costs that is the real influence on expenditures per pupil, that is, the number of students in the district. The exploratory nature of such an analysis may obscure underlying information about cause and effect. (See Section 2.8, Exploratory Data Analysis.)

[5] Id. at 187.

§8.4.2   Dummy Variables

Quantitative as well as qualitative variables may be analyzed using regression equations. Dollars of profit, years of age, pounds of effluent, minutes of television advertising, numbers of individuals executed for murder, cubic feet of gas reserves — all are measurable units that can take on many values and are examples of quantitative variables. The value of a *qualitative* or *categorical variable* cannot be measured because an observation will merely place an item in a category. Race and gender are categorical variables because observing an individual results in a categorization according to race or gender rather than a measurement. Gender is a *dichotomous* categorical variable, which means that it can take one of only two possible values, male and female. Race might be a dichotomous variable if there are only two categories, such as white and nonwhite, but is not necessarily true, because one may be black, Anglo, Asian, or Hispanic. Race is still a categorical variable because the observation of an individual's race leads not to a numerical measurement but to a categorization. For the same reason occupation, state of residence, and season of the year are also categorical variables.

In order to use categorical variables in a regression analysis it is necessary to assign numerical values to the observations. For a dichotomous categorical variable 1 and 0 are assigned to indicate that the observation falls in one or the other of the two possible categories. The assigned values are used as data in calculating the regression statistics. (See Section 7.4, Correlations Involving Dichotomous Variables.) When a categorical variable is converted into a quantitative variable, it is often referred to as a *dummy variable*.

The assignment of 1 and 0 is arbitrary, but it is essential in interpreting regression results to know which category was assigned which value. Equation 8.4.2(a) is a bivariate regression equation taken from *Paxton v. Union National Bank.*[6]

$$\text{Earnings} = \$854.42 - \$213.35(\text{Race})$$

8.4.2(a)

In this example blacks were assigned the value 1, and nonblacks were assigned the value 0. If we use this equation for prediction, the esti-

[6] 519 F. Supp. 136, 163 (E.D. Ark. W.D. 1981).

mate of monthly earnings for a black employee, $641.07, will be calculated as in Equation 8.4.2(b), where 1 is the value of the race variable.

$$\text{Black's Earnings} = \$854.42 - \$213.35(1) = \$641.07$$

8.4.2(b)

The estimate for nonblacks, $854.42, is calculated with 0 as the value of the independent variable in the Equation 8.4.2(c).

$$\text{Nonblack's Earnings} = \$854.42 - \$213.35(0) = \$854.42$$

8.4.2(c)

The estimated earning for blacks is lower than for nonblacks by the amount of b, $-\$213.35$.

Had we assigned nonblacks the value 1 and blacks the value 0, the regression results would appear as in Equation 8.4.2(d), with Equations 8.4.2(e) and (f) showing the estimates for blacks and nonblacks, respectively.

$$\text{Earnings} = \$641.07 + \$213.35(\text{Race})$$

8.4.2(d)

$$\text{Black's Earnings} = \$641.07 + \$213.05(0) = \$641.07$$

8.4.2(e)

$$\text{Nonblack's Earnings} = \$641.07 + \$213.05(1) = \$854.42$$

8.4.2(f)

The estimates do not change regardless of which group is assigned the value 1. The b value, which indicates the differential between the categories, has changed from a minus to a plus because in the original formulation the individuals in the group assigned the value 1 (blacks) earned $213.35 *less,* but the revised formulation shows the individuals in the group assigned the value 1 (nonblacks) earning $213.35 more. Thus the absolute value of b stayed the same; only the sign changed. Note that the value of the intercept, a, did change. The intercept is interpreted as a base salary, which is adjusted by the value of b, the sign of which depends on the group assigned the value 1. These statements regarding the effect and interpretation of *b* in the dummy variable context apply to regression equations with numerous independent variables as well.

Presseisen v. Swarthmore College:[7] The plaintiff's regression equation for salary included gender as a dummy variable together with variables for age, years since highest degree, and years at Swarthmore (all quantitative variables) as well as degree and division (categorical variables). The coefficients for the independent variables were calculated using 1971 data and again separately each year for 1972 through 1976. The coefficients for gender for those six years were 0 in 1971, −$340 in 1972, −$292 for 1973, −$153 for 1974, −$303 for 1975, and −$211 for 1976, illustrating the estimated average difference in salary between men and women who were otherwise similar in age, years since highest degree, years at Swarthmore, degree, and division. Had men been assigned the value 1 and women 0 the signs on the *b*'s for gender would change but their absolute magnitude would remain the same. For the dummy variable "degree," if the value 1 is assigned, indicating that a faculty member possessed the degree in question, e.g., Ph.D., then a 0 would indicate the absence of a degree. The coefficient for degree would then indicate the incremental effect on salary of having the Ph.D.

Chicken Antitrust Litigation:[8] Plaintiffs used a regression equation in this antitrust suit to illustrate the impact of the activities of the defendant, National Broiler Marketing Association, on market prices for chicken. While some of the independent variables, such as production levels, were continuously measured quantitative variables, there was a PCB scare during 1972 that was likely to have affected the demand for chicken. The study of price changes over time included a dummy variable that took one value during the period of the scare and another before and after the scare. The coefficient for this dummy variable estimated the effect on the price level that was due to the scare.

The use of dummy variables for categorical variables that are not dichotomous is also common. In *Presseisen* the variable "division" could represent more than two academic groupings within the college. If there are numerous categories within a variable, it is possible to estimate the effect of being in each separate category by including numerous dummy variables in the regression equation. Equation

---

[7] 442 F. Supp. 593, 616-617 (E.D. Pa. 1977), *aff'd*, 582 F.2d 1275 (3d Cir. 1982).
[8] 560 F. Supp. 963, 993 (N.D. Ga. 1980).

8.4.2(g) is a model of salary determination that assumes salary is a function of gender, represented by G, academic division (represented by several dummy variables), and other influences (all embodied in the regression intercept, a).

$$\text{Salary} = a + b_1 x_1 + b_2 x_2 + b_3 x_3 + b_4 x_4$$

8.4.2(g)

The academic divisions in this example are arts (ART), social sciences (SS), humanities (HUM), and hard sciences (HS). The variable x_1 stands for gender, with a 1 assigned to males and a 0 to females. The variable x_2 stands for arts. If the jth faculty member in the sample is in the arts division, $x_{2,j}$ gets a value of 1; if not, $x_{2,j}$ gets a value of 0. The variable x_3 stands for social sciences, with a 1 assigned if a faculty member is in the social science department, 0 if not. The variable x_4 stands for humanities, with a 1 indicating a faculty member in the humanities division. In this way the categorical variable is broken down into a series of dichotomous dummy variables. There is no variable for the hard sciences. The regression equation recognizes the faculty member from the hard sciences by recording zeros in each of the dummy variables representing the other divisions. As a general rule, there is one fewer dichotomous dummy variable for a particular categorical variable, such as division, than there are categories. For the variable "division," there are four categories, therefore there are three dichotomous dummy variables capturing the effect of being in different divisions. The effect of the fourth classification is embodied in the regression intercept, a, which captures all influences not represented by chosen independent variables.

If the regression results are as shown in Equation 8.4.2(h) we can predict the salary of a faculty member of either gender in any division and estimate the effect of being a particular gender or being in a particular division, as shown in Exhibit 8.4.2(a).

$$\text{Salary} = 15,860 + 275 x_1 + 1500 x_2 - 2700 x_3 + 3500 x_4$$

8.4.2(h)

EXHIBIT 8.4.2(a)
Prediction from and Interpretation of Equation
with Dummy Variables

Gender	Division	($) Salary
Male	ART	$15860 + 275(1) + 1500(1) - 2700(0) + 3500(0) = 17{,}635$
Female	ART	$15860 + 275(0) + 1500(1) - 2700(0) + 3500(0) = 17{,}360$
Male	SS	$15860 + 275(1) + 1500(0) - 2700(1) + 3500(0) = 13{,}435$
Male	HUM	$15860 + 275(1) + 1500(0) - 2700(0) + 3500(1) = 19{,}635$
Male	HS	$15860 + 275(1) + 1500(0) - 2700(0) + 3500(0) = 16{,}135$

Adjustment due to Classification

Division
ART	$+1500 = b_2$
SS	$-2700 = b_3$
HUM	$+3500 = b_4$
HS	0

Gender
Male	$+275 = b_1$
Female	0

Exhibit 8.4.2(a) illustrates that males make \$275 more on average than females, b_1 equals \$275, that compared to hard scientists, faculty members of the same gender in arts make \$1500 more (b_2), in social sciences make \$2700 less (b_3), and in humanities make \$3500 more (b_4). Other comparisons of pairs are possible. Faculty members in the arts make \$4200 more on average than those of the same gender in the social sciences ($b_2 - b_3 = \$1500 - (-\$2700) = \$4200$), and those in the social sciences make \$6200 less on average than those of the same gender in humanities ($b_3 - b_4 = -\$2700 - \$3500 = -\$6200$).

Presseisen v. Swarthmore College:[9] The purpose of including dummy variables for academic divisions was to eliminate from the gender variable any effect that was due to the fact that some divisions paying higher average salaries contained mostly males. The defendant's expert testified as follows:

> Let's suppose that one area, let me choose physics, is predominantly a male area, that the situation for hiring in physics and promotion is highly competitive, that is to say that the college competes for a scarce resource and must not only pay high initially but must raise rates rapidly and contrast that to another area, let us suppose English, where there are a great many candidates, the competition that the college faces for recruit-

[9] 442 F. Supp. 593, 616-617 (E.D. Pa. 1977), *aff'd*, 582 F.2d 1275 (3d Cir. 1982).

ment is not so heavy, and they might not raise people as rapidly in that area.

If it were the case that in the departments such as physics that were male-dominated and in departments such as English that were more mixed, then the differences between policies as regards physics and English would show up in this analysis as affecting males and females, and that I would describe as a bias in the analysis as given.

The inclusion of dummy variables for divisions draws out of the gender coefficient any difference due to division. The defendant's expert testified that once division was included in the regression analysis, the alleged difference between men and women shrank to zero. The plaintiffs did not respond to this testimony.

Categorical variables with numerous categories appear in other substantive law areas as well.

Improvements to UHF Television Reception:[10] In an effort to improve the quality of television viewing, the Federal Communications Commission instituted several rules designed to make UHF channel selection systems more nearly comparable to VHF tuning systems. Evidence had shown that people would be more likely to watch more UHF stations if the UHF channel selector dial on the television set were easier to use. A survey of 4000 households provided the data for a regression analysis with dummy variables used to evaluate the particular effect on UHF viewing (the dependent variable, measured perhaps in hours per day) of each of six types of channel selector knobs. This analysis allowed the Commission to compare the relative effects of the style of channel selection system.

The examples presented in this section have all shown the use of dummy variables to represent explanatory factors. It is also possible to use a dummy variable as the dependent variable. If we were interested in predicting the probability of being hired given various qualifications, the prediction for any given applicant would range between 0% and 100%. The information would come from applicants, some of whom had been hired, some not hired. The data would reflect the result of an individual's application, with 1 indicating an applicant who was hired and 0 indicating an applicant who was not. Equation 8.4.2(i) presents the hypothetical results of such an equation.

---

[10] 90 F.T.C. 1121, 1132-1134 (1982).

Probability of Being Hired =

.05 + .13 (Race) + .003 (Age) + .15 (B.A. Degree)

1 if white   1 if yes

0 if nonwhite   0 if no

8.4.2(i)

For a 30-year-old white man with no college degree, the probability of being hired is .05 + .13 (1) + .003 (30) + .15 (0), which equals .27 or 27%. The individual regression coefficients are interpreted as indicating the change in the probability of being hired as a result of having the characteristic indicated by the value 1 for the independent variable.[11]

> **McCleskey v. Zant:**[12] Researchers testifying in support of defendant's habeas corpus petition attempted to model the process by which those convicted of murder were sentenced. With the hope of showing that race of the defendant had an influence on the probability of getting the death penalty, a regression analysis used several hundred independent variables in addition to the race of the defendant to determine the relevant explanatory factors. The dependent variable was the probability of receiving the death penalty. The regression coefficient of .06 associated with the race of the defendant variable is interpreted as indicating that the probability of getting the death penalty is six percentage points higher for black defendants than for white defendants when other measured characteristics were identical.

B. SIGNIFICANCE TESTING FOR INDIVIDUAL REGRESSION STATISTICS

Regression coefficients and intercepts calculated from sample data are estimates of relationships in the population from which the sample was drawn. Their precision can be described by confidence intervals similar to those used for sample means and proportions in Sections 6.7 and 6.8. A two-tailed confidence interval describes a

---

[11] Such an approach was used to determine whether gender and race affected the probability of being hired as a professional in Vuyanich v. Republic Natl. Bank, 505 F. Supp. 224, 330 (N.D. Tex. 1980), *judgment vacated and remanded,* 723 F.2d 1195 (5th Cir. 1984).

[12] 580 F. Supp. 338 (N.D. Ga. 1984).

range within which the population parameter is likely to fall, and a one-tailed interval yields a limit below or above which the population parameter is likely to fall. Using a t test it is possible to test the statistical significance of a sample regression statistic in order to determine the probability that any difference between the sample statistic and zero (or any other chosen value) is due to the random selection of items included in the sample from which the statistic was calculated. Section 8.5 discusses the importance of significance testing of sample regression coefficients. Section 8.6 discusses the standard error of the regression coefficient used for both constructing confidence intervals, the subject of Section 8.7, and direct significance testing, the subject of Section 8.8. Section 8.9 discusses the application and interpretation of significance testing for sample regression intercepts. The detailed discussions of both confidence intervals and significance testing in Chapter 6 are applicable in many ways to regression analysis. The discussion in this chapter is therefore somewhat abbreviated and reference back to appropriate portions of Chapter 6 is encouraged. Cross-references have been supplied to assist in that process.

§8.5 The Relevance of Significance Testing for Individual Regression Statistics

A sample regression coefficient describes the relationship between a particular independent variable and the dependent variable. Because the coefficient is only an estimate, there exists the possibility that any correspondence observed was due to random selection of items for the sample rather than the presence of a relationship in the population. Thus the regression coefficient that appears to show a strong correspondence between variables may just be due to chance, and the coefficient that shows only a small correspondence between variables may, on the other hand, be due not to chance but to an actual relationship in the population. Significance testing yields a p-value indicating the probability that an observed correspondence, whether large or small, is due to chance.

The hypothesis related to individual regression coefficients is often that there is no relationship between the independent variable and the dependent variable. We reject this hypothesis if the regression coefficient, b, is significantly different from zero. The b is statistically significant if there is a low enough probability, indicated by the p-value, that the correspondence it measures occurred by chance.

In each of the examples discussed in Section 8.3 the statistical significance of the regression coefficients should be tested before any reliance is placed on those estimates. Thus it would be imprudent to conclude that there is any statistical evidence that tire use is related to increasing tread wear, that changing the racial composition of school classes affects test performance, that blacks or women have a lower salary, on average, than whites or men, that productivity factors explain salary differentials, that audience size affects advertising rates, that engaging in certain production processes affects effluent discharge, that race is a factor considered in sentencing, or that the death penalty deters crime, unless an appropriate test of the statistical significance of the sample regression coefficient indicates a sufficiently low p-value associated with the alternative hypothesis.

§8.6   The Standard Error of the Regression Coefficient

The *standard error of the regression coefficient, se_b,* measures how much estimated regression coefficients from different samples of the same population are likely to differ from one another. One standard error of the regression coefficient measures the typical deviation among sample regression coefficients calculated from repeated samples from the same population. For large samples, most regression coefficients will be close to the population value, with decreasing frequency of sample estimates further from the population value. Thus, for large samples, the distribution of sample regression coefficients around the population coefficient is approximately normal. (See Section 4.13 regarding the normal distribution.) Sample regression coefficients may deviate from the population coefficient just by chance, that is, due to the particular observations selected for the sample. The greater the typical deviation is, the greater will be the standard error. Significance testing using the standard error of the regression coefficient is similar to significance tests using the standard error of the mean discussed in Chapter 6. (See Sections 6.6 through 6.10.)

§8.7   Confidence Intervals for Regression Coefficients

Regression coefficients and standard errors of regression coefficients are generally calculated by computer since the formulas require numerous, repetitive mathematical manipulations. Once the sample coefficient associated with a particular independent variable and its standard error are computed, however, a t Table such as the one appearing in the Appendix of Tables at the end of this book can be used to construct confidence intervals for the coefficient. The confidence interval can be used to estimate a range within which the population coefficient is likely to fall, to estimate an upper limit above which or a lower limit below which the population coefficient is unlikely to fall, or to test whether the estimated coefficient is significantly greater than or less than a chosen value.

It is useful to calculate a confidence interval when we are interested in the size of the population regression coefficient. The confidence interval indicates the precision of the sample regression coefficient as an estimate of the population coefficient and indicates a range within which that parameter is likely to fall.

South Dakota Public Utility Commission v. Federal Energy Regulatory Commission:[1] Regression analysis was used to determine when the gas reserves in a particular field would run out. A bivariate regression equation with annual additions to reserves as the dependent variable and time (measured in years) as the independent variable indicates the average rate of change in annual additions to reserves each year. The coefficient for the variable "years" -160.16 billion cubic feet, indicates a decline of 160.16 billion cubic feet per year. The precision of this estimate can be determined by calculating the standard error of the coefficient and a two-tailed confidence interval around the coefficient that for 95% confidence runs from -327.35 billion to 7.03 billion cubic feet. Since this range includes zero, one cannot reject the hypothesis that there is no relationship between annual additions to reserves and time at a .05 level of significance with a two-tailed interval.

A one-tailed interval can be used to test the hypothesis that the annual additions to reserves do not *decline* over time. A one-tailed approach indicates that we can be 95% certain that the coefficient is less than -25.31 billion cubic feet and can reject the hypothesis that there is no decline at a .05 level of significance. (These calculations appear in Section 8.18.)

The procedure for calculating confidence intervals for sample regression coefficients of dummy variables and for multivariate equations is the same for quantitative variables in a bivariate regression equation, as is their interpretation. This is illustrated by examining the coefficient on race from *Paxton v. Union National Bank.* Exhibit

§8.7   [1] 643 F.2d 504 (8th Cir. 1981).

8.7(a) is a reproduction of the defendant's very readable exhibit presenting regression results for salary and various explanatory factors. The regression coefficients and the intercept are clearly presented, as well as the sample size information necessary to calculate the critical t value used for both confidence interval calculation and direct significance testing. The standard errors associated with the various coefficients appear in parentheses under each coefficient. Using the t Table and formulas from Section 8.18, a two-tailed confidence interval indicates that we can be 95% confident that, on average, black employees earn between $88.41 more and $96.79 less than comparable white employees. A one-tailed interval indicates that we can be 95% confident that, on average, the amount by which black employees' earnings *exceed* white employees' earnings is less than $73.35. These results hardly present convincing evidence of discrimination against blacks.[2]

---

[2] Note that Exhibit 8.7(a) also displays the mean value of the observations of each variable for each race. This information helps to explain why the coefficient on race in Equation (1), $-$213.35$, decreased to $-$4.19$ in Equation (2) where other relevant explanatory variables were included. Whites appear to be more highly qualified in terms of education, seniority, and experience, as is illustrated by their higher mean values.

EXHIBIT 8.7(a)
Defendant's Regression Results
Paxton v. Union National Bank

	Mean Value		Regression Dependent Variable = Earnings (Standard Error in Parentheses)	
Variable	*Whites*	*Blacks*	*(1)*	*(2)*
Race (work force = 17.9% black)	0.0	1.0	−$213.35 (64.92)	−$ 4.19 (46.77)
Years of Schooling	13.5	13.1		27.51 (15.24)
B.A. Degree (1 if yes)	0.22	0.11		98.19 (69.98)
M.A. Degree (1 if yes)	0.03	0.00		135.54 (132.06)
Months of Seniority	64.6	28.4		40.80 (3.93)
Part-time work (1 if no, i.e., if full-time)	0.06	0.13		126.57 (69.48)
Months of Bank Management Experience	2.7	0.0		83.44 (12.79)
Months of Other Management Experience	6.0	0.0		89.73 (8.43)
Months of Computer Spec. Experience	1.1	0.5		77.16 (18.07)
Months of Accounting Experience	0.7	0.0		36.23 (24.07)
Months of Collector Experience	0.8	0.1		88.34 (22.29)
Months of Professional/ Technical Experience	2.9	.03		24.21 (12.99)
Y-Intercept			854.24	
R^2 (adjusted)			.02	.52
Number of Employees			402	402
Adjust B/W Earnings Ratio (%)				99.5%

§8.8   Direct Significance Testing for
Individual Regression Coefficients

The statistical significance of individual regression coefficients can be evaluated directly using the t test. The two-tailed t test allows one to determine whether the coefficient is significantly different from some hypothesized value while the one-tailed t test can be used in two ways, either to determine whether the coefficient is significantly greater than some value or, alternatively, to determine whether the coefficient is significantly less than some value. (See Section 4.14, which explains the difference between the one- and two-tailed tests.)

The approach parallels that developed for sample means and proportions in Sections 6.10 and 6.12. A calculated t statistic is obtained by calculating the disparity between the estimated coefficient and the comparison value (such as zero, in which case the disparity, $b_i - 0$, is equal to the magnitude of the estimated coefficient, b_i) and dividing the disparity by the estimated standard error of the regression coefficient, se_b. The calculated t value is then compared to appropriate critical t values on the t Table that indicate a p-value associated with the disparity. The p-value indicates the probability that a disparity at least as great as the one observed could occur by chance. The mathematical procedures involved and the use of the t Tables are discussed in Section 8.19.

Paxton v. Union National Bank:[1] Equation 8.8(a) summarizes the regression results in a traditional fashion, showing the estimated standard errors of the regression coefficients in parentheses under their associated coefficients.

$$\text{Earnings} = -4.19R + 27.51YS + 98.19BA + 135.54MA +$$
$$(se_b) \quad (46.77) \quad (15.24) \quad (69.98) \quad (132.06)$$

$$40.80S + 126.57PT + 83.44BMX + 89.73OMX + 77.16CSX +$$
$$(3.93) \quad (69.48) \quad (12.79) \quad (8.43) \quad (18.07)$$

$$36.23AX + 88.34CX + 24.21PTX$$
$$(24.07) \quad (22.29) \quad (12.99)$$

8.8(a)

§8.8   [1]519 F. Supp. 136, 163 (E.D. Ark. W.D. 1981).

These are the same results as depicted in Equation 8.7(a), with abbreviations for the variables. The p-value for the hypothesis that race has no effect on earnings is determined by dividing the coefficient, -4.19, by the standard error, 46.77. This gives a calculated t value of $-.09$. Comparison to critical t values shows a p-value greater than .90, or 90%, which is the probability that the difference between the estimated coefficient and zero occurred by chance. By almost any standard we would not reject the hypothesis. The variable "months of accounting experience," AX, by comparison, has a calculated t value of 1.51 and a p-value of .20. If we were to reject the hypothesis that there is no relationship between earnings and months of accounting experience we would face a 20% chance of a type 1 error. (See Section 2.10.3 regarding type 1 and type 2 errors.) Using a one-tailed approach, we calculate a p-value of .05 for rejecting the hypothesis that increasing years of schooling does not increase earnings and for the hypothesis that working full-time does not increase earnings relative to working part-time. These calculations are discussed in Section 8.19.

§8.9 Significance Testing for Regression Intercepts

The *regression intercept* summarizes the average effect on the dependent variable of those variables not specified in the regression equation. It provides a baseline that is adjusted by the variations in the independent variables. If one is interested in the precision of the estimate of the baseline that is embodied in the calculated intercept, the t statistic is an appropriate way to estimate a confidence interval around the intercept or to test hypotheses regarding that intercept directly.

If the calculated intercept is \$9500 in an annual salary equation where the seven independent variables are various experience factors, it is possible to test whether this baseline salary is significantly greater than zero by dividing \$9500 by the estimated standard error of the intercept, se_a, which yields a calculated t value of 3.78 if the standard error is \$2513. If the sample size underlying the estimate is 92, using an appropriate critical t value we can calculate a 99% confidence interval from \$2815.42 to \$16,184.58. Since zero does not fall in this range we may reject, at a .01 level of significance, the hypothesis that a is not significantly different from zero. A two-tailed direct significance test indicates that we can reject the hypothesis of no difference with a p-value of .001 because the calculated t of 3.78 exceeds the critical t of 3.373. Similarly, a one-tailed confidence interval with a 99% confidence level would be evidence that the population intercept is *greater* than $3493.93, and one could reject the hypothesis that the intercept is not *greater* than zero at a significance level of .0005. The computations appear in Section 8.20.

If one desired to know whether the population baseline salary was greater than the poverty level for a family of two, assumed here to be $6100, the difference between *a* and this external standard, $3400, would be divided by the estimated standard error of the intercept to get the calculated *t*. For an intercept of $9500 and an associated standard error of $2513, the disparity of $3400 divided by the standard error would give a calculated *t* of 1.35, indicating a significance level of .10 for this one-tailed test.

The same approach works with an equation with a dichotomous dependent variable. In an equation such as that used in *Vuyanich v. Republic National Bank of Dallas*,[1] where the probability of being hired as a professional is the dependent variable (see Section 8.4.2), the intercept is interpreted as the baseline probability of being hired into a professional job, i.e., of being hired into a position without regard to the job qualifications variables included in the regression equation. An intercept of .07 would suggest a 7% probability of being hired as a professional even without regard to the enumerated qualifications. A confidence interval or direct significance test employing the estimated standard error of the intercept could be used to determine whether this intercept is significantly different from zero.

C. ANALYZING THE EXPLANATORY POWER OF THE ESTIMATED REGRESSION LINE

Predictions based on estimated regression statistics appear to have a surface validity due to their being derived from an arcane process involving occasionally complex mathematical manipulations. Such predictions are, however, prone to the vagaries of chance and human error and machination just as other statistical estimates are. This section describes three approaches to analyzing the reliability of predictions based on regression analysis. The first is a guide of the practical

§8.9   [1] 505 F. Supp. 224, 335 (N.D. Tex. 1980), *judgment vacated and remanded*, 723 F.2d 1195 (5th Cir. 1984).

significance of the estimates as a predictive tool. The coefficient of multiple determination, R^2, discussed in Section 8.10, is very much like the coefficient of determination, r^2, discussed in Section 7.17. This coefficient indicates how much of the variation in the dependent variable is accounted for by variations in all of the independent variables included in the regression equation. The other approaches test the statistical significance of the results. Confidence intervals for the predicted values of dependent variables are discussed in Section 8.11. Direct significance testing using the F test is discussed in Section 8.12. The F test is used to analyze the statistical significance of many coefficients simultaneously in the same way the t test, discussed in Section 8.7, tests the statistical significance of individual regression coefficients.

The most significant means of analyzing the explanatory power of regression estimates and predictions may be neither the coefficient of multiple determination, the confidence interval, nor the F test, but common sense. Regression analysis is based on a set of background assumptions that must be met (or approximated) before any legal significance should be attached to regression results. These approaches, however, like those in previous sections, assume that the background requirements have been met. The effect of failing to meet background requirements is discussed in Parts D and E of this chapter. The general purpose of those sections is to catalog a variety of reasons why regressions of the sort presented in the previous sections may give misleading estimates.

§8.10 The Coefficient of Multiple Determination

The *coefficient of multiple determination* describes the proportion of variation in the dependent variable that is accounted for by variations in the independent variables included in a regression equation. The coefficient of multiple determination, given the symbol R^2, takes a value between zero and one. An R^2 of zero indicates that none of the variation in the dependent variable is accounted for by the variation in the independent variables. Such a case would arise if the values of the independent variables selected showed no systematic relationship to the value of the dependent variable. A low R^2 frequently indicates that relevant explanatory variables have been omitted from the regression equation.

Paxton v. United National Bank:[1] A bivariate regression analysis with a dependent salary variable resulted in a regression coefficient of $213.35 on the independent variable, race of employee. See Exhibit 8.7(a). The R^2 for this equation was .02, indicating that 2% of the fluctuation in salary was accounted for by race. The defendant's expert also calculated regression results for a multivariate equation that included 11 other independent variables one would expect to influence salary, such as education, seniority, and experience variables. The inclusion of these additional factors increased the R^2 for the equation as a whole to .52, indicating that these variables taken together accounted for 52% of the variation in salary.

An R^2 of one indicates that all of the variation in the dependent variable can be accounted for by variation in the independent variables. But an R^2 equal to one does not mean that all of the relevant variables having a causal influence on the dependent variable have been included in the regression equation. An equation with head circumference as the dependent variable and hat size as the independent variable would have an R^2 very close to one, and might be taken to suggest that hat size accounts for all of the variation in head size. It is clear beyond peradventure that the circumference of one's head does not change very much in response to the acquisition of a larger or smaller hat. Neither the R^2 nor the regression coefficient itself tells the analyst anything about causation, but the R^2 correctly specifies a relationship between head circumference and hat size. Indeed, hat size for men is determined by dividing the circumference of the top of the head by 3.1415. But head size is almost certainly due more to genetic factors than to one's hat size.

Northshore School District No. 417 v. Kinnear:[2] The state school finance system was challenged because the revenue raising mechanism allegedly created unequal educational opportunity as measured by expenditures per pupil across school districts. The state's statistical expert, after examining a variety of factors that might be expected to have a strong relationship to the dependent variable, expenditure per pupil, presented an equation with two independent variables, certificated staff per 1000 students and average pay for certificated staff, that had an R^2 of .75. Relying in part on the statistical evidence that these two independent variables explained 75% of the variation in expenditures, the court concluded that it was not the allegedly unconstitutional financing sys-

§8.10 [1] 519 F. Supp. 136, 163 (E.D. Ark. W.D. 1981).
[2] 530 P.2d 178, 187 (Wash. 1974).

tem that created differences. The court's reliance may have been inappropriate. Even though these apparently innocuous independent variables explained 75% of the variation, the issue of what caused expenditures to vary in value is not addressed. While there was some suggestion that the rural nature of some school districts causes higher staff per student ratios, it is quite plausible that the financing system also allows wealthier school districts to pay more to teachers or to hire more teachers per pupil. The statistician's proof, without more, does not demonstrate the lack of a relationship between the financing system and the alleged inequities. If all three variables in this equation were caused by a fourth factor, the financing scheme, perhaps the regression results should not exonerate the state.

Regression analyses in which the purpose is to estimate the influence of particular independent variables rather than to predict the value of the dependent variable also make use of the coefficient of multiple determination as a guide to whether there may be additional relevant explanatory variables that have not been included in the equation. One example is the *Paxton* case discussed above. Inclusion of additional independent variables in the salary equation not only raised the R^2 from .02 to .52, it reduced the coefficient associated with the race of the employee from $-\$213.35$ to $-\$4.19$, indicating a smaller (in fact, statistically insignificant) effect of race on salary. The reason that inclusion of additional variables reduced the estimated influence of race on salary is that those variables were strong predictors of salary and were themselves related to race. For instance, the coefficient associated with "months of seniority" is $40.80, suggesting that for each additional month an employee had worked at Union National Bank, monthly earnings were an average of $40.80 higher. This coefficient is statistically significant at a .0005 level of significance.[3] The relationship to race was that whites had an average seniority of 64.8 months while blacks had only 28.4 months. Given that seniority is a significant factor in earnings, it is not surprising that blacks earn less. Once the seniority element is removed from race, the influence of race itself is diminished. The low R^2 when only race was included as an explanatory variable was a clue that relevant variables might have been omitted. Their inclusion would affect the estimation of the effect of race on salary if they had some relationship to both race and salary, otherwise, their inclusion would not have added in-

[3] The calculated t value for the "months of seniority" variable was 10.38. See Exhibit 8.7(a).

formation to the resolution of this particular legal issue since there was no prediction involved.

> **McCleskey v. Zant:**[4] Plaintiff's experts attempted to use regression analysis to explain the influence of the race of the victim and the race of the defendant on the probability of a murderer getting the death penalty. One regression estimate presented by the plaintiff's experts was based on an equation with 230 variables and resulted in an R^2 of .48. The court recognized the R^2 as a measure of how successfully the regression model predicts death penalty sentencing but concluded, "As the 230-variable model does not predict the outcome in half of the cases and none of the other models produced by the petitioner has an R^2 even approaching .5, the court is of the opinion that none of the models are sufficiently predictive to support an inference of discrimination."[5]

The court's conclusion in *McCleskey* fails to recognize that a high R^2 is not required for the coefficient on the race variables to be statistically significant. In fact both the race-of-victim and race-of-defendant coefficients were statistically significant (at the .01 level) for this 230-variable equation. The primary purpose of this regression was not prediction but rather estimation of the coefficients.

It was not inappropriate, however, for the *McCleskey* court to look at the size of R^2. A low R^2 does suggest that some explanatory variables have been omitted, and in some cases this might make a difference. The *Paxton* example illustrates that the inclusion of additional variables that are correlated to the race variables may reduce both the absolute magnitude of the regression coefficient on the race variables and their statistical significance. The Appendix to the *McCleskey* decision includes a chart indicating how the effect of the race of victim and statistical significance decreased as more explanatory variables were included by petitioner's experts in the many regressions they estimated.[6] Those findings are reproduced in Exhibit 8.10(a). The regression coefficient for the race of the victim, b_v, measures the increase in death sentencing rate associated with having a white victim for the various equations estimated by the plaintiff's experts. The court was apparently impressed with the decline in b_v as the equation was expanded: "The teaching of this chart has a universal lesson for courts. That lesson is that where there is a multitude of factors in-

---

[4] 580 F. Supp. 338 (N.D. Ga. A.D. 1984).
[5] Id. at 361.
[6] Id. at 403.

fluencing the decision-maker, a court cannot rely on tests of statistical significance to validate the data unless it is first shown that the statistical model is sufficiently predictive."[7] This lesson is overstated by the court. The R^2 is relevant to significance testing of individual coefficients only if additional variables are likely to be correlated with the variables of interest. This chart gives little support to the notion that the additional variables are highly correlated to both the probability of receiving the death penalty and race. One of petitioner's experts focused attention on the regressions with ten or more variables. The size of b_v and its statistical significance decline very little for those equations. Petitioner's expert was of the opinion that it would require an enormous number of variables to make the coefficient insignificant.[8] Moreover, the increased probability of black murderers receiving the death penalty is almost constant and always statistically significant (at the .05 level of significance) regardless of the number of independent variables included in the equation. From these data *McCleskey* appears to be a contrary example to the *Paxton* case.

[7] Id. at 362 n. 2.
[8] Id. at 362.

EXHIBIT 8.10(a)
Impact of Expanding Regression Size
McCleskey **Example**

Dependent Variable = Probability of Death Penalty

Number of Independent Variables	Regression Coefficient* Independent Variable	
	Race of Victim	Race of Defendant
1	.17 (.001)	.10 (.01)
2	.09 (.0001)	.05 (.03)
9	.07 (.001)	.04 (.10)
10	.07 (.0014)	.04 (.09)
13	.06 (.001)	.05 (.01)
14	.06 (.001)	.06 (.001)
44	.07 (.0002)	.06 (.0004)
83	.10 (.001)	.07 (.01)
136	.07 (.01)	.06 (.01)
230	.06 (.01)	.06 (.01)
250	.04 (.04)	.04 (.05)

*p-values appear in parentheses under the regression coefficients.

Some analysts prefer to rely on a version of the coefficient of multiple determination that is referred to as the *corrected* or *adjusted* R^2. The R^2 is corrected or adjusted for the sample size and the number of independent variables that are included in the equation (see Section 8.21 for the formula for converting R^2 into the adjusted R^2. The reason for the adjustment is that often the inclusion of variables that are irrelevant from a causal viewpoint will increase the predictive power of the equation just because of chance correspondence between the irrelevant variable and the dependent variable. (See Section 8.16, Omitted Variables — Overspecification.) The adjusted R^2 is smaller than the regular R^2 by an amount that compensates for the inclusion of additional variables. The effect of the adjustment is significant if the number of independent variables is large relative to the size of the sample from which the regression statistics are calculated.

§8.11 *Confidence Intervals for Predicted Values*

Once the regression statistics have been calculated for a regression equation, the results can be used to predict a value of the independent variable that will occur given knowledge of the values of all the dependent variables. It is useful to construct an interval around the predicted value to indicate the precision of the estimate (see Chapter 6, Part F, regarding the difference between precision and accuracy). There are two useful types of predictions resulting from regression analysis.[1] The first type of predicted value is an estimate of the population mean value that the dependent variable will have given specified values for each of the independent variables. A confidence interval around this predicted value will indicate a range within which the population mean value for the dependent variable is likely to fall when the independent variables take the values specified.

B. F. Goodrich and Co. v. Department of Transportation:[2] Automobile tire quality grading standards were established using a bivariate regression equation with tread depth the dependent variable predicted by miles of use, the independent variable. Using regression statistics from test results of a sample of different tires one could predict the average tread depth that would be remaining after any given amount of use. Using the hypothetical equation tread depth = 714 − .0155 (miles of use), one would predict that there would be a tread depth of 94 mils after 40,000 miles of use (714 − .0155 (40,000) = 94). The remaining tread depth for different tires will vary, so the prediction is the estimate of the average remaining tread depth. Since 94 mils is approximately 3/32 of an inch, barely enough to pass the motor vehicle inspection in some states, it would be nice to know how precise this estimate is. A

---

§8.11 [1] See T. Wonnacott & R. Wonnacott, Regression: A Second Course in Statistics 42-47 and 442-444 (1981) regarding the distinction between these types of predictions.
[2] 541 F.2d 1178, 1194 (6th Cir. 1976).

confidence interval around this estimate would give a range within which the population average tread depth after 40,000 miles would be likely to fall.

The second type of predicted value is an estimate of a particular value for a dependent variable rather than the mean value. Instead of predicting the average amount of tread remaining on tires after a given number of miles of use as in the *B. F. Goodrich* example, we might interpret the prediction as estimating how much tread will be remaining on a particular tire using test results from that tire. The interval around this type of estimate is often referred to as a *prediction interval* to indicate how the predicted value of the dependent variable is being interpreted.[3]

American Telephone and Telegraph Co.:[4] In this rate regulation case, AT&T used regression analysis based on data from past years to predict that the dependent variable, rate of return on invested capital, would equal 12.62% in a particular future period, assuming various specified values for the independent variables, including prices they would charge for their services and measures of the demand for their services. Because the expected rate of return is crucial to stockholders and creditors, the prediction interval would allow one to estimate a range within which the rate of return for that particular period was likely to fall. A one-tailed interval would allow one to calculate a minimum rate of return above which the rate of return could be expected to fall with a specified level of certainty. The FCC chastised AT&T for failing to include intervals in its rate request[5] and ordered that future filings include intervals and standard errors of estimated values of dependent variables.

To calculate confidence and prediction intervals one must obtain critical t values from the t Table and calculate the standard error of the estimated value of the dependent variable. The *standard error of the estimate, se_{y*},* is a measure of the variation one would expect among estimates calculated from regression analyses of repeated samples of the same population.[6] Once the standard error is determined, the

---

[3] See, e.g., T. Wonnacott & R. Wonnacott, Regression: A Second Course in Statistics 443 (1981).

[4] 86 F.C.C. 956, 965-966 (1981).

[5] Id. at n. 46.

[6] Because there are two types of estimates one may obtain from regression statistics, there are two formulas for the standard error of the estimate. See T. Wonnacott & R. Wonnacott, Regression: A Second Course in Statistics 443 (1981).

procedures for calculating the interval resemble that for other confidence intervals.

B. F. Goodrich Co. v. Department of Transportation:[7] The predicted tread depth for automobile tires with 40,000 miles of use was estimated as 94 mils by solving the equation $y_j^* = 714 - .0155\,(40{,}000)$. If the standard error of this estimate were 1.5 mils for a sample of 22 trials, a 90% confidence interval around this estimate would reveal that we could be 90% confident that the average amount of remaining tread after 40,000 miles of use lies between 91.41 and 96.59 mils.

American Telephone and Telegraph Co.:[8] The predicted rate of return on capital invested for a particular period based on specified price and demand factors was .1262 or 12.62%. If the standard error of the estimate was .0300 for a sample size of 12 years of AT&T's operating history and there were seven explanatory variables, a 95% prediction interval around this estimate would range from .0429 to .2524. Investors or creditors could be 99% certain that the rate of return would be above 1.38% and there is only a .5% chance that it will exceed 26.43%. These calculations are shown in Section 8.22.

§8.12 Direct Significance Testing for Predictions

Significance tests may be used to calculate p-values for hypotheses related to predictions. A typical hypothesis is that there is no relationship between the dependent variable and all of the independent variables combined. This is roughly equivalent to a test of the hypothesis that the R^2 in the population is zero or that the coefficients on all of the independent variables are simultaneously zero, both of which results would be interpreted as evidence that there is no relationship between the dependent variable and the independent variables. If there is no statistically significant relationship, then one might conclude that the variables chosen have no reliable predictive or explanatory power.

The test statistic for evaluating the statistical significance of numerous independent variables is the F statistic. In application it is very much like the t statistic in that one calculates an F for the regression equation and then compares the calculated F to a critical F value

[7] 541 F.2d 1178, 1194 (6th Cir. 1976).
[8] 86 F.C.C. 956, 965-966 (1981).

given by an F Table. F Tables for the common significance levels of
.05 and .01 appear in the Appendix of Tables at the end of this book.
The F statistic is usually calculated by computer, but the F value can
be calculated from the R^2 as shown in Section 8.23.

> **Northshore School District No. 417 v. Kinnear:**[1] The state used
> regression analysis to determine what factors explained variations in
> school expenditures per pupil across school districts. The equation with
> two independent variables, certificated staff per 1000 students and av-
> erage pay for certificated staff, accounted for 75% of the per pupil
> expenditures; the R^2 was .75. The calculated F for this regression equa-
> tion was 476. The F Table reveals a critical F, for a .01 significance level
> of 4.79 for the appropriate number of degrees of freedom. Because the
> calculated F is larger than the critical F we can reject the hypothesis that
> these variables have no cumulative explanatory power at a .01
> significance level.

In Section 8.10 it was noted that the inclusion of additional variables in the regression equation often increases the R^2 for the equation, suggesting increased explanatory power. The adjusted R^2 was
recommended as one way of compensating in changes between the
added independent variables and the dependent variables. The F test
may also be used to examine whether the additional explanatory
power due to the inclusion of additional variables is statistically
significant.

One approach to testing the hypothesis that some subset of the
independent variable adds nothing to its explanatory power is to calculate an F value for the difference between the R^2 values for two
equations: the full equation, with all independent variables included,
and a reduced equation, the equation without the independent variables whose explanatory value is questionable. This F test might be
interpreted as a test of the hypothesis that the difference between the
R^2 values for the two equations is not greater than zero, which would
only occur if the contribution of the additional variables to the statistical significance of the reduced regression equation's predictions was
negligible. An example of how this test might be used is presented in
Section 8.15, Multicollinearity, where the question involved is
whether to include in the equation two independent variables whose
relationship to one another violates one of the background assump-

§8.12   [1] 530 P.2d 178, 187 (Wash. 1974).

tions underlying regression analysis. The calculations for this application of the F test appear in Section 8.24.

Whenever there are individual regression coefficients that are statistically significant, the F test indicates that there is a statistically significant relationship between the dependent variable and the independent variables. Surprisingly, the F test may show that a regression equation is statistically significant at a given significance level even though none of the individual regression coefficients are. This occurs because some combination of the independent variables taken together do have some explanatory power. While this may indeed indicate that the equation produces statistically reliable predictions, it may also be an indicator that there is some correlation among the independent variables that may mean that the individual regression coefficients are unreliable.[2] Whether this is a problem depends on the use made of the regression results. See the discussion of *McCleskey v. Zant* in Sections 8.10 and 8.15.

D. NONLINEAR REGRESSION ANALYSIS

The regression equations discussed to this point have described only linear relationships between independent and dependent variables. A linear relationship between two variables can be described by a b value showing a constant rate of increase (or decrease) in the values of one variable as values of the other variable change. For many purposes, a straight line with the general form $y = a + bx$ provides the best summary of the relationship between two such variables. See Section 8.1. A careful conceptualization of the likely relationship between two variables or an examination of sample data may indicate that there is no constant rate of change between the variables, that a straight line does not give an accurate description of the relationship.

If nonlinear relationships are modeled by linear formulas such as those discussed to this point, a significance test of a regression coefficient or of the regression equation as a whole may lead one to conclude incorrectly that there is no relationship between the variables or that the independent variables have little explanatory power. The mathematical techniques underlying ordinary least squares estima-

---

[2] See S. Chatterjee & B. Price, Regression Analysis by Example 64 (1977).

tions of regression statistics can still be used in many nonlinear cases, however, by discerning the nature of the nonlinear relationship and transforming the data appropriately. For other cases of nonlinear relationships, regression techniques other than ordinary least squares must be used.[3] (See Section 8.1.1 for a discussion of least squares.)

This part of the chapter presents a brief discussion of nonlinear regression analysis. Section 8.13 discusses methods by which nonlinear relationships might be detected. Section 8.14 presents several examples of how nonlinear relationships may be estimated by ordinary least squares techniques and how statistics for nonlinear relationships are interpreted.

§8.13   Indicators of Nonlinearity

It is possible in some cases to detect nonlinear relationships by a commonsense consideration of how the variables interrelate or by plotting data for two variables to see whether or not they fall along a more or less straight line. A third method is plotting the errors in prediction to see whether they follow a pattern. These three methods are discussed in this section.

In Section 8.4.1 we described the process of choosing variables for a regression equation as being a conceptual one. It is useful for the investigator to have an idea of how a system operates before choosing variables in order to avoid interpreting random statistical correspondences as being indicative of causation. The same logic applies to choosing between a linear and a nonlinear model to represent the underlying relationships between variables. It may not be realistic, for instance, to expect that the total number of dollars of income going to all lawyers will continue to rise at a constant rate for each additional lawyer graduating from law school; eventually the supply of lawyers may outstrip the demand for their services and some law graduates will have to settle for lower-paying jobs. Thus the total income to all lawyers may rise at a rapid rate as the profession expands, but once it reaches a certain size that rate of increase may slow down. Such a relationship would be nonlinear because the rate is not constant. If total income going to lawyers is the dependent variable and the num-

---

[3]The problem of nonlinear relationships between variables is also discussed in general terms in Section 7.23, The Problem of Nonlinear Correspondences, which provides some general references to solutions to nonlinear correspondences in estimating correlation coefficients.

ber of lawyers is the independent variable, a straight line might not provide an accurate description of the relationship.

It was only a theoretical perspective that led us to expect a non-linear relationship between the number of lawyers and the total income of lawyers. It is often the case that plotting the data from a sample will illustrate that the relationship is best described as non-linear. Exhibit 8.13(a) presents a scatter plot for hypothetical data on earnings as it relates to the age of workers. Having plotted this data, it becomes apparent that there is not a constant rate of increase in salary as one ages. For some reason very old and very young workers have lower than average wages. A linear regression equation such as that depicted by the line $y = a + bx$ in Exhibit 8.13(a) shows a constant increase in earnings. The R^2 for such an equation might be very low, however, suggesting that variations in age account for little of the variation in earnings. In addition, the standard error of the regres-

EXHIBIT 8.13(a)
Nonlinear Relationship Between Earnings and Age

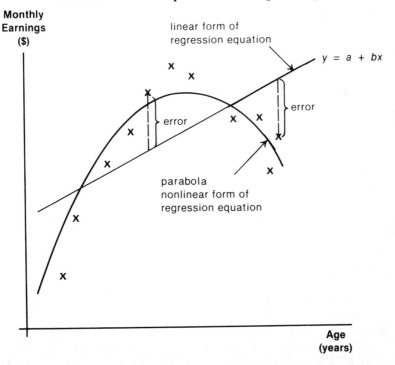

sion coefficient might be large relative to b, perhaps large enough to lead us to conclude that the coefficient is not significantly different from zero. Both of these results would be surprising if we suspect, a priori, that a strong relationship exists or if the scatter plot reveals a systematic relationship between the variables. Closer scrutiny might be called for in order to determine why older and younger workers earn less than middle-aged workers; examining the labor market might reveal that more young and old employees work part-time or that they work less overtime. A nonlinear estimation, such as the parabola indicated in Exhibit 8.13(a), might capture these subtleties and result in statistically significant regression statistics.

A third indicator of nonlinearity relies on the fact that estimated regression equations do not always give perfect predictions of the values of their dependent variables; the estimated y_j^* for a specified set of observed values for the independent variables is not always equal to the observed y_j that corresponded to those observed x values. The difference between y_j^* and y_j is referred to as the *error*, e, or sometimes as the *residual error* or *residual*. The formula for the error is given in Equation 8.13(a).

$$e_j = y_j^* - y_j$$

8.13(a)

Since the general equation for predicting y_j^* is written as $y_j^* = a + b_1 x_{i,j} + b_2 x_{2,j} + \ldots + b_m x_{m,j}$, and the difference between y_j^* and y_j is the error, e_j, the formula for y_j is sometimes written to include the error, to take into account the inaccuracy in prediction, as shown in Equation 8.13(b).

$$y_j = a + b_1 x_{1,j} + b_2 x_{2,j} + \ldots + b_m x_{m,j} + e_j$$

8.13(b)

If a nonlinear relationship is being estimated by a linear model, the errors may display a pattern that reveals the nonlinearity. Given a regression estimate of the relationship between two variables, one can calculate the error in prediction for each observation of the dependent variable. If the errors for prediction of y values for each of the observed values of x are plotted on a graph, visual examination of the plot may reveal the pattern.

As an example, consider the hypothetical relationship between age and earnings described earlier in this section. The data in Exhibit

8.13(a) suggest that young people tend to have low monthly earnings and that increasing age is associated with increasing earnings up to the point where increased age becomes associated with declining monthly earnings. If this curvilinear relationship is estimated by a straight line, such as $y = a + bx$ in Exhibit 8.13(a), the errors between observed values (marked by x's) and predicted values (on the straight line) will follow a pattern. Since the error, e_j, is the difference between the observed y_j and predicted y_j^*, the errors on Exhibit 8.13(a) appear as the vertical distances between the observed values and the regression line, $y = a + bx$. For young and old people, the errors are predictably positive because the line overestimates their earnings, and for those of middle age they are negative because the line underestimates their earnings. If one were to graph the errors, they would display the pattern shown in Exhibit 8.13(b). This kind of graph is

EXHIBIT 8.13(b)
Plot of Residuals from Linear Regression of Age on Earnings

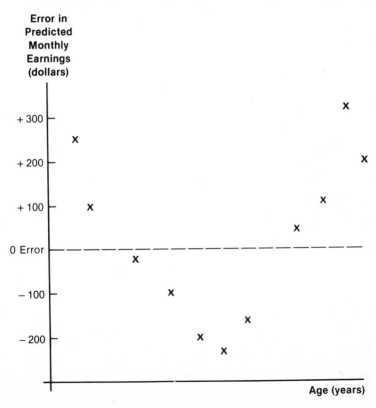

457

sometimes referred to as a *plot of residuals*. If the errors are randomly distributed around the regression line, the plotted residuals will be arrayed around the "0 Error" line in a random fashion rather than in a pattern as shown. This pattern suggests that a nonlinear specification of the regression equation might be appropriate.

The F test for R^2 may be used to test whether one specified equation has a greater ability than another to explain variations in the dependent variable. This test may assist in the choice between a linear and nonlinear specification.

§8.14 Examples of Nonlinear Specifications

To calculate regression statistics for nonlinear equations one starts with the general formula for the type of curvilinear relationship suspected. There are general formulas in statistics and mathematics books for many curves, including the parabolic (or, more generally, polynomial) curve in Exhibit 8.13(a). Having identified the appropriate general formula for a curve that appears to fit the data, the analyst modifies the data from which the regression statistics are to be calculated to fit the formula, a process referred to as *linear transformation* in this regression context. Using transformed data, estimated regression statistics can be calculated using the same ordinary least squares technique introduced in Section 8.1. For some transformations the statistics may then be tested for statistical significance by the t and F tests described in Sections 8.8 and 8.12.

The following examples illustrate two common transformations used in litigation and interpretation of the results. There are many more types of available transformations than are discussed here.[1] Some relationships are strictly nonlinear and cannot be transformed into linear forms. For these relationships other types of regression estimation techniques are needed.

Agarwal v. Arthur G. McKee & Co.:[2] The plaintiff, an Asian-Indian engineer, alleged that the defendant-employer discriminated

---

§8.14 [1] Useful descriptions and discussions of a variety of available transformations appear in S. Chatterjee & B. Price, Regression Analysis by Example 29 (1977); R. Winkler & W. Hays, Statistics: Probability, Inference, and Decision, 2d ed. 701 (1975); and K. Smillie, An Introduction to Regression and Correlation 78 (1966) on polynomial transformations.
[2] 19 Fair Empl. Prac. Cas. (BNA) 503 (N.D. Cal. 1977).

against minorities in setting salaries. The plaintiff's salary equation included independent variables for minority status, total years of education, number of years since receipt of highest degree, age of employee, type of professional registration held by the employee, years of prior experience, years of experience at McKee, and the number of years of any break in service at McKee. The theory underlying the regression equation was that all of the variables had linear relationships with salary except for two, age and years of experience at McKee.

Plaintiff's theory with respect to the independent variable "years of experience at McKee" must have been that the effect of this experience on salary changes over time — specifically, that in mid-career the beneficial effects of longevity diminish and longevity turns into a detriment. This kind of nonlinear relationship is similar to the one depicted in Exhibit 8.13(a). The general formula for a parabola like the curve in this Exhibit is shown in Equation 8.14(a).

$$y = a + b_1 x + b_2 x^2 + e$$

8.14(a)

In this equation there is one dependent variable, y (salary), and one independent variable, x (years of experience at McKee). There are, however, two regression coefficients: b_1, which is associated with the number of years of experience at McKee, x, and b_2, which is associated with the number of years of experience at McKee *squared*, x^2.

The data used to calculate the two b's were collected from McKee's employment files, where years of experience were recorded. The values of x used to calculate b_2 are squared before the coefficient is computed, hence, the data entered into the computer appear as shown in Exhibit 8.14(a). The computer treats x^2 as if it were a different variable from x and computes a coefficient for x^2, using the data appearing in the third column of the exhibit. The result is an estimated equation such as that in Equation 8.14(b), with two regression coefficients, b_1 equal to 1500 and b_2 equal to -40, which estimate the effect of experience on salary.

$$\text{Salary} = 10,000 + 1500x - 40x^2 + e$$

8.14(b)

EXHIBIT 8.14(a)
Hypothetical Data for Nonlinear Regression
***Agarwal* Example**

y *Salary*	x *Experience (years)*	x^2 *Experience (years squared)*
$25,050	5	25
$10,500	3	9
$17,920	4	16
.	.	.
.	.	.
.	.	.

Prediction with an estimated nonlinear equation such as the one in the *Agarwal* example is fairly straightforward. A value for the independent variable, such as x_j equals six years of experience, is entered into the equation, squared where appropriate, and used to compute salary, as in Equation 8.14(c).

Predicted Salary for Six Years Experience $= 10,000 +$
$1500(6) - 40(6)^2 = 10,000 + 1500(6) - 40(36) = \$17,560$

8.14(c)

If there are additional independent variables, regression coefficients for those are calculated as well and values for those variables must be specified in order to make a prediction. Because the effect of the independent variable in the *Agarwal* salary equation changes the longer one works at the company, the *b* for this equation is not as readily interpretable as the b_j's in linear regression models. However, it is possible to test whether variation in experience has a significant effect on variation in salary. In the bivariate case, such as where experience is the only independent variable in a salary equation, the R^2 and the *F* test on the whole equation will provide a guide to practical significance and a test of the statistical significance between the variables, respectively. If there are numerous independent variables in the equation, as in *Agarwal,* an *F* test that compares the predictive reliability of the equation with and the equation without the experience-at-McKee variable will be a guide to the statistical significance of the contribution of experience at McKee to explaining salary. This *partial F* test is referred to in Section 8.12. An application of the *F* test for a subset of variables is presented in the discussion of multicol-

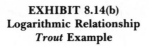

EXHIBIT 8.14(b)
Logarithmic Relationship
Trout **Example**

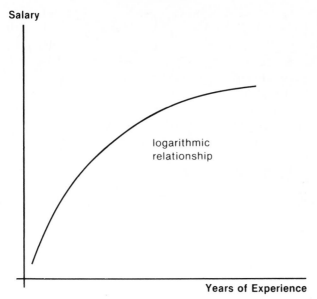

linearity in Section 8.15 and in Section 8.24. That approach is directly applicable to the problem presented by the need to calculate the statistical significance of experience at McKee in the polynomial equation in *Agarwal*.

Trout v. Hidalgo:[3] The plaintiffs alleged that the Department of the Navy had discriminated against women in promotion to higher salary grades. The proof consisted primarily of multiple regression analyses of statistical data from Naval personnel records. The salary equations were logarithmic in nature rather than polynomial, as in *Agarwal*. While the exact nature of the changes is unclear from the opinion, one frequent transformation is to convert all of the data into their common logarithms[4] in order to produce a curve like that in Exhibit 8.14(b).

---

[3] 517 F. Supp. 873, 879 (D.D.C. 1981).
[4] A *logarithm* is a transformation based on exponents. The common logarithm of any number is the power to which ten must be raised to equal the number. Thus, since ten equals 10^1, 100 equals 10^2, and 1000 equals 10^3, the common logarithms of 10, 100, and 1000 are 1.0, 2.0, and 3.0 respectively. Logarithms, commonly referred to as

The relationship between salary and experience and productivity variables often are estimated based on the form of the curve shown in Exhibit 8.14(b), instead of the polynomial form in Exhibit 8.13(a), when there is no expectation that eventually salary will decline. The theory underlying this model is that salary will rise quickly at first as one acquires more experience but later increases in increments due to an additional year of experience get smaller.

The first step in transforming data discussed in the *Trout* example is to find the common log of each piece of data. For a salary of $18,200, for instance, the common log is 4.260, while for a level of experience of six years the common log is .778.[5] The data actually used by the computer to calculate the regression statistics are the log equivalents of the observed values rather than the observed data themselves. Exhibit 8.14(c) illustrates some of the observed and the transformed data used to find the regression statistics for the non-linear regression equation shown in Equation 8.14(d), which is substituted for the linear form in Equation 8.14(e).

$$\log (\text{Salary}) = \log a + b \log (\text{Experience})$$

8.14(d)

$$\text{Salary} = a + b\text{Experience}$$

8.14(e)

The result of this calculation will be an equation like that in Equation 8.14(f).

$$\log y = 3.85 + 0.6 \log x$$

8.14(f)

"logs," were developed more than 3000 years ago to simplify the process of multiplication and long division.
[5] Many hand-held calculators give these transformations.

EXHIBIT 8.14(c)
Logarithmic Transformation of Data Points

Equation: $\log y = \log a + b \log x$

y (Salary in dollars)	x (Experience in years)	log y	log x
25,050	5	4.399	0.699
10,500	3	4.024	0.477
17,920	4	4.253	0.602
18,200	6	4.260	0.778
.	.	.	.
.	.	.	.
.	.	.	.

To predict salary with a logarithmic equation such as that in the *Trout* example for a given level of experience, one first converts the number of years of experience to its common log equivalent. For 15 years of experience, for instance, the common log is 1.176. The effect of experience on salary is given by the estimated regression coefficient, *b*, which equals 0.6 times the common log of experience, here 0.6 × 1.176, or 0.706. The experience effect is added to the baseline salary, measured in logs, 3.85, to get the common log of the predicted salary, 4.556 (= 3.85 + 0.706). To find what this salary is in regular dollars one converts the log equivalent back to decimal numbers. The decimal equivalent of 4.556 is 35,974, so the predicted salary is $35,974 for 15 years of experience.

For logarithmic equations such as the one discussed in the *Trout* example, the *t* test can be used to evaluate the statistical significance of each estimated regression coefficient (without any conversion) and the *F* test can be used to test the statistical significance of the entire regression equation in the same manner as for linear regression equations. (See Sections 8.8 and 8.12.) The R^2 also has the same interpretation as for linear equations (see Section 8.10).

It may appear to the reader that nonlinear approaches present too many complications to be worthwhile. For the polynomial equations, prediction was fairly straightforward but significance testing of the relevant regression coefficients was somewhat more difficult. For logarithmic equations, significance testing is straightforward but interpretation of the results is slightly complicated. Explaining the results of nonlinear estimation to the factfinder may present special difficulties. The goal of regression, however, is to present an accurate model of the process under consideration and nonlinear estimations may present more accurate descriptions of relationships than those that are linear. The tests of statistical significance can be used to evaluate whether there is any improvement in the explanatory power of a regression equation or coefficient by using one technique rather than another. The lawyer will want to compare the benefits of changing model specification to the costs of difficulty in interpretation.

E. COMMON DIFFICULTIES
IN REGRESSION ANALYSIS

As discussed in Section 2.10.2, a set of background assumptions underlie most inferential statistical methods. In Sections 8.15 through 8.17 three background assumptions for regression analysis are examined. The first assumption is that the independent variables included in a regression equation are not correlated with each other. The problem arising from correlated independent variables, called *multicollinearity,* is that individual estimated regression coefficients may inaccurately measure the influences of their associated independent variables on the dependent variable. In addition, significance tests for individual regression coefficients may be unreliable if multicollinearity is present. Multicollinearity is discussed in Section 8.15.

The second background assumption is that all relevant explanatory variables have been included in the model, but no irrelevant variables have been included. Omitting relevant variables may affect the size of the regression coefficient on one or more of the independent variables as well as the precision of predicted values of the dependent variable and therefore may change the conclusions one draws from the regression analysis. Overspecification of an equation by including irrelevant variables may also lead to erroneous conclusions. These two problems are discussed in Section 8.16.

The third background assumption discussed here is that the variance of the errors does not change systematically over observations. This problem, referred to as *heteroscedasticity,* may result in misleading confidence intervals and significance tests for the regression statistics. Heteroscedasticity is discussed in Section 8.17.

§8.15   Correlated Independent Variables: Multicollinearity

An underlying assumption of regression analysis is that no independent variable included in a regression equation is correlated with any other independent variable or set of them. A significant correlation between two variables may be revealed by the calculation and significance testing of a correlation coefficient between them (see Section 7.1). If there is a relationship between one independent variable and some collection of the other independent variables, a regression equation using one of these as the dependent variable and the others as explanatory variables may reveal this relationship.

It is difficult to state absolutely when the presence of correlations among independent variables becomes a problem, but statisticians agree that the correlation must be high. One source suggests that the correlation coefficient, r, between two independent variables must exceed .8 for there to be a serious multicollinearity problem. If such a high correlation is not found then one proceeds as if there were no multicollinearity.[1] Similarly, if the correlation is between an independent variable and a collection of other independent variables, the R^2 must be very high for a regression equation describing the relationship between the variables. The key to avoiding multicollinearity is to be vigilant in the search for associations between the independent variables. The computer is a handy tool for running through all permutations and combinations to find these relationships, but one must keep in mind that multicollinearity is not a serious concern unless the correspondences are very high. Ordinary least squares is a tool that is *robust,* which means that it gives reliable results unless the departures from the background assumptions are quite severe.

Correlated independent variables cause problems for interpretation of regression coefficients for those variables because the coefficient purportedly separates the influence of one variable from those of all other variables: a high correlation between them makes it difficult to separate their respective influences on the dependent variable. If one tried to predict a lawyer's annual earnings (the dependent variable) on the basis of annual billable hours and total hours spent in the office (two independent variables), it might be difficult to separate these two influences because there is considerable correlation between

§8.15   [1] M. Lewis-Beck, Applied Regression: An Introduction 60 (1983).

them. The correlation between them is not perfect; some lawyers spend a lot of time in the office spinning wheels, getting coffee, or engaged in work for clients that is not billed at an hourly rate. But if the correlation between the variables is very high, ordinary least squares will be unable to separate their independent influences on annual earnings.

> **Presseisen v. Swarthmore College:**[2] The plaintiff alleged that the college discriminated against women in several respects, including promotions policy and salary determination. Since salary is determined at least in part by academic rank, it seems proper to include rank in the multiple regression equation used to explain salary. Plaintiff claimed, however, that rank was correlated with gender and that to include both rank and gender in the salary equation would raise the problem of multicollinearity.

One of the results of multicollinearity is that the standard errors of the regression coefficients of the correlated variables are larger than they would be otherwise. Because the standard error is critical to their significance testing, a larger standard error for a given coefficient increases the likelihood that it will be found not statistically significant. This is a problem for plaintiffs in discrimination suits because the correlation between gender (or race) and other important explanatory variables may make the coefficients on some or all of the variables statistically insignificant, leading to the conclusion that gender (or race) has no effect on hiring, promotion, or salary. In *Presseisen* the plaintiff's salary equations, which did not include rank along with the gender variable, showed a statistically significant coefficient on gender while the defendant's, which did include rank, showed a coefficient on gender that was not statistically significant.

> **Presseisen v. Swarthmore College:**[3] Following the rule that multicollinearity is not a problem unless the correlation is very high, one can analyze the proper approach to deciding whether rank should be included in an equation used to decide whether gender is a significant factor in salary determination. The court analyzed the relationship between rank and gender before examining salary. The court examined the differences in mean salaries between men and women of the same rank and found that the plaintiff had not borne her burden of showing

---

[2] 442 F. Supp. 593 (E.D. Pa. 1977), *aff'd*, 582 F.2d 1275 (3d Cir. 1982).
[3] 442 F. Supp. 593 (E.D. Pa. 1977).

that there was a significant statistical disparity. This amounted to a finding that gender and rank were not substantially related. With this finding in hand, the court concluded that rank should be included in the salary equation.

The reasoning behind inclusion of rank in *Presseisen* is quite proper and nicely summarized in *Craik v. Minnesota State University Board*,[4] where dissenting Judge Swygert concludes:

> The plaintiffs make more spirited arguments, however, against the inclusion of rank [as an independent variable in the salary equation for teachers]. They argue that rank should be omitted because it is highly correlated to sex, and therefore poses a multicollinearity problem, threatening to mask as rank differences disparities actually due to sex. This argument stands or falls with their arguments that rank is determined discriminatorily; because I consider those arguments to have been properly rejected, there is no reason not to include rank as an independent variable in the regression.

The defendant's argument for inclusion of the rank variable was buttressed in *Craik* by evidence that compared each female class member to at least five, and often more, men of similar education, rank, experience, and academic department during the relevant years. The judge found no significant differences between the salaries of similar men and women.[5]

When multicollinearity is not serious, ordinary least squares usefully separates the individual influences of the correlated independent variables.

Paxton v. Union National Bank:[6] A bivariate earnings equation with race as the independent variable showed a statistically significant coefficient on race. The expansion of this equation to include experience and educational variables resulted in a coefficient on race that was not statistically significant. There was a correlation between race and many of the experience and educational variables (see Section 8.2) but these were legitimate explanatory factors for earnings, as the defendant was unlikely to have caused the differences in educational attainment among the racial groups. In the bivariate regression that made race appear to be a significant factor, the race of the employee was really

---

[4] 34 Fair Empl. Prac. Cas. (BNA) 649, 695 (8th Cir. 1984).
[5] Id. at 696.
[6] 519 F. Supp. 136, 163 (E.D. Ark. W.D. 1981).

capturing a lot of the effect of experience and education, legitimate exculpatory factors, rather than the effect of race alone, an inculpatory factor. The court appropriately recognized that this diminished statistical significance suggested a lack of proof of discrimination in pay practices.

One result of the large estimated standard errors for correlated estimated regression coefficients that may result from multicollinearity is that the coefficients may appear, contrary to expectation, to be statistically insignificant. If an analyst is confronted with a particular equation in which two variables whose effects on the dependent variable was thought a priori to be large but whose coefficients are both statistically insignificant, a *partial F test* may be a useful indicator of the presence of multicollinearity. The partial F test can be used to determine whether the two variables combine to have a statistically significant explanatory effect on the dependent variable. If the combined effect is statistically significant but the individual effect of each as measured by the regression coefficient is not, then multicollinearity should be suspected. An example where this occurs and a description of the partial F calculation appear in Section 8.24.

Other informal tests for multicollinearity require a prior notion of the sizes (and relative sizes) of the estimated regression coefficients. Because multicollinearity may cause unexpectedly large or small coefficients, such a result might cause suspicion. Similarly, repeating the calculations with data from a different sample or the deletion of a few observations from a given sample might lead to abnormally large changes in the sizes of the estimated coefficients if multicollinearity is severe. Often the lawyer does not have the luxury of comparing several samples, so some of these indicators may be of less utility than others in litigation applications.

Multicollinearity is not a problem if the purpose of the equation is to predict the value of the dependent variable rather than to evaluate the statistical significance of a particular independent variable. The explanatory power of all independent variables is included in the predictive equation even if, due to multicollinearity, the individual coefficients are not significant. Because the R^2 and F tests are based on errors in prediction rather than on the estimated standard errors of the coefficients (which may be inflated due to multicollinearity), the R^2 and F tests are unaffected by the presence of multicollinearity.

Note that only the coefficients and standard errors for the collinear variables in an equation are affected by multicollinearity. The coefficients and significance testing for other independent variables are unaffected.

The problem of multicollinearity is not limited to employment cases. Avoidance of multicollinearity is important in any application of regression analysis where attention is focused on the practical or statistical significance of individual regression coefficients.

> **McCleskey v. Zant:**[7] In this habeas corpus case, the petitioner's experts submitted multiple regression evidence to demonstrate the influence of racial factors, particularly the race of the murder victim and of the defendant, on the probability of being sentenced to death, the dependent variable. The various equations had as many as 230 variables, including variables that represented the aggravating circumstances surrounding the murder. In his opinion, Judge Forrester expressed concern about the correlation between the race of the victim and the presence or absence of aggravating and mitigating circumstances. The regression coefficient on race of victim calculated by petitioner showed a six percentage point increase in the probability of getting the death penalty if the victim was white. The respondent argued, however, that white-victim cases were generally more aggravated than black-victim cases. Of 25 types of aggravating circumstances, 23 occurred at a statistically significant higher proportion in white- than in black-victim cases. Similarly, it appeared that mitigating circumstances appeared more frequently in black-victim cases. If there was a high correlation between race of victim and the aggravated nature of the crime then it could be the nature of crime rather than race of the victim that was explaining the imposition of the death penalty on a defendant. Judge Forrester concluded that "[t]he presence of multicollinearity substantially diminishes the weight to be accorded to the circumstantial statistical evidence of racial disparity."[8]

The validity of the criticism of petitioner's regression results in *McCleskey* depends partially on whether the coefficient on race of the victim was statistically significant. One effect of multicollinearity is to reduce the statistical significance of the regression coefficient. If the coefficient on race of victim remains statistically significant despite alleged collinearity with variables included in the equation, that is evidence that there is indeed a statistically significant relationship between the dependent variable and that independent variable. In fact, the coefficient on race of victim was statistically significant in

[7] 580 F. Supp. 338, 363 (N.D. Ga. A.D. 1984).
[8] Id. at 364.

McCleskey, and for various samples and models the size of the coefficient stayed about the same. See Exhibit 8.10(a).

On the other hand, if there was multicollinearity between race of victim and some of the included independent variables that legitimately justify a harsher sentence, there might be a collinear relationship between race of victim and significant explanatory variables omitted from the equation. The inclusion of these other variables might reduce both the size and statistical significance of the coefficient on race of victim. See the discussion of *Paxton v. Union National Bank* in Section 8.3 and a more detailed discussion of this evaluation of the *McCleskey* case in Section 8.10.

§8.16   Omitted Variables/Overspecification

Difficulty in interpretation of regression results may arise from the omission of relevant variables from the regression equation or the inclusion of irrelevant variables in the equation. Such improper specification of a regression model may affect the size and interpretation of the regression coefficients or the predicted values of the dependent variable. The problem of omitting relevant variables may be more serious and is therefore treated first.

Failure to include in the regression equation an independent variable that has a statistically significant relationship to the dependent variable will decrease the predictive power of the regression equation. The R^2 measures the variation in the dependent variable that is accounted for by variation in the independent variables (see Section 8.10). Because the R^2 captures the variations of only those variables included in the equation, the explanatory power of an omitted variable is missing from the prediction and not included in R^2. A low R^2 may be indicative of failure to include relevant explanatory factors.

Failure to include in the regression equation an independent variable that has a statistically significant relationship to the dependent variable will give an unreliable estimate of the regression coefficients for variables that are included only if those variables are correlated with the omitted variable. *Paxton v. Union National Bank*[1] is a classic illustration of the effect on the coefficient for an independent variable of omitting correlated independent variables from the equa-

§8.16   [1]519 F. Supp. 136, 163 (E.D. Ark. W.D. 1981).

tion. In the bivariate estimate of the effect of race on earnings the coefficient for race was −$213.35, indicating that black employees earned $213.35 less on average than white employees. When previously omitted independent variables were added to the equation, the coefficient on race fell to −$4.19, because the race coefficient had picked up part of the explanatory power of such variables as level of educational achievement and experience that were correlated to race. If omitted independent variables are not correlated to the included variables, the coefficients on the included variables will be unbiased even though the explanatory power of the equation may be low. Thus including additional variables will not improve the accuracy of the estimated regression coefficient associated with a variable of interest if the additional variables are not correlated with that variable.

Rosario v. New York Times Co.:[2] The plaintiffs, classes of non-white and Hispanic persons, alleged discrimination in the areas of wages and training by the defendant daily newspaper. The defendant moved for summary judgment claiming, inter alia, that the plaintiffs' regression analyses omitted too many variables, such as news judgment, writing ability, and managerial capability. The judge considered the possibility that these skills were just as prevalent in the nonwhite-Hispanic population as in the white-nonHispanic population, in which case inclusion of the omitted variables would have no effect on the included variables. If these skills are randomly distributed among races there would be only chance correlations between the race variable and a quantifiable measure of these skills. The judge prudently ordered a trial to resolve the issue of the effect of the missing variables.

One might wonder about the propriety of adding to an equation an omitted independent variable that is correlated to an included independent variable given the problem of multicollinearity discussed in Section 8.15. The first answer to this is that multicollinearity is a problem only when the correspondence between the two variables is high. A second answer is that multicollinearity is not a problem if the equation is used for prediction rather than estimating the effect of a particular independent variable. If it is necessary to explain the effect of particular factors, it may be necessary to find another regression technique to analyze the data. A regression technique referred to as *two-stage least squares* has been suggested as one possible approach to this problem. This technique uses a regression estimate of the rela-

[2] 84 F.R.D. 626, 630 (S.D.N.Y. 1979).

tionship between two correlated, independent variables to aid in the identification of the accurate, unbiased effect of each variable on the dependent variable. Discussions of two-stage least squares appear in most econometric texts.[3]

Inclusion of irrelevant variables is less of a problem than omitting relevant variables unless it results in multicollinearity between one of the irrelevant variables and a variable whose coefficient is of importance to the analysis. In such a case, it may be best to omit the potentially irrelevant variable. The question of whether a variable is irrelevant must be answered on a conceptual level but the basic problem is no different from deciding whether a particular piece of evidence is relevant to a particular issue.

Because the existence of multicollinearity presents no particular problem when a regression is to be used for prediction, overinclusion of variables does not bias the prediction. The R^2 can be adjusted to take into account the number of independent variables (see Section 8.10).

For significance testing and construction of confidence and prediction intervals, whether for the regression as a whole or for particular regression statistics, the inclusion of irrelevant independent variables will have an effect on the number of degrees of freedom used to determine critical t and F values. This effect will be less for large sample sizes than small, as an examination of the tables of critical values reveals.

The analyst choosing between omitting and including a variable for which data are available may wish to opt in favor of inclusion except where the probability of multicollinearity is high because the problems with overinclusion are less severe. This is particularly true when the number of degrees of freedom for significance testing is large.

§8.17   *Variance in Errors: Heteroscedasticity*

The final background assumption for regression analysis to be considered here is that the variance of the error does not change in a systematic way over observations.[1] For it to do so, the variance of the

---

[3] See e.g., T. Wonnacott & R. Wonnacott, Regression: A Second Course in Statistics 319 (1981).
§8.17   [1] The errors are the differences between predicted and observed values for

errors for one subset of observations would have to be significantly different from that for another subset. If, for instance, large values of the independent variables had relatively large errors while for small values the errors were relatively small, this would be a systematic variation in the size of the errors. The subgroup of large observations of the dependent variables would have errors with a larger variance than would the errors for the subgroup of small observations. This is an example of *heteroscedastic* errors. This property of errors is referred to as *heteroscedasticity*.

Exhibits 8.17(a) and (b) illustrate two of the ways in which the variances of errors may change systematically. Exhibit 8.17(a) illustrates the relationship between annual earnings for 39 law school graduates chosen at random. It appears that recent graduates have some variation in their salaries but not nearly as much as lawyers who have been practicing for a long time. Estimating the regression statistics for a bivariate regression would give a least squares estimate of the relationship between years out of school and annual income. The errors would be the differences between predicted values, on the estimated regression line, $y = a + bx$, and the observed values, marked by x's. The greater variation in earnings for lawyers who have been out of law school longer leads to greater errors for that group and, consequently, a larger variance for those errors.

Exhibit 8.17(b) illustrates variations in salary for law professors with different amounts of law teaching experience. It appears that there is considerable variation and large predictive errors for law professors with little teaching experience, probably because they have come from a variety of prior work experiences both in terms of length of practice and type of experience. For seasoned law professors there is less variation as they reach the top of the salary scale at a university. Salary predictions for professors with more law-teaching experience will generally have smaller errors.

In both exhibits the variance of the errors changes systematically over observations; increasing as the values of the independent variable increase in Exhibit 8.17(a) and decreasing as the values increase in Exhibit 8.17(b). Both of these examples illustrate the presence of heteroscedasticity.

The primary practical effect of heteroscedasticity is on confi-

---

the dependent variable, as shown in Equation 8.13(a). The variance of the errors is the sum of the squared deviations of the errors from their mean divided by the sample size minus one (see Section 4.21.2).

EXHIBIT 8.17(a)
Scatter Plot of Heteroscedastic Data
Lawyers' Income

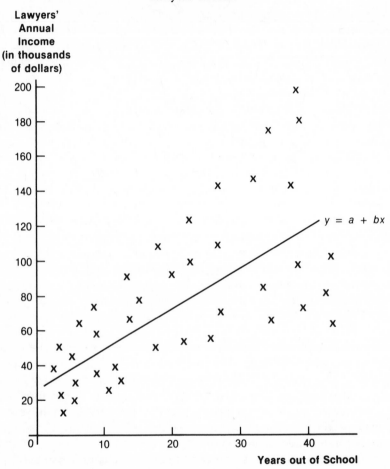

dence and prediction intervals and on significance testing, all of which may be misleading when heteroscedasticity is present. One can see by viewing the exhibits that the equations give reliable predictions for earnings or salaries for some of the individuals because the errors for some, the younger ones in Exhibit 8.17(a) and the older ones in Exhibit 8.17(b), are small. That being the case, the prediction intervals for the predictions should be small, the confidence intervals for the regression coefficient on the independent variables should be small,

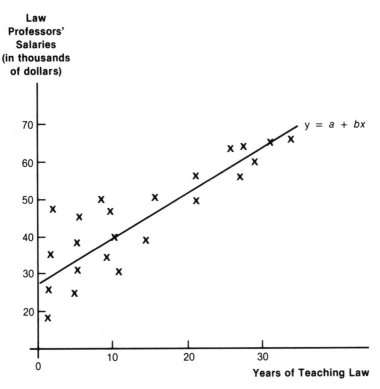

EXHIBIT 8.17(b)
Scatter Plot of Heteroscedastic Data
Law Professors' Salaries

and both the t and F tests should show a high level of statistical significance. Just the opposite is true for those people who have been out of law school for a long time or those who have just started teaching. There is a greater amount of error in prediction, the regression coefficient on the independent variable should be less statistically significant, and the resulting confidence intervals should be broader. Significance tests and calculated test statistics do not, however, reveal this difference in precision for different values of the independent variable; they provide average values that overestimate the statistical significance of those statistics and predictions for observations associated with large errors and understate the statistical significance for observations with smaller errors. Thus tests of statistical significance are unreliable when heteroscedasticity is present.

One solution to the problem of heteroscedasticity is to transform the data so as to reduce the errors to uniform size. The processes of transformation are analogous to those described in Section 8.14. An alternative is to use a regression technique called *weighted least squares,* which substitutes the principle of weighted least squares for ordinary least squares.[2] The regression estimates are obtained by minimizing the sum of squared *weighted* errors rather than minimizing the sum of squared errors, as is done for the ordinary least squares regression technique. The weights may be assigned in a variety of ways, such as in inverse proportion to the variance of the errors in order to de-emphasize the large errors. The transformation and weighted least squares approaches are equivalent to one another for some transformations and weights but may present problems in interpretation for the court. While they do give precise estimates with reliable significance testing, their nature may be difficult to explain to the factfinder.

F. COMPUTATIONS RELATED TO REGRESSION ANALYSIS

The following notation is used in the formulas included in this chapter. The numbers in parentheses following each definition indicate the section where the term was first introduced. Note that upper case letters indicate population values while lower case letters indicate sample values. A symbol in parentheses following a similar symbol to be defined is the sample equivalent of a population symbol.

A (a) — the population (sample) intercept or constant term in a regression equation (8.1)

$a*$ — a standard to which an estimated regression intercept is compared to determine the statistical significance of a difference between them (8.9)

B (b) — the population (sample) regression coefficient for a particular independent variable (8.1)

b_i — the regression coefficient associated with the independent variable x_i (8.1.2)

$b*$ — a standard to which an estimated regression coefficient is compared to determine the statistical significance of a difference between them (8.8)

---

[2] See T. Wonnacott & R. Wonnacott, Regression: A Second Course in Statistics 209 (1981), where these methods are discussed in greater detail.

d.f. — the number of degrees of freedom for tests of statistical significance of regression statistics (8.18)

e_j — the error associated with the prediction of the jth value of the dependent variable (8.1.1)

F — a test statistic used in significance testing for predictions from regression equations (8.12)

k — the number of independent variables in the regression equation (8.18)

n — the size of the sample from which statistics are calculated (8.18)

OLS — ordinary least squares, a method for estimating regression statistics (8.1)

R^2 — the coefficient of multiple determination (8.10)

se_a — the estimated standard error of the population regression intercept (8.9)

se_b — the estimated standard error of the population regression coefficient (8.6)

se_{y*} — the standard error of the estimated values of the dependent variable, y; when squared, the explained variance in the observed y values (8.21)

t — a test statistic used in significance testing for individual regression statistics (8.7)

x_i — one of several independent variables (8.12)

x_j — the jth observed value of the independent variable, x (8.1.1)

$x_{i,j}$ — the jth observed value of the ith independent variable (8.12)

y_j — an observed value of the dependent variable, y

y_j^* — a predicted value for the dependent variable based on specified values for the independent variables and the estimated regression statistics (8.1.1)

§8.18 Confidence Intervals for Regression Coefficients — Calculations

Using Equation 8.18(a),[1] a two-tailed confidence interval can be calculated for an estimated regression coefficient once it and its standard error have been calculated.

§8.18 [1] See T. Wonnacott & R. Wonnacott, Regression: A Second Course in Statistics 37, 89 (1981).

$$\text{confidence interval }(b) = b \pm t_{\text{critical}} \times se_b$$

8.18(a)

The corresponding formulas for a one-tailed interval designed to show the maximum value the coefficient is likely to reach at a given level of confidence is shown in Equation 8.18(b), while that for a minimum value is shown in Equation 8.18(c).

$$\text{upper limit} = b + t_{\text{critical}} \times se_b$$

8.18(b)

$$\text{lower limit} = b - t_{\text{critical}} \times se_b$$

8.18(c)

See Sections 6.6 and 6.22 for more detailed discussion of the use and construction of confidence intervals. The estimated regression coefficient, b, and its standard error, se_b, are almost always calculated by computer, and their formulas are not shown here.[2]

The critical t value is obtained by examining the t Table for the appropriate number of degrees of freedom, the desired confidence level, and the desired type of interval, one-tailed or two-tailed. See Section 6.22 for a more detailed discussion of the use of the t Table. The formula for degrees of freedom for a confidence interval (or a direct significance test) for a regression coefficient obtained by the ordinary least squares method is shown in Equation 8.18(d).[3]

$$d.f. \text{ (OLS regression, } t \text{ test)} = n - k - 1$$

8.18(d)

The n in this formula stands for the sample size; k stands for the number of *independent* variables.[4]

Using Equation 8.18(a) we can calculate the 95% confidence in-

[2] See Section 8.1 note 1.

[3] T. Wonnacott & R. Wonnacott, Regression: A Second Course in Statistics 89 (1981).

[4] Sometimes statistics texts state that the degrees of freedom is calculated as $n - k$ instead of $n - k - 1$. Whenever that convention is used, k is always defined as the total number of variables, independent variables plus the one dependent variable. With this definition, the two approaches give exactly the same results.

terval for the *South Dakota Public Utility Commission* example discussed in Section 8.7 as shown in Exhibit 8.18(a). The $t_{critical}$ is chosen for $n - k - 1 = 10 - 1 - 1 = 8$ degrees of freedom, a 95% confidence level, and a two-tailed interval.

EXHIBIT 8.18(a)
Two-Tailed Confidence Interval for Regression Coefficient
***South Dakota* Example**

$b = -160.16$ billion cubic feet
$se_b = 72.5$ billion cubic feet
$t_{8d.f., 95\%, \text{two-tailed}} = 2.306$

$$\text{interval} = b \pm t_{critical} \times se_b$$
$$= -160.16 \pm 2.306 \times 72.5$$
$$= -160.16 \pm 167.19$$
$$= -327.35 \text{ to } 7.03 \text{ billion cubic feet}$$

Equations 8.18(b) and (c) as applied in Exhibit 8.18(b) indicate that we can be 95% confident that the population regression coefficient is less than -25.31 billion cubic feet or 95% confident that it is greater than -295.01 billion cubic feet for the one-tailed approaches.

EXHIBIT 8.18(b)
One-Tailed Confidence Intervals for Regression Coefficient
***South Dakota* Example**

$b = -160.16$ billion cubic feet (bcf)
$se_b = 72.5$ bcf
$t_{8d.f., 95\% \text{ confidence, one-tailed}} = 1.860$

Interval to estimate maximum value the population
coefficient is likely to take
$$= b + t_{critical} \times se_b$$
$$= -160.16 + 1.860 \times 72.5$$
$$= -160.16 + 134.85 = -25.31$$
95% confidence that B is less than -25.31 bcf

Interval to estimate minimum value the population
coefficient is likely to take
$$= b - t_{critical} \times se_b$$
$$= -160.16 - 1.860 \times 72.5$$
$$= -160.16 - 134.85 = -295.01 \ bcf$$
95% confidence that B is greater than -295.01 bcf

479

§8.19 Direct Significance Testing for Individual Regression Coefficients — Calculations

The calculated t value for direct significance testing of regression coefficients is shown in Equation 8.19(a), where b^* is the value to which the estimated regression coefficient, b, is compared.

$$t_{calculated} = \frac{b - b^*}{se_b}$$

8.19(a)

The hypothesis tested is often stated as "b is not different from zero" or "b is not greater than zero" or "b is not less than zero." In each of these cases b^* equals zero, so the t is calculated as shown in Equation 8.19(b).[1]

$$t_{calculated} = \frac{b}{se_b}$$

8.19(b)

The calculated t value is compared to critical t values from the t Table for a one- or two-tailed test and an appropriate number of degrees of freedom, given by Equation 8.18(d) as equal to $n - k - 1$, where n is the sample size and k is the number of independent variables in the regression equation.

For the *Paxton* example in Section 8.7, the appropriate number of degrees of freedom is $n - k - 1 = 402 - 12 - 1 = 389$. Following the rule that the next lower number of degrees of freedom appearing on the Table is consulted whenever the exact number is not shown, the critical t values for 120 degrees of freedom are used. A portion of the t Table for 120 degrees of freedom is reproduced in Exhibit 8.19(a).

---

§8.19 [1] T. Wonnacott & R. Wonnacott, Regression: A Second Course in Statistics 91 (1981).

EXHIBIT 8.19(a)
Critical *t* Values for 120 Degrees of Freedom

Significance Level

Degrees of Freedom	One-Tailed Test												
	.45	.40	.35	.30	.25	.20	.15	.10	.05	.025	.01	.005	.0005
	Two-Tailed Test												
	.90	.80	.70	.60	.50	.40	.30	.20	.10	.05	.02	.01	.001
120	.126	.254	.386	.526	.677	.845	1.041	1.289	1.658	1.980	2.358	2.617	3.373

Using the formula in Equation 8.19(b), we find the calculated t values for four of the independent variables in the regression equation in *Paxton* as shown in Exhibit 8.19(b).

EXHIBIT 8.19(b)
Calculated t Values
Paxton Example

Variable	b	se_b	b/se_b = *calculated* t
Race	−4.19	46.77	−.09
Months of Accounting Experience	36.23	24.07	1.51
Years of Schooling	27.51	15.24	1.81
Part Time Work	126.57	69.48	1.82

The critical t value associated with a calculated t is that which is closest to yet not greater than the absolute value of the calculated t value. The p-value associated with a critical t value is shown on the top of the t Table above the appropriate critical t value. Thus for race, where the absolute value of the calculated t is .09, the associated critical value is even less than the smallest one shown for 120 degees of freedom, .126, and thus the p-value is even greater than .90 for a two-tailed test. For months of accounting experience, the critical t value of 1.289 is the one closest to yet not greater than 1.51, the calculated t value, so the associated two-tailed p-value is .20. For years of schooling and part-time work the associated critical t value is 1.658 and the one-tailed p-value is .05.

When comparing an observed coefficient, such as the estimated regression coefficient of \$135.54 associated with the variable "M.A. Degree" in *Paxton,* with a value other than zero, such as a figure of \$200 per month (which might make acquiring a Master's Degree worthwhile in terms of its return in salary), Equation 8.19(c) is appropriate.

$$t_{calculated} = \frac{b - b^*}{se_b} = \frac{135.54 - 200}{132.06} = -.488$$

8.19(c)

The b equals 135.54 while the b^*, which is the value for comparison, equals 200, and the standard error of b equals 132.06 (see Exhibit 8.7(a)). The calculated t value is −.488, as shown in Equation 8.19(c).

To calculate the probability that the difference between 135.44 and 200 is due to random selection of items to include in the sample, we find the critical t value closest to yet not greater than .488, which is .386 for 120 degrees of freedom. If the hypothesis is that there is no difference between the population coefficient for M.A. Degree and the $200 comparison value, then a two-tailed test is appropriate, and the p-value associated with a critical t of .386 is .70. There is a 70% chance of a Type 1 error if we reject this hypothesis. If the hypothesis is that the population coefficient is not less than the comparison value, a one-tailed test is appropriate, and the associated p-value is .35.

§8.20 Significance Testing for Regression Intercepts — Calculations

Using Equation 8.20(a),[1] a two-tailed confidence interval can be calculated for a regression intercept once the a and its standard error have been calculated.

$$\text{confidence interval } (a) = a \pm t_{\text{critical}} \times se_a$$

8.20(a)

Formulas for one-tailed tests involving a appear in Equations 8.20(b) (for determining a value above which the population A is unlikely to fall) and 8.20(c) (for determining a value below which it is unlikely to fall).

$$\text{upper limit} = a + t_{\text{critical}} \times se_a$$

8.20(b)

$$\text{lower limit} = a - t_{\text{critical}} \times se_a$$

8.20(c)

The values of the estimated intercept, a, and its standard error, se_a, are almost always calculated by computer and therefore their formulas are omitted here.[2]

---

§8.20 [1] See T. Wonnacott & R. Wonnacott, Regression: A Second Course in Statistics 37 (1981).
[2] See Section 8.1 note 1.

The critical t value is determined as for the confidence intervals involving estimated regression coefficients, discussed in Section 8.18.

Calculated t values are computed by the formula in Equation 8.20(d), with a^* indicating the value to which the estimated intercept, a, is compared.

$$t_{\text{calculated}} = \frac{a - a^*}{se_a}$$

8.20(d)

The calculated t is compared to the critical t from the t Table for $n - k - 1$ degrees of freedom, and the significance level and type of test (one- or two-tailed) chosen.

For the salary equation example discussed in Section 8.9 the estimated intercept was \$9500 and its standard error, \$2513. The sample size, n, was 92 persons and there were seven independent variables. Using Equation 8.18(d), one calculates the number of degrees of freedom as being equal to $n - k - 1 = 92 - 7 - 1 = 84$. The t Table does not show critical values for 84 degrees of freedom, so the next lower number of degrees of freedom, 60, is used. For a 99% confidence interval, the two-tailed critical t value is 2.660 and the one-tailed critical t value is 2.390. Using Equations 8.20(a), (b), and (c), two-tailed and one-tailed intervals are computed in Exhibit 8.20(a).The two-tailed interval shows that the population baseline salary is unlikely to fall outside the range of \$2815.42 to \$16,184.58. The first one-tailed interval shows that the population baseline salary is unlikely to be below \$3493.93; the second shows that it is unlikely to exceed \$15,506.07.

EXHIBIT 8.20(a)
Confidence Intervals for Regression Intercepts
Salary Equation Example

$a = \$9500$

$se_a = \$2513$

$t_{60\ d.f.,\ 99\%\ \text{confidence, two-tailed}} = 2.660$

$t_{60\ d.f.,\ 99\%\ \text{confidence, one-tailed}} = 2.390$

Two-tailed 99% confidence interval for A

interval $= a \pm t_{\text{critical}} \times se_a$
$= \$9500 \pm 2.660 \times \$2513 = \$9500 \pm \$6684.58$
$= \$2815.42 \text{ to } \$16,184.58$

One-tailed interval to find a value below which A is unlikely to fall.

$= a - t_{\text{critical}} \times se_a$
$= \$9500 - 2.390 \times \$2513 = \$9500 - \$6006.07$
$= \$3493.93$

One-tailed interval to find a value above which A is unlikely to fall.

$= a + t_{\text{critical}} \times se_a$
$= \$9500 + 2.390 \times \$2513 = \$9500 + \$6006.07$
$= \$15,506.07$

Direct significance testing is illustrated in Exhibit 8.20(b), where the t test is used to calculate p-values. In each case the calculated t value depends on the value to which the estimated intercept is compared. The first hypothesis is that the population intercept is not different from zero, a two-tailed test, the second is that it is not greater than $6100, a one-tailed test, and the third is that it is not less than $11,000, a one-tailed test. For each example, Equation 8.20(d) is used to find the calculated t value.

EXHIBIT 8.20(b)
t Tests for Regression Intercept
One and Two-Tailed Tests

$$a = \$9500$$
$$se_a = \$2513$$

(1) HYPOTHESIS: $A = 0$

$$t_{\text{calculated}} = \frac{a - a^*}{se_a} = \frac{\$9500 - 0}{\$2513} = 3.780$$

$t_{\text{critical for 60 } d.f., \text{ two-tailed, } .001} = 3.460$

Reject hypothesis at significance level $= .001 = p$-value

(2) HYPOTHESIS: $A < \$6100$

$$t_{\text{calculated}} = \frac{a - a^*}{se_a} = \frac{\$9500 - \$6100}{\$2513} = 1.35$$

$t_{\text{critical for 60 } d.f., \text{ one-tailed, } .10} = 1.296$

Reject hypothesis at significance level $= .10 = p$-value

(3) HYPOTHESIS: $A > \$11,000$

$$t_{\text{calculated}} = \frac{a - a^*}{se_a} = \frac{\$9500 - \$11,000}{\$2513} = -0.597$$

$t_{\text{critical for 60 } d.f., \text{ one-tailed, } .30} = .527$

Reject hypothesis at significance level $= .30 = p$-value

§8.21 The Coefficient of Multiple Determination — Calculations

The coefficient of multiple determination, R^2, indicates the percentage of total variation in the dependent variable accounted for by the variation in the independent variables. The regression coefficients for the independent variables are used to calculate estimated values of the dependent variable for each set of observed values of the independent variables. The formula for a particular predicted value of the dependent variable, y_j^*, is shown in Equation 8.21(a) for an equation with m independent variables.

$$y_j^* = a + b_1 x_{1,j} + b_2 x_{2,j} + \ldots + b_m x_{m,j}$$

8.21(a)

The variance of the estimated y values, $se_{y^*}^2$, is a measure of the amount of variation in y accounted for by the independent variables and is sometimes referred to as the *explained variance*. See Section 4.6 for a general discussion of the variance. When the explained variance is divided by the *total variance* in the dependent variable, se_y^2, the result is the percentage of total variance in the dependent variable that is explained by variations in the independent variables, that is, R^2. The formula for R^2, derived by dividing the explained variance by the total variance is simplified in Equation 8.21(b).[1]

$$R^2 = \frac{\Sigma(y_j^* - m_y)^2}{\Sigma(y_j - m_y)^2}$$

8.21(b)

Exhibit 8.21(a) illustrates the calculation of an R^2 for a bivariate regression equation from the *South Dakota Public Utilities* example discussed in Section 8.0.

§8.21 [1] See T. Wonnacott & R. Wonnacott, Regression: A Second Course in Statistics 180 (1981).

EXHIBIT 8.21(a)
Calculation of R^2
South Dakota Public Utilities Example

Bivariate Regression $y = 317,294 - 160.16x + e$

y_j Annual Additions to Reserves (in billion cubic feet)	x_j Time (measured in years)	$y_j^* = 317,294 - 160.16x_j$ (predicted y values) (in billion cubic feet)	$(y_j - m_y)^2$	$(y_j^* - m_y)^2$
3,307	1967	2,252	3,154,176	519,841
984	1968	2,092	299,209	314,721
1,107	1969	1,932	179,776	160,801
2,012	1970	1,771	115,600	57,600
1,871	1971	1,611	123,904	6,561
1,883	1972	1,451	1,296	57,600
1,567	1973	1,291	153,664	160,000
1,139	1974	1,131	547,600	313,600
791	1975	971	776,161	519,841
650	1976	810		

$\Sigma y_j = \overline{15,311}$

$\Sigma y_j / n = 1531.1 = m_y$

$\Sigma(y_j - m_y)^2 = \overline{5,351,386}$

$\Sigma(y_j^* - m_y)^2 = \overline{2,110,565}$

$$R^2 = \frac{\Sigma(y_j^* - m_y)^2}{\Sigma(y_j - m_y)^2} = \frac{2,110,565}{5,351,386} = .39$$

The corrected or adjusted R^2 is computed by the formula given in Equation 8.21(c).[2]

$$R^2_{\text{corrected}} = \left(R^2 - \frac{k}{n-1}\right)\left(\frac{n-1}{n-k-1}\right)$$

8.21(c)

Thus, for the regression equation in *McCleskey* with 230 independent variables ($k = 230$) based on a sample of 2500 defendants ($n = 2500$), an R^2 of .48 would be adjusted to .43 as shown in Equation 8.21(d).

$$R^2_{\text{corrected}} = \left(.48 - \frac{230}{2500-1}\right)\left(\frac{2500-1}{2500-230-1}\right) = .43$$

8.21(d)

The R^2 of .75 in *Northshore*, with two independent variables based on a sample of measurements in 320 districts would be adjusted to .748, as shown in Equation 8.21(e).

$$R^2_{\text{corrected}} = \left(.75 - \frac{2}{320-1}\right)\left(\frac{320-1}{320-2-1}\right) = .748$$

8.21(e)

For a given R^2, a smaller sample size or a larger number of independent variables will result in a greater correction.

§8.22 Confidence Intervals for Predicted Values — Calculations

Confidence intervals for predicted values of dependent variables are calculated using formulas in Equations 8.22(a), (b), and (c) for two-tailed intervals, values above and below which the population value is unlikely to fall, respectively.[1]

confidence or prediction interval $(y_j^*) = y_j^* \pm t_{\text{critical}} \times se_{y}.$

8.22(a)

[2] Id. at 181.
§8.22 [1] See T. Wonnacott & R. Wonnacott, Regression: A Second Course in Statistics 442-443 (1981).

$$\text{upper limit} = y_j^* + t_{\text{critical}} \times se_{y^*}$$

8.22(b)

$$\text{lower limit} = y_j^* - t_{\text{critical}} \times se_{y^*}$$

8.22(c)

Degrees of freedom for critical t values are calculated according to Equation 8.22(d), where n is the sample size and k is the number of independent variables in the regression equation from which the prediction is calculated.

$$d.f. \text{ (confidence or prediction interval)} = n - k - 1$$

8.22(d)

For the *B. F. Goodrich* example in Section 8.11, we can calculate the two-tailed 90% confidence interval for the predicted average tread depth of 94 mils, as shown in Exhibit 8.22(a), using Equation 8.22(a) and critical t value for $n - k - 1 = 22 - 1 - 1$ equals 20 degrees of freedom.

EXHIBIT 8.22(a)
Two-tailed Confidence Interval
***B. F. Goodrich* Example**

$y_j^* = 94$ mils
$se_{y^*} = 1.5$ mils
$t_{20\ d.f.,\ 90\%,\ \text{two-tailed}} = 1.725$

$$\begin{aligned}
\text{interval} &= y_j^* \pm t_{\text{critical}} \times se_{y^*} \\
&= 94 \pm 1.725 \times 1.5 \\
&= 94 \pm 2.59 \\
&= 91.41 \text{ to } 96.59 \text{ mils}
\end{aligned}$$

The one- and two-tailed prediction intervals for the AT&T example are calculated in Exhibit 8.22(b) for $(12 - 7 - 1 =)$ 4 degrees of freedom.

EXHIBIT 8.22(b)
One- and Two-Tailed Prediction Intervals
AT&T Example

$$y_j^* = .1262$$
$$se_{y^*} = .03$$

Two-tailed interval

$t_{critical} = 2.776$ for 95% confidence, 4 $d.f.$, two-tailed

$$\begin{aligned}
\text{interval} &= y_j^* \pm t_{critical} \times se_{y^*} \\
&= .1262 \pm 2.776 \times .03 \\
&= .1262 \pm .08328 \\
&= .0429 \text{ to } .2524
\end{aligned}$$

One-tailed intervals (99%)

To obtain a value below which the population value
$t_{critical} = 3.747$ for 99% confidence, 4 $d.f.$, one-tailed

$$\begin{aligned}
\text{lower boundary} &= y_j^* - t_{critical} \times se_{y^*} \\
&= .1262 - 3.747 \times .03 \\
&= .1262 - .1124 = .0138 \text{ or } 1.38\% \text{ return}
\end{aligned}$$

To obtain a value above which Y_j is unlikely to fall:
$t_{critical} = 3.747$ for 99% confidence, 4 $d.f.$, one-tailed

$$\begin{aligned}
\text{maximum value} &= y_j^* + t_{critical} \times se_{y^*} \\
&= .1262 + 3.747 \times .03 \\
&= .1262 + .1124 = .2386 \text{ or } 23.86\%
\end{aligned}$$

If we can be 99% confident that $Y_j < .2386$,
then there is a 1% chance that $Y_j > .2386$.

While the formulas for the standard errors of the estimates for predictions of population means and individual values of the dependent variable are different from one another (see Section 8.11 note 5), the standard errors are usually calculated by computer, so the formulas are omitted here.

§8.23   Direct Significance Tests for Predictions — Calculations

The F statistic is calculated either from the formula in Equation 8.23(a), which relies on the variances of the estimated y_j^* values and of the observed y_j values or from the formula in Equation 8.23(b), which calculates the F value from the coefficient of multiple determination R^2.[1]

$$F_{calculated} = \frac{\Sigma(y_j^* - m_y)^2}{\Sigma(y_j - m_y)^2 - \Sigma(y_j^* - m_y)^2} \times \frac{n - k - 1}{k}$$

8.23(a)

$$F_{calculated} = \frac{R^2}{1 - R^2} \times \frac{n - k - 1}{k}$$

8.23(b)

Both give the same result as illustrated in Exhibit 8.23(a), which utilizes the statistics from the *South Dakota Public Utility Commission* data in Exhibit 8.21(a).

EXHIBIT 8.23(a)
Calculation of an *F* Value
***South Dakota* Example**

Bivariate Regression $y = 317{,}294 - 160.16x$

y = annual additions to gas reserves (in billion cubic feet)
x = time (in years)
$\Sigma(y_j^* - m_y)^2 = 2{,}110{,}565$
$\Sigma(y_j - m_y)^2 = 5{,}351{,}386$
$n = 10$ (sample size)
$k = 1$ (number of independent variables)
$R^2 = .3944$

$$F_{calculated} = \frac{\Sigma(y_j^* - m_y)^2}{\Sigma(y_j - m_j)^2 - \Sigma(y_j^* - m_y)^2} \times \frac{n - k - 1}{k}$$

$$= \frac{2{,}110{,}565}{5{,}351{,}386 - 2{,}110{,}565} \times \frac{10 - 1 - 1}{1} = 5.21$$

$$F_{calculated} = \frac{.3944}{1 - .3944} \times \frac{10 - 1 - 1}{1} = 5.21$$

§8.23   [1] These formulas appear in matrix algebra notation in T. Wonnacott & R. Wonnacott, Regression: A Second Course in Statistics 460 (1981). The logic of these formulas is also explained in R. Pfaffenberger & J. Patterson, Statistical Methods for Business and Economics 549 (1977). See also D. Barnes, Statistics as Proof: Fundamentals of Quantitative Evidence 356 (1983), where these formulas are discussed.

The F test is performed by comparing the calculated F value to a critical F value obtained from an F Table for an appropriate number of degrees of freedom for the F test, which is influenced by sample size, n, and the number of independent variables, k. There are two calculations necessary to determine the appropriate number of degrees of freedom for the F test, the number in the numerator and the number in the denominator. The fraction referred to by the words *numerator* (the top number of a fraction) and *denominator* (the bottom number, or divisor, of a fraction) is shown in Equation 8.23(c).

$$d.f. \text{ (F test of entire regression)} = \frac{k}{n - k - 1}$$

$$8.23(c)$$

Thus the number of degrees of freedom in the numerator is equal to k and the degrees of freedom in the denominator is equal to $n - k = 1$ as summarized in Equations 8.23(d) and (e).[2]

$$d.f. \text{ (numerator, F test of entire regression)} = k$$

$$8.23(d)$$

$$d.f. \text{ (denominator, F test of entire regression)} = n - k - 1$$

$$8.23(e)$$

In order to show critical F values for various significance levels an F Table would have to have three dimensions, one each for degrees of freedom in the numerator, degrees of freedom in the denominator, and significance level. Limitations of the printed page result in a different F Table for each significance level. Included in the Appendix of Tables at the end of this book are F Tables for the common significance levels of .05 and .01. The appropriate critical F value for a particular significance level is found in the column beneath the correct number of degrees of freedom in the numerator (which appear across the top of the table) and in the row to the right of correct number of degrees of freedom in the denominator (which appear along the left side of the Table). Exhibit 8.23(b) illustrates the application of the F test to the regression equation in *Northshore School District,*

---

[2] See T. Wonnacott & R. Wonnacott, Regression: A Second Course in Statistics 460. See also note 1 above.

discussed in Section 8.12. Since $F_{calculated} > F_{critical}$, i.e., 476 > 6.85, one would reject the hypothesis that there is no relationship between the dependent and independent variables at a .01 level of significance.

EXHIBIT 8.23(b)
F Test
***Northshore School District* Example**

Expenditures per pupil =
b_1 (Average Pay) + b_2 (Staff per 1000 Students)

$R^2 = .75$
n = 320 (number of school districts in the sample)
k = 2 (number of independent variables)

$$F_{calculated} = \frac{R^2}{1 - R^2} \times \frac{n - k - 1}{k} = \frac{.75}{1.75} \times \frac{320 - 2 - 1}{2} = 476$$

$F_{critical}$ = 6.85 for k = 2 degrees of freedom in the numerator and $n - k - 1 = 320 - 2 - 1 = 317$ degrees of freedom in the denominator and a significance level of .01

§8.24 Partial F Test to Detect Multicollinearity — Calculations

The presence of serious multicollinearity between two independent variables whose estimated regression coefficients are not statistically significant can be detected by a comparison of F values for two regression equations, one of which includes the two variables and the other of which omits them. A significant difference in the F values suggests that these variables have a significant effect on the dependent variable despite the appearance of insignificance from a t test on their coefficients. This anomaly is explained by the fact that independently they appear to have no effect due to multicollinearity but that together they do.

Detection of whether there is a statistically significant difference between F values for the two equations is simplified by the partial F test, which is a test for the significance of that difference and yields a p-value associated with the difference that estimates the probability that the difference could have occurred by chance. It tests the hypothesis of no difference between the explanatory power of the equations. The formula for the calculated F for the partial F test appearing in Equation 8.24(a)[1] involves the calculation of the coefficient of multiple determination for the full equation including the collinear variables, R^2_{full}, and for the partial equation in which the collinear variables are omitted, $R^2_{partial}$.

$$\text{(partial) } F_{calculated} = \frac{R^2_{full} - R^2_{partial}}{(1 - R^2_{full})} \times \frac{n - k_{full} - 1}{k_{full} - k_{partial}}$$

$$\text{8.24(a)}$$

The number of independent variables in the full equation is designated as k_{full}, while the number of independent variables remaining after the collinear variables are removed is $k_{partial}$. The sample size is n.[2]

The calculated F statistic is compared to critical F values on an F Table for the number of degrees of freedom given by Equations 8.24(b) and (c).

$$d.f. \text{ (numerator, partial } F \text{ test)} = k_{full} - k_{partial}$$

$$\text{8.24(b)}$$

$$d.f. \text{ (denominator, partial } F \text{ test)} = n - k_{full} - 1$$

$$\text{8.24(c)}$$

Exhibit 8.24(a) illustrates an application of the partial F test to a hypothetical salary equation for lawyers. Formally, this partial F statistic is used to test the hypothesis that the two collinear variables, gender and partnership status (1 = partner, 0 = not a partner) together have no relationship to the dependent variable. A failure to reject the hypothesis leads one to disregard suspicions of multicollinearity, because it means that the combined explanatory power of both influences has no statistical significance and is consistent with finding that the individual regression coefficients are not statistically significant. A rejection of the hypothesis lends credence to one's suspicions of multicollinearity because it suggests that despite the lack of statistical significance of the individual regression coefficients, there is some explanatory power embodied in the relationship between them.

§8.24 [1] See T. Wonnacott & R. Wonnacott, Regression: A Second Course in Statistics 184 (1981).
[2] Id. at 185.

EXHIBIT 8.24(a)
Application of the Partial F Test
Salary Equation Example

Full Equation

$$\text{Salary} = \$20,500 + \$270(G) + \$5,900(PS) + \$52(A) + \$22(C)$$

se_b		267	9,520	13	5
calculated t		(1.01)	(0.62)	(3.97)	(4.4)

$$R^2 = .47$$

Partial Equation

$$\text{Salary} = \$22,950 + \$52(A) + \$22(C)$$

se_b	13	5
calculated t	(3.97)	(4.4)

$$R^2 = .39$$

Significance Test

$$k_{\text{full}} = 4$$
$$k_{\text{partial}} = 2$$
$$n = 45$$

$F_{\text{critical}} = 3.23$ [for 2 $d.f.$ numerator ($k_{\text{full}} - k_{\text{partial}} = 4 - 2 = 2$),
5 $d.f.$ denominator ($n - k_{\text{full}} - 1 = 45 - 4 - 1$
$= 40$), and .05 significance level]

$$\text{calculated } F = \frac{R^2_{\text{full}} - R^2_{\text{partial}}}{1 - R^2_{\text{full}}} \times \frac{n - k_{\text{full}} - 1}{k_{\text{full}} - k_{\text{partial}}}$$

$$= \frac{.47 - .39}{1 - .47} \times \frac{45 - 4 - 1}{4 - 2}$$

$$= 3.01 < F_{\text{critical, .05}}$$

Thus do not reject the hypothesis of no relationship between salary and the dependent variables, gender and partnership status.

Key:
(G) = Gender
(PS) = Partnership Status
(A) = Age
(C) = Number of Clients

CHAPTER NINE

Presenting and Attacking Statistical Evidence

§9.0 Introduction

This chapter deals with a number of practical problems that a lawyer is likely to encounter in trying a case involving statistical evidence. Some of these problems are evidentiary while others are tactical. This chapter does not purport to be either a detailed treatise on the law of evidence or a comprehensive trial tactics manual. Its purpose is, rather, to identify some of the evidentiary issues that have arisen most frequently in statistical cases and to comment on some of the tactical decisions that are of particular significance in such cases. The discussion will draw on the case law, the collective experience of the authors, and the growing literature on the scientific study of the trial process.

The presentation of statistical evidence is the subject of Sections 9.1 through 9.6. Sections 9.1 and 9.2 review a number of psychological principles that should be carefully considered in planning and presenting the testimony of a statistical expert. Sections 9.3 and 9.4 deal with evidentiary problems likely to arise in statistical cases. Section 9.3 discusses several general problems that have arisen in the case law, while Section 9.4 offers practical and procedural suggestions on the use of demonstrative evidence to support a statistical case. Sections 9.5 and 9.6 present two sets of recommended pretrial procedures that may obviate many evidentiary disputes and thereby shorten and simplify the trial of a case that turns on statistical evidence. Section 9.7 treats the topic of attacking statistical evidence on cross-examination and discusses several substantive legal and factual issues likely to be of particular importance in statistical cases. Section 9.8 deals with issues of strategy and style in the cross-examination of a statistical expert.

A.   COMMON THEMES IN PRESENTING STATISTICAL EVIDENCE

The lawyer who is about to offer statistical proof should begin with two sobering assumptions. These are (1) that the trier of fact will rarely have any prior knowledge of statistical techniques, and (2) that the trier of fact will probably be unsympathetic to the general concept of statistical proof.

The validity of the first assumption is self-evident. Select 12 people off the street and it is unlikely that any of them will have taken a statistics course; it is even more unlikely that any who have will have remembered much of it. The same is true to a somewhat lesser extent for judges. Few state or federal judges encountered by the authors have an academic background in quantitative science. Some, particularly federal judges, may have heard cases involving statistical proof or even have attended a seminar on statistical evidence. Statistical proof is still sufficiently rare, however, that the lawyer should not assume such experience and should in no event assume that the prior experience was educational in a meaningful way. With either judge or jury, then, the lawyer must consider the slate blank until explicitly advised to the contrary.

The validity of the second assumption is less obvious. It has never been demonstrated empirically[1] but is amply confirmed by the experience of the authors. First-time jurors typically come to court with exaggerated expectations about the drama of the courtroom confrontation. At the very least, they will expect an opportunity to scrutinize fellow human beings under pressure and to draw conclusions about credibility and character. They are also likely to presume, and in any event will be reminded by the judge, that they should bring their common sense and good judgment into the courtroom with them. It may be unsettling or worse to suggest to them that they should decide whether an employer has discriminated, whether someone has committed a forgery, or the value of someone's working life by reference to mathematical models rather than their own common sense and their perceptions of the character of the witnesses.

Add to this expectation factor some of the negative public perceptions of statistics as a science, and the problem is exacerbated. Some jurors may recoil at the sight of numbers and symbols in the belief that they are beyond their comprehension. Others will sense manipulation in the introduction of complex proof into what they may view as a simple problem of human behavior and may conclude that a party's reliance on statistical proof is merely an effort to hide a weak case. Finally, some jurors may be conversant with such statistical disasters as recent government economic forecasts and may vent their frustration at any form of statistical evidence.[2]

---

§9.0 [1] Substantial research has been done, however, on the broader subject of the development and modification of attitudes. Such research suggests generally that witnesses will come to court with pre-existing attitudes about many matters, and that they will be most receptive to evidence that does not challenge those attitudes. Changing juror attitudes is a complex process that combines persuasion on both logical and personal levels. For a concise review of the literature in the field, see Vinson, Litigation: An Introduction to the Application of Behavioral Science, 15 Conn. L. Rev. 767, 784-795 (1983).

[2] The generalizing process described in the text is analogous to the psychological process of trait clustering, which takes place when one person perceives that another possesses a particular trait and then automatically draws the conclusion that the person possesses other traits generally associated with the first. See Vinson, supra note 1 at 781-782.

Judges can be expected to be less swayed by subjective considerations. Where the applicable law provides that statistical evidence is admissible and may be probative, most trial judges can be counted on not to take a reversible position out of sheer hostility to quantitative science. Nonetheless, statistical evidence is merely evidence, to be weighed at the discretion of the trier of fact, and judges are as susceptible as anyone to cultural biases against statistics. In a recent sex discrimination case tried in a federal court, to take an extreme example, the trial judge admitted the plaintiff's regression analysis and seemed to be following the testimony until the plaintiff's expert said that some elements of his analysis were expressed in logarithms. At that point, the judge interrupted and said that he would not have logarithms in his court and would not credit an analysis that included such esoteric nonsense. He was not moved by a showing that this form of analysis required logarithms and that the defendant's expert had used exactly the same method.[3] Although this instance may be extreme, it does serve to emphasize that part of the burden of proof in a statistical case is to persuade the trier of fact, whether judge or jury, of the essential validity of statistical methodology. Sections 9.1 and 9.2 discuss strategies for persuading the trier of fact of the validity of the statistical argument. Section 9.1 focuses on establishing a bond or rapport between the lawyer and the jury or judge as factfinder. Section 9.2 focuses on methods of presentation of expert testimony.

§9.1　Statistics and Solidarity

A partial solution to the problems just discussed is found in the anthropological concept of *solidarity*. In studying how and why people form groups and develop consensus, anthropologists have long observed that bonds develop between those who share certain beliefs and cultural attributes. People feeling such cultural commonality will see and define themselves as a group vis-à-vis others who do not share the attributes in question.[1] Many cultural groups, for example, have a

---

[3] American Lawyer, Jul./Aug. 1983, 100, col. 4.

§9.1　[1] See F. Bailey, Stratagems and Spoils (1968). In the view of many anthropologists, shared language is both a cause and an effect of cultural integrity. An enormously influential if much criticized theory, the Sapir-Whorf hypothesis, holds that the way in which members of a culture organize the world is determined by the structure of their language, and not vice-versa. See E. Sapir, Culture, Language and Personality 1-44 (8th ed. 1966). A logical corollary of the Sapir-Whorf hypothesis is that

shared belief about their origin, a belief that typically establishes them as the chosen people of their deity. In accordance with this belief, they call themselves by a name that means *"the people"* ("Navaho" is an example of such a name),[2] at once constituting themselves a group and defining outsiders by reference to the shared creation mythology. This feeling of commonality is termed *solidarity*.

Solidarity can be as important to the trial lawyer as it is to the anthropologist. In the face of unfamiliar and perhaps threatening technical testimony, members of a jury may rally around their shared scientific naivete, constitute themselves a transient cultural entity, and begin to defend their borders against any intrusion by the expert witness.[3] A judge may experience a similar reaction, arriving at the same point of resistance through a somewhat different mental process. A trial lawyer's task is two-fold: to persuade the judge or jurors that the perceived boundary between them and the expert is artificial at best, and ultimately to maneuver them into a position of solidarity *with the expert*.

The trial lawyer can most effectively blur the boundary by demonstrating his or her ability to go back and forth across it with apparent ease. This is best done by skillful use of language, initially in the opening statement and later in the examination and cross-examination of experts.[4] If the lawyer shows himself to be comfortable with the technical jargon of the expert and is then able to translate that jargon to the jury in a simple, comprehensible yet non-condescending way, the message will be conveyed that any initial knee-jerk antistatistical reaction may have been unjustified. If well executed, the lawyer's demonstration of linguistic facility can bring the judge or jurors at least to a point of neutrality, from which the second and more difficult part of the persuasive effort can be launched.

---

two people with some linguistic common ground are more likely to have congruent world views than two people who come from entirely different linguistic backgrounds.

[2] See, e.g., C. Kluckhohn & D. Leighton, The Navaho 197-208 (1948).

[3] The anthropological findings discussed in the text are consistent with the psychological principle that members of a group such as a jury tend to listen as a group. See Vinson, Litigation: An Introduction to the Application of Behavioral Science, 15 Conn. L. Rev. 767, 789 (1983).

[4] For discussions of the significance of language style in the courtroom, see W. O'Barr, Linguistic Evidence 1-13 (1982); Conley, O'Barr, Lind, & Erickson, The Power of Language: A Multi-Disciplinary Study of Language in the Courtroom, 1978 Duke L. J. 1375; Conley, Language in the Courtroom: Form over Substance? 15 Trial 32 (1979); Lett, The Influence of Dialect and Accent in the Courtroom, 19 Intl. Socy. of Barristers Q. 334 (1984); E. Loftus, Eyewitness Testimony (1979).

The ultimate objective is to elicit a strongly affirmative reaction by making the judge and jurors feel like participants in the almost magical process of science. The goal is to establish a feeling of solidarity between the trier of fact and the expert, and the means to this end is again language. If the judge and jurors are given even a passing familiarity with some of the key statistical terminology in the case, they can be made to feel as if they have some intellectual common ground with the expert, common ground not shared by the rest of the world. Being thus co-opted into a feeling of solidarity, they may, to some extent at least, close ranks behind the expert in the face of attacks on the validity of his or her testimony. Having gained temporary admission to the expert's inner circle, the judge and jurors may be ready to defend it as their own.[5]

The teaching process begins in the opening statement,[6] during which some specific burdens are imposed on the lawyer. First, statistical jargon cannot be avoided. Statistical terminology is in the case, for better or worse; if the lawyer treats it as a foreign language, the judge and jurors will too, and the impact of the statistical case is likely to be lost. Second, the lawyer must not only confront the technical terminology, but must make progress toward explaining it. He or she should not take the common approach of treating the technology as a "black box," the contents of which is beyond the understanding of anyone but the experts. Too much skepticism has arisen about the role of science in our society for the lawyer to say simply "I can't understand this any more than you can; you'll have to trust the expert just as I do." By doing so the lawyer not only risks reinforcing whatever prejudices the trier of fact may have about statistical evidence but also forfeits the opportunity to take an important affirmative step.

The process begun in the opening statement continues throughout the expert's testimony. The expert should not shy away from technical terms but should use them whenever appropriate, pausing immediately to explain each term in straightforward language (there are other reasons for doing this, having to do with the expert's credi-

---

[5] Psychologically, the lawyer's objective must be to develop a positive attitude toward the expert on the part of the factfinder. This can be accomplished by subtly suggesting to the judges and jurors that the expert is a person with whom they share attitudes, values, and beliefs. See Vinson, supra note 3, at 786-787 (1983). One means of achieving this latter objective is to create some intellectual common ground between the expert and the factfinder through the sharing of language. See note 1 supra.

[6] Psychologists have demonstrated that jurors find it easier to recall the opening and closing portions of a trial than the middle. See Vinson, supra note 3, at 793.

bility, which will be discussed in the Section 9.2).[7] Nonmathematical analogies and visual aids can facilitate the process.[8]

An obvious question is how practical it is to attempt to give the trier of fact a meaningful education. Where a case is tried to a judge, it is probably realistic to expect him or her to be willing and able to understand explanations of terms and concepts at least on the level presented in the first chapter of this book. Experience suggests that it may also be realistic to expect one or two members of a 12-member panel, particularly in a metropolitan area, to be willing and able to function at a similar level. The anticipated success rate should be higher where the task is defined more narrowly as merely to get the jurors to recognize and have a rudimentary understanding of some of the more important statistical terms in the case. This alone may be enough to achieve the psychological objectives just outlined.

The short answer to the question, however, is that there is no alternative to making the attempt. If the effort is not made, any strongly negative feelings toward statistical evidence will remain unchallenged. If it is implied that the evidence is beyond the comprehension of the trier of fact,[9] such as by the substitution of a simplistic and artificial alternative terminology, those feelings are likely to be strengthened. If, on the other hand, the complexity of the evidence is dealt with squarely, the worst that can happen is that the

---

[7] The suggestions made in the text are collaterally supported by recent research on jury instructions. Many lawyers assume, for the most part correctly, that jury instructions are not well understood by jurors. It is further assumed that this lack of understanding is due to a combination of the inherent complexity of legal concepts and the incomprehensibility of legal jargon. It has been demonstrated convincingly, however, that lack of comprehension by jurors is due not so much to these factors but to the sentence structure, syntax, and lexicon traditionally used in the instructions. The understanding of legal concepts and terms can be significantly improved if the form of the language used to explain them is closer to ordinary conversational English. See Charrow & Charrow, Making Legal Language Understandable: A Psycholinguistic Study of Jury Instructions, 79 Colum. L. Rev. 1306 (1979).

[8] See Section 9.4, where demonstrative evidence is discussed.

[9] It should be acknowledged that there is a substantial body of opinion that much scientific evidence *is* beyond the comprehension of a typical jury. The Supreme Court has expressed concern about "the practical abilities and limitations of juries." Ross v. Bernhard, 369 U.S. 531, 538 n. 10 (1970). On occasion, lower federal courts have indicated that the problems arising from complex evidence may override the Seventh Amendment right to a jury trial. See e.g., Bernstein v. Universal Pictures, Inc., 79 F.R.D. 59 (S.D.N.Y. 1978); In re Boise Cascade Sec. Litig., 420 F. Supp. 99, 104 (W.D. Wash. 1978). See generally Imwinkelried, The Standard for Admitting Scientific Evidence: A Critique from the Perspective of Juror Psychology, 28 Vill. L. Rev. 554, 563-564 (1983).

judge and/or jurors will retain the attitudes they had at the start of the case; the proponent of the evidence is at least likely to get some points for trying.[10]

§9.2 Maximizing the Persuasiveness of the Statistical Expert

In the preceding section it was argued that for tactical reasons the lawyer and the statistical expert must make a straightforward effort to introduce the trier of fact to statistical terminology and concepts. The question then becomes how to maximize the persuasive impact of this effort. On the substantive side, the key has already been suggested: explanations must be put in simple yet nonpatronizing terms,[1] and every effort must be made to explain unfamiliar statistical methods by analogy to events and processes with which judges and jurors are more likely to be comfortable. The Yankee Stadium hypothetical in Section 1.13, through which the concepts of sampling and chance explanation were introduced, is an example of the type of illustration that is contemplated.

It is abundantly clear, however, that the style in which the statistical expert testifies is as important as the substance. A detailed experimental study of language in the courtroom in which one of the authors participated demonstrated convincingly that jurors are influenced in their evaluation of witnesses by such features of language style as word choice, intonation, relative assertiveness, and degree of reliance on the lawyer for prodding.[2] A number of the findings from that study are directly relevant to the testimony of statistical experts.

First, the witness should be prepared to testify under direct examination with virtually no assistance from the lawyer and to speak independently about his or her research and findings. The lawyer

---

[10] If the lawyer is given some credit for forthrightness in dealing with complex evidence, the credit is likely to redound to the benefit of his or her case. Experimental evidence suggests that jurors are influenced in their evaluations by what they perceive to be the proponent lawyer's attitude toward the evidence presented. See Conley et al., supra note 7, at 1389. Accordingly, if the members of the jury infer that the lawyer thinks that a body of complex evidence is worth understanding, they may be more inclined to make the effort themselves.

§9.2 [1] See W. O'Barr, Linguistic Evidence 83-87 (1982) and sources cited therein.

[2] See Conley, O'Barr, Lind, & Erickson, The Power of Language: A Multi-Disciplinary Study of Language in the Courtroom, 1978 Duke L.J. 1375; O'Barr, supra note 1.

should intervene with questions only to the extent necessary to satisfy the trial judge that the testimony is indeed an examination and not a speech. Narrative testimony will have four effects, all salutary: (1) it will enhance the judge and jury's perception of the witness's credibility, expertise and degree of preparation; (2) it will lead the trier of fact to infer that the lawyer has confidence in the witness; (3) it will cause the testimony to conform to the probable expectation of lay jurors that a scientific expert is brought into court to teach and that his testimony should therefore take a different form from that of fact witnesses; and (4) for the academic expert, the teaching format will help the witness by removing some of the unfamiliarity and consequent discomfort from the process of testifying.[3]

Second, the witness must not deviate from his or her normal professional speech habits and demeanor, however nonjudicial they may seem to the lawyer. There are few circumstances under which an expert should be encouraged to adopt any new patterns of behavior, whether verbal or nonverbal, that the lawyer or witness may feel are more appropriate to the courtroom. The strongest finding that has emerged from the study of language in the courtroom is that jurors make very rapid evaluations of a witness's background and status and then form expectations about the type of linguistic behavior that is appropriate for that witness. When these expectations are confounded, the jurors are likely to react negatively, even punitively.[4] They will prefer, at least on a subconscious level, a witness who speaks in a natural and thus appropriate style to one who alters his or her natural speaking style to conform to someone else's standards. It is significant that human listeners in general apparently are very accurate in their perceptions of what constitutes a natural style for a particular speaker.[5]

Applied to statistical experts, this means that the witness should consider the judge and jury to be competent but inexperienced stu-

---

[3] For a discussion of the effect on jurors of narrative testimony, see O'Barr, supra note 1, at 76-83.

[4] See Conley et al., supra note 2, at 1389-1390; O'Barr, supra note 1, at 83-87. See also H. Giles & P. Powesland, Speech Style and Social Evaluation 37-46 (1975); W. Labov, The Social Stratification of English in New York City (1966).

[5] The general sensitivity of listeners to variations in speech style is illustrated by an experiment performed by one of the authors. The purpose of the experiment was to assess whether the subject jurors were influenced in evaluating a lawyer and a witness by the extent to which the two interrupted each other. The experiment showed that the listeners were influenced by differences in the amount of interruption that were so subtle that they could not be consciously perceived by people who had been instructed to look for them. See Conley et al., supra note 2, at 1390-1391.

dents. The expert should not alter his or her natural demeanor, appearance, tone of voice, or rate of speaking, as any such variations are likely to be noticed and to elicit an adverse reaction. Judges and jurors will expect the statistician to display some mastery of the terminology in the field, so when new concepts or methods are initially introduced, they should be given their real names, which should be used throughout. Consistent with the suggestions made in the preceding section, of course, each time a new term or concept is introduced, it should be explained thoroughly.

In summary, if the judge and jurors have been introduced to a professor of statistics, the presentation should be professorial in style. If the natural style of the professor is irredeemably obscure, or if the professor cannot simplify without taking a condescending approach, the proponent's lawyer is advised not to try to modify the expert's linguistic personality but to get a new expert.

B. EVIDENTIARY PROBLEMS IN PRESENTING STATISTICAL EVIDENCE

The testimony of a statistical expert is likely to be complicated enough without introducing further confusion in the form of frequent objections, bench conferences, and voir dire examinations. The simplest way to minimize such confusion is to identify in advance and plan for those problems that are likely to arise. Much of this will be a matter of standard evidentiary law and practice; a review of that broad topic is beyond the scope of this book. The purpose of this part of Chapter 9 is to treat in some detail a few of the evidentiary issues that have proven to be particularly troublesome in statistical cases. Section 9.3 discusses a number of general issues that recur in the statistical evidence case law, and Section 9.4 is devoted to the single topic of demonstrative evidence, which is treated from both a legal and tactical perspective.

§9.3   General Evidentiary Considerations

On the surface, statistical testimony is simply a variety of expert testimony and is therefore subject to the provisions of Article VII of the Federal Rules of Evidence.[1] The fundamental requirements are set forth in Rule 702, which provides that expert testimony is appropriate in a case in which "scientific, technical or other specialized knowledge will assist the trier of fact to understand the evidence or to determine a fact in issue." In such a case, Rule 702 further provides that expert opinions may be expressed by one "qualified as an expert by knowledge, skill, experience, training, or education."

Rule 703 governs the foundation required for expert testimony and substantially liberalizes the prior common law rules. The facts or data that form the basis of the expert's opinion need not themselves be admissible, as long as they are "of a type reasonably relied upon by experts in the particular field in forming opinions or inferences upon the subject." In addition, the expert need not acquaint himself with the facts beforehand, since he is entitled to rely on "those perceived by or made known to him at or before the hearing." The expert may, for example, listen to and comment on the testimony of an opposing or corroborating expert or may respond to old-fashioned hypothet-

---

§9.3   [1] The full text of Fed. R. Evid. 702-705 is as follows:

Rule 702.   Testimony by Experts

If scientific, technical, or other specialized knowledge will assist the trier of fact to understand the evidence or to determine a fact in issue, a witness qualified as an expert by knowledge, skill, experience, training, or education, may testify thereto in the form of an opinion or otherwise.

Rule 703.   Bases of Opinion Testimony by Experts

The facts or data in the particular case upon which an expert bases an opinion or inference may be those perceived by or made known to him at or before the hearing. If of a type reasonably relied upon by experts in the particular field in forming opinions or inferences upon the subject, the facts or data need not be admissible in evidence.

Rule 704.   Opinion on Ultimate Issue

Testimony in the form of an opinion or inference otherwise admissible is not objectionable because it embraces an ultimate issue to be decided by the trier of fact.

Rule 705.   Disclosure of Facts or Data Underlying Expert Opinion

The expert may testify in terms of opinion or inference and give his reasons therefor without prior disclosure of the underlying facts or data, unless the court requires otherwise. The expert may in any event be required to disclose the underlying facts or data on cross-examination.

The lengthy Advisory Committee Notes following these rules discuss the ways in which they deviate from common law practice.

ical questions. Further departures from the common law are contained in Rule 704, which permits opinions on the ultimate issue to be decided by the trier of fact, and Rule 705, which permits an expert to state an opinion and the reasons for it without reference to the underlying facts or data, subject to the discretion of the court and, of course, to cross-examination.

Perhaps it is predictable that these rules have not been given literal application where statistical evidence is at issue. Many trial judges, while paying lip service to the liberal provisions of the rules, impose far stricter requirements on the proponents of statistical evidence. In many of the cases in which such evidence has been limited, the problem has arisen from the fact that statistical experts have tended to rely heavily on electronic data processing in sorting out the facts and reaching an opinion.

There should be no question about admissibility when the expert bases his or her opinion on computerized data that were compiled prior to litigation in the ordinary course of business (as when, for example, an expert in an employment discrimination case relies on the compilations and analyses in the defendant's affirmative action reports). Such data are admissible in their own right under Rule 803(6) as "Records of regularly conducted activity." This rule specifically includes "data compilations" "if kept in the course of a regularly conducted business activity." The cases have been nearly unanimous for more than 15 years that admissibility is not impaired solely because the compilations are generated electronically.[2] Moreover, the authenticating witness is generally not required to be personally familiar with the data processing techniques employed.[3]

As the Court of Appeals for the Eighth Circuit has noted, however, "computer-generated evidence requires a more substantial evidentiary foundation than is normally offered under the business records exception."[4] In one criminal case, for example, the court required the proponent of a computer-generated business record to show

(1) what the input procedures were, (2) that the input procedures and printouts were accurate within 2 percent, (3) that the computer was

---

[2] See, e.g., United States v. Orozco, 590 F.2d 789 (9th Cir.), *cert. denied,* 442 U.S. 920 (1979).

[3] See Merrick v. U.S. Rubber Co., 440 P.2d 314 (Ariz. App. 1968) (decided under Arizona analog to the federal business records rule).

[4] United States v. Scholle, 553 F.2d 1109, 1125 (8th Cir.), *cert. denied,* 434 U.S. 940 (1977).

tested for internal programming errors on a monthly basis, and (4) that the printouts were made, maintained and relied on by the [proponent] in the ordinary course of its business activities.[5]

It has also been held, again largely in the criminal context, that the proponent of computerized evidence bears a greater burden to permit pretrial review by his or her adversary. In one criminal tax case, for example, the defendant objected on appeal to the prosecution's reliance on an Internal Revenue Service computer printout of nonfiling taxpayers. In reversing the conviction, the Court of Appeals for the Third Circuit held that the IRS was required to give the defendant access to the following prior to the retrial:

(a) all the relevant IRS handbooks documenting the procedures, machine operations, and other relevant information pertaining to its electronic data processing system; (b) statistical analyses relating to the Service's ability to discover and report accurately failures to file returns; (c) an expert familiar with all aspects of the non-filing lists; (d) an expert familiar with all aspects of the processing of work through the Mid-Atlantic Service Center; and (e) an expert who has made studies on the reliability of the Service's data processing systems.[6]

The burdens of proof and disclosure discussed in the preceding paragraphs are extreme and are unlikely to be imposed in civil cases. Nonetheless, the idea that use of computerized evidence imposes a heightened burden on its proponent is also present in the civil case law.

In *Perma Research and Development v. Singer Co.*,[7] a contract case, the plaintiff claimed that the defendant had breached an agreement to develop and market an automotive antiskid device for which the plaintiff had obtained a patent. The key to the plaintiff's successful case was the testimony of two expert witnesses that the device as patented could have been made workable and marketable by the defendant. The testimony of both these witnesses was ultimately based on a computer simulation of the hypothetical device in operation. The validity of the simulation was questioned on appeal, but the Second Circuit held only that "[t]he trial judge did not abuse his

---

[5] United States v. Weatherspoon, 581 F.2d 595, 598 (7th Cir. 1978) (computer printouts introduced by government in fraud case).
[6] United States v. Liebert, 519 F.2d 542, 550 (3rd Cir. 1975).
[7] 542 F.2d 111 (2d Cir. 1976).

discretion in allowing the experts to testify as to this particular basis for their ultimate conclusion."[8]

In a dissenting opinion, however, Judge Van Graafeiland offered an incisive analysis of the dangers that inhere in mathematical modeling in particular and computerized evidence generally. First he questioned the extent to which the simulation of the operation of the antiskid device reflected reality. Noting that "[e]xperts are not exempt from the rules of evidence . . . and their testimony must be based upon established facts," Judge Van Graafeiland criticized the trial court for its failure to insist that the expert's model accurately simulate the device in operation.[9] This is, of course, the same type of criticism to which the plaintiff's analysis was properly subjected in the *Corrugated Container* litigation (see Section 1.12). The problem is endemic to mathematical modeling: regardless of the care taken, any mathematical model is a representation of its creator's view of reality, and its accuracy is thus dependent on the judgments and assumptions made by its creator. Accordingly, the criticism that a particular model is speculative is always available, and the question is merely one of degree.

Judge Van Graafeiland went on to consider the problems arising from the fact that the plaintiff's simulations were done on a computer. While acknowledging that business records should not be suspect merely because they are computerized, he argued that "[w]here . . . a computer is programmed to produce information specifically for purposes of litigation, an entirely different picture is presented."[10] Citing the computer's unique ability "to package hearsay and erroneous or misleading data in an extremely persuasive format," and warning that "[a]n error in programming can be repeated time after time," he suggested that in civil as well as criminal cases the court should require computer inputs and outputs, as well as the analytical program itself, to be made available to the opposing party long in advance of trial.[11]

The concerns expressed by Judge Van Graafeiland about mathematical modeling and computerized evidence are clearly justified, even if somewhat overstated. The rules of evidence provide no simple solution to the difficulties he raises. It is true that expert opinions

[8] Id. at 115.
[9] Id. at 122-123.
[10] Id. at 125.
[11] Id. at 125-126. Judge Van Graafeiland quoted at length from Roberts, A Practitioner's Primer on Computer-Generated Evidence, 41 U. Chi. L. Rev. 254 (1974).

must ultimately be premised on facts; to the extent that the trial judge finds the factual foundation to be inadequate, Judge Van Graafeiland was correct in stating that he has discretion to exclude the opinion.[12] The best way to defeat such objections is to discover and resolve them well in advance of the testimony, through the use of specialized pretrial procedures. These procedures are the subject of Sections 9.5 and 9.6.

§9.4 Demonstrative Evidence

Virtually every presentation of statistical evidence will involve the use of charts, graphs, slides, or some other form of demonstrative evidence. The purpose of this section is, first, to discuss the practical rationale for making extensive use of demonstrative evidence in statistical cases; second, to describe how such evidence can be introduced most effectively; and third, to review those principles of evidence law that will govern its use. The general concerns reviewed in the preceding section are, of course, equally applicable to demonstrative evidence, and this section should therefore be considered in conjunction with Section 9.3.

Psychologists have amply demonstrated the significance of visual cues in the learning process. Research in a variety of contexts has confirmed that in conveying information, a picture may indeed be worth a thousand words.[1] The current popularity of computer learning programs that utilize video display terminals is a variation on this theme.

Many of the reasons for the impact of visual displays are self-evident. First, in a setting where the communication is otherwise oral, a newly introduced visual display attracts attention simply because of its novelty.[2] Second, a visual display is generally far more selective than an oral or written presentation in the information that it attempts to convey. The audience is therefore likely to make the assumption, at least subconsciously, that the information being

---

[12] For useful reviews of the case law on computerized evidence, see Horning, Electronically Stored Evidence, 41 Wash. & Lee L. Rev. 1335 (1984); Fleming, A Guide to the Use of Computers to Estimate Damages in Complex Litigation, 2 Computer L.J. 863 (1980).

§9.4 [1] See generally Vinson, Litigation: An Introduction to the Application of Behavioral Science, 15 Conn. L. Rev. 767, 768-770 (1983).

[2] See id. at 775 (1983).

displayed is of special significance and to give it appropriate attention.[3] Third, it is often far simpler to describe relationships among
people or things in graphic form than it is to describe them verbally.
This principle applies a fortiori when the relationships to be described are mathematical, as when formulas and the results of computations must be presented. Fourth, when a visual display is presented
as a summary of or an adjunct to the written or spoken word, the
entire presentation benefits from what linguists term redundancy.
Natural speech is replete with overlap, repetition, cross-referenc-
ing, adumbration and recapitulation; this redundancy insures the
speaker against imprecise utterances and lapses of attention on the
part of the listener.[4] When natural conversation is reduced to writing
or transformed into formal rhetoric, much of this natural redundancy tends to be lost. Combining visual and oral cues can rein-
troduce this helpful element in a way that is likely to be inoffensive to
the listener. Finally, visual displays have the virtue of relative perma-
nency. Once missed by the listener, the spoken word cannot be retrieved, but when a visual display is permitted to sit before the
audience it is possible for the viewer to assimilate information that was
initially missed, to dwell on material not initially understood, and to
review points of apparent significance. In addition, a visual display
that remains before the members of the audience provides a focus for
their attention if they lose interest during the subsequent verbal presentation.[5]

All of these considerations are directly applicable to statistical
evidence. Without visual cues the explanation of even the simplest
mathematical relationship can be convoluted. The conceptual basis
for a particular statistical method can often be conveyed simply and
effectively in graphic form; this representation will give the listener
an anchor that will hold fast even when the detailed presentation of
the analysis begins to drift away. And when the analysis generates
results that are numerically compelling (e.g., that women were paid
32% less than comparably qualified men in a given year), those results
should not be spoken and forgotten but should remain before the
factfinder for as long as the court will permit.

---

[3] For a discussion of selective attention and perception, see id. at 770-772 and
sources cited therein.
[4] See J. Lyons, Introduction to Theoretical Linguistics 84-90 (1971 ed.).
[5] The human attention span is limited and is thought by many not to exceed 20
minutes. Vinson, Psychological Anchors: Influencing the Jury, 8 Litig. 20-22 (1982).

Specifically, the demonstrative evidence in a statistical case should typically include at least the following categories of exhibits:

1. *A summary of the data base.* In a plaintiff's employment discrimination case, for example, this exhibit might consist of a blowup of one of the defendant's employment records, with each of the items of information that the plaintiff has extracted underlined and briefly defined. This exhibit will emphasize to the trier of fact the completeness of the plaintiff's data collection effort and will assist in shifting to the defendant the burden of accounting for any apparent lacunae in the data (as when, for example, the plaintiff has not used "undergraduate major" as an independent variable in a regression analysis designed to predict salary because it was not regularly recorded in the defendant's records).

2. *An outline of the method of analysis to be employed.* An outline of the plaintiff's regression analysis described in Section 1.12 (the *Corrugated Container* litigation), for example, might take the form depicted in Exhibit 9.4(a). Its purpose would be to demonstrate the historical basis for the predictive use of the analysis and to dramatize the plaintiff's view of the "but for" effect of the alleged conspiracy on price trends.

3. *A glossary of a few essential terms.* The glossary should be limited to those technical terms that recur and are truly necessary to an appreciation of the statistical case. The glossary will serve to underscore the importance of the terms included, will provide the judge and jurors with a means to reacquaint themselves with particular terms as they are reintroduced into the testimony, and will assist in the process of developing solidarity between the expert and the trier of fact, as described in Section 9.1. Each time a technical term is used, the availability of the glossary will remind the judge and jury that the expert (and by extension, his or her proponent) has invited them to share the information

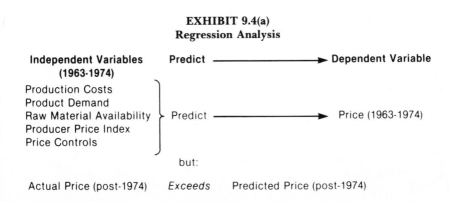

EXHIBIT 9.4(a)
Regression Analysis

EXHIBIT 9.4(b)
Average Salary — Men v. Comparably Qualified Women
1978-1980

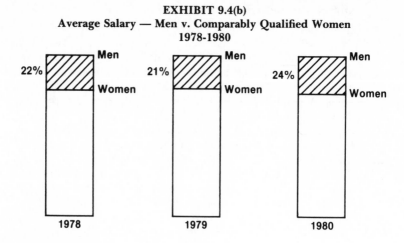

that is the key to the expert's identity and the source of his or her power.

4. *A summary of results.* The utility of keeping favorable results before the trier of fact requires no explanation. Pay close attention, however, to the form in which results are presented. A regression analysis in an employment discrimination case, for example, may show that women received 78% of the pay given to comparably qualified men. It is equally accurate and perhaps more effective, however, to say that women received 22% less pay. It may be even more effective — but still accurate — to state the results in terms of the pay gap between comparably qualified men and women, as depicted in Exhibit 9.4(b). (See also Section 2.7.3, where various types of graphics are discussed.)

Finally, a general word about the form in which statistical exhibits are presented: it is recommended that the principal exhibit in each of the four categories be presented in the form of a large chart, slide, or overhead projection transparency. These methods of presentation offer three advantages: (1) they make a striking visual impression; (2) their use disrupts the normal and expected sequence of events in the courtroom because the witness is required to move about the courtroom to discuss the exhibits, thus drawing attention to the testimony; and, (3) with an academic expert, the use of such teaching aids will strike a familiar chord and facilitate the process of acclimating the witness to the courtroom.

In preparing a graph or other display, the goals are to make it simple and at the same time to make it stand out against the visual and verbal background. Considerations of simplicity generally dictate that no more than one concept or idea be presented on a single exhibit. For the same reason, unnecessary detail should be avoided. Thus, if the point to be conveyed is that in a given year women made an average of $3,200 less than comparably qualified men, that information and that information alone should be presented. The statistical details underlying that conclusion will have a place in the testimony, but not on the key exhibit that presents the conclusion.

Judges and jurors quickly adapt to the level of stimulation they are receiving in the courtroom at any given moment; this level forms the background against which new stimuli are perceived. To some extent, any visual aid will distinguish itself from that background, since most courtroom stimuli are verbal. This inherent distinctiveness can be enhanced in several ways, however. First, the selective use of color to highlight key points is particularly effective, since colored documents are an endangered species in this age of photocopying. Second, the size of a visual display is correlated with the amount of attention it initially receives; important points should be stated in large letters. And third, where mathematically permissible, graphs should be designed to convey a sense of motion and thus of urgency. A jagged line, for example, is likely to be more persuasive than a smooth curve as an illustration of change.[6]

It is also recommended that all exhibits be reproduced on eight and one-half by eleven inch paper and included in a looseleaf binder that is distributed to the judge and jurors. The use of such exhibit books is at the discretion of the trial judge, and the practice is increasingly tolerated, if not encouraged. Many judges are also now willing to permit note-taking in complex cases.[7] If so, the jurors should be instructed on any limits that the court will place on the use of notes, and blank paper should be provided in the exhibit book. These matters should be taken up with the court and decided at the pretrial stage.

Whatever method of presentation is chosen, the admissibility of demonstrative evidence should be clarified as much as possible before the expert testifies (see Section 9.5). Statistical evidence is complicated enough; its intrinsic complexity need not be exacerbated by distract-

---

[6] For a discussion of adaptation level and stimulus perception in the courtroom, see Vinson, supra note 1, at 776-778.

[7] See generally Note, Taking Note of Note-Taking, 10 Colum. J.L. & Soc. Prob. 565 (1974).

ing sequences of objections, responses, and rulings.[8] The local rules of many federal courts require that the parties exchange and attempt to stipulate to the admissibility of exhibits prior to trial; provision is also made for the court to rule on those items that remain in dispute.[9] In the absence of such a local rule, or in addition to whatever relief the rule may give, either party may move for a pretrial conference pursuant to Rule 16 of the Federal Rules of Civil Procedure. Among the items that are appropriate for discussion at a Rule 16 conference is "the possibility of obtaining admissions of fact and of documents which will avoid unnecessary proof."

If a stipulation or ruling in limine cannot be obtained, Rule 1006 of the Federal Rules of Evidence provides the most direct route to the admission of most demonstrative evidence in statistical cases. That rule, captioned "Summaries," provides that "[t]he contents of voluminous writings, recordings or photographs which cannot conveniently be examined in court may be presented in the form of a chart, summary, or calculation," provided that the underlying documents are made available for inspection.[10] Rule 1006 is literally applicable to exhibits that summarize the results of statistical analyses embodied in pages of notes and computer printouts. (The use of Rule 1006 presumes that the data being summarized are themselves admissible, or that they are being disclosed, although not necessarily admitted, as sources of the expert's opinion under Rule 705. See Section 9.3.) Most courts will require only that the expert testify as a matter of personal knowledge that the chart accurately summarizes the underlying calculations.[11] Rule 1006 is less obviously applicable to glossaries and exhibits that outline methods of analysis. Nonetheless, courts will often

---

[8] It is widely believed that objections call attention to the evidence being objected to, but the impact of objections on jurors has not been studied in detail. See W. O'Barr, Linguistic Evidence 102-104 (1982); R. Keeton, Trial Tactics and Methods 167 (2d ed. 1973).

[9] See, e.g., M.D. Tenn. Local Rules 11(a)(6-7), 12(c)(1-4).

[10] The text of Fed. R. Evid. 1006 is as follows:

Rule 1006. Summaries

The contents of voluminous writings, recordings, or photographs which cannot conveniently be examined in court may be presented in the form of a chart, summary, or calculation. The originals, or duplicates, shall be made available for examination or copying, or both, by other parties at reasonable time and place. The court may order that they be produced in court.

[11] For a detailed discussion of the use of Rule 1006, see Manual for Complex Litigation (West 1982) §2.71.

treat these exhibits as being covered by the rule, on the theory that they condense otherwise lengthy testimony based in part on the personal knowledge of the witness and in part on sources on which statisticians regularly rely. Again, if the Rule 1006 theory is used, federal judges will typically require foundation testimony to the effect that the exhibit accurately summarizes the views of the expert.

Alternatively, recourse can be had to Rule 901, which deals with authentication and identification. Authentication is, as the Advisory Committee Note to Rule 901 indicates, "a special aspect of relevancy." To the extent that the entire line of expert testimony is relevant, exhibits summarizing the expert's views, premises, and results should also be relevant, subject to authentication. Pursuant to Rule 901(a), this requires only "evidence sufficient to support a finding that the matter in question is what its proponent claims." More specifically, Rule 901(b)(1) provides that this general requirement may be satisfied by testimony of a "witness with knowledge" "that a matter is what it is claimed to be." In the context of expert exhibits, the requirement can usually be met by testimony that the expert is personally familiar with the contents of the exhibit and with the information that underlies it, has supervised the preparation of the exhibit, and can state on personal knowledge that it is a fair and accurate representation of the underlying information.

C. PRETRIAL PROCEDURES FOR STATISTICAL EVIDENCE

The preceding sections highlighted several evidentiary pitfalls a lawyer is likely to encounter in presenting a statistical case. In a number of contexts, it was suggested that these pitfalls can be avoided by the use of pretrial procedures specially tailored to statistical cases. This part of the chapter describes a pretrial program that may reduce delays during trial, improve the quality of the presentations being made to the trier of fact, and improve the effectiveness of the trial judge's management of the case. Section 9.5 deals with several recommendations made by the Federal Judicial Center in its Manual for Complex Litigation that are particularly appropriate for use in statistical cases. Section 9.6 reviews a series of procedural "protocols" for statistical cases and offers practical suggestions for their implementation.

§9.5 The Manual for Complex Litigation

A number of generally useful pretrial procedures are described in the Manual for Complex Litigation, which is used in the trial of complex and multidistrict cases in the federal courts. In preparing the Manual, the Federal Judicial Center gave careful consideration to the problems posed by computerized evidence. In §2.7.1 of the manual, entitled Proof of Facts in Complex Cases, a series of recommendations are made concerning the introduction of scientific evidence. The first, fourth, fifth, and sixth recommendations relate directly to computerized evidence, and their use may help to solve many of the evidentiary problems discussed in Section 9.3 and 9.4.[1]

The first recommendation is that voluminous or complicated data that are themselves of an admissible character should be presented in the form of summaries, charts, or graphs. This recommendation is made on the authority of Rule 1006 of the Federal Rules of Evidence and is conditioned on disclosure of underlying data to opposing counsel well in advance of trial. The manual advises that underlying data not be placed in evidence at all.[2]

The fourth recommendation is that in appropriate circumstances the use and admissibility of computer-maintained records and com-

---

§9.5 [1] The second and third recommendations deal with the specific problem of using polls and samples as evidence or the basis for conclusions put in evidence. They provide as follows:

   Second Recommendation. Scientifically designed samples and polls, meeting the tests of necessity and trustworthiness, are useful adjuncts to conventional methods of proof and may contribute materially to shortening the trial of the complex case.
   Third Recommendation. The underlying data, method of interpretation employed, and conclusions reached in polls and samples should be made available to the opposing party far in advance of trial, and, if possible, prior to the taking of the poll or sample. [Federal Judicial Center, Manual for Complex Litigation (West 1982)] §2.712-3 at 112, 117.

As should be evident from the substantive chapters of this book, samples are often used in statistical analyses, and specific reference should be made to these recommendations in preparing and presenting such analyses.

[2] First Recommendation. Voluminous or complicated data of an admissible character should, whenever possible, be presented through written or oral summaries, tabulations, charts, graphs, or extracts. The underlying data, together with the proposed exhibits or summary testimony, should be made available to opposing counsel well in advance of the time they are to be offered, to permit all objections to be raised and if possible resolved prior to the offer. Underlying data should not be placed in evidence in the ordinary case. [Id. §2.711 at 110 (footnote omitted).]

puter analyses of raw data "should be promoted and facilitated."[3] Again, admissibility will be conditioned on advance disclosure of "[c]omputer inputs and outputs, the underlying data, and the program methods employed."[4] The fifth recommendation suggests that extensive discovery should be permitted concerning these required disclosures.[5]

The sixth recommendation, which specifies the form in which the disclosures are to be made, is in several respects an elaboration of the fourth.[6] Its basic premise is that computer-generated records should generally be admissible, regardless of whether they are kept in the ordinary course of business or prepared specifically for use at trial, as long as they are probative and certain disclosure procedures have been followed. These procedures call for the offering party to do a series of things "well in advance of trial":

(a) demonstrate that the procedures for input of the data base conform to the practice in the business or profession of the person from whom the evidence is obtained;

(b) in the case of a printout prepared especially for trial, demonstrate that the data base was used in making a business or professional judgment within a reasonable time prior to the preparation of the printout to be introduced;

---

[3] Fourth Recommendation. When computer-maintained records and computer analyses of raw data are valuable sources of evidence, their use and admissibility should be promoted and facilitated. Computer inputs and outputs, the underlying data, and the program method employed should be made available to the opposing party in advance of trial as a condition of admissibility. [Id. §2.714 at 117.]

[4] Id.

[5] Fifth Recommendation. Discovery requests relating to the computer and its programs, inputs, and outputs should be processed using methods consistent with the approach used in discovery of other types of information. [Id. §2.715 at 118.]

[6] Sixth Recommendation. Computer-maintained records kept in the regular course of business and printouts prepared especially for litigation should be admitted if the court finds that reliable computer equipment and techniques have been used and that the material is of probative value. The court should therefore require, well in advance of trial, that (a) the offering party demonstrate that the input procedures conform to the standard practice of persons engaged in the business or profession of the party or person from whom the printout is obtained; (b) in the case of a printout prepared especially for trial, the offering party demonstrate that the person from whom the printout is obtained relied on the data base in making a business or professional judgment within a reasonably short period of time before producing the printout sought to be introduced; (c) the offering party provide expert testimony that the processing program reliably and accurately processes the data in the data base; and (d) the opposing party be given the opportunity to depose the offeror's witness and to engage a witness of its own to evaluate the processing procedure. [Id. §2.716 at 121.]

(c) provide an expert opinion that the program that has been used reliably and accurately processes the data in the data base;

(d) make available for deposition the witness through whom the computerized evidence will be introduced.[7]

Taken together, the fourth, fifth, and sixth recommendations contemplate a procedure that will obviate most objections, and in any event permit them to be ruled on in limine. In the absence of an agreement or stipulation, the Manual suggests, the foundation testimony at trial should consist of statements by the person who supervised the data processing concerning the validity of the methods used, the reliability of the computer, the accuracy of the inputs, the validity of the programming, and the accuracy and completeness of the outputs.[8]

While the Manual for Complex Litigation applies only to a limited number of cases, an informal version of its recommended procedures can be urged on the court in any case involving computerized evidence. The experience of the authors suggests that such a recommendation is likely to be received enthusiastically because of the potential for shortening and simplifying the trial. Several other procedures that relate specifically to statistical evidence can be recommended on the same basis.

§9.6 Finkelstein's Protocols

In two important law review articles, Michael Finkelstein, a leading practitioner of statistical evidence, has advocated a series of "protocols" to be used in cases involving complex statistical proof.[1] The protocols consist of both conceptual suggestions and concrete recommendations for procedural improvements. Although his protocols were developed in the context of administrative proceedings, they are readily extensible to judicial matters.[2] As will be seen, their use com-

---

[7] See id.

[8] Id. §2.714 at 118.

§9.6 [1] Finkelstein, Regression Models in Administrative Proceedings, 86 Harv. L. Rev. 1442 (1973), reprinted in M. Finkelstein, Quantitative Methods in Law, ch. 7 (1978); Finkelstein, The Judicial Reception of Multiple Regression Studies in Race and Sex Discrimination Cases, 80 Colum. L. Rev. 737 (1980).

[2] The thrust of Finkelstein's protocols is embodied in a set of proposed litigation procedures drafted by a committee of the Bar of the City of New York. Special Committee on Empirical Data in Legal Decision Making, Recommendations on Pretrial

plements perfectly the use of the recommendations in the Manual for Complex Litigation discussed in the preceding section.

The protocols are as follows (in italics), with comments concerning their applicability to statistical evidence:

1. *A decisionmaker* [judge or administrative body] *should (1) specify the data of such relevance and importance that he finds merit econometric* [or, by extension, other statistical] *analysis, and (2) require that econometric* [statistical] *presentations begin with those data and incorporate other data on a separate basis only when necessary for purposes of accuracy or refinement.*[3] That is, at an early conference, the judge should agree with the parties on what the appropriate data base is, and then direct that the parties focus their analytical efforts on it. Such an approach will minimize irrelevant and thus potentially misleading statistical analysis, will shorten and simplify the trial, and will avoid the all too common problem of the parties trying two different cases because they believe two different sets of data to be significant.

Key v. The Gillette Company:[4] The plaintiff was certified as a representative of a class comprising women who held salaried positions with Gillette in Massachusetts during the years 1968-1975, inclusive. At trial, the plaintiff's expert presented a regression analysis that purported to show that in each of the class years women were paid approximately 20% less than men who were equivalent on all of the qualifications reflected in Gillette's records. The plaintiff's analysis excluded only those employees for whom the records were incomplete. Gillette countered with a regression analysis that was similar in method but that for a variety of reason excluded the first four years of the class period and focused on employees in a limited number of technical jobs. In an opinion that was vacated by the court of appeals, the district court, perhaps confused by the conflicting data bases, decertified the class and declined even to consider the merits of the plaintiff's statistics-based claim of classwide discrimination.

2. *(1) A party objecting to an econometric* [statistical] *model introduced by another party should demonstrate the numerical significance of his objec-*

Proceedings in Cases with Voluminous Data, 30 The Record of the Assoc. of the Bar of the City of New York 49 (1984).

[3] M. Finkelstein, Quantitative Methods in Law 232-233 (1978).

[4] No. 75-4934-C (D. Mass. June 21, 1982) *vacated* and *remanded*, No. 82-1601 (1st Cir. Jan. 1, 1983). There has been no further action since the court of appeals vacated the district's order decertifying the class. There is thus no decision yet on the merits of the class claims. The district court's interlocutory order on class certification, the only reported opinion in the case, appears at 90 F.R.D. 606 (D. Mass. 1981).

tions whenever possible, and (2) A party objecting to an econometric [statistical] model of data designated by the decisionmaker for econometric [statistical] analysis should produce a superior alternative analysis of those data.[5] The first branch of this protocol requires two things: that objections to the adversary's analysis be stated in concrete and quantitative rather than speculative terms and that an objecting party produce a better alternative. The first point is reasonably self-evident and has been made in a number of cases. Simply put, a number of courts have required that a party seeking to overcome the prima facie effect of a statistical analysis must state as precisely as possible what *is* wrong with the analysis and cannot prevail by suggesting that a number of things *might be* wrong with it.[6] The second branch provides that when certain data have been designated for analysis by the court, a party cannot prevail merely by criticizing the other party's model; it must present an alternative. The true significance of this requirement is found in the third protocol.

3. *In any case in which the decisionmaker resorts to significant use of econometric [statistical] findings, he should select the model that most usefully describes the data and should base his findings on that model.*[7] This means that a statistical case should not be treated in the way that real estate valuation cases frequently are, with the trier of fact merely selecting the value midway between those proposed by the two experts. The reason for this is that competing statistical analyses typically do not differ because of the inclusion of divergent subjective judgments about the value of something. Rather, they differ in discrete ways because the two sides have made differing assumptions about the data and/or have chosen different analytical approaches. Accordingly, two divergent statistical analyses will tend to be more comparable to an apple and an orange than to two oranges of different sizes. For a court arbitrarily to pick the midpoint between the two, Finkelstein argues, would be a rejection of the whole rational scientific process on which the use of statistical evidence is premised. If a court permits statistical evidence to be used, he contends, it must be ready, willing, and able to play by the rules of the statistical game.[8]

[5] M. Finkelstein, supra note 3, at 238.
[6] E.g., Trout v. Hidalgo, 517 F. Supp. 873, 881 (D.D.C. 1981), *modified sub nom.* Trout v. Lehman, 702 F.2d 1094 (D.C. Cir. 1983); Mecklenburg v. Montana State Bd. of Regents, 13 Empl. Prac. Dec. ¶11,438 at 6495 (D. Mont. 1976). See generally Teamsters v. United States, 431 U.S. 324, 360 (1977).
[7] M. Finkelstein, supra note 3, at 244.
[8] Id. at 245-246.

CAB Fare Case:[9] In the era of regulated airline fares, one of the factors that the Civil Aeronautics Board was required to consider was the likely effect of a proposed fare increase on air traffic. In the 1971 industrywide fare setting proceeding, the Board's Bureau of Economics introduced two statistical studies of the impact of fares on traffic, each based on different data. The first showed that air travel would decline by about 1.25% for every 1% increase in fares; the second showed a 1.27% decline for each 1% fare increase. Two of the largest airlines attacked these studies with analyses of their own. TWA's study showed a decline of only .57% and United's, a decline of .58%.

The board rejected all of the competing models. It settled instead on a compromise figure of .7%. While such a midpoint compromise may have intuitive appeal to the layperson, Finkelstein argues, "[t]he choice of a value that lies between the estimates of two different models . . . is in reality consistent with the assumptions of neither, so that the compromise would lack any evidentiary support."[10]

(4) *A finding resting in substantial part on data which have been analyzed econometrically* [statistically] *should be no more precise than the finding which the decisionmaker is prepared to accept on the basis of the econometric* [statistical] *analysis.*[11] This means that the court should never purport to make a finding which is any more precise or definite than those proposed in the analyses submitted by the parties. If the court is concerned about the precision or accuracy of the competing analyses, then a fortiori it should not use a less refined, more intuitive method to arrive at a conclusion more precise than those that it has rejected.

CAB Fare Case:[12] In the fare-setting case just discussed, an expert for the airlines could reasonably have argued that in the future the decrease in traffic resulting from a 1% increase in fares was likely to be somewhat less than the 1.25% suggested by the Board's Bureau of Economics. The basis for such an argument would have been that in 1971 it seemed likely that rail passenger service would continue to deteriorate, but this factor was not considered by the Board. Under the reasoning of the fourth protocol, however, such an expert opinion would not be an adequate basis for choosing any particular percentage figure between those proposed by the bureau and those proposed by

---

[9] Domestic Passenger Fare Investigation Phase 7, No. 21866-7 (C.A.B., April 9, 1971). This proceeding is discussed in M. Finkelstein, supra note 3, at 240-245.
[10] Id. at 243.
[11] Id. at 247.
[12] Domestic Passenger Fare Investigation Phase 7, No. 21866-7 (C.A.B., April 9, 1971).

the airlines. If the omitted variable seems to be of substantial practical significance, the only statistically reasonable solution is to create a new model that includes the variable.

While Finkelstein's protocols may prove too detailed for a particular case, their general premises, taken in the context of the evidentiary points already discussed, support a number of suggestions that should prove helpful in all cases involving statistical evidence. *First*, as early in the case as possible counsel should jointly request a pretrial conference for the purpose of introducing the court to the contemplated statistical evidence. At the conference they should disclose the fact that they will be relying on statistical evidence, and should describe in qualitative terms the nature of the analyses being performed. Both sides can use this conference to assess the court's experience with and receptivity to statistical analysis.

Second, at a similarly early stage of the case, the opposing attorneys should take up between themselves the issue of the data base. It is often useful to include the experts in these discussions. Ideally, the two sides can agree that a precisely defined body of data is the relevant one. Absent such an agreement, there are at least two options. Under the authority of Rule 16 of the Federal Rules of Civil Procedure, a further pretrial conference can be held, and the parties can request the court to listen to arguments in support of the competing data bases and then to issue an order limiting the evidence to analysis of one of them. Although it is often difficult for courts to schedule lengthy pretrial conferences, this conference can eliminate considerable trial time and greatly simplify the process of decision. On this basis, the court should be strongly urged to listen briefly to the statisticians for the two sides and to ask them questions.

As an alternative to or perhaps prior to a conference on the scope of the data, the issue can be focused and sometimes even obviated by the careful use of requests to admit under Rule 36 of the Federal Rules of Civil Procedure. A plaintiff in an employment discrimination case, for example, can request the defendant employer to admit (a) that the personnel records that have been turned over in discovery are complete and accurate, and (b) that there are no sources or compilations of the information contained in those records other than the ones that have been made available. Such admissions will force the defendant to take a position on the question of the adequacy of its records and will foreclose objections that the plaintiff has relied on an inferior source of employment information when he or she could readily have discovered a more adequate source. If the data are reasonably concise, the plaintiff can take the process a step further by compiling the data in a form suitable for analysis and by then requesting that the defendant admit the accuracy of the compilation. Since Rule 36 requires considerable specificity in a party's responses, the rule can be used to identify or eliminate purely factual objections to a proposed data base, thereby leaving for the court only questions of legal relevancy.[13] The defendant employer can of course use the same process to compel the plaintiff to identify what, if any, inaccuracies he or she has discovered in the employer's records.

Third, if the case will turn on competing statistical analyses, the parties should urge on the court Finkelstein's point that an intuitively based compromise would be unsupported by the evidence. This can be done by suggestion and argument at a pretrial conference, and also in several more formal ways. If the case is to be tried to the court, the parties should agree that proposed findings of fact and conclusions of law and proposed forms of judgment should be couched only in terms of the results dictated by the competing analyses. The parties might even enter a stipulation that judgment be entered only in the form recommended by one of them. In a jury case the same effect can be achieved if the parties agree upon or the court otherwise provides a set of jury instructions and a special-verdict form that require the jury to accept one of the two analyses or reject both, with no room for compromise.[14]

Achieving an agreement on the third set of recommendations may be difficult. From the perspective of the plaintiff's counsel, acceding to these recommendations may be at odds with the traditional view that plaintiffs should ask for the highest figure reasonably supported by the evidence and hope for a compromise on a lesser but still substantial award. The third set of recommendations calls for an all-or-nothing approach.

[13] Fed. R. Civ. P. 36(a) imposes the following requirements on a party answering a request for admission:

> The answer shall specifically deny the matter or set forth in detail the reasons why the answering party cannot truthfully admit or deny the matter. A denial shall fairly meet the substance of the requested admission, and when good faith requires that a party qualify his answer or deny only a part of the matter of which an admission is requested, he shall specify so much of it as true and qualify or deny the remainder. An answering party may not give lack of information or knowledge as a reason for failure to admit or deny unless he states that he has made reasonable inquiry and that the information known or readily obtainable by him is insufficient to enable him to admit or deny.

[14] Under Fed. R. Civ. P. 49, the court may require the jury to return a special verdict that contains a specific written finding on each issue of fact or may require a general verdict supported by answers to specific interrogatories.

Before rejecting these recommendations, however, the plaintiff's counsel should consider an important factor. Experienced trial lawyers will be familiar with the general reluctance of factfinders to give litigants exactly what they are asking for; this tendency is consistent with the adage that every claim or defense is worth something. Under the recommended approach, however, a judge or jury that is persuaded of the existence of discrimination or other proscribed conduct has no choice but to accept the plaintiff's calculation of damages, and the opportunity to win precisely the relief sought is thus enhanced.

D. ATTACKING STATISTICAL EVIDENCE: CROSS-EXAMINATION

Previous sections have dealt with a number of substantive and stylistic considerations to be taken into account when planning and presenting a case based on statistical evidence. This part of the chapter examines similar issues from the perspective of a lawyer who must attack a statistical case through cross-examination.

The general theory of cross-examination is amply if not exhaustively covered in the trial practice literature, and is well beyond the scope of this book. Several principles take on special significance, however, when the subject of the cross-examination is a statistical expert. These principles are the subject of the sections that follow. The purpose of the sections that follow is to alert the cross-examiner to a number of potential opportunities and, by negative implication, to warn the expert of a number of potential pitfalls. The suggestions made fall into two categories: Section 9.7 reviews substantive considerations, which relate to the background and preparation of the expert and the content of his or her testimony; while Section 9.8 reviews considerations of form, which relate to the manner in which substantive opportunities can be most effectively exploited. Section 9.9 summarizes the cross-examination of statistical experts.

§9.7 Considerations of Substance

In the cross-examination of experts, much emphasis has traditionally been placed on qualifications, adequacy of preparation, consistency between testimony and prior statements, errors in methodology, and the appropriate breadth of the opinions offered.[1] Each of these factors may have particular significance in a statistical case.

§9.7.1 Qualifying an Expert

Pursuant to Rule 702 of the Federal Rules of Evidence, qualification an expert depends on "knowledge, skill, experience, training, or education."[2] As discussed in Section 9.3, the standard is a broad one; the rule should be and tends to be liberally construed in favor of qualification.[3] Where there is serious question about an expert's qualifications, and where the testimony will be harmful, the appropriate response is for the opponent to ask for a voir dire or preliminary cross-examination on the issue prior to the rendering of the opinion and then to seek a preliminary ruling from the court.[4] More typically, however, opposing counsel will conclude that the expert is less than ideally qualified, but probably sufficiently so to satisfy Rule 702. Under such circumstances, the opponent will surely want to bring the qualification issue to the attention of the trier of fact, even though there is limited likelihood of precluding or striking the testimony. A tactical question then arises as to whether to attack the expert's qualifications in a preliminary examination limited to that issue or during the course of a full cross-examination after the expert has testified.

If there is little realistic hope of disqualifying the witness and the objective of the inquiry is therefore to impeach, deferring the inquiry until full cross-examination would seem to be the more prudent choice in almost all circumstances. An ultimately unsuccessful preliminary examination is likely to have three effects on the trier of fact,

---

§9.7 [1] See generally T. Mauet, Fundamentals of Trial Techniques 288-290 (1980); J. Conley & J. Marcellino, The Computer Professional as Expert Witness 11-12 (Monograph published by Nat. Computer Conference, Las Vegas, Nev., 1984); Goldstein Trial Technique, ch. 16 (2d ed. 1969 and 1983 Supp., I. Goldstein & F. Lane, eds.); R. Keeton, Trial Tactics and Methods 155-162 (2d ed. 1973).

[2] Fed. R. Evid. 702. The full text of the rule reads: "If scientific, technical, or other specialized knowledge will assist the trier of fact to understand the evidence or to determine a fact in issue, a witness qualified as an expert by knowledge, skill, experience, training, or education, may testify thereto in the form of an opinion or otherwise."

[3] See Fed. R. Evid. 702, Notes of Advisory Committee on Proposed Rules.

[4] See Goldstein Trial Technique, supra note 1, §11.17.

all of them undesirable, according to the theory of courtroom communication that has been advanced in Sections 9.1 and 9.2. First, in a jury case if the preliminary inquiry is done in the presence of the jurors, it will be different from anything they have experienced with other witnesses, and it will therefore stand out against the background. The expert's testimony as a whole is thus likely to receive a mental asterisk in the minds of the jurors.

Second, the preliminary inquiry will almost inevitably result in multiple repetition. Experience suggests that in a preliminary examination, since the very survival of the expert is at issue, the court is likely to be liberal in allowing statement and restatement of qualifications the expert deems relevant. The judge is thus likely to permit the expert to be expansive in responding to hostile questions and to allow the expert's proponent ample opportunity to ask redirect questions. If some of the expert's accomplishments are individually impressive, even if arguably inadequate when taken together to qualify him or her to testify, opposing counsel will presumably wish to avoid such repetition.

Third, and perhaps most important in a jury case, if the court concludes that the expert is indeed qualified, it will do so against the background of an unusual and thus memorable dispute. Such a judgment is likely to have a greater impact on jurors than a perfunctory ruling on qualification after an uncontested tender of the expert. As the expert then moves into the substance of his or her testimony, he or she will do so wearing the mantle of one who has been tested and officially approved.[5]

If the decision is made to defer the qualification issue until full cross-examination, questioning should be limited to those areas in which the expert has a demonstrable shortcoming. The cross-examination literature directs the attention of the cross-examiner to such matters as academic background, jobs held, the nature of the work performed in those jobs, publications, and honors received.[6] These factors may be highly significant in a statistical case, and certainly should not be neglected.

In a statistical case, however, the most significant opportunities

---

[5] This is another aspect of the concept of solidarity discussed in Section 9.1. The jurors' evaluation of the expert will surely be enhanced if they sense that there is some solidarity between the expert and the court. Having the court state that the expert has been found to be qualified can only help to create such an impression.

[6] See Goldstein Trial Technique, supra note 1, §16.26; J. Conley & J. Marcellino, supra, note 1, at 11-12; R. Keeton, supra note 1, at 159-162.

for cross-examination may arise from a single problem, that being the enormity of the task imposed on the expert. As the reader should now appreciate, the ability to perform a complex analysis (as opposed to the ability to try a case involving such an analysis) presupposes a broad knowledge of statistical theory and substantial experience with its manifold applications. Except in unusual circumstances, the requisite ability is likely to be possessed only by one who is engaged full-time in the business of statistics, whether in academics or industry. The corollary of this proposition is that one who has the appropriate statistical capabilities will be most unlikely to have personal knowledge of the business of the client. While any good expert will insist on some acquaintance with the realities underlying the statistics, most will have to admit that their analyses are designed to shed some light on behavior that they have had little or no opportunity to observe firsthand.

Where these circumstances obtain, the expert will be faced with a difficult dilemma; concomitantly, of course, the cross-examiner will have an important opportunity. Consider the example of a statistician testifying on behalf of an automobile manufacturer in an employment discrimination case. Even though she is an eminent university professor, the statistician has never been employed in the automobile industry; her only relevant practical experience has been as a consumer and an occasional home repair person. Knowing this, the cross-examiner might begin by asking the witness to assent to the proposition that she is dealing only in statistical abstractions, and does not know whether the defendant, through its officers and employees, has engaged in any specific discriminatory acts. If the answer is in the affirmative, the opportunities for closing argument are obvious. Presumably, the expert will resist, saying that although she is unable to probe people's minds, the results she has observed would be most unlikely to have occurred in the absence of discrimination. The cross-examiner will then suggest that the expert, under the guise of probability, is in effect passing judgment on the behavior of people whose character, performance, and work environment she has never actually observed.[7]

---

[7] A comparable exchange occurred between the plaintiff's counsel and the defendant's expert in the trial of the case of Key v. The Gillette Co. The defendant's expert ultimately admitted, "I'm expressing no opinion at all about discrimination at Gillette." Key v. The Gillette Co., No. 82-1601 (1st Cir., January 1, 1983), appendix at 673. This statement played a prominent part in the plaintiff's posttrial brief, request for findings and rulings, and appellate brief.

The only reported opinion in this case is the district court's interlocutory order

Given the limited purpose of statistical evidence, such a line of questioning is in one sense unfair; its potential, however, particularly in a jury case, is equally obvious. While the authors are aware of no relevant empirical studies, recent electoral history alone would suggest that Americans are becoming increasingly resistant to the notion of their lives being influenced, if not controlled, by distant and impersonal managers of information. An independent statistician can easily be cast as just such a villain.

From the expert's perspective, there are no simple answers to this line of questioning. The expert must adhere to a proper definition of the role of statistical evidence and not claim the ability to do more than draw inferences. Any negative effects of such necessary candor must be neutralized elsewhere in the case. First, whenever possible, and whether representing a plaintiff or a defendant, a lawyer should avoid making statistical evidence the only evidence in a case. Any evidence of individual acts of discrimination that is available to the plaintiff should be offered; similarly, allegedly discriminating officials who protest their innocence should be given a chance to defend themselves in court. In each case, the purpose is to prevent a contest between a statistical inference and the sworn testimony of a human being. As a theoretical matter, it is not the purpose of statistics to prove that a particular witness is not telling the truth; as a practical matter, common sense suggests that the human being will usually win the contest. It is more consistent with the limited purpose of statistical evidence and far preferable from a practical standpoint if, for example, an inculpatory statistical inference (that the observed salary discrepancies are most unlikely to have occurred in a nondiscriminatory environment) and individual testimony about alleged acts of discrimination can be presented as mutually corroborating evidence.[8]

It should also be emphasized that the cross-examiner's ability to portray the statistical expert as a manipulative outsider will be limited

---

certifying the class. 90 F.R.D. 606 (D. Mass. 1981). After trial the district court issued an opinion in which it decertified the class but reached no judgment on the merits of the class claims. No. 75-4934-C (D. Mass. June 21, 1982). This opinion was vacated and remanded by the First Circuit in the opinion cited above.

[8] For an interesting example of the interaction between statistical and individual evidence, see Marsh v. Eton Corp., 639 F.2d 328 (6th Cir. 1981). The majority found discrimination on the basis of statistics alone, even though the sample size in the analysis was suspect, while one dissenting judge pointed out that there was no evidence of discrimination against any particular individual. Id. at 330. For a general discussion of the same topic, see A. Larson & L. Larson, Employment Discrimination §50.80-81 (1983 ed.).

by the success that the expert's proponent has had in achieving the goals discussed earlier in this chapter. It was suggested that the expert must demystify the science of statistics, be candid about its limitations, and, through the appropriate use of language, invite the trier of fact to participate in the workings of science (see Section 9.1). To the extent that this effort has been successful, there should be some reluctance on the part of the fact finder to repudiate the newly established solidarity with the expert and return to the presumption that statistics is an arcane, impenetrable, and thus untrustworthy art. If the proponent of the expert has been entirely successful, there may even be a tendency on the part of the judges and jurors to treat the cross-examiner's attack on the expert as an attack on themselves as well and to react punitively.

§9.7.2 Inadequacy of Data

The importance to any statistical analysis of an adequate data base was discussed at length in Chapter 2. Moreover, it has been repeatedly emphasized that sample size and randomness are important considerations in most tests of statistical significance. (See generally Chapter 6.) The size and makeup of an expert's sample are therefore critical from a purely statistical standpoint. This is also an area where weaknesses are particularly susceptible of exploitation by a skillful cross-examiner. The statistician must therefore be prepared to explain the absence of any data that might strike the lay observer as relevant and probative. Since law and logic are not always synonymous with sound statistical methodology, the expert must be prepared to defend omissions that have no effect on the validity of the results, and even omissions that are beyond his or her control.

Key v. The Gillette Co.:[9] In this class action the plaintiff alleged that the defendant discriminated against women by paying them less than their comparably qualified male counterparts over an eight-year period. The plaintiff's expert performed a regression analysis in which he included as independent variables (factors that should influence salary) all categories of information that were systematically maintained in the defendant's personnel files. These variables were age (thought to be an approximation of experience), sex, seniority, highest level of

---

[9] No. 82-1601 (1st Cir. January 1, 1983). For the procedural history of this case see note 7 supra.

education attained (expressed in years), and the Gillette facility at which the individual worked. The expert included information about anyone employed at Gillette during any portion of the class period as defined by the court, subject only to the exclusion of incomplete personnel files. On the basis of this analysis, the expert offered an opinion that there were statistically significant discrepancies between the salaries of men and comparably qualified women.

The defendant's expert performed a similar analysis, but, as instructed by his client, excluded data for certain of the class years, based on Gillette's view that the court had erroneously interpreted the statute of limitations in deciding on the class period. He also focused his analysis on only certain job categories, again on the basis of his client's view of the proper legal scope of the action.

On cross-examination, the plaintiff's expert was heavily criticized for excluding such seemingly relevant factors as job-related pre-Gillette experience and college major. The defendant's expert was criticized for allowing the scope of his analysis to be determined by nonstatistical factors — namely, his client's view of the law. The district court's judgment repeated the criticism of the plaintiff's expert but made no mention of the suggested shortcomings in the defendant's analysis.

The *Key* case suggests three important points about cross-examination and the adequacy of the data base. First, the expert must be prepared to explain and defend the absence of any data that the intelligent lay person might expect to be included, even when the absence is due to factors beyond the expert's control. In *Key* both the defendant and the court criticized the plaintiff's failure to use as independent variables several factors that in the abstract one might assume to have an important influence on salary. The plaintiff's expert's answer to the criticism was that he simply could not include as variables factors that Gillette had not deemed sufficiently important to record regularly in its personnel files. In fact, the expert might have continued, to hold him responsible for the absence of such data would be to invite employers to avoid liability simply by keeping poor records.[10] Apparently the cross-examiner got the better of the exchange on this point, as the explanation failed to persuade the district judge.

---

[10] A number of courts have refused to hold plaintiffs responsible for gaps in the data that are attributable to a defendant's record-keeping practices. E.g., Trout v. Hidalgo, 517 F. Supp. 873, 882-883 (D.D.C. 1981), *modified sub nom.* Trout v. Lehman, 702 F.2d 1094 (D.C. Cir. 1983). Cf. Valentino v. United States Postal Serv., 674 F.2d 56 (D.C. Cir. 1982) (plaintiffs repeatedly criticized for failure to utilize available information).

Second, cross-examiners must be alert for, and experts must be extremely wary of, exclusions of data dictated by other than statistical considerations. In *Key*, Gillette's expert was repeatedly reminded on cross-examination that he had excluded a considerable amount of potentially relevant data not on the basis of his own professional judgment, but simply because his client told him to. Although the district court did not comment on this issue in its opinion, a reading of the transcript suggests that the point made was a telling one. Presumably, if it can be shown that the expert has followed instructions in deciding what data are relevant, it can be plausibly suggested that he may have been similarly influenced in performing the analysis and interpreting the results. Other courts have reacted more strongly to comparable evidence of exclusion.[11]

Third, on cross-examination as well as direct, the trial lawyer must never lapse into taking for granted the attention and understanding of the trier of fact. A reader of the *Key* transcript having some statistical sophistication would probably be surprised by the court's reactions to the points made on cross-examination. The only reasonable inference to be drawn is that the parties, particularly the plaintiff, either failed in their initial burden of education or, having brought the factfinder to a point of basic literacy, moved mechanically through the remainder of the case without continually reassessing the court's level of understanding and interest.

§9.7.3 Methodology Used by the Expert

In reviewing the expert's statistical methodology, the lawyer should be particularly aware of two situations that may present special opportunities for cross-examination: the use of a plainly inappropriate method or the choice of a method whose use is the subject of dispute among statisticians.

Examples of an inappropriate method include the uncorrected use of a chi-square test of significance when one of the categories being evaluated contains fewer than five cases (see Section 5.7) and the use of the chi-square test to assess differences among multiple categories that can be ranked in order of preferability (see Section 5.2). In cases involving competetent experts, such errors should be

---

[11] E.g., Valentino v. United States Postal Serv., 511 F. Supp. 917, 944 n. 21 (D.D.C. 1981), *aff'd*, 674 F.2d 56 (D.C. Cir. 1982).

rare. Forcing an admission of error on cross-examination should, however, have enormous persuasive power. It is difficult to imagine a greater demonstration of competence on the part of the cross-examining lawyer than to show that he or she has greater command of a pertinent statistical technique than the expert.

In spite of this potential, the cross-examiner should be cautious in attacking an apparent methodological error. First, the error may be apparent rather than real, and the expert may be able to expose the lawyer's lack of understanding and dispense with the criticism as mere cavil. In other circumstances, the theoretical error may be real, but it may have no practical effect. An example of this would be a comparison across numerous categories where a Fisher Exact Test would be more methodologically sound than a chi-square test, but where the number of cases in the categories is sufficiently large that the two tests yield virtually identical results (see Section 5.9.1). In such a situation an improvident attack may give the expert a forum to demonstrate the breadth of his or her knowledge, with the cross-examiner's relatively insignificant point lost in the process.

Far more common are cases in which a chosen methodology is the subject of contention among statisticians. In such cases, an expert who does not deal forthrightly with the disputed methodology may be vulnerable on cross-examination.

Key v. The Gillette Co.:[12] In this class action the plaintiff alleged that the defendant paid women less than comparably qualified men. The disputed methodological point was whether or not to include the company's job group designation as an independent variable in a regression analysis in which salary was the dependent variable. The company divided most of its salaried employees into 12 job groups. Each group included all employees within a certain salary range, regardless of function. Thus a single group might include patent lawyers, accountants, and chemists whose salaries were within about $4,000 of each other.

The experts agreed that seniority, experience, and facility at which a person was employed were appropriate independent variables (that is, factors one would expect to influence salary). The defendant's expert also included job group as an independent variable in his regression analysis. His rationale was twofold. First, he suggested that as a matter of common sense one ought not to compare paralegals with senior patent lawyers; in comparing employees in order to evaluate the in-

----

[12] No. 82-1601 (1st Cir. January 1, 1983). For the history of this case see note 7 supra.

fluence of sex on salary, the comparison should be limited to people whose jobs had something in common (at least to the extent that such commonality would be reflected by similarities in salary). Second, he pointed out that his regression analysis yielded a much higher R^2, or coefficient of multiple determination, than did the plaintiff's analysis, which did not include job group as an independent variable. As a statistical matter, he concluded, his analysis was superior because it explained more of the observed salary variation than did the plaintiff's analysis. For the various years of the class period he found few discrepancies in male and female salaries that attained statistical significance.

In his primary analysis, the plaintiff's expert did not include job group as an independent variable. He testified that, although including job group yielded a regression equation that explained more of the observed variation, he excluded it for logical reasons. In his view, job group was nothing more than a somewhat imprecise synonym for salary: to say that job group is a factor that influences salary is to say nothing more than that people in the same salary range will have similar salaries. For this reason, he believed, job group, while from a statistical standpoint a powerful explanatory factor, shed no light on the question of what employee characteristics Gillette considered in setting salary. For the various class years he found differences of approximately 20% between male and female salaries; these differences were highly significant.

In recognition of the competing arguments, the plaintiff's expert also performed a regression analysis in which he included job group as an independent variable. He found statistically significant differences in salary between men and women who were comparably qualified and who were in the same job group, although these differences were in the range of only a few percent.

The methodological dispute that arose in *Key* has occurred in several reported cases, and the results have varied. Those courts that have held job group to be a necessary and proper independent variable perceived a certain illogic in comparing people whose salaries and jobs differed widely, while those that excluded job group tended to see its inclusion as an exercise in circular reasoning.[13] Of particular interest here is the vulnerability of each position to cross-examination.

---

[13]Compare Trout v. Hidalgo, 517 F. Supp. 873, 883 (D.D.C. 1981), *modified sub nom.* Trout v. Lehman, 702 F.2d 1094 (D.C. Cir. 1983) and Mecklenburg v. Montana State Bd. of Regents, 13 Empl. Prac. Dec. ¶11,438 at 6496 (D. Mont. 1976) (both rejecting job group as an independent variable) with Valentino v. United States Postal Serv., 674 F.2d 56, 69, 71 n. 23 (D.C. Cir. 1982) (criticizing plaintiff for failure to consider "occupational classification").

In *Key*, the defendant's expert chose not to raise the methodological issue on direct examination beyond citing the logical and statistical reasons for his decision to include job group. Two important points were made by the cross-examiner. First, an analogy was made to a regression analysis that sought to account for the weights of prize fighters. The expert agreed that one would reasonably include among the independent variables such factors as the height of the fighters, the height and weight of their parents, the average height and weight for their ethnic group, and some measure of their nutritional history, all of which would presumably have an influence on their weights. One might also consider including as an independent variable the weight class in which the boxer fought — for example, welterweight (135-147 pounds) or middleweight (147-160 pounds). If this were done, the expert concurred, the explanatory power of the regression analysis would be greatly enhanced; in fact it would probably explain virtually all of the observed variation in fighters' weights. However, he agreed, the inclusion of that variable would add nothing to our understanding of what factors influenced the weight of individual fighters and in what relative proportions; we would merely have increased the coefficient of determination by including on the other side of the equation a variable that was roughly synonymous with the dependent variable being studied. The defendant's expert was ultimately forced to admit that the inclusion of job group was virtually indistinguishable from the inclusion of weight class. The plaintiff's counsel was then in a position to argue that the expert had engaged in statistical legerdemain.

It is even more significant that the expert was forced to confront the practical implications of his methodological choice. Specifically, he was asked whether, if his method were to become the legal standard, any employer who wished to discriminate against women could do so simply by placing all women, regardless of qualifications, in lower-paying job groups, and then paying them the same as the men in those groups. He was forced to acknowledge that if his approach were the law, a defendant who discriminated in such a fashion would escape liability.

A reading of the transcript suggests that the plaintiff's expert was considerably less vulnerable. On direct examination, he had partially defused the issue by acknowledging the difference of opinion and then explaining the logical justification for the choice he had made. Furthermore, in deference to the viewpoint of the defendant's expert, he had performed an exploratory analysis using his opponent's methodology (see Section 2.8 for a general discussion of exploratory analysis). The results, although perhaps of limited practical significance, did reach statistical significance. He was able to offer a cautious conclusion that an evaluation of the situation from the opposing perspective did not cause him to reject his conclusion, but in fact tended to corroborate the results of his primary analysis.

The fate of the two experts on cross-examination suggests a number of strategic lessons. First, an expert should never deal with a point of disputed methodology by simply presenting one of the competing viewpoints and assuming that the opposing lawyer will be unaware of or unable to articulate the other one. The converse of this point, of course, is that the opposing lawyer should make the effort, with the aid of his or her expert, to understand and be able to take advantage of the issue. Where the methodological point has been ignored on direct examination, the cross-examiner has the opportunity to present the issue on his or her terms, choosing both the emphasis it is to be given and the logical and linguistic framework in which it is to be discussed.

Second, the expert not only should deal with the dispute on direct examination, but should do so in a comprehensive fashion. The expert should explain both methodological options, should discuss the arguments advanced in favor of each, and then should state the reasons for the choice made. The impression conveyed to the trier of fact should be one of broad knowledge of the subject, independence, and fairmindedness. By the time the issue is reached on cross-examination, the trier of fact will have been educated to expect it, and, as is often the case in the student-teacher context, the students will have adopted many of the biases of the teacher.[14] Contrast this with the situation in which the cross-examiner achieves a dramatic revelation, compels the expert to admit that an important methodological point has been ignored, and then, through the use of leading questions, educates the jury about the point in terms of his or her choosing.

A final and more difficult question is whether experts facing methodological disputes should routinely perform the disfavored version of the analysis, as did the plaintiff's expert in the *Key* case. In

---

[14]One psychological study suggests that jurors tend to consider the lawyer's attitude toward a witness in forming judgments about that witness. See Conley, O'Barr, Lind, & Erickson, The Power of Language: A Multi-Disciplinary Study of Language in the Courtroom, 1978 Duke L.J. 1375, 1386-1389.

that case the statistician was fortunate enough to obtain results that tended to corroborate his own findings. The expert who does not perform the competing analysis will be subject to cross-examination on the basis that he or she did not adequately consider the alternative methodology; the response must be that, for reasons that should have been advanced on direct examination, a judgment was made that the alternative analysis would shed no light on the ultimate issue. Where the alternative analysis is performed and the results are adverse, it may become an albatross. Under ideal circumstances, the expert can use the divergent results to illustrate the manner in which the disfavored methodology distorts the problem.[15] More often, the expert will be forced to defend himself against charges of doing two equally plausible analyses and choosing the one that yields the right answer.

Given the great importance of creating an image of fairness and of choosing the terms on which the issue is debated, a presumption should probably be exercised in favor of performing the competing analysis. (It goes almost without saying that if the alternative analysis is performed, its results should be disclosed on direct examination, whether good, bad, or indifferent.) This presumption will be strengthened where the expert's a priori judgment is that the alternative analysis will tend to support his or her conclusion or will provide a vehicle for illustrating the shortcomings of the competing methodology. In either event, the expert should be fully prepared to explain whatever choice is made on cross-examination.

§9.7.4 Prior Statements by the Expert

In virtually all jurisdictions, prior statements by the witness that are inconsistent with his or her trial testimony are admissible for purposes of impeachment of the witness.[16] For impeachment purposes, a prior inconsistent statement may take the form of an oral remark or a written statement. Under Rule 801(d)(1)(a) of the Federal Rules of Evidence, a prior inconsistent statement is also admis-

---

[15] Consider the problem with the use of job group as an independent variable, discussed previously in connection with the *Key* case. In some instances the inclusion of job group will lead to a coefficient of multiple determination that is almost 1. See Section 8.10. A skillful expert can use such an unusually high coefficient to illustrate the point that including job group as an independent variable merely puts a synonym for salary on the other side of the regression equation.

[16] See generally McCormick on Evidence 73-85 (Cleary ed., 3d ed. 1984).

sible as substantive evidence if it was made under oath.[17] Since people qualified to testify as statistical experts tend to have generated substantial written output during their careers and often testify regularly, the prior inconsistent statement issue merits particular attention in a statistical case.

In preparing to cross-examine a statistical expert, the opposing lawyer, aided by his or her expert, should pay particular attention to the methodological choices that are embodied in the anticipated testimony. These choices should then be compared with reports the expert has generated in connection with the litigation, and positions the expert has taken in prior litigation and in publications, in order to determine whether he or she has previously rejected or criticized the options chosen in the present case. A resume including a list of publications will presumably have been obtained in discovery and can be supplemented by use of the computerized bibliographies that are available in most scientific disciplines. Notes, comments, and draft reports prepared by the expert in connection with the case at hand are often available in discovery.[18] Even if such documents have not been discovered, their disclosure can sometimes be compelled on cross-examination under Rule 705 of the Federal Rules of Evidence.[19] Such documents can often be a fertile source of conflicting statements about the merits of competing methodologies. Computerized legal research systems such as Lexis and Westlaw now permit a lawyer to enter the name of an expert and generate every judicial opinion in which he or she has been mentioned. This capability permits a quick and thorough examination of positions taken by the expert in prior litigation.

[17] Fed. R. Evid. 801(d)(1)(A) provides as follows:

Statements Which Are Not Hearsay. A statement is not hearsay if —
  1. Prior Statement by Witness. Declarant testifies at the trial or hearing and is subject to cross-examination concerning the statement, and the statement is (A) inconsistent with his testimony, and was given under oath subject to the penalty of perjury at a trial, hearing, or other proceeding, or in a deposition . . . .

[18] The availability in discovery of documents prepared by experts in preparation for litigation is a complex issue that involves work product immunity under Fed. R. Civ. P. 26(b)(3) and the general discoverability of experts' work under Rule 26(b)(4). The outcome often turns on whether the expert will be testifying at trial and whether the documents in question contain facts on which the expert will rely in testifying. See generally 8 C. Wright & A. Miller, Federal Practice and Procedure §§2029-2034 (1970).
  [19] Fed. R. Evid. 705 provides as follows: "The expert may testify in terms of opinion or inference and give his reasons therefor without prior disclosure of the underlying facts or data, unless the court requires otherwise. The expert may in any event be required to disclose the underlying facts or data on cross-examination."

A corollary point is that each expert, with the assistance of counsel, should be doing the very same research. Few of us have instant recall of every statement that we have ever made on a particular topic. The expert should anticipate that there will be cross-examination along the lines suggested above and should therefore be aware of and prepared to deal with statements that may be a source of vulnerability. Particular attention should be paid to prior litigation in which a contrary position has been taken on an issue of methodology. It is difficult to imagine anything more damaging than an unexplained showing that the expert has consistently chosen one option when representing plaintiffs and another when representing defendants.

§9.7.5 Overstatements and Statistical Fallacies

Exaggerated statements of the importance of statistical findings are another major source of vulnerability for experts. Most overstatements are derived from either of two fundamental fallacies: (1) that statistics can be used to *prove* things, and (2) that numbers can be subjected to statistical analysis without any thought about what gave rise to them. The first fallacy has been repeatedly discussed throughout this book. As the reader should now appreciate, statistical analysis does not prove things; it merely assesses the likelihood of the chance occurrence of observed phenomena. The second is somewhat less obvious. Another way to make the point is to say that statisticians must never take leave of their common sense and critical faculties. The second fallacy can be illustrated by the failure to distinguish adequately between practical and statistical significance.

> **In re National Commission on Egg Nutrition:**[20] In this case the Federal Trade Commission considered whether statements made by a trade association concerning the nutritional value of eggs were unfair or deceptive. In evaluating the statements, one piece of evidence was a finding based on World Health Organization data from 30 countries that there was a correlation of .67 between the coronary death rate and the average daily intake of eggs. The correlation yields a p-value that satisfies the most widely used conventions for statistical significance. An expert might therefore testify on the basis of this evidence alone that it would be most unlikely for the available data to have yielded such a correlation as a matter of chance.

[20] 88 F.T.C. 89 (1976).

The temptation, of course, is to take the additional step and conclude, on the basis of the finding of statistical significance, that there is a causal relation between egg consumption and heart disease, but this conclusion would ignore some fairly obvious practical considerations. Statistical significance merely excludes chance as a reasonably probable explanation for the observed correlations; it does not exclude any other possible explanations. Statistical and practical significance will be roughly synonymous where there are no other conceivable explanations for the correlation besides chance and the suspected causal relationship. Here, however, alternative practical explanations are readily available. It might be the case, for example, that egg consumption is correlated with consumption of meat and other fatty foods, with cigarette smoking, or with high-stress lifestyles. If so, it is equally plausible that one of these other factors is the true causal agent and that egg consumption is merely an innocent bystander suffering guilt by association. Under such circumstances, an attempt to equate statistical significance with practical significance would be an invitation to a cross-examination in which the expert was portrayed as a scientist who had lost touch with reality.

Overstatements also tend to result from findings of marginal statistical significance, particularly where the sample size is small. Assume, for example, that the expert has chosen a p-value of .05 as his criterion of significance. The analysis yields a p-value of .05, and the expert testifies that chance has been excluded as a potential cause of the observed discrepancy or relationship. By thus treating significance as a discrete rather than a continuous phenomenon, the expert becomes vulnerable to quick calculations by the opposing expert disclosing that a change in a limited number of observations would have caused the result to be insignificant. The smaller the sample size, the fewer the number of observations that will be needed to tip the balance. The cross-examiner may then be in a position to compel an admission that if one, two, three, or however many observations had turned out differently, the expert would have reached an entirely different conclusion. The cross-examiner can further suggest that a limited number of errors in making or coding observations would have had the same effect (see Section 2.3 concerning the likelihood of such errors).

The overall point is that the expert must be careful never to overstate either directly or by implication what the statistical method can accomplish. The problem is particularly acute where the expert's findings are marginal even by statistical standards. Conversely, the cross-examining lawyer must be alert for and ready to take advantage of any such overstatements.

§9.8 Considerations of Form

The ultimate purpose of cross-examination is to exploit any substantive weaknesses in the expert's testimony, including those discussed in Section 9.7. To achieve maximum effect, however, mastery of the substantive points alone is not enough. The difficulty of the subject matter requires careful attention to form; that same difficulty creates a great opportunity for the cross-examiner who can frame the inquiry in appropriate terms.

In developing a style for cross-examination of statistical experts, the lawyer should keep in mind three goals: first, to paint himself or herself as a credible mediator between the scientific and lay worlds; second, to continue the education of the judge and jury, presumably begun in opening argument, concerning those statistical concepts that the lawyer deems most relevant to the case; and third, to undermine whatever confidence the trier of fact may have developed in the competing expert.

The first of these goals can most effectively be achieved by the use of the communication techniques recommended for opening statement and direct examination (see Section 9.1): the lawyer must demonstrate an ability both to use the technical jargon of statistics and to explain it in a straightforward way. The cross-examining lawyer can greatly enhance his or her perceived competency by choosing a limited area in which the opposing expert will be forced to deal with the lawyer as an equal. In the *Key* case, for example, the cross-examining lawyer's ability to debate the defendant's expert on a narrow point of methodology presumably enhanced his standing as an authority worth listening to concerning other statistical issues in the case. In any such display of statistical mastery, however, counsel must always be mindful of playing the role as intermediary between the scientist and the trier of fact. Consistent with the suggestions made earlier, whenever technical terms are used in the course of cross-examination, the questions should embody a straightforward definition until it is clear that the trier of fact has fully assimilated the jargon.

The second goal is that of education. In a substantive sense, this means that the trier of fact must be told about certain terms and concepts. As important as the fact of educating, however, is the manner in which it is done. Any fact or event is capable of being described in a number of ways that are all literally "accurate," but, as social scientists have repeatedly demonstrated, the impact of the description will vary widely according to the descriptive style chosen.[1]

This principle becomes relevant on cross-examination when the lawyer has an opportunity to raise an important issue that the opposing expert has neglected or understated on direct examination. As was discussed above in reference to methodological disputes (see Section 9.7.3), the cross-examiner will not only transmit substantive information to the judge and jury, but will shape their reception of the information by choosing the stylistic context in which it is presented. Consider again the example of the inclusion of job group as an independent variable by the defendant's expert in *Key v. The Gillette Co.*[2] Had he given more attention on direct examination to the inclusion of that variable, he presumably would have emphasized that under widely accepted statistical standards its inclusion caused the regression equation to assume far greater explanatory power. For this reason, he might have added, his regression analysis was in a statistical sense a better fitting model of the actual salary data than the plaintiff's analysis.

As it turned out, however, the cross-examiner, with his ability to use leading questions, was able to set the agenda for the discussion. He was able to lend a pejorative tone to this initial discussion of the issue by associating the defendant's position with the patently specious example of the boxers' weights and by reiterating, with the concurrence of the defendant's expert, that job group was not an "independent" variable in the sense of a characteristic of the employee that an employer might reasonably consider in selecting a position and setting a salary. The fact of increased explanatory power did emerge, but it was cast as a statistical artifact not grounded in the external world.

The third goal is that of undermining the credibility of the opposing expert. Substantively, of course, this is accomplished by the

---

§9.8 [1] W. O'Barr, Linguistic Evidence 1-13 (1982); Conley, O'Barr, Lind, & Erickson, The Power of Language: A Multi-Disciplinary Study of Language in the Courtroom, 1978 Duke L.J. 1375; Conley, Language in the Courtroom: Form over Substance? 15 Trial 32 (1979); Lett, The Influence of Dialect and Accent in the Courtroom, 19 Intl. Socy. of Barristers Q. 334 (1984); E. Loftus, Eyewitness Testimony (1979).

[2] No. 82-1601 (1st Cir. January 1, 1983). See Section 9.6.

traditional means of exposing errors, omissions, and inconsistencies. The cross-examining lawyer should also bear in mind two related stylistic points. Where the opposing expert has shown an ability to present his or her point of view in terms that are at once statistically appropriate and comprehensible to the trier of fact, the cross-examiner should be particularly careful to employ questions that do not admit of extensive narrative answers.[3] Conversely, where the expert has shown himself to be confusing or condescending, such tendencies should be encouraged. Consider again the example of the job group variable in *Key*. Had the defendant's expert been subject to the stylistic weakness just described, it would have been appropriate for the cross-examiner to use leading questions to make the substantive point in his own terms, and then to tolerate or even elicit an explanation from the expert through the use of less structured questions. Under such circumstances, the expert's linguistic behavior would presumably have tended to confirm the cross-examiner's suggestion that the defendant's analysis was a statistical stratagem at variance with common sense.

§9.9 Cross-Examination Summary

In its substantive aspects, the cross-examination of a statistical expert has much in common with that of any other witness. As has been suggested, there are substantive points that are of particular importance in statistical cases and that therefore merit particular attention on the part of the cross-examiner. Moreover, because statistical experts think and speak in terms that are foreign to most people who sit as judges or jurors, questions of language and style may assume as much importance as substantive issues. In cross-examination, just as in direct examination and in argument, lawyers and witnesses must be alert for opportunities to enhance the credibility of their case through the appropriate use of language. Conversely, they must be equally alert for situations in which the use of inappropriate language can vitiate an important substantive point.

---

[3] Narrative answers have been shown to be particularly persuasive. See Conley et al., supra note 1, at 1386-1389.

CHAPTER TEN

Cases Involving Statistical Evidence

§10.0   Introduction

Thus far this book has been organized along statistical lines. Individual chapters deal with particular concepts and methods, and within the various chapters pertinent cases are discussed to illustrate their application. The organization of this chapter is quite different, since its purpose is to present examples of how statistics have been used in a number of important substantive law areas.

Each of the sections in this chapter deals with a single substantive area, such as torts, antitrust, or unfair competition, and each section contains a number of cases that illustrate how statistical methods have been used in the area of law under discussion. The presentation of each case consists of a synopsis of the facts and a brief analysis of the statistical methods used. The methods are italicized and followed by cross references to the sections of the book in which they are discussed. The cases come from a variety of courts and administrative tribunals and are selected more for their practical explanatory value than for their precedential significance.

This chapter is not intended to be an exhaustive compilation of cases involving statistical evidence; its more limited purpose is to illustrate the wide range of applications of statistical methods in court. A reader with some background in statistical theory who is confronting a specific legal problem might well choose to begin with this final chapter in order to find examples of statistical techniques that have been used in the relevant substantive law area. He or she can then refer to the specific sections of the book that cover those techniques.

For other readers, it is hoped that this chapter will lend a concluding note of realism to the study of statistics and the law. All readers should note a significant contrast between many of the cases discussed in this chapter and those introduced in earlier chapters. The cases in earlier chapters have not only been chosen for their explanatory value but are often edited or expanded upon to permit a comprehensive treatment of the statistical point under discussion: missing numbers are sometimes added, assumptions about the techniques used are sometimes made, and further analyses not referred to in the case are occasionally suggested. The reader who examines the full reports of the cases presented in this chapter will see immediately that courts' discussions of statistical methods are often cryptic and that conclusions drawn from statistical evidence are often stated without supporting analysis. Thus it is frequently difficult to determine from the reports what statistical methods were used. Determining whether the techniques used have been correctly chosen and applied almost always requires that we make assumptions about the data or about the specifics of the statistical methods employed in order to reconstruct the analysis. In large part, the cases discussed in this chapter are different from those discussed in previous chapters.

§10.1 Tort Law

Practicing tort lawyers will be aware that statistical evidence is becoming commonplace in the trial of tort cases. Statistical techniques are used increasingly to demonstrate relationships between defendants' acts and plaintiffs' injuries and to project lost earnings and profits, but appellate opinions that address issues involving statistical evidence in tort cases are still rare.

The cases reviewed in this section are grouped into two categories. Section 10.1.1 presents a series of cases in which statistical evidence is used to prove tort liability, generally by showing a statistical relationship between an injury and an allegedly tortious act. Those discussed in Section 10.1.2 illustrate various statistical approaches to the proof of tort damages.

§10.1.1 Statistical Proof of Tort Liability

Three environmental cases illustrate the use of statistics to prove tort liability. The first, *Orchard View Farms, Inc. v. Martin Marietta Aluminum, Inc.*,[1] was a trespass case in which the plaintiff attempted to prove that pine tree blight on its property was caused by fluoride emissions from the defendant's manufacturing plant. The plaintiff introduced evidence that "scorching" of needles was far more extensive in forests near the plant than in those farther from the plant. The plaintiff also introduced evidence of a *correlation coefficient* (Section 7.1) of + .50 between amount of scorching and fluorine content of the pine needles. This degree of correlation was shown to be significant at the .05 level. Based on this and other evidence of damage to vegetation as well as the defendant's poor record in monitoring and control-

§10.1 [1] 500 F. Supp. 984 (D. Or. 1980).

ling its effluents, the court found for the plaintiff and awarded punitive damages.

Lea Co. v. North Carolina Board of Transportation[2] was an inverse condemnation case in which the plaintiff sought compensation for flooding damage to its property allegedly resulting from highway construction by the defendant state agency. Shortly after completion of the construction, there was an unusually bad flood in a nearby stream. The plaintiff alleged that the flooding was exacerbated by the construction, with consequent damage to its property. After a trial verdict for the plaintiff, one of the issues on appeal was whether the natural flooding had been reasonably foreseeable at the time the construction was begun.

In affirming the judgment, the Supreme Court of North Carolina cited a statistical analysis performed by an expert hydrologist. He constructed a *regression model* (Section 8.1) of water flow in the affected stream. Using the model, he predicted "the frequency with which any particular level of flooding at the construction site was statistically likely to return."[3] This analysis provided the basis for findings that the serious flood was a foreseeable event and that some of the increased water flow that occurred at the time was the direct and foreseeable result of the highway construction.

The statistical analysis itself was not described in detail. The case does, however, suggest a novel use for regression analysis. The expert hydrologist constructed a model of the flooding in which various characteristics of stream flow were the *independent variables* and water level was the *dependent variable*. The court apparently accepted the argument that if a well-constructed model predicted that a flood would occur with a reasonable frequency (every 100 years in this case), then such a flood could be described as reasonably foreseeable.

The final example in this category is *Dow Chemical Co. v. Blum*.[4] Although not actually a tort case, it does suggest how statistics can be used in products liability cases. The case was brought by a herbicide manufacturer seeking reversal of an EPA order banning two of its herbicides. In issuing an emergency ban order, the EPA relied in part on statistical evidence that showed: (1) that the 1972-1977 rate of spontaneous abortions in areas sprayed with the suspect herbicide was significantly higher than the rate in a control area; (2) that there was

---

[2] 308 N.C. 603 (1983).
[3] Id. at 612.
[4] 469 F. Supp. 892 (E.D. Mich. 1979).

a statistically significant seasonal cycle in the abortion index in the sprayed areas; and (3) that there was a statistically significant correlation between the cycle in the abortion rate and the timing of the spraying in the affected areas.

The district court provided little detail on the statistical studies, with the exception of a reference to a *chi-square test* (Section 5.2) that demonstrated a statistically significant relationship between spontaneous abortions and spraying. The court also noted that Dow had criticized the studies on the grounds: (1) that the results were skewed by an aberrational number of abortions during one of the months in the study period; (2) that the correlation between spraying patterns and the abortion cycle could be attributed to such factors as a greater proportion of women of childbearing age residing in the affected areas and an influx of temporary residents during the months when the abortion rate peaked; and (3) that the study used data based on estimated rather than actual births. Notwithstanding these criticisms, the court upheld the EPA's order as being "not a clear error of judgment or completely without foundation."[5]

§10.1.2 Statistical Proof of Tort Damages

A personal injury case, two wrongful death cases, and a business tort action illustrate the use of statistical evidence to prove tort damages.

In its 1983 decision in *Jones & Laughlin Steel Corp. v. Pfeifer*,[6] the Supreme Court established standards for proving lost future income in cases under the federal Longshoremen's and Harbor Workers' Compensation Act. While no specific statistical methods are mentioned in the opinion, the guidelines laid down by the Court clearly contemplate the introduction of statistical evidence. The Court said that the proof of lost future income should proceed in three stages. First, the lost stream of income should be estimated by starting with the worker's annual wage at the time of injury and adjusting it for future years to reflect such "individual factors" as foreseeable promotions and such "societal factors" as foreseeable productivity changes within the worker's industry.[7] Second, the income stream should be

[5] Id. at 905.
[6] 462 U.S. 523 (1983).
[7] Id. at 536.

discounted to its present value, which involves calculating that lump sum amount that, if invested prudently as of the time of injury, would yield an income stream equivalent to what the worker might have earned but for the injury.[8] Finally, the calculations should be adjusted to insure that the value of the award is not diminished over time by inflation. The Court reviewed a number of econometric approaches to the prediction of inflation but found the economic evidence "distinctly unconvincing"; for reasons that are not entirely clear, it concluded that a trial court should not be reversed "if it adopts a rate of between one and three percent and explains its choice."[9]

A variety of quantitative techniques might be appropriate at each of the Court's three stages. The determination of the lost income stream will require a number of economic assumptions on which mathematical calculations will be based, while discounting to present value is, as the Court observed, the subject of a widely used formula.[10] The final step in the process, the prediction of inflation rates, is a matter of sophisticated econometric forecasting.

United States v. English[11] was a wrongful death action under the Federal Tort Claims Act brought by the widow of a contractor killed in an electrical accident on government property. At issue on appeal was the propriety of an award to the plaintiff of her interest in the deceased's lost future earnings. The court of appeals agreed with the government that the trial court should have reduced the decedent's stream of income to its present value. Rejecting another government argument, the court of appeals refused to criticize the trial court for taking inflationary trends into account in calculating future income.

The plaintiff's expert calculated lost future income by applying a projected increase of 7.5% per year to the decedent's earnings over the course of his expected working life. The 7.5% factor was derived from a *regression model* (Section 8.1) of earnings of persons employed in contract construction. The court of appeals commented favorably on the regression analysis, and pointed out that since it was based on "past earnings and past increases in earnings which were themselves affected by inflationary pressures," it would automatically "result in a future projection which incorporates the assumption that there will be future inflation similar to that of the past several years."[12] That is,

[8] Id. at 536-537 & n. 21.
[9] Id., 548-549.
[10] Id. at 537 n. 21.
[11] 521 F.2d 63 (9th Cir. 1975).
[12] Id. at 71 n. 5.

since one of the independent variables (past earnings) was influenced by inflation, the dependent variable (future earnings) would also necessarily reflect that influence.

Krohmer v. Dahl[13] was another survivorship and wrongful death action, brought against a funeral home by the father of a young man who had been killed while working there. The defendant appealed from an $85,000 verdict. One of the issues considered by the Montana Supreme Court was the admissibility of certain testimony by an economist named Dr. Heliker concerning the decedent's prospective earnings.

Dr. Heliker "testified to the possible earnings of classes of people of the same type as the decedent if they had survived through their normal life expectancy."[14] He used data obtained from the United States Census Bureau, which in turn had been obtained "by a 25 percent *random sample* [(Section 6.2)] of the population of Montana." The analysis was not otherwise described.

The defendants objected to the Heliker study because the decedent had been a student at the time of his death and no showing had been made that he was preparing for any particular occupation or profession. The court affirmed the judgment, relying on guidelines suggested in an earlier case by the Supreme Court of New Mexico:[15]

> No general rule can be formulated that would properly control the admission of evidence to prove a man's future earning capacity. It must be arrived at largely from probabilities; and any evidence that would fairly indicate his present earning capacity, and the probability of its increase or decrease in the future are to be admitted.

The use of statistical evidence to prove lost profits resulting from a business tort is illustrated by *ABC Trans National Transport, Inc. v. Aeronautics Forwarders, Inc.*[16] Several key employees of ABC walked off the job and went to work for Aeronautics, allegedly bringing a number of ABC's customers along with them. ABC alleged that Aeronautics had conspired with the former employees to bring about their departure and the attending diversion of customers. ABC sought injunctive relief and damages in the form of lost profits. The

---

[13] 145 Mont. 207, 402 P.2d 979 (1973).
[14] 402 P.2d at 981.
[15] Id. at 982, referring to the case of Turietta v. Wyche, 212 P.2d 1041, 1047 (N.M. 1949).
[16] 90 Ill. App. 3d 817 (1980).

appellate court affirmed the trial court's denial of injunctive relief and its limited damage award, with some modifications. The appellate court rejected ABC's argument that the lost profits awarded by the trial court were "manifestly inadequate."[17]

At trial, ABC had introduced a *linear regression analysis* (Section 8.2) performed by a financial analyst. Its purpose was to project the profits that ABC would have enjoyed in 1979 and 1980 had the walk-out and subsequent loss of business not occurred. The regression analysis was intended to be corroborative of other, qualitative expert testimony. Unfortunately, the reported appellate opinion provides no further information about the regression.

The trial court awarded damages far below what the plaintiff's experts had recommended. With reference to the statistical evidence that was apparently rejected, the appellate court commented: "While the plaintiff's economic evidence and theories demonstrate commendable preparation on the part of counsel, the trial court was not impelled to adopt the estimates of plaintiff's expert witnesses."[18] The appellate court directed several criticisms at the plaintiff's evidence of lost profits: (1) the plaintiff greatly overstated the period during which defendant's tortious activities affected its profits; (2) the plaintiff's analysis assumed that, absent the defendant's misconduct, the key employees would have remained indefinitely at ABC; and (3) the analysis further assumed that the customers who were allegedly diverted would also have remained with ABC indefinitely.

The appellate court summarized its findings as follows:[19]

> Plaintiff's economic theory provides one viable way of calculating these losses, yet defendants challenged certain underlying assumptions of that calculation. . . . Economic data can be interpreted in different ways for different purposes. As useful as a particular accounting technique may be in predicting a company's financial future, it cannot be regarded as conclusive proof of legal damages; the judge or jury must be free to draw their own inferences from the evidence presented.

§10.2 Unfair Competition and Trade Regulation

The cases falling under this broad heading can be grouped into two major categories: trademark infringement and deceptive adver-

[17] Id. at 834.
[18] Id.
[19] Id., 835-836.

tising and labeling. Many of the cases in both categories involve the use of *surveys* to determine consumer attitudes (Sections 2.1, 2.2, and 6.14). In the infringement cases surveys were used to determine whether the alleged infringement resulted in consumer confusion. In some of the deceptive advertising and labeling cases, they were used in a similar fashion to assess the impact of alleged misrepresentations on consumers. In other cases in this category, a variety of statistical techniques were used to assess the truth of claims about product efficacy.

§10.2.1 Trademark Infringement

Typical of the infringement cases is *Amstar Corp. v. Domino's Pizza, Inc.*[1] The plaintiff, Amstar, alleged that the defendant's use of the name "Domino" infringed its trademark on Domino Sugar. Both sides presented survey evidence on the question of whether the defendant's use of the name "Domino" tended to create confusion among consumers.

The plaintiff's study involved personal interviews of a *random sample* (Sections 6.2 and 6.3) of 525 people in ten cities in the eastern United States. Upon being shown a Domino's Pizza box, 44.2% of those interviewed indicated that they believed that the company that made the pizza made other products, and 72% of that group and 31.6% of all 525 respondents believed that the pizza company also made sugar. In finding for the plaintiff, the district court took this as evidence of "substantial confusion between Domino's Pizza and Domino Sugar," and gave this evidence "substantial weight as evidence of confusion among the consuming public."[2]

The defendant also presented a survey. This survey purported to show that few consumers were confused as to the source of Domino's Pizza or were influenced by the possibility that it might be a product of the same company that marketed Domino Sugar. The district court rejected this survey evidence. First, the survey was not the work of an independent statistical expert, since the defendant's lawyers helped to formulate the questionnaire. Second, the sample of people interviewed was not random, since it was drawn from a list of people who had recently placed orders for Domino's Pizza, who, the court believed, could be expected to be more aware of the independent status

---

§10.2   [1] 205 U.S.P.Q. 128 (N.D. Ga. 1979), *rev'd*, 205 U.S.P.Q. 969 (5th Cir. 1980).
[2] 205 U.S.P.Q. at 140.

of Domino's Pizza than the public at large. Third, the court criticized the manner in which the interviews were conducted. Many of the interviewers suspected the identity of the client and knew the purpose of the survey. They were also assisted by employees of Domino's Pizza who were aware of the results desired. Finally, the court found the locations where the interviews were held to be "contaminated."[3] Some were conducted in Domino's Pizza stores, and others were conducted in the subjects' homes but in the presence of Domino's pizza employees.

The court of appeals ultimately rejected both surveys. It agreed with the district court with respect to the defendant's survey, but also found the plaintiff's survey defective. First, the people surveyed by the plaintiff did not "include a fair sampling of those purchasers most likely to partake of the alleged infringer's goods or services,"[4] since eight of the ten cities in which the survey was conducted had no Domino's Pizza outlet. Second, the persons interviewed consisted entirely of women found at home during the day who identified themselves as the member of the household responsible for grocery buying. Such people, the court concluded, were much more likely to have been exposed to the plaintiff's trademark than to the defendants'. Finally, the survey "neglected completely defendants' primary customers — young, single, male college students."[5] Given these defects, the court of appeals found that the plaintiff had failed to meet its burden to show that the use of the mark "Domino's Pizza" was likely to confuse, mislead or deceive the public.[6]

Related survey problems were identified by the court in *Dreyfus Fund, Inc. v. Royal Bank of Canada.*[7] The plaintiff investment fund sought to enjoin an advertising campaign by the defendant bank because of alleged trademark infringement. The plaintiff introduced the results of a survey intended to show consumer confusion. A number of questions "were posed to a random group of persons likely to see the bank's advertisements and likely to consider procuring investment services."[8] The survey indicated that a high proportion of two subgroups of those polled (readers of the New York Times and The Wall Street Journal) associated the picture of a lion used by the Royal

[3] Id. at 141.
[4] Id. at 979.
[5] Id.
[6] Id.
[7] 525 F. Supp. 1108 (S.D.N.Y. 1981).
[8] Id. at 1116

Bank in its advertising campaign with Dreyfus. The court declined to give the survey any weight, however, because the plaintiff's expert admitted a number of methodological flaws. In particular, he testified that the questionnaires were not administered according to his instructions and that as many as half of the respondents had not been selected in a manner designed to ensure *random sampling* (Section 6.2).[9]

In *Nestlé Co. v. Chester's Market, Inc.,*[10] the issue was whether the defendant had infringed the plaintiff's trademark by using the phrase "Toll House cookie." The defendant brought a motion for summary judgment, arguing that the alleged trademark had become a generic term. Both plaintiff and defendant submitted extensive *survey* evidence (sections 2.1, 2.2, 6.14) on the issue of consumer attitudes toward the phrase in dispute. The plaintiff's surveys tended to show that consumers viewed "Toll House" as a descriptive term for a certain type of chocolate chip cookie, while the defendant's experts interpreted their results as suggesting that consumers " 'perceive Toll House to be a trademark relied on for quality.' "[11] In the course of evaluating the competing surveys, the court presented what may be the best available review of the evidentiary questions raised by consumer opinion surveys.[12] It criticized the defendant's survey on a variety of grounds, including the failure of one expert to disclose the questions asked,[13] the use of leading questions by another,[14] and the failure of both surveys to address directly the issue of genericness,[15] and granted the defendant's motion.

Finally, in *Levi Strauss & Co. v. Blue Bell, Inc.,*[16] both sides introduced surveys on the issue of whether consumers were confused by shirtpocket label tabs used by Levi's and Wrangler (Blue Bell). Defendant Blue Bell commissioned a survey of 1,256 randomly selected adult women in households throughout the continental United States who had purchased a child's shirt during the preceding 12 months. This sample was characterized as "a fully adequate number for making projections . . . to the population."[17] Ninety-five percent

---

[9] Id.
[10] 571 F. Supp. 763 (D. Conn. 1983).
[11] Id. at 772.
[12] Id., 772-775.
[13] Id. at 775.
[14] Id. at 777.
[15] Id. at 779.
[16] 216 U.S.P.Q. 606 (N.D. Cal. 1982), *modified,* 221 U.S.P.Q. 525 (9th Cir. 1984).
[17] 216 U.S.P.Q. at 614.

confidence intervals for the sample proportion (Section 6.8) of those correctly identifying the merchandise revealed that the estimates were very *precise* (Ch. 6 Part F).[18] The study indicated that "the overwhelming majority" of respondents who used the pocket tab in identifying the maker of a shirt were correct in their identification, prompting the inference that the tabs were not a source of confusion.

A similar survey offered by Levi's suggested that in some cities as many as 20% of the respondents who used the tabs in identifying shirts mistook Wrangler shirts for a Levi Strauss product. The district court found this survey considerably less credible than Blue Bell's, however, for several reasons. First, Blue Bell's survey was nationwide, while Levi Strauss' was limited to two major metropolitan areas. Second, the court had "doubts" concerning the accuracy of projecting results of the Levi Strauss survey to the population from which the respondents were drawn because of questions about the randomness of the selection of respondents and the adequacy of the representation of "certain portions of the population surveyed."[19] Third, while the Levi Strauss survey was too narrow in some respects, it was too broad in the sense that it included respondents who were not necessarily purchasers of shirts; and fourth, the court believed that the questions used by Levi Strauss were likely to have influenced answers.

On the basis of this comparison of the competing surveys, the district court found that plaintiff Levi Strauss had failed to make a case of consumer confusion. The Ninth Circuit affirmed the judgment for the defendant on the trademark issue, substantially adopting the district court's critique of the surveys.

§10.2.2   Deceptive Advertising and Labeling

Many deceptive advertising cases have involved claims based on survey results. In determining whether the suspect advertisement is deceptive, the initial question is whether the claims made are true. This determination requires an evaluation of the survey on which the claims are based.

In re Litton Industries, Inc.[20] involved advertisements that said that repairmen preferred Litton microwave ovens. This claim was based

---

[18] Id.
[19] Id. at 615.
[20] 97 F.T.C. 1 (1981), *modified*, 100 F.T.C. 457 (1982).

on a *survey* (Sections 2.1, 2.2, and 6.14) conducted by Litton. The Federal Trade Commission found that the survey was defective and that the representation made in the advertisement was thus unsubstantiated. The first problem identified was that the survey supposedly included only independent service companies, but in fact included some Litton dealers who would presumably be biased toward the brand they sold. Second, the survey excluded independent service companies who serviced Litton microwaves but were not on Litton's authorized service list. Litton was ordered to desist from making the unsubstantiated representation and to keep accurate records of future studies and surveys.

Comparable questions about the validity of a survey arose in *In re MacMillan, Inc.*[21] The complaint alleged that LaSalle Extension University, owned by MacMillan, had misrepresented the success achieved by its graduates in its advertising. The complaint sought restitution of tuition money.

The principal evidence introduced in support of the complaint was a survey "designed to measure the success of LaSalle's vocationally motivated graduates."[22] It purported to show that few LaSalle graduates had improved their employment situations as a result of taking LaSalle courses. While the Commission found that much of LaSalle's advertising did have a tendency to deceive, it rejected the survey and declined to order restitution.

The first significant defect in the survey procedure was the use of a cover letter on the stationery of the Commission's Bureau of Consumer Protection. The Commission found that "as a whole, the letter suggested that LaSalle was under investigation for illegal practices injurious to consumers."[23] A second and related problem concerned self-selection by respondents: as a general proposition, the Commission noted, dissatisfied persons are more likely to respond to a survey than those who are satisfied. The effect of the cover letter, according to the Commission, was to exacerbate this factor.

In addition, many of the key questions in the survey were found to be leading, and many of the multiple choice answers were also suspect because the narrow list of choices provided may have enhanced the likelihood of answers adverse to LaSalle. Finally, the "success" factor that the survey purported to measure was flawed because

---

[21] 96 F.T.C. 208 (1980).
[22] Id. at 306.
[23] Id. at 308.

the survey gave no consideration to the degree of effort expended by the respondent in improving his or her job situation. The analysis of the survey concludes with a thorough discussion of the general standards for the acceptance of survey evidence.[24]

A survey of grocery prices was rejected by the FTC in *In re Kroger Co.*[25] Kroger had advertised the results of its "Price Patrol Survey," claiming that it demonstrated that shopping at Kroger cost less than shopping at other stores. The Commission found these advertisements to be misleading, in part because the "Price Patrol Survey" did not include a representative mix of grocery products.

The Commission also considered an analysis of the Kroger survey done by a public interest group, which compared the number of items in the survey whose prices had just been decreased to the number of those whose prices had just been increased. Using a *chi-square test* (Section 5.1), the group demonstrated that the survey included more items whose prices had just been decreased than would have been expected on the basis of chance.[26] The inference drawn was that there seemed to be some association between an item's presence on a particular Price Patrol Survey list and a change in price immediately prior to its inclusion.

In another line of deceptive advertising cases, statistical analyses have been used to assess the validity of claims about product efficacy. *In re Warner Lambert Co.*[27] is typical of this line of cases. The FTC considered a study purportedly substantiating a claim that Listerine was effective in the prevention of colds. In this study, students gargled with either a colored water rinse or Listerine. Subjects who contracted cold symptoms were then examined by doctors who quantified the severity of the symptoms. The Commission rejected the study because of a lack of *blindness,* among other reasons (Section 6.17). Specifically, the doctors' findings could have been biased because an examining doctor would have been able to detect Listerine on the breath of a student complaining of cold symptoms. In addition, students themselves could tell from the flavor whether they were gargling with Listerine or water and could also have been exposed to Listerine advertising on television.

---

[24] Id., 309-312.
[25] 98 F.T.C. 639 (1981), *modified,* 100 F.T.C. 573 (1982).
[26] 98 F.T.C. at 692.
[27] 86 F.T.C. 1398 (1975), *modified,* 562 F.2d 749 (D.C. Cir. 1977), *cert. denied,* 435 U.S. 950 (1978).

At issue in *In re Pfizer, Inc.*[28] were advertisements concerning the pain-relieving capabilities of a Pfizer topical anesthetic. In its attempt to show the truth of the claim, Pfizer introduced, among other evidence, a study in which either the Pfizer product or a placebo had been administered to experimental subjects with minor burns. The test was conducted by a physician, and the results were subsequently analyzed by a statistician. The physician concluded "that the active ingredients were more effective than the placebo." He described the study as "an adequate and well-controlled scientific test which substantiates the claim."[29] The statistician used a *t test* (Section 6.10) to determine whether the results of the physician's study were attributable to chance. He concluded that "there was considerably less than a five percent chance that the results found by the study were due to chance."[30]

The administrative law judge relied on the study as evidence "that it was much more probable than not that [the anesthetic] was more effective than its base materials in relieving sunburn pain"[31] and recommended dismissal of the complaint. In affirming the dismissal the full Commission expressed no view on the adequacy of the study; it found it irrelevant since it had been conducted after the alleged misrepresentation was made.

In *In re National Commission on Egg Nutrition*,[32] the issue was whether advertisements about health benefits of eating eggs were misleading. In ordering the respondents to cease from disseminating a number of claims about the healthful properties of eggs, the FTC relied on several medical studies that demonstrated links between heart disease and eggs and other sources of cholesterol. In particular, it cited studies that showed a *correlation coefficient* (Section 7.1) of $+.83$ between average daily dietary cholesterol intake and heart disease mortality rate in several countries, a correlation coefficient of $+.762$ between average daily intake of dietary cholesterol and heart disease rate in another sample of countries, and a correlation coefficient of $+.66$ between egg consumption and heart disease mortality rate in a sample of 30 countries. These findings were described as "significant" or "highly significant."[33] The results were found to be consistent with

[28] 81 F.T.C. 23 (1972).
[29] Id. at 46.
[30] Id. at 49.
[31] Id. at 56.
[32] 88 F.T.C. 89 (1976), *modified*, 570 F.2d 157 (7th Cir. 1977), *cert. denied*, 439 U.S. 821 (1978).
[33] 88 F.T.C. at 133.

a number of other epidemiological studies and with an extensive body of clinical, pathological, and experimental evidence.

The final case involving the use of statistical evidence to assess the validity of product efficacy claims is *In re American Home Products Corp.*[34] The complaint alleged that American Home was making misleading claims about the relative efficacy of Anacin, Arthritis Pain Formula, and other nonprescription drug products, including statements in televised advertisements that Anacin's pain relieving performance was superior to that of aspirin. Among the evidence introduced by American Home was expert testimony to the effect that the recommended dose of Anacin does indeed have greater pain-killing power than a comparable dose of standard aspirin, because it contains more of the active aspirin ingredients. This finding was premised on the existence of a "dose response curve." This curve purportedly showed that the painkilling effect increases in proportion to the amount of aspirin taken. "This relationship was found to be statistically significant at the 95% *confidence level.*"[35] (Section 1.13 note 4.) American Home's expert inferred from this curve that a recommended dose of Anacin, with its 650-milligram aspirin content, would have substantially more painkilling effect than a standard 500-milligram dose of aspirin. The Commission rejected this testimony, finding that "the evidence regarding the existence of an ascending dose response curve for aspirin" was "equivocal," particularly in the dosage range being studied.[36]

The Commission next addressed a claim that the caffeine contained in Anacin and Arthritis Pain Formula worked in conjunction with the aspirin to enhance the pain-relieving effect. American Home introduced a study that purported to show that two tablets of a combination of pain reliever containing aspirin, caffeine, and a third substance were more effective than a comparable dose of aspirin alone. American Home's expert testified that "this difference was statistically significant at the 99% confidence level [.01 level of significance], indicating caffeine may have increased or added to the analgesic effect."[37] The Commission rejected this study because it "did not compare aspirin with and without caffeine, but rather aspirin versus a combina-

---

[34] 98 F.T.C. 136 (1981), *modified,* 101 F.T.C. 698 (1983), *reopened,* 103 F.T.C. 528 (1984).
[35] 98 F.T.C. at 209.
[36] Id. at 211.
[37] Id. at 214.

tion" of aspirin, caffeine, and a third substance.[38] The Commission's point was that when more than one experimental condition is changed, one cannot legitimately draw inferences about the source of any change in the experimental results. Finally, the Commission reviewed a number of consumer surveys designed to assess whether American Home's advertising had resulted in a consumer perception that its products were indeed more effective. The Commission concluded that consumers did think of the American Home pain relievers as more effective than aspirin and that the unsubstantiated advertising claims therefore did tend to mislead the public. A cease and desist order was entered.

Another FTC proceeding illustrates an inventive use of *standard deviations* (Section 4.7) and *coefficients of variation* (Section 4.8) to evaluate a claim of false labeling. In *In re Forte-Fairbairn, Inc.*,[39] it was alleged that the respondent sold fibers labeled as "baby llama" fibers that were actually baby alpaca fibers. In an effort to determine the true origin of the fibers that had been shipped, the experts for the two sides made a statistical comparison of the suspect fibers with known samples of alpaca and llama fibers. Measurements of the known samples of alpaca fibers yielded a coefficient of variation of 18 to 25% and an average coefficient of variation of 22%. The known samples of llama fibers yielded coefficients of variation in the range of 28 to 35%. Samples drawn from the suspect fibers yielded an average coefficient of variation in excess of 30%. "Both experts agreed that their observations of the [suspect] fiber samples in terms of coefficient of variation agreed with known samples of baby llama, but did not agree with their observations of known samples of baby alpaca."[40] These statistical findings agreed completely with a microscopic examination of diagnostic features of fiber morphology. Relying in part on this evidence, the Commission dismissed the complaint.

§10.2.3 Summary

Two types of problems appropriate for statistical treatment are most common in the unfair trade practices area. Where the issue is consumer attitude, the task will be to select an appropriate sample of consumers, to design and administer a survey questionnaire that gen-

[38] Id. at 215.
[39] 62 F.T.C. 1146 (1963).
[40] Id., 1168-1169.

erates relevant and unbiased information about their attitudes, and then to assess the significance of any patterns or relationships that are observed. Other cases require assessment of the truth of particular claims and representations. The particular statistical method chosen here will depend on the nature of the claim. As the foregoing cases illustrate, the statistical analyses undertaken range from comparisons of the variability within two samples to assessing correlations between health problems and consumption of particular substances.

§10.3 Communication Law

The Federal Communications Commission has frequently received statistical studies as evidence in its rule-making proceedings. The Commission's rules of evidence deal specifically with the introduction of statistical evidence: "In the case of every kind of statistical study, the following items shall be set forth clearly: The formulas used for statistical estimates, standards and test statistics, the description of statistical tests, plus all related computations, computer programs and final results."[1] The Commission has relied on statistical evidence in three major categories of cases: inquiries into the effect of its rules and policies, assessments of the potential effects of proposed technological changes, and rate-setting proceedings. The statistical techniques include standard deviations, regression analyses, standard errors of sample means, and confidence intervals. The three sections that follow present examples from each of the three major categories of cases.

§10.3.1 Review of FCC Policies

Three cases illustrate the use of statistical evidence in the assessment of FCC policies. A *regression analysis* (Section 8.1) was introduced in each case. In the first, *Amendment of §73.34, 73.240 and 73.636 of the Commission's Rules Relating to Multiple Ownership of Standard, FM, and Television Broadcast Stations*[2], one of the issues was the impact on programming decisions of joint ownership of newspapers and broadcast stations. The FCC performed a regression analysis in which the de-

§10.3 [1] 47 C.F.R. §1.363.
[2] 50 F.C.C.2d 1046 (1975).

pendent variable was the number of minutes of certain types of local and public affairs programs broadcast by a particular station. The independent variables included channel type (VHF or UHF), network affiliation, station revenue, number of competitors in the market, and newspaper joint ownership. The Commission inferred from the results of the analysis that there was "an undramatic but nonetheless statistically significant superiority in newspaper owned television stations in a number of program particulars."[3]

In *In re AM-FM Program Duplication,*[4] the Commission amended an existing rule in order to restrict the duplication of AM programming on FM stations. One of the commissioners, Glen O. Robinson, concurred with the general principle of limiting duplication, but felt that the amendment adopted did not go fast or far enough. In his opinion Commissioner Robinson pointed out that the Commission had ignored evidence tending to show that duplication was not necessary to the economic welfare of FM stations. He pointed in particular to a regression analysis performed by the FCC staff that measured the effect of duplication (as an independent variable) on station revenues and expenses (as dependent variables). The analysis showed that the presence of duplication had a statistically significant effect on both revenues and expenses. The relationship was negative, however, because the presence of duplication resulted in a decrease of similar proportions in both. Since savings seemed to be canceled out by revenue losses, Commissioner Robinson concluded, "the elimination of duplication does not significantly affect FM station viability."[5] His use of the regression results is particularly interesting because it demonstrates clearly the relationship between the concepts of *statistical significance* and *practical significance* (Section 1.14).

In *Inquiry into the Economic Relationship Between Television Broadcasting & Cable Television,*[6] the Commission reported a variety of data on the impact of cable TV on conventional broadcast stations. The report was part of a broader assessment of rules relating to the carriage of distant signals by cable systems. Included as an appendix was a Rand Corp. study on the diversion of viewers from local broadcast stations by these distant signals.

The Rand study began with the premise that cable households

[3] Id. at 1078 n. 26.
[4] 59 F.C.C.2d 147 (1976).
[5] Id. at 162.
[6] 71 F.C.C.2d 632 (1979).

had been shown to watch more television than noncable households. The study used the technique of *least squares regression analysis* (Section 8.1) in an effort to determine what factors contributed to this observed effect. Two proposed explanations were that the improved reception cable provides promotes more frequent viewing and that people who subscribe to cable are more avid television viewers in the first instance. One regression equation estimated the respective effects of six independent variables on the dependent variable "total home television use," using data from 121 counties. The independent variables included measures of cable versus conventional television viewing in the households studied (as an indication of the influence of signal superiority), cable availability (included as part of the effort to assess the self-selection factor), and the number of stations received by cable and noncable households (included to assess the impact of wider choice on overall viewing frequency). A second analysis was performed in which the dependent variable was the audience share for cable and conventional stations in the relevant areas. The results of the analyses were characterized as "weak, but not conclusive, evidence that cable leads to increased viewing because of better reception."[7] On the basis of this and other studies, the Commission concluded that "the effect on local station audiences of eliminating the signal carriage rules appears small."[8]

§10.3.2 Assessment of Technology

Four cases illustrate the use of statistical techniques to assess the efficacy or impact of particular communications technologies. In the first case, the question was whether there was a relationship between types of channel selectors and the amount of UHF viewing. In *In re Improvements to UHF Television Reception*,[9] the *t* test and *F* test were used to test "assertions that channel selectors have a substantial effect on UHF viewing." The *t* test (Section 6.10) was used to indicate the significance of a difference in VHF viewing habits between viewers with two different types of channel selectors. A *regression equation* (Section 8.1) was designed to estimate the different effects on viewing of six different types of channel selectors. An F *test* (Section 8.12) was

---

[7] Id. at 724.
[8] Id. at 687.
[9] 90 F.C.C.2d 1121 (1982).

employed to test the hypothesis that the regression coefficients of the channel selector variables were all zero, indicating that viewing was unaffected by the type of selector on the television set. The tests yielded p-values greater than .05, leading analysts and the Commission to the conclusion that the effects of selector choice on viewing habits were negligible.[10]

In a second case, *Application of WLCY-TV, Inc.*,[11] the issue was whether increasing the height of one station's antenna would have an economic impact on two other stations. The potentially affected stations offered expert testimony from an economist who expressed the opinion that both stations would suffer substantial loss of viewers. His opinion was corroborated by that of a second expert, who refined the first witness's estimates of audience shares for the three competing stations. The second witness calculated 95% *confidence intervals* for each of the shares, which the Commission described as the intervals within which "the actual share will fall . . . 95% of the time."[12] The Commission rejected this evidence of market impact as overstating the problem, however, and allowed the proposed antenna change.

Two additional cases illustrate the special role assigned to estimates of the *standard error of the mean* (Section 6.6) in determining whether TV signals are "significantly viewed," and thus required to be carried by cable systems. The applicable regulation provides that "[s]ignificant viewing . . . may be demonstrated by an independent professional audience survey of non-cable television homes that covers at least two weekly periods . . . ."[13] If two or more surveys are taken, "they shall include samples sufficient to assure that the combined surveys result in an average [viewing level] figure at least one standard error above the required viewing level."[14]

In *In re Clearview Cable TV, Inc.*,[15] the Commission found that Clearview had failed to satisfy the requirements of the applicable regulation, because the margin of error in its survey of viewing levels had not been stated. This deficiency was remedied in a subsequent proceeding.[16] The Commission also commented on an applicant's

[10] Id. at 1134 n. 33.
[11] 69 F.C.C.2d 335 (1975).
[12] Id. at 360 n. 37.
[13] 47 C.F.R. §76.54(b).
[14] Id.
[15] 69 F.C.C.2d 1186, 1189 (1978).
[16] 71 F.C.C.2d 1133, 1136 n. 8 (1979). The applicable regulation was 47 C.F.R. §76.54(b).

failure to calculate the standard error as required by regulation in *Applications of Lebanon Valley TV Cable, Inc.*[17]

§10.3.3   Rate Setting

Two cases involving the permissible rate of return on investment for AT&T illustrate the use of *standard deviations* (Section 4.7) and *regression analysis* (Section 8.1) in FCC rate setting proceedings. In the first, *In re American Telephone and Telegraph Co.*,[18] AT&T petitioned for a modification of its rate of return for interstate and foreign service. One piece of evidence discussed by the Commission was a comparison of AT&T's rate of return on investment to that offered by a group of utilities and two groups of industrial companies. AT&T's expert used the standard deviation of the rate of return for each of the groups as a partial measure of investment risk. The theory was that since the "standard deviation measures the dispersion in the market rate of return on the investment," a higher standard deviation would reflect more fluctuation in rate of return, and hence higher risk.[19] The Commission gave the comparison "scant weight," citing "serious limitations in measuring comparability of risk" that were acknowledged by "all parties."[20]

In the second case, *In re American Telephone and Telegraph Co. [II]*,[21] the Commission considered whether implementation of certain rate increases proposed by AT&T would cause it to exceed its authorized rate of return. In order to predict the effect of the increases on rate of return, AT&T had to estimate future demand for and projected revenues from its services. AT&T introduced two *regression models* (Section 8.1). Each model included two regression equations, one using future demand (measured in terms of messages transmitted) as the dependent variable and one using projected revenue (measured in terms of average revenue per message). The Commission criticized the models and ordered AT&T to reconsider them because of its concern about one of the independent variables used in both models. Both models included as an independent variable an estimate

---

[17] Again, the applicable regulation was 47 C.F.R. §76.54(b). 61 F.C.C.2d 53, 54 n. 3 (1976).
[18] 86 F.C.C.2d 257 (1981).
[19] Id. at 276 n. 10.
[20] Id. at 276.
[21] 86 F.C.C.2d 956 (1981).

of price elasticity of demand, as measured by the extent to which changes in rates would influence demand. The Commission expressed concern that AT&T "may have overstated the price elastic nature of demand," and thus understated demand and revenue.[22] The Commission further criticized AT&T for developing the elasticity estimates in the context of one model and then transferring them to the other, even though the economic assumptions underlying the two were quite different.[23]

§10.3.4 Summary

As the cases in the three preceding sections illustrate, the use of statistical evidence is common in FCC proceedings, and the Commission's staff has considerable expertise in dealing with statistics. In assessing the impact of its rules and policies, the Commission has considered and responded critically to evidence involving a wide range of statistical techniques (Section 10.3.1). A number of statistical methods, some of them specified by the Commissions' rules, are regularly used to evaluate the feasibility and potential effects of new technology (Section 10.3.2). Statistical evidence also plays a vital role in making the forecasts and comparisons necessary in setting rates for carriers regulated by the Commission (Section 10.3.3). In all cases, the FCC's statistical expertise creates both an opportunity and an obligation for lawyers and statisticians: an opportunity to make novel and creative use of statistical evidence, and an obligation to use extreme care in designing and carrying out quantitative analyses.

§10.4 Environmental Law

Because of the nature of the issues involved, environmental cases often require an interdisciplinary approach. The decisionmaker must frequently listen to expert testimony and resolve complex questions of scientific fact before the relevant legal standards can be applied. This section presents several cases in which statistical techniques were used to analyze environmental problems. Since statistical analysis is becoming the rule rather than the exception in these cases, the exam-

---

[22] Id. at 966.
[23] Id. at 967.

ples represent only a sample of a much larger body of law. The cases in Section 10.4.1 illustrate the use of statistical evidence in setting and enforcing environmental standards; those in Section 10.4.2 illustrate the use of statistics in assessing responsibility for observed environmental effects.

§10.4.1 Environmental Standards

The Environmental Protection Agency and other agencies with environmental responsibilities frequently consider statistical evidence in assessing the prospective impact of standards, rules, and policies. Under the Clean Air Act,[1] for example, the EPA is required to determine whether an alleged pollutant causes adverse health effects and if so, what pollution concentration level will be permitted. Several air pollution cases and a water pollution case illustrate the use by the EPA of a variety of statistical techniques in setting and enforcing environmental standards.

In *Ethyl Corp. v. EPA*,[2] the agency considered the question of whether airborne lead would endanger the public health. The EPA was required to determine whether lead in the air was likely to *cause* public health problems. Since statistical evidence cannot be used to prove causation directly, the EPA considered studies addressed to the more limited question of whether there was a statistically significant *correlation* (Section 7.4) between airborne lead and particular health problems. In finding that such a correlation did exist and then inferring from this finding that the public health was indeed endangered, the EPA relied on a number of clinical studies, but rejected one offered by the petroleum industry because of differences among testing areas in nonairborne sources of lead.[3] The EPA's conclusions were affirmed by the court of appeals.

Once airborne lead has been found to endanger the public health, the next step is to control it by setting ambient air concentration standards. The EPA's standards were challenged by an industry group in *Lead Industries Association v. EPA*.[4] The EPA determined that one- to five-year-old children constituted the most vulnerable group

§10.4 [1] 42 U.S.C. §§7401 et seq. (1982).
[2] 541 F.2d 1 (D.C. Cir. 1976), *cert. denied*, 426 U.S. 941 (1976).
[3] 541 F.2d, 55-63.
[4] 647 F.2d 1130, 1141-1145 (D.C. Cir.), *cert. denied*, 449 U.S. 1042 (1980).

and then established for this group a maximum safe level of 30 micrograms of lead per deciliter of blood. Its goal was to ensure that 99.5% of the target population had blood levels below the maximum. Relying on studies that showed that blood level response to lead levels in the ambient air is variable, and that the *logarithms* (Section 8.14) of blood levels are *normally distributed* (Section 4.13) in the population, the EPA used the *standard deviation* (Section 4.7) of the logarithm of blood level response to determine the maximum allowable blood level that would ensure that 99.5% of the target population fell below the maximum safe level. The agency then made certain assumptions about the respective contributions of ambient air and nonair lead to blood levels and calculated a maximum allowable ambient air level. The court of appeals upheld the standard in the face of an industry challenge to the validity of some of the assumptions on which the calculations rested. The case is particularly interesting because it illustrates the use of findings of *statistical significance* in making judgments about *practical* and *legal significance* (Section 1.14), and the role that assumptions play in the process of statistical inference.

The health risks of occupational exposure to arsenic were at issue in *Asarco, Inc. v. OSHA*,[5] in which members of the smelting industry unsuccessfully challenged regulations promulgated by the Occupational Safety and Health Administration. In the course of reviewing the epidemiological evidence, the court considered a study of exposure risks offered by the industry and rejected by OSHA. The court concurred with OSHA, criticizing the study for its "low statistical power," which it defined as a quantification of "the ability of a study to detect an excess risk that truly exists."[6] It also noted other common errors in epidemiological studies, including low significance levels (Section 1.14) and poor sampling techniques (Section 6.2).[7]

In *Cleveland Electric Illuminating Co. v. EPA*,[8] the EPA considered the adequacy of a state plan to control sulphur dioxide emissions from power plants. The EPA relied on a *regression* model (Section 8.1) in setting limits on the amount of sulphur dioxide that each power plant would be allowed to emit. For each plant, the model analyzed the effect on sulfur dioxide concentrations in the ambient air of such variables as plant capacity, smokestack height, surrounding terrain,

---

[5] 746 F.2d 483 (9th Cir. 1984).
[6] Id. at 493 & n. 19.
[7] Id.
[8] 572 F.2d 1150 (6th Cir. 1978), *cert. denied*, 439 U.S. 910 (1978).

and weather conditions. The result was a set of predictions about the effects of permitting particular emission levels. These predictions formed the basis of the EPA's decision, which was affirmed by the court of appeals after a review of the adequacy of the regression model.

A more recent case involving a challenge to sulphur dioxide standards set by the EPA is *Kamp v. Hernandez*,[9] in which the Court of Appeals for the Ninth Circuit upheld Arizona's Clean Air Act implementation plan over the objections of environmentalists. While the case turned largely on disputed interpretations of various provisions of the Act, the court did address itself to one major statistical issue, the *probability* (Section 1.15) of the maximum emission standard being exceeded more than once in any given year. The court calculated that probability at 0.2643,[10] but made no reference to any further analysis of the question.

In the final air pollution case, *Reserve Mining Co. v. EPA*,[11] an initial issue was the amount of asbestos being discharged into the air by Reserve's plant. Although the case did not involve an established legal standard, the method of measurement employed was one frequently used in setting and enforcing legal standards. The analysis began with the recognition that one cannot actually count all the particles of asbestos in the air at a given place. The EPA's expert therefore collected a number of samples from the air around the plant. The expert then averaged the asbestos fiber concentration in the various samples and calculated a 95% *confidence interval* (Section 6.7) around the average. This confidence interval represented a range of concentrations within which the actual concentration of asbestos was likely to fall 95% of the time. Had the lower end of the interval been greater than an established legal maximum, one could be 95% confident, based on a *two-tailed test* (Section 6.7), that the average concentration of asbestos in the air around the plant exceeded that standard.

The use of confidence intervals in setting legal standards is illustrated by a water pollution case, *Marathon Oil Co. v. EPA*.[12] Marathon challenged effluent limits that had been set for their offshore oil and gas platforms. The EPA had based the limits on data collected from

[9] 752 F.2d 1444 (9th Cir. 1985).
[10] Id. at 1450 & n. 4.
[11] 514 F.2d 492 (8th Cir. 1975).
[12] 564 F.2d 1253 (9th Cir. 1977).

installations using the "best practicable control technology currently available."[13] The agency sampled effluent levels at a number of such plants, computed a mean level of effluent, then calculated a 99% confidence interval for the mean. The EPA established the upper end of the confidence interval as the legal maximum, on the theory that it represented the effluent level below which that installation using the best available technology could expect to fall 99% of the time. The court of appeals approved the method but remanded the specific standard for further consideration. Its principal concern was that the EPA, in calculating averages and confidence intervals, had failed to take samples during events such as breakdowns and maintenance shutdowns. Because such events are inevitable even at the best-equipped installations and because they result in high effluent levels, the court reasoned, the EPA's confidence interval gave an unrealistic picture of the level of effluent control that was actually achieved 99% of the time.[14]

§10.4.2 Causation

Environmental cases, like tort cases, often require a showing that a party's conduct is the cause of a particular event or effect. Statistical evidence, of course, cannot be used to prove causation directly. It can be used, however, to exclude chance as a plausible explanation for a particular relationship or discrepancy. When chance has been excluded, the trier of fact may consider other explanations for the event in question, including those which place responsibility on one or more of the parties.

This reasoning process is illustrated by the case of *Orchard View Farms v. Martin Marietta Aluminum Corp.*,[15] a trespass case also discussed in Section 10.1.1. The plaintiff attempted to prove that fluoride emissions from the defendant's plant were the cause of pine tree blight on its property. The evidence showed that needle damage was far more extensive in pine trees near the plant than in those farther away. There was also a positive correlation between fluorine content of the pine needles and needle damage; the *correlation coefficient* (Section 7.1) was +.50. Because this correlation was

---

[13] Id. at 1266.
[14] Id. at 1268.
[15] 500 F. Supp. 984 (D. Or. 1980).

significant at the .05 level, the court was able to exclude chance as a plausible explanation for the apparent relationship among needle damage, plant proximity, and fluorine concentration. On the basis of this statistical evidence and other evidence concerning vegetation damage and the defendant's conduct, the court assigned responsibility for the environmental damage to the defendant and awarded punitive damages to the plaintiff.

The role of statistical correlation as a necessary step in the process of inferring causation was also noted in *Mision Industrial, Inc. v. EPA*,[16] in which the court of appeals upheld Puerto Rico's clean air implementation plan against a challenge by several groups. In discussing planned limitations on sulphur emissions, the court observed that the demonstrated correlation between the level of sulphur emissions and the level of sulphur dioxide pollutants in the ambient air provided a reasonable basis for imposing such limits.[17]

Finally, in *Dow Chemical Co. v. Blum*,[18] a case that is also discussed in Section 10.1.1, the court rejected a challenge to an emergency EPA ban on two herbicides. In imposing the ban the EPA had relied on "a series of highly complex statistical analyses"[19] that showed a statistically significant correlation between spontaneous abortions and herbicide spraying in certain geographic areas. Although the authors of the analyses emphasized that their studies showed only correlation and disclaimed any effort to prove causation, the court found the EPA's reliance reasonable and upheld the ban.

§10.5 Food and Drug Law

The regulations of the Food and Drug Administration make frequent reference to statistical methods. These regulations prescribe or approve particular statistical techniques for use in testing the quality and purity of food products or the safety and efficacy of drugs. In the reported cases and administrative decisions, however, references to statistical evidence are relatively uncommon. Section 10.5.1 reviews several examples in the FDA's regulations. Section 10.5.2 then presents a series of cases and administrative proceedings in which tech-

---

[16] 547 F.2d 123 (1st Cir. 1976).
[17] Id. at 130 n. 6.
[18] 469 F. Supp. 892 (E.D. Mich. 1979).
[19] Id. at 897.

niques such as random sampling, standard deviation, and regression analysis are used in the analysis of these issues.

§10.5.1 Food and Drug Administration Regulations

Several sections of Title 21 of the Code of Federal Regulations make reference to statistical methods to be used in food and drug evaluation. *Standard deviations* (Section 4.7), for example, are mentioned in many sections dealing with food and drugs. Pursuant to 21 C.F.R. §§620.4(e)-(f) (1984), standard deviations of certain measures of potency are to be calculated in testing the potency of vaccines. Section 660.103(2)-(4) also requires the calculation of standard deviations in estimating drug potency, and pursuant to 21 C.F.R. §556.380, standard deviations must be calculated in determining the amount of chemical residue present in beef tissue. *Coefficients of variation* (Section 4.8) are mentioned in §§1020.30-31, which deal with diagnostic x-ray systems. The first of these sections defines the coefficient of variation in the relevant context; the second requires that the coefficient of variation for radiation exposure fall within specified limits. Finally, §152.126 is typical of a number of sections that make reference to *random samples* (Section 6.2).

§10.5.2 Food and Drug Case Law

As the citations in the preceding section illustrate, statistical evidence is viewed as acceptable and often essential in complying with FDA regulations: many are very specific in describing the types of statistical analysis necessary to comply with certain requirements. It is therefore surprising that statistical evidence is discussed relatively infrequently in the reported food and drug case law. This section reviews several of the cases that do make reference to statistical evidence. The techniques discussed include random sampling, chi-square analysis, and regression analysis.

Random sampling (Section 6.2) is often discussed in connection with determinations of the quality of regulated substances. In *T. J. Stevenson & Co. v. 81,913 Bags of Flour*,[1] for example, the issue was the amount of insect infestation in a large quantity of flour. Since it would

---

§10.5 [1] 449 F. Supp. 84 (S.D. Ala. 1976), *modified,* 629 F.2d 338 (5th Cir. 1980).

not have been feasible to inspect the entire contents of all 81,913 bags, a sampling procedure was devised. Two percent of the bags (20 per 1,000) were randomly selected for inspection. Ten ounces of flour were then culled from each 100-pound bag and inspected. As the court noted, this procedure resulted in less than one part per 5,000 being inspected. In addition, the random removal of flour may have been inappropriate, since the insects tended to rise to the tops of the bags. The court approved the sampling procedure, however, because it was generally accepted in the trade.[2]

Sampling played a somewhat different role in *United States v. Morton-Norwich Products, Inc.*,[3] in which one of the issues was the definition of drug sterility. The defendant's experts used a definition premised on probabilistic testing of random samples prior to shipment. The court rejected this approach, holding that its use "would obliterate the standard of absolute liability imposed by the FDA."[4]

In *Smithkline Corp. v. FDA*,[5] a drug manufacturer appealed from the FDA's summary refusal to approve its new weight-loss drug. The FDA had based its original decision on the manufacturer's failure to submit the results of "well-controlled investigations"[6] of the drug's safety and efficacy. The court of appeals expressed uncertainty about the meaning of the phrase "well-controlled investigations" in the context of the case and remanded it for further proceedings to clarify an incomplete and ambiguous evidentiary record. One aspect of the evidence the court discussed in some detail was a set of clinical trials conducted by the manufacturer. These trials included a study comparing weight loss while using the new drug with weight loss while using a reducing agent of known effectiveness. The manufacturer reported the raw average weight losses associated with the two drugs as well as the average weight losses adjusted by a *multiple regression equation* (Section 8.1). The court was "unable to grasp" whether this analysis met the "well controlled investigation" standard.[7]

In *Certified Color Manufacturers' Assn. v. Mathews*,[8] the manufacturers of Red Dye No. 2 sought to have this food additive returned to the FDA's approved list. In an effort to determine whether the dye

[2] 449 F. Supp. at 95.
[3] 461 F. Supp. 760 (N.D.N.Y. 1978).
[4] Id. at 764.
[5] 587 F.2d 1107 (D.C. Cir. 1978).
[6] Id. at 1111 (quoting 21 C.F.R. §314.111(a)(5)(ii)).
[7] 587 F.2d at 1120 n. 31.
[8] 543 F.2d 284 (D.C. Cir. 1976).

was a carcinogen, an expert studied its effects on rats. One group of rats was given a high dosage, a second group a low dosage. Some of the high-dosage groups showed a higher incidence of cancer. A *chi-square test* (Section 5.1) was performed on the results, and it was found for some of the groups of high and low dosage rats that the difference in cancer rates was statistically significant at the .05 level. Since the study did not support the hypothesis that Red Dye No. 2 dosages were not correlated with cancer rates, the court found, the FDA had a rational basis for refusing to approve it.

Finally, a variety of statistical methods were mentioned in *United States v. Premo Pharmaceutical Laboratories, Inc.*[9] The issue in *Premo* was whether the defendant's new generic drugs, which contained many of the same active ingredients as other drugs already approved by the FDA, should be allowed to be marketed without further approval. The court granted the government's motion for a preliminary injunction halting marketing because it found the products in question were "new drugs" that were "not generally recognized as safe and effective by qualified experts."[10]

The court reviewed at length the defendant's efforts to prove that the new and existing drugs had equivalent "bioavailability," which it defined as "the rate and extent to which the active drug ingredient . . . is absorbed from a drug product and becomes available at the site of drug action."[11] In its introductory findings the court noted that a statistical comparison of bioavailability must meet two criteria. First, the court stated, "one determines whether the test shows that with a 95% degree of confidence (i.e., 95 times out of 100) the two products have not been shown to differ from each other."[12] Second, it is necessary to determine the *power* of the test (see Section 2.10.2), which the court defined as the test's sensitivity in detecting small differences in the bioavailability of the drugs being compared.[13] The court later commented on expert testimony to the effect that an F *test* (Section 8.12) could be used in evaluating the power of a bioavailability test.[14]

Premo's bioavailability studies were rejected for a variety of reasons. The work of one expert, for example, was criticized because of

---

[9] 511 F. Supp. 958 (D.N.J. 1981).
[10] Id. at 973.
[11] Id. at 962 (quoting 21 C.F.R. §320.1(a)).
[12] 511 F. Supp. at 986.
[13] Id.
[14] Id. at 1015.

the absence of a power analysis.[15] Another expert had stricken certain results that he believed to be more than two *standard deviations* (Section 4.10) from the mean, but the court found his calculations to be in error. This cast suspicion on the entire study, the court found, even though the expert testified that the discrepancies were "extremely small, and . . . would not affect the conclusions reached in his analysis."[16] The court also noted that Premo had relied on *in vitro* (test tube) tests instead of the preferred *in vivo* (live) tests without demonstrating any statistical *correlation* (Section 7.1) between the two types of tests.[17]

Although the court did not describe any of the statistical analyses in detail, the *Premo* case is remarkable both for the volume of statistical evidence that the court examined and the care with which it did so. In few reported opinions has the court given such attention to the methodological arguments of the competing experts and rendered such an informed judgment about their relative merits. An important general lesson emerging from the case is that the proponent of a statistical analysis is the likely loser if an interested judge is unable to understand the evidence fully.

§10.6   Antitrust Law

The Sherman[1] and Clayton[2] antitrust acts prohibit combinations and conspiracies in restraint of trade, monopolization, attempted monopolization, and mergers that may tend to lessen competition. In monopoly and merger cases, it is often necessary to define the relevant market and to determine the market shares held by the companies involved. Where combinations or conspiracies in restraint of trade are alleged, the market impact of the allegedly anticompetitive practices is often useful evidence that the restraint is unreasonable. Statistical evidence has been relied on in resolving many issues relevant to antitrust liability and has been used in the calculation of antitrust damages. The sections that follow present cases in which such evidence has been used to define the relevant market (Section 10.6.1),

---

[15] Id. at 1005.
[16] Id.
[17] Id. at 1007.
§10.6   [1] 15 U.S.C. §§1 et seq.
[2] 15 U.S.C. §§12 et seq.

to assess market shares (Section 10.6.2), to evaluate the effect of anti-competitive practices (Section 10.6.3), and to calculate antitrust damages (Section 10.6.4).

§10.6.1 Relevant Market Determination

In determining the market power wielded by an antitrust defendant or in assessing the effect on competition of a proposed merger, it is first necessary to define the market within which the analysis will be carried out. This market is termed the *relevant market*. It has two components: the relevant product market, which consists of those product lines in which the defendant and other affected companies are actual or potential competitors; and the relevant geographic market, which is the portion of the country in which the defendant and other affected companies do business or readily could do business. Generally, antitrust defendants strive to define the relevant markets broadly in order to dilute their own market shares, while plaintiffs seek a narrower definition.

An important concept in defining the relevant product market is cross-elasticity of demand. The relevant product market is often said to include products actually sold by the defendant as well as any additional ones that consumers view as reasonable substitutes for the defendant's. Additional products are deemed to be reasonable substitutes if demand for them is responsive to the same factors that influence demand for the defendant's products. Under such circumstances, demand for the two sets of products is said to be cross-elastic.

Statistical evidence was introduced on the issue of cross-elasticity of demand in *In re Beatrice Foods Co.*,[3] an investigation by the Federal Trade Commission of the competitive effects of Beatrice's acquisition of Tropicana, the country's largest producer of chilled, ready-to-serve orange juice. The question was whether, as Beatrice argued, the relevant product market should include both chilled orange juice (COJ) and frozen concentrated orange juice (FCOJ). Commissioner Douglas noted in a concurring opinion that, "[i]ntuitively, one would expect demand for FCOJ and COJ to be highly correlated because of their highly similar taste and use characteristics."[4] This intuition was contradicted, however, by the findings of a *regression analysis* (Section 8.1).

[3][1984] Trade Reg. Rep. (CCH) ¶22,035 (May 26, 1983).
[4]Id. at 22,637.

Two regression equations were particularly influential. In the first, the dependent variable was per capita consumption of chilled juice, while the independent variables included the prices of frozen concentrate and other juice products. The relevant *regression coefficient* (Section 8.1) showed that movements in the price of frozen concentrate had little effect on demand for chilled juice; the coefficient was not significantly different from zero. In the second equation, consumption of frozen concentrate was the dependent variable; the prices of chilled orange juice and other juice products were independent variables. This equation demonstrated no convincing relationship between chilled juice price and frozen concentrate consumption, as the relevant regression coefficient differed from zero at only a marginally significant level (p-value $= .10$).[5] On the basis of this study the Commission concluded "that there are no statistically significant substitutes for COJ, including FCOJ . . . and that consumer demand for COJ is relatively price inelastic."[6] It therefore limited the relevant product to chilled juice but permitted the merger nonetheless because of Beatrice's small pre-merger share of that market.

Although he concurred in the Commission's conclusion, Commissioner Douglas questioned the extent of its reliance on the regression analysis. He noted that a colleague of the expert who performed the analysis testified that the reliability of the underlying data was suspect. He also identified a problem of *multicollinearity* (Section 8.15), which he defined as the tendency of "several independent variables . . . to move together."[7] When this occurs, he pointed out, "it is difficult to determine whether the value of a given coefficient for any one of those variables actually measures the effect of that variable (e.g., the cross-elasticity of demand between FCOJ and COJ), or instead simply reflects the strong influence of other related independent variables."[8] Finally, Commissioner Douglas observed that the fact that the regression coefficient between two variables does not differ significantly from zero does not prove that there is no practical relationship between the two: "the fact that the statistical test failed to *reject* the null hypothesis does not allow one to conclude that the null hypothesis is true and that the cross-elasticity of demand must be zero."[9]

[5] Id. at 22,638.
[6] Id., 22,619-22,620.
[7] Id. at 22,638.
[8] Id.
[9] Id. at 22,638.

The use of statistical evidence to delineate relevant geographic markets is illustrated by *In re Weyerhaeuser Co.*[10] In that case a Federal Trade Commission administrative law judge denied the FTC's request that Weyerhaeuser be ordered to divest itself of a recently acquired paper mill and dismissed the Commission's complaint. One of the issues considered was the scope of the relevant geographic market. The Commission argued that it should be limited to eleven western states, but the judge found that it was national. In so holding, he relied on price data from the eastern and western markets, which reflected a *correlation* (Section 7.1) between prices in the two markets: "simply looking at the pricing history of this industry is almost enough to convince one that the eastern and western . . . prices are competitively inter-related."[11]

§10.6.2 Market Share Determination

In both monopoly and merger cases, once the relevant market has been defined, the next step is often to calculate the defendant's share of that market. It is necessary in merger cases to look at the division of the market before and after the merger in order to assess the impact on competition. In such cases, market shares are invariably quantified, but statistical analysis of the market share data is rare.

In *In re Pillsbury Co.*,[12] for example, the Federal Trade Commission considered the competitive effect on the frozen pizza market of Pillsbury's acquisition of another frozen pizza manufacturer. The Commission found that the merger had caused Pillsbury's market share to increase from 15.4% to 17.1%, while the shares held by the four largest competitors had increased from 60% to 62%. Without assessing the statistical significance of these changes in market share allocation, the Commission determined that they had no practical significance and dismissed the complaint.

Rebuttal of market share data usually involves an attack on the methods used to collect and compile the data. In an earlier case involving the same company, *In re Pillsbury Mills, Inc.*,[13] the FTC ordered divestiture of a flour company that Pillsbury had acquired.

---

[10] [1984] Trade Reg. Rep. (CCH) ¶22,087 (Oct. 11, 1983).
[11] Id. at 22,778.
[12] 93 F.T.C. 966 (1979).
[13] 57 F.T.C. 1274 (1960).

Interestingly, the market share data that the Commission relied on were quite similar to those that led to a different result in the later case. Here Pillsbury introduced its own data, which tended to show that the industry was less concentrated than the Commission believed. Pillsbury's data were rejected because the Commission identified a number of flaws in collection and compilation.

Pillsbury's expert relied on *surveys* (Sections 2.1 and 2.2) of consumer flour use in estimating market shares. These surveys, which measured household consumption, were found to be "not projectionable as to quantities or as to market shares [because] they were not designed and, in fact, were not conducted for that purpose."[14] The Commission found also that the expert had not been consistent in his procedures for incorporating survey data into market share estimates and that his analytical procedures permitted far too many judgments to be made by the analyst.

In a third merger case, *In re Diamond Alkali Co.*,[15] the Commission found that the respondent's share of the portland cement market had increased from 27% to 43% as a result of the merger. Rather than attacking these findings on their own merits, the respondent sought to undercut their practical significance by offering a survey of cement buyers' perceptions of the post-merger market. The survey was conducted by University of Chicago law professor Hans Zeisel; the principal finding was that "[n]inety-nine and six-tenths percent of all consumers stated that they had not experienced any adverse effects from the acquisition."[16] Although it did not criticize the methodology, the Commission apparently gave no weight to the Zeisel survey in ordering divestiture.

§10.6.3   Anticompetitive Practices

Statistical evidence has sometimes been used to show that antitrust defendants have engaged in such anticompetitive practices as price fixing, market allocation, and attempting to monopolize. Often the evidence consists of raw numerical data that become the subject of expert commentary. In *In re Kellogg Co.*,[17] for example, the FTC

[14] Id. at 1365.
[15] 72 F.T.C. 700 (1967).
[16] Id. at 733.
[17] 99 F.T.C. 8 (1982).

charged several cereal manufacturers with a variety of practices that had the effect of maintaining a highly concentrated, noncompetitive market structure in the production and sale of ready-to-eat cereals. One FTC witness presented several years of pricing data from the respondent manufacturers and "purported to find pricing coordination among a number of products."[18] "Coordination" was "loosely defined . . . in terms of price levels and the amount of price moves of the pairs of products being studied."[19] The expert's general point was that price changes tended to follow a pattern, with Kellogg raising prices first and other manufacturers following suit after a predictable interval.

The same FTC expert also presented a detailed study of 16 "rounds" of price increases[20] he examined to determine the *correlation* (Section 7.1) between the prices of Kellogg, the alleged industry leader, and the prices of its competitors. His theory was apparently that a high correlation would be evidence of a coordinated pricing policy. The administrative law judge rejected the study as evidence of price collusion, since "[o]ne would expect a degree of correlation over time for products that are closely related in terms of condition of supply and demand."[21]

Perhaps the best illustration of the use of statistical analysis in an attempt to prove anticompetitive behavior is found in the *In re Corrugated Container Antitrust Litigation.*[22] The plaintiffs, who were purchasers of corrugated cardboard containers, alleged that the manufacturers had conspired to keep prices artificially high during the period from 1963 to 1975. The plaintiffs' expert created a *regression model* (Section 8.1) of prices during the alleged conspiracy period. This model was then used to predict prices in the post-conspiracy period. The predicted prices proved to be higher than the actual prices. The plaintiffs inferred from this finding that a factor present during the conspiracy period but absent in the post-conspiracy period — that is, the conspiracy — must have influenced prices in the earlier period.

The defendant then introduced a regression model of its own, a model of prices during the post-conspiracy, presumably competitive

[18] Id. at 97.
[19] Id.
[20] Id. at 111.
[21] Id. at 112.
[22] 441 F. Supp. 921 (J.P.M.D.L. 310, 1977). See the discussion of this case in Section 1.12.

period. This model was then used to predict prices during the conspiracy period. The actual prices during the conspiracy period were found to be considerably *lower* than the prices predicted by the model. The defendant concluded that the prices during the reign of the alleged conspiracy were even lower than would have been expected under competitive circumstances. The jury found for the defendant, and it is tempting to speculate that the verdict was influenced by the defendant's success in confounding the plaintiffs' statistical analysis.

§10.6.4 Antitrust Damages

Had there been a finding for the plaintiff buyers in *In re Corrugated Container Antitrust Litigation*,[23] discussed in the preceding section, a *regression model* (Section 8.1) could have been used to calculate damages. Recall that the models both purported to predict prices. Regression statistics based on data from competitive periods could have been used to predict the prices that would have been charged in the absence of a conspiracy. Actual prices during the conspiracy period would presumably have been higher than competitive prices. The difference between the actual and predicted prices would have provided some measure of the economic impact of the alleged conspiracy.

A similar approach was taken in *Spray-Rite Service Corp. v. Monsanto Corp.*[24] In that case, the court of appeals and, ultimately, the Supreme Court, affirmed a jury finding that the defendant herbicide manufacturer had terminated the plaintiff distributor in furtherance of a conspiracy with other distributors to fix the resale price of its herbicides. Spray-Rite's evidence of damages included a regression analysis performed by an expert economist. The expert created a model of Spray-Rite's sales performance before the termination and used it in conjunction with an analysis of general industry trends and of Spray-Rite's costs to predict Spray-Rite's future performance had it not been terminated.[25] The court of appeals accepted the method and

---

[23] Id.

[24] 684 F. 2d 1226 (7th Cir. 1982), *aff'd*, 104 S. Ct. 1464, *reh'g denied*, 104 S. Ct. 2378 (1984). The Supreme Court's opinion dealt with the evidence required to prove a price-fixing conspiracy and did not discuss the damage issue.

[25] 684 F.2d at 1241.

affirmed almost the entire award (the Supreme Court did not discuss the damage issue).

§10.7 Tax Law

Federal tax cases in which statistical evidence has been used fall into two categories. In the first category of cases, discussed in Section 10.7.1, statistical analysis has been used to determine the reasonable value of certain assets and expenses. The subjects of analysis have included the reasonableness of compensation paid to corporate executives, the fair market value of securities, and the amount of unreported income reasonably attributable to employees who receive tips. In the second category, discussed in Section 10.7.2, statistical evidence has been introduced in an effort to prove that assets such as network television contracts and utility easements have determinable useful lives and are therefore depreciable.

§10.7.1 Valuation of Assets and Liabilities

In order to determine the amount of tax due or the deduction allowable with respect to a particular asset or liability, it is necessary to establish the value of the asset or liability. In a number of tax cases statistical evidence has been introduced to assist in the valuation process.

In *News Publishing Co. v. United States*[1] the corporate taxpayer sought to deduct the $127,000 in compensation that it paid to its chief executive officer. The Internal Revenue Service contended that this amount was excessive and thus not entirely deductible. A government expert presented a *regression model* (Section 8.1) of compensation paid to chief executives in the publishing industry that predicted a salary range of $39,000 to $49,000 for executives of companies similar in size to the taxpayer. The court accepted the analysis and disallowed the deduction for compensation in excess of the predicted range.[2]

The fair market value of unregistered securities was at issue in *Campbell v. United States*.[3] The administrators of a trust claimed a

---

§10.7 [1] 81-1 Tax Cas. (CCH) ¶9435 (Ct. Cl. 1981).
[2] Id. at 87, 217-218.
[3] 661 F.2d 209 (Ct. Cl. 1981).

refund because securities that had been acquired were worth less than originally reported. In deciding to discount the securities 43% below their market price, the court relied on a regression analysis that attempted to capture the influence on value of such factors as earning patterns and the risk inherent in unregistered stock.

In *Learner v. Commission*[4] there was a dispute over the fair market value of shares in a closely held corporation as of a particular date. The Service argued that the stock should be valued by comparison to the stock of similar companies, and introduced a regression model based on data derived from other allegedly similar corporations. The court rejected the regression analysis because of insufficient comparative data and found for the taxpayer. In a useful footnote, the court discussed some of the problems inherent in performing regression analyses under such circumstances.[5]

In *Davies v. Commissioner*[6] statistical evidence was relied on in deciding how much unreported tip income could be reasonably attributed to casino blackjack dealers. The Service had come into possession of a diary kept by one of the dealers in which he had recorded his daily tips. A statistical analyst plotted the tip data on graphs for each day of the week and used a *least squares linear regression analysis* (Section 8.1) to predict daily tips for other dealers. These predictions were discounted by 10% to allow for variation.[7] The court held that this method of valuing tips was "rationally based and presumptively correct."[8]

Finally, in *Selig v. United States*[9] the taxpayer had purchased a professional baseball team for $10.8 million. Of that amount, he allocated $10.2 million to player contracts, which are depreciable assets, and $.5 million to franchise cost, which is not depreciable (the allocation of $100,000 to equipment costs was not disputed). The Service disputed the allocation, arguing that more should have been allocated to the franchise cost. It supported its argument with a complex regression model of the value of player contracts. The court analyzed the model at some length and concluded that the contract values arrived at were economically reasonable. It rejected the Service's position, however, because it refused to accept the basic premise of the

[4] 45 T.C.M. (CCH) 922 (1983).
[5] Id. at 933 n. 20.
[6] 42 T.C.M. (CCH) 768 (1981).
[7] Id., 771-772.
[8] Id. at 775.
[9] 565 F. Supp. 524 (E.D. Wis. 1983), *aff'd*, 740 F.2d 572 (7th Cir. 1984).

model — that purchase price can be allocated between player contracts and franchise costs in an economically reasonable manner.[10] The court also criticized both the quality and quantity of the data used in creating the regression model. The taxpayer's allocation was ultimately accepted.

§10.7.2 Determination of Useful Life

Under the Internal Revenue Code and Regulations[11] a deduction is permitted for the depreciation in value of property used in a trade or business. In order to qualify for a depreciation deduction, however, the property in question must have a determinable useful life. In *Indiana Broadcasting Corp. v. Commissioner*[12] the taxpayer claimed that affiliation contracts between its television stations and the networks had determinable useful lives and were therefore depreciable assets and in support of its position offered a statistical analysis of the contracts' life expectancies based on years of network experience.[13] The Tax Court found for the taxpayer, but the Seventh Circuit held the Tax Court's acceptance of the analysis to be clearly erroneous and reversed. The appellate court was particularly concerned that the statistical analysis seemed to ignore some important realities in the industry, including the general "state of flux" and the contract renewal policy of one of the major networks.[14] The opinion of the court of appeals might be read as a refusal to attribute *practical significance* to findings that achieved *statistical significance* (Section 1.10).

The use of statistical methods to prove the life expectancy of an asset has been accepted in other cases. One approved method, the actuarial method, was discussed in *Chesapeake and Ohio Railway Co. v. Commission.*[15] In that case, the railroad sought to prove that certain gradings and tunnel bores were depreciable assets with determinable useful lives. The method involves the calculation of a "survivorship ratio," defined as the ratio of assets that actually survive for a certain time period to the number that could have been retired.[16] This ratio is

---

[10] 565 F. Supp., 537-541.
[11] I.R.C. §167(a)(1) (1983); Treas. Reg. §1.167(a)-1.
[12] 41 T.C. 793 (1964), *rev'd*, 350 F.2d 580 (7th Cir. 1965).
[13] 41 T.C., 811-812.
[14] 350 F.2d, 584-586.
[15] 64 T.C. 352 (1975).
[16] Id., 372-373.

useful to calculate a "survivor curve" designed to represent the probable average life of the asset.[17] When survivorship data are incomplete, the survivorship curves may be extended artificially by means of projections known as "Iowa curves."[18] Iowa curves, according to the Tax Court, are "developed on the premise that retirements of physical property follow general mathematical equations to an extent which permits the retirement of industrial properties to be classified into patterns."[19] While concerned about the "borderline character of the reliability of extrapolation" in the circumstances of the case, the court concluded that the statistical evidence was adequate to show that the assets in question had a determinable useful life.[20]

A similar actuarial method was employed unsuccessfully in *Burlington Northern, Inc. v. United States*,[21] where the issue was once again whether railroad gradings had determinable useful lives. The court did not reject the method itself but found it to be inappropriately applied to the facts of the case. In particular, the court noted, the use of Iowa curve projections requires that the asset in question show an increasing rate of retirement with increasing age. The court held that, in contrast to the *Chesapeake* case, the data in the case at hand did not reflect that characteristic.[22]

§10.8 Employment Discrimination Law

Statistical evidence has had its most elaborate development in the area of employment discrimination law. In its 1971 decision in *Griggs v. Duke Power Co.*[1] the Supreme Court held that Title VII of the Civil Rights Act[2] prohibits not only overt discrimination but testing and other practices that are fair on their face but have a discriminatory impact. This holding eliminated the need to prove intent in the traditional, qualitative fashion and suggested the possibility of a numerical showing that a protected group had fared less well than the majority under the suspect procedure. This suggestion was confirmed six years

---

[17] Id. at 373.
[18] Id.
[19] Id. at 374.
[20] Id. at 380.
[21] 80-2 Tax Cas. (CCH) ¶9781 (Ct. Cl. 1980).
[22] Id. at 85,577.
§10.8 [1] 401 U.S. 424 (1971).
[2] 42 U.S.C. §§2000e et seq.

later in *Hazelwood School District v. United States*,[3] where the Court held that appropriate statistical evidence could be sufficient to make a prima facie case that the defendant had engaged in a pattern or practice of discrimination. The same year, in *Teamsters v. United States*[4] the Court held that once a prima facie statistical case had been established, the burden fell to the defendant to refute the plaintiff's statistical proof.

The Supreme Court's explicit approval of statistical proof is unique to the discrimination area. Perhaps as a result, both the quantity and the quality of the opinions discussing statistical evidence far exceed what is found in any other area of the law. In fact, almost every statistical method discussed in this book appears in at least one discrimination case. This section will present a small sample of this case law in an effort to illustrate its range. The material is organized according to the nature of the entity alleged to have discriminated. Section 10.8.1 discusses discrimination cases brought against educational institutions, Section 10.8.2, cases brought against private employers, and Section 10.8.3, cases brought against governmental entities. Virtually every recognized method of statistical proof is illustrated in each of the three categories.

§10.8.1 Discrimination Involving Educational Institutions

One of the first cases that involved numerical proof of employment discrimination was *Davis v. Cook*,[5] in which black school teachers and principals alleged that they were paid less than their white counterparts by the Atlanta Board of Education. The plaintiffs' expert compared the two black principals in the system to a sample of white principals. The expert's report included *sample means* (Section 6.5) for the two groups on such variables as age, years in service, and salary. The expert found salary discrepancies that went beyond what could reasonably be attributed to objective factors. The district court agreed and found that the discrepancies were due to discrimination. The court of appeals reversed on procedural grounds without reaching the merits of the statistical evidence.

---

[3] 433 U.S. 299 (1977).
[4] 431 U.S. 324, 342-343 & nn. 23-24 (1977).
[5] 80 F. Supp. 443 (N.D. Ga. 1948), *rev'd*, 178 F.2d 595 (5th Cir. 1949), *cert. denied*, 340 U.S. 811 (1950).

In *Davis* a substantial amount of statistical data was introduced, and comparisons were made between data sets, but the discrepancies observed were apparently not tested for statistical significance. The more recent educational institution case law illustrates the use of a wide range of significance tests. In *Caulfield v. Board of Education*,[6] for example, both the *chi-square test* (Section 5.1) and the Z-*test* (Section 4.14) were employed. The plaintiffs challenged an agreement between the defendant Board and the Department of Health, Education and Welfare that was intended to eliminate discrimination in the hiring and assignment of teachers. In finding that the agreement was reasonable, the district court cited a variety of statistics that tended to show widespread discrimination requiring a remedy. One study showed that for the 1973-1974 school year, blacks were substantially underrepresented in one of the two pools from which the Board hired teachers.[7] A Z test indicated that this underrepresentation was statistically significant in four of the five teacher categories studied. The district court also cited the disparate impact on blacks of a number of pass-fail examinations used by the Board in hiring. The significance of differences between black and white pass rates on 16 tests was assessed using a combination of chi-square tests, sometimes adjusted by means of the *Yates correction* (Section 5.7), and Z tests.[8]

In *Love v. Alamance County Board of Education*[9] the plaintiff, a black female teacher, alleged that the Board had discriminated against her by turning her down for numerous promotions. A statistician testifying for the defendant analyzed the Board's applicant flow and hiring data over a nine-year period. She compared the relative success of black and white applicants using the *binomial test* (Section 4.15). She substituted *Fisher's Exact Test* (Sections 4.17 and 5.9.1) as a test of significance "[w]hen the raw data involved small pools."[10] Her conclusion was that "there is no statistical support for the existence of non-neutral policy or of a pattern or practice of discrimination against blacks or females."[11] The plaintiff did not dispute these statistical findings, a factor that influenced the court in finding for the defendant.

---

[6] 486 F. Supp. 862, *aff'd*, 632 F.2d 999 (2d Cir. 1980), *cert. denied*, 450 U.S. 1030 (1981).
[7] 486 F. Supp. at 900.
[8] Id. at 903.
[9] 581 F. Supp. 1079 (M.D.N.C. 1984).
[10] Id. at 1084.
[11] Id.

A final case involving faculty hiring and promotion is *Presseisen v. Swarthmore College*,[12] a class action in which the plaintiff female faculty members alleged that they were discriminated against in hiring, salary, and promotion. In support of their salary claim, the plaintiffs introduced a *regression analysis* (Section 8.1). The *dependent variable* (Section 8.1) in the analysis was salary. The *independent variables* (Section 8.1) included sex, age, years at Swarthmore, years since highest degree, and division. The plaintiffs' expert excluded job rank as an independent variable, on the theory that it was not a truly independent variable because it was *correlated* with gender and thus another manifestation of Swarthmore's allegedly discriminatory practices. The analysis showed that when the other independent variables were held constant, female faculty members were paid less than their male counterparts by statistically significant amounts.[13]

The district court declined to accept the plaintiff's analysis. Its principal concern was that the analysis ignored a number of factors, such as scholarship, teaching ability, and quality of publications that, while difficult to quantify, are presumably important in personnel decisions. The court observed that the plaintiff's expert, although eminently well qualified as a statistician, did not claim any expertise in college administration.[14] The defendant also offered its own regression analysis, which was virtually identical to the plaintiffs' except that job rank was included as an independent variable. The defendant's expert found no statistically significant salary differences between comparably qualified men and women.[15] After viewing a number of shortcomings in both analyses, the court concluded that "[i]n essence, they have destroyed each other, and the Court is, in effect, left with nothing."[16] Since the plaintiffs bore the burden of proof, judgment was entered for the defendant.

§10.8.2 Discrimination by Private Employers

The range of the statistical methods used is equally broad in cases involving private employers. In *Capaci v. Katz & Besthoff, Inc.*,[17] for

---

[12] 442 F. Supp 593 (E.D. Pa. 1977), *aff'd*, 582 F.2d 1275 (3d Cir. 1978).
[13] 442 F. Supp. at 614-615.
[14] Id., 615-616.
[15] Id., 616-619.
[16] Id. at 619.
[17] 711 F.2d 647 (5th Cir. 1983), *cert. denied*, 104 S. Ct. 1709 (1984).

example, the court of appeals reversed a district court finding that the defendant drugstore chain had not discriminated on the basis of gender in hiring manager trainees. The appellate court considered a number of issues, "the most important of which concern the use and abuse of statistical techniques by the parties in the trial below."[18]

The Equal Employment Opportunity Commission, which had intervened before trial, offered extensive statistical evidence. On the issue of discrimination in the hiring of trainees, the EEOC's expert analyzed the respective success rates of male and female applicants for trainee positions. He found that 37.37% of the male applicants had been hired during the relevant time period, versus only 15.96% of the female applicants. Applying a *chi-square test* of significance (Section 5.1), the expert found this discrepancy to be statistically significant at the .001 level.[19] The defendant responded with qualitative testimony from a labor psychologist to the effect that women would be unlikely to apply for the jobs in question; this self-selection, the psychologist concluded, invalidated the plaintiffs' statistical evidence.[20] The court of appeals characterized this and related defense evidence as an attempt to "raise theoretical objections to the data or statistical approach taken," and reminded the defendant that it was required to "demonstrate how the errors affect the results . . . particularly in cases where the plaintiff has demonstrated gross disparities."[21]

The EEOC's expert also compared the percentage of women among the newly hired trainees to the percentage of women among those holding comparable positions in the local labor market. He relied on *census reports* (Section 2.2) as his source of local labor market data. The defendant criticized the use of census data on the ground that they were not sufficiently refined to permit precise comparisons between its workforce and the external market. Rejecting that criticism, the court of appeals held that it was unreasonable to "require refinements beyond that available in published statistics."[22] As the court put it, "[a] perfect statistical model is not required."[23]

In *EEOC v. H. S. Camp & Sons, Inc.,*[24] the defendant meat packer was alleged to have discriminated against blacks and females in hir-

---

[18] 711 F.2d at 651.
[19] Id. at 652 & n. 3.
[20] Id. at 653.
[21] Id. at 654.
[22] Id. at 653.
[23] Id.
[24] 542 F. Supp. 411 (M.D. Fla. 1982).

ing, compensation, promotion and job assignment, and terms and conditions of employment. Both sides introduced statistical evidence. On the hiring issue, the EEOC's expert collected applicant flow data for the relevant years that showed for each year how many blacks and women applied for jobs and how many members of each group were hired. The expert performed an analysis (not described in the opinion) of the female data and found "a very strong statistical disparity"[25] between the observed and expected numbers of women in the defendant's workforce. He also introduced the data for racial disparities but did not analyze their significance. The defendant's expert was asked to perform such an analysis on cross-examination, however, and did so. He calculated the *standard deviation* (Section 4.7) of the number of black employees and found that the observed number differed from the expected number by 5.78 standard deviations.[26] While recognizing that other courts had been persuaded by lesser disparities, the court rejected the EEOC's entire hiring case because of deficiencies in its expert's data collection and sampling techniques.[27]

The EEOC supported its claim of racial discrimination in job assignment by showing that at various relevant times the defendant had maintained entire departments that had no black employees. In rebuttal the defendant's expert introduced a *confidence interval* (Section 6.8) analysis of each department. Initially he established a black availability figure for the defendant's workforce. He chose the percentage of blacks in the relevant local labor pool, implicitly assuming that everyone in this pool was qualified for employment in all of the suspect departments, and then calculated a 95% confidence interval around that figure. This represented the interval within which samples drawn randomly from the relevant labor pool should fall 95% of the time. Thus, if the actual percentage of blacks in a given department fell within the interval, one could be reasonably certain that the assignment had been random and therefore nondiscriminatory.[28] He concluded that the defendant had in fact assigned employees randomly during the years studied. If, however, he derived his availability figure from the defendant's applicant flow data rather than from census data, he was forced to conclude "that it was highly unlikely that

---

[25] Id. at 424.
[26] Id. at 423.
[27] Id., 444-445.
[28] Id. at 427.

the employees were randomly assigned to departments."[29] The court found that the EEOC had made a prima facie case and that the defendant's inconclusive analysis constituted an inadequate rebuttal.[30]

In a final case involving a private defendant, *Commonwealth of Pennsylvania v. Local Union 542*,[31] it was alleged that a union and a number of contractors had discriminated against minority construction workers in the areas of membership, referrals, and wages and hours. A statistical expert testified for the plaintiffs on the referral issue. He developed a series of "selection lists" that showed the order in which unemployed workers had been referred to jobs. He compared the actual order of referral to the order in which the workers were listed on "out-of-work lists," which reflected the order in which unemployed workers were supposed to be recalled.[32] He performed this comparison by calculating *rank correlation coefficients* (Section 7.11). A strong positive correlation would have indicated that proper recall procedures were being followed. The expert found that the coefficients were positive but very low, suggesting that factors other than priority on the work lists were influencing the order of recall. To confirm this suggestion he calculated the *coefficient of determination* (Section 7.17) for each pair of lists. This coefficient measured the amount of the variance in the selection list rankings that could be explained by the worklist rankings. He found that "the average for all lists indicates that 82.5% of variance is the result of factors *other than* order on the out-of-work list."[33] The district court found that this analysis corroborated the plaintiffs' allegations "in the sense that it proves there is much room for arbitrary and standardless selection."[34] On the basis of this and other statistical evidence, the district court found discrimination.

§10.8.3　Discrimination by Government Entities

In this area, as in those discussed in the preceding two sections, the case law is voluminous and the range of statistical techniques used

---

[29] Id.

[30] Id. at 446.

[31] 469 F. Supp. 329 (E.D. Pa. 1978), *aff'd mem.*, 648 F.2d 922 (3d Cir. 1981), *rev'd sub nom.* General Bldg. Contractors Assn. v. Pennsylvania, 458 U.S. 375 (1982) (the Supreme Court reversed on the issue of the burden of proof under 42 U.S.C. §1981 and did not reach the statistical evidence).

[32] 469 F. Supp. at 355.

[33] Id. at 356 (emphasis in original).

[34] Id. at 357.

is broad. In the first illustrative case, *Jurgens v. Thomas,*[35] the Equal Employment Opportunity Commission was forced to defend its own affirmative action policy against a charge that the policy discriminated against white males. Both sides introduced extensive statistical evidence in support of their positions. Both parties, for example, compared the promotion rates for white males with those for other groups.[36] The plaintiffs' expert performed a single analysis that aggregated employees in all job grades. Using a *chi-square test* (Section 5.1) of significance, he found a highly significant disparity between all men and all women ($p = .0001$) and a marginally significant disparity between white males and all others. The EEOC expert compared white males to all others in a few selected job categories. Using a Z *test* (Section 4.14), he found that the observed white male promotion rate was not significantly lower than the expected rate. He also did an aggregate analysis and found again that the observed promotion rate for white males was not significantly lower than the expected rate. The two experts argued, apparently inconclusively, over whether *Fisher's Exact Test* (Sections 4.17 and 5.9.1) would have been a more appropriate test of significance.

The case discusses a number of other statistical issues. References to data collection and sampling procedures, for example, appear throughout the opinion. The case is perhaps most valuable, however, as an illustration of the shifting burden of persuasion in an employment discrimination case. The plaintiffs presented statistical evidence sufficient to create a prima facie case. The EEOC responded not with generalities but with specific criticisms of the plaintiff's analyses and with statistical alternatives to many of them. While the court accepted many of the EEOC's arguments, it concluded that its practices had in fact had a discriminatory impact on white males.[37]

In *Ensley Branch, NAACP v. Seibels,*[38] the issue was whether tests administered to applicants for police and fire positions had a disparate impact on blacks. A number of statistical analyses were discussed by the court. The plaintiffs introduced summary statistics showing that the proportion of blacks on the police and fire departments was substantially less than the proportion of blacks in the local population. In an effort to validate the tests that had led to this underrepresenta-

---

[35] 30 Empl. Prac. Dec. (CCH) ¶33,090 (N.D. Tex. 1982).
[36] Id. at 27,299.
[37] Id. at 27,307.
[38] 13 Emp. Prac. Dec. (CCH) ¶11,504 (N.D. Ala. 1977).

tion, two experts employed by the defendant calculated sample *means* (Section 4.21.1) and *standard deviations* (Section 4.7) for test scores achieved by black and white candidates, and then used the *t* test (Section 6.12) to assess the significance of the differences found. Many of the differences between blacks and whites were significant. They calculated the same statistics for the academy scores and performance ratings achieved by black and white officers.

Next, the defendant's experts calculated *correlation coefficients* (Section 6.2) for test scores and various measures of performance on the job. Comparing the correlation coefficients for the two racial groups, they found no significant differences between blacks and whites with respect to the extent to which test scores correlated with job performance. Finally, they performed *regression analyses* (Section 8.1) to measure to what extent test scores accurately predicted job performance for each group. Differences between the regression lines for the two groups were evaluated for significance using the F-*test* (Section 8.12). The net result, the court concluded, was that the tests that had been studied in this manner did not appear to predict job performance any less accurately for blacks than for whites.[39] Nonetheless, the court found that the defendant had not fully explained the gross disparities relied on by the plaintiffs and ordered remedial hiring measures.[40]

In *EEOC v. Federal Reserve Bank of Richmond*,[41] the defendant bank was alleged to have discriminated against blacks in promotion policies. The district court found discrimination in two pay grades, but the court of appeals reversed. One of the statistical issues discussed by the court of appeals was the calculation of the number of *standard deviations* (Section 4.11) by which the observed numbers of black promotions differed from the expected numbers. The plaintiffs' expert, in testimony accepted by the district court, used a formula associated with the *hypergeometric distribution* (Section 4.17) in calculating standard deviations. Citing statistical texts, the court of appeals noted that the hypergeometric formula is appropriate "when small numbers are involved and when these numbers are 'finite' . . . without replacements."[42] After reviewing the samples from which the

[39] Id., 6798-6802.
[40] Id. at 6808.
[41] 698 F.2d 633 (4th Cir. 1983), *rev'd*, 104 S. Ct. 2794 (1984). The Supreme Court's opinion dealt only with the issue of whether the class judgment was res judicata of individual actions and did not reach the statistical evidence.
[42] 698 F.2d at 650.

standard deviations were calculated, the court found that neither of the reasons for selecting the hypergeometric formula obtained, and thus a formula associated with the *binomial distribution* (Section 4.15) should have been used. The error was a material one, the court emphasized, because the hypergeometric calculations led to higher standard deviations, which were more favorable to the plaintiffs.

The final case in this category is the Supreme Court's often cited decision in *Castaneda v. Partida.*[43] The case arose when a Mexican-American prisoner filed a habeas corpus petition alleging that Texas discriminated against Mexican-Americans in choosing grand juries, including the one that had indicted him. The petitioner's most important evidence was the fact that over an 11-year period only 39% of the grand jurors in the relevant county had been Mexican-American even though the population of the county was 79% Mexican-American. In a lengthy footnote[44] the Court pointed out that the variable of interest, number of Mexican-American grand jurors, was binomially distributed. It noted that the observed number of Mexican-American grand jurors was 339, versus an expected number of 688. The Court then calculated the *standard deviation* (Section 4.21.3) of the binomial variable, and found "[a] difference between the expected and observed number of Mexican-Americans of approximately 29 standard deviations."[45] It stated that "[a]s a general rule for such large samples, if the difference between the expected value and the observed number is greater than two or three standard deviations, then the hypothesis that the jury drawing was random would be suspect to a social scientist."[46] The Court went on to conclude that the petitioner had made out a prima facie case, and that the qualitative, anecdotal evidence offered by the state was not an adequate rebuttal. The "two or three standard deviation" guideline mentioned in the footnote has been repeatedly cited by the lower courts.[47]

---

[43] 430 U.S. 482 (1977).
[44] Id. at 496 n. 17.
[45] Id.
[46] Id.
[47] See Section 4.11 on the history of this rule.

APPENDIX A

Standard Statistical Tables

Z Table

Z	0.00	0.01	0.02	0.03	0.04	0.05	0.06	0.07	0.08	0.09
0.0	.0000	.0040	.0080	.0120	.0160	.0199	.0239	.0279	.0319	.0359
0.1	.0398	.0438	.0478	.0517	.0557	.0596	.0636	.0675	.0714	.0753
0.2	.0793	.0832	.0871	.0910	.0948	.0987	.1026	.1064	.1103	.1141
0.3	.1179	.1217	.1255	.1293	.1331	.1368	.1406	.1443	.1480	.1517
0.4	.1554	.1591	.1628	.1664	.1700	.1736	.1772	.1808	.1844	.1879
0.5	.1915	.1950	.1985	.2019	.2054	.2088	.2123	.2157	.2190	.2224
0.6	.2257	.2291	.2324	.2357	.2389	.2422	.2454	.2486	.2517	.2549
0.7	.2580	.2611	.2642	.2673	.2704	.2734	.2764	.2794	.2823	.2852
0.8	.2881	.2910	.2939	.2967	.2995	.3023	.3051	.3078	.3106	.3133
0.9	.3159	.3186	.3212	.3238	.3264	.3289	.3315	.3340	.3365	.3389
1.0	.3413	.3438	.3461	.3485	.3508	.3531	.3554	.3577	.3599	.3621
1.1	.3643	.3665	.3686	.3708	.3729	.3749	.3770	.3790	.3810	.3830
1.2	.3849	.3869	.3888	.3907	.3925	.3944	.3962	.3980	.3997	.4015
1.3	.4032	.4049	.4066	.4082	.4099	.4115	.4131	.4147	.4162	.4177
1.4	.4192	.4207	.4222	.4236	.4251	.4265	.4279	.4292	.4306	.4319
1.5	.4332	.4345	.4357	.4370	.4382	.4394	.4406	.4418	.4429	.4441
1.6	.4452	.4463	.4474	.4484	.4495	.4505	.4515	.4525	.4535	.4545
1.7	.4554	.4564	.4573	.4582	.4591	.4599	.4608	.4616	.4625	.4633
1.8	.4641	.4649	.4656	.4664	.4671	.4678	.4686	.4693	.4699	.4706
1.9	.4713	.4719	.4726	.4732	.4738	.4744	.4750	.4756	.4761	.4767

z	.00	.01	.02	.03	.04	.05	.06	.07	.08	.09
2.0	.4773	.4778	.4783	.4788	.4793	.4798	.4803	.4808	.4812	.4817
2.1	.4821	.4826	.4830	.4834	.4838	.4842	.4846	.4850	.4854	.4857
2.2	.4861	.4864	.4868	.4871	.4875	.4878	.4881	.4884	.4887	.4890
2.3	.4893	.4896	.4898	.4901	.4904	.4906	.4909	.4911	.4913	.4916
2.4	.4918	.4920	.4922	.4925	.4927	.4929	.4931	.4932	.4934	.4936
2.5	.4938	.4940	.4941	.4943	.4945	.4946	.4948	.4949	.4951	.4952
2.6	.4953	.4955	.4956	.4957	.4959	.4960	.4961	.4962	.4963	.4964
2.7	.4965	.4966	.4967	.4968	.4969	.4970	.4971	.4972	.4973	.4974
2.8	.4974	.4975	.4976	.4977	.4977	.4978	.4979	.4979	.4980	.4981
2.9	.4981	.4982	.4983	.4983	.4984	.4984	.4985	.4985	.4986	.4986
3.0	.4987	.4987	.4987	.4988	.4988	.4989	.4989	.4989	.4989	.4990
3.1	.4990	.4991	.4991	.4991	.4992	.4992	.4992	.4992	.4993	.4993
3.2	.4993	.4993	.4994	.4994	.4994	.4994	.4994	.4995	.4995	.4995
3.3	.4995	.4995	.4996	.4996	.4996	.4996	.4996	.4996	.4996	.4997
3.4	.4997	.4997	.4997	.4997	.4997	.4997	.4997	.4997	.4997	.4998
3.5	.4998	.4998	.4998	.4998	.4998	.4998	.4998	.4998	.4998	.4998
3.6	.4998	.4998	.4999	.4999	.4999	.4999	.4999	.4999	.4999	.4999
3.7	.4999	.4999	.4999	.4999	.4999	.4999	.4999	.4999	.4999	.4999
3.8	.4999	.4999	.4999	.4999	.4999	.4999	.4999	.4999	.4999	.5000
3.9	.5000	.5000	.5000	.5000	.5000	.5000	.5000	.5000	.5000	.5000

Source: R. Fisher and F. Yates, Statistical Tables for Biological, Agricultural and Medical Research 45 (Table II) (6th ed. 1963). Reprinted with permission of Oliver and Boyd, Edinburgh.

Table of Critical Values of Z

Significance Level

One-Tailed Test												
.45	.40	.35	.30	.25	.20	.15	.10	.05	.025	.01	.005	.0005

Two-Tailed Test												
.90	.80	.70	.60	.50	.40	.30	.20	.10	.05	.02	.01	.001
.126	.253	.385	.524	.674	.842	1.036	1.282	1.645	1.960	2.326	2.576	3.291

Random Number Table

03528	28071	97041	45167	35421	71345	47286	83567	94170
49761	39465	52683	82093	09867	06982	10359	49102	65328
80219	29485	85093	45687	32579	52867	70851	03621	51490
43657	70361	24176	30129	48016	03194	29463	94587	32768
36524	07561	67820	20739	69045	54978	90317	64529	57319
97801	98234	13459	58146	13782	36102	48562	78301	64802
56913	06289	64527	30265	43209	84152	69183	01278	41973
84027	51734	80193	49718	81675	69307	47250	39546	25068
70523	83297	81239	05913	75206	18350	81623	59327	08317
68194	60541	06745	68742	38491	67924	07549	64081	56492
59208	56078	74268	54981	12573	51246	43985	04628	54670
13674	31492	09351	27630	68490	38097	27160	97531	32918
40329	15237	65897	18693	43709	10783	41237	72168	87194
71568	98604	13402	20547	58612	95426	89605	35904	23506
78136	62531	92143	28935	98410	78059	76901	24618	85102
09452	84097	05876	46107	75236	61432	35482	57093	93647
58236	29871	53107	50762	47103	81973	35716	83924	21593
10974	64350	89264	41839	69852	65042	42089	67501	40678
83417	26179	19562	71358	78542	72896	74312	57346	16248
29065	45038	38704	90246	13069	43105	85960	82019	97305
48210	25789	52193	36489	82167	01325	52839	25301	24150
79365	31460	04687	17502	49053	74896	70614	78649	63987
67439	45961	21035	64530	84067	32516	57819	23461	15894
10285	80723	64789	81972	51923	07498	04623	80957	06723
25481	69345	02391	32647	27845	92017	82401	95342	02538
70963	17820	68574	85091	16093	64538	93756	01786	67419
59816	13897	31250	32940	28754	48721	31748	43960	93028
47023	45260	47896	68751	61039	63905	96250	78521	54176
03957	87529	60895	27615	21875	74590	90758	29064	57408
84612	61403	23714	40839	69403	31286	34621	87513	63219

Source: R. Fisher and F. Yates, Statistical Tables for Biological, Agricultural and Medical Research 140 (Table XXXIIIi) (6th ed. 1963). Reprinted with permission of Oliver and Boyd, Edinburgh.

Cumulative Binomial Table

n	x	.05	.10	.15	.20	.25	P .30	.35	.40	.45	.50
2	1	.0975	.1900	.2775	.3600	.4375	.5100	.5775	.6400	.6975	.7500
	2	.0025	.0100	.0225	.0400	.0625	.0900	.1225	.1600	.2025	.2500
3	1	.1426	.2710	.3859	.4880	.5781	.6570	.7254	.7840	.8336	.8750
	2	.0072	.0280	.0608	.1040	.1562	.2160	.2818	.3520	.4252	.5000
	3	.0001	.0010	.0034	.0080	.0156	.0270	.0429	.0640	.0911	.1250
4	1	.1855	.3439	.4780	.5904	.6836	.7599	.8215	.8704	.9085	.9375
	2	.0140	.0523	.1095	.1808	.2617	.3483	.4370	.5248	.6090	.6875
	3	.0005	.0037	.0120	.0272	.0508	.0837	.1265	.1792	.2415	.3125
	4	.0000	.0001	.0005	.0016	.0039	.0081	.0150	.0256	.0410	.0625
5	1	.2262	.4095	.5563	.6723	.7627	.8319	.8840	.9222	.9497	.9688
	2	.0226	.0815	.1648	.2627	.3672	.4718	.5716	.6630	.7438	.8125
	3	.0012	.0086	.0266	.0579	.1035	.1631	.2352	.3174	.4069	.5000
	4	.0000	.0005	.0022	.0067	.0156	.0308	.0540	.0870	.1312	.1875
	5	.0000	.0000	.0001	.0003	.0010	.0024	.0053	.0102	.0185	.0312
6	1	.2649	.4686	.6229	.7379	.8220	.8824	.9246	.9533	.9723	.9844
	2	.0328	.1143	.2235	.3447	.4661	.5798	.6809	.7667	.8364	.8906
	3	.0022	.0158	.0473	.0989	.1694	.2557	.3529	.4557	.5585	.6562
	4	.0001	.0013	.0059	.0170	.0376	.0705	.1174	.1792	.2553	.3438
	5	.0000	.0001	.0004	.0016	.0046	.0109	.0223	.0410	.0692	.1094
	6	.0000	.0000	.0000	.0001	.0002	.0007	.0018	.0041	.0083	.0156

n	x										
7	1	.3017	.5217	.6794	.7903	.8665	.9176	.9510	.9720	.9848	.9922
	2	.0444	.1497	.2834	.4233	.5551	.6706	.7662	.8414	.8976	.9375
	3	.0038	.0257	.0738	.1480	.2436	.3529	.4677	.5801	.6836	.7734
	4	.0002	.0027	.0121	.0333	.0706	.1260	.1998	.2898	.3917	.5000
	5	.0000	.0002	.0012	.0047	.0129	.0288	.0556	.0963	.1529	.2266
	6	.0000	.0000	.0001	.0004	.0013	.0038	.0090	.0188	.0357	.0625
	7	.0000	.0000	.0000	.0000	.0001	.0002	.0006	.0016	.0037	.0078
8	1	.3366	.5695	.7275	.8322	.8999	.9424	.9681	.9832	.9916	.9961
	2	.0572	.1869	.3428	.4967	.6329	.7447	.8309	.8936	.9368	.9648
	3	.0058	.0381	.1052	.2031	.3215	.4482	.5722	.6846	.7799	.8555
	4	.0004	.0050	.0214	.0563	.1138	.1941	.2936	.4059	.5230	.6367
	5	.0000	.0004	.0029	.0104	.0273	.0580	.1061	.1737	.2604	.3633
	6	.0000	.0000	.0002	.0012	.0042	.0113	.0253	.0498	.0885	.1445
	7	.0000	.0000	.0000	.0001	.0004	.0013	.0036	.0085	.0181	.0352
	8	.0000	.0000	.0000	.0000	.0000	.0001	.0002	.0007	.0017	.0039
9	1	.3698	.6126	.7684	.8658	.9249	.9596	.9793	.9899	.9954	.9980
	2	.0712	.2252	.4005	.5638	.6997	.8040	.8789	.9295	.9615	.9805
	3	.0084	.0530	.1409	.2618	.3993	.5372	.6627	.7682	.8505	.9102
	4	.0006	.0083	.0339	.0856	.1657	.2703	.3911	.5174	.6386	.7461
	5	.0000	.0009	.0056	.0196	.0489	.0988	.1717	.2666	.3786	.5000
	6	.0000	.0001	.0006	.0031	.0100	.0253	.0536	.0994	.1658	.2539
	7	.0000	.0000	.0000	.0003	.0013	.0043	.0112	.0250	.0498	.0898
	8	.0000	.0000	.0000	.0000	.0001	.0004	.0014	.0038	.0091	.0195
	9	.0000	.0000	.0000	.0000	.0000	.0000	.0001	.0003	.0008	.0020

Linear interpolation will be accurate at most to two decimal places.

Cumulative Binomial Table (*continued*)

n	x	.05	.10	.15	.20	.25	.30	.35	.40	.45	.50
10	1	.4013	.6513	.8031	.8926	.9437	.9718	.9865	.9940	.9975	.9990
	2	.0861	.2639	.4557	.6242	.7560	.8507	.9140	.9536	.9767	.9893
	3	.0115	.0702	.1798	.3222	.4744	.6172	.7384	.8327	.9004	.9453
	4	.0010	.0128	.0500	.1209	.2241	.3504	.4862	.6177	.7340	.8281
	5	.0001	.0016	.0099	.0328	.0781	.1503	.2485	.3669	.4956	.6230
	6	.0000	.0001	.0014	.0064	.0197	.0473	.0949	.1662	.2616	.3770
	7	.0000	.0000	.0001	.0009	.0035	.0106	.0260	.0548	.1020	.1719
	8	.0000	.0000	.0000	.0001	.0004	.0016	.0048	.0123	.0274	.0547
	9	.0000	.0000	.0000	.0000	.0000	.0001	.0005	.0017	.0045	.0107
	10	.0000	.0000	.0000	.0000	.0000	.0000	.0000	.0001	.0003	.0010
11	1	.4312	.6862	.8327	.9141	.9578	.9802	.9912	.9964	.9986	.9995
	2	.1019	.3026	.5078	.6779	.8029	.8870	.9394	.9698	.9861	.9941
	3	.0152	.0896	.2212	.3826	.5448	.6873	.7999	.8811	.9348	.9673
	4	.0016	.0185	.0694	.1611	.2867	.4304	.5744	.7037	.8089	.8867
	5	.0001	.0028	.0159	.0504	.1146	.2103	.3317	.4672	.6029	.7256
	6	.0000	.0003	.0027	.0117	.0343	.0782	.1487	.2465	.3669	.5000
	7	.0000	.0000	.0003	.0020	.0076	.0216	.0501	.0994	.1738	.2744
	8	.0000	.0000	.0000	.0002	.0012	.0043	.0122	.0293	.0610	.1133
	9	.0000	.0000	.0000	.0000	.0001	.0006	.0020	.0059	.0148	.0327
	10	.0000	.0000	.0000	.0000	.0000	.0000	.0002	.0007	.0022	.0059
	11	.0000	.0000	.0000	.0000	.0000	.0000	.0000	.0000	.0002	.0005

n	x										
12	1	.9998	.9992	.9978	.9943	.9862	.9683	.9313	.8578	.7176	.4596
	2	.9968	.9917	.9804	.9576	.9150	.8416	.7251	.5565	.3410	.1184
	3	.9807	.9579	.9166	.8487	.7472	.6093	.4417	.2642	.1109	.0196
	4	.9270	.8655	.7747	.6533	.5075	.3512	.2054	.0922	.0256	.0022
	5	.8062	.6956	.5618	.4167	.2763	.1576	.0726	.0239	.0043	.0002
	6	.6128	.4731	.3348	.2127	.1178	.0544	.0194	.0046	.0005	.0000
	7	.3872	.2607	.1582	.0846	.0386	.0143	.0039	.0007	.0001	.0000
	8	.1938	.1117	.0573	.0255	.0095	.0028	.0006	.0001	.0000	.0000
	9	.0730	.0356	.0153	.0056	.0017	.0004	.0001	.0000	.0000	.0000
	10	.0193	.0079	.0028	.0008	.0002	.0000	.0000	.0000	.0000	.0000
	11	.0032	.0011	.0003	.0001	.0000	.0000	.0000	.0000	.0000	.0000
	12	.0002	.0001	.0000	.0000	.0000	.0000	.0000	.0000	.0000	.0000
13	1	.9999	.9996	.9987	.9963	.9903	.9762	.9450	.8791	.7458	.4867
	2	.9983	.9951	.9874	.9704	.9363	.8733	.7664	.6017	.3787	.1354
	3	.9888	.9731	.9421	.8868	.7975	.6674	.4983	.2704	.1339	.0245
	4	.9539	.9071	.8314	.7217	.5794	.4157	.2527	.0967	.0342	.0031
	5	.8666	.7721	.6470	.4995	.3457	.2060	.0991	.0260	.0065	.0003
	6	.7095	.5732	.4256	.2841	.1654	.0802	.0300	.0053	.0009	.0000
	7	.5000	.3563	.2288	.1295	.0624	.0243	.0070	.0013	.0001	.0000
	8	.2905	.1788	.0977	.0462	.0182	.0056	.0012	.0002	.0000	.0000
	9	.1334	.0698	.0321	.0126	.0040	.0010	.0002	.0000	.0000	.0000
	10	.0461	.0203	.0078	.0025	.0007	.0001	.0000	.0000	.0000	.0000
	11	.0112	.0041	.0013	.0003	.0001	.0000	.0000	.0000	.0000	.0000
	12	.0017	.0005	.0001	.0000	.0000	.0000	.0000	.0000	.0000	.0000
	13	.0001	.0000	.0000	.0000	.0000	.0000	.0000	.0000	.0000	.0000

Cumulative Binomial Table (*continued*)

						P					
n	x	.05	.10	.15	.20	.25	.30	.35	.40	.45	.50
14	1	.5123	.7712	.8972	.9560	.9822	.9932	.9976	.9992	.9998	.9999
	2	.1530	.4154	.6433	.8021	.8990	.9525	.9795	.9919	.9971	.9991
	3	.0301	.1584	.3521	.5519	.7189	.8392	.9161	.9602	.9830	.9935
	4	.0042	.0441	.1465	.3018	.4787	.6448	.7795	.8757	.9368	.9713
	5	.0004	.0092	.0467	.1298	.2585	.4158	.5773	.7207	.8328	.9102
	6	.0000	.0015	.0115	.0439	.1117	.2195	.3595	.5141	.6627	.7880
	7	.0000	.0002	.0022	.0116	.0383	.0933	.1836	.3075	.4539	.6047
	8	.0000	.0000	.0003	.0024	.0103	.0315	.0753	.1501	.2586	.3953
	9	.0000	.0000	.0000	.0004	.0022	.0083	.0243	.0583	.1189	.2120
	10	.0000	.0000	.0000	.0000	.0003	.0017	.0060	.0175	.0426	.0898
	11	.0000	.0000	.0000	.0000	.0000	.0002	.0011	.0039	.0114	.0287
	12	.0000	.0000	.0000	.0000	.0000	.0000	.0001	.0006	.0022	.0065
	13	.0000	.0000	.0000	.0000	.0000	.0000	.0000	.0001	.0003	.0009
	14	.0000	.0000	.0000	.0000	.0000	.0000	.0000	.0000	.0000	.0001
15	1	.5367	.7941	.9126	.9648	.9866	.9953	.9984	.9995	.9999	1.0000
	2	.1710	.4510	.6814	.8329	.9198	.9647	.9858	.9948	.9983	.9995
	3	.0362	.1841	.3958	.6020	.7639	.8732	.9383	.9729	.9893	.9963
	4	.0055	.0556	.1773	.3518	.5387	.7031	.8273	.9095	.9576	.9824
	5	.0006	.0127	.0617	.1642	.3135	.4845	.6481	.7827	.8796	.9408
	6	.0001	.0022	.0168	.0611	.1484	.2784	.4357	.5968	.7392	.8491
	7	.0000	.0003	.0036	.0181	.0566	.1311	.2452	.3902	.5478	.6964
	8	.0000	.0000	.0006	.0042	.0173	.0500	.1132	.2131	.3465	.5000
	9	.0000	.0000	.0001	.0008	.0042	.0152	.0422	.0950	.1818	.3036
	10	.0000	.0000	.0000	.0001	.0008	.0037	.0124	.0338	.0769	.1509

11	.0592	.0255	.0093	.0028	.0007	.0001	.0000	.0000	.0000	.0000
12	.0176	.0063	.0019	.0005	.0001	.0000	.0000	.0000	.0000	.0000
13	.0037	.0011	.0003	.0001	.0000	.0000	.0000	.0000	.0000	.0000
14	.0005	.0001	.0000	.0000	.0000	.0000	.0000	.0000	.0000	.0000
15	.0000	.0000	.0000	.0000	.0000	.0000	.0000	.0000	.0000	.0000
16										
1	1.0000	.9999	.9997	.9990	.9967	.9900	.9719	.9257	.8147	.5599
2	.9997	.9990	.9967	.9902	.9739	.9365	.8593	.7161	.4853	.1892
3	.9979	.9934	.9817	.9549	.9006	.8029	.6482	.4386	.2108	.0429
4	.9894	.9719	.9349	.8661	.7541	.5950	.4019	.2101	.0684	.0070
5	.9616	.9147	.8334	.7108	.5501	.3698	.2018	.0791	.0170	.0009
6	.8949	.8024	.6712	.5100	.3402	.1897	.0817	.0235	.0033	.0001
7	.7228	.6340	.4728	.3119	.1753	.0796	.0267	.0056	.0005	.0000
8	.5982	.4371	.2839	.1594	.0744	.0271	.0070	.0011	.0001	.0000
9	.4018	.2559	.1423	.0671	.0257	.0075	.0015	.0002	.0000	.0000
10	.2272	.1241	.0583	.0229	.0071	.0016	.0002	.0000	.0000	.0000
11	.1051	.0486	.0191	.0062	.0016	.0003	.0000	.0000	.0000	.0000
12	.0384	.0149	.0049	.0013	.0003	.0000	.0000	.0000	.0000	.0000
13	.0106	.0035	.0009	.0002	.0000	.0000	.0000	.0000	.0000	.0000
14	.0021	.0006	.0001	.0000	.0000	.0000	.0000	.0000	.0000	.0000
15	.0003	.0001	.0000	.0000	.0000	.0000	.0000	.0000	.0000	.0000
16	.0000	.0000	.0000	.0000	.0000	.0000	.0000	.0000	.0000	.0000

Cumulative Binomial Table (*continued*)

n	x	.05	.10	.15	.20	.25	P .30	.35	.40	.45	.50
17	1	.5819	.8332	.9369	.9775	.9925	.9977	.9993	.9998	1.0000	1.0000
	2	.2078	.5182	.7475	.8818	.9499	.9807	.9933	.9979	.9994	.9999
	3	.0503	.2382	.4802	.6904	.8363	.9226	.9673	.9877	.9959	.9988
	4	.0088	.0826	.2444	.4511	.6470	.7981	.8972	.9536	.9816	.9936
	5	.0012	.0221	.0987	.2418	.4261	.6113	.7652	.8740	.9404	.9755
	6	.0001	.0047	.0319	.1057	.2347	.4032	.5803	.7361	.8529	.9283
	7	.0000	.0008	.0083	.0377	.1071	.2248	.3812	.5522	.7098	.8338
	8	.0000	.0001	.0017	.0109	.0402	.1046	.2128	.3595	.5257	.6855
	9	.0000	.0000	.0003	.0026	.0124	.0403	.0994	.1989	.3374	.5000
	10	.0000	.0000	.0000	.0005	.0031	.0127	.0383	.0919	.1834	.3145
	11	.0000	.0000	.0000	.0001	.0006	.0032	.0120	.0348	.0826	.1662
	12	.0000	.0000	.0000	.0000	.0001	.0007	.0030	.0106	.0301	.0717
	13	.0000	.0000	.0000	.0000	.0000	.0001	.0006	.0025	.0086	.0245
	14	.0000	.0000	.0000	.0000	.0000	.0000	.0000	.0005	.0019	.0064
	15	.0000	.0000	.0000	.0000	.0000	.0000	.0000	.0001	.0003	.0012
	16	.0000	.0000	.0000	.0000	.0000	.0000	.0000	.0000	.0000	.0001
	17	.0000	.0000	.0000	.0000	.0000	.0000	.0000	.0000	.0000	.0000
18	1	.6028	.8499	.9464	.9820	.9944	.9984	.9996	.9999	1.0000	1.0000
	2	.2265	.5497	.7759	.9009	.9605	.9858	.9954	.9987	.9997	.9999
	3	.0581	.2662	.5203	.7287	.8647	.9400	.9764	.9918	.9975	.9993
	4	.0109	.0982	.2798	.4990	.6943	.8354	.9217	.9672	.9880	.9962
	5	.0015	.0282	.1206	.2836	.4813	.6673	.8114	.9058	.9589	.9846

6	.0002	.0064	.0419	.1329	.2825	.4656	.6450	.7912	.8923	.9519
7	.0000	.0012	.0118	.0513	.1390	.2783	.4509	.6257	.7742	.8811
8	.0000	.0002	.0027	.0163	.0569	.1407	.2717	.4366	.6085	.7597
9	.0000	.0000	.0005	.0043	.0193	.0596	.1391	.2632	.4222	.5927
10	.0000	.0000	.0001	.0009	.0054	.0210	.0597	.1347	.2527	.4073
11	.0000	.0000	.0000	.0002	.0012	.0061	.0212	.0576	.1280	.2403
12	.0000	.0000	.0000	.0000	.0002	.0014	.0062	.0203	.0537	.1189
13	.0000	.0000	.0000	.0000	.0000	.0003	.0014	.0058	.0183	.0481
14	.0000	.0000	.0000	.0000	.0000	.0000	.0003	.0013	.0049	.0154
15	.0000	.0000	.0000	.0000	.0000	.0000	.0000	.0002	.0010	.0038
16	.0000	.0000	.0000	.0000	.0000	.0000	.0000	.0000	.0001	.0007
17	.0000	.0000	.0000	.0000	.0000	.0000	.0000	.0000	.0000	.0001
18	.0000	.0000	.0000	.0000	.0000	.0000	.0000	.0000	.0000	.0000
19 1	.8228	.8649	.9544	.9856	.9958	.9989	.9997	.9999	1.0000	1.0000
2	.2453	.5797	.8015	.9171	.9690	.9896	.9969	.9992	.9998	1.0000
3	.0665	.2946	.5587	.7631	.8887	.9538	.9830	.9945	.9985	.9996
4	.0132	.1150	.3159	.5449	.7369	.8668	.9409	.9770	.9923	.9978
5	.0020	.0352	.1444	.3267	.5346	.7178	.8500	.9304	.9720	.9904
6	.0002	.0086	.0537	.1631	.3322	.5261	.7032	.8371	.9223	.9682
7	.0000	.0017	.0163	.0676	.1749	.3345	.5188	.6919	.8273	.9165
8	.0000	.0003	.0041	.0233	.0775	.1820	.3344	.5122	.6831	.8204
9	.0000	.0000	.0008	.0067	.0287	.0839	.1855	.3325	.5060	.6762
10	.0000	.0000	.0001	.0016	.0089	.0326	.0875	.1861	.3290	.5000

Cumulative Binomial Table (*continued*)

n	x	.05	.10	.15	.20	P .25	.30	.35	.40	.45	.50
19	11	.0000	.0000	.0000	.0003	.0023	.0105	.0347	.0885	.1841	.3238
	12	.0000	.0000	.0000	.0000	.0005	.0028	.0114	.0352	.0871	.1796
	13	.0000	.0000	.0000	.0000	.0001	.0006	.0031	.0116	.0342	.0835
	14	.0000	.0000	.0000	.0000	.0000	.0001	.0007	.0031	.0109	.0318
	15	.0000	.0000	.0000	.0000	.0000	.0000	.0001	.0006	.0028	.0096
	16	.0000	.0000	.0000	.0000	.0000	.0000	.0000	.0001	.0005	.0022
	17	.0000	.0000	.0000	.0000	.0000	.0000	.0000	.0000	.0001	.0004
	18	.0000	.0000	.0000	.0000	.0000	.0000	.0000	.0000	.0000	.0000
	19	.0000	.0000	.0000	.0000	.0000	.0000	.0000	.0000	.0000	.0000
20	1	.6415	.8784	.9612	.9885	.9968	.9992	.9998	1.0000	1.0000	1.0000
	2	.2642	.6083	.8244	.9308	.9757	.9924	.9979	.9995	.9999	1.0000
	3	.0755	.3231	.5951	.7939	.9087	.9645	.9879	.9964	.9991	.9998
	4	.0159	.1330	.3523	.5886	.7748	.8929	.9556	.9840	.9951	.9987
	5	.0026	.0432	.1702	.3704	.5852	.7625	.8818	.9490	.9811	.9941
	6	.0003	.0113	.0673	.1958	.3828	.5836	.7546	.8744	.9447	.9793
	7	.0000	.0024	.0219	.0867	.2142	.3920	.5834	.7500	.8701	.9423
	8	.0000	.0004	.0059	.0321	.1018	.2277	.3990	.5841	.7480	.8684
	9	.0000	.0001	.0013	.0100	.0409	.1133	.2376	.4044	.5857	.7483
	10	.0000	.0000	.0002	.0026	.0139	.0480	.1218	.2447	.4086	.5881
	11	.0000	.0000	.0000	.0006	.0039	.0171	.0532	.1275	.2493	.4119
	12	.0000	.0000	.0000	.0001	.0009	.0051	.0196	.0565	.1308	.2517
	13	.0000	.0000	.0000	.0000	.0002	.0013	.0060	.0210	.0580	.1316
	14	.0000	.0000	.0000	.0000	.0000	.0003	.0015	.0065	.0214	.0577
	15	.0000	.0000	.0000	.0000	.0000	.0000	.0003	.0016	.0064	.0207

16	.0059	.0015	.0003	.0000	.0000	.0000	.0000	.0000	.0000	.0000
17	.0013	.0003	.0000	.0000	.0000	.0000	.0000	.0000	.0000	.0000
18	.0002	.0000	.0000	.0000	.0000	.0000	.0000	.0000	.0000	.0000
19	.0000	.0000	.0000	.0000	.0000	.0000	.0000	.0000	.0000	.0000
20	.0000	.0000	.0000	.0000	.0000	.0000	.0000	.0000	.0000	.0000
21										
1	1.0000	1.0000	1.0000	.9999	.9994	.9976	.9908	.9671	.8906	.6594
2	1.0000	.9999	.9997	.9996	.9944	.9810	.9424	.8450	.6353	.2830
3	.9999	.9994	.9976	.9914	.9729	.9255	.8213	.6295	.3516	.0849
4	.9993	.9969	.9890	.9660	.9144	.8083	.6296	.3887	.1520	.0189
5	.9967	.9874	.9630	.9076	.8016	.6326	.4140	.1975	.0522	.0032
6	.9867	.9611	.9043	.7991	.6373	.4334	.2307	.0827	.0144	.0004
7	.9608	.9036	.7998	.6433	.4495	.2564	.1085	.0287	.0033	.0000
8	.9054	.8029	.6505	.4635	.2770	.1299	.0431	.0083	.0006	.0000
9	.8083	.6587	.4763	.2941	.1477	.0561	.0144	.0020	.0001	.0000
10	.6682	.4883	.3086	.1632	.0676	.0206	.0041	.0004	.0000	.0000
11	.5000	.3210	.1744	.0772	.0264	.0064	.0010	.0001	.0000	.0000
12	.3318	.1841	.0849	.0313	.0087	.0017	.0002	.0000	.0000	.0000
13	.1917	.0908	.0352	.0108	.0024	.0004	.0000	.0000	.0000	.0000
14	.0946	.0379	.0123	.0031	.0006	.0001	.0000	.0000	.0000	.0000
15	.0392	.0132	.0036	.0007	.0001	.0000	.0000	.0000	.0000	.0000
16	.0133	.0037	.0008	.0001	.0000	.0000	.0000	.0000	.0000	.0000
17	.0036	.0008	.0002	.0000	.0000	.0000	.0000	.0000	.0000	.0000
18	.0007	.0001	.0000	.0000	.0000	.0000	.0000	.0000	.0000	.0000
19	.0001	.0000	.0000	.0000	.0000	.0000	.0000	.0000	.0000	.0000

Cumulative Binomial Table (continued)

n	x	.05	.10	.15	.20	.25	.30	.35	.40	.45	.50
21	20	.0000	.0000	.0000	.0000	.0000	.0000	.0000	.0000	.0000	.0000
	21	.0000	.0000	.0000	.0000	.0000	.0000	.0000	.0000	.0000	.0000
22	1	.6765	.9015	.9720	.9926	.9982	.9966	.9999	1.0000	1.0000	1.0000
	2	.3018	.6608	.8633	.9520	.9851	.9959	.9990	.9998	1.0000	1.0000
	3	.0948	.3800	.6618	.8455	.9394	.9793	.9399	.9984	.9997	.9999
	4	.0222	.1719	.4248	.6680	.8376	.9319	.9755	.9924	.9980	.9996
	5	.0040	.0621	.2262	.4571	.6765	.8355	.9284	.9734	.9917	.9978
	6	.0006	.0182	.0999	.2674	.4832	.6866	.8371	.9278	.9729	.9915
	7	.0001	.0044	.0368	.1330	.3006	.5058	.6978	.8416	.9295	.9738
	8	.0000	.0009	.0114	.0561	.1615	.3287	.5264	.7102	.8482	.9331
	9	.0000	.0001	.0030	.0201	.0746	.1865	.3534	.5460	.7236	.8569
	10	.0000	.0000	.0007	.0061	.0295	.0916	.2084	.3756	.5650	.7383
	11	.0000	.0000	.0001	.0016	.0100	.0387	.1070	.2281	.3963	.5841
	12	.0000	.0000	.0000	.0003	.0029	.0140	.0474	.1207	.2457	.4159
	13	.0000	.0000	.0000	.0001	.0007	.0043	.0180	.0551	.1328	.2617
	14	.0000	.0000	.0000	.0000	.0001	.0011	.0058	.0215	.0617	.1431
	15	.0000	.0000	.0000	.0000	.0000	.0002	.0015	.0070	.0243	.0669
	16	.0000	.0000	.0000	.0000	.0000	.0000	.0003	.0019	.0080	.0262
	17	.0000	.0000	.0000	.0000	.0000	.0000	.0001	.0004	.0021	.0085
	18	.0000	.0000	.0000	.0000	.0000	.0000	.0000	.0001	.0005	.0022
	19	.0000	.0000	.0000	.0000	.0000	.0000	.0000	.0000	.0001	.0004
	20	.0000	.0000	.0000	.0000	.0000	.0000	.0000	.0000	.0000	.0001

21	.0000	.0000	.0000	.0000	.0000	.0000	.0000	.0000	.0000	.0000
22	.0000	.0000	.0000	.0000	.0000	.0000	.0000	.0000	.0000	.0000

23	1	1.0000	1.0000	1.0000	1.0000	.9997	.9987	.9941	.9762	.9114	.6926
	2	1.0000	1.0000	.9999	.9993	.9970	.9884	.9602	.8796	.6849	.3206
	3	1.0000	1.0000	.9990	.9957	.9843	.9508	.8668	.6920	.4080	.1052
	4	.9998	.9988	.9948	.9819	.9462	.8630	.7035	.4604	.1927	.0258
	5	.9987	.9945	.9810	.9449	.8644	.7168	.4993	.2560	.0731	.0049
	6	.9947	.9814	.9460	.8691	.7312	.5315	.3053	.1189	.0226	.0008
	7	.9827	.9490	.8760	.7466	.5601	.3463	.1598	.0463	.0058	.0001
	8	.9534	.8848	.7627	.5864	.3819	.1963	.0715	.0152	.0012	.0000
	9	.8950	.7797	.6116	.4140	.2291	.0903	.0273	.0042	.0002	.0000
	10	.7976	.6364	.4438	.2592	.1201	.0408	.0089	.0010	.0000	.0000
	11	.6612	.4722	.2871	.1425	.0546	.0149	.0025	.0002	.0000	.0000
	12	.5000	.3135	.1636	.0682	.0214	.0046	.0006	.0000	.0000	.0000
	13	.3388	.1836	.0813	.0283	.0072	.0012	.0001	.0000	.0000	.0000
	14	.2024	.0937	.0349	.0100	.0021	.0003	.0000	.0000	.0000	.0000
	15	.1050	.0411	.0128	.0030	.0005	.0001	.0000	.0000	.0000	.0000
	16	.0466	.0153	.0040	.0008	.0001	.0000	.0000	.0000	.0000	.0000
	17	.0173	.0048	.0010	.0002	.0000	.0000	.0000	.0000	.0000	.0000
	18	.0053	.0012	.0002	.0000	.0000	.0000	.0000	.0000	.0000	.0000
	19	.0013	.0002	.0000	.0000	.0000	.0000	.0000	.0000	.0000	.0000
	20	.0002	.0000	.0000	.0000	.0000	.0000	.0000	.0000	.0000	.0000
	21	.0000	.0000	.0000	.0000	.0000	.0000	.0000	.0000	.0000	.0000
	22	.0000	.0000	.0000	.0000	.0000	.0000	.0000	.0000	.0000	.0000
	23	.0000	.0000	.0000	.0000	.0000	.0000	.0000	.0000	.0000	.0000

Cumulative Binomial Table (*continued*)

n	x	.05	.10	.15	.20	.25	.30	.35	.40	.45	.50
24	1	.7080	.9202	.9798	.9953	.9990	.9998	1.0000	1.0000	1.0000	1.0000
	2	.3391	.7075	.8941	.9669	.9910	.9978	.9995	.9999	1.0000	1.0000
	3	.1159	.4357	.7202	.8855	.9602	.9881	.9970	.9993	.9999	1.0000
	4	.0298	.2143	.4951	.7361	.8850	.9576	.9867	.9965	.9992	.9999
	5	.0060	.0851	.2866	.5401	.7534	.8889	.9578	.9866	.9964	.9992
	6	.0010	.0277	.1394	.3441	.5778	.7712	.8956	.9600	.9873	.9967
	7	.0001	.0075	.0572	.1889	.3926	.6114	.7894	.9040	.9636	.9887
	8	.0000	.0017	.0199	.0892	.2338	.4353	.6425	.8081	.9137	.9680
	9	.0000	.0003	.0059	.0362	.1213	.2750	.4743	.6721	.8270	.9242
	10	.0000	.0001	.0015	.0126	.0547	.1528	.3134	.5109	.7009	.8463
	11	.0000	.0000	.0003	.0038	.0213	.0742	.1833	.3498	.5461	.7294
	12	.0000	.0000	.0001	.0010	.0072	.0314	.0942	.2130	.3849	.5806
	13	.0000	.0000	.0000	.0002	.0021	.0115	.0423	.1143	.2420	.4194
	14	.0000	.0000	.0000	.0000	.0005	.0036	.0164	.0535	.1341	.2706
	15	.0000	.0000	.0000	.0000	.0001	.0010	.0055	.0217	.0648	.1537
	16	.0000	.0000	.0000	.0000	.0000	.0002	.0016	.0075	.0269	.0758
	17	.0000	.0000	.0000	.0000	.0000	.0000	.0004	.0022	.0095	.0320
	18	.0000	.0000	.0000	.0000	.0000	.0000	.0001	.0005	.0028	.0113
	19	.0000	.0000	.0000	.0000	.0000	.0000	.0000	.0001	.0007	.0033
	20	.0000	.0000	.0000	.0000	.0000	.0000	.0000	.0000	.0001	.0008
	21	.0000	.0000	.0000	.0000	.0000	.0000	.0000	.0000	.0000	.0001
	22	.0000	.0000	.0000	.0000	.0000	.0000	.0000	.0000	.0000	.0000
	23	.0000	.0000	.0000	.0000	.0000	.0000	.0000	.0000	.0000	.0000
	24	.0000	.0000	.0000	.0000	.0000	.0000	.0000	.0000	.0000	.0000

25

x										
1	.7226	.9282	.9828	.9962	.9992	.9999	1.0000	1.0000	1.0000	1.0000
2	.3576	.7288	.9069	.9726	.9930	.9984	.9997	.9999	1.0000	1.0000
3	.1271	.4629	.7463	.9018	.9679	.9910	.9979	.9996	.9999	1.0000
4	.0341	.2364	.5289	.7660	.9038	.9668	.9903	.9976	.9995	.9999
5	.0072	.0980	.3179	.5793	.7863	.9095	.9680	.9905	.9977	.9995
6	.0012	.0334	.1615	.3833	.6217	.8065	.9174	.9706	.9914	.9980
7	.0002	.0095	.0695	.2200	.4389	.6593	.8266	.9264	.9742	.9927
8	.0000	.0023	.0255	.1091	.2735	.4882	.6939	.8464	.9361	.9784
9	.0000	.0005	.0080	.0468	.1494	.3231	.5332	.7265	.8660	.9461
10	.0000	.0001	.0021	.0173	.0713	.1894	.3697	.5754	.7576	.8852
11	.0000	.0000	.0005	.0056	.0297	.0978	.2288	.4142	.6157	.7878
12	.0000	.0000	.0001	.0015	.0107	.0442	.1254	.2677	.4574	.6550
13	.0000	.0000	.0000	.0004	.0034	.0175	.0604	.1538	.3063	.5000
14	.0000	.0000	.0000	.0001	.0009	.0060	.0255	.0778	.1827	.3450
15	.0000	.0000	.0000	.0000	.0002	.0018	.0093	.0344	.0960	.2122
16	.0000	.0000	.0000	.0000	.0000	.0005	.0029	.0132	.0440	.1148
17	.0000	.0000	.0000	.0000	.0000	.0001	.0008	.0043	.0174	.0539
18	.0000	.0000	.0000	.0000	.0000	.0000	.0002	.0012	.0058	.0216
19	.0000	.0000	.0000	.0000	.0000	.0000	.0000	.0003	.0016	.0073
20	.0000	.0000	.0000	.0000	.0000	.0000	.0000	.0001	.0004	.0020
21	.0000	.0000	.0000	.0000	.0000	.0000	.0000	.0000	.0001	.0005
22	.0000	.0000	.0000	.0000	.0000	.0000	.0000	.0000	.0000	.0001
23	.0000	.0000	.0000	.0000	.0000	.0000	.0000	.0000	.0000	.0000
24	.0000	.0000	.0000	.0000	.0000	.0000	.0000	.0000	.0000	.0000
25	.0000	.0000	.0000	.0000	.0000	.0000	.0000	.0000	.0000	.0000

Source: CRC Handbook of Tables for Probability and Statistics 195-202 (W. Beyer ed., 2d ed. 1968). Copyright © 1968 by The Chemical Rubber Co., CRC Press, Inc. Reprinted with permission.

Chi-Square Table

Degrees of Freedom	Significance Level (p)										
	.90	.80	.70	.50	.30	.20	.10	.05	.02	.01	.001
1	.0158	.0642	.148	.455	1.074	1.642	2.706	3.841	5.412	6.635	10.827
2	.211	.446	.713	1.386	2.408	3.219	4.605	5.991	7.824	9.210	13.815
3	.584	1.005	1.424	2.366	3.665	4.642	6.251	7.815	9.837	11.345	16.266
4	1.064	1.649	2.195	3.357	4.878	5.989	7.779	9.488	11.668	13.277	18.467
5	1.610	2.343	3.000	4.351	6.064	7.289	9.236	11.070	13.388	15.086	20.515
6	2.204	3.070	3.828	5.348	7.231	8.558	10.645	12.592	15.033	16.812	22.457
7	2.833	3.822	4.671	6.346	8.383	9.803	12.017	14.067	16.622	18.475	24.392
8	3.490	4.594	5.527	7.344	9.524	11.030	13.362	15.507	18.168	20.090	26.125
9	4.168	5.380	6.393	8.343	10.656	12.242	14.684	16.919	19.679	21.666	27.877
10	4.865	6.179	7.267	9.342	11.781	13.442	15.987	18.307	21.161	23.209	29.588
11	5.578	6.989	8.148	10.341	12.899	14.631	17.275	19.675	22.618	24.725	31.264
12	6.304	7.807	9.034	11.340	14.011	15.812	18.549	21.026	24.054	26.217	32.909
13	7.042	8.634	9.926	12.340	15.119	16.985	19.812	22.362	25.472	27.688	34.528
14	7.790	9.467	10.821	13.339	16.222	18.151	21.064	23.685	26.873	29.141	36.123
15	8.547	10.307	11.721	14.339	17.322	19.311	22.307	24.996	28.259	30.578	37.697

16	9.312	11.152	12.624	15.338	18.418	20.465	23.542	26.296	29.633	32.000	39.252
17	10.085	12.002	13.531	16.338	19.511	21.615	24.769	27.587	30.995	33.409	40.790
18	10.865	12.857	14.440	17.338	20.601	22.760	25.989	28.869	32.346	34.805	42.312
19	11.651	13.716	15.352	18.338	21.689	23.900	27.204	30.144	33.687	36.191	43.820
20	12.443	14.578	16.266	19.337	22.775	25.038	28.412	31.410	35.020	37.566	45.315
21	13.240	15.445	17.182	20.337	23.858	26.171	29.615	32.671	36.343	38.932	46.797
22	14.041	16.314	18.101	21.337	24.939	27.301	30.813	33.924	37.659	40.289	48.268
23	14.848	17.187	19.021	22.337	26.018	28.429	32.007	35.172	38.968	41.638	49.728
24	15.659	18.062	19.943	23.337	27.096	29.553	33.196	36.415	40.270	42.980	51.179
25	16.473	18.940	20.867	24.337	28.172	30.675	34.382	37.652	41.566	44.314	52.620
26	17.292	19.820	21.792	25.336	29.246	31.795	35.563	38.885	42.856	45.542	54.052
27	18.114	20.703	22.719	26.336	30.319	32.912	36.741	40.113	44.140	46.963	55.476
28	18.939	21.588	23.647	27.336	31.391	34.027	37.916	41.337	45.419	48.278	56.893
29	19.768	22.475	24.577	28.336	32.461	35.139	39.087	42.557	46.693	49.588	58.302
30	20.599	23.364	25.508	29.336	33.530	36.250	40.256	43.773	47.962	50.892	59.703

Source: R. Fisher and F. Yates, Statistical Tables for Biological, Agricultural and Medical Research 47 (Table IV) (6th ed. 1963). Reprinted with permission of Oliver and Boyd, Edinburgh.

t Table

	Significance Level												
	One-Tailed Test												
Degrees of Freedom	.45	.40	.35	.30	.25	.20	.15	.10	.05	.025	.01	.005	.0005
	Two-Tailed Test												
	.90	.80	.70	.60	.50	.40	.30	.20	.10	.05	.02	.01	.001
1	.158	.325	.510	.727	1.000	1.376	1.963	3.078	6.314	12.706	31.821	63.657	636.619
2	.142	.289	.445	.617	.816	1.061	1.386	1.886	2.920	4.303	6.965	9.925	31.598
3	.137	.277	.424	.584	.765	.978	1.250	1.638	2.353	3.182	4.541	5.841	12.924
4	.134	.271	.414	.569	.741	.941	1.190	1.533	2.132	2.776	3.747	4.604	8.610
5	.132	.267	.408	.559	.727	.920	1.156	1.476	2.015	2.571	3.365	4.032	6.869
6	.131	.265	.404	.553	.718	.906	1.134	1.440	1.943	2.447	3.143	3.707	5.959
7	.130	.263	.402	.549	.711	.896	1.119	1.415	1.895	2.365	2.998	3.499	5.408
8	.130	.262	.399	.546	.706	.889	1.108	1.397	1.860	2.306	2.896	3.355	5.041
9	.129	.261	.398	.543	.703	.883	1.100	1.383	1.833	2.262	2.821	3.250	4.781
10	.129	.260	.397	.542	.700	.879	1.093	1.372	1.812	2.228	2.764	3.169	4.587
11	.129	.260	.396	.540	.697	.876	1.088	1.363	1.796	2.201	2.718	3.106	4.437
12	.128	.259	.395	.539	.695	.873	1.083	1.356	1.782	2.179	2.681	3.055	4.318
13	.128	.259	.394	.538	.694	.870	1.079	1.350	1.771	2.160	2.650	3.012	4.221
14	.128	.258	.393	.537	.692	.868	1.076	1.345	1.761	2.145	2.624	2.977	4.140
15	.128	.258	.393	.536	.691	.866	1.074	1.341	1.753	2.131	2.602	2.947	4.073

16	.128	.258	.392	.535	.690	.865	1.071	1.337	1.746	2.120	2.583	2.921	4.015
17	.128	.257	.392	.534	.689	.863	1.069	1.333	1.740	2.110	2.567	2.898	3.965
18	.127	.257	.392	.534	.688	.862	1.067	1.330	1.734	2.101	2.552	2.878	3.922
19	.127	.257	.391	.533	.688	.861	1.066	1.328	1.729	2.093	2.539	2.861	3.883
20	.127	.257	.391	.533	.687	.860	1.064	1.325	1.725	2.086	2.528	2.845	3.850
21	.127	.257	.391	.532	.686	.859	1.063	1.323	1.721	2.080	2.518	2.831	3.819
22	.127	.256	.390	.532	.686	.858	1.061	1.321	1.717	2.074	2.508	2.819	3.792
23	.127	.256	.390	.532	.685	.858	1.060	1.319	1.714	2.069	2.500	2.807	3.767
24	.127	.256	.390	.531	.685	.857	1.059	1.318	1.711	2.064	2.492	2.797	3.745
25	.127	.256	.390	.531	.684	.856	1.058	1.316	1.708	2.060	2.485	2.787	3.725
26	.127	.256	.390	.531	.684	.856	1.058	1.315	1.706	2.056	2.479	2.779	3.707
27	.127	.256	.389	.531	.684	.855	1.057	1.314	1.703	2.052	2.473	2.771	3.690
28	.127	.256	.389	.530	.683	.855	1.056	1.313	1.701	2.048	2.467	2.763	3.674
29	.127	.256	.389	.530	.683	.854	1.055	1.311	1.699	2.045	2.462	2.756	3.659
30	.127	.256	.389	.530	.683	.854	1.055	1.310	1.697	2.042	2.457	2.750	3.646
40	.126	.255	.388	.529	.681	.851	1.050	1.303	1.684	2.021	2.423	2.704	3.551
60	.126	.254	.387	.527	.679	.848	1.046	1.296	1.671	2.000	2.390	2.660	3.460
120	.126	.254	.386	.526	.677	.845	1.041	1.289	1.658	1.980	2.358	2.617	3.373
∞	.126	.253	.385	.524	.674	.842	1.036	1.282	1.645	1.960	2.326	2.576	3.291

Source: **R.** Fisher and F. Yates, Statistical Tables for Biological, Agricultural and Medical Research 46 (Table III) (6th ed. 1963). **Reprinted with** permission.

r Table

Number of Pairs	Significance Level One-Tailed Test .05	.025	.01	.005	.0005
	Two-Tailed Test .10	.05	.02	.01	.001
3	.98769	.99692	.999507	.999877	.9999988
4	.90000	.95000	.98000	.990000	.99900
5	.8054	.8783	.93433	.95873	.99116
6	.7293	.8114	.8822	.91720	.97406
7	.6694	.7545	.8329	.8745	.95074
8	.6215	.7067	.7887	.8343	.92493
9	.5822	.6664	.7498	.7977	.8982
10	.5494	.6319	.7155	.7646	.8721
11	.5214	.6021	.6851	.7348	.8471
12	.4973	.5760	.6581	.7079	.8233
13	.4762	.5529	.6339	.6835	.8010
14	.4575	.5324	.6120	.6614	.7800
15	.4409	.5139	.5923	.6411	.7603
16	.4259	.4973	.5742	.6226	.7420
17	.4124	.4821	.5577	.6055	.7246
18	.4000	.4683	.5425	.5897	.7084
19	.3887	.4555	.5285	.5751	.6932
20	.3783	.4438	.5155	.5614	.6787
21	.3687	.4329	.5034	.5487	.6652
22	.3598	.4227	.4921	.5368	.6524
27	.3233	.3809	.4451	.4869	.5974
32	.2960	.3494	.4093	.4487	.5541
37	.2746	.3246	.3810	.4182	.5189
42	.2573	.3044	.3578	.3932	.4896
47	.2428	.2875	.3384	.3721	.4648
52	.2306	.2732	.3218	.3541	.4433
62	.2108	.2500	.2948	.3248	.4078
72	.1954	.2319	.2737	.3017	.3799
82	.1829	.2172	.2565	.2830	.3568
92	.1726	.2050	.2422	.2673	.3375
102	.1638	.1946	.2301	.2540	.3211

Source: R. Fisher and F. Yates, Statistical Tables for Biological, Agricultural and Medical Research 63 (Table VII) (6th ed. 1963). Reprinted with permission.

Spearman r Table

	Significance Level One-Tailed Test			
	.05	.025	.01	.005
Number	Two-Tailed Test			
of Pairs	.10	.05	.02	.01
5	0.900	——	——	——
6	0.829	0.886	0.943	——
7	0.714	0.786	0.893	——
8	0.643	0.738	0.833	0.881
9	0.600	0.683	0.783	0.833
10	0.564	0.648	0.745	0.794
11	0.523	0.623	0.736	0.818
12	0.497	0.591	0.703	0.780
13	0.475	0.566	0.673	0.745
14	0.457	0.545	0.646	0.716
15	0.441	0.525	0.623	0.689
16	0.425	0.507	0.601	0.666
17	0.412	0.490	0.582	0.645
18	0.399	0.476	0.564	0.625
19	0.388	0.462	0.549	0.608
20	0.377	0.450	0.534	0.591
21	0.368	0.438	0.521	0.576
22	0.359	0.428	0.508	0.562
23	0.351	0.418	0.496	0.549
24	0.343	0.409	0.485	0.537
25	0.336	0.400	0.475	0.526
26	0.329	0.392	0.465	0.515
27	0.323	0.385	0.456	0.505
28	0.317	0.377	0.448	0.496
29	0.311	0.370	0.440	0.487
30	0.305	0.364	0.432	0.478

Source: N. Johnson and F. Leone, 1 Statistics and Experimental Design in Engineering and the Physical Sciences 547 (2d ed. 1977). Reprinted with permission.

z' Transformation of r Table

z	.00	.01	.02	.03	.04	.05	.06	.07	.08	.09
.0	.0000	.0100	.0200	.0300	.0400	.0500	.0599	.0699	.0798	.0898
.1	.0997	.1096	.1194	.1293	.1391	.1489	.1586	.1684	.1781	.1877
.2	.1974	.2070	.2165	.2260	.2355	.2449	.2543	.2636	.2729	.2821
.3	.2913	.3004	.3095	.3185	.3275	.3364	.3452	.3540	.3627	.3714
.4	.3800	.3885	.3969	.4053	.4136	.4219	.4301	.4382	.4462	.4542
.5	.4621	.4699	.4777	.4854	.4930	.5005	.5080	.5154	.5227	.5299
.6	.5370	.5441	.5511	.5580	.5649	.5717	.5784	.5850	.5915	.5980
.7	.6044	.6107	.6169	.6231	.6291	.6351	.6411	.6469	.6527	.6584
.8	.6640	.6696	.6751	.6805	.6858	.6911	.6963	.7014	.7064	.7114
.9	.7163	.7211	.7259	.7306	.7352	.7398	.7443	.7487	.7531	.7574
1.0	.7616	.7658	.7699	.7739	.7779	.7818	.7857	.7895	.7932	.7969
1.1	.8005	.8041	.8076	.8110	.8144	.8178	.8210	.8243	.8275	.8306
1.2	.8337	.8367	.8397	.8426	.8455	.8483	.8511	.8538	.8565	.8591
1.3	.8617	.8643	.8668	.8692	.8717	.8741	.8764	.8787	.8810	.8832
1.4	.8854	.8875	.8896	.8917	.8937	.8957	.8977	.8996	.9015	.9033

	.0	.1	.2	.3	.4	.5	.6	.7	.8	.9
1.5	.9051	.9069	.9087	.9104	.9121	.9138	.9154	.9170	.9186	.9201
1.6	.9217	.9232	.9246	.9261	.9275	.9289	.9302	.9316	.9329	.9341
1.7	.9354	.9366	.9379	.9391	.9402	.9414	.9425	.9436	.9447	.9458
1.8	.94681	.94783	.94884	.94983	.95080	.95175	.95268	.95359	.95449	.95537
1.9	.95624	.95709	.95792	.95873	.95953	.96032	.96109	.96185	.96259	.96331
2.0	.96403	.96473	.96541	.96609	.96675	.96739	.96803	.96865	.96926	.96986
2.1	.97045	.97103	.97159	.97215	.97269	.97323	.97375	.97426	.97477	.97526
2.2	.97574	.97622	.97668	.97714	.97759	.97803	.97846	.97888	.97929	.97970
2.3	.98010	.98049	.98087	.98124	.98161	.98197	.98233	.98267	.98301	.98335
2.4	.98367	.98399	.98431	.98462	.98492	.98522	.98551	.98579	.98607	.98635
2.5	.98661	.98688	.98714	.98739	.98764	.98788	.98812	.98835	.98858	.98881
2.6	.98903	.98924	.98945	.98966	.98987	.99007	.99026	.99045	.99064	.99083
2.7	.99101	.99118	.99136	.99153	.99170	.99186	.99202	.99218	.99233	.99248
2.8	.99263	.99278	.99292	.99306	.99320	.99333	.99346	.99359	.99372	.99384
2.9	.99396	.99408	.99420	.99431	.99443	.99454	.99464	.99475	.99485	.99495
	.0	.1	.2	.3	.4	.5	.6	.7	.8	.9
3	.99505	.99595	.99668	.99728	.99777	.99818	.99851	.99878	.99900	.99918
4	.99933	.99945	.99955	.99963	.99970	.99975	.99980	.99983	.99986	.99989

Source: R. Fisher and F. Yates, Statistical Tables for Biological, Agricultural and Medical Research 63 (Table VIIi) (6th ed. 1963). Reprinted with permission of Oliver and Boyd, Edinburgh.

F Tables (Significance Level = .05)

Degrees of Freedom in Denominator (= n − k − 1)	Degrees of Freedom in Numerator (= k)								
	1	2	3	4	5	6	7	8	9
1	161.4	199.5	215.7	224.6	230.2	234.0	236.8	238.9	240.5
2	18.51	19.00	19.16	19.25	19.30	19.33	19.35	19.37	19.38
3	10.13	9.55	9.28	9.12	9.01	8.94	8.89	8.85	8.81
4	7.71	6.94	6.59	6.39	6.26	6.16	6.09	6.04	6.00
5	6.61	5.79	5.41	5.19	5.05	4.95	4.88	4.82	4.77
6	5.99	5.14	4.76	4.53	4.39	4.28	4.21	4.15	4.10
7	5.59	4.74	4.35	4.12	3.97	3.87	3.79	3.73	3.68
8	5.32	4.46	4.07	3.84	3.69	3.58	3.50	3.44	3.39
9	5.12	4.26	3.86	3.63	3.48	3.37	3.29	3.23	3.18
10	4.96	4.10	3.71	3.48	3.33	3.22	3.14	3.07	3.02
11	4.84	3.98	3.59	3.36	3.20	3.09	3.01	2.95	2.90
12	4.75	3.89	3.49	3.26	3.11	3.00	2.91	2.85	2.80
13	4.67	3.81	3.41	3.18	3.03	2.92	2.83	2.77	2.71
14	4.60	3.74	3.34	3.11	2.96	2.85	2.76	2.70	2.65
15	4.54	3.68	3.29	3.06	2.90	2.79	2.71	2.64	2.59
16	4.49	3.63	3.24	3.01	2.85	2.74	2.66	2.59	2.54
17	4.45	3.59	3.20	2.96	2.81	2.70	2.61	2.55	2.49
18	4.41	3.55	3.16	2.93	2.77	2.66	2.58	2.51	2.46
19	4.38	3.52	3.13	2.90	2.74	2.63	2.54	2.48	2.42
20	4.35	3.49	3.10	2.87	2.71	2.60	2.51	2.45	2.39
21	4.32	3.47	3.07	2.84	2.68	2.57	2.49	2.42	2.37
22	4.30	3.44	3.05	2.82	2.66	2.55	2.46	2.40	2.34
23	4.28	3.42	3.03	2.80	2.64	2.53	2.44	2.37	2.32
24	4.26	3.40	3.01	2.78	2.62	2.51	2.42	2.36	2.30
25	4.24	3.39	2.99	2.76	2.60	2.49	2.40	2.34	2.28
26	4.23	3.37	2.98	2.74	2.59	2.47	2.39	2.32	2.27
27	4.21	3.35	2.96	2.73	2.57	2.46	2.37	2.31	2.25
28	4.20	3.34	2.95	2.71	2.56	2.45	2.36	2.29	2.24
29	4.18	3.33	2.93	2.70	2.55	2.43	2.35	2.28	2.22
30	4.17	3.32	2.92	2.69	2.53	2.42	2.33	2.27	2.21
40	4.08	3.23	2.84	2.61	2.45	2.34	2.25	2.18	2.12
60	4.00	3.15	2.76	2.53	2.37	2.25	2.17	2.10	2.04
120	3.92	3.07	2.68	2.45	2.29	2.17	2.09	2.02	1.96
∞	3.84	3.00	2.60	2.37	2.21	2.10	2.01	1.94	1.88

10	12	15	20	24	30	40	60	120	∞
241.9	243.9	245.9	248.0	249.1	250.1	251.1	252.2	253.3	254.3
19.40	19.41	19.43	19.45	19.45	19.46	19.47	19.48	19.49	19.50
8.79	8.74	8.70	8.66	8.64	8.62	8.59	8.57	8.55	8.53
5.96	5.91	5.86	5.80	5.77	5.75	5.72	5.69	5.66	5.63
4.74	4.68	4.62	4.56	4.53	4.50	4.46	4.43	4.40	4.36
4.06	4.00	3.94	3.87	3.84	3.81	3.77	3.74	3.70	3.67
3.64	3.57	3.51	3.44	3.41	3.38	3.34	3.30	3.27	3.23
3.35	3.28	3.22	3.15	3.12	3.08	3.04	3.01	2.97	2.93
3.14	3.07	3.01	2.94	2.90	2.86	2.83	2.79	2.75	2.71
2.98	2.91	2.85	2.77	2.74	2.70	2.66	2.62	2.58	2.54
2.85	2.79	2.72	2.65	2.61	2.57	2.53	2.49	2.45	2.40
2.75	2.69	2.62	2.54	2.51	2.47	2.43	2.38	2.34	2.30
2.67	2.60	2.53	2.46	2.42	2.38	2.34	2.30	2.25	2.21
2.60	2.53	2.46	2.39	2.35	2.31	2.27	2.22	2.18	2.13
2.54	2.48	2.40	2.33	2.29	2.25	2.20	2.16	2.11	2.07
2.49	2.42	2.35	2.28	2.24	2.19	2.15	2.11	2.06	2.01
2.45	2.38	2.31	2.23	2.19	2.15	2.10	2.06	2.01	1.96
2.41	2.34	2.27	2.19	2.15	2.11	2.06	2.02	1.97	1.92
2.38	2.31	2.23	2.16	2.11	2.07	2.03	1.98	1.93	1.88
2.35	2.28	2.20	2.12	2.08	2.04	1.99	1.95	1.90	1.84
2.32	2.25	2.18	2.10	2.05	2.01	1.96	1.92	1.87	1.81
2.30	2.23	2.15	2.07	2.03	1.98	1.94	1.89	1.84	1.78
2.27	2.20	2.13	2.05	2.01	1.96	1.91	1.86	1.81	1.76
2.25	2.18	2.11	2.03	1.98	1.94	1.89	1.84	1.79	1.73
2.24	2.16	2.09	2.01	1.96	1.92	1.87	1.82	1.77	1.71
2.22	2.15	2.07	1.99	1.95	1.90	1.85	1.80	1.75	1.69
2.20	2.13	2.06	1.97	1.93	1.88	1.84	1.79	1.73	1.67
2.19	2.12	2.04	1.96	1.91	1.87	1.82	1.77	1.71	1.65
2.18	2.10	2.03	1.94	1.90	1.85	1.81	1.75	1.70	1.64
2.16	2.09	2.01	1.93	1.89	1.84	1.79	1.74	1.68	1.62
2.08	2.00	1.92	1.84	1.79	1.74	1.69	1.64	1.58	1.51
1.99	1.92	1.84	1.75	1.70	1.65	1.59	1.53	1.47	1.39
1.91	1.83	1.75	1.66	1.61	1.55	1.50	1.43	1.35	1.25
1.83	1.75	1.67	1.57	1.52	1.46	1.39	1.32	1.22	1.00

(*continued*)

F Tables (*continued*) (Significance Level = .01)

Degrees of Freedom in Denominator ($= n - k - 1$)	Degrees of Freedom in Numerator ($= k$)								
	1	2	3	4	5	6	7	8	9
1	4052	4999.5	5403	5625	5764	5859	5928	5982	6022
2	98.50	99.00	99.17	99.25	99.30	99.33	99.36	99.37	99.39
3	34.12	30.82	29.46	28.71	28.24	27.91	27.67	27.49	27.35
4	21.20	18.00	16.69	15.98	15.52	15.21	14.98	14.80	14.66
5	16.26	13.27	12.06	11.39	10.97	10.67	10.46	10.29	10.16
6	13.75	10.92	9.78	9.15	8.75	8.47	8.26	8.10	7.98
7	12.25	9.55	8.45	7.85	7.46	7.19	6.99	6.84	6.72
8	11.26	8.65	7.59	7.01	6.63	6.37	6.18	6.03	5.91
9	10.56	8.02	6.99	6.42	6.06	5.80	5.61	5.47	5.35
10	10.04	7.56	6.55	5.99	5.64	5.39	5.20	5.06	4.94
11	9.65	7.21	6.22	5.67	5.32	5.07	4.89	4.74	4.63
12	9.33	6.93	5.95	5.41	5.06	4.82	4.64	4.50	4.39
13	9.07	6.70	5.74	5.21	4.86	4.62	4.44	4.30	4.19
14	8.86	6.51	5.56	5.04	4.69	4.46	4.28	4.14	4.03
15	8.68	6.36	5.42	4.89	4.56	4.32	4.14	4.00	3.89
16	8.53	6.23	5.29	4.77	4.44	4.20	4.03	3.89	3.78
17	8.40	6.11	5.18	4.67	4.34	4.10	3.93	3.79	3.68
18	8.29	6.01	5.09	4.58	4.25	4.01	3.84	3.71	3.60
19	8.18	5.93	5.01	4.50	4.17	3.94	3.77	3.63	3.52
20	8.10	5.85	4.94	4.43	4.10	3.87	3.70	3.56	3.46
21	8.02	5.78	4.87	4.37	4.04	3.81	3.64	3.51	3.40
22	7.95	5.72	4.82	4.31	3.99	3.76	3.59	3.45	3.35
23	7.88	5.66	4.76	4.26	3.94	3.71	3.54	3.41	3.30
24	7.82	5.61	4.72	4.22	3.90	3.67	3.50	3.36	3.26
25	7.77	5.57	4.68	4.18	3.85	3.63	3.46	3.32	3.22
26	7.72	5.53	4.64	4.14	3.82	3.59	3.42	3.29	3.18
27	7.68	5.49	4.60	4.11	3.78	3.56	3.39	3.26	3.15
28	7.64	5.45	4.57	4.07	3.75	3.53	3.36	3.23	3.12
29	7.60	5.42	4.54	4.04	3.73	3.50	3.33	3.20	3.09
30	7.56	5.39	4.51	4.02	3.70	3.47	3.30	3.17	3.07
40	7.31	5.18	4.31	3.83	3.51	3.29	3.12	2.99	2.89
60	7.08	4.98	4.13	3.65	3.34	3.12	2.95	2.82	2.72
120	6.85	4.79	3.95	3.48	3.17	2.96	2.79	2.66	2.56
∞	6.63	4.61	3.78	3.32	3.02	2.80	2.64	2.51	2.41

Source: E. Pearson and H. Hartley, eds., I Biometrika Tables for Statisticians 159 (Table 18) (1958). Reprinted with permission of the Biometrika Trustees.

10	12	15	20	24	30	40	60	120	∞
6056	6106	6157	6209	6235	6261	6287	6313	6339	6366
99.40	99.42	99.43	99.45	99.46	99.47	99.47	99.48	99.49	99.50
27.23	27.05	26.87	26.69	26.60	26.50	26.41	26.32	26.22	26.13
14.55	14.37	14.20	14.02	13.93	13.84	13.75	13.65	13.56	13.46
10.05	9.89	9.72	9.55	9.47	9.38	9.29	9.20	9.11	9.02
7.87	7.72	7.56	7.40	7.31	7.23	7.14	7.06	6.97	6.88
6.62	6.47	6.31	6.16	6.07	5.99	5.91	5.82	5.74	5.65
5.81	5.67	5.52	5.36	5.28	5.20	5.12	5.03	4.95	4.86
5.26	5.11	4.96	4.81	4.73	4.65	4.57	4.48	4.40	4.31
4.85	4.71	4.56	4.41	4.33	4.25	4.17	4.08	4.00	3.91
4.54	4.40	4.25	4.10	4.02	3.94	3.86	3.78	3.69	3.60
4.30	4.16	4.01	3.86	3.78	3.70	3.62	3.54	3.45	3.36
4.10	3.96	3.82	3.66	3.59	3.51	3.43	3.34	3.25	3.17
3.94	3.80	3.66	3.51	3.43	3.35	3.27	3.18	3.09	3.00
3.80	3.67	3.52	3.37	3.29	3.21	3.13	3.05	2.96	2.87
3.69	3.55	3.41	3.26	3.18	3.10	3.02	2.93	2.84	2.75
3.59	3.46	3.31	3.16	3.08	3.00	2.92	2.83	2.75	2.65
3.51	3.37	3.23	3.08	3.00	2.92	2.84	2.75	2.66	2.57
3.43	3.30	3.15	3.00	2.92	2.84	2.76	2.67	2.58	2.49
3.37	3.23	3.09	2.94	2.86	2.78	2.69	2.61	2.52	2.42
3.31	3.17	3.03	2.88	2.80	2.72	2.64	2.55	2.46	2.36
3.26	3.12	2.98	2.83	2.75	2.67	2.58	2.50	2.40	2.31
3.21	3.07	2.93	2.78	2.70	2.62	2.54	2.45	2.35	2.26
3.17	3.03	2.89	2.74	2.66	2.58	2.49	2.40	2.31	2.21
3.13	2.99	2.85	2.70	2.62	2.54	2.45	2.36	2.27	2.17
3.09	2.96	2.81	2.66	2.58	2.50	2.42	2.33	2.23	2.13
3.06	2.93	2.78	2.63	2.55	2.47	2.38	2.29	2.20	2.10
3.03	2.90	2.75	2.60	2.52	2.44	2.35	2.26	2.17	2.06
3.00	2.87	2.73	2.57	2.49	2.41	2.33	2.23	2.14	2.03
2.98	2.84	2.70	2.55	2.47	2.39	2.30	2.21	2.11	2.01
2.80	2.66	2.52	2.37	2.29	2.20	2.11	2.02	1.92	1.80
2.63	2.50	2.35	2.20	2.12	2.03	1.94	1.84	1.73	1.60
2.47	2.34	2.19	2.03	1.95	1.86	1.76	1.66	1.53	1.38
2.32	2.18	2.04	1.88	1.79	1.70	1.59	1.47	1.32	1.00

APPENDIX B

Mathematical Symbols

The following notation is used in this book. The section numbers in parentheses following each definition indicate where in each chapter the notation is first employed. Note that upper-case letters indicate population values, while lower-case letters indicate sample values. A lower-case symbol in parentheses that follows a similar symbol being defined is the sample equivalent of a population symbol.

A (a) — the population (sample) regression intercept or constant term (8.1).

$a*$ — a standard to which an estimated regression intercept is compared to determine the statistical significance of a difference between them (8.9).

B (b) — the population (sample) regression coefficient (8.1).

b_i — the sample regression coefficient associated with the independent variable x_i (8.12).

$b*$ — a standard to which an estimated regression coefficient is compared to determine the statistical significance of a difference between them (8.8).

χ^2 — the chi-square value (5.18).

$d.f.$ — the number of degrees of freedom (6.22.1) (7.22) (8.18).

E_j — the expected value for the jth type of observation (5.18).

e_j — the error associated with the prediction of the jth value of the dependent variable (8.1.1).

F — a test statistic used in significance testing for multiple regression results (8.12).

k — in Chebychef's inequality, the number of standard deviations between the observed value and the mean (4.22).

— in regression analysis, the number of independent variables in a regression equation (8.18).

M_X (m_x) — the mean of a population (sample) of possible observations of the variable X (x) (4.21.1) (6.20.1) (7.21).

M_Y (m_y) — the mean of a population (sample) of possible observations of the variable Y (y) (4.21.1) (7.21).

m_{y_0} — the mean of those observations of the continuous variable that are paired with observations belonging to one of the two groups represented by the dichotomous variable (7.24).

m_{y_1} — the mean of those observations of the continuous variable that are paired with observations belonging to the second of the two groups represented by the dichotomous variable (7.24).

N (n) — the number of numbers or items in the population (sample) (4.21.1) (6.20.1) (7.21) (8.18).

N_1 — in the hypergeometric formula, the number of items in the population from which the sample was drawn that possess the characteristic of interest (4.25).

— in calculating a sample proportion, p, the number of observations in a sample possessing a particular characteristic (6.20).

n_1 — the number of observations in the first sample (6.21.3).

N_2 — in the hypergeometric formula, the number of items in the population from which the sample was drawn that do not possess the characteristic of interest (4.25).

— in calculating a sample proportion, q, the number of observations in a sample not possessing a particular characteristic (6.20).

n_2 — the number of observations in the second sample (6.21.3).

O_j — the observed value for the jth type of observation (5.18).

OLS — ordinary least squares, a method for estimating regression statistics (8.1).

P (p) — the proportion of observations in the population (sample) that possess a particular characteristic (4.21.1) (6.20.2) (7.24).

p_0 — an observed proportion of observations that possess a particular characteristic (4.24).

p_1 — the proportion of observations in the first sample that possess a particular characteristic (6.21.3).

p_2 — the proportion of observations in the second sample that possess a particular characteristic (6.21.3).

Q (q) — the proportion of observations in the population (sample) that do not possess a particular characteristic (4.21.1) (6.20.3) (7.24).

Appendix B

q_1 — the proportion of observations in the first sample that do not possess a particular characteristic (6.21.3).

q_2 — the proportion of observations in the second sample that do not possess a particular characteristic (6.21.3).

r — the Pearson product moment correlation coefficient (7.1).

R^2 — The coefficient of multiple determination (8.10).

r^2 — the coefficient of determination (7.17).

r_{pb} — the point biserial correlation coefficient (7.8).

r_S — the Spearman rank correlation coefficient (7.11).

Rx_i — the rank of the ith observation of the variable X (7.25).

Ry_i — the rank of the ith observation of the variable Y (7.25).

Σ — the arithmetic summation of the terms that follow (4.21.1) (5.18) (6.20) (7.21).

SD (sd) — the population (sample) standard deviation (6.20.3).

sd_1 — the standard deviation of the first sample (6.21.3).

sd_2 — the standard deviation of the second sample (6.21.3).

SD^2 (sd^2) — the variance of a population (sample) (4.21.2).

SD_X (sd_x) — the population (sample) standard deviation of the variable X (4.21.3) (7.21).

SD_Y (sd_y) — the population (sample) standard deviation of the variable Y (4.21.3) (7.21).

se_a — the estimated standard error of the population regression intercept (8.9).

se_b — the estimated standard error of the population regression coefficient (8.6).

$se_{diff.\,m.}$ — the standard error of the difference between sample means (6.21.3).

$se_{diff.\,p.}$ — the standard error of the difference between sample proportions (6.21.3).

se_m — the standard error of the sample mean (6.21.1).

se_p — the standard error of the sample proportion (6.21.2)

se_r — the standard error of the Pearson product moment correlation coefficient (7.22).

se_{y*} — the standard error of the estimated values of the dependent variable, y. When squared, the explained variance in the observed y values (8.21).

t — a test statistic used in significance testing (6.22.1) (7.5) (8.7).

X (x) — a variable that takes on numerical values (4.21.1) (7.21).

X_i (x_i) — the ith value in a sequence of observations of X (x) (4.21.1) (6.20.1) (7.21).

— in regression analysis, one of several independent variables (8.12).

x_j — the jth observed value of the independent variable x (8.1.1).

$x_{i,j}$ — the jth observed value of the ith independent variable (8.12).

x_0 — an observed frequency with which a particular characteristic appears as a result of n successive trials (4.23).

Y (y) — a variable that takes on numerical values (4.21.1) (7.21).
— in regression analysis, the dependent variable (8.1).

Y_i (y_i) — the ith value in a sequence of observations of Y (y) (4.21.1) (7.21).

y_j — the jth value in a sequence of observations of the dependent variable, y (8.1.1).

y_j^* — a predicted value for the dependent variable based on specified values for the independent variables and the estimated regression statistics (8.1.1).

Z — a number of standard deviations between an observed and expected value. Also, an inferential test statistic, referred to as a Z score. (4.13) (4.22).

Z_{X_i} (Z_{x_i}) — the Z score associated with the ith value from the list of observations of the variable X (7.21).

Z_{Y_i} (Z_{y_i}) — the Z score associated with the ith value from the list of observations of the variable Y (7.21).

z' — the Fisher z-prime, used in estimating a confidence interval for the Pearson product moment correlation coefficient (7.23).

! — the factorial sign indicating tht the number preceding it is to be multiplied by every positive integer less than that number (4.23).

APPENDIX C

Selected Equations

$$\text{mean (finite population)} = M_X = \frac{\Sigma X_i}{N}$$

4.21.1(a)

$$\text{mean (sample)} = m_x = \frac{\Sigma x}{n}$$

4.21.1(b)

$$\text{mean (binomially distributed random variable)} = M_X = nP$$

4.21.1(c)

$$\text{mean (hypergeometrically distributed random variable)} =$$
$$M_X = \frac{nN_1}{N_1 + N_2} = n\frac{N_1}{N}$$

4.21.1(d)

$$\text{variance (finite population)} = SD^2 = \frac{\Sigma(X_i - M_X)^2}{N}$$

4.21.2(a)

$$\text{variance (sample)} = sd^2 = \frac{\Sigma(x_i - m_x)^2}{n - 1}$$

4.21.2(b)

$$\text{(binomial) } SD^2 = nPQ$$

4.21.2(c)

$$\text{(hypergeometric) } SD^2 = \left(\frac{N-n}{N-1}\right) n \frac{N_1}{N} \frac{N_2}{N}$$

4.21.2(d)

$$SD = \sqrt{SD^2} = \sqrt{\frac{\Sigma(X_i - M_X)^2}{N}}$$

4.21.3(a)

$$\text{(sample) } sd = \sqrt{sd^2} = \sqrt{\frac{\Sigma(x_i - m_x)^2}{n-1}}$$

4.21.3(b)

$$\text{(binomial) } SD = \sqrt{SD^2} = \sqrt{nPQ}$$

4.21.3(c)

$$\text{(hypergeometric) } SD = \sqrt{SD^2} = \sqrt{\left(\frac{N-n}{N-1}\right) n \frac{N_1}{N} \frac{N_2}{N}}$$

4.21.3(d)

$$\text{(binomial) } sd \text{ as percentage of group size} = \frac{sd}{n} = \frac{\sqrt{nPQ}}{n} = \sqrt{\frac{PQ}{n}}$$

4.21.3(e)

$$CV = \frac{SD}{M} \times 100\% \text{ or } \frac{sd}{m} \times 100\%$$

4.21.4(a)

$$\text{binomial probability of } x_0 = \frac{n!}{x_0!\,(n-x_0)!}P^{x_0}Q^{(n-x_0)}$$

$$\textbf{4.23(a)}$$

$$\text{binomial } p\text{-value (one-tail)} =$$

$$\sum \frac{n!}{x!\,(n-x)!}P^{x}Q^{(n-x)} \text{ for all } x \text{ from } x_0 \text{ to } n$$

$$\textbf{4.23(b)}$$

$$\text{binomial } p\text{-value (one-tail)} =$$

$$\sum \frac{n!}{x!\,(n-x)!}P^{x}Q^{(n-x)} \text{ for all } x \text{ from } 0 \text{ to } x_0$$

$$\textbf{4.23(c)}$$

$$\text{binomial } p\text{-value (two-tail)} = \sum \frac{n!}{x!\,(n-x)!}P^{x}Q^{(n-x)}$$

$$\text{for all } x \text{ from } 0 \text{ to } (M_X - |x_0 - M_X|) \text{ and from } (M_X + |x_0 - M_X|) \text{ to } n$$

$$\textbf{4.23(g)}$$

$$\text{hypergeometric probability of } x_0 =$$

$$\frac{\dfrac{N_1!}{x_0!\,(N_1 - x_0)!} \times \dfrac{N_2!}{(n - x_0)!\,(N_2 - (n - x_0))!}}{\dfrac{N!}{n!\,(N - n)!}}$$

$$\textbf{4.25(a)}$$

$$\text{hypergeometric } p\text{-value } (x_0 < M_X) \text{ (one-tailed test)} =$$

$$\sum \frac{\dfrac{N_1!}{x!\,(N_1 - x)!} \times \dfrac{N_2!}{(n - x)!\,(N_2 - (n - x))!}}{\dfrac{N!}{n!\,(N - n)!}}$$

$$\text{for all } x \text{ from } 0 \text{ to } x_0$$

$$\textbf{4.25(b)}$$

hypergeometric p-value ($x_0 > M_X$) (one-tailed test) =

$$\sum \frac{\dfrac{N_1!}{x! \, (N_1 - x)!} \times \dfrac{N_2!}{(n - x)! \, (N_2 - (n - x))!}}{\dfrac{N!}{n! \, (N - n)!}}$$

for all x from x_0 to N_1 or n (whichever is smaller)

4.25(c)

hypergeometric p-value (two-tailed test) =

$$\sum \frac{\dfrac{N_1!}{x! \, (N_1 - x)!} \times \dfrac{N_2!}{(n - x)! \, (N_2 - (n - x))!}}{\dfrac{N!}{n! \, (N - n)!}}$$

for all x from 0 to $(M_X - |x_0 - M_X|)$

and from $(M_X + |x_0 - M_X|)$ to N_1 or n (whichever is smaller)

4.25(d)

$$\chi^2 = \sum \frac{(O_j - E_j)^2}{E_j}$$

5.18(a)

$$\text{Yates corrected } \chi^2 = \sum \frac{(|O_j - E_j| - 1/2)^2}{E_j}$$

5.20(a)

$$\text{sample proportion} = p = \frac{N_1}{N_1 + N_2}$$

6.20(b)

$$se_m = \sqrt{\frac{SD^2}{n}} \cong \sqrt{\frac{sd^2}{n}}$$

6.21.1(a)

Appendix C

$$se_p = \sqrt{\frac{PQ}{n}} \cong \sqrt{\frac{pq}{n}}$$

6.21.2(a)

$$se_{\text{difference between means}} = se_{\text{diff.m.}} =$$
$$\sqrt{\frac{(n_1 - 1)sd_1^2 + (n_2 - 1)sd_2^2}{(n_1 - 1) + (n_2 - 1)}} \times \sqrt{\frac{1}{n_1} + \frac{1}{n_2}}$$

6.21.3(a)

$$se_{\text{difference between proportions}} = se_{\text{diff.p.}} = \sqrt{\frac{p_1 q_1}{n_1} + \frac{p_2 q_2}{n_2}}$$

6.21.3(b)

$$\text{confidence interval (means)} = m \pm t_{\text{critical}} \times se_m$$

6.22.1(a)

$$\text{degrees of freedom (conf. int. for mean)} = d.f. = n - 1$$

6.22.1(b)

$$\text{confidence interval (means)} = m \pm Z_{\text{critical}} \times se_m$$

6.22.1(c)

$$\text{confidence interval (proportion)} = p \pm Z_{\text{critical}} \times se_p$$

6.22.2(a)

$$\text{confidence interval (difference between means)} =$$
$$\text{difference} \pm t_{\text{critical}} \times se_{\text{diff.m.}}$$

6.22.3(a)

$$\text{confidence interval (difference between means)} =$$
$$\text{difference} \pm Z_{\text{critical}} \times se_{\text{diff.m.}}$$

6.22.3(b)

confidence interval (difference between proportions) =
difference $\pm Z_{\text{critical}} \times se_{\text{diff.p.}}$

6.22.3(c)

degrees of freedom (difference between two sample means) =
$n_1 + n_2 - 2$

6.22.3(d)

$$\text{calculated } t = \frac{\text{sample estimate}}{\text{estimated standard error of sample estimate}}$$

6.23(a)

$$\text{calculated } Z = \frac{\text{sample estimate}}{\text{standard error of sample estimate}}$$

6.23(b)

$$\text{calculated } t = \frac{\text{sample estimate} - \text{external standard}}{\text{estimated standard error of sample estimate}}$$

6.23(c)

$$\text{calculated } Z = \frac{\text{sample estimate} - \text{external standard}}{\text{standard error of sample estimate}}$$

6.23(d)

$$\text{sample size} = n = \left(\frac{Z_{\text{critical}} \times SD}{\text{desired range}}\right)^2 \cong \left(\frac{Z_{\text{critical}} \times sd}{\text{desired range}}\right)^2$$

6.24(a)

$$\text{sample size} = n =$$
$$\left(\frac{Z_{\text{critical}}}{\text{desired range}}\right)^2 \times PQ \cong \left(\frac{Z_{\text{critical}}}{\text{desired range}}\right)^2 \times pq$$

6.24(b)

Appendix C

$$r = \frac{\Sigma(Z_{x_i} \times Z_{y_i})}{n - 1}$$

7.21(a)

$$Z_{x_i} = \frac{x_i - m_x}{sd_x}$$

7.21(b)

$$Z_{y_i} = \frac{y_i - m_y}{sd_y}$$

7.21(c)

$$r = \frac{\Sigma(x_i - m_x)(y_i - m_y)/(n - 1)}{sd_x sd_y}$$

7.21(f)

$$r = \frac{\Sigma(x_i - m_x)(y_i - m_y)}{\sqrt{\Sigma(x_i - m_x)^2 \Sigma(y_i - m_y)^2}}$$

7.21(g)

$$r = \frac{n\Sigma x_i y_i - \Sigma x_i \Sigma y_i}{\sqrt{(n\Sigma x_i^2 - (\Sigma x_i)^2)(n\Sigma y_i^2 - (\Sigma y_i)^2)}}$$

7.21(h)

$$t_{calculated} = r/se_r$$

7.22(a)

$$se_r = \sqrt{\frac{1 - r^2}{n - 2}}$$

7.22(b)

$$t_{\text{calculated}} \text{ (Pearson } r) = \frac{r\sqrt{n-2}}{\sqrt{1-r^2}}$$

7.22(c)

$$d.f. \text{ (}t \text{ test for } r) = n - 2$$

7.22(d)

$$se_{z'} = \frac{1}{\sqrt{n-3}}$$

7.23(a)

$$z' \pm Z_{\text{critical}} \times se_{z'}$$

7.23(b)

$$r_{pb} = \frac{(m_{y_1} - m_{y_0})\sqrt{pq}}{sd_y}$$

7.24(a)

$$r_{phi} = \frac{BC - AD}{\sqrt{(A+B)(C+D)(A+C)(B+D)}}$$

7.24(b)

$$r_S = 1 - \frac{6\Sigma(Rx_i - Ry_i)^2}{n(n^2-1)}$$

7.25(a)

$$t_{\text{calculated}} \text{ (Spearman } r) = r_S\sqrt{\frac{n-2}{1-r_S^2}}$$

7.26(a)

$$\text{confidence interval } (b) = b \pm t_{\text{critical}} \times se_b$$

8.18(a)

Appendix C

$$d.f. \text{ (OLS regression, } t \text{ test)} = n - k - 1$$

8.18(d)

$$t_{\text{calculated}} = \frac{b - b^*}{se_b}$$

8.19(a)

$$t_{\text{calculated}} = \frac{b}{se_b}$$

8.19(b)

$$\text{confidence interval } (a) = a \pm t_{\text{critical}} \times se_a$$

8.20(a)

$$t_{\text{calculated}} = \frac{a - a^*}{se_a}$$

8.20(d)

$$R^2 = \frac{\Sigma(y_j^* - m_y)^2}{\Sigma(y_j - m_y)^2}$$

8.21(b)

$$R^2_{\text{corrected}} = \left(R^2 - \frac{k}{n - 1}\right)\left(\frac{n - 1}{n - k - 1}\right)$$

8.21(c)

$$\text{confidence or prediction interval } (y_j^*) = y_j^* \pm (t_{\text{critical}} \times se_{y^*})$$

8.22(a)

$$d.f. \text{ (confidence or prediction interval)} = n - k - 1$$

8.22(d)

$$F_{\text{calculated}} = \frac{\Sigma(y_j^* - m_y)^2}{\Sigma(y_j - m_y)^2 - \Sigma(y_j^* - m_y)^2} \times \frac{n - k - 1}{k}$$

8.23(a)

$$F_{\text{calculated}} = \frac{R^2}{1 - R^2} \times \frac{n - k - 1}{k}$$

8.23(b)

$$\textit{d.f.} \ (F \text{ test of entire regression}) = \frac{k}{n - k - 1}$$

8.23(c)

$$\textit{d.f.} \ (\text{numerator, } F \text{ test of entire regression}) = k$$

8.23(d)

$$\textit{d.f.} \ (\text{denominator, } F \text{ test of entire regression}) = n - k - 1$$

8.23(e)

$$(\text{partial}) \ F_{\text{calculated}} = \frac{R^2_{\text{full}} - R^2_{\text{partial}}}{(1 - R^2_{\text{full}})} \times \frac{n - k_{\text{full}} - 1}{k_{\text{full}} - k_{\text{partial}}}$$

8.24(a)

$$\textit{d.f.} \ (\text{numerator, partial } F \text{ test}) = k_{\text{full}} - k_{\text{partial}}$$

8.24(b)

$$\textit{d.f.} \ (\text{denominator, partial } F \text{ test}) = n - k_{\text{full}} - 1$$

8.24(c)

Table of Cases

643

Table of Cases

Index

(References are to section numbers)

Index

Index